Compensation Committee Handbook

COMPENSATION COMMITTEE HANDBOOK

Third Edition

JAMES F. REDA
STEWART REIFLER
LAURA G. THATCHER

BICENTENNIAL
1807
WILEY
2007
BICENTENNIAL

John Wiley & Sons, Inc.

Library of Congress Cataloging-in-Publication Data:

Reda, James F.
Compensation committee handbook / James F. Reda, Stewart Reifler, Laura G. Thatcher.—3rd ed.
 p. cm.
 Includes bibliographical references and index.
 ISBN 978-0-470-17131-8 (cloth)
 1. Compensation management–United States–Handbooks, manuals, etc.
 2. Wages–Law and legislation–United States–Handbooks, manuals, etc.
 I. Reifler, Stewart. II. Thatcher, Laura G. III. Title.
 HF5549.5.C67R435 2008
 658.3′2—dc22

2007028031

Printed in the United States of America
10 9 8 7 6 5 4 3 2 1

The authors dedicate this book to their spouses for all
of their patience and continued support.
Deborah Reda
Sheryl Reifler
Brad Thatcher

Contents

Foreword

Not too long ago, the general consensus among independent directors was that the chairman of the audit committee had the most challenging position in the boardroom. That consensus has unraveled as, post-Sarbanes-Oxley, the necessary and appropriate audit committee tasks have become more widely agreed to and the committee member qualifications more demanding.

The compensation committee chair is now widely considered the most difficult role on the board. One reason is that the compensation committee chair and committee members may often find themselves in a difficult tug-of-war with management on pay matters. In the worldwide hunt for executive talent, the compensation committee needs to be vigilant in assuring that management is adequately compensated. But as trustees or fiduciaries for the shareholders, the task of the compensation committee is to get the best management and the best business results at the least cost to the shareholders. Managements, of course, for themselves and their families, seek the highest pay they can get. As a result, and inevitably, compensation committees and managements will at least start out with different points of view when approaching executive compensation issues. If the compensation committee is performing its duties to the shareholders, it may, at some point, have to tell management "no." That is no fun even if management is not performing at a high level; it is tougher by far if management is doing well. The proper and necessary back and forth between the compensation committee and management can sometimes make board and committee meetings stressful and unhappy events.

Another reason why the compensation committee's task is challenging is that there are few road maps for deciding what compensation is "right." Audit committee members can at least refer to voluminous and detailed (though often ambiguous) rules stating how books and records should be kept and how transactions should be accounted for. However, there is no equivalent body of "generally accepted compensation principles" to guide the work of the compensation committee. While nearly everyone can agree on compensation questions at a very high level of generality— "pay for performance," for example—application of that bromide to a specific company at a specific time in its history and with a particular management in place is another matter entirely. Not only are there few concrete guideposts in reaching pay decisions, there are no compensation police to curb the wilder inclinations of the compensation outliers. Audit firms are overseen by the Public Company Accounting Oversight Board (PCAOB), the Securities and Exchange Commission (SEC), and state bodies; in contrast, no one in particular oversees the compensation consultants on which compensation committees have come to so heavily rely. The *Grasso* case attracts attention precisely because it is one of a very small set. Contrast the number of cases concerning compensation brought by any regulatory authority with, for example, the cases brought relating to accounting matters. Without firm principles to guide them, compensation committees are at hazard of drifting into some very muddy waters.

If this is enough to make the compensation committee's job hard, public attention to compensation issues has continued to increase—from activist shareholders legitimately concerned about pay levels and practices and special interest groups using compensation matters to hide other agendas, to the sensationalistic business and general media, and politicians eager to score easy points with their constituents. Even compensation committees made up of hard-working, thoughtful board members who understand their responsibilities can find themselves on the wrong end of an ugly controversy about pay decisions.

The consequences of making bad compensation decisions can be severe. They range from ill-advised legislative initiatives to shareholder revolts. How should directors who want to do the right things with executive pay proceed? Two rules are preeminent:

1. Don't join a compensation committee unless you are willing to do the necessary work. Much of the effort of the compensation committee requires great attention to what may appear to be (and often are) mind-numbing details. If a director isn't willing to engage, work hard, and learn the details of compensation matters, he or she shouldn't be on the compensation committee. For example, is a director willing to read and understand the details of the CEO's employment contract? Has he or she read and understood the stock option plan that the shareholders are being asked to approve? Has the compensation committee member analyzed the data that the committee's consultant has offered up? Does he or she know what Sections 162(m), 409A, and 280G are, or what FAS 123R is? Directors answering "no" to such questions should consider seeking another committee assignment or going back to school.

2. Don't join a compensation committee unless you understand your role on that committee. Too many directors are unwilling or unable to challenge management or their fellow directors over compensation issues. From one point of view, this is completely understandable: few people enjoy conflict, particularly with individuals whom they may generally like, respect, and need to work with on a continuing basis. And board members should support and encourage ethical, intelligent, and hardworking managements. The boardroom and committee room culture is generally one of compromise and consensus, and there is much to be said on behalf of collegiality. But it is possible to both disagree with someone and support them. Some directors, unfortunately, act as if their only task on the compensation committee were to make management happy and avoid conflict, rather than to get the best performance from management at a reasonable cost.

Though we have little hard data, my guess would be that nearly every recent compensation mess in public companies—from backdated stock options to some outstandingly ill-advised CEO pay and severance packages—leads back to directors who were too eager to please management or their fellow directors, too unwilling to challenge the assumptions underlying compensation plans, too busy with their Black-Berries, or too distracted by other obligations to delve into the details of compensation plans, and too careless with the shareholders' money. Though the vast majority of compensation committees appear to be made up of intelligent and hardworking direc-tors, unfortunately, the minority of compensation committees that don't perform their job reasonably end up attracting negative public comment and shareholder reaction to all compensation committees. At the moment, the public may not be up in arms over executive compensation, but small sparks can sometimes set off large explosions, and—though we hardly need reminding—the quadrennial presidential election cycle circus is well under way. The counterproductive legislative and ill-thought-through activist compensation agendas harm all public corporations by limiting their flexibility and distracting them from more urgent tasks at hand.

All of us—managements and compensation committees—have failed to do the ne-cessary work of helping the politicians and the media, not to mention our shareholders and employees, understand the compensation realities we face, and the rationales for our compensation decisions. The 2007 SEC executive compensation disclosure re-quirements, which almost predictably have led to prolix, confusing, and "apples and oranges" presentations, haven't helped. It is unrealistic to expect managements to be persuasive advocates for their own compensation, given their self-interested status. Compensation committees must lead this effort, but leadership can be based only on credible work, which on its face justifies its determinations. Unless directors involved in compensation decision making can articulate their views in a plain and reasonable fashion to regulators, shareholders, the media, and employees—instead of just to the beneficiaries of their efforts—it is unlikely the pressures on compensa-tion committees will recede.

Which brings us to this *Handbook*. It is designed to help the compensation com-mittee member understand his or her duties and role, and to remind him or her of both the general and technical determinants of good compensation committee decision making. No compensation committee will make the right decisions all the time, but a good compensation committee should make the right decisions on average over the long term, and should always make sensible and defensible decisions, even if in hindsight they may appear to be disadvantageous. This *Handbook* will help willing compensation committee members end up at the right place. It will make good com-pensation committees better and will help the rest catch up.

Philip R. Lochner Jr.

Philip R. Lochner Jr. is a former commissioner of the U.S. Securities and Exchange Commission. He serves or has served on the boards of directors and compensation committees of a variety of public companies, including Adelphia Communications Corporation; Solutia, Inc.; Apria Healthcare Group, Inc.; CLARCOR, Inc.; CMS Energy Corporation; Crane Co.; GTech Holdings, Inc.; and Monster Worldwide, Inc. He has also served as a member of the Board of Governors of the National Association of Securities Dealers and of the American Stock Exchange, as a member of the Legal Advisory Committee of the New York Stock Exchange, and as a member of the boards of directors of the Investor Responsibility Research Center and the National Association of Corporate Directors. He was Vice President, General Counsel, and Secretary of Time Incorporated and later was Senior Vice President and Chief Administrative Officer of Time Warner Inc.

Preface

Concern about executive pay is hardly a new phenomenon. Historically, it has tended to ebb and flow with overall economic conditions. Attention tends to decline in periods of economic plenty—as long as most Americans perceive themselves as doing well, they worry less that chief executive officers (CEOs) might be doing better still. Likewise, as general economic fortunes subside, the relatively large earnings of corporate leaders invoke public ire.

True to form, at the end of the bull market of the 1990s, we saw a swing of the pendulum from an attitude of "anything goes" to widespread negative attention on executive pay. Adding to the sense of public distrust was the round of high-profile corporate failures and fraud that took place in the early 2000s. Even though at the time of this writing we find ourselves once again in a robust domestic economy, with the Dow Jones Average ascending to historic highs, the backlash from the burst of the dot-com bubble and the notable corporate failures early in this century retain momentum even today.

The Sarbanes-Oxley Act of 2002, the new Public Company Accounting Oversight Board, and new rules from the stock exchanges responded to the notorious corporate failures by focusing on measures that make it more difficult for corporate officers to commit fraud and that strengthen the ability of corporate boards to detect misconduct. New accounting rules requiring expensing of stock options, an expansive principles-based compensation disclosure regime, a new overlay of laws regulating deferred compensation, and a push for various "say-on-pay" proposals round out the corporate reforms started in the early 2000s.

Public policy makers, public and private oversight bodies, and shareholder groups continue to focus on enhancing the ability of corporate boards of directors to ensure that businesses operate ethically and effectively. The Conference Board, the National Association of Corporate Directors, the Society of Corporate Secretaries and Governance Professionals, the Business Roundtable, the Council of Institutional Investors, and a variety of institutional investor advisory groups have all provided very thoughtful comments and leadership on issues of executive compensation and the role of the compensation committee. Furthermore, some major U.S. public corporations have contributed to the good-governance movement and have themselves provided leadership in this area. We rely substantially on this leadership to provide the best practice guidance throughout this *Handbook*. While recognizing that there is no single "correct" model for executive pay that will fit every business organization, there is an identifiable set of evolving "best practices" that compensation committees and boards of directors can apply. The practices discussed in this new edition reflect current and pending regulations, including new rules by the Securities and Exchange Commission, the Internal Revenue Service, the Financial Accounting Standards Board, the New York Stock Exchange, and The Nasdaq

Stock Market. They also reflect the experience of compensation committee members and the knowledge gained in careers as business executives, government officials, corporate board members, governance experts, compensation consultants, and academics engaged in the study of business history and practices. Our hope is that this *Handbook* will stimulate useful and vigorous dialogue within compensation committees and boards of directors on valid measurements of executive performance, the appropriate level of compensation, and the proper mix of compensation elements and incentives, including base pay, performance bonuses, equity grants, retirement benefits, welfare benefits, perquisites, and other benefits.

We also hope that the best practices identified in this *Handbook* will encourage compensation committees to establish a set of values that guides compensation discussions. This process should include identifying the goals that the pay package is designed to achieve, carefully examining each element of compensation, and considering the potential costs of the package in a variety of scenarios. Our fundamental point is that every company should have a compensation system based on a core set of clearly established principles, not one based on ad hoc decision making. However, more important than any best practice is the attitude and rigor that the compensation committee brings to its task. What is needed most is courage, leadership, and a spirit of independence—the willingness to ask uncomfortable questions, test the assumptions that underlie traditional past practices, strengthen accepted practices that work, say "no" when the situation warrants, and chart new courses when the rationale for old habits falls short. These characteristics, combined with the best practices discussed in this *Handbook*, will ensure best-in-class performance for compensation committees.

Acknowledgments

Each of the authors would like to thank certain individuals who contributed to this third edition of the *Compensation Committee Handbook*.

Laura Thatcher sends special thanks to her husband Brad, who engaged in serious debate of corporate governance principles while tending the horses and running the farm. She also acknowledges with admiration and appreciation the assistance and counsel of her colleagues Kim Phillips and Kerry Tynan, who spent many hours reviewing this book. Lastly, she thanks her law firm of 28 years, Alston & Bird, for encouraging her to embark on this engaging and professionally rewarding adventure.

Stewart Reifler expresses his appreciation to all of the boards of directors, compensation committees, chief executive officers, chief operating officers, chief financial officers, general counsels, senior human resource executives, and other executives whom he has advised over the years, and who have indirectly but immeasurably contributed to this book. In addition, he wishes to thank the executive compensation attorneys at Vedder Price who have all—in one way or another—directly affected the observations, commentary, analysis, and substance of this book. Finally, he particularly wants to thank Kevin Hassan for his time and attention spent in meticulously reviewing selected chapters of this *Handbook*.

Jim Reda thanks his wife, Deborah Reda, who has supported him in every way over the past 16 years, as well as to Laura Thatcher and Stewart Reifler, who agreed to revise the second and third editions of this *Handbook*. He would also like to thank outstanding directors and compensation committee chairs such as Jane Pfeiffer, Earnest Deavenport, William Walters, Donald McHenry, Sam Gibara, Mike Ullman, and Burl Osborne, who have made Corporate America a better place with their time and energy in designing and implementing shareholder-friendly performance plans that encourage outstanding corporate performance. The knowledge gained in working with these outstanding directors is the basis of this *Handbook* and his consulting practice.

Finally, the authors want to thank Tim Burgard at John Wiley & Sons for all of his time and effort in making possible this third edition of this *Handbook*.

About the Authors

JAMES F. REDA
Founder and Managing Director, James F. Reda & Associates, LLC
Mr. Reda has served for more than 20 years as advisor to the top managements and boards of major corporations in the United States and abroad in matters of executive compensation, performance, organization, and corporate governance. Mr. Reda has played an integral role in the field of executive compensation and the formation of the role of the compensation committee. As a recognized authority on corporate governance, he also serves as expert witness in executive compensation litigation and is typically retained by compensation committees as an outside independent advisor. Mr. Reda has a BS in industrial engineering from Columbia University, and an SM in management from Massachusetts Institute of Technology, Sloan School of Management. He is a member of the American Society of Corporate Secretaries; WorldatWork; The National Association of Stock Plan Professionals; National Association of Corporate Directors (NACD); and the New York Society of Security Analysts, for which he serves on the corporate governance committee. He is past chair of the Atlanta Chapter of NACD and was a commissioner member of the NACD Blue Ribbon Commission entitled "Executive Compensation and the Role of the Compensation Committee."

STEWART REIFLER
Shareholder, Vedder, Price, Kaufman & Kammholz, PC
Stewart Reifler is a shareholder of Vedder, Price, Kaufman & Kammholz, PC, and heads its executive compensation practice in New York. He has extensive experience in representing companies, their boards, and their executives, both as an attorney with Weil, Gotshal & Manges and the Law Offices of Joseph E. Bachelder and as a compensation consultant with PricewaterhouseCoopers. He is a member of the executive compensation steering committee of the American Institute of Certified Public Accountants. He has been quoted in *BusinessWeek, Fortune, Journal of Accountancy, International Tax Review,* and *Practical Accountant,* and he is a frequent speaker on executive compensation topics. His articles have appeared in the *National Law Journal, Metropolitan Corporate Counsel, The Tax Executive, Journal of Compensation and Benefits, Mergers and Acquisitions, Director's Monthly, Directors & Boards, Securities Regulatory Update, Corporate Business Taxation Monthly, Estate Tax Planning Advisor,* and *Journal of Taxation of Employee Benefits.* He currently serves on the Advisory Board of *Corporate Business Taxation Monthly.*

LAURA G. THATCHER
Partner, Alston & Bird LLP

Laura Thatcher heads Alston & Bird LLP's executive compensation practice and serves as special executive compensation counsel to many U.S. and international publicly traded companies. She serves on the Editorial Board of the *Journal of Deferred Compensation,* the Advisory Board of the Certified Equity Professional Institute of Santa Clara University (CEPI), and chairs the Board of Review for a multidisciplinary initiative spearheaded by CEPI to create a series of "white papers" to provide industry guidance as to areas of risk and appropriate controls in equity compensation. Ms. Thatcher is also chair of the compensation committee of a southeast regional commercial construction and real estate development company. A frequent speaker and author on topics relating to executive compensation, Ms. Thatcher's articles and interviews have appeared in numerous national publications and media including the *Wall Street Journal, Financial Times, Washington Post, USA Today,* MSNBC.com, the *Drudge Report, Directors & Boards,* and various publications of the Bureau of National Affairs (BNA), including the *BNA Corporate Accountability Report, BNA Daily Tax Report,* and *BNA Executive Compensation Library.*

All three of the authors are members of the CompensationStardards.com Executive Compensation Task Force.

Part One

The Modern Compensation Committee

Chapter 1

The Compensation Committee

One of the most important determinants of a successful corporate strategy is the quality of the compensation committee. The committee is charged with designing and implementing a compensation system that effectively rewards key players and encourages direct participation in the achievement of the organization's core business objectives.

Outstanding, well-integrated compensation strategy does not just happen. Rather, it is the product of the hard work of independent, experienced compensation committee members. The most effective pay strategies are simple in design, straightforward in application, and easy to communicate to management and investors. The pay program for the chief executive officer (CEO) should be in line with pay programs for the company's other executives and with its broad-based incentive programs. In other words, there should be no conflict in the achievement of objectives, and the potential rewards should be as meaningful to all participants as to the CEO.

The United States is unique in its vast number of high-earning entrepreneurs, entertainers, athletes, lawyers, consultants, Wall Street traders, bankers, analysts, investment managers, and other professionals. Yet, it is the pay levels of corporate executives, in particular CEOs, that stir the most heated debate and controversy. It is estimated that the bull market of the 1990s created over 10 million new millionaires whose wealth was derived almost solely from stock options. During this period, many CEOs made hundreds of millions in option gains and other compensation—often making as much as 400 times the earnings of the average workers in their companies. Beginning in late 2001, the business world changed dramatically. Now, with the public's and investors' direct focus on corporate governance and compensation philosophy, and recent changes in accounting rules affecting equity-based compensation, CEOs and other executives should not expect to sustain historic rates of wealth accumulation, absent substantial performance that is no longer linked solely to the price of the company's stock.

While the proxy statement compensation tables provide historical information and raw data about the company's compensation of its top executive officers, the new Compensation Discussion and Analysis (CD&A) provides a window into the company's compensation philosophy and a means for investors to assess whether and how closely pay is related to performance. A thoughtfully prepared CD&A is good evidence of a well-functioning compensation committee that takes its work seriously.

Among the topics covered in this chapter are:

- Board and board committee structure
- Independence measures
- Compensation committee size
- Compensation committee charter
- Role of the compensation committee and its chair
- Duties and responsibilities
- Precepts for responsible performance
- Compensation benchmarking
- The importance of meeting minutes

BOARD STRUCTURE: THE FOCUS ON INDEPENDENCE

Much of the recent public scrutiny of corporate governance issues has focused on structural issues as they relate to corporate boards—questions related to independence from management; separation of the chair and CEO positions; issues related to the composition and function of board committees; and renewed efforts to create a framework in which outside directors can obtain impartial advice and analysis, free of undue influence from corporate management.

While it has always been desirable to have a healthy complement of outside directors on the board, corporate governance rules adopted by the New York Stock Exchange (NYSE) and The Nasdaq Stock Market (NASDAQ) in 2003 require that a majority of a listed company's board consist of independent directors and, with limited exceptions, that such board appoint fully independent compensation, audit, and nominating/corporate governance committees. The NYSE and NASDAQ rules also prescribe standards for determining the independence of individual directors, which, when layered over the director independence standards under Section 162(m) of the Internal Revenue IRC (IRC) and Rule 16b-3 of the Securities Exchange Act of 1934 (Exchange Act), make the nomination and selection of compensation committee members a challenging exercise.

COMPENSATION COMMITTEE COMPOSITION AND MULTIPLE INDEPENDENCE REQUIREMENTS

When selecting directors to serve on the compensation committee of a public company, the nominating committee should choose only those persons who meet all the relevant independence requirements that will permit the committee to fulfill its intended function. For example, a compensation committee member must be an "independent director," as defined under NYSE or NASDAQ rules, where applicable. In addition, a public company is well served to have a compensation committee consisting solely of two or more directors who meet (1) the definitional requirements of "outside director" under IRC Section 162(m), and (2) the definitional requirements of "non-employee director" under Rule 16b-3 of the Exchange Act. This often leads to a lowest common denominator approach of identifying director candidates who satisfy the requirements of all three definitions. Unfortunately, the three tests are not identical, and it is indeed possible to have a director who meets one or more independence tests but not another.

NYSE/NASDAQ INDEPENDENCE TESTS

Under the 2003 NYSE listing rules, an independent director is defined as a director who has no material relationship with the company. NASDAQ defines independence as the absence of any relationship that would interfere with the exercise of independent judgment in carrying out the director's responsibilities. In both cases, the board has a responsibility to make an affirmative determination that no such relationships exist. The rules list specific conditions or relationships that will render a director nonindependent. These are summarized in Exhibit 5.1 in Chapter 5.

RULE 16b-3 INDEPENDENCE TEST

Awards of stock options and other equity awards to directors and officers of a public company, generally referred to as "Section 16 insiders," are exempt from the short-swing profit provisions of Section 16 of the Exchange Act if such awards are made by a compensation committee consisting solely of two or more "non-employee directors" (as defined in Rule 16b-3 under the Exchange Act). In addition to such compensation committee approval, there are three alternative exemptions under Rule 16b-3: (1) such awards to Section 16 insiders can be preapproved by the full board of directors, (2) the awards can be made subject to a six-month holding period (measured from the date of grant), or (3) specific awards can be ratified by the shareholders (which alternative is, for obvious reasons, rarely taken).

Disadvantages of relying on full board approval for the Rule 16b-3 exemption are that (1) it is administratively awkward to single out awards to Section 16 insiders for special full board approval, and (2) if the full board takes on that role, the CD&A may need to address that anomaly. Therefore, prevalent practice is for the compensation committee to be staffed exclusively with directors who meet the Rule 16b-3 definition of "non-employee director," and to have the compensation committee approve all equity awards to Section 16 insiders.

To qualify as a "non-employee director" under Rule 16b-3, a director cannot (1) be a current officer or employee of the company or a parent or subsidiary of the company; (2) receive more than $120,000 in compensation, directly or indirectly, from the company or a parent or subsidiary of the company for services rendered as a consultant or in any capacity other than as a director; or (3) have a reportable transaction under Regulation S-K Item 404(a) of the Securities and Exchange Commission (SEC), as outlined in Exhibit 1.1.

Exhibit 1.1   Regulation S-K Item 404(a) Transactions with Related Persons

What	Any financial transaction, arrangement, or relationship, including indebtedness or guarantee of indebtedness
When	Occurred in last fiscal year or is currently proposed
Between Whom	(1) The company or its subsidiaries, and (2) the director or nominee or his or her immediate family member
Threshold Amount	$120,000
Nature of Interest	Direct or indirect material interest in the transaction or other entity
Exceptions	Instructions provide guidance as to whether an indirect interest is material

IRC SECTION 162(m) INDEPENDENCE TEST

For any performance-based compensation granted to a public company's CEO, or its next three (or four) most highly compensated executive officers ("covered employees") to be excluded from the $1 million deduction limit of IRC Section 162(m), such compensation must have been approved in advance by a compensation committee consisting solely of two or more "outside directors" (as defined under the IRC Section 162(m) regulations). (See Chapter 8 for detail about the evolving definition of *covered employee* under IRC Section 162(m).) Full board approval of such compensation will not suffice for this purpose, unless all directors who do not qualify as outside directors abstain from voting. Therefore, prevalent practice is for the compensation committee to be staffed exclusively with directors who meet the IRC Section 162(m) definition of "outside director," and to have such compensation committee approve all performance-based awards to executive officers and others who might reasonably be expected to become *covered employees* during the life of the award.

To qualify as an "outside director" under IRC Section 162(m), a director (1) cannot be a current employee of the company, (2) cannot be a former employee of the company who receives compensation for services in the current fiscal year (other than tax-qualified retirement plan benefits), (3) cannot be a current or former officer of the company, and (4) cannot receive compensation from the company, directly or indirectly, in any capacity other than as a director. Exhibit 1.2 outlines the IRC Section 162(m) independence test, including a summary of what constitutes "indirect" compensation.

STATE LAW INTERESTED DIRECTOR TEST

To further complicate the analysis, the concept of independence is also applied in determining whether a director is "interested" in a particular transaction under consideration by the board or the committee. A director who meets all of the regulatory definitions of independence under the NYSE/NASDAQ rules, Rule 16b-3 and IRC Section 162(m), can still have a personal interest in a particular transaction that can interfere with his or her ability to render impartial judgment with respect to that transaction. This type of nonindependence will not render the director unsuitable to

Exhibit 1.2 Outside Director Requirements under IRC §162(m) Regulations

Current Employee	The director cannot be a current employee of the publicly held company.
Former Employee	The director cannot be a former employee of the publicly held company who receives compensation for services in the current fiscal year (other than tax-qualified retirement plan benefits).
Officer	The director cannot be a current or former officer of the publicly held company.
Remuneration	The director cannot receive remuneration from the company, directly or indirectly, in any capacity other than as a director. See categories 1–4 for what constitutes "indirect" remuneration.
Category 1	If remuneration is paid directly to the director, he or she is disqualified. No *de minimis* exception.
Category 2	If remuneration is paid to an entity of which the director is a 50% or greater beneficial owner, he or she is disqualified. No *de minimis* exception.
Category 3	If remuneration (other than a *de minimis* amount) was paid in the last fiscal year to an entity in which the director beneficially owns between 5% and 50%, he or she is disqualified. See below for definition of a *de minimis* amount.
Category 4	If remuneration (other than *de minimis* amount) was paid in the last fiscal year to an entity by which the director is employed (or self-employed) other than as a director, he or she is disqualified. See below for definition of *de minimis* amount.
***De minimis* amount other than for personal services**	Payments not for personal services are *de minimis* if they did not exceed 5% of the gross revenue of the other entity for its last fiscal year ending with or within the company's last fiscal year.
***De minimis* amount for personal services**	Payments for personal services are *de minimis* if they do not exceed $60,000.
Personal Services	Remuneration is for personal services if it (1) is paid to an entity for personal services consisting of legal, accounting, investment banking, or management consulting services (or similar services) and is not for services that are incidental to the purchase of goods or nonpersonal services; and (2) the director performs significant services (whether or not as an employee) for the corporation, division, or similar organization (within the third-party entity) that actually provides the legal, accounting, investment banking, or management consulting services (or similar services) to the company, or more than 50% of the third-party entity's gross revenues are derived from that corporation, division, subsidiary, or similar organization.
Former Officer Defined	A director is not precluded from being an outside director solely because he or she is a former officer of a corporation that previously was an affiliated corporation of the publicly held corporation. For example, a director of a parent corporation of an affiliated group is not precluded from being an outside director solely because that director is a former officer of an affiliated subsidiary that was spun off or liquidated. However, an outside director would cease to be an outside director if a corporation in which the director was previously an officer became an affiliated corporation of the publicly held corporation.

serve on the compensation committee, but he or she may need to be excused from voting on the particular matter. An example of this might be a situation in which the compensation committee is determining whether to hire a particular consulting firm to advise the committee with respect to a particular matter and one of the committee members has a relative at such consulting firm. This relationship would not necessarily bar the committee member from satisfying any of the regulatory definitions of independence (particularly if the amount of the consultant's fee is less than $120,000), but the director might have a personal interest in having the committee hire that consulting firm over another. In that case, the interested director should disclose the nature of his or her interest in the matter and abstain from voting on the hiring question. Once that consulting firm has been hired to represent the committee, the matter is over, and the originally interested director may resume active participation in the business of the committee.

FULL DISCLOSURE OF PERTINENT INFORMATION

The SEC's proxy rules require disclosure of relevant background information about each director that is intended to give shareholders an indication of the director's unique qualifications and any relationships or affiliations that might affect his or her judgment or independence. For example, disclosure is required regarding:

- All positions and offices the director holds with the company
- Any arrangement or understanding between the director and any other person pursuant to which he or she is to be selected as a director or nominee
- The nature of any family relationship (by blood, marriage, or adoption, not more remote than first cousin) between the director and any executive officer or other director
- The director's business experience during the past five years
- Any other public company directorships held by the director
- The director's involvement in certain legal proceedings
- The director's compensation from the company for the last completed fiscal year, in the form of a summary compensation table and related narrative disclosures, similar to the Summary Compensation Table for executive officers
- Any financial transaction, arrangement, or relationship, including indebtedness or guarantee of indebtedness, occurring in the last year or currently proposed, to which the company or any of its affiliates is party, in which the amount involved exceeds $120,000 and in which the director has, or will have, a direct or indirect material interest
- Any failure by the director to make a timely filing of any Section 16 report during the last fiscal year
- Any director interlocking relationships

DIRECTOR INTERLOCKS

As a reflection of the insistence on unbiased, independent analysis in setting executive pay, there is a special sensitivity to so-called "director interlocks." A director interlock exists where there are any of the following relationships:

- An executive officer of the company serves as a member of the compensation committee of another entity, one of whose executive officers serves on the compensation committee of the company.

- An executive officer of the company serves as a director of another entity, one of whose executive officers serves on the compensation committee of the company.

- An executive officer of the company serves as a member of the compensation committee of another entity, one of whose executive officers serves as a director of the company.

- NYSE/NASDAQ description—A director of the listed company is, or has a family member who is, employed as an executive officer of another entity where at any time during the last three years any executive officers of the listed company served on the compensation committee of such other entity.

While not prohibited as a legal matter, director interlocks are suspect due to the possibility that they could engender a "you scratch my back, I'll scratch yours" influence or other *quid pro quo* situation affecting executive compensation decisions. For that reason, a director who has an interlock of the nature described under applicable NYSE or NASDAQ rules will not be deemed an independent director until three years after such interlocking employment relationship has terminated. During that time, he or she would not be eligible to serve on the compensation committee.

An interlocking relationship will be evident to the public. The SEC's rules for public companies require disclosure in the proxy statement, under the specific caption "Compensation Committee Interlocks and Insider Participation," of each person who served as a member of the compensation committee (or board committee performing equivalent functions) during the last fiscal year, indicating each committee member who is or was an employee or officer of the company, had a disclosable interest or transaction with the company, or had an interlocking relationship.

COMPENSATION COMMITTEE SIZE

State law has little to say about the size of a board of directors, and even less about the size of its oversight committees such as the compensation committee. The Revised Model Business Corporation Act (Model Act), on which a majority of states base their corporation laws, provides that a board must consist of one or more individuals, with the number to be specified or fixed in accordance with the corporation's charter or bylaws. Under the Model Act, a company's charter or bylaws may fix a minimum and maximum number of directors and allow the actual number of directors within the range to be fixed or changed from time to time by the shareholders or the board. Delaware, which does not follow the Model Act but is the state of incorporation for many U.S. companies, has similar requirements for determining the size of the board.

Corporations should attempt to assemble a board that reflects a diversity of viewpoints and talents, but is not so large as to frustrate the accomplishment of business at meetings. Smaller boards (those with 12 or fewer members) may allow more free interchange among directors who might otherwise be reticent to express their views in a larger group. However, when considering the appropriate size for a public company board, it is important to include a sufficient number of independent directors to staff the audit, compensation, and nominating/corporate governance committees, each of which is now required by applicable rules to consist solely of independent directors.

Given the interplay of three separate independence requirements for compensation committee members, as discussed previously, it is unusual for a public company's compensation committee to have more than five members. A compensation committee of three to five members should provide an adequate forum for a useful exchange of ideas and healthy debate.

COMPENSATION COMMITTEE CHARTER

The compensation committee (whether it is called such or by some other name—e.g., the human resources committee) generally is established through a formal board resolution, in accordance with applicable state corporate law, the company's articles/certificate of incorporation, and/or the company's bylaws. In the past, some compensation committees had a written charter, while others did not. However, today most compensation committees have a written charter, largely due to recent changes in stock exchange listing rules. As discussed in more detail later, rules at the NYSE require that both the audit committee and the compensation committee have a written charter, while the NASDAQ rules only require that audit committees have a written charter. Nevertheless, most compensation committees at public companies have a written charter since it is viewed as an element of good corporate governance and companies must disclose in their proxy statements whether or not they have a charter. In addition, there may be other federal or state statutory or regulatory requirements for such a charter with respect to specific regulated industries.

Some companies use a short-form charter (often less than a page) that grants the compensation committee authority in very broad strokes. Others adopt a long-form charter that spells out the duties and responsibilities of the committee, the procedures to be followed, and a variety of other specifications and requirements (such as number of members, number of scheduled meetings per year, and so forth).

While the long-form charter is often favored as providing an aura of good corporate governance practice, one drawback is that the details in the charter must in fact be followed. For example, if the charter provides that the committee shall meet at least once every quarter, then the committee must do so or be in violation. Another consequence of the long-form charter is the need for more frequent review and adjustment. Any adjustments must follow an appropriate amendment procedure and will require subsequent disclosure.

See Appendix D for an annotated form of a compensation committee charter and selected examples of compensation committee charters at NYSE and NASDAQ companies.

NYSE COMPENSATION COMMITTEE REQUIREMENTS

Under NYSE rules, the compensation committee must have a written charter that addresses the committee's purpose and responsibilities and requires an annual performance evaluation of the committee. The compensation committee of an NYSE listed company must, at a minimum, have direct responsibility to:

- Review and approve corporate goals and objectives relevant to CEO compensation, evaluate the CEO's performance in light of those goals and objectives, and, either as a committee or, if the board so directs, together with the other independent directors, determine and approve the CEO's compensation level based on that evaluation. The committee is free to discuss CEO compensation with the board generally, as long as the committee shoulders these absolute responsibilities.

- Make recommendations to the board with respect to (1) compensation of the company's executive officers other than the CEO, (2) incentive compensation plans, and (3) equity-based plans.

- Produce a compensation committee report on executive compensation as required by the SEC to be included in the company's annual proxy statement or annual report on Form 10-K filed with the SEC. (This is now just a very short-form report under the SEC's 2007 disclosure rules, stating that the committee has reviewed and discussed with management the CD&A and recommends, or not, that it be included in the proxy statement and annual report. Therefore, the committee's review and discussion of the CD&A is now indirectly part of the NYSE requirement.)

The compensation committee charter should also address: (1) committee member qualifications, (2) committee member appointment and removal, (3) committee structure and operations (including authority to delegate to subcommittees), and (4) committee reporting to the board.

If a compensation consultant is to assist in the evaluation of director, CEO, or senior executive compensation, the compensation committee charter should give that committee sole authority to retain and terminate the consulting firm, including sole authority to approve the firm's fees and other engagement terms.

NASDAQ COMPENSATION COMMITTEE REQUIREMENTS

Under NASDAQ rules, compensation of the CEO and all other executive officers of the company must be determined, or recommended to the board for determination, either by a majority of the independent directors, or a compensation committee comprised solely of independent directors. The CEO may not be present during voting or deliberations with respect to his or her own compensation.

Unlike the NYSE, NASDAQ rules do not specifically require the compensation committee to have and publish a charter. However, it is generally a matter of good corporate governance that a charter be established and followed. The first model compensation committee charter appearing in Appendix D is annotated to conform to both the NYSE and NASDAQ rules as currently in effect.

ROLE OF THE COMPENSATION COMMITTEE

Over time, the role of the compensation committee as a core oversight committee of the board has crystallized. As indicated previously, the NYSE and NASDAQ corporate governance rules require all listed companies to have a compensation committee (or a committee having that function, regardless of the name) composed entirely of independent directors.

The tenets of sound corporate governance embodied in the NYSE and NASDAQ rules should be heeded by any company, whether public or private. The NYSE and NASDAQ rules set out minimum standards governing the deliberative process of the compensation committee. A good committee will not stop there. As discussed more fully in Chapter 5, a host of influential business and investor groups have published their own concepts of best practices for the compensation committee. While none is binding or has the force of law, and while one might not agree with all the views in each report, these best practice guidelines are a "must read" for every compensation committee member who seriously undertakes to consider the proper role of the committee.

The basic role of the compensation committee is twofold. First is to be the "owner" of the company's executive and director compensation philosophy and programs. Second is to provide the primary forum in which core compensation issues are fully and vigorously reviewed, analyzed, and acted upon (either by the committee itself or by way of recommendation to the full board or the independent directors as a group). The decisions and actions of the compensation committee may make the difference between mediocre and outstanding corporate performance.

The more defined role of the compensation committee varies from company to company, and is contingent on various factors such as ownership structure, concerns of shareholders (and perhaps stakeholders—as broadly defined), director capabilities, board values, market dynamics, the company's maturity and financial condition, and other intrinsic and extrinsic factors. The compensation committee, more than any other oversight committee, is charged with the all-important task of balancing the interests of shareholders with those of management. The essential conflict between these two interests is generally not over pay levels, but rather the relationship of pay to performance. Shareholders favor a compensation plan strongly tied to corporate performance, while managers could prefer a compensation plan with maximum security.

Exhibit 1.3 illustrates a typical division of responsibilities among the full board, the nominating committee, and the compensation committee relative to certain

Exhibit 1.3   Board/Compensation Committee Responsibility Matrix

	Approval/Review Required	
	Full Board	Committee
Corporate Organization		
• Certificate of Incorporation (adoption or amendment)	X	
• Corporate bylaws (adoption or amendment)	X	
• Stock: all authorization to issue or buy back shares	X	
Board Organization		
• Board membership qualification		Nominating
• Board committee memberships		Nominating
• New member selection		Nominating
Compensation Matters: Base Salary		
• Salaries of CEO and executive officers		Compensation
Officer Employment Agreements		
• Severance agreements	X	Compensation
• Retention agreements	X	Compensation
• Change in control agreements	X	Compensation
Fringe Benefits		
• Establishment of new plans or amendments to existing plans	X	Compensation
Incentive Compensation		
• All arrangements for corporate officers		Compensation
• Approval of specific financial targets		Compensation
• Determination of payouts		Compensation
Long-Term (Cash) Incentive Plans		
• Establishment of performance targets		Compensation
• Award sizing		Compensation
Stock Plans		
• Establishment of, or amendment to, equity compensation plans	X	Compensation
• Administration of stock plans		Compensation
• Grants under all stock plans		Compensation

matters. Where the responsibilities overlap, it generally implies committee recommendation followed by board ratification.

ROLE OF THE COMPENSATION COMMITTEE CHAIR

The chair's role is to lead the committee and initiate its agenda. The chair of the compensation committee may be selected by the members of the compensation committee, by the nominating committee, or as otherwise provided in the committee's charter. The responsibilities of the chair might appropriately include:

• Suggesting the calendar and overall outline of the annual agenda for the committee
• Convening and preparing the agenda for regular and special meetings
• Presiding over meetings of the committee, keeping the discussion orderly and focused, while encouraging questions, debate, and input from all members on each topic under discussion
• Providing leadership in developing the committee's compensation philosophy and policy
• Counseling collectively and individually with members of the committee and the other independent directors
• Interviewing, retaining, and providing interface between the committee and outside experts, consultants, and advisors

DUTIES AND RESPONSIBILITIES OF THE COMPENSATION COMMITTEE

The fundamental task of the compensation committee is to establish the compensation philosophy of the company. Having done so, it should design programs to advance that philosophy. In almost all cases, this will require the advice of outside experts, to assure that specific performance metrics and performance goals are established that promote desired performance and that pay is in line with such performance.

The compensation committee should assume primary responsibility for the following general areas:

• Compensation philosophy and strategy
• Compensation of the CEO and other executive officers
• Compensation of nonexecutive officers (or the oversight of such compensation if delegated to others)

- Compensation of directors (this function is sometimes housed at the board level or with the governance committee)
- Management development and succession (this function is sometimes placed with the full board or the governance committee)
- Equity compensation plans
- Retirement plans, benefits, and perquisites (this function is sometimes shared with, or performed by, a separate benefits plan committee):
  - Qualified retirement plans, profit sharing, and savings plans
  - Nonqualified plans such as supplemental executive retirement plans (SERPs), nonqualified deferred compensation, and pension restoration plans
  - Welfare benefits, including medical, life insurance, accidental death, and disability insurance
  - Executive benefits such as supplemental medical coverage and supplemental life and/or disability insurance
  - Perquisites
- Contractual arrangements with management, including employment and severance agreements
- For public companies, preparation of the CD&A, or a least review and discussion of the CD&A with management, for inclusion in the company's proxy statement and annual report

The decision as to how far compensation committee oversight should be extended depends on various factors, including the corporate culture, strength of management, the size of the committee, the regulatory environment in which the company operates, and prior corporate performance in these areas.

Exhibit 1.4 contains a checklist covering typical duties of the compensation committee.

SIX PRECEPTS FOR RESPONSIBLE COMMITTEE PERFORMANCE

To execute its duties responsibly, the compensation committee must be able to efficiently synthesize highly technical information and apply sound business judgment. As the field of executive compensation becomes increasingly complex and more in the focus of public attention, the committee's job grows more and more challenging. Adherence to the following six precepts will pave the way to optimal performance by the committee:

1. Get organized
2. Get and stay informed

Exhibit 1.4   Checklist for the Compensation Committee

- Ensure disinterest and independence from management
- Retain and maintain direct access to outside experts/consultants
- Establish and periodically review/update compensation philosophy
- Establish a compensation strategy (including pay plans) consistent with overall compensation philosophy and corporate objectives
- Ensure that shareholder and corporate economic values are prime drivers of the executive pay program
- Be sensitive to external pressures
- Be mindful of controversial pay practices
- Balance fixed versus variable rewards
- Define equity participation strategy
- Understand and coordinate all elements of executive pay
- Assess the real dollar value/cost of executives' total pay packages
- Carefully select recognized industry index and/or an appropriate peer group for the performance group
- Compare pay programs with relevant peer group
- Link payments with performance goals
- Set goals for CEO, evaluation performance against such goals, and set CEO pay levels

3. Keep an eye on the big picture
4. Return to reason
5. Consider the shareholders' perspective
6. Communicate effectively

1. GETTING ORGANIZED

Set the agenda. As noted previously, many topics generally fall within the purview of the compensation committee. To make sure that all are considered in a timely and effective manner, the compensation committee chair should at the beginning of the fiscal year prepare a schedule of meetings for the whole year, along with a tentative agenda for each meeting. To accommodate new topics arising over the ensuing months, a specific agenda should be prepared and circulated before each meeting. An example of such an annual schedule, along with possible recurring agenda items, is shown in Exhibit 1.5.

Provide timely information. It is best to provide written materials to each committee member at least a week before each meeting so that he or she will have ample

Exhibit 1.5 Illustrative Compensation Committee Agenda

Event	Meeting Date	Recurring Agenda Items
End of calendar/ fiscal year in December	Late February	• Approve minutes of prior meeting
		• Review prior year operating results presented as required by bonus plan criteria
		• Evaluate performance of CEO for prior year, and review and approve recommended bonus plan payments
		• Review and approve recommendations related to current year participation in bonus plan
		• Review and approve current year bonus plan targets for organization units and plan participants
		• Review and approve personal goals of CEO for current year
		• Review and discuss draft of CD and A for inclusion in proxy
		• Review executive compensation disclosures for inclusion in proxy
		• Review new plan proposals for inclusion in proxy
After annual shareholders' meeting and approval of stock-related plans	June/July or September/ October	• Approve minutes of prior meeting
		• Review and approve recommendations for annual equity grants
		• Review and approve mid-year promotions, new hires
		• Receive consultant's report on fringe benefits and benefit costs, competitive practices and recommended changes and costs
		• Receive annual management development and succession planning overview from CEO
		• Engage outside studies for various matters
		• Review performance of outside advisors
Late in year	November/ early December	• Approve minutes of prior meeting
		• Review consultant's report on compensation levels and competitive pay practices
		• Review and approve recommended changes in salary structure and bonus plan provisions
		• Approve additions and removals from bonus plan participation

(Continued)

Exhibit 1.5   (Continued)

- Review executive compensation budget, and approve annual salary increases for next year
- New ideas session (planning session for new ideas, plans, and programs)
- Discuss incentive measures for upcoming year
- Annual review of executive severance plans
- Review corporate compensation philosophy and pay strategy

opportunity to review them in advance and will be able to come to the meeting fully prepared to ask pertinent questions and move the discussion forward. Such materials should include minutes of the prior meeting, and materials and information pertinent to the agenda for the current meeting—such as copies of any plans or agreements to be considered by the committee, reports and analysis from outside experts, internally prepared information relevant to the matter, and proposed resolutions.

Engage outside experts. Issues faced by compensation committees today involve sophisticated techniques and require a facile understanding of financial measures and tax and accounting applications. The "level playing field" that resulted from stock option expensing has increased the use of alternative types of equity compensation vehicles, many of which may be less familiar to compensation committee members. The array of choices alone can be bewildering. Moreover, the role of the committee itself is becoming imbued with an overlay of regulatory requirements and legal nuances, while trends in shareholder litigation underscore the importance of relying on the advice of outside experts. Delaware courts in the well-publicized *Disney* and *Cendant* cases focused on the alleged failure of those compensation committees to seek expert advice in advance of important compensation decisions.

For these and other reasons, it is all but essential that the compensation committee look to competent outside compensation consultants and legal advisors. While it may be appropriate for the committee to engage its own legal counsel for special assignments, the relationship with the compensation consultant should be of an ongoing nature. It is axiomatic and essential that it should be the committee, and not management, that interviews and hires outside experts. The allegiance of such experts should be to the committee, and ultimately to the company, rather than to management.

Establish a meaningful CEO evaluation program. The compensation committee should create and adhere to an effective CEO evaluation program. NYSE and NASDAQ corporate governance rules require the compensation committee to review the CEO's performance on an annual basis, but this should be done regardless of any regulatory requirement. Such an evaluation is essential for the proxy statement CD&A, and provides a basis for determining whether the company's executive incentive compensation programs are achieving intended results. Chapter 3 addresses the CEO evaluation process.

Exhibit 1.6 Sample Form for Board Evaluation

Rate the following statements in relation to our board of directors

Topic	Description	Rating*
1.	The board knows and understands the company's beliefs, values, philosophy, mission, strategic plan, and business plan, and reflects this understanding on key issues throughout the year.	
2.	The board has and follows procedures for effective meetings.	
3.	Board meetings are conducted in a manner that ensures open communication, meaningful participation, and timely resolution of issues.	
4.	Board members receive timely materials for consideration prior to meetings.	
5.	Board members receive accurate minutes.	
6.	The board reviews and adopts annual capital and operating budgets.	
7.	The board monitors cash flow, profitability, net revenue and expenses, productivity, and other financially driven indicators to ensure the company performs as expected.	
8.	The board monitors company performance with industry comparative data.	
9.	Board members stay abreast of issues and trends affecting the company, and use this information to assess and guide the company's performance not just year to year, but in the long term.	
10.	Board members comprehend and respect the difference between the board's policy-making role and the CEO's management role.	
11.	The board acts to help the CEO by setting clear policy.	
12.	Board goals, expectations, and concerns are honestly communicated with the CEO.	

*Rating 1 to 3, with 1 for "meets expectations" to 3 for "exceed expectations"

Establish annual compensation committee (and perhaps board) evaluation programs. NYSE corporate governance rules require an annual self-performance evaluation by the compensation committee. If board compensation is within the purview of the compensation committee rather than the nominating/governance committee, it may also make sense for the compensation committee to implement the board evaluation program. The program should include feedback solicited from other directors, the CEO, other senior executives, and other interested parties. See Exhibit 1.6 for a sample board evaluation form.

2. GETTING AND STAYING INFORMED

Understand the context. The committee cannot make valid compensation decisions in a vacuum. Even where the committee does not have direct oversight or responsibility for all aspects of compensation and benefits, it is imperative that the committee have an understanding of how all the pieces of the puzzle fit together. The committee should have access to information necessary to calculate the value of an executive's total compensation arrangement at any given time. For example, if the committee is considering one element of pay for the CEO, such as a long-term equity award, it must be able to do so in the context of the CEO's total pay, including all forms of compensation and benefits (such as base salary, short-term incentive opportunity, qualified and nonqualified deferred compensation, SERPs, perquisites, severance arrangements, and other previously granted long-term incentives), to ensure that the total compensation is reasonable and not excessive.

Naturally, not all elements of pay will be considered at a single committee meeting, and not all information before the committee at a given time will be presented with equal detail or emphasis. However, as baseline contextual information, the committee should insist on regularly being provided with the senior executives' total compensation tallies—perhaps in the form of a simple spreadsheet showing each element of pay and benefits, a brief summary of how each pay program operates, and an estimate of current rates, benefit levels, or balances.

Understand each element of the compensation program. The compensation committee, not management or the human resources department, is the "owner" of the company's executive compensation and employment plans, programs, and arrangements. As such, it is the compensation committee's duty to thoroughly understand all compensation programs, both simple and complex.

There is no one "correct" way to conduct this review, as long as it results in a full and thorough examination of each program. Generally, this review will involve management (including the human resources department), the company's auditors, and the committee's independent advisors. Only when the committee has its arms around all aspects of each program can it make informed and appropriate decisions in implementing (and perhaps restructuring) the overall compensation strategy.

Regularly review and quantify the impact of termination and change-in-control provisions in all compensation plans and programs. Change-in-control (CIC) arrangements have become quite commonplace for senior executives at many public companies. At some companies, CIC agreements or policies extend protections deeper into employee ranks, and in some cases, cover all employees. The committee must keep sight of the estimated aggregate cost of all such CIC protections, including tax gross-ups and lost deductions, under various circumstances. Because circumstances change and compensation programs can dramatically affect the cost of CIC arrangements in not-so-obvious ways, this exercise should be undertaken on a regular basis to guard against surprises if and when an actual CIC situation arises. In assessing the potential cost, the committee should consider that aggregate CIC payments of 1 percent to 3 percent of the transaction amount are generally within standard practice, at least with respect to large public companies.

The SEC's new executive compensation disclosure rules require a public company to quantify in the proxy statement the amount that each named executive officer would receive from the company if he or she had terminated employment on the last day of the prior fiscal year, assuming termination under a variety of circumstances, including termination in connection with a change in control. This new specific disclosure requirement will necessitate a disciplined and detailed analysis of all compensation plans and arrangements at least annually.

3. KEEPING AN EYE ON THE BIG PICTURE

Compensation plans and programs should be consistent with the achievement of corporate strategy. This is especially true with incentive-based compensation. It makes little sense for the compensation programs to be motivating executives to achieve goals that do not help to achieve the company's business objectives.

The committee must take an active hand in the process. For example, with the aid of management and outside advisors, each member of the committee should learn and understand the financial measures that are most relevant to the company's success and design incentive programs on the basis of those measures. The committee should understand how any year-end financial reporting adjustments (or other events) might affect such measures and thereby affect compensation based on those measures. Where feasible, performance compensation programs should be designed to minimize the possibility of manipulation to achieve certain results—not on the assumption that management would do so, but more as evidence of a sound and reliable program.

The compensation committee should be prepared to explain to investors in the CD&A how the short-term and long-term incentive programs for executive officers relate specifically to and complement the company's overall strategy. Moreover, the committee should be thoughtful in setting and explaining goals for incentive compensation. For example, setting "stretch" or very demanding goals and being prepared to pay commensurate with achieving this level of performance, can be an effective driver of performance.

4. RETURNING TO REASON

There is no denying that executive compensation in the 1990s soared to unsustainable levels. Fueled by the seemingly endless bull market, the investing public's "irrational exuberance" (as dubbed by Alan Greenspan as early as 1996) and perhaps even unintentionally by the then-prevailing benchmarking practices of compensation consultants in which all executives were slated for above-average pay levels, executive compensation simply got out of hand. In the sobering post-scandal environment of the mid-2000s, boards and management alike recognize that something dramatic must be done to restore investor confidence and return compensation to sensible, sustainable levels. If the private sector cannot be disciplined and effective in achieving this, it is all but certain that Congress will intervene. We are already seeing this in the form of sweeping legislation passed in 2004 to regulate and control deferred compensation (IRC Section 409A, as discussed in Chapter 8), and other populist proposals such as (1) the "Say on Pay" legislation pending in Congress as of the time of this writing, which (if signed into law) would allow shareholders at public companies a nonbinding advisory vote on executive compensation as disclosed in the CD&A, summary compensation tables, and related material, and on any severance agreements that are reached while a company is considering a takeover proposal or merger, and (2) various Congressional revenue-raising proposals to impose an annual $1 million cap on deferred compensation and significantly expand the reach of IRC Section 162(m).

Steering the correction course requires the attention, support, and serious direction of the compensation committee. Consultants and advisors should be given free reign and encouragement to give an honest review and assessment of the company's pay practices and to speak up when changes are in order. The compensation committee must then be prepared to make hard decisions or negotiate with management if cutbacks on existing compensation are recommended in one area or another. Evidence of real negotiations with management can be of evidentiary importance in future shareholder litigation.

All this is not to say that executive pay is evil or unnecessary. It is, of course, still true that competitive compensation is needed to attract and retain the best executive talent. The compensation committee will continue to need to understand the "market" for executive compensation, both in form and levels of pay. Independent compensation specialists are best equipped to provide this information. However, the common practice of setting pay based on benchmarking for comparable positions gleaned from survey data is one of the main culprits for runaway compensation in the 1990s. This is because so many companies targeted executive pay at the 75th percentile of the selected peer group. It is easy to see, in hindsight, that this annual ratcheting effect—where this year's 75th percentile becomes the next year's 50th percentile—led to unrealistically high competitive data. Moreover, there is considerable room for manipulation of such studies, by cherry picking the peer companies, for example, to include those that recently experienced aberrational strong performance, those that emphasize one element of pay over others, or those that are not appropriate peers of the company based on revenue, market cap, or other factors. While the committee need not turn away from considering objective outside data as a legitimate measure of competitive practice, it can safeguard the process by making sure its consultants understand the committee's expectation of candor and objectivity, and by asking the right questions about how and why the data were selected. The mechanical process of compensation benchmarking is discussed later in this chapter.

5. CONSIDERING THE SHAREHOLDERS' PERSPECTIVE

The compensation committee must consistently ask the question, "Is this in the shareholders' best interests, and how will shareholders view it?" In today's business environment, shareholders are taking a greater interest than ever before in matters of executive compensation. While this does not change the duty or allegiance of the committee, it does provide a useful focus to its deliberations.

Shareholder value is paramount. In general, executive compensation should be accretive to shareholder value. Existing and new programs should be considered by the compensation committee in this context. The committee should analyze each compensation program with a view to its potential effects on financial results and shareholder dilution, and whether such effects can be managed or mitigated. For example, in the case of an equity-based compensation plan, the source of shares to pay participants (i.e., newly issued shares or repurchases in the market) can affect the dilution analysis.

Understand and consider institutional investor concerns. Institutional investors have been making their voices heard loud and clear, aided by a number of factors, including the post-Enron NYSE and NASDAQ rules that require shareholder approval for all new or materially modified equity compensation plans, new rules that prohibit brokers from voting street-name shares on compensation plan proposals without the express direction of the beneficial owners, and the increasingly high approval rate of shareholder proposals in recent proxy seasons. Shareholder activism has matured considerably from its roots in the 1970s. Independent research firms such as IRRC Institute for Corporate Responsibility glean, organize, and make available information on corporate governance and social responsibility issues affecting investors. IRRC does not advocate on any side of the issues it covers. A host of institutional investor advisory groups, such as Institutional Shareholder Services, Glass, Lewis & Co., and the Council of Institutional Investors, as well as large investor pension funds such as the Teachers Insurance and Annuity Association–College Retirement Equities Fund (TIAA-CREF), the California Public Employees' Retirement System (CalPERS), the State of Wisconsin Investment Board (SWIB), and the New York City Employees' Retirement System (NYCERS), and large mutual funds such as Fidelity Investments, take a more confrontational stance on issues. Most have formulated complex models for assessing the potential dilution and "value transfer" of proposed compensation plans. Together or individually, these groups make possible powerful voting and economic blocks that cannot be ignored.

The compensation committee should be proactive in anticipating institutional investor concerns. Corporate governance issues, such as the independence of directors, organization of the board, incentive plans and programs, CEO selection and succession, employment agreements, executive stock ownership, insider trading actions, compensation levels, and other related issues are fair game for shareholder comment. It is usually productive to seek the input of the company's largest institutional investors on compensation proposals well in advance of putting them up for shareholder vote. Often, it is possible to adjust proposed plan provisions in a way that will make the difference in the plan being approved or voted down.

6. COMMUNICATING EFFECTIVELY

Take control of the CD&A. The CD&A that appears in the annual proxy statement provides the best window into the work of the committee. The amount of candor, care, and detail that goes into that report speaks volumes about how seriously the committee takes its role and responsibility. The preparation of this report should not be relegated to management, the compensation consultant, or legal counsel. Rather, it should reflect the independent and thoughtful analysis of the committee, even if others participate in the drafting. In a shift of focus from prior years, the CD&A is "company disclosure" rather than a report of the compensation committee, and it is deemed "filed" with the SEC rather than "furnished." This means that the company has liability for the CD&A under applicable securities laws and the CD&A is covered by the CEO and CFO certifications required by the Sarbanes-Oxley Act of 2002. Because of these new, more stringent standards, it is expected and appropriate for the preparation of the CD&A to be a collaborative effort, involving management, finance, human resources, internal legal staff, and outside advisors. But the compensation committee, as the architect of the company's compensation philosophy and programs, should be a primary and active participant in the process. A straightforward and thorough explanation of the committee's actions and philosophy is critical to a meaningful report.

See Appendix E for sample CD&As taken from several 2007 proxy statements, the first year for such reports.

COMPENSATION BENCHMARKING

Compensation committees are constantly examining whether the compensation levels of the top executives are reasonable, both from an external perspective and an internal perspective. This is done for two reasons. First is to ensure that the pay levels are competitive, because if they are not (otherwise referred to as "below market"), another company may try to raid the executive talent pool. Second is to ensure that the compensation levels are neither too high nor too disproportionate (i.e., there is reasonable balance between salary, annual bonus, long-term incentives, pension, and so on).

This examination generally entails two processes. First is to collect and review recent and reputable surveys (usually published by compensation consulting or accounting firms). These surveys must be carefully reviewed to determine the methodology used and the quality of the data. For example, a survey might say that the median salary of CEOs in the biotechnology industry is $400,000; however, upon closer review, it may be discovered that only three companies were included, and that one of the companies has a founder CEO who receives a nominal salary. Accordingly, these surveys are helpful but cannot—in and of themselves—be used to set executive compensation levels.

The second process is to prepare a benchmarking or comparison study. This can be done in-house, but most companies prefer to use outside advisors. The most important aspect of these studies is to construct a peer group of companies that both the compensation committee and management agree represents "market." In addition, there should be a minimum of 10 peer companies. Generally, 15 to 30 companies would be preferred to ensure that any anomaly (known as an "outlier" or a "red circle") would not significantly impair the overall results. With the development of sophisticated databases, it is not uncommon for some companies to have peer groups in excess of 50 companies.

Peer companies generally are selected based on similarities to the subject company in terms of revenues, market capitalization, and/or industry, oftentimes using Standard Industrial Classification (SIC) codes that are the same as or similar to the subject company. Sometimes, other aspects are considered, such as geography, company age, financial performance, and so forth. No matter what and how many characteristics are used to construct the peer group, the key is for all parties to agree that the peer group is representative of an appropriate "market."

After the peer group is finalized, the next step is to collect and collate executive compensation data, either from private databases or culled from publicly filed documents, such as proxy statements and Form 10-Ks. Of course, each data point must be reviewed to ensure that it is correct. For example, some benchmarking studies will mingle different fiscal years. Other benchmarking studies may mechanically cull data from a proxy statement without any analysis, and thus could, for example, use an "annual salary" amount that actually is for a partial year. Other benchmarking studies may apply inconsistent valuation methodologies (such as valuation of stock options or other long-term incentive awards). In addition, more and more benchmarking studies are including performance analysis of each peer company. This is then used to determine whether the compensation level should be set at, below, or above the peer group's median level. For example, if the subject company is performing below the median of the peer group, then arguably the compensation levels should also be below the median of the peer group.

Finally, after all the data are collected, reviewed, and otherwise "scrubbed," it is placed into a model that typically shows quartiles and what percentile levels apply to the company's existing executives or candidates. An example of such a model is shown in Exhibit 1.7.

These models also typically show ratios, such as between target annual bonus and salary, long-term incentives (LTI) and salary, and LTI and total compensation. In addition, some companies use ratios to set executive compensation levels below the CEO (e.g., the chief operating officer's salary level is set at 75 percent of the CEO's salary level).

While many companies have used these benchmarking studies as a rigid guide to setting executive compensation, the better practice is to apply both an objective and subjective analysis of the data. In other words, the data are first quantitatively reviewed and then qualitatively reviewed. The reason for this is that each company has its own particular set of facts and circumstances, and square pegs should not be forced into round holes. For example, assume a company wants to pay its CEO at "market median," that the median CEO salary of the peer group is determined to be $500,000, and the salary of the subject company's CEO is $650,000. The compensation committee, however, when it hired the CEO, agreed to the $650,000 salary level because that was the CEO's salary level at the previous employer. Accordingly, the salary level will be in the upper quartile, and the compensation committee will most

Exhibit 1.7 CEO Benchmarking Study Template

Company	CEO	Salary	Target Bonus	Total Actual Bonus	Total Cash Comp	Stock Awards	Stock Options	Other LTI	Total LTI	Other Comp	Total Comp
1											
2											
3											
...											
20											
Subject company											
Minimum											
25th percentile											
50th percentile											
75th percentile											
Maximum											
Average											

likely need to adjust other components of this CEO's compensation (but not the salary) to bring it within "market median."

THE IMPORTANCE OF COMPENSATION COMMITTEE MEETING MINUTES

Today's heightened focus on corporate governance in general, and executive compensation in particular, justifies a close review of the processes of the compensation committee, and its documentation of the same. It has always been customary corporate practice to keep minutes of committee meetings. However, it is important to recognize that minutes, which are easily attainable by shareholders, are as important in what they don't say as what they do say.

Historically, many companies have taken the view that perfunctory, bare-bones minutes were adequate and even preferred—a means of satisfying minimum corporate procedural requirements without airing dirty laundry in the form of dissenting opinions or serious debate that might suggest lack of unanimity or weakness of resolve. However, recent shareholder litigation and apparent trends in judicial review, as discussed more fully in Chapter 5, suggest that the better approach favors thoughtful minutes that reflect in detail the ultimate action taken, discussion of each topic, the time devoted to the discussion, the alternatives reviewed, the consideration of relevant materials and outside advice, and the rationale for each decision reached. Two well-publicized Delaware court cases illustrate how the quality of minutes can make a difference very early in the litigation process.

In 2003, the Delaware Chancery Court refused to dismiss a complaint by shareholders in *In re Walt Disney Co. Derivative Litigation*, 825 A.2d 275 (Del Ch. 2003), alleging that Disney's directors breached their fiduciary duties when they approved an employment agreement with its president, Michael Ovitz, which ultimately resulted in an award to him allegedly exceeding $140 million after barely one year of employment. The court focused heavily on what was reflected in the minutes of the compensation committee, from which it appeared that:

- No draft employment agreement was presented to the compensation committee for review before the meeting.

- The committee received only a summary of the employment agreement, and no questions were asked about the agreement.

- No expert consultant was present to advise the compensation committee.

- The compensation committee met for less than an hour and spent most of its time on two other topics, including the compensation of one director for helping secure Ovitz's employment.

- No time was taken to review the documents for approval.

- The committee approved the hiring in principle but directed Michael Eisner, Disney's CEO and Ovitz's close friend, to carry out the negotiations with regard to certain still unresolved and significant details.

Referring to the board meeting that followed the compensation committee meeting, the court further noted that less than 2 of 15 pages of minutes were devoted to discussions of hiring the new president and that, so far as such minutes reflected, no presentations were made to the board regarding the terms of the draft agreement, no questions were raised, and no expert consultant was present to give advice.

The *Disney* court concluded that the alleged facts, if true, could support a determination that the defendant directors' action went beyond a mere breach of the duty of care to amount to a lack of good faith, such that their action would not be protected by the business judgment rule or by the company's director exculpation provision in its charter. If so, the directors could be held personally liable and unindemnifiable. Ultimately, after a full trial on the merits, the Delaware court in *Disney* determined that the directors did not breach their duties of care or good faith, although the process they followed fell short of current best practices. The lesson from the early phase of the *Disney* case remains intact: that thoughtfully prepared minutes can make the difference as to whether a well-pled fiduciary duty claim survives a motion to dismiss.

Also to the point is the April 2004 settlement of shareholder litigation against Cendant Corporation. The complaint alleged the directors breached their fiduciary duties in approving an amendment to the CEO's employment agreement that would have provided, among other things, an uncapped annual bonus stated as a percentage of the company's pretax earnings, $100 million of life insurance for the rest of his life, and severance benefits that could have exceeded $140 million. According to the complaint, the minutes of the compensation committee reflected:

- No analysis of the potential cost to Cendant of the new agreement
- No discussion of the committee's deliberation on various aspects of the proposed changes to the agreement
- No advice from outside advisors, such as compensation experts or independent legal advisors
- No questions raised about the financial consequences to the company under various severance scenarios
- No involvement by any member of the compensation committee in the negotiation of the agreement

Even if the directors did in fact exercise more care and deliberation than alleged, the quick settlement of this lawsuit (the month after it was filed) might indicate the defendants' recognition of the damning potential of scant minutes on their ability to establish adequate proof to the contrary.

The lesson from these cases and others sure to come is this: Adherence to fiduciary duties is an absolute requirement, and keeping minutes that reflect the proper amount of attention, deliberation, and consideration of compensation decisions can be of pivotal evidentiary value in shielding directors from personal liability.

Accordingly, compensation committee meeting minutes should reflect:

- Each discussion topic and the approximate time that the matter was considered
- Whether outside advisors were present or consulted and the extent of their involvement
- The committee's consideration of any cost analyses for specific proposals, such as financial modeling of employment and severance contracts under various scenarios
- Whether questions were asked, about what in general, and by whom (but minutes need not, and should not, be at the level of a transcript of the meeting)
- Due consideration by the committee of the reasonableness of the particular element of pay being voted on, when viewed in context with the executive's overall compensation package

CALL TO ACTION

The work of the modern compensation committee is serious business. Much progress has been made over the course of the last five years since the monumental corporate failures that set in motion a deluge of corporate reform measures. Compensation committees, for the most part, have exhibited a sincere effort to restore the trust of corporate America, but it is not an overnight task. As difficult as it has been in the last three years to grapple with the sea change in accounting rules and tax and securities legislation that affect all aspects of executive pay, the compensation committee cannot afford to take a breather. Until there is widespread perception that the excesses of prior years are under control, we can expect to see more pressure brought to bear from all quarters: Congress, shareholder advocates, and the mainstream media. The groundwork has been laid, the paving has begun, and the road stretches out before us.

Chapter 2

Selecting and Training Compensation Committee Members

For purposes of this chapter, it will be assumed that the company seeks new independent directors to round out the board and staff its core oversight committees, including the compensation committee. The chapter will first discuss the processes the nominating committee should follow to identify and attract qualified independent individuals who are best suited to serve as independent directors for their particular company. Later, the chapter will discuss the orientation and training of the individuals who are selected to fill that role.

As discussed in Chapter 1, independence is the core requirement for the compensation committee. However, independence is not the sole determinant of its success. Particularly now, as compensation programs are under public scrutiny and have evolved well beyond the historical reliance on "plain vanilla" stock options and cash bonuses, it is imperative that compensation committee members have a facile understanding of the evolving landscape of executive pay and the expanding array of compensation vehicles available to shape desired results. They must be able to use this knowledge to devise programs that are straightforward, transparent, and effective. To this end, the committee should receive continuing training and employ the advice of independent experts and advisors.

THE ROLE OF THE NOMINATING COMMITTEE

The New York Stock Exchange (NYSE) and The Nasdaq Stock Market (NASDAQ) recognize that a fully independent nominating committee is central to the effective functioning of the board, and that director and board committee nominations are among the board's most important functions. NYSE-listed companies must have a nominating/corporate governance committee that is made up exclusively of independent directors. This committee is charged with identifying individuals qualified to become board members, consistent with criteria approved by the board, and to select, or to recommend that the board select, the director nominees for the next annual meeting of shareholders. Under NASDAQ rules, director nominees must be selected, or recommended for the full board's selection, either by a nominating committee comprised solely of independent directors or by a majority of the independent directors.

The rationale for this is that an independent nominating committee enhances the independence and quality of the nominees. This notion holds true for nonlisted companies as well. Given today's focus on sound corporate governance principles, it makes sense for private and other nonlisted companies to take advantage of the careful thought that has been applied to these issues by the NYSE, NASDAQ, the Securities and Exchange Commission (SEC), and influential business and investor groups.

While the nominating committee may be separate from a corporate governance committee, those functions are often combined in a single committee under a combined designation. Either such committee (or the combined committee) may be assigned to periodically review and make recommendations regarding the size of the board, committee structure and committee assignments, and frequency of regular board and committee meetings. In some cases, the nominating or corporate governance committee also specifies the roles and responsibilities of each board committee, in keeping with the corporate charter and bylaws and the specific requirements for the composition and function of committees as imposed by the NYSE, NASDAQ, and the SEC, where applicable. Management's input to these decisions may be considered, but predominant and best practice is to leave the ultimate decisions to the independent nominating or corporate governance committee.

NOMINATION AND SELECTION OF NEW COMPENSATION COMMITTEE MEMBERS

Finding and selecting qualified outside directors is one of the most challenging and rewarding dimensions of building an effective compensation committee. Before beginning the search for new directors, the company should develop a board prospectus. The board prospectus can be a helpful tool in recruiting director candidates, and can assist the company in networking with lenders, advisors, and others who might know of attractive director candidates. A sample board prospectus is shown in Exhibit 2.1.

Exhibit 2.1   Sample Board Prospectus

We seek one independent director to round out our board of directors and help us manage the future of our successful corporation. We believe our business and industry will face new issues more complex and challenging than we have confronted before. We believe a board consisting of a majority of qualified independent and experienced directors to be an invaluable resource to aid in providing the very best return to our shareholders. The following describes our company and the roles and purpose we envision for our board.

Our Company

We are the largest company of its kind in the southeastern part of the United States. We have 25 locations and a significant investment in real estate through three real-estate

---

holding companies. We have several separate but related lines of business. In all, we are a $450-million enterprise with 3,200 employees.

We provide the highest quality and broadest line of high-end products and services to our customers. We are proud to have recently received the very first "Blue Ribbon" award in our industry. We reach our customers through a valued 100-year-old reputation and well-managed public relations. Market reputation in this business, however, can be overturned by only one year of poor performance.

The Immediate Needs of the Board

The company's local and traditional market has matured. The changing attitudes of consumers to our industry and products require major changes to our company. Recent federal legislation will greatly affect the structure of our industry and how firms in our industry compete. The company must invent new ways of designing, manufacturing, distributing, selling, and servicing our products. To do this, we need to refocus the company's business while at the same time raise significant capital.

The Purpose of the Board

The primary purpose of the board is to help management to increase shareholder value. The company will benefit from successful independent directors who bring their diverse experience to bear on the best interests of the company.

The board will help management evaluate the key issues and decisions facing our business. The board will offer a forum to discuss important and strategic decisions, while bringing a fresher perspective that will encourage corporate management to consider additional alternatives.

The Nature of the Board

Our board will be comprised of eight members: the CEO and seven outside directors. You will be replacing a 62-year-old director who is not standing for renomination. Of the six other outside directors, four are current or former CEOs of their own businesses, one is the president of a major local university, and one is the managing partner of a large, local law firm.

Our board will formally meet four times per year at a morning meeting. The day usually begins very early at 7:30 A.M., and ends in mid-afternoon. Each independent director will serve on one or more of the following committees: audit, compensation, and nominating/corporate governance. Committees meet an average of four times a year.

Conclusion

We believe an additional experienced independent director will assist corporate management in this challenging time in the company's evolution.

The board prospectus should describe clearly the purpose and goals of the board. It should convey the qualities and capabilities the board is seeking in directors, and describe the board structure, director compensation, and anticipated time demands on members. The board prospectus should convey the business, culture, philosophy, and values of the company. This prospectus usually includes the information in Exhibit 2.2.

Exhibit 2.2   Typical Elements of a Board Prospectus

I. Overview of the Company
   A. Industry
   B. Most important products and types of consumers
   C. Size
   D. Major shareholders

II. Board Profile
   A. Character of business
     • Stage of life cycle (start-up, rapidly growing, mature)
     • Relative strengths or weaknesses (highest quality producer in the region, need to develop more cost-conscious culture)
     • Strategic thrust (developing an international presence, seeking to grow by acquisition, committed to increasing market share)
   B. Relationship of the board with management
   C. Personal criteria of candidates
     • Desired background, personal characteristics, and experience of board candidates

III. Structure of the Board
   A. Number of independent directors and management/investor directors on the board
   B. Committee structure
   C. Number of meetings (board and committee)
   D. Time commitment
   E. Compensation
   F. Director indemnification and insurance
   G. Term of office
   H. Mandatory retirement age or term limitations

The search for new directors begins typically with the nominating committee, which may request recommendations from the chief executive officer (CEO) and other directors. Whatever the source of the recommendation, the nominating committee should carefully evaluate each candidate. Politics, bolstering egos, repaying debts, conveying thanks, rewarding performance, and satisfying interest groups should not play a role in selecting directors. The nominating committee should select new board members—and renominate existing board members—with one purpose in mind: to meet the specific needs and best interests of the company as they evolve over time.

A typical search for independent directors begins with an overview of the needs of the board—representation that may be lacking or need more emphasis. For example, the company may seek greater diversity on its board, or may seek a new director with experience in a particular sector (e.g., academic, public service, business, nonprofit) or area of useful expertise. Perhaps the board would benefit from directors with more time availability or higher profile in the company's industry or community.

The following sections illustrate possible strengths and weaknesses of various categories of outside board candidates.

COMPETITORS

Directors or officers of current or potential competitors generally do not make ideal candidates because of their inherent conflict of interest. This is another reason to seek directors from other industries so as to take advantage of their fresh perspectives and new insights, rather than an affirmation of what management already knows. Often, the best place to find such insight is from directors with backgrounds in different industries facing analogous challenges and problems.

CONSULTANTS

Paid advisors are not usually good candidates for board service. Such status would render them nonindependent under NYSE and NASDAQ rules and ineligible to serve on any core committees of the board. The services of outside consultants are readily available to the board in any event; as directors, they bring to the boardroom an inherent conflict of interest. The board can always invite trusted advisors to attend board sessions—it is not necessary to make them directors to reap the benefits of their knowledge.

Where technical "independence" is not a requirement, some boards may make an exception for advisors who have broad exposure to top executives in a wide range of companies. These professionals often develop executive skills and can be a valuable resource, even if they lack first-hand executive experience.

FRIENDS

Directors should never be selected on the basis of friendships with management or existing directors. Such personal ties can lead to allegations of cronyism (whether or not true) and jeopardize the independence and effectiveness of the board. Moreover, the candid exchange of viewpoints needed from directors can put a strain on friendships. Even at the recruitment stage, it may be difficult to objectively interview and assess the references of such candidates.

RETIREES

Retired executives from other industries often make promising director candidates. For example, many retirees enjoy high visibility, generous time availability, and useful experience. However, there can be drawbacks. A retiree may eventually lose touch with the mainstream of business or become overly enamored with board service as a source of retirement income, ego support, or stimulation. If a retiree becomes beholden to management and the other directors to maintain his or her seat on the board, it may compromise the independent contribution he or she might otherwise make.

ACADEMICS

Academics can be good director candidates for the right board. They provide an excellent source of intellectual capital, tend to have reasonable time availability, and often are skillful in consensus building and tactful interaction among those having divergent viewpoints. However, they may lack the "real world" experience that can be useful in a profit-driven business environment.

PEOPLE WHO HOLD OTHER DIRECTORSHIPS

People who serve on other boards make tempting director candidates, due to their relevant experience. However, serving on too many boards at once can curtail the effectiveness of directors.

OTHER CEOS, ENTREPRENEURS, OR BUSINESS OWNERS

Experienced peers often make excellent outside directors. Executives from other companies who have weathered crises at their own companies can provide invaluable counsel to the board facing similar or even dissimilar business challenges. However, the nominating committee should avoid creating interlocking relationships where, for example, any of the company's executive officers serve on the candidate's board. As discussed in Chapter 1, overlapping (or interlocking) directorships can compromise a director's independence, causing him or her to temper decisions and comments to protect the other relationship. Another issue to guard against in selecting directors who are CEOs of another company is the so-called "kindred spirit" phenomenon, in which the director may be disinclined to be critical of management because he or she sympathizes with the discomfort of dealing with a "difficult" board.

TIME COMMITMENT

At a minimum, attendance at four board meetings per year, including preparation and travel time, would take about eight days per year. However, all outside directors will most likely serve on one or more oversight committees, which require a substantially greater time commitment in terms of preparation for and attendance at meetings, interaction with management and outside advisors, ongoing training, and taking a leadership role in special projects. In that case, the minimum time commitment can quickly balloon to 30 days per year.

A key issue to consider in the selection of board members is time availability. Directors who do not have time to attend and adequately prepare for board meetings and devote concentrated effort to committee work will not contribute to an effective board. Spreading committee assignments effectively among board members can alleviate the time commitment required of well-qualified directors.

Ideally, all directors will have equal time and energy to devote to the business of the board and committees on which they serve. However, in the real world, some will have more time availability and others will provide more value for other characteristics. In selecting outside directors, the nominating committee would do well to acknowledge and plan for this. For example, outside directors who have full-time positions elsewhere or serve on a number of other boards may make invaluable contributions but may have minimal time to devote to the company's board, while directors who are retired or are in academia may have more time. If possible, the nominating committee should try to balance the board and its committee assignments accordingly to provide the most effective allocation of director resources.

In the nomination process, it is important that all candidates fully understand and buy into the notion that they must be prepared to devote the time, regardless of personal or professional inconvenience, to meet their responsibilities to the board, particularly in times of unexpected activity such as major litigation, responding to a takeover proposal, or considering strategic business alternatives for the company.

DIVERSITY

Diversity of the board and its compensation committee allows for a variety of experiences and knowledge to bring to bear on the issues under consideration by the committee. A diverse board or committee is in a position to make better decisions, because issues must be considered from a variety of perspectives. The move toward organizational diversity begins with commitment and open-mindedness.

As companies demand more of their board members, both in terms of time and technical expertise, and as shareholders become more active in governance, the pressures are intensifying to diversify and broaden board and committee membership. More and more major institutional investors are citing diversity as a criterion in making or maintaining investment positions.

ATTRACTING CANDIDATES

Quality boards and quality companies attract quality directors. Having excellent outside advisors available to the board (auditors, legal advisors, and compensation consultants) will serve to allay any concerns that a good director candidate may have about personal liability arising from legal or accounting irregularities. A healthy diversity of industries represented on the board may also help attract director candidates who are senior executives from outside of the company's industry. For example, a CEO from another industry serving on the company's board can profit personally from the exchange of ideas among fellow board members hailing from industries other than his or her own.

In general, the following factors attract good directors:

- Quality of management
- Ethics of the company
- Prospect of serving with respected peers
- Opportunity to learn
- Opportunity to make a difference—to make an impact on the future direction of an organization in a measurable way
- Opportunity to use his or her own knowledge and expertise
- Opportunity to network with top business leaders
- Opportunity to serve in a prestigious position
- Compensation—to a limited degree
- Entrepreneurial spirit, an opportunity to create something special
- Personal challenge

A proactive, enthusiastic approach to the director search goes a long way to attracting superlative directors.

CONDUCTING THE SEARCH

Conducting a successful search for directors is a time-consuming process, including researching and educating potential candidates and conducting initial and callback interviews. Using a professional search firm can be an effective and efficient way to guide the process, although not inexpensive. In general, the company should be prepared to pay up to the equivalent of one year's director's fees for the service.

In practice, large public companies tend to use professional search firms to find new directors, particularly now that there is high demand for independent directors who have an advanced level of expertise in one or more substantive areas. Small to mid-sized firms and private companies use such firms more sparingly. These companies most often select directors who are personally known to current board members. Other prevalent sources of referral are directors of other companies and professional trade organizations.

Professional trade organizations, such as the National Association of Corporate Directors (NACD) and Catalyst, local chambers of commerce, business roundtables, and other similar organizations can be a useful starting place for a search for appropriate director candidates. These organizations typically keep biographies of their members, which can be prescreened by the company for promising director candidates. The NACD, for example, makes available a confidential directory service for companies recruiting directors.

Whatever search method is employed, a typical search may result in consideration of 20 to 25 candidates to derive a list of three to five finalists who are acceptable for board service. The nominating committee should review the list to cull out any who may be unacceptable, for one reason or another. Then, the nominating committee, perhaps with the CEO and/or search firm representative, should meet with the finalists for more in-depth interviews.

A search for new board members can take several months. This process can be shortened if board recruiting is an ongoing process. The nominating committee should always have three to five promising candidates in mind should there be a need to replace directors or expand the board.

Using an outside search firm allows the nominating committee to select among prequalified, available candidates, best using the committee's time to focus on the culture, the fit, and the vision. The following are some of the other advantages of using a competent outside recruiter:

- Allows the company to proactively recruit to its strategic plan and critical issues
- Gives access to the broadest spectrum of targeted, qualified candidates
- Allows the search to extend beyond the board's own circle of influence
- Provides a more extensive choice among highly qualified candidates
- Validates the board to potential director candidates
- Validates the board to the company's constituents (shareholders, senior officers, alliance partners)
- Provides an objective point of reference and interview process
- Promotes integrity, confidentiality, and discretion in the director search
- Increases the efficiency of the search by eliminating less qualified candidates early in the process
- Promotes the goodwill of the CEO, candidates, directors, and constituents

HOW TO APPROACH CANDIDATES

Once a list of qualified candidates has emerged, the focus shifts to seeking information from the candidates to narrow the field to those with the best fit. Some of the following questions can solicit useful information from the candidates:

- Why do you want to serve on the board of this company?
- What is your opinion of the company? (Does he or she have knowledge of how the company competes, how it markets, who its competition is, who its customers are, what its critical issues are?)
- How will you contribute to the board? (Ask for clear and simple examples of how the candidate can contribute.)
- What are your specific areas of expertise? How will your expertise add value to the board?

- What is your financial acumen? (Each director should have the ability to read and understand financial analysis, but need not have a professional financial or accounting background.)
- On how many other boards do you serve? (List for-profit and not-for-profit separately.) What role do you play on those boards?
- What is your view of the role of the board and corporate governance?
- What has been your most rewarding experience as a director?
- How specifically have you added value to the boards on which you serve?
- What has been your most difficult experience as a director?
- Are you willing and able to commit to the level of participation we require?
- What are your concerns?

CEO INVOLVEMENT IN THE SELECTION PROCESS

Current NYSE and NASDAQ rules require a nominating committee of independent directors to take the lead in nominating and renominating directors. That duty often includes assigning directors to oversight committees, such as the compensation committee, and selecting committee chairs. However, management, and in particular the CEO, should have an opportunity to provide input to these decisions. It is important that all key constituents (nominating committee, other board members, management, and the new director) be comfortable with the process. If managed well, the new board member should begin on a positive footing, knowing that he or she has the backing of several constituencies participating in the selection.

MAKING THE FINAL SELECTION

In screening director candidates, some of the most important qualities to consider are also the simplest. At a minimum, the candidate should exhibit integrity and the ability to make thoughtful and sometimes difficult decisions.

The candidate should show candor, an eagerness to learn, and a lively interest in the business and work of the board and the committees on which he or she is likely to serve. The candidate should demonstrate courage of conviction, readiness to express his or her viewpoint, and the kind of personality that can be effective in a boardroom setting—an ability to be a team player, for instance.

With respect to each serious candidate for director, the nominating committee should conduct a personal interview and a comprehensive review of his or her background and experience and compare the findings with the needs of the board. A successful board selection process can make the difference in the company's ability to recruit other qualified directors. Every director nominated to the board serves as an incentive or disincentive for other prospective directors to serve.

In identifying and selecting directors for an effective board, the following criteria should be considered and weighed as appropriate:

- *Availability*. With the increased focus on corporate governance, serving as a director, particularly a director of a public company, requires a serious time commitment, as discussed previously. The days are gone for "social" director-ships, in which the primary time commitment is for perfunctory quarterly meetings followed by an afternoon of golf and dinner. Even the best qualified directors will not be effective if they do not have the time to devote serious attention to the business of the board and the committees on which they serve.

- *Intelligence*. Intelligence is a baseline requirement, but it comes in many different forms. One aspect is the director's ability to offer a fresh look at an old problem, even in an area in which he or she lacks practical experience. For directors who are not experienced in the company's business sector or with board service in general, the company can provide education and training opportunities to make them more effective directors. Director training sessions are offered by many educational institutions, including Harvard, Wharton, University of Chicago, Stanford, Yale, and Duke University, and by independent business groups such as the NACD.

- *Reputation*. A director's high-profile reputation in the business community can be especially important for the board of an emerging company, a company in a turnaround situation, or a company moving toward a broadly held shareholder base. Often, however, there is a trade-off between a director's reputation and availability, which should be taken into consideration. Reputation is always hard to measure, and can be favorable or unfavorable. A review of the candidate's own publications and references to the candidate in the media can be enlightening in assessing his or her business or professional reputation. It is also useful to check the references of the candidate with peers in his or her respective field.

- *Communication skills*. The ability to communicate effectively—especially extemporaneously in a group setting—is an important quality for a corporate director. Personal interviews with the candidate can be particularly instructive as to this ability. It is not always true that a polished public speaker is also an effective communicator in a give-and-take setting, such as the boardroom.

- *Experience*. Relevant experience can be an important determinant of the effec-tiveness of a potential director, whether it be:
  - Direct experience in the company's industry
  - Prior experience as a director in other companies
  - Executive managerial experience in another company

- *Leverage*. Leverage denotes the ability of the director to use his or her pro-fessional affiliations to expand the company's relationships (such as the ability of an investment banker director to introduce the company into the capital markets), and to provide additional management expertise in areas identified as lacking on the board (such as the ability of a director experienced in marketing to provide insight to an industrial company seeking to expand into consumer products). In some cases, especially for emerging companies or companies undergoing a transformation, a director's leverage can be an important factor.

The weight placed on each of these factors should be guided by the company's needs, the strengths and shortcomings of other board members, and the urgency of finding a new board member. To organize an evaluation of several director candidates, the company should rank the criteria and then rank the candidates.

An illustration of such an evaluation appears in the following paragraphs and in Exhibit 2.3.

A middle-market public company is searching for an outside director to fill the role of the retiring chairman of the compensation committee. The company's current board is comprised of a majority of high-profile, independent directors drawn from locally based, large public companies. The retiring director noted as one reason for her retirement from the board her lack of adequate time to devote to the business of the compensation committee.

A primary focus of the nominating committee, therefore, is that the new director has available time to serve as chairman of the compensation committee. In addition, the nominating committee is seeking a candidate ranking high in intelligence, communication skills, and professional reputation, but experience and leverage are not strong criteria in the search.

The candidates making the final cut are:

- *Candidate A.* The new CEO of the retiring board member's company. This candidate comes from outside of the company's industry and outside of the local area. He is very well regarded professionally and gets high marks for relevant experience.

- *Candidate B.* A business school professor in her mid-40s. She has a reasonably successful academic career, and has a Ph.D in economics from Stanford University.

Exhibit 2.3 Illustration of a Candidate Evaluation Summary

	Outside Director Candidates				
	Weight	A	B	C	D
Availability	10	4	10	7	9
Communication skills	10	8	6	8	7
Intelligence	8	6	10	10	6
Reputation	7	8	4	7	7
Experience	4	10	4	6	8
Leverage	2	8	3	7	4
Total weighted score		280	290	317	297

She has little relevant experience other than her role as a department chairperson at her business school.

- *Candidate C.* A local lawyer who does no work for the company and specializes in intellectual property law (a particularly important matter with the company). This lawyer also serves on the board of another publicly held company. She is a Rhodes Scholar who graduated first in her class at Harvard University. She also has served as head of her law firm's executive committee.

- *Candidate D.* A prematurely retired senior executive from a large local company. After his retirement, this executive went on to run an emerging company for two years, and has since left that firm. He is in his late 50s, currently serves on two boards, and wants to serve on one more to round out his work schedule.

According to Exhibit 2.3, candidate C is the best qualified closely followed by candidates B and D. While candidate C does not have as much availability as B and D, her high ranks in intelligence and communication skills and moderately high rank in professional reputation make her the first choice overall.

HOW TO SAY NO

For every candidate who is ultimately selected for the board, there are others who will need to be rejected. This task can be made easier if the process is managed responsibly. For example, a thorough prescreening process will reduce the number of candidates who reach the final stages of consideration. The board should not let the screening process go too far unless there is strong interest in the candidate. It would be a mistake, for example, to set up more than one meeting with a candidate or ask him or her to the company to "meet and greet" the board and senior executives unless the nominating committee considers the person a serious and well-qualified contender for the position.

When the time comes to end the solicitation of a particular candidate, the best approach is to emphasize the goals communicated at the outset of the screening process—to select a complementary group of people with a mix of backgrounds and expertise to match the needs of the company.

WHAT IF THE NEW DIRECTOR DOES NOT WORK OUT?

Despite the favorable odds associated with a well-planned and thorough director search or committee assignment, boards sometimes make mistakes in selecting or assigning directors. Errors usually do not become clear immediately. It may take as much as a year or two for a board to conclude that a particular director is not making an adequate contribution. Annual director performance evaluations will hasten the determination and allow corrections to be made on a more timely basis.

Once mistakes are discovered, boards should act promptly to make corrections or reassignments, however uncomfortable that process may be. Most often, the best way to deal with the problem is for the chair of the nominating committee (or other appropriate board representative) to approach the nonperforming director directly and explain that he or she will not be nominated for reelection (or in some cases to ask for an early resignation), and the reason for that decision. Sometimes, the explanation may be that the needs of the business are changing and the board needs new directors having skills and backgrounds different from his or her own. Other times, the explanation must be more direct, but can still be delivered in a nonthreatening and congenial manner.

In most cases, an underperforming but honest director will be asked to serve out the remainder of his or her current term and not stand for reelection. The company's public relations team can help to manage communications about the reason for the director's departure from the board.

The nominating committee may turn to professional advisors, such as director search firms, in reconfiguring the company's board, particularly if more than one director needs to be removed. In addition to assisting with the director assessment, such firms can also meet with the soon-to-be removed director to lessen the tension in a delicate situation.

BENEFITS OF AN EDUCATED BOARD

The most effective directors understand the specific business concerns of the company or the committees they serve, and the overall economic, political, and social environment in which the company exists and competes. All directors should be prepared to consider and discuss a multitude of complex issues in the appropriate context. Membership on a board, particularly in today's environment, is more than just a position of honor—it is a position of public trust. Effective participation on a board can be enhanced through training and continuing education on topics ranging from new technologies and developments in the company's particular business, to new approaches in effective organizational leadership and corporate governance.

Through systematic and appropriately focused training, board members can enhance their own leadership skills and competencies and increase their knowledge. A skilled and knowledgeable board results in an organization better able to serve its shareholders, employees, and community.

ORIENTATION OF NEW MEMBERS

While the director recruitment process serves as an initial stage of orientation, the process should not stop there. A proper board orientation program should entail more than introductions to other board members and management and a summary of the logistics of board meetings. New board members should be instructed as to the organization's mission, goals, products, and services, and the company's expectations of its board of directors. Some organizations conduct orientation sessions for prospective members; others hold them for new members only once they join the board. In either case, a primary purpose of board orientation is to give new members information about the organization's operations and their roles as board members.

Directors who serve on core committees, such as the compensation committee, should receive ongoing topical training of relevance to the mission of the committee. Compensation committees are encouraged to engage outside consultants and advisors (independent of management) to assist the committee in understanding and designing compensation programs that effectively drive performance, while reflecting current compensation philosophies and evolutions in relevant legal and accounting rules.

Some companies maintain a checklist for new board members whereby the director must spend time with various executives throughout the company, such as executives in the legal and human resources departments and the corporate secretary. Other companies provide paid educational opportunities for directors in programs offered by major universities and organizations such as the NACD.

A planned, systematic approach to orientation is most effective. Exhibit 2.4 suggests one orientation approach that can be modified to suit different circumstances.

Exhibit 2.4   Suggestions for Director Orientation Program

I. Plan the Orientation Program

   A. During recruitment, prospects should have learned what is generally expected of them as members of the board of directors. The board's written job description should include a statement that participation in orientation is mandatory, so it will not come as a surprise when one or two days (not necessarily consecutive) are spent on orientation activities.

   B. Plan the distribution of materials in accordance with each orientation activity. Too much written material too soon is overwhelming.

   C. Use the background data gathered during recruitment to tailor presentations according to a new member's personal and professional interests.

   D. Consider assigning a sponsor—an experienced board member—to each new director, making sure the purpose of this relationship is clear to both.

II. Orient New Members to the Organization

   A. Schedule a meeting with the CEO to give the new board member an opportunity to ask specific questions about the organization's operations, culture, and most important current issues. For the CEO, meeting with new board members provides a chance to establish a good working relationship early on.

   B. Board members will be called upon to make decisions regarding the company's physical plant and employees, so onsite visits are vital to the role of the director. With this in mind, plan a tour of a representative sample of the company's various facilities (e.g., factory, headquarters building, training facility, sales office, distribution warehouse, etc.). Even if the organization is not a facilities-based business, a visit to the main office where the organization conducts its business is highly recommended.

   C. Prepare a brief two- or three-page synopsis of key organizational demographics: customers, employees, suppliers, company milestones, major changes over the past five years, executive officer roster (with photos and detailed biographies), trends, and other appropriate data to supplement oral presentations.

D. Arrange for new members to attend an executive staff meeting or briefing session by the CEO's staff. The new directors should have the opportunity to meet key personnel, learn about their respective areas of responsibility, and ask questions.

III. Orient Members to the Board

A. Have the board chair make a welcoming call or visit to all new members.

B. Distribute a biographical sketch of the new members to the full board, including members' terms and committee assignments, places and positions of employment, contact information, and other relevant information.

C. Hold an informal social function to help integrate new members with the rest of the board.

D. Schedule a meeting for all new board members with the executive committee and other committee chairs. This gives newcomers an opportunity to become acquainted with the board's leadership and with the activities of the committees. A discussion of board procedures, directors' roles, responsibilities and liabilities, and major issues facing the organization provides new members with useful perspectives on the whole organization.

E. Distribute the board manual (or briefing book), which should include some or all of the following information to the new directors, as relevant:
- Company organization chart with officer biographies
- Mission statements
- Strategic plans
- Most recent proxy statement and annual report to shareholders
- Core strategies
- Company history
- Board materials, including the board charter, structure, needs matrix, directors' biographies, meeting dates, locations, committee assignments, summaries and processes, and profiles for any open board seats
- Marketing materials
- Customer profiles
- Articles and information sources on the industry
- Competition data
- Financial statements
- Insider trading policy
- Analyst reports
- Corporate bylaws and committee charters
- Corporate calendar
- Board and committee meeting minutes
- Director compensation package
- Director evaluation program
- Management succession plan
- Short-term and long-term incentive plans

(Continued)

F. Provide time for a debriefing among the new members, board chair, and CEO so any questions and concerns can be clarified. Debriefing sessions also can be an opportunity to ask new board members which parts of the orientation were most helpful, which were the least helpful, and how future board orientations might be improved.

ONGOING TRAINING

Initial board orientation should be followed by systematic and focused training opportunities, including regularly scheduled retreats or renewal sessions, and occasional training programs or workshops on special topics.

Some companies charge the nominating/corporate governance committee with the oversight responsibility for board education. Others may select an ad hoc committee to plan board educational activities. Either type of planning group can more effectively fulfill its function by adhering to the following principles of board development:

- Carefully formulate a purpose for all board development activities.
- Set realistic training objectives.
- When planning an activity, consider the unique needs and interests of all members of the board.
- Consider different types of development activities, such as in-house training, guest speakers or consultants, and workshops or conferences.
- Evaluate each educational activity.

The full board should be involved in the selection of issues to be addressed in board development training. The committee should set specific training objectives, decide on appropriate content and formats, manage the logistics, and perform other related tasks. Approaching board development in this way increases the likelihood of full participation.

In addition to helping a board learn how to operate more effectively, a good program of board development sustains members' interest in the organization and in the board. When board members are well informed and trained to carry out the board's primary functions, they are more comfortable with, and are more likely to remain committed to, their roles.

An organized development program for a board sends a positive message to its members that the organization values the directors' contributions enough to invest time and resources to their continuing excellence. Development programs give board members an opportunity for self-renewal and for quality time away from business as usual. In short, the ongoing education of a board is an excellent strategy for keeping board members motivated, focused, and energetic.

A development program might include the introduction of an outside advisor/ expert at each board meeting. For example, in a typical meeting schedule over the course of a year, the board might schedule presentations from the following types of outside groups:

January	Executive compensation consultant
April	Outside legal counsel
June	Outside auditor engagement partner
September	Leading expert on corporate governance
November	Prominent business school professor

OUTSIDE EXPERTS AND ADVISORS

While boards have for decades sought the advice of outside consultants and advisors, the concerns of spiraling executive pay and allegations of executive malfeasance over the last few years have led to an insistence that boards exercise autonomy in the hiring and firing of such outside advisors.

A primary concern for shareholders is whether the board makes executive compensation decisions independent of management influence. One key ingredient in the compensation committee's independent decision-making is having truly independent compensation advisors. In a 2006 report entitled *The Evolving Relationship between Compensation Committees and Consultants,* The Conference Board's Global Corporate Governance Research Center recommends that compensation committees consider independence from management as the crucial question in selecting and using compensation consultants.

NYSE rules require that if the compensation committee uses a compensation consultant to assist in the evaluation of director, CEO, or other senior executive compensation, the compensation committee must have sole authority to retain and terminate the consulting firm and to approve its fees. These rules are designed to avoid even the appearance of undue influence by the payee over his or her own compensation. While outside advisors should have access to management and other corporate resources, such as the human resources department, for input and consultation, the advisors' allegiance and reporting relationship should be to the compensation committee alone.

Many diversified human resources (HR) consulting firms provide compensation advice to compensation committees, but have significant economic incentives to cross-sell additional unrelated services to the company, such as outsourcing of HR processes, retirement and benefits consulting, insurance and underwriting, and information technology consulting, from which they derive a significant portion or perhaps a majority of their revenue. This can present a conflict of interests similar to that addressed in the Sarbanes-Oxley Act of 2002 with respect to outside auditors providing audit and non-audit services to the company.

In selecting an appropriate outside compensation consultant, the compensation committee should look for the following criteria:

- *Independence from management.* Advisors engaged solely by the compensation committee are more likely to provide objective advice consistent with the board's responsibility to shareholders. According to The Conference Board report on consultant independence referenced earlier, without control of the committee-consultant relationship, directors risk impairing their own independence and thus violating their fiduciary duties.

- *Industry expertise.* This expertise should include a solid understanding of the overall industry in which the company is engaged, its competitive market forces, key dynamics that influence individual company and overall industry perform-ance, and the competitive talent pools.

- *Direct and relevant experience.* Advisors should be highly experienced and have successful track records in assisting similar companies. Generally speaking, the prospective consultant should have several years of executive compensation consulting experience.

- *Executive compensation consulting resources.* The consulting firm should have an extensive survey library, data resources, and secondary consulting resources in the event that the lead consultant is not available.

- *Visibility and good reputation.* Particularly for large companies, the consulting firm and its lead consultants should be nationally recognized and well-regarded.

- *Seamless integration of resources.* The lead consultant and consulting firm should be able to deliver, or arrange for, accounting, tax, actuarial, pension, and financial advice in a seamless manner.

- *Nationwide and worldwide coverage.* A company with internationally based executive officers should also look for international consulting capabilities.

- *Proficiency in all elements of total compensation.* The consulting firm and its consultants should have knowledge of salary; short-term and long-term incentive programs; and pension-benefit, welfare-benefit, employment, severance and change-in-control agreements, and executive perquisite programs. A consultant who is not personally proficient in all elements of total compensation should be able to recognize issues and access expertise in all such areas.

- *Business goals and executive compensation strategy alignment.* The philosophy of the consulting firm should be compatible with the company's philosophy. Some consultants have a specific philosophy and approach toward compensation and may be reluctant to or unable to acknowledge the merits of a different but legitimate approach favored by the compensation committee. This would be a poor fit.

- *Performance measurement expertise.* The consultant must be expert at interpreting financial statements and correctly applying financial ratios and measures in light of the company's industry and business plan and other pertinent facts and circumstances.

- *Creativity and capability to create custom designs.* The consulting firm should be able to provide creative solutions in the context of shifting economic trends and business models.

Different types of advisors serve different purposes, ranging from advice with respect to developments in corporate governance, accounting rules or securities compliance and disclosure issues, to specific advise on peer group competitive practices. The following is a summary of some of the broad types of outside advisors a compensation committee might choose to consult. In many cases, the fields of expertise overlap or complement one another.

LAW FIRM

It is becoming increasingly common for the compensation committee to engage its own legal counsel in addition to the compensation consultant. A law firm with a broad business practice can generally provide a compensation committee advice with respect to historic practices and recent developments in the areas of corporate governance and board duties and responsibilities, securities compliance and disclosure, tax, special concerns and planning opportunities in the context of mergers and acquisitions, and executive employment and severance arrangements. Unlike executive compensation consultants, law firms generally do not have access to databases or survey data to be used in developing specific compensation programs. Because compensation consultants are not usually lawyers, the two disciplines frequently work together to assist a compensation committee in developing and implementing a sound compensation strategy and program in keeping with current legal parameters.

SPECIALIZED EXECUTIVE COMPENSATION CONSULTING FIRM

Executive compensation consulting firms generally focus on current issues in executive compensation practices. Using extensive databases and survey data, they can help the compensation committee identify appropriate trends and design a compensation program that will drive desired performance, encourage retention, and manage shareholder dilution. While generally well versed in governmental and regulatory trends and issues, most consulting firms do not render legal or tax advice.

HUMAN RESOURCES/GENERAL COMPENSATION AND BENEFITS FIRM

These diversified HR consulting firms provide actuarial, benefits, compensation, organizational dynamics, and pension plan advice, outsourcing of HR functions, and employee communications. Such firms tend not to be highly specialized in technical/regulatory areas and generally do not provide tax or legal advice. Compensation committees who rely on a diversified HR consulting firm for executive compensation advice should be aware of the nature of other work the firm may be providing to the company and bear in mind any potential conflict of interest that such other work might present, as discussed previously in this chapter.

INSURANCE SPECIALIST

Insurance specialists often offer innovative approaches to specific needs. Because their solutions are typically oriented to the sale of various types of insurance products, the focus is somewhat narrow. While they can play a valuable role, it is not likely that an insurance specialist would be equipped to provide the broad range of advice that a compensation committee needs to design and implement a total compensation program. Again, the compensation committee should be sensitive to potential conflicting interests situations,

ACCOUNTING FIRM

The Sarbanes-Oxley Act imposes significant limitations on a company's ability to use the non-audit services of its outside auditor. However, accounting firms can be an outstanding source of technical know-how, as they typically have subject matter experts in all aspects of business and commerce, with a focus on accounting and tax rules. More and more frequently, public companies are using one major accounting firm for auditing services and a competitor firm for nonaudit services, including compensation advice. Again, most accounting firms do not render legal advice.

Chapter 3

CEO Succession and Evaluation

The most important responsibility of a board of directors is management succession, particularly for the chief executive officer (CEO) position. While the CEO often takes the lead for hiring and succession of other management personnel, it is the board of directors—and often the compensation committee—that is tasked with the responsibility of CEO succession and evaluation.

CEO succession planning must be in place in case the CEO dies, is disabled, or quits. In addition, there must be a succession plan in case the CEO loses the confidence of the board and/or the company's constituents. Thus, CEO evaluations must be done to determine whether the CEO's employment should be continued. Accordingly, proper and timely CEO evaluations are critical to the company and its shareholders, since the evaluation often will trigger the initial implementation of the CEO succession plan.

While succession planning and CEO evaluation are the responsibilities of the entire board, these responsibilities typically fall on the shoulders of the compensation committee, the governance committee, or on a committee that usually includes all or most of the members of the compensation committee.

SUCCESSION PLANNING

In its *Corporate Governance Best Practices: A Blueprint for the Post-Enron Era*, released in 2003, The Conference Board stated that a successful succession planning process should:

- Be a continuous process
- Be driven and controlled by the board
- Involve CEO input
- Be easily executable in the event of a crisis
- Consider succession requirements based on corporate strategy
- Be geared toward finding the right leader at the right time
- Develop talent pools at lower levels
- Avoid a "horse race" mentality that may lead to the loss of key deputies when the new CEO is chosen

These generalizations apply both to CEO and other management succession. There is no standard "one-size-fits-all" succession plan. Instead, each board must determine the processes and methods that will produce such a plan and shape it into the best plan for its purposes. Generally, this will involve developing the existing executive talent pool of the company and the use of executive recruiting firms, directors' personal contacts, and an overall "ear-to-the-ground" approach. No matter what, the most important point is that there be a CEO succession plan in place at all times.

CEO EVALUATION

Companies listed on the New York Stock Exchange (NYSE) are required to adopt corporate governance guidelines that include succession planning policies and principles for CEO selection and performance review, as well as policies regarding succession in the event of an emergency or the retirement of the CEO. NYSE rules do not require that the results of CEO evaluations be disclosed or that they even be in writing. As discussed later, there are pros and cons to having a written evaluation process, and in many instances an evaluation process that mixes oral and written elements is the best course.

Listing requirements of The Nasdaq Stock Market (NASDAQ) do not include a specific requirement for succession planning and CEO performance reviews. However, most NASDAQ-listed companies would do so as a matter of sound corporate governance.

The executive compensation disclosure rules issued by the Securities and Exchange Commission (SEC) require discussion of pay decisions with respect to the company's top executive officers. However, there is no requirement that a CEO evaluation be completed or that the results be publicly disclosed. Thus, CEO evaluations generally remain private and confidential, unless disclosure is required by subpoena or other imposed discovery process.

A meaningful CEO evaluation process should have the following attributes:

• Regular executive sessions culminating in a formal annual evaluation
• Carefully planned framework for evaluation
• Objective analysis
• Effective tying of the evaluation to the CEO's pay package

CEO evaluations are closely linked with director evaluations and, when properly conducted, can help engender a sense of teamwork between the board and the CEO. Good chemistry between the board and the CEO is important. It starts with an attitude that fosters a sense of respect, worthiness, and direct and clear communication. Once the board and the CEO "bond," they can more easily share their visions of the future and get a buy-in from one another. This meeting of the minds goes a long way in keeping the company on track under adversity and conflict.

To open and maintain the channels of communication, the board or lead director of the board should meet with the CEO on a regular basis to go over the evaluation and the evaluation process. These evaluation sessions should be a scheduled part of the board process, and not hurried or shortened.

Too often, directors have limited interaction with the CEO, usually occurring only during board or committee meetings. Observations of the CEO by the directors are important for that part of the evaluation based on qualitative and personal traits. In other words, it is difficult for directors to fairly evaluate a CEO when they have not observed the CEO performing his or her daily work. Accordingly, it is important for each director involved in the evaluation process to interact with the CEO outside of board and committee meetings.

BARRIERS TO EFFECTIVE CEO EVALUATION

A number of factors can inhibit the effectiveness of a CEO evaluation:

- *Discomfort.* Some board members find evaluating the CEO neither enjoyable nor comfortable. The majority of CEOs feel the same way.
- *Misunderstood purpose.* Some directors misuse the evaluation to find fault rather than use the process for constructive purposes.
- *Ambiguity.* This can be a major impediment to an effective CEO evaluation process. Ambiguity can come from a failure to fairly articulate the organization's strategic goals, the CEO's job description and goals, how the evaluation process is designed, or the way in which evaluation results are shared with the CEO.
- *Low priority.* The CEO evaluation should be given a high priority, and a sufficient amount of time and energy must be dedicated to the process.
- *Objective measurements.* There is often difficulty in rating the CEO on qualitative or subjective factors, such as the CEO's ability to develop the leadership pipeline.
- *Being critical of the CEO.* Some boards fear that being critical in an evaluation could jeopardize the CEO's overall effectiveness.

These factors, of course, should not inhibit the CEO evaluation process, and directors must take appropriate action to ensure that they do not.

CEO EVALUATION PROCESS

An appropriate CEO evaluation has two important components: the process itself and the evaluation criteria.

The evaluation process includes laying out the evaluation approval authority, the administration of the evaluation (including the form of the summary report), the type of evaluation (oral versus written), the disposition of the evaluation worksheets, the timing of the evaluation, and most important, the feedback to the CEO. Furthermore, there is a direct connection between the board evaluation process and the CEO evaluation process and measurement criteria. These sets of criteria and processes should be integrated to ensure a smooth evaluation process and to avoid disconnects between the board and management.

To make the evaluation process more objective, the board should create a job description for the CEO and a solid basis for performance measures and targets. The performance targets should be finalized during the first fiscal quarter of each year. That will provide an objective reference to evaluate the CEO once the year is complete. Progress against these objective reference points will be used to provide feedback to the CEO.

The CEO's job description should explicitly state what the board expects from the CEO. A basic CEO job description not only sets out the executive's duties, responsibilities, and powers, but should also prescribe a set of priorities. Essentially, the job description will provide a solid footprint for a performance evaluation system. Exhibit 3.1 shows a sample job description.

CONFIDENTIALITY IS PARAMOUNT

The CEO evaluation should be conducted with utmost confidentiality. Completed evaluation forms should be returned only to the director in charge of the evaluation, who should then arrange to compile a summary of the responses. An outside consultant (perhaps the same organization that is assisting with the director evaluation program) can help manage this process. It is best that management (especially the CEO) not see the raw information, as it may be taken out of context and have an unintended effect on the CEO's performance or perception.

To assure confidentiality and to encourage an objective evaluation and associated comments, worksheet forms should be destroyed after the evaluations are summarized. The retention of notes and comments relating to the CEO's performance—just like handwritten notes on board materials—may be misinterpreted when reviewed out of context.

There is no requirement that this information be retained or disclosed to shareholders. Moreover, requiring such retention or disclosure would make the evaluation process more cumbersome than necessary.

ORAL VERSUS WRITTEN PROCESS

To sidestep the issue of document retention, it is possible for the outside directors to conduct an oral evaluation of the CEO. This process would be similar to the recommended process for written evaluations. For example, there would still be a

Exhibit 3.1   Sample CEO Job Description

Major Task	Benchmark for Achievement
Corporate leader	Lead the innovative process that takes the company into new, more profitable markets. Lead the business planning process.
Chief communicator	Be the chief representative for the company. Keep visions, values, and missions in front of the public, shareholders, stock analysts, employees, suppliers, and alliance members. Promote quality communication within the company. Be able to express ideas, plans, strategies, and reasons for change in a clear, persuasive, concise, and effective manner.
Attitude leader	The CEO should have a positive attitude toward the board, with a particular emphasis on the need to engage the board. Behaviors that encourage good board relations are: • Providing enough information for board members to be effective and timely in their input. • Staying in touch with the board. • Fostering honesty, candor, frankness, and openness in communications with all board members. • Responding to the board's advice in a clear and convincing manner. If the CEO and the board agree on something to be done, the CEO should make sure it happens. • Being willing to be held accountable. • Share in the credit with the board, when the company is successful.
Cultural leader	Set the tone of the company's culture by example. Encourage behavior that will grow the business, such as entrepreneurial spirit, as well as accountability for results.
Executive team leader	Lead the executive team. Demand success and be willing to reorganize executive team based on results.
Corporate resource manager	Use corporate resources effectively and efficiently. Strike an optimum balance between long-term and short-term needs. Pay particular attention to human resources issues, especially with regard to executive succession planning. Ensure that proper measurement and control processes are in place, especially the performance appraisal system.

(Continued)

Exhibit 3.1   (Continued)

Major Task	Benchmark for Achievement
Continual learner	Seek ways to improve the company, as reflected in improved corporate results. Always seek feedback for the purpose of positive change and improvement.
Strategic planner	Form the company's structure and processes to fit the strategy and culture sought by the board. Encourage various corporate sectors to work together for a common, strategic goal. Be willing to restructure the company, when necessary, based on clear strategic needs.

CEO evaluation form outlining goals and objectives, and the CEO would discuss his or her performance before the full board. The full board would ask the CEO questions about his or her performance and then meet in executive session to discuss the CEO's performance. The results of these discussions would be summarized and shared with the CEO shortly after the executive session. This discussion typically would not be conducted by the full board, but by one or two directors.

The primary advantage of an oral-based CEO evaluation process is that the interplay between directors is conducted in executive session without written comments that may be misunderstood. Moreover, group discussion may help some directors articulate and refine their own evaluations of the CEO. Also, oral evaluation generally takes less time than written evaluations.

The disadvantage of an oral-based CEO evaluation process is that a few very vocal directors may unduly influence other directors, which can undermine a fair and objective evaluation of the CEO. Another problem with an oral process is that it may not allow for in-depth review of the performance, since the evaluation usually occurs all at one meeting.

The following are pointers for a well-organized oral CEO evaluation:

- Before the process begins, the board should agree to a list of objectives and goals to guide the discussion. This typically is the same guide that the CEO used for discussion of his or her performance before the board. Generally, it is difficult to have a meaningful evaluation if the discussion jumps to and from various sections of the evaluation.

- The board discussion should be organized, managed, and controlled. Typically, one board member leads the discussion, and the chairs of the compensation and corporate governance committees are consulted at the end of each section of the CEO's performance that is discussed.

- All members of the board should be given an opportunity to contribute to the discussion. To promote this objective, different outside directors could lead the discussion for different sections of the evaluation. Providing the opportunity for active participation by all directors is important to the integrity of the evaluation process.

To counteract some of the disadvantages of an oral process, many companies use written CEO evaluations that—even though destroyed when the evaluation process is completed—nevertheless were in writing. The discipline of putting one's thoughts in writing generally contributes to a more orderly process.

RESPONSIBILITY FOR PROCESS AND EVALUATION TIMETABLE

As mentioned earlier, the CEO evaluation process usually is "owned" by the compensation committee, the corporate governance committee, or the full board.

While, as noted before, the CEO evaluation is handled differently by different boards, some have devised an approval authority flow similar to the following:

- A lead evaluation director (the same person who gives the feedback to the CEO) is appointed by the board. This need not be the "lead director" of the board.
- All outside directors complete the CEO evaluation form.
- The CEO also completes the self-assessment form.
- These forms are then provided to the chairs of the compensation and corporate governance committees.
- The committee chairs agree on some points and "agree to disagree" on other points.
- The CEO evaluation is then discussed in executive session at the next compensation and/or corporate governance committee meetings.
- A final review of the evaluation is made, and the full board (excluding the CEO) finalizes the evaluations at the same meeting.
- An appointment is made with the CEO (usually sometime after the meeting).
- The chair of the compensation or corporate governance committee (singly or jointly) typically gives the feedback. It is important that this meeting be conducted in person, as body language and facial expressions convey significant meaning in these types of discussions.
- The evaluation is then used, in conjunction with financial results, to award the CEO his or her bonus at the next compensation committee meeting.
- The work papers associated with the evaluation are destroyed. This includes notes taken at the board meeting (standard practice at most companies).

Having a lead evaluation director is key to this process, as he or she serves as a personal link between the CEO and the evaluation committee and/or full board. In addition, having a lead evaluation director allows for utmost confidentiality and integrity of the process.

EVALUATION CRITERIA

In determining the criteria to be used for evaluating the CEO, directors should focus on the following questions:

- Is our CEO the best for our company—at this time and this place? Why?
- Are there gaps in expectations, goals, and commitments? If so, is the CEO addressing them?
- Does the CEO understand the gaps in expectations, goals, and commitments, and respond to them?
- Has the board specifically discussed the performance measurement criteria with the CEO?
- What does the CEO have to do to succeed? Is he or she doing it?
- Is there a strong succession plan in place? Do we pay enough attention to succession issues?
- Are the proper strategies in place?
- What two or three strategies can most affect the company, such as price increases, changes in the product mix, adding value to products?
- Are things getting better or worse?
- Where is the new top line growth in the company going to come from?
- Does the CEO develop, attract, retain, and motivate an effective management team?
- Is there high-quality, cost-effective management of operations?

Generally, most directors prefer that a portion of the CEO's annual bonus be based on qualitative and/or nonfinancial criteria. For example, criteria that some boards select as nonfinancial goals to be taken into account in determining the annual bonus are leadership development and succession planning. How well is the CEO grooming his or her successor, and how much talent is there in the pipeline? As with most qualitative criteria, it is sometimes difficult to accurately measure this performance, but the collective subjective assessments by all participating directors generally can provide a fairly accurate picture. However, many CEO incentive compensation programs must satisfy the "performance-based compensation" requirements of Internal Revenue Code (IRC) Section 162(m) or else the compensation will be non-deductible (see discussion later in this chapter).

The following should be taken into account in designing an evaluation form:

- Type of evaluation:
  - Self-evaluation
  - Peer evaluation (board only)
  - 360-degree evaluation (board, certain executive officers, rank-and-file employees, and shareholders)

- Rating system:
  - Letter grades (e.g., A through F) with comments
  - Number grades (e.g., 1 through 5; 1 through 10) with comments
  - No ratings with comments
- Measurement criteria:
  - Qualitative
  - Quantitative financial
  - Quantitative nonfinancial
- Linkage between evaluation process and bonus decision

It is recommended that a combination self-evaluation and board evaluation be completed. The self-evaluation will allow the CEO to focus on his or her performance and may uncover facts and accomplishments that have not come to the attention of the board. The 360-degree approach generally takes six to eight weeks to complete, may be counterproductive, and does not necessarily lead to an improved or different rating than a board evaluation. However, a review of the leadership survey that covers those constituencies may be used as input to a CEO evaluation. This leadership survey might capture actions and activity that the board does not see directly, such as nurturing positive relationships with senior executives. Leadership surveys typically work well in organizations where the culture is healthy, trust is deep, and the CEO invites this type of feedback.

Use of a numerical rating scale (e.g., 1 through 6) is recommended, with identifying characteristics for each number (e.g., "always exceeds expectations," "meets expectations," "below expectations"). Use of letter grades (A, A−, B+, etc.) can have a negative connotation associated with doing poorly in school. A rating scale can also require that the board answer each question with comments. Directors should be encouraged to comment on each criterion; however, a rating focuses the director and can be tabulated and summarized. See Exhibit 3.2 for a sample CEO evaluation form, and Exhibit 3.3 for a sample evaluation form from The Conference Board that was contained in Appendix 6 of *Corporate Governance Best Practices: A Blueprint for the Post-Enron Era*.

The next step is to weight these criteria. It should be made clear to the CEO that certain criteria may be more important than others. Several sections of the evaluation may have equal weight. In any event, it is imperative that the criteria and the weighting of the criteria be clearly understood at the beginning of the performance period. Exhibit 3.4 provides a summary of the CEO evaluation process, and Exhibit 3.5 provides sample questions to include in the evaluation.

LINKING THE EVALUATION TO CEO INCENTIVE COMPENSATION

The last but most important part of the evaluation process is to link the evaluation process to the CEO's pay package. It is important to ensure that CEO pay is in line with

Exhibit 3.2   Illustrative CEO Evaluation Form

Section	Major Topics and Description	Weight Rating[*]
1.	**Strategic Planning** • Ensures the development of a long-term strategy • Establishes objectives and plans that meet the needs of shareholders, customers, employees, and all other corporate stakeholders, and ensures consistent and timely progress toward strategic objectives • Obtains and allocates resources consistent with strategic objectives. Reports regularly to the board on progress toward strategic plan milestones	10
2.	**Leadership** • Develops and communicates a clear and consistent vision of the company's goals and values • Ensures that this vision is well understood, widely supported, and effectively implemented within the organization • Fosters a corporate culture that encourages, recognizes, and rewards leadership, excellence, and innovation • Ensures a culture that promotes ethical practice, individual integrity, and cooperation to build shareholder value	10
3.	**Financial Results** • Establishes and achieves appropriate annual and longer-term financial performance goals • Ensures the development and maintenance of appropriate systems to protect the company's assets and assure effective control of operations	15
4.	**Management of Operations** • Ensures high-quality, cost-effective management of the day-to-day business affairs of the company • Promotes continuous improvement of the quality, value, and competitiveness of the company's products and business systems • Encourages and rewards creative solutions to business and management solutions	4
5.	**Management Development** • Develops, attracts, retains, and motivates an effective and unified senior management team • Ensures that programs for management development and succession planning have the required resources and direction to grow the future leaders of the company	10

6.   Human Resources   6
     - Ensures the development of effective programs for the recruitment, training, compensation, retention, and motivation of employees
     - Ensures that adequate human resources are available to meet the needs of the company
     - Establishes and monitors programs to promote workplace diversity
     - Provides for appropriate recognition of the achievements of individuals and groups

7.   Communications   7
     - Serves as chief spokesperson for the company, communicating effectively with shareholders, prospective investors, employees, customers, suppliers, and consumers
     - Effectively represents the company in relationships with industry, the government, and the financial community, including major investor groups and financial services firms

8.   Board Relations   10
     - Works closely with the board to keep directors informed on the state of business on critical issues relating to the company
     - Works closely with the board to keep the directors informed on the company's programs toward the achievement of operating plan and strategic plan milestones
     - Provides effective support for board operations, including board materials, and advisory services

---

* Note: The numeric ranking system is:
1. Substantially Below Expectations
2. Slightly Below Expectations and Progressing Toward Meeting Expectations
3. Meets Expectations
4. Well Above Expectations
5. Clearly Exceeds Expectations in the Most Important Aspects of Section
6. Substantially Exceeds Expectations in All Aspects of Section

corporate performance. For example, care should be taken to avoid large stock grants, bonus payments, salary increases, and other compensation increases that could be viewed as windfalls at a time of employee layoffs or poor corporate performance.

Too often in the past, the CEO evaluation process has not been linked to the CEO bonus decision. The bonus is usually determined using quantitative financial criteria such as earnings per share (EPS) growth, or earnings before interest, taxes, depreciation, and amortization (EBITDA). As mentioned previously, the CEO evaluation form generally is more qualitative than quantitative, and contains nonfinancial criteria, such as leadership, communications, board relations, and

---

Exhibit 3.3   The Conference Board Sample CEO Evaluation Form

---

Process:

- Evaluation sheet distributed (date) to active independent board members
- Completed evaluation sheets returned to xxx by (date)
- Xxx will summarize input and pass on anonymously to yyy
- Yyy will circulate to the board and preview with zzz, adding his own feedback
- Active independent board members discuss evaluation with zzz at (date) board meeting

Evaluation:

Your name: ——————————————————————— (will be removed by xxx)
Please return to xxx prior to (date)

Section A: Primary Responsibilities of the CEO

Consider the factors listed below when forming your evaluation. Provide relevant examples when possible.

1. Development of the primary strategy and objectives of the company

- Appropriateness given the external environment
- Clarity and consistency of the strategy
- Process that encourages effective strategic planning

Grade (check one) ☐ Outstanding ☐ Good ☐ Needs Improvement
Comments/examples:

_____
_____
_____

2. Tone and structure of how the company operates

- Appropriateness of organizational structure to the primary strategy
- Alignment of management with the strategy
- Clearly communicated with a process for identifying and measuring progress toward the strategy
- Timely adjustments in strategy when necessary
- Fosters a culture of ethical behavior that includes effective compliance programs, strong auditing, and financial controls

Grade (check one) ☐ Outstanding ☐ Good ☐ Needs Improvement
Comments/examples:

_____
_____
_____

3. Leadership and development of the management team

- Succession planning in place at higher levels that includes an effective plan for developing candidates for the long term
- Turnover of management
- Energy of management team
- Motivates and inspires employees to realize the company's vision
- Effective role model for the organization

Grade (check one) ☐ Outstanding ☐ Good ☐ Needs Improvement
Comments/examples:
_____
_____
_____

4. Relationship with the board

- Keeps the board fully informed of important aspects of the company
- Practices and encourages open, honest, and timely communication
- Effective presentations
- Ability to raise and explain key issues
- Ability to draw on past experiences in issues facing the corporation

Grade (check one) ☐ Outstanding ☐ Good ☐ Needs Improvement
Comments/examples:
_____
_____
_____

Section B: Performance to (company) values

The CEO should set the tone by role modeling (company) values. Please consider the CEO's strengths, areas for development, and the factors listed below. Provide relevant examples when possible.

1. Results orientation

- Sets challenging and competitive goals
- Focuses on output
- Assumes responsibility
- Constructively confronts and solves problems
- Executes flawlessly

Grade (check one) ☐ Outstanding ☐ Good ☐ Needs Improvement
Comments/examples:
_____
_____
_____

(Continued)

2. Risk taking

- Fosters innovation and creative thinking
- Embraces change and challenges the status quo
- Listens to all ideas and viewpoints

Grade (check one) ☐ Outstanding ☐ Good ☐ Needs Improvement
Comments/examples:

_____

_____

_____

3. Discipline

- Conducts business with uncompromising integrity and professionalism
- Makes and meets commitments
- Properly plans, funds, and staffs projects
- Learns from our successes and mistakes

Grade (check one) ☐ Outstanding ☐ Good ☐ Needs Improvement
Comments/examples:

_____

_____

_____

4. Quality

- Strives to achieve the highest standards of excellence
- Does the right things right
- Continuously learns, develops, and improves

Grade (check one) ☐ Outstanding ☐ Good ☐ Needs Improvement
Comments/examples:

_____

_____

_____

5. Customer orientation

- Listens and responds to our customers, suppliers, and stakeholders
- Clearly communicates mutual intentions and expectations
- Delivers innovative and competitive products and services

Grade (check one) ☐ Outstanding ☐ Good ☐ Needs Improvement
Comments/examples:

6. Great place to work

- Style: open and direct
- Works as a member of a team with respect and trust for each other

- Recognizes and rewards accomplishments
- Manages performance fairly and firmly
- Makes (company) an asset to our communities worldwide

Grade (check one) ☐ Outstanding ☐ Good ☐ Needs Improvement
Comments/examples:
_____
_____
_____

Section C: Overall summary

   1. Greatest strength as a CEO
Comments/examples:
_____
_____
_____

   2. Major highlights and lowlights of the past 12 months
Comments/examples:
_____
_____
_____

   3. Words of advice to the CEO
Comments/examples:
_____
_____
_____

   4. Overall performance
Grade (check one) ☐ Outstanding ☐ Good ☐ Needs Improvement
Comments/examples:
_____
_____
_____

management development. Appropriately, companies are now tending to link these two evaluation processes.

Qualitative criteria should be used in the CEO evaluation process. Unfortunately, for public companies, IRC Section 162(m), which caps the deduction of non-performance-based compensation paid to top executives at $1 million, requires quantitative—not qualitative—performance goals. Thus, many public companies avoid using qualitative CEO evaluations as a performance metric for the annual cash bonus. It is preferable to use qualitative goals to determine the size of equity-based incentive compensation grants that still are subject to other time-based or performance-based conditions. Thus, if the grant satisfies the IRC Section 162(m) performance requirements (such as an

---

Exhibit 3.4   CEO Evaluation Process Checklist

These questions are designed to help boards assess their CEO evaluation process and determine if any improvements are necessary.

Questions

1. Does the CEO have a current, written position description that is clear and comprehensive? This job description can be based on traits and characteristics of the position.
2. Does the CEO have an employment agreement that, among other items, includes severance benefits?
3. Has the board established a written policy statement covering the policy statement, a formal CEO goal setting and appraisal process?
4. Has the board formed an effective and independent compensation committee and corporate governance committee? Do these committees have charters?
5. Do both the CEO and board members perceive the executive evaluation process as constructive and objective?
6. Does the CEO receive clear and useful feedback on the board's expectations and evaluation of his or her performance?
7. Do all members of the board have sufficient input into establishing the CEO's goals and evaluating performance? How is this input obtained:
   - Via a written questionnaire?
   - Conversations with the board chair?
   - Interviews conducted by an independent third party who summarizes findings?
   - Other means?
8. Does the executive evaluation committee make a summary report of its work to the full board so all members can be confident that an effective evaluation process is in place, and so they are aware of the CEO's current goals?
9. Do all board members understand and honor the confidential nature of any personnel evaluation, including executive appraisal?
10. Are the CEO's performance goals both quantitative and qualitative, and do they reflect all important aspects of the organization's mission, strategic vision, and major priorities, not only financial and business objectives? Qualitative factors such as the CEO's ability to develop the leadership pipeline, and a continuously learning organization should be included.
11. Is the CEO performance evaluation effectively linked to executive compensation in a way that rewards the CEO for effective performance?
12. If challenged by shareholders, employees, the public, media, or governmental agencies, can members of the board clearly articulate a policy and rationale for the CEO's compensation and benefits package?

---

at-the-money stock option or stock appreciation right) and the other IRC Section 162(m) requirements, the underlying compensation should be fully deductible under IRC Section 162(m) even though subjective factors were considered in determining the size of the award.

Exhibit 3.5 CEO Question Reference Guide

Suggested areas for investigation and performance traits with related questions in six major areas of CEO expertise: strategy, leadership, organizational issues, building and maintaining relationships, functional knowledge, and integrity and ethics.

Part I. Strategy

A. Company's business model: Knowledge of how and where an organization makes its profits and its revenues in relationship to its suppliers and customers.

   1. How well does the CEO understand the business model and critical success factors?

   2. Is the CEO able to come up to speed quickly with a business model that he or she may not have had previous exposure to?

   3. Does this individual appreciate the interrelationship of suppliers, value creation, and customer needs?

B. Corporate strategy formulation: Knowledge of alternative strategies and knowledge of the strengths and weaknesses of different strategy alternatives. Knowledge of a company's customer base and trends within differing customer segments that may offer strategic opportunities.

   1. How strategic is the CEO in his or her thought processes? Do the questions he or she asks reflect appreciation of the importance of clear strategic thinking?

   2. Have you observed incidents in which the CEO has strongly influenced or made a significant contribution to strategic direction or its determination in a company or board setting?

   3. Does the CEO respond to critical questions to investigate the depth of management's analysis and thinking on strategic alternatives?

C. Competition: Knowledge of key competitors (their strategies, core competencies, leadership) as well as knowledge of potential competitors who might enter an industry due to shifts in the market or technology.

   1. How externally focused and knowledgeable is the CEO regarding existing and potential competitors within the company's competitive universe?

   2. Does the CEO add value to a board discussion of competitive threats to a company?

   3. Does the CEO have previous exposure to companies that are or may become competitors?

D. Global markets: Understanding existing and potential international markets for the company and fundamental knowledge about national economies and government relations in those markets.

   1. Does the CEO have a multinational frame of reference based on experience and/or interest?

   2. Does the CEO have knowledge of and/or experience in regions of the world in which the company is operating or wishes to expand into?

(Continued)

3. How sensitive is the CEO to cultural differences and beliefs, and are there illustrative specific examples?

Part II. Leadership

A. Senior executive coaching: Skills in coaching senior executives and helping them set goals for self-development and personal growth.

1. Does the CEO have a record of accomplishment of successful coaching and mentorship?

2. Do you have information regarding the CEO's reputation with subordinates?

3. Does the CEO ask questions in a board setting that display an interest in succession and people development?

B. Senior executive development: Ability to transfer knowledge about a business, suggests learning experiences, and provides meaningful feedback to senior executives about their behavior.

1. Do you believe the CEO can establish a strong advisory and trusting relationship with senior management? Are there any examples?

2. Would the CEO be willing to counsel a senior executive regarding inappropriate personal behaviors that are negatively affecting the CEO's effectiveness?

3. Has a member of the board sought out the CEO for advice? Frequently?

Part III. Organizational Issues

A. Strategy implementation: Understanding how strategic plans need to be implemented through organizational systems with appropriate deployment of resources. Demonstrate an understanding of initiatives that build on a company's core competencies.

1. How astute is the CEO in understanding the need to bring along people to initiate and execute strategies?

2. Does the CEO follow up in subsequent board meetings to ensure that proposed and agreed-upon strategies were tried and/or implemented?

3. Is the CEO realistic and practical regarding the company's capability to actually implement strategic proposals and new ways of doing business?

B. Change management: Knowledge of basic change processes, such as communications strategies, tactics to overcome resistance, dedicated change management teams, and the use of benchmarks.

1. Has the CEO led significant organizational change?

2. How sophisticated is the CEO's understanding of the inherent obstacles to change?

3. Does the CEO hold senior management accountable for implementing required organizational change?

C. Group effectiveness: Understanding of information about how groups best do knowledge sharing and how the board can effectively get information to assist in key strategic decisions.

1. Are you aware of the CEO's exposure and/or appreciation of the need for a knowledge-sharing mentality in a learning-oriented company?

2. Does the CEO work well with senior management and the board for the best interest of the company?

3. Does the CEO's ego get in the way of his or her effectiveness with others?

D. Organizational design: Understanding of alternative organizational designs, their strengths and weaknesses, and how they affect and relate to business strategy.

1. Have you observed the CEO's knowledge and experience with alternative organizational structures?

2. Does the CEO share appropriate insights regarding organizational alternatives that display experience and knowledge of these considerations in a board setting?

3. Are you aware if the CEO has learned from a significant mistake in organizational design?

Part IV. Building and Maintaining Relationships

A. Governments: Understanding of how to deal with governmental entities in terms of regulatory approval and financial management.

1. Have you observed or do you know about the CEO's record of accomplishment in working effectively with governmental agencies?

2. Any reason to be concerned about the CEO's reputation with governmental agencies that have oversight or interest in the company's business?

B. Investors, financial analysts, and the media: Knowledge about communicating effectively with investor groups, analysts, and media representatives.

1. Have you observed the CEO's communications ability in public forums such as with analysts, media, or other external constituencies?

2. Does the CEO alienate or turn people off by his or her communication style? Does he or she win people over with persuasive and sincere communications?

C. Communities and the environment: Knowledge of key communities in which the company has its headquarters and major operations. Understanding of legal and social issues concerning the environmental impact of the company's operations.

1. How sensitive is the CEO to interest groups or community groups that require attention?

2. Does the CEO consider community service an integral part of a senior executive's role in a significant leadership position?

Part V. Functional Knowledge

A. Finance: Understanding of alternative sources of capital and acquisitions, mergers, and divestitures.

(Continued)

   1. Is the CEO comfortable with financial and capital analysis and external reporting requirements to be an effective director?

   2. Has the CEO raised capital for his or her own enterprise and/or does he or she appreciate the intricacies of this process?

   3. Is the CEO well known and respected in the capital markets?

B. Audit: Comprehension of financial statements and auditing procedures.

   1. Is the CEO familiar with generally accepted accounting principles and appropriate standards for public company financial reporting?

C. Technical expertise: Knowledge of the key core competencies in the organization with respect to how they are obtained and managed.

   1. Does the CEO understand the core organizational competencies required for an organization to be successful?

D. Legal issues: Understanding of the particular legal issues that the organization faces in its business, from both a business and regulatory perspective.

   1. Does the CEO have significant experience with legal requirements of his or her own business or of a company on whose board he or she serves?

   2. Are there any legal difficulties that the CEO has been affected by that might lead to embarrassment or difficulty for the company?

E. Human resources: Understanding of the critical talent issues of the organization and, if relevant, understanding of labor relations.

   1. To your knowledge, does the CEO value the need for outstanding talent? Are there particular initiatives that the CEO has implemented or insisted on in a board role?

   2. Has the CEO ever been involved in a particularly contentious labor dispute or been subject to criticism for his or her treatment of people?

F. Information technology: Particular focus on the impact of enterprise information systems and the Internet on the company from the point of view of internal management and with regard to the capability of these systems to provide effective interfaces with customers and suppliers.

   1. How knowledgeable is the CEO in the areas of information technology utilization in the company?

   2. Does the CEO appreciate the need for technology to achieve competitive strategic advantage?

   3. How comfortable is the CEO in critically evaluating the need for significant capital investment in information systems and other technological improvements?

G. Marketing: Understanding of and information about the company's markets and the ability to structure the organization to interface effectively with its markets.

1. Does the CEO bring strong general management appreciation of the role of marketing to the success of the overall enterprise?

2. How comfortable is the CEO in evaluating marketing initiatives?

3. Does the CEO add value to board discussions regarding marketing programs and expenditures?

Part VI. Integrity and Ethics

A. Ethical responsibilities: Ability to identify and raise key ethical issues concerning the activities of the company and of senior management as they affect the business community and society.

1. Are you aware of any issues in the CEO's background, experience, or behavior that indicate anything less than the highest standards of personal integrity?

2. Is integrity and ethical behavior a strong personal value of the CEO?

3. To your knowledge, has the CEO had to deal with unethical situations?

Another method that some companies might use to incorporate qualitative performance goals into an arrangement that qualifies for deductibility under IRC Code Section 162(m) involves using a concept known as "negative discretion." This is done by reasonably "oversizing" the incentive compensation target and then reducing that amount based on the achievement of the qualitative goals. For example, assume that a CEO has an annual bonus target of 100 percent of base salary based on achieving specified EBITDA goals. The compensation committee would like to pay an additional 50 percent of base salary if 100% of the qualitative goals are achieved, 20 percent if between 75 percent and 100 percent of the qualitative goals are achieved, and 0 percent if the CEO does not achieve at least 75 percent of the qualitative goals. The compensation committee then sets the annual bonus target at 150 percent of base salary, still based on achieving the EBITDA goals. Assuming the EBITDA goals were achieved, the committee then determines whether the qualitative goals were achieved, and to what degree. If all of the qualitative goals were achieved, then the bonus is not reduced (i.e., 150 percent of base salary). If only 80 percent of the qualitative goals were achieved, then the bonus is reduced by 20 percent (i.e., 120 percent of base salary). If less than 75 percent of the qualitative goals were achieved, then the bonus is reduced by 33⅓ percent (i.e., 100 percent of base salary).

Regardless of the method used to link CEO performance to CEO incentive pay, the important point is to link the CEO evaluation process to the design and execution of the CEO incentive pay program.

Chapter 4

Director Compensation

This chapter discusses the compensation of directors and the role compensation committees typically play in determining the types and levels of such compensation.

OVERVIEW

In most instances, members of boards of directors who are not employees or major shareholders of the corporation are paid for their services as directors. For purposes of this chapter, the assumption is that only outside/independent directors are paid director compensation and that employee-directors and/or major shareholder-directors are paid nothing with respect to their director services.

In the past, director's fees tended to be meaningful but relatively modest amounts, primarily due to the limited amount of time that directors devoted to such service. For example, for many years the estimated annual service time for a director was thought to be approximately 100 hours. Thus, assuming $250 per hour, the annual total amount that would be paid to a director would be $25,000; at $500 per hour, it would be $50,000 per year. Again, these are meaningful compensation amounts but relatively small when compared to the annual compensation of many actively employed directors. For those directors who were retired from their life careers, director's fees usually represented an ancillary "stipend" for board service that the retiree director relished for its prestige and honor, not for its pay. Of course, there were some directors who served on five, six, or even 10 boards, and the aggregate of that compensation made for quite a tidy sum. However, it can be safely said that most directors—whether they were active chief executive officers (CEOs), retired CEOs, investors, law firm partners, professors, physicians, or politicians—do not serve on a board of directors of a public corporation for the compensation.

Much has happened to change the nature of corporate board service over the last decade. In the post-Enron era, new federal and state legislation, new Securities and Exchange Commission (SEC) regulations, new stock exchange listing rules, a new sense of public outrage toward perceived corporate excesses, and a new fear of shareholder litigation have caused directors to work harder, longer, and—more importantly—more carefully than ever before. It would not be unusual for some directors at public companies to now devote 200 to 300 service hours a year to a single board.

In addition, directors are being limited in the number of boards on which they may serve. Service on too many boards is negatively perceived by the public and the investment community. The view is that the director is stretched too thin for effective performance. Moreover, the increased annual time commitment required for board service in today's environment will, for most directors, serve as a practical limit against serving on many boards. Accordingly, it is expected that directors most likely will serve on no more than four boards, with a typical number being two or three.

The combination of the reduction in the number of boards on which a director can serve, the increase in hours devoted to board service, the new emphasis on training and expertise, and the pressure of increased accountability has fueled changes in director compensation over the past few years. Accordingly, director fees have been substantially increasing. Recent surveys report that director fees have generally increased over 50 percent between 2001 and 2006. While these surveys examined different company or industry groups, and thus produced different results, there is no question that compensation for board service is and will continue to increase until these new workload requirements and service arrangements level out.

In most cases, boards rely on the compensation committee to review director compensation and recommend appropriate compensation levels applicable to all directors. In some cases, review and setting of director compensation is a joint effort between the compensation committee and the corporate governance committee. In almost every case, however, the ultimate committee recommendation is presented to the full board for discussion and approval. Typically, director compensation is reviewed every two or three years, although more frequent review has been the rule during this period where the very structure of director compensation has been undergoing wholesale reconfiguration.

ELEMENTS OF DIRECTOR COMPENSATION

Generally, most directors receive elements of both cash-based and equity-based compensation, such as stock options, restricted stock, and/or restricted stock units (RSUs). The impact of the changes in the accounting for director equity-based compensation is discussed later in this chapter. In addition, in the past, directors often had additional benefits and perquisites, such as pension or deferred compensation arrangements, health and life insurance coverage, and/or company-paid charitable contributions made at the direction of the director. However, these programs have fallen out of favor with shareholders and the public, and most companies have phased out and discontinued these programs.

The most typical elements of director compensation include some or most of the following:

- Board member annual retainer, usually paid in cash, equity, or a combination of both

- Board chair annual retainer, usually paid in cash, but sometimes paid in both cash and equity

- Lead/presiding director special fees, paid in equity and/or cash
- Board member in-person meeting fee, usually paid in cash
- Board member telephonic meeting fee, usually paid in cash, but sometimes ignored, particularly if the telephonic meeting was short and informal, and/or no minutes were recorded
- Board chair in-person meeting fee, usually paid in cash
- Committee member annual retainer, usually paid in cash
- Committee chair annual retainer, usually paid in cash
- Committee member in-person meeting fee, usually paid in cash
- Committee member telephonic meeting fee, usually paid in cash but sometimes ignored, particularly if the telephonic meeting was short and informal, and/or no minutes were recorded
- Committee chair in-person meeting fee, usually paid in cash
- Special one-time initial (or sign-on/sign-up) fee, usually paid in equity
- Other special project or per diem fees, usually paid in cash

In addition, expenses incurred by the directors for board service (e.g., travel, office services, continuing director education) are normally reimbursed by the company. Finally, it should be noted that some companies do not differentiate between in-person meetings and telephonic meetings.

The preceding elements of director compensation are neither uniform nor consistent from industry to industry nor from company to company. For example, some companies may pay a high annual retainer and small (or no) meeting fees. Other companies may pay a small (or no) annual retainer and high meeting fees. Some companies pay no additional compensation for committee service, while others pay additional compensation (both as an annual retainer and meeting fees) for committee service. Some companies provide new directors a "sign-on" or "sign-up" equity grant as an inducement to join the board.

As is the case with executive compensation, the equity-based compensation practices for outside directors historically were guided in large part by accounting considerations. Thus, prior to 2005, because almost all companies used Accounting Principles Bulletin Opinion No. 25 (APB 25) as their equity-based compensation accounting standard, equity-based compensation for directors usually was in the form of "at-the-money" stock options (i.e., stock options with an exercise price equal to the fair market value of the stock on the date of grant). Common practice, along with the accounting interpretation provided in Financial Accounting Standards Board (FASB) Interpretation No. 44 (FIN 44), treated at-the-money stock options granted to non-employee directors as resulting in no compensation expense. Some companies did use stock, stock units, restricted stock, or RSUs in lieu of or in addition to stock options; but this, of course, resulted in a compensation charge under APB 25. However, almost no company granted stock appreciation rights (SARs), as this type of equity-based compensation produced "variable accounting" under APB 25 and FASB Interpretation No. 28 (see Chapter 9 for more detail).

Today, all director equity-based compensation is subject to expensing under Statement of Financial Accounting Standards No. 123, revised 2004 (FAS 123R), which requires that a grant-date "fair value" of the award be treated as a compensation expense and recorded in the company's financial statements. FAS 123R continued the concept under APB 25 of treating non-employee directors the same as employees for purposes of equity-based compensation accounting. Thus, while the "advantage" of using stock options over restricted stock or RSUs has greatly diminished, equity-based compensation still has an accounting advantage over the use of cash. In addition, using a company's stock to pay its directors has an appeal to shareholders. Accordingly, most director compensation programs will continue to include a meaningful portion of equity-based compensation.

Many companies grant equity-based compensation with some vesting requirements, which do vary from company to company. Some companies imposed a vesting schedule of only one year, while others imposed three-, four-, or five-year pro-rata vesting schedules. And, of course, some companies imposed no vesting restrictions on directors' equity awards.

Because FAS 123R now requires a compensation charge for stock option grants, and because the deferred compensation rules under Internal Revenue Code (IRC) Section 409A affects director compensation, many companies have been rethinking their director equity-based compensation programs. While some companies have continued to use at-the-money director stock options (or more recently, SARs payable only in stock), based on the notion that such awards are purely performance based, many others have switched to "full-value" stock awards, deferred stock units, restricted stock, or RSUs, based on the notion that the equity award is in lieu of cash and does contain a performance upside/downside element. In addition, as part of this "rethink," companies are now considering using restricted stock and not RSUs in order to avoid subjecting the grant to IRC Section 409A.

It has been customary for directors' equity-based compensation to vest immediately upon a change in control (similar to the accelerated vesting of equity-based compensation granted to executives and other employees). While this acceleration feature could present a potential conflict of interest (tempting a director to unduly favor a proposal that would accelerate the vesting of his or her awards), most companies reasoned that the accelerated vesting provision of director equity grants was not meaningful enough to negatively impact a director's decision regarding a change in control. However, given the focus on director independence in the post-Enron era, this reasoning should be revisited by each board that grants equity awards to its directors that accelerate on a change in control.

Many companies have or are contemplating implementing some type of program that requires executives to either maintain specified company stock ownership levels and/or prevents executives from selling compensatory shares received through option exercise, vesting of restricted stock, or delivery of shares underlying RSUs. Similarly, some companies have imposed these programs with respect to director equity-based compensation. In some instances, new directors are required to buy and hold a specified number of shares or dollar amount of company stock, or simply to hold all shares granted as director compensation. While in the past this program often included a company-provided loan arrangement, such loan arrangements are now prohibited by Section 402 of the Sarbanes-Oxley Act of 2002. Thus, these "mandatory purchase" arrangements have become less popular since the company loan feature has not been available. In other instances, directors are required to hold all or substantially all of their compensatory shares of company stock until they leave the board. However, this kind of program may seem too onerous and might impair director-recruiting activities.

Generally, some minimum level of company share ownership is desired for all directors, but the appropriate level is largely dependent on the type and dollar amount of the director compensation program. Director equity-based compensation generally is granted under a company stock or incentive compensation plan. Under old SEC rules regarding the exemption of equity-based compensation from short-swing profit liability under Section 16(b) of the Securities Exchange Act of 1934, only "disinterested" directors (as then defined) were eligible to grant exempt awards to Section 16 insiders. To preserve the "disinterested" status of directors for this purpose, they could only receive equity awards pursuant to a formula plan that did not allow any discretion about the timing or amount of such awards to the directors. Therefore, companies commonly maintained separate formula plans for awards to outside directors. This rule, however, was changed in 1996 by eliminating the concept of "disinterested" director status. It was replaced by a different concept of director independence embodied in the definition of a "non-employee" director, as discussed more fully in Chapter 1, which does not depend on the source or manner of making equity awards to such director. Thus, equity-based compensation may now be granted to both employees and directors under the same plan. Nevertheless, whether director awards are made from a separate plan or under the company's employee equity plan, many institutional investors prefer to see grants to outside directors made pursuant to an established formula, program, or policy, in order to avoid any implication that directors might be making grants to themselves on a discretionary basis. This makes good sense from a corporate governance perspective. See Chapter 7 for a more detailed discussion of the Section 16 short-swing profit rules.

Finally, there has been discussion regarding whether director compensation arrangements should be solely tied to performance goals, such as earnings targets or growth, similar to an executive annual bonus or long-term cash compensation program. In 2006, the Coca-Cola Company announced that it would be implementing such a program, which is described in its 2007 proxy statement as follows:

> In 2006 the Board of Directors adopted the Directors' Plan in order to link the pay of the Directors more closely with the interests of shareowners. Under the Directors' Plan, each Director was credited with the number of share units equal to the number of shares of Common Stock which could be purchased on February 16, 2006 with

$175,000. On each dividend date the number of units was adjusted as though the dividends had been reinvested. In February 2009 performance for the three-year period 2006–2008 will be certified. If the performance target is met, the units will be paid in cash equal to the number of units multiplied by the fair market value of the shares of Common Stock. If the performance target is not met, the Directors will receive nothing. For the first three-year performance period the Board set a target of 8% compound annual growth in earnings per share. The Company's 2005 earnings per share of $2.17 (after considering items impacting comparability) is used as the base for this calculation. No meeting, attendance or committee chair fees are paid under the Directors' Plan. The Board of Directors has the discretion to make a one-time cash award to any new Director.

While there may be a few examples of companies like Coca-Cola that have done this, most companies seem to avoid this type of director compensation arrangement, probably due to the apparent inherent conflicts it engenders. Simply put, these kinds of arrangements most likely are best suited for management, who run the day-to-day business of the company, and therefore have more direct effect on the attainment of particular financial performance measures. Many practitioners believe that it is more appropriate that long-term stock price movements be the primary performance measure impacting director compensation because it directly aligns directors' interests with the interests of shareholders.

DISCLOSURE

Compensation arrangements for directors of public companies must be disclosed. This disclosure typically is found in a company's annual proxy statement, but it could be found in a special proxy statement, or in a Form 10-K, Form S-1, or Form S-4.

The SEC's new executive compensation disclosure rules issued in 2006 now require a "Director Compensation Table" that must include the following for all directors who are not "named executive officers":

- The aggregate dollar amount of all fees earned or paid in cash for services as a director, including annual retainer fees, committee and/or chairmanship fees, and meeting fees.

- For awards of stock, the aggregate grant-date fair value computed in accordance with FAS 123R, and for awards of stock options, with or without tandem SARs (including awards that subsequently have been transferred), the aggregate grant-date fair value computed in accordance with FAS 123R, and for each director, disclosure by footnote to the appropriate column of the aggregate number of stock awards and the aggregate number of option awards outstanding at fiscal year end.

- The dollar value of all earnings for services performed during the fiscal year pursuant to "nonequity incentive plans" and all earnings on any outstanding awards.

- The sum of (1) the aggregate change in the actuarial present value of the director's accumulated benefit under all defined benefit and actuarial pension plans (including supplemental plans) from the pension plan measurement date used for financial statement reporting purposes with respect to the company's audited financial statements for the prior completed fiscal year to the pension plan measurement date used for financial statement reporting purposes with respect to the company's audited financial statements for the covered fiscal year plus (2) above-market or preferential earnings on compensation that is deferred on a basis that is not tax-qualified, including such earnings on nonqualified defined contribution plans.

- All other compensation for the covered fiscal year that the company could not properly report in any other column of the Director Compensation Table.

- The dollar value of total compensation for the covered fiscal year.

The "All Other Compensation" column of the Director Compensation Table includes, but is not limited to, the following:

- Perquisites and other personal benefits, or property, unless the aggregate amount of such compensation is less than $10,000; perquisites and personal benefits may be excluded as long as the total value of all perquisites and personal benefits for a director is less than $10,000; however, if the total value of all perquisites and personal benefits is $10,000 or more for any director, then each perquisite or personal benefit, regardless of its amount, must be identified by type. If perquisites and personal benefits are required to be reported for a director pursuant to this rule, then each perquisite or personal benefit that exceeds the greater of $25,000 or 10 percent of the total amount of perquisites and personal benefits for that director must be quantified and disclosed in a footnote. Perquisites and other personal benefits are valued on the basis of the aggregate incremental cost to the company. With respect to the perquisite or other personal benefit for which footnote quantification is required, the company is required to describe in the footnote its methodology for computing the aggregate incremental cost. Reimbursements of taxes owed with respect to perquisites or other personal benefits must also be included and are subject to separate quantification and identification as tax reimbursements, even if the associated perquisites or other personal benefits are not required to be included because the total amount of all perquisites or personal benefits for an individual director is less than $10,000 or are required to be identified but are not required to be separately quantified.

- All gross-ups or other amounts reimbursed during the fiscal year for the payment of taxes.

- For any security of the company or its subsidiaries purchased from the company or its subsidiaries (through deferral of salary or bonus, or otherwise) at a discount from the market price of such security at the date of purchase, unless that discount is available generally, either to all security holders or to all salaried employees of the company, the compensation cost, if any, computed in accordance with FAS 123R.

- The amount paid or accrued to any director pursuant to a plan or arrangement in connection with (1) the resignation, retirement, or any other termination of such director, or (2) a change in control of the company.

- Company contributions or other allocations to vested and unvested defined contribution plans.

- Consulting fees earned from, or paid or payable by, the company and/or its subsidiaries (including joint ventures).

- The annual costs of payments and promises of payments pursuant to director legacy programs and similar charitable award programs. Programs in which the company agrees to make donations to one or more charitable institutions in a director's name, payable by the company currently or upon a designated event, such as the retirement or death of the director, are charitable awards programs or director legacy programs. The company is required to provide footnote disclosure of the total dollar amount payable under the program and other material terms of each such program.

- The dollar value of any insurance premiums paid by, or on behalf of, the company during the covered fiscal year with respect to life insurance for the benefit of a director.

- The dollar value of any dividends or other earnings paid on stock or option awards, when those amounts were not factored into the grant date fair value required to be reported for the stock or option award columns.

In addition, any item reported for a director in the All Other Compensation column that is not a perquisite or personal benefit and whose value exceeds $10,000 must be identified and quantified in a footnote to the column.

The rules do allow that two or more directors may be grouped in a single row in the Director Compensation Table if all elements of their compensation are identical; however, the names of the directors for whom disclosure is presented on a group basis should be clear from the table. In addition, the company is required to provide a narrative description of any material factors necessary to an understanding of the director compensation disclosed in the Director Compensation Table. While material factors will vary depending on the facts, examples of such factors may include, in given cases, among other things:

- A description of standard compensation arrangements (such as fees for retainer, committee service, service as chairman of the board or a committee, and meeting attendance)

- Whether any director has a different compensation arrangement, identifying that director, and describing the terms of that arrangement

Finally, if the company is presenting a new compensation plan for shareholder approval, the SEC requires that a "New Plan Benefits Table" be included in the proxy statement. This table must disclose the aggregate of the proposed benefits or amounts to be paid or granted under the new plan to the "current directors who are not executive officers as a group."

TRENDS IN DIRECTOR COMPENSATION

As mentioned previously, director compensation is undergoing two fundamental changes. First, the overall level of director compensation is increasing due to the additional workload and the fact—to some degree—that directors can no longer serve on many boards at the same time. Second, the changes in the accounting rules regarding equity-based compensation are impacting the type and form of equity awards companies use to compensate directors. Together, these changes are causing most boards to reexamine the director compensation structure and levels. This reexamination is likely to be done on an annual basis, at least until patterns stabilize, and it makes sense to get back to a more typical review schedule of every two to three years.

Over the past few years, most surveys have shown that director compensation increasing in the double-digit range. The 2006 Director Compensation Report released by the National Association of Corporate Directors (NACD) stated that major trends in director compensation are:

- Double-digit increases in board pay levels across all revenue groups over the past few years
- Significant growth in the use and value of share awards, alongside stagnant or declining stock option use and values
- Increased popularity of premium pay structure for service on major board committees
- Increased use of fee/retainers for committee chairs
- More frequent meetings of audit, compensation, and governance/nominating committees
- Sharp increases in adoption of board share ownership and retention guidelines

In addition, the NACD report showed that median levels for total pay, based on proxy statements filed by companies with fiscal year ends between February 1, 2005, and January 31, 2006, were as follows:

- $74,332 for companies with annual revenues between $50 million and $500 million
- $110,500 for companies with annual revenues between $500 million and $1 billion

- $132,760 for companies with annual revenues between $1 billion and $2.5 billion
- $157,165 for companies with annual revenues between $2.5 billion and $10 billion
- $204,975 for the top 200 companies (based on annual revenues)

Certain specific trends are unmistakable. One is the payment of additional fees to audit committee chairs and/or members that are over and above what other committee chairs and/or members receive. Another is the payment of additional amounts to nonexecutive board chairs and presiding/lead directors. Also, as mentioned previously, the replacement of stock option grants with full-value equity awards is expected to continue.

Of perhaps a less universal nature is the emerging practice of "bundling" all director compensation (i.e., annual retainers, meeting fees, committee fees) into a single amount that applies to all directors. The rationale for this is that it simplifies the fee structure and administration. The drawback is that this "one-size-fits-all" approach presumes that all directors provide equal service to the company, which in many circumstances is not the case. Payment of this universal fee usually is in a combination of cash and equity. Thus, for example, a company may have a fixed annual fee of $150,000, of which $75,000 is paid in cash and $75,000 is paid in equity.

The equity portion may be allocated between restricted stock/RSUs and stock options/SARs, or it may be paid all in restricted stock/RSUs or all in stock options/ SARs. Since all equity-based compensation will result in a compensation charge, this leaves room for design creativity in determining whether the grant should be a full-value award (such as restricted stock/RSUs) or an appreciation award (such as options/SARs) and, in either case, whether it should be fully vested as of the grant date or subject to vesting (by continued service or other performance measures).

A variation of bundling is to provide a variety of fee levels, based on the position or positions of each individual director. For example, a board might pay a base retainer to all directors, plus varying supplemental retainers to directors who serve as (1) board chair or lead director, (2) chair of the audit committee, (3) chair of any other committee, and/or (4) member of the audit committee. The layering of these different fees for service will result in individual directors' being paid different amounts, but it has the advantage of allocating the overall director compensation budget on the basis of work and responsibility.

For those companies that do not favor a fixed-fee approach, the trend may be to substantially increase board and committee meeting fees and to maintain or slightly increase annual retainers. The rationale here is that the compensation is paid for actual service—service in a board position that requires meetings once a month should be compensated at a higher level than a position that entails meetings held once a quarter. Whatever approach is followed, because the audit committee has assumed at least the appearance of heightened importance and public scrutiny, the fees relating to service on the audit committee most likely will become and continue to be higher than for service on other committees. Moreover, as compensation committee service continues to attract public focus and require greater expertise, fees relating to service on the compensation committee may similarly be higher than fees for service on the governance/nominating and other board committees.

Finally, the practice of making an initial equity grant, in a meaningful amount, to induce new directors to join the board probably will increase, since many people who might otherwise have considered board service may be dissuaded by the increased workload and perceived level of exposure. The initial sign-up award most likely will be in the form of restricted stock/RSUs, and with some kind of vesting requirement.

Ultimately, the decisions as to director compensation (as to both types and levels) will vary from company to company, based on company size, industry, culture, and simply the makeup of the board itself. How the board divides its labors will be a major consideration. Some companies may strive to balance the work so that service is equally shared among all independent directors, while others may have one or two independent directors who shoulder the lion's share. Since there is no magic formula, many companies and boards will perform selected benchmarking studies to help design and construct an appropriate director compensation program. However, in that context, care should be taken not to allow the benchmarking exercise to lead to the exploding compensation phenomenon observed in the recent past with respect to executive compensation, where companies pegged compensation in each year to the 75th percentile of market. As long as the benchmarking is used to discern market trends in director program design, and rational discipline is applied to the overall compensation levels, this type of market survey approach can be a useful tool.

CONDUCTING A DIRECTOR COMPENSATION STUDY

Conducting a director compensation study is very similar to conducting an executive compensation study. One useful resource is published surveys produced by compensation consulting firms, executive search firms, and corporate-advisory organizations such as the NACD, The Conference Board, investor advisory services, and executive compensation consulting firms. A second useful exercise is to observe the director programs at a peer group of companies that would serve well for comparison (usually due to size and/or industry). The information from these two sources would then be compared to the company's current board practices.

While the SEC new director compensation disclosure provides a "one-stop" tabular peek into the level of total compensation paid to any one director, the Director Compensation Table does not, in and of itself, provide the exact type or form that is used to pay such compensation. For example, two directors listed in the table might be paid different amounts due to a wide variety of reasons not apparent from the table (e.g., different meeting attendance levels, committee memberships, chairing committees, etc.) Accordingly, the narrative that accompanies the Director Compensation Table remains a vital source for understanding director compensation arrangements at peer companies.

A wide range of discretion can be applied in selecting appropriate peer companies in a director compensation study, due to the similarities in the nature of director service for public companies across different industries, revenue ranges, and stock exchanges. Because not all companies pay the same types of director compensation, a minimum of 15 companies, preferably 20 to 30, should be selected in order to provide a useful comparator group. For example, if only 10 peer companies are used, and only half pay committee chair annual retainers, the data may not be statistically reliable. However, if 30 or more companies are selected, the incidence of those that pay committee chair annual retainers is likely to be higher and provide a better base for comparison. While increasing the number of peer companies to 50 would produce even more "hits" on a particular type of compensation used, the statistical relevance of the difference between groups of 30 or 50 companies is not likely to be as meaningful as the difference between groups of 10 and 30 companies.

The study should break down the components of director compensation into various types, and measure the level of each type. In addition, the study should determine total director compensation paid in the aggregate to all directors, and determine a per-director annual compensation level. For purposes of comparison, an assumption as to the number of board meetings and committee meetings is necessary. For example, it is typical to assume that a board will meet four times per year, and each committee will meet six times per year. A study may be more complicated if the subject company has more committees than the typical three oversight committees (compensation, audit, and governance/nominating) for which it intends to pay special compensation.

The following is an example of applying these assumptions at Company 1 of a peer group of 15 companies:

Assumptions

- Full board meets four times per year.
- Compensation committee meets six times per year.
- Audit committee meets six times per year.
- Corporate governance committee meets six times per year.
- There are no telephonic meetings.

Fees

- Cash annual board retainer of $20,000 per year
- $2,000 for each board meeting
- $1,500 for each committee meeting
- Additional audit committee member retainer of $5,000 per year
- Additional audit committee chair retainer of $10,000 per year
- 2,000 shares of restricted stock per year, valued at $35,000

Results

- Each director receives:
  - $20,000 as a cash annual retainer

- ◦ $35,000 as an equity annual retainer
- ◦ $8,000 for attendance at board meetings

for a total of $63,000.

- Each committee member receives:
  - ◦ $63,000 as a board member
  - ◦ $9,000 for committee meetings

for a total of $72,000.

- Each audit committee member receives:
  - ◦ $63,000 as a board member
  - ◦ $9,000 for committee meetings
  - ◦ $5,000 as an audit committee member cash annual retainer

for a total of $77,000.

- The audit committee chair receives:
  - ◦ $63,000 as a board member
  - ◦ $9,000 for committee meetings
  - ◦ $10,000 as an audit committee chair cash annual retainer

for a total of $82,000.

These assumptions are similarly applied to the other 14 peer companies. Next, a model is built to show each data point for each component of director compensation, whether or not such component is used at the peer company or the subject company, using the previously stated assumptions, and then combining all components to determine a relativistic total compensation figure for each company. See Exhibit 4.1 for a director compensation benchmarking study template.

These models should be reviewed both quantitatively and qualitatively. For example, a company may want to know what should be the level of sign-on/sign-up grants. The median may be $100,000, but if only two companies out of 30 pay such grants, then two conclusions could be reached. First is that most companies do not use this type of director compensation. Second is that this compensation—while it may not have been paid as a sign-on grant—may have been paid in another form (e.g., higher annual equity grants). Therefore, it would be necessary to examine other types and totals. In other words, director compensation studies do not typically allow an "apples-to-apples" comparison. Accordingly, boards must examine not only what the numbers are, but also what the numbers actually mean. Only after a complete review and proper consideration of the data, and perhaps after consultation with outside advisors, can the compensation committee make optimal use of such a study in preparing recommendations of the types and levels of director compensation appropriate for the company.

Exhibit 4.1 Director Compensation Benchmarking Study Template

Company	(1) Board Cash Annual Retainer	(2) Board Equity Annual Retainer	(3) Board In-Person Meeting Fee	(4) Board Teleph. Meeting Fee	(5) Board Chair Annual Retainer	(6) Board Chair Meeting Fee	(7) Lead Director Annual Retainer	(8) Lead Director Meeting Fee
Co. 1								
Co. 2								
…								
Co. 5								
Minimum								
25th Percentile								
Median								
75th Percentile								
Maximum								
Average								
Subject Co.								Continued….

Company	(9) Chair Audit Cmte Cash Annual Retainer	(10) Chair Audit Cmte Meeting Fees	(11) Chair Comp Cmte Cash Annual Retainer	(12) Chair Comp Cmte Meeting Fees	(13) Chair Gov Cmte Cash Annual Retainer	(14) Chair Gov Cmte Meeting Fees	(15) other	(16) other
Co. 1								
Co. 2								
….								
Co. 15								
Minimum								
25th Percentile								
Median								
75th Percentile								
Maximum								
Average								
Subject Co.							other	Continued…

85

(Continued)

Exhibit 4.1 (Continued)

Company	(17) Audit Cmte Cash Annual Retainer	(18) Audit Cmte Meeting Fees	(19) Comp Cmte Cash Annual Retainer	(20) Comp Cmte Meeting Fees	(21) Gov Cmte Cash Annual Retainer	(22) Gov Cmte Meeting Fees	(23) Other	(24) Other	Continued...
Co. 1									
Co. 2									
...									
Co. 15									
Minimum									
25th Percentile									
Median									
75th Percentile									
Maximum									
Average									
Subject Co.									

Company	(25) Total Board Chair	(26) Total Lead Director	(27) Total Board Member	(28) Total Chair Audit Cmte	(29) Total Chair Comp Cmte	(30) Total Chair Gov Cmte	(31) Total Member Audit Cmte	(32) Total Member Comp Cmte	(33) Total Member Gov Cmte
Co. 1									
Co. 2									
...									
Co. 15									
Minimum									
25th Percentile									
Median									
75th Percentile									
Maximum									
Average									

Part Two

Legal and Regulatory Framework

Chapter 5

Corporate Governance

This chapter discusses matters of corporate governance that should be of particular interest to compensation committees. The chapter begins with a discussion of the fiduciary duties of loyalty and care, and the evolving role of good faith, owed by corporate directors to the corporation on whose board they serve. The next section addresses practical applications of director fiduciary duties of compensation committee members in specific contexts. The section "Self-Regulatory Organization Corporate Governance Rules and 'Best Practice' Recommendations" covers the New York Stock Exchange (NYSE) and The Nasdaq Stock Market (NASDAQ) corporate governance rules and "best-practices" recommendations published by various business interest groups, including The Conference Board Commission on Public Trust and Private Enterprise, the Business Roundtable, Institutional Shareholder Services (ISS), and the Teachers Insurance and Annuity Association–College Retirement Equities Fund (TIAA-CREF).

FIDUCIARY DUTIES OF DIRECTORS

A corporate director stands in a fiduciary relationship to the corporation he or she serves and, as such, has certain duties to the corporation. A fiduciary duty claim brought against a director of a corporation is governed by the law of the state where the corporation is incorporated. For purposes of this chapter, we will assume that the applicable state's business corporation statute is based on the Model Business Corporation Act developed by the Committee on Corporate Laws of the Section of Business Law of the American Bar Association (the Model Act). This chapter will also refer to the corporation law of the State of Delaware, whose business code does not follow the Model Act but is the jurisdiction widely recognized as having the most fully developed body of corporation law.

Model Act Section 8.30 specifically imposes three duties on a director:

> A director shall discharge his duties as a director, including his duties as a member of a committee:
>
> (a) In good faith;
>
> (b) With the care an ordinarily prudent person in a like position would exercise under similar circumstances; and
>
> (c) In a manner the director reasonably believes to be in the best interests of the corporation.

Delaware has no statute that sets out the standard of conduct for corporate directors. However, through its reported decisions, the Supreme Court of Delaware has recognized the distinct duties of loyalty and due care, and in November 2006, at long last, definitively characterized the observance of good faith as a necessary condition of the duty of loyalty rather than an independent fiduciary duty that stands on the same footing as the duties of loyalty and care.

DUTY OF LOYALTY

In the leading case of *Guth v. Loft, Inc.,* 5 A.2d 503 (Del. 1939), the Delaware Supreme Court held that the rule requiring undivided and unselfish loyalty from a director to the corporation "demands that there shall be no conflict between duty and self-interest." A basic principle of Delaware corporate law is that directors are subject to the fundamental fiduciary duty of loyalty and that directors may not derive any personal benefit through self-dealing.

However, for corporate fiduciaries, the mere existence of a conflict of interest does not automatically lead to liability for a breach of fiduciary duty. Having a conflict of interest is not something someone is "guilty of"; it is simply a state of affairs. In fact, introductory remarks to the Model Act acknowledge that "a corporation and its shareholders may secure major benefits from a transaction despite the presence of a corporate fiduciary's conflicting interest." Consistent with this view, the Model Act provides a statutory safe harbor for certain director conflict-of-interest transactions.

In 2006, the Delaware Supreme Court clarified that "the fiduciary duty of loyalty is not limited to cases involving financial or other cognizable fiduciary conflict of interest. It also encompasses cases where the fiduciary fails to act in good faith . . . [A] director cannot act loyally towards the corporation unless she acts in the good faith belief that her actions are in the corporation's best interest" *Stone v. Ritter,* 911 A.2d 362 (Del. 2006).

DUTY OF CARE

When corporate directors exercise discretionary authority by making a business decision on behalf of the corporation, they must do so with due care. The analysis focuses on care with respect to the *process* by which the decision was reached (e.g., was all material information reasonably available taken into consideration), as opposed to the *substance* of the decision itself (e.g., was a reasonably careful, or risk free, course of action selected). This focus on process is due to the reluctance of courts to second-guess corporate decisions made by an informed board that followed appropriate procedures, a concept known as the "business judgment rule," which is discussed below.

Under Delaware law, the adequacy of the decision-making process is measured by concepts of gross negligence. Some states, however, have applied concepts of ordinary negligence in application of the fiduciary duty of care. In light of the "ordinarily prudent person" language of the standard of care set forth in Model Act

Section 8.30, it is likely that a court undertaking a business judgment rule analysis under a Model Act state would measure the adequacy of the decision-making process by concepts of ordinary negligence.

THE EVOLVING ROLE OF GOOD FAITH

The "duty" of good faith is not susceptible to concise definition. It is a broad principle that applies to all aspects of the conduct of corporate fiduciaries. According to the American Law Institute (ALI), "a director or officer violates the duty to perform his or her functions in good faith if he or she knowingly causes the corporation to disobey the law." The Official Comments to the Model Act provide, "[c]onduct involving knowingly illegal conduct that exposes the corporation to harm will constitute action not in good faith, and belief that decisions made (in connection with such conduct) were in the best interests of the corporation will be subject to challenge as well."

Another perspective on the duty of good faith is provided by the following Official Comment to the Model Act:

> Where conduct has not been found deficient on other grounds, decision-making outside the bounds of reasonable judgment—an abuse of discretion perhaps explicable on no other basis—can give rise to an inference of bad faith. That form of conduct (characterized by the court as "constructive fraud" or "reckless indifference" or "deliberate disregard" in the relatively few case precedents) giving rise to an inference of bad faith will also raise a serious question whether the director could have reasonably believed that the best interests of the corporation would be served.

The Delaware Supreme Court has recently exerted a renewed effort to provide guidance about the role of good faith in the realm of fiduciary duties of directors under Delaware law. In its June 2006 decision, *In Re The Walt Disney Company Derivative Litigation*, 906 A. 2d 27 (Del. 2006), the court attempted to bring focus to evolving speculation about the scope of the requirement to act in good faith, but stopped short of a definitive and categorical definition. It identified three different categories of fiduciary behavior that are "candidates for the 'bad faith' pejorative label." These run from (1) subjective bad faith, which is fiduciary conduct motivated by an actual intent to do harm, at one extreme, to (2) a lack of due care—that is, fiduciary action taken solely by reason of gross negligence and without any malevolent intent, at the other end of the spectrum. Notably, the court soundly rejected the notion that gross negligence (including a failure to inform oneself of available material facts), without more, can constitute bad faith.

> From a broad philosophical standpoint, that question [i.e., whether gross negligence alone can ever constitute bad faith] is more complex than would appear, if only because (as [the Court of Chancery], and others have observed) "issues of good faith are (to a certain degree) inseparably and necessarily intertwined with the duties of care and loyalty. . . ." But, in the pragmatic, conduct-regulating legal realm, which calls for more precise conceptual line drawing, the answer is that grossly negligent conduct, without

more, does not and cannot constitute a breach of the fiduciary duty to act in good faith. The conduct that is the subject of due care may overlap with the conduct that comes within the rubric of good faith in a psychological sense, but from a legal standpoint those duties are and must remain quite distinct. Both our legislative history and our common law jurisprudence distinguish sharply between the duties to exercise due care and to act in good faith, and highly significant consequences flow from that distinction.

In between subjective bad faith and gross negligence is a third category of fiduciary conduct identified by the *Disney* court as a candidate for "bad faith": intentional dereliction of duty or a conscious disregard for one's responsibilities. The court concluded that this type of misconduct is properly treated as a failure to act in good faith, which is not entitled to exculpation or indemnification under Delaware law. In coming to this conclusion, the court noted that "the universe of fiduciary misconduct is not limited to either disloyalty in the classic sense (i.e., preferring the adverse self-interest of the fiduciary or of a related person to the interest of the corporation) or gross negligence." The Supreme Court in *Disney* upheld as legally appropriate, but not exclusive, the three examples of bad faith that were originally articulated in the Delaware Chancery Court opinion:

> The good faith required of a corporate fiduciary includes not simply the duties of care and loyalty, in the narrow sense that [such duties are discussed earlier in the decision], but all actions required by a true faithfulness and devotion to the interests of the corporation and its shareholders. A failure to act in good faith may be shown, for instance, where the fiduciary intentionally acts with a purpose other than that of advancing the best interests of the corporation, where the fiduciary acts with the intent to violate applicable positive law, or where the fiduciary intentionally fails to act in the face of a known duty to act, demonstrating a conscious disregard for his duties. There may be other examples of bad faith yet to be proven or alleged, but these three are the most salient.

For many years, scholars have engaged in intellectual debate about whether, under Delaware law, there is an independent duty of good faith from which liability can arise apart from the duties of care and loyalty. While *Disney* confirmed that a failure to exercise due care (expressed in terms of gross negligence) does not translate per se into a lack of good faith, thus implying that there may indeed be a separate duty of good faith, the Delaware Supreme Court some three months later seemingly put the issue to rest in the case of *Stone v. Ritter.* In *Stone*, a case that focused on a board's oversight duties (discussed below), the court ruled that the obligation to act in good faith is subsumed within the duty of loyalty and is not itself a separate source of liability.

> The phraseology used in [*In re Caremark International Inc. Derivative Litigation*] and that we employ here—describing the lack of good faith as a "necessary condition to liability"—is deliberate. The purpose of that formulation is to communicate that a failure to act in good faith is not conduct that results, *ipso facto*, in the direct imposition

of fiduciary liability. . . . The failure to act in good faith may result in liability because the requirement to act in good faith "is a subsidiary element[,]" i.e., a condition, "of the fundamental duty of loyalty" [*Guttman v. Huang*, 823 A.2d 492 (Del. Ch. 2003)]. It follows that because a showing of bad faith conduct, in the sense described in *Disney* and *Caremark*, is essential to establish director oversight liability, the fiduciary duty violated by that conduct is the duty of loyalty.

This view of a failure to act in good faith results in two additional doctrinal consequences. First, although good faith may be described colloquially as part of a "triad" of fiduciary duties that includes the duties of care and loyalty, the obligation to act in good faith does not establish an independent fiduciary duty that stands on the same footing as the duties of care and loyalty. Only the latter two duties, where violated, may directly result in liability, whereas a failure to act in good faith may do so, but indirectly. The second doctrinal consequence is that the fiduciary duty of loyalty is not limited to cases involving a financial or other cognizable fiduciary conflict of interest. It also encompasses cases where the fiduciary fails to act in good faith. As the Court of Chancery aptly put it in *Guttman*, "[a] director cannot act loyally towards the corporation unless she acts in the good faith belief that her actions are in the corporation's best interest."

See the discussion later in this chapter about how these evolving notions of the role of good faith should be of particular interest to directors serving on compensation committees.

THE BUSINESS JUDGMENT RULE

The "business judgment rule" is a judicially created rebuttable presumption that limits the ability to second-guess board decisions made honestly and in good faith. The Delaware Supreme Court in the *Disney* case has articulated the business judgment rule as follows:

> Our law presumes that "in making a business decision the directors of a corporation acted on an informed basis, in good faith, and in the honest belief that the action taken was in the best interests of the company." [*Aronson v. Lewis*, 473. A. 2d 805 (Del. 1984)] Those presumptions can be rebutted if the plaintiff shows that the directors breached their fiduciary duty of care or of loyalty or acted in bad faith. If that is shown, the burden then shifts to the director defendants to demonstrate that the challenged act or transaction was entirely fair to the corporation and its shareholders.

Thus, directors' decisions will be respected by courts unless the directors are interested or lack independence relative to the decision, do not act in good faith, act in a manner that cannot be attributed to a rational business purpose, or reach their decision by a grossly negligent process that includes the failure to consider all material facts reasonably available [*Brehm v. Eisner*, 746 A.2d 244, 264 n.66 (Del. 2000)].

When a plaintiff challenging a director's decision succeeds in rebutting the presumption of the business judgment rule, the judicial deference to director decision making afforded by the rule disappears and the burden shifts to the defendant director to prove the entire fairness of the challenged decision.

Even if a director makes a good faith, impartial business decision in a manner that satisfies the duty of care due process, the business judgment rule will not protect a decision that cannot be attributed to any rational business purpose. Put another way, irrationality is the outer limit of the business judgment rule. However, the limited substantive review of a business decision contemplated by this outer limit of the business judgment rule (i.e., is the decision "irrational") may really be a way of inferring bad faith, and thus may have little or no significance independent of the good faith element of the business judgment rule.

In summary, the business judgment rule protects the business decisions of corporate directors who act in good faith, on an informed basis, and without a conflict of interest so long as the decisions can be attributed to a rational business purpose. Nevertheless, as previously indicated, there are limits on the degree of judicial deference afforded to the business judgments of corporate directors.

When the business judgment rule does not apply due to the directors having an interest in the matter being approved, the entire fairness standard is a formidable hurdle, as illustrated by the 2007 Delaware Chancery Court decision in *Valeant Pharmaceuticals International v. Jerney,* Del. Ct. Ch. New Castle No. 19947 (March 1, 2007). The "entire fairness" analysis has two nonindependent components: fair dealing and fair price. The fair dealing aspect addresses the questions of when the transaction was timed, how it was initiated and negotiated, how it was disclosed to the directors, and how approvals were obtained. The fair price element of the analysis examines the economic and financial considerations. In *Valeant*, outside directors who approved a transaction bonus for themselves and management were not entitled to the business judgment rule due to their self-interest in the matter. The Chancery Court was highly critical of the process followed by the compensation committee in approving the bonuses and in its reliance on the report of an outside compensation consultant that had initially been selected by management. Among other things, this case illustrates the limitations of Section 141(e) of the Delaware corporation code, which provides that a director will be "fully protected" in relying on experts chosen with reasonable care, particularly in situations in which the business judgment rule is not applicable.

BOARD OVERSIGHT DUTIES

The role of a corporate director includes two principal functions: a decision-making function and an oversight function. The decision-making function generally involves action taken at a particular point in time, while the oversight function generally involves ongoing monitoring of the corporation's business and affairs over a period of time.

Proper discharge of the board's oversight responsibility has two principal components: (1) a duty to monitor by undertaking reasonable efforts to remain attentive to and informed of the corporation's business and affairs; and (2) a duty to inquire when indications of potential problems, or "red flags," arise. As explained by the drafters of the Model Act, the board's oversight function:

> refers to concern with the corporation's information and reporting systems and not to proactive inquiry searching out system inadequacies or noncompliance. While directors typically give attention to future plans and trends as well as current activities, they should not be expected to anticipate the problems which the corporation may face except in those circumstances where something has occurred to make it obvious to the board that the corporation should be addressing a particular problem. The standard of care associated with the oversight function involves gaining assurances from management and advisers that systems believed appropriate have been established coupled with ongoing monitoring of the systems in place, such as those concerned with legal compliance or internal controls—followed up with a proactive response when alerted to the need for inquiry.

Duty to Monitor

The duty of a board of directors to monitor corporate affairs is well established. The failure to discharge this duty, where found actionable, has typically been characterized by the courts in terms of abdication or sustained inattention, not a brief distraction or temporary interruption (Model Act Section 8.31). The ALI notes that courts have generally recognized the dangers inherent in making *post hoc* judgments about the care exercised by directors and officers and have allowed them considerable leeway. Nevertheless, according to the ALI, sustained patterns of inattention to obligations by directors or officers or unreasonable blindness to problems that later cause substantial harm will create exposure to liability. Cases illustrative of directors being found liable for breaching the duty to monitor include *Francis v. United Jersey Bank,* 432 A.2d 814 (N.J. 1981) and *Hoye v. Meek,* 795 F.2d 893 (10th Cir. 1986).

When directors do remain actively engaged and attentive to corporate affairs, courts have been more reluctant to hold them liable for breach of the duty to monitor notwithstanding their failure to detect and prevent misconduct occurring within the corporation. Notable Delaware cases illustrative of this include *Graham v. Allis-Chalmers Manufacturing Co.,* 188 A.2d 125 (Del. 1963), *In re Caremark International Inc. Derivative Litigation,* 698 A.2d 959 (Del. Ch. 1996), and most recently, *Stone v. Ritter,* discussed above in the context of the evolving analysis of the role of good faith, in which the Delaware Supreme Court said:

> We hold that *Caremark* articulates the necessary conditions predicate for director oversight liability: (a) the directors utterly failed to implement any reporting or information system or controls; *or* (b) having implemented such a system or controls, consciously failed to monitor or oversee its operations thus disabling themselves from being informed of risks or problems requiring their attention. In either case, imposition

of liability requires a showing that the directors knew that they were not discharging their fiduciary obligations. Where directors fail to act in the face of a known duty to act, thereby demonstrating a conscious disregard for their responsibilities, they breach their duty of loyalty by failing to discharge that fiduciary obligation in good faith.

In summary, courts have generally been reluctant to impose liability on directors for failing adequately to monitor corporate affairs absent some form of sustained inattention or abdication of duty. Courts have acknowledged that actively engaged boards will not always be able to detect and prevent misconduct occurring within the corporation. Thus, as long as reasonable efforts are undertaken to remain attentive to and informed of the corporation's business and affairs, directors generally will be found to have discharged their duty to monitor, even if loss-creating activities go unnoticed.

Duty to Inquire

The second prong of the duty of oversight is the duty to inquire when, in the course of monitoring corporate affairs, red flags arise indicating a potential problem that merits more in-depth attention. As stated by the drafters of the Model Act in Section 8.31:

> [E]mbedded in the oversight function is the need to inquire when suspicions are aroused. This duty is not a component of ongoing oversight, and does not entail proactive vigilance, but arises when, and only when, particular facts and circumstances of material concern (*e.g.*, evidence of embezzlement at a high level or the discovery of significant inventory shortages) suddenly surface.

Thus, in addition to remaining informed generally of corporate affairs through on going monitoring, directors must exercise reasonable care to recognize and inquire about circumstances that awaken suspicion. The circumstances surrounding a duty of inquiry can affect the manner and scope of inquiry that is appropriate.

Two cases illustrating the duty to inquire are *McCall v. Scott,* 239 F.3d 808 (6th Cir.), *amended,* 250 F. 3d 997 (6th Cir. 2001) and *In re Abbott Laboratories Derivative Shareholders Litigation,* 325 F.3d 795 (7th Cir. 2003).

DIRECTOR EXCULPATION

Since 1986, almost all states have adopted statutes permitting a corporation to include in its charter a provision limiting the personal liability of the corporation's directors for monetary damages to the corporation or its stockholders for breaches of fiduciary duty as a director, within certain public policy limits. These so-called "exculpation" statutes go a long way toward providing protection of directors, but the shield from liability is not absolute. All such exculpation statutes carve out certain types of liability for which the directors cannot be exculpated. In the Model Act and in Delaware those limitations include liability: (1) for any breach of the director's duty of loyalty to the corporation, (2) for acts or omissions not in good faith or that involve intentional misconduct or a knowing violation of law, (3) for approving unlawful distributions under state law, or (4) for any transaction from which the director derived an improper personal benefit.

The carve-out for "acts or omissions not in good faith or that involve intentional misconduct or a knowing violation of law" leaves room for a finding of liability in breaches of the duty of oversight. In this regard, it is noteworthy that the *Caremark* and *Stone* courts characterized its test for liability in the oversight context (i.e., "sustained or systematic failure of a director to exercise reasonable oversight") as conduct that lacks good faith. Accordingly, a failure to monitor that amounts to sustained inattention or abdication is not likely to be protected by a customary director exculpation provision.

A breach of the duty to inquire may be similarly vulnerable. As discussed earlier, when "red flags" arise in the course of monitoring corporate affairs, directors have an affirmative duty to respond to those red flags by making further inquiry. Under many states' laws, a negligent failure to recognize and respond to red flags may breach this duty. However, when a director exculpation provision applies (such as that in the Model Act or the Delaware code), a director's failure to respond to red flags must amount to conduct "not in good faith" or must involve "intentional misconduct" or "a knowing violation of law" in order to establish liability. Where, as under two leading cases regarding the duty to inquire (*McCall* and *Abbott*), a failure to respond to red flags amounts to a "conscious disregard of known risks," this could constitute conduct not in good faith and, if so, would not be protected by a director exculpation provision.

PRACTICAL APPLICATIONS OF FIDUCIARY DUTY RULES FOR THE COMPENSATION COMMITTEE IN SPECIFIC CONTEXTS

THE INCREASING FOCUS ON THE DUTIES OF DUE CARE AND THE ROLE OF GOOD FAITH IN MAKING COMPENSATION DECISIONS

For the first time in decades, the role of good faith in the context of board decisions galvanized public attention in 2003, when the Delaware Court of Chancery denied a motion to dismiss a complaint alleging that the directors of The Walt Disney Company had breached their fiduciary duty of good faith in connection with the hiring and later dismissal of Michael Ovitz [*In re Walt Disney Co. Derivative Litigation,* 825 A.2d 275 (Del. Ch. 2003)]. That procedural action led to widespread speculation that, in the post-Enron environment, Delaware corporate law might somehow be evolving so as to blur the distinction between the duty of care and the duty of good faith. This touched close to home in boardrooms across America, because a finding of lack of good faith not only deprives directors of the protection of the business judgment rule, but also renders them unindemnifiable and ineligible for exculpation from monetary damages under state law, and most likely bars recovery under director and officer liability insurance policies. Although the Delaware courts ultimately determined that the Disney directors' conduct did not amount to bad faith or even a lack of due care, the case raised the bar for procedural best practices in the context of compensation decisions.

The Disney directors' deliberations took place in an era that predated the current focus on executive compensation and post-Enron corporate governance. That may have played a role in the court's finding on the issue of due care. Whether it did or not, the court specifically found that the directors' conduct fell short of current best practices, and listed specific things that the board should have done better. The court specifically recommended the practice of using a spreadsheet (or what we would refer to now as a *tally sheet*) when considering management employment and/or severance agreements. The tally sheet should:

- Be prepared by or with the assistance of a compensation expert, showing the amount the executive would receive under various foreseeable circumstances (such as termination with or without "cause"; resignation with or without "good reason"; termination in connection with a change in control, retirement, and so on)

- Be explained to the committee members, either by the expert who prepared it or by a fellow committee member similarly knowledgeable about the agreement and its consequences

- Be attached as an exhibit to the minutes of the committee meeting at which it was discussed

- Form the basis for the deliberations and the decision by the committee

It is also a good practice to have the presentation and the decision take place at separate meetings, so that the committee will have ample time to assimilate the information and exercise independent, informed judgment. The use of tally sheets in this context should be second nature to compensation committees today. In fact, the new compensation disclosure rules of the Securities and Exchange Commission (SEC) require a company to describe and quantify in the annual proxy statement the amounts that would be received by each of the top executive officers in connection with a hypothetical termination of employment as of the end of the prior year, including termination by resignation, severance, retirement, or constructive termination, or a change in control. This disclosure requirement in effect codifies the "best practice" of preparing annual tally sheets to inform the board of this detailed information.

HEIGHTENED SCRUTINY IN CHANGE IN CONTROL CONSIDERATIONS

Compensation committees should be particularly mindful of the increased scrutiny that may be accorded their decisions about executive compensation or employment/

severance agreements in anticipation of a "hostile" change in control of the company (such as a tender offer or unsolicited merger proposal).

Directors faced with a takeover attempt are inherently endowed with competing interests. On one hand, they must, as always, act in the best interests of the corporation and its shareholders, complying with the familiar duties of care and loyalty, and the overarching requirement of good faith. But a change in control of the corporation often portends a change in management, including directors, thus feeding the directors' (particularly management directors') self-interest in preserving their positions with the company. Recognizing this inherent conflict, the Delaware judiciary introduced a notion of heightened scrutiny for board decisions made in defensive situations. Under this so-called "Unocal" standard (referring to *Unocal Corp. v. Mesa Petroleum Co.*, 493 A.2d 946 (Del. 1985)), the business judgment rule will not apply to protect the board's defensive action unless (1) the directors can show that they had reasonable grounds for believing that a danger to corporate policy and effectiveness existed because of another person's stock ownership, and (2) any defensive measure taken is reasonable in relation to the threat posed.

Once in a defensive situation, the Unocal standard would apply, for example, to decisions to approve change-in-control severance agreements for management or to approve generous executive compensation packages, both of which can have a deterrent effect to the acquirer. Having a majority of independent directors making the decision materially enhances the board's ability to satisfy the Unocal standard.

Whether or not in a defensive situation, the clear lesson from *Disney* (and now widely accepted best practice) is that, when considering employment, severance, or retirement agreements for management, the compensation committee should insist on reviewing numerical illustrations of the effect of the proposed benefits under various scenarios. An understanding of the magnitude of the arrangement is a baseline for the committee's ability to form a reasonable belief that it is in the best interest of shareholders. For example, while it is not uncommon to see agreements with full change-in-control tax gross-up protection for executive officers, the committee should fully understand the practical effects and hypothetical costs of such provisions before approving them. In order to appreciate the potential cost of such provisions, it is necessary to understand the nature and operation of the so-called "golden-parachute" excise tax. For a more technical discussion of these tax rules, see Chapter 8.

FIDUCIARY DUTIES IN THE CONTEXT OF OPTION GRANT PRACTICES

Notwithstanding the final resolution of the *Disney* case (absolving the directors from liability), any notion that the so-called duty of good faith might recede quietly into the background was short-lived. A scant eight months later, the Delaware Court of Chancery reintroduced the specter that a compensation committee might step across the line into bad faith in the context of option grant practices. Two decisions issued on the same day, *Ryan v. Gifford*, C.A. No. 2213-N (Del. Ch. Feb. 6, 2007) and *In Re Tyson Foods, Inc. Consolidated Shareholder Litigation*, C.A. No. 1106-N

(Del. Ch. Feb. 6, 2007), were each in the nature of denials of motions to dismiss claims in shareholder derivative suits, prior to any discovery having taken place. However, they give cogent insight into the views of the Delaware courts on option grant practices, as well as the renewed emphasis on the role of good faith in everyday board actions.

Ryan v. Gifford is an options backdating case in which it is alleged that the board of Maxim Integrated Products, Inc. allowed at least nine options to be backdated over the course of 1998 to 2002. It should come as little surprise that the Court of Chancery would view the intentional backdating of options as being inconsistent with the requirement to act in good faith. In the opinion, Chancellor William Chandler wrote:

> Based on the allegations of the complaint, and all reasonable inferences drawn there-from, I am convinced that the intentional violation of a shareholder approved stock option plan, coupled with fraudulent disclosures regarding the directors' purported compliance with that plan, constitute conduct that is disloyal to the corporation and is therefore an act in bad faith. Plaintiffs allege the following conduct: Maxim's directors affirmatively represented to Maxim's shareholders that the exercise price of any option grant would be no less than 100% of the fair value of the shares, measured by the market price of the shares on the date the option is granted. Maxim shareholders, possessing an absolute right to rely on those assurances when determining whether to approve the plans, in fact relied upon representations and approved the plans. Thereafter, Maxim's directors are alleged to have deliberately attempted to circumvent their duty to price the shares at no less than market value on the option grant dated by surreptitiously changing the dates on which the options were granted. To make matters worse, the directors allegedly failed to disclose this conduct to their shareholders, instead making false representations regarding the option dates in many of their public disclosures.
>
> I am unable to fathom a situation where the deliberate violation of a shareholder approved stock option plan and false disclosures, obviously intended to mislead shareholders into thinking that the directors complied honestly with the shareholder-approved option plan, is anything but an act of bad faith. It certainly cannot be said to amount to faithful and devoted conduct of a loyal fiduciary. Well-pleaded allegations of such conduct are sufficient, in my opinion, to rebut the business judgment rule and to survive a motion to dismiss.

If the plaintiffs in this case are able to rebut the business judgment rule, and the defendants are then unable to prove that their actions were entirely fair to the corporation, this case will add to the already significant headaches faced by directors who are involved in an options backdating review. As we know from the discussions earlier in this chapter, a finding of lack of good faith, and consequently a breach of the duty of loyalty, will strip the directors of their ability to be indemnified or insured and of the protection of exculpation provisions in the corporation's charter, leaving them entirely vulnerable for unreimbursable personal liability.

In Re Tyson Foods involves, among other things, the alleged propitious timing of option grants to precede the release of positive news (a practice sometimes referred to as "spring-loading"). Chancellor Chandler's comments on this practice are more thought provoking, given that many people—including notably at least one member of the SEC—view this practice as being within the realm of benign, or even astute, business judgment. The court recognized the more nuanced analysis in this context, stating:

> Whether a board of directors may in good faith grant spring-loaded options is a somewhat more difficult question than that posed by options backdating, a practice that has attracted much journalistic, prosecutorial, and judicial thinking of late. At their heart, all backdated options involve a fundamental, incontrovertible lie: directors who approve an option dissemble as to the date on which the grant was actually made. Allegations of spring-loading implicate a much more subtle deception.

> Granting spring-loaded options, without explicit authorization from shareholders, clearly involves an indirect deception. A director's duty of loyalty includes the duty to deal fairly and honestly with the shareholders for whom he is a fiduciary. It is inconsistent with such a duty for a board of directors to ask for shareholder approval of an incentive stock option plan and then later to distribute shares to managers in such a way as to undermine the very objectives approved by shareholders. This remains true even if the board complies with the strict letter of a shareholder-approved plan as it relates to strike prices or issue dates.

> The question before the Court is not, as plaintiffs suggest, whether spring-loading constitutes a form of insider trading as it would be understood under federal securities law. The relevant issue is whether a director acts in bad faith by authorizing options with a market-value strike price, as he is required to do by a shareholder-approved incentive option plan, at a time when he *knows* those shares are actually worth more than the exercise price. A director who intentionally uses inside knowledge not available to shareholders in order to enrich employees while avoiding shareholder-imposed requirements cannot, in my opinion, be said to be acting loyally and in good faith as a fiduciary.

Moreover, the *Tyson* court ruled that the directors' alleged actions were sufficient to toll the statute of limitations on the basis of equitable tolling and fraudulent concealment.

> It is difficult to conceive of an instance, consistent with the concept of loyalty and good faith, in which a fiduciary may declare that an option is granted at "market rate" and simultaneously withhold that both the fiduciary and the recipient knew at the time that those options would quickly be worth much more. Certainly at this stage of the litigation, plaintiffs are entitled to the reasonable inference of conduct inconsistent with a fiduciary duty.

Both substantively and procedurally, the focus of the court in *Tyson* was on the deceptive nature of spring-loaded grants, rather than on the fact that they could result in lower-than-market exercise prices (assuming that discounted options are not prohibited by the shareholder-approved plan). Because directors are quite often, if not most of the time, aware of nonpublic information that could affect the price of the company's stock, it is a sobering thought that the grant of an option at any time could in hindsight be viewed as spring-loading—particularly if the consequence of such practice is unindemnifiable personal liability. Should it make a difference to the "deception" analysis that the shareholder-approved equity plan contemplates the grant of restricted stock, which is in essence a zero-priced option? Whatever the outcome, Chancellor Chandler's comments in the *Tyson* motion-to-dismiss decision will likely compel compensation committees to adopt option grant policies that limit the grant of options to the period shortly after the release of earnings.

PUBLIC DISCLOSURE OF COMPENSATION POLICIES AND DECISIONS

Beginning with the 2007 proxy season, public companies are required to produce a Compensation Discussion and Analysis (CD&A) that serves as an overview of the company's overall executive compensation policies and decisions, the material compensation decisions made under those programs and policies with respect to the company's top executive officers, and the most important factors considered in making those decisions. This report appears in the proxy statement for meetings at which directors are elected and in the company's annual report on Form 10-K. For more information on the nature of this required report, see Item 402(b) of Regulation S-K of the SEC, which is discussed in Chapter 6 and included in full in Appendix A.

Whenever corporate fiduciaries communicate publicly or directly with stockholders, they must do so honestly, candidly, and completely in all material respects. This standard of disclosure arises out of the more general fiduciary duties of care and loyalty. A leading case for this proposition is *Malone v. Brincat,* 722 A.2d 5 (Del. 1998), in which the Delaware Supreme Court found an implied duty of accurate and honest disclosure whenever directors communicate publicly on behalf of the corporation, stating:

> Whenever directors communicate publicly or directly with shareholders about the corporation's affairs, with or without a request for shareholder action, directors have a fiduciary duty to shareholders to exercise due care, good faith and loyalty. It follows *a fortiori* that when directors communicate publicly or directly with shareholders about corporate matters the *sine qua non* of directors' fiduciary duty to shareholders is honesty.

Malone was directly addressing disclosures that have a direct impact on the financial condition of the company. As such, it may not bear as directly on a discussion of compensation policy and decisions such as is contained in the CD&A. Certainly, this does not excuse the company and its compensation committee from being forthright, thoughtful, and honest in the CD&A. However, the scrutiny applied to the CD&A from a fiduciary duty standpoint may not be quite as intense as for disclosure of a more factual nature that could affect the financial condition of the company.

Nevertheless, unlike the prior years' compensation committee report included in the proxy statement, the new CD&A is soliciting material and is deemed "filed" with the SEC, which makes it subject to the liabilities of Section 18 of the Securities Exchange Act of 1934. In addition, to the extent that the CD&A and any of the other disclosure regarding executive officer and director compensation or other matters are included or incorporated by reference into a periodic report, the disclosure is covered by the certifications that principal executive officers and principal financial officers are required to make under the Sarbanes-Oxley Act of 2002. Likewise, a company's disclosure controls and procedures apply to the preparation of the company's proxy statement and Form 10-K, including the CD&A.

SUMMARY

Disney, Ritter, and *Tyson* provide an important lesson for compensation committees in Delaware and elsewhere: Following best practices is more important today than ever before. Blind reliance on the business judgment rule is not warranted, especially in matters as fundamental to the compensation committee's charge as considering and approving management compensation and severance arrangements, granting equity compensation, and explaining the rationale for compensation decisions to the company's owners. The recent emphasis on good faith as an integral element of the duty of loyalty should be uppermost in the minds of all directors as they apply themselves to the business at hand.

SELF-REGULATORY ORGANIZATION CORPORATE GOVERNANCE RULES AND "BEST PRACTICE" RECOMMENDATIONS

NASDAQ AND NYSE RULES

In November 2003, the SEC approved significant changes to the listing standards of the NYSE and NASDAQ that were intended to enhance corporate governance and bolster investor confidence following a number of well-publicized corporate failures among U.S. public companies. These listing standards supplement, rather than replace, the corporate governance reforms adopted by the SEC pursuant to Sarbanes-Oxley Act of 2002.

Without going into detail here about all aspects of these corporate governance listing standards, Exhibit 5.1 gives a brief overview and comparison of the NYSE and NASDAQ rules.

Exhibit 5.1 NYSE and NASDAQ Governance Rules

	NYSE Standards	NASDAQ Standards
Composition of board of directors	• Must have a majority of independent directors.	• Must have a majority of independent directors and identify them in the proxy statement.
Definition of director independence	• Board must affirmatively determine that the director has no material relationship with the company. The following persons *cannot* be considered independent: • A director who is or was in the last three years an employee of the company, or whose immediate family member is or was in the last three years an executive officer of the company. • A director who, or whose immediate family member, received in the last three years more than $100,000 per year in direct compensation from the company. • A director who is or was in the last three years affiliated with or employed by, or whose immediate family member is or was in the last three years affiliated with or employed in a professional capacity by, a present or former internal or external auditor of the company. • A director who, or whose immediate family member, is or was in the last three years employed as an executive officer of another company where any of the listed company's present executives serve on the compensation committee of the other company. • A director who is an executive officer or employee of, or whose immediate family member is an executive officer of, another company that makes payments to or receives payments from the company for property or services in an amount that in any single fiscal year exceeds the greater of $1 million or 2% of the other company's consolidated gross revenues, is not independent until three years after falling below such threshold.	• Board must affirmatively determine that the director has no relationships that would interfere with the exercise of independent judgment. • The following persons *cannot* be considered independent: • A director who is or was in the last three years an employee of the company or an affiliate; or • A director who, or whose family member, accepted in the last three years payments in excess of $100,000 from the company or an affiliate; or • A director with any family member who is or was in the last three years an executive officer of the company or an affiliate; or • A director who is, or has a family member who is, a partner, controlling shareholder, or executive officer of any organization to which the company made, or from which the company received, payments for property or services in the last three years, that exceeded the greater of $200,000 or 5% of the recipient's consolidated gross revenues for the year in which the payments were made; or • A director who is, or who has a family member who is, employed as an executive officer of another entity where at any time during the current or past three years any of the executive officers of the listed company served on the compensation c-ommittee of such other entity; or • A director who is, or whose family member is, a current partner of the company's outside auditor, or was a partner or employee of the company's outside auditor who worked on the company's

Nonmanagement director executive sessions	• Nonmanagement directors (which may include directors who do not qualify as "independent") must meet in regularly scheduled executive sessions without management present.
	• An executive session of only "independent" directors should be held at least once a year.
	• Independent directors must regularly meet in executive sessions at which only they are present.
Nominating/corporate governance committee	Company must have a nominating/corporate governance committee composed entirely of independent directors. The committee must have and publish a written charter.	• A nominating committee comprised solely of independent directors or a majority of the independent directors must select, or recommend for the board's selection, director nominees.
		The company must certify that it has adopted a formal written charter or board resolution addressing the nominations process.
Compensation committee	• Must be composed entirely of independent directors. The committee must adopt and publish a written charter. The charter must be included on the company's web site, and the Form 10-K must state that the charter is available on the web site and in print to any shareholder who requests it.	• CEO compensation must be determined, or recommended to the board for determination, either by a compensation committee comprised solely of independent directors or a majority of the independent directors, and the CEO may not be present during voting or deliberations. Compensation of all other executive officers must be determined in the same manner, except that the CEO may be present.
		If the compensation committee has at least three members, one nonindependent director (who is not an officer or employee or a family member of an officer or employee) may serve on the committee (for no more than two years) if the board, under exceptional and limited circumstances, determines it is the company's and the shareholders' best interests. The nature of such non-independent director's relationship with the company and the reasons for the board's determination must be disclosed in the next annual proxy statement or in its Form 10-K if a proxy statement is not filed.

(Continued)

Exhibit 5.1 (Continued)

	NYSE Standards	NASDAQ Standards
Audit committee member qualifications	• *Independence.* Company must have an audit committee with a minimum of three members, who each satisfy the independence requirements under both the NYSE and Exchange Act Rule 10A-3(b)(1). • *Financial Literacy.* Each member of the audit committee must be financially literate or must become financially literate within a reasonable period of time after appointment to the committee. At least one member also must have accounting or related financial management expertise.	• *Independence.* Company must have an audit committee consisting of at least three directors who each satisfy the independence requirements under NASDAQ and Exchange Act Rule 10A-3(b)(1) *and* have not participated in the preparation of the financial statements of the company or any current subsidiary of the company at any time during the past three years. • *Financial Literacy.* Members must be able to read and understand financial statements. The company must certify that at least one audit committee member is financially sophisticated (as defined).
Audit committee charter and internal audit function	• Audit committee must adopt and publish a written charter. The company must also establish an internal audit function, which may be outsourced to a firm other than its independent auditor. • The company must include the audit committee charter on its website, and the Form 10-K must state that the information is available on the website and in print to any shareholder who requests it.	• Audit committee must adopt a written charter. • The company must conduct an appropriate review of all related-party transactions (as defined in Item 404 of Regulation S-K) on an on-going basis and all such transactions shall be approved by the audit committee or another independent body of the board of directors.
Shareholder approval of equity compensation plans	• See Chapter 7 for a discussion of these rules.	• See Chapter 7 for a discussion of these rules.
Corporate governance guidelines	• Company must adopt and disclose corporate governance guidelines.	• No requirements

Codes of business conduct and ethics	• Company must adopt and disclose a code of business conduct and ethics for directors, officers and employees. Only the board of directors or a board committee may waive provisions of the code for executive officers or directors, and such waivers must be promptly disclosed to the company's shareholders.	• Company must have a publicly available code of conduct that complies with the definition of a Code of Ethics under the Sarbanes-Oxley Act and which is applicable to all directors, executive officers and employees. Only the board of directors may grant waivers of compliance with the code for executive officers and directors, and all such waivers, as well as the reason for the waiver, must be disclosed on a Form 8-K within five days.
Certifications	• CEOs of listed companies must certify to the NYSE each year that, as of the date of the certification, he or she is not aware of any violation by the listed company of the NYSE corporate governance listing standards.	• No requirement
Enforcement	• NYSE may issue public reprimand letters, suspend trading or delist a company for violations of listing standards.	• NASDAQ may deny relisting to a company based on a corporate governance violation that occurred while that company's appeal of the delisting was pending. A material misrepresentation or omission by an issuer to NASDAQ may form the basis for delisting.

BUSINESS GROUPS WEIGH IN WITH "BEST PRACTICES" RECOMMENDATIONS REGARDING EXECUTIVE COMPENSATION

Conference Board Report

The Conference Board's 12-member Commission on Public Trust and Private Enterprise was formed in 2002 to address the circumstances that led to the well-publicized corporate scandals of that era and the resulting decline of confidence in corporations, their leaders and America's capital markets. The first of the Commission's three reports was published in September 2002, entitled *Executive Compensation: Principles, Recommendations and Specific Best Practice Suggestions.* The Commission first identified certain factors related to executive compensation that it believed contributed to the corporate implosion, including overuse of fixed-price stock options in the face of a sustained bull market, an imbalance between unprecedented levels of executive compensation and the relationship to long-term company performance, lack of independent and vigorous oversight by compensation committees, and the lack of downside risk in compensation vehicles. The report sets out seven principles that are intended to guide compensation committees to restore good corporate governance, followed in each instance by specific practice suggestions.

The second report, entitled *Corporate Governance: Principles, Recommendations and Specific Best Practice Suggestions,* was published in January 2003. In this report, the Commission presents certain corporate governance practices that it believes should be upheld in order to prevent shareholders' diminishing trust in, and respect of, the corporate form. These factors include long-term ownership focus, appropriate balance between executive officers and the board of directors, an independent nominating/corporate governance committee, and self-evaluations by the board of directors. The report sets out nine principles that are intended to guide compensation committees to restore good corporate governance.

The third of the Commission's three reports, entitled *Audit and Accounting: Principles, Recommendations and Specific Best Practice Suggestions,* also was published in January 2003. This report provides seven principles that it believes will strengthen shareholders' confidence in audited financial statements.

These three reports, along with those that follow below, are suggested reading for all directors who serve on compensation committees. They can be found on The Conference Board's web site at www.conference-board.org/pdf_free/SR-03-04.pdf.

Breeden Report on MCI: *Restoring Trust*

This report arose out of the bankruptcy of WorldCom in 2002, which followed accusations of accounting fraud and executive malfeasance by former CEO Bernie Ebbers. The court appointed Richard Breeden (a former chairman of the SEC) to serve as corporate monitor to investigate corporate practices at WorldCom and issue a report of recommendation. Published in August 2003, the Breeden Report contains 78 detailed recommendations dealing with board governance. All of these were accepted unanimously by the new MCI Board. Of the 78 specific recommendations, nine relate to executive compensation practices, five to director compensation, and nine to the compensation committee itself.

While the Breeden Report is specific to MCI, generally speaking, its recommendations are very conservative positions when compared to historical practices. Some of the more controversial recommendations are a mandatory 10-year term limit for directors, a requirement to change accounting firms every 10 years, an absolute prohibition on granting stock options, and the requirement that compensation limit be housed in the corporate charter or bylaws. Some of the other recommendations may be useful for consideration. The Breeden Report is of interest primarily as an example of decided backlash from the era of corporate scandals.

Business Roundtable Report

The Business Roundtable is an association of chief executive officers of leading U.S. corporations with a combined workforce of 10 million employees and over \$4.5 trillion in annual revenues. It is recognized as an authoritative voice on matters affecting U.S. business corporations, and as such has an interest in improving corporate governance practices. In January 2007, the Business Roundtable published its updated *Report on Executive Compensation: Principles and Commentary,* containing and discussing a list of seven corporate governance principles relating to executive compensation. Short and to the point, they are as follows:

1. Executive compensation should be closely aligned with the long-term interests of stockholders and with corporate goals and strategies. It should include significant performance-based criteria related to long-term stockholder value and should reflect upside potential and downside risk.
2. Compensation of the CEO and other top executives should be determined entirely by independent directors, either as a compensation committee or together with the other independent directors based on the committee's recommendations.
3. The compensation committee should understand all aspects of executive compensation and should review the maximum payout and all benefits under executive compensation arrangements. The compensation committee should understand the maximum payout under multiple scenarios, including retirement, termination with or without cause, and severance in connection with business combinations or sale of the business.
4. The compensation committee should require executives to build and maintain significant continuing equity investment in the corporation.
5. The compensation committee should have independent, experienced expertise available to provide advice on executive compensation arrangements and plans. The compensation committee should oversee consultants to ensure that they do not have conflicts that would limit their ability to provide independent advice.
6. The compensation committee should oversee its corporation's executive compensation programs to see that they are in compliance with applicable laws and regulations and aligned with best practice.

7. Corporations should provide complete, accurate, understandable, and timely disclosure to stockholders concerning all elements of executive compensation and the factors underlying executive compensation policies and decisions.

Commentary on each of these principles is contained in the longer report, which can be found at www.businessroundtable.org/pdf/ExecutiveCompensationPrinciples.pdf.

Institutional Shareholder Services (ISS) Policies

ISS believes that, while independent directors bear much of the responsibility to ensure good corporate governance, shareholders also play a critical role in the governance process. ISS issues proxy voting and corporate governance guidelines to institutional investors and corporations. In January 2007, ISS published its report, *ISS US Corporate Governance Policy 2007 Updates*. The report discusses ISS's current and new policy positions on a number of corporate governance issues and addresses the rationale behind its evolving policies with respect to particular issues. There are over 15 corporate governance issues identified and discussed in the 2007 report, including performance tests for directors, "burn rates" and equity awards, poor executive pay practices, options backdating, board independence, performance-based stock options and other equity awards the lack of a nominating committee, the definition of *independent director*, and equity-based compensation plans. Given the increased focus on shareholders' interests, compensation committee members should find this report instructive for anticipating reactions of institutional shareholders with respect to corporate governance and executive compensation issues.

In addition, based on information contained in public filings and corporate web sites and press releases, ISS calculates for many publicly traded companies a Corporate Governance Quotient score, or CGQ. The CGQ reflects the governance practices of a public company based on numerous criteria, including board and committee composition and executive and director compensation. Companies are given an overall score and a ranking relative to the market and a peer group. ISS calculates these rankings regardless of whether a company chooses to be ranked, in order to assist institutional shareholders in evaluating the quality of a company's governance practices. Boards of directors should seek to be cognizant of their CGQ and ranking and the specific elements that determine the CGQ. Taking action to follow many of the "best practices" set forth in these reports and addressed elsewhere in this book may improve a company's CGQ and ranking.

TIAA-CREF Policy Statement

The fifth edition of the policy statement on corporate governance by TIAA-CREF was issued in March 2007 and reflects its policies and guidelines in light of recent change in the corporate governance and equity compensation arena. The statement discusses

TIAA-CREF's policies and guidelines with respect to the following aspects of corporate governance:

- Shareholder rights
- Director elections
- The board of directors
- Board structure and processes
- Executive compensation
- Governance of companies domiciled outside the United States
- Environmental and social responsibility issues

Their policies regarding executive compensation have been updated to reflect expectations on CD&A, and TIAA-CREF makes clear that they support the SEC's new disclosure rules. these policies can be found at www.tiaa-cref.org/pubs/pdf/governance_policy.pdf.

Chapter 6

Disclosure of Executive and Director Compensation

This chapter begins with a detailed summary of the rules on disclosure of executive and director compensation and transactions with management, which were completely overhauled in 2006. The chapter then reviews some of the preexisting disclosure requirements that relate to equity-based compensation plans, and concludes with a very brief description of selected items of Regulation S-K which are relevant to officer and director compensation and transactions. The full text of each of these selected items is included in Appendix A.

BACKGROUND

In August 2006, after what proved to be the most fruitful comment period in recent history, the Securities and Exchange Commission (SEC) adopted new rules relating to the disclosure of executive and director compensation and related matters. The rules prescribed in the 436-page release detailed a new regime for disclosure of executive and director compensation at a level that had been long awaited by the investing community. The new rules also address disclosures of related-person transactions, director independence, corporate governance, and other similar matters.

While the rules are thorough and comprehensive, the SEC made it clear that it is not in the practice of judging the propriety of a company's executive compensation program. Rather, its purpose is to provide investors with the tools necessary to make informed decisions. The new rules are drafted with that in mind, and require descriptive "principles-based" disclosure regarding a company's compensation program.

The historical disclosure regime was based on a relatively narrow rules-based approach, requiring in most areas strict adherence to tabular presentation of prescribed elements of compensation, augmented by footnotes and other explanations where required or deemed useful. In 1992, when the old rules were adopted, this tabular focus was an intentional departure from the then prevalent free-form narrative description of compensation plans and benefits, which more often than not resulted in muddled information that defied comparability analysis. While it has not come full circle with the new rules, the SEC's current focus is on a more balanced "principles-based" approach to compensation disclosure. This approach melds the familiar tabular presentation of specific compensation elements with a requirement for supporting narrative discussion that reaches beyond the mere presentation of numbers, to explain the purpose, function, and rationale for the different elements comprising the whole executive compensation program. While the old rules had been outpaced by evolving compensation practices that in some instances allowed significant compensation to fall outside of the disclosure net, the new rules are designed to be nimble—requiring disclosure of *all* elements of compensation, in whatever form they may take.

COMPENSATION DISCUSSION AND ANALYSIS

The most striking addition to the disclosure scheme is the new Compensation Discussion and Analysis (CD&A) section, which replaces the traditional compensation committee report. The CD&A is *not* a report of the compensation committee, it does not address the meetings and discussions of the compensation committee, and it is not made "over the names" of individual compensation committee members as under the old rules for the compensation committee report. Rather, the CD&A is company disclosure that is deemed "filed" with the SEC as part of the proxy statement and any other filings in which it is included. As such, the CD&A is subject to the liabilities of Section 18 of the Securities Exchange Act of 1934 (Exchange Act) and covered by the chief executive officer (CEO) and chief financial officer (CFO) certifications required to be made under the Sarbanes-Oxley Act of 2002.

The CD&A borrows from the tradition of Management's Discussion and Analysis of Financial Condition and Results of Operations (MD&A) under Item 303 of Regulation S-K, in that it calls for a frank, accountable, and individualized discussion of information relevant to investors. The CD&A serves as an overview of the company's overall executive compensation policies and decisions, the material compensation decisions made under those programs and policies with respect to the company's top executive officers, and the material factors considered in making those decisions. The CD&A should address (but not repeat) the information contained in the accompanying compensation tables. However, the CD&A disclosure is not limited to the company's last fiscal year. Any relevant actions taken after the last fiscal year-end should be disclosed, as well as any information from prior years if such information provides context to the discussion. Boilerplate disclosure is roundly discouraged, and the report must be presented in "plain English."

The CD&A must address at a minimum the following six items:

1. The objectives of the company's compensation program
2. What the compensation program is designed to reward
3. Each element of compensation
4. Why the company chooses to pay each element
5. How the company determines the amount (and, where applicable, the formula) for each element of compensation
6. How each compensation element and the company's decisions regarding that element fit into the company's overall compensation objectives and affect decisions regarding other elements

In addition to these six main areas that must be addressed in the CD&A, the rules list 15 supplemental issues that should be addressed to the extent they are relevant to an understanding of the company's compensation program. Selected examples of such additional information include:

- The policies for allocating between long-term and currently paid-out compensation, and between cash and noncash compensation
- How the determination is made as to when awards are granted, including awards of equity-based compensation such as options
- What specific items of corporate performance are taken into account in setting compensation policies and making compensation decisions
- How specific forms of compensation are structured and implemented to reflect corporate or individual performance
- How prior compensation is considered in setting future compensation (e.g., how gains from prior option or stock awards are considered in setting retirement benefits)
- The impact of the accounting and tax treatments of particular forms of compensation
- The company's stock ownership requirements or guidelines, and any policies regarding hedging the economic risk of such ownership
- The role of executive officers in determining executive compensation

Despite the level of specific discussion required, the instructions to the CD&A provide that companies are not required to disclose target levels with respect to quantitative or qualitative performance-related factors, or any factors or criteria involving confidential commercial or business information, the disclosure of which would result in competitive harm to the company. The standard to use in making a determination to omit confidential information is the same as would apply when requesting confidential treatment of information in a registration statement or periodic report, but companies are not required to submit a confidential treatment request in this context. Target levels cannot be omitted if the information is otherwise publicly disclosed. A company may be required to demonstrate to the SEC that omitted information would result in competitive harm if disclosed. Also, the CD&A must discuss the significance of the undisclosed target levels, so that an investor could understand, for example, the relative degree of difficulty in achieving the target levels.

THE TABULAR DISCLOSURES

Following the CD&A, detailed disclosure of executive compensation is organized into three broad categories, each as discussed in more detail later in this chapter:

- *Historical compensation.* Compensation paid currently or deferred with respect to the last three fiscal years continues to be reflected in a Summary Compensation

Table, but in a revised and reorganized format that includes a new column requiring disclosure of a single figure for total compensation. The three-year disclosure is phased in over 2006, 2007, and 2008. The Summary Compensation Table is followed by a supplemental table providing backup information for grants of plan-based awards.

- *Equity holdings.* Holdings of equity interests that relate to compensation or are potential sources of future gains, and information regarding recent realization of gains upon the exercise or vesting of equity awards, is disclosed in two new tables.

- *Retirement and postemployment payments and benefits.* Retirement benefits, including pension benefits and nonqualified deferred compensation, are reflected in two new tables. Disclosure as to other potential postemployment benefits, such as those payable in the event of a change in control or constructive termination, are required in narrative rather than tabular form, although companies are free to add tables if that would improve the clarity of the disclosure.

NAMED EXECUTIVE OFFICERS

As in the past, the disclosures for officers focus exclusively on the company's so-called "named executive officers." Historically, a company's named executive officers included its CEO and the four most highly compensated executive officers, excluding the CEO. The new rules add the principal financial officer to the list of "named executive officers," and the number of additional highly compensated executive officers is reduced from four to three.

Note that the new rules use the terms *principal* executive officer and *principal* financial officer, rather than *chief* executive officer and *chief* financial officer. Accordingly, the tables refer to the PEO and PFO, rather than CEO and CFO.

Historically, the determination of the most highly compensated executive officers was based only on total annual salary and bonus for the last fiscal year. The new rules revise this requirement so that the determination is made on the basis of *total compensation* for the most recent fiscal year, minus (1) the actuarial present value of accumulated pension plan benefits and (2) above-market earnings on nonqualified deferred compensation. For purposes of determining these three other named executive officers, the new rules eliminate the historical exception for compensation that is "not recurring and unlikely to continue" because of the SEC's concern that such exception was susceptible to manipulation. However, the historical exception for payments attributable to overseas assignments was retained.

The new rules retain the historical requirement to include up to two additional individuals for whom disclosure would have been required but for the fact that they were no longer serving as executive officers at the end of the last completed fiscal year.

One result of the change in the definition of *named executive officer* is that the number of officers who could potentially make the list is larger and more unpredictable than in past years.

SUMMARY COMPENSATION TABLE

The Summary Compensation Table continues to serve as the principal disclosure vehicle regarding executive compensation. Consistent with historical requirements, the table requires disclosure of compensation for the company's named executive officers for each of the last three completed fiscal years, whether or not actually paid out. Because the new rules significantly change the mix of information required by the table, however, the three-year disclosure is phased in, so that a company's 2007 proxy statement was required to include disclosure covering only 2006, and the 2008 proxy statement will include disclosure for 2006 and 2007; in 2009 and thereafter, three years of historical compensation data will once again be included in the table.

The reconfigured Summary Compensation Table includes eight columns. These are discussed briefly below, because the information they call for, in some cases, is not obvious:

1. *Salary.* The salary column includes salary earned in the year, as well as salary that was earned but deferred.
2. *Bonus.* The traditional bonus column is retained, but includes only bonus amounts that are not performance based (such as discretionary or guaranteed bonuses). Annual cash bonuses that are earned based on performance are reflected in the Non-Equity Incentive Plan Compensation column, which is a departure from historical practice. This column proved to be an area of some confusion in the first year under the new rules, because it is not always clear whether a bonus is discretionary or performance based, where the committee retains discretion to adjust a performance-based award up or down based on subjective assessments.
3. *Stock Awards.* This column reflects the amount expensed by the company for financial accounting purposes in the designated year for stock awards, regardless of the year of grant. Therefore, it may include expense recognized in the latest year for awards made in prior years. For purposes of the disclosure rules, the term *stock awards* means equity awards such as restricted stock, restricted stock units, phantom stock, phantom stock units, common stock equivalent units, or other similar instruments that do not have option-like features (sometimes referred to in other contexts as "full-value" awards).
4. *Option Awards.* Just as for stock awards, this column reflects the amount expensed by the company for financial accounting purposes in the designated year for option awards, regardless of the year of grant. Therefore, it may include expense recognized in the latest year for awards made in prior years. For purposes of the disclosure rules, the term *option awards* means stock options, stock appreciation rights, and similar stock-based compensation instruments that have option-like features (sometimes referred to in other contexts as "appreciation-type" awards).

   Where the earnings on outstanding stock awards and option awards are not included as part of the fair value calculation for accounting purposes, the earnings on such awards are required to be reported in the All Other Compensation column. For example, dividends or dividend equivalents paid on stock awards are typically included in the grant date fair value calculation for the stock award and would not be separately reported as earnings. It is less typical for option awards to have dividend equivalent rights or other types of earnings.

5. *Non-Equity Incentive Plan Compensation.* A new Non-Equity Incentive Plan Compensation column shows the dollar value, including earnings, of any awards granted under an incentive plan where the relevant performance measure is not based on the price of the company's equity securities and the award may not be settled by issuance of the company's equity securities. Awards must be disclosed in this column in the year in which the relevant performance criteria are satisfied and the compensation earned, regardless of whether payment is actually made to the named executive officer in that year.

6. *Change in Pension Value and Nonqualified Deferred Compensation Earnings.* Companies must disclose in this column the aggregate change in actuarial present value to the named executive officer of defined-benefit and actuarial plans accrued during the year and any above-market or preferential earnings on nonqualified deferred compensation. The company must identify and quantify the full amount of each element in a footnote.

7. *All Other Compensation.* This column serves as a catch-all for disclosure of all other compensation not required to be disclosed in any other column. It includes, but is not limited to, the following items:

   • *Perquisites and other personal benefits.* The value of perquisites and other personal benefits must be disclosed unless the aggregate amount of such compensation is less than $10,000. Note that this threshold for disclosure is considerably lower than the threshold under the old rules of $50,000 or 10 percent of salary and bonus. If disclosure of perquisites is required, then each perquisite must be *identified* in a footnote and, if it is valued at the greater of $25,000 or 10 percent of total perquisites and other personal benefits, its *value* must be disclosed. The new rules do not provide a definition of perquisites or personal benefits. As discussed below, the adopting release does, however, provide interpretive guidance regarding how to determine whether an item is a perquisite or other personal benefit.

   • *Additional items.* The All Other Compensation column also includes, but is not limited to, the following items: amounts paid or accrued pursuant to a plan or arrangement in connection with any termination of employment or change in control, annual company contributions to defined contribution plans, dollar value of any insurance premiums paid by the company with respect to life insurance for the benefit of the named executive officer, tax gross-ups and other reimbursements, and compensation relating to purchases of securities from the company at a discount.

8. *Total Compensation.* The Total Compensation column is a hallmark of the new rules. A simple mathematical sum of the other columns in the Summary Compensation Table, it is intended to provide a succinct picture of an executive's *aggregate* compensation for the year and to facilitate comparability analysis from

company to company. However, as discussed later, the total compensation column is based in part on the accounting cost to the company of options and stock awards, rather than the grant-date value or the value the executive may ultimately receive from those awards.

PERQUISITES

The SEC's adopting release for the new rules contains welcome guidance regarding the identification of perquisites, an area that has long been shrouded in mystery. The release provides that an item is not a perquisite or personal benefit if it is *integrally and directly related* to the performance of the executive's duties, but the SEC warns that this standard should be narrowly construed. Otherwise, an item is a perquisite or personal benefit if it confers a direct or indirect benefit that has a personal aspect, without regard to whether it may be provided for some business reason or for the convenience of the company, unless it is generally available on a non-discriminatory basis to all employees.

Examples of items requiring disclosure as perquisites or personal benefits include club memberships not used exclusively for business entertainment purposes, personal financial or tax advice, personal travel using vehicles owned or leased by the company, personal travel otherwise financed by the company, personal use of other property owned or leased by the company, housing and other living expenses (including but not limited to relocation assistance and payments for the executive or director to stay at his or her personal residence), security provided at a personal residence or during personal travel, commuting expenses (whether or not for the company's convenience or benefit), and discounts on the company's products or services not generally available to employees on a nondiscriminatory basis.

Companies must value perquisites based on the aggregate incremental cost to the company, which reflects the SEC staff's guidance in the past, and companies must also disclose in a footnote the methodology for computing such aggregate incremental cost.

GRANTS OF PLAN-BASED AWARDS TABLE

A new table follows and supplements the Summary Compensation Table to give more detail about compensation awards. This Grants of Plan-Based Awards Table shows the following information with respect to awards granted in the most recently completed fiscal year:

- The grant date, and, if such grant date is different from the date on which the board or compensation committee took action to grant such award, the date of such board or committee action

- Estimated future payouts at threshold, target, and maximum levels under both nonequity and equity incentive plan awards

- The number of shares of stock granted in the fiscal year and the number of securities underlying options that are not required to be disclosed in the preceding columns.

- The per-share exercise price of options granted in the fiscal year, and if such exercise price is less than the *closing market price* of the stock on the date of grant, the closing market price on the date of grant.

- The full grant-date fair value of the award calculated under current equity-based compensation accounting rules.

The footnotes to the table contain a description of the material terms of the grants.

It is noteworthy that the rules use the *closing market price on the grant date* as being the assumed determinant of "fair market value" on the grant date. Historically, it has been very common for option plans to define fair market value as of the grant date as the closing price of the stock on the last trading day before the grant date, or as the average of the high and low trading prices on the grant date. If a company's plan contains one of these alternate definitions of fair market value (or another one), it must footnote the table and explain why it uses a convention other than closing market price on the grant date. Because of this peculiarity of the new rules, many companies have or are considering changing the plan definitions to conform to the SEC's preferred definition.

Companies must provide narrative disclosure of any additional material factors necessary to an investor's understanding of the information disclosed in the Summary Compensation Table and the Grants of Plan-Based Awards Table. This narrative disclosure should focus on and provide context to the quantitative disclosure in the tables. Material factors will vary depending on the facts, but might include descriptions of:

- The material terms in the named executive officers' employment agreements

- Repricings or other material modifications of any outstanding option or other stock-based award

- Award terms relating to data provided in the Grants of Plan-Based Awards Table, which could include, for example, performance criteria and/or formulas, vesting schedules, whether dividends or other amounts would be paid, the applicable rate, and whether that rate is preferential

- An explanation of the amount of salary and bonus in proportion to total compensation

EQUITY HOLDINGS

Two new tables are required to provide investors with an understanding of previously awarded, outstanding equity compensation, including amounts realized during the last fiscal year as a result of the vesting or exercise of equity awards.

- *Outstanding Equity Awards at Fiscal Year-End Table.* This new table provides information relating to outstanding stock options, stock appreciation rights, restricted stock awards, and other equity incentive plan awards as of the end of the most recently completed fiscal year.

  - With respect to appreciation-type awards (which would include time-based and performance-based options and stock appreciation rights, for example), the following information must be disclosed:
    - → The number of securities underlying unexercised, *exercisable* time-based awards
    - → The number of securities underlying unexercised, *unexercisable* time-based awards
    - → The number of securities underlying unexercised, unearned *performance-based* awards
    - → The exercise price of each such award
    - → The expiration date of each such award
  - With respect to stock awards (which would include time-based and performance-based restricted stock and restricted stock units awards, for example), the following information must be provided:
    - → The number of unvested shares or units of stock
    - → The market value of unvested shares or units of stock
    - → The number of unvested, unearned shares, units or other performance-based rights held under equity incentive plans
    - → The market payout value of unvested, unearned performance-based shares or units of stock held under equity incentive plans
    Footnotes should contain certain additional information, including the vesting dates of awards held at fiscal year-end.

- *Option Exercises and Stock Vesting Table.* This new table provides information relating to amounts realized by each named executive officer upon exercise of option awards or the vesting of stock awards in the last fiscal year.

RETIREMENT AND POSTEMPLOYMENT PAYMENTS AND BENEFITS

The new rules incorporate three main changes regarding disclosure of postemployment compensation:

1. Tabular and narrative disclosure of defined-benefit pension plans replaces the historical pension plan table.
2. Tabular and narrative disclosure of information regarding nonqualified defined-contribution plans and other deferred compensation is a new requirement.

3. Disclosure requirements regarding compensation arrangements triggered upon a termination of employment or change in control have been revised.

- *Pension Benefits Table.* This table discloses estimated annual retirement payments under defined-benefit plans for each named executive officer, including the following information: (1) the plan name, (2) the number of years of credited service, (3) the actuarial present value of accumulated benefit, and (4) any payments during the last fiscal year. A narrative description is required of material factors necessary to an understanding of each plan disclosed in the table, such as:

  - The material terms and conditions of benefits available under the plan, including the plan's retirement benefit formula and eligibility standards

  - Early retirement arrangements, including identification of any named executive officer who is currently eligible for early retirement

  - The specific elements of compensation, such as salary and various forms of bonus, included in applying the benefit formula, identifying each such element

  - Regarding participation in multiple plans, the reasons for each plan

  - Company policies with regard to such matters as granting extra years of credited service

- *Nonqualified Deferred Compensation Table.* This table discloses contributions, earnings and balances under nonqualified defined contribution and other deferred compensation plans, specifically: (1) the dollar value of executive contributions in the last fiscal year, (2) the dollar value of the company's contributions in the last fiscal year, (3) the aggregate earnings in the last fiscal year (not limited to preferential earnings as in the Summary Compensation Table), (4) aggregate withdrawals/distributions, and (5) aggregate balance at the end of the last fiscal year. Again, a narrative description is required of material factors necessary to an understanding of each plan disclosed in the table, such as:

  - The types of compensation permitted to be deferred, and any limitations (by percentage of compensation or otherwise) on the extent to which deferral is permitted

  - The measures of calculating interest or other plan earnings (including whether such measures are selected by the named executive officer or the company and the frequency and manner in which such selections may be changed), quantifying interest rates, and other earnings measures applicable during the company's last fiscal year

  - Material terms with respect to payouts, withdrawals, and other distributions

- *Potential postemployment payments.* Companies now must provide narrative disclosure of the specific aspects of any written or unwritten arrangement that provides for payments at, following, or in connection with the resignation, severance, retirement, or other termination (including constructive termination) of a named executive officer, a change in his or her responsibilities, or a change in control of the company, including:

○ The specific circumstances that would trigger payments under the termination or change-in-control arrangements or the provision of other benefits

○ The estimated dollar value of payments and benefits that would be provided in each termination circumstance, including tax gross-up payments, and whether they would or could be lump sum or annual, disclosing the duration and by whom they would be provided

○ How the appropriate payment and benefit levels are determined under the various circumstances that would trigger payments or provision of benefits

○ Any material conditions or obligations applicable to the receipt of payments or benefits, including but not limited to noncompete, nonsolicitation, nondisparagement, or confidentiality covenants, including the description of the duration and provisions regarding waiver of breach of these agreements

○ Any other material features necessary for an understanding of the provisions

Companies must provide *quantitative* disclosure of estimated termination payments and benefits using the following assumptions: (1) the triggering event took place on the last business day of the company's last completed fiscal year, and (2) the price per share of the company's securities is the closing market price as of that date. In the event that uncertainties exist, companies must make reasonable estimates and disclose material assumptions underlying such estimates. This disclosure is considered forward-looking information, as appropriate, that falls within the safe harbor for disclosure of such information.

OPTION GRANT PRACTICES

In his introductory remarks to the SEC's open meeting to adopt the new rules, SEC Chairman Christopher Cox noted that the new rules intend to provide investors with "a clear and complete picture of how their company uses options to compensate executives." While the SEC intentionally avoided the use of colloquial terms such as *backdating* or *spring-loading*, the new rules address option grant practices in several ways.

First, the Grants of Plan-Based Awards Table that supplements the Summary Compensation Table shows the date of grant of an option, the closing market price on the grant date if it is greater than the exercise price, the methodology for determining the exercise price if it is different than the closing price of the company's stock on the grant date, and the date the compensation committee or board of directors took action to approve the grant if that date is other than the grant date. These new information requirements should be sufficient to enable investors to readily identify any instance of granting "discounted" options. Moreover, the narrative disclosure that follows the table should be used to explain the rationale for such grants.

Second, the CD&A requires disclosures about the company's programs, plans, and practices concerning the timing of equity grants in coordination with the release of material nonpublic information. Companies are called upon to analyze and discuss, as appropriate, material information such as the reasons the company selects particular grant dates for awards or the methods the company uses to select the terms of awards, such as the exercise prices of stock options. The SEC's release provides questions to discuss in the CD&A that are intended to elicit detailed information about the company's option grant practices:

- Does the company have any program, plan, or practice to time option grants to its executives in coordination with the release of material nonpublic information?

- How does any program, plan, or practice to time option grants to executives fit in the context of the company's program, plan, or practice, if any, with regard to option grants to employees more generally?

- What was the role of the compensation committee in approving and administering such a program, plan, or practice? How did the board or compensation committee take such information into account when determining whether and in what amount to make those grants? Did the compensation committee delegate any aspect of the actual administration of a program, plan, or practice to any other persons?

- What was the role of executive officers in the company's program, plan, or practice of option timing?

- Does the company set the grant date of its stock option grants to new executives in coordination with the release of material non-public information?

- Does the company plan to time, or has it timed, its release of material nonpublic information for the purpose of affecting the value of executive compensation?

It is relevant to note that the SEC does not in its release condemn or condone any particular grant practices. The focus is on full disclosure, so that the effect of a company's grant practices will be determined by market forces.

DIRECTOR COMPENSATION

Under the old rules, a company was required to provide a narrative description of any compensation arrangements with its directors. The new rules require a Director Compensation Table, which resembles the Summary Compensation Table but provides information only with respect to the most recently completed fiscal year.

The new Director Compensation Table must set forth for each director:

- The dollar amount of any fees earned or paid in cash
- The amount expensed by the company in the last year for any stock awards or option awards held by the director
- The dollar amount of any non–stock incentive plan compensation
- Any change in pension value and nonqualified deferred compensation earnings
- The dollar amount of all other compensation received
- The dollar value of the total amount of compensation received

Once again, any material factors necessary to an understanding of the table must be described in the accompanying narrative disclosure. In addition, the aggregate number of equity awards outstanding at fiscal year end must be disclosed in a footnote to the appropriate column of the table.

For more information about director compensation disclosure, see Chapter 4.

FORM 8-K

Since August 2004, Item 1.01 of Form 8-K has required companies to report, within four business days, the entry into a material contract "outside of the ordinary course of business" or an amendment of such a contract that is material to the company. Before the 2006 rules went into effect, these requirements under Item 1.01 specifically included compensatory plans, contracts and arrangements with any director or named executive officer (regardless of the amount involved), and with any other executive officer unless immaterial in amount or significance.

With its revisions to the Form 8-K rules in August 2004, the SEC intended to increase the "real-time" disclosure of presumptively material events relating to executive compensation. As it happened, the SEC got more than it bargained for. Interpreting the standards for disclosure conservatively, companies flooded the market with compensation information that arguably was below the intended materiality threshold, which tended to obscure the material information that was duly reported.

In the 2006 rules, the SEC narrowed the scope of executive compensation disclosures on Form 8-K with the intent to elicit unquestionably or presumptively material information and to limit "real-time" disclosure of information that falls below that threshold. Specifically, the new rules eliminate the requirement to report pursuant to Item 1.01 the entry into or the material amendment of compensatory plans, contracts and arrangements with directors and executive officers, as well as the requirement to report, pursuant to Item 1.02, the termination of any such contracts.

The filing of this information was largely shifted to Item 5.02 of Form 8-K by expanding that item. Item 5.02 continues to require disclosure (1) when a new director is elected or resigns or refuses to stand for re-election and (2) when certain designated officers (principal executive officer, president, principal financial officer, principal accounting officer, and principal operating officer) are appointed, retire, resign, or are terminated. This list of officers is expanded in the new rules to include any person who was a named executive officer as of the end of the last completed fiscal year. The requirement for disclosure as to other executive officers is eliminated entirely.

In addition to the above information, Item 5.02 also requires a brief description of the terms and conditions of any new or materially amended compensatory plan, contract or arrangement with a named executive officer, and any grant or award made thereunder, unless such grant or award is consistent with previously disclosed plans or arrangements. Revised Item 5.02 also requires disclosure if the salary and bonus of a named executive officer were not calculable as of the time of the last proxy statement, but there is a subsequent payment, grant, award, decision, or other occurrence which results in such amounts being calculable in whole or in part. Material contracts still must be filed pursuant to Regulation S-K Item 601(b)(10), discussed later in this chapter.

BENEFICIAL OWNERSHIP REPORTING

The 2006 disclosure rules amended Item 403(b) of Regulation S-K to require footnote disclosure of the number of shares pledged as security for indebtedness by named executive officers, directors, and director nominees. This disclosure provides further transparency into the share ownership of management and how management could be influenced by the risks and contingencies associated with that share ownership.

DISCLOSURE OF RELATED PERSON TRANSACTIONS

The SEC adopted significant revisions to Item 404 of Regulation S-K, "Certain Relationships and Related Transactions," in order to "streamline and modernize this disclosure requirement, while making it more principles-based." The changes focused on four sections:

1. Revised Item 404(a) contains a general disclosure requirement for related person transactions, including those involving indebtedness.
2. Revised Item 404(b) requires disclosure regarding the company's policies and procedures for the review, approval or ratification of related person transactions.
3. Revised Item 404(c) requires disclosure regarding promoters of a company.
4. New Item 407 consolidates former corporate governance disclosure requirements and requires disclosure regarding the independence of directors.

Item 404(a) requires disclosure regarding any transaction since the beginning of the company's last fiscal year, or any currently proposed transaction, in which (1) the company was or is to be a participant, (2) the amount involved exceeds $120,000, and (3) any related person had, or will have, a direct or indirect material interest.

In an effort to clarify the disclosure requirements for certain relationships and related transactions, the SEC adopted a principles-based approach to such disclosure and eliminated certain presumptions regarding materiality. In adopting such an approach, the SEC intended to focus the disclosure analysis on the significance of the information to investors in light of all of the circumstances, including the significance of the interest to the person having the interest, the relationship of the related persons to the transaction, and with each other, and the amount involved in the transaction.

Although Section 402 of the Sarbanes-Oxley Act generally prohibits loans to officers and directors of public companies, it does not apply to all related persons (as defined in Item 404) of an issuer. As a result, the new rules change some situations in which indebtedness disclosure is required:

- Disclosure of indebtedness transactions is now required for significant share-holders who are related persons.

- Disclosure is required of all material indirect interests in indebtedness trans-actions of related persons, including significant shareholders and immediate family members.

The SEC adopted a new requirement for disclosure of the policies and procedures established by a company and its board of directors regarding related person transactions. Specifically, the new rules require a description of the company's policies and procedures for the review, approval or ratification of any transaction required to be reported under Item 404(a). The description must include the material features of such policies and procedures such as:

- The types of transactions that are covered
- The standards to be applied
- The persons or groups of persons on the board of directors or otherwise who are responsible for applying such policies and procedures, which for listed compa-nies would in most cases be the audit committee of the board of directors
- Whether such policies and procedures are in writing and, if not, how they are evidenced

The new rules also require identification of any transactions required to be reported under Item 404(a) where the company's policies and procedures did not require review, approval, or ratification or where such policies and procedures were not followed.

CORPORATE GOVERNANCE AND INDEPENDENCE OF DIRECTORS

New Item 407 consolidates disclosure requirements regarding director independence and corporate governance under a single disclosure item and updates director independence disclosure requirements to reflect current Exchange Act requirements and current stock exchange listing standards. Under the old rules, each company listed on an exchange determined whether its directors and committee members were independent based upon company adopted definitions, which, at a minimum, must comply with the listing standards applicable to the company. The 2006 rules require a company to identify its independent directors (and, in the case of disclosure in proxy or information statements, nominees for director) under the applicable definition of board independence and also any members of the compensation, nominating, and audit committee that are not independent under the applicable definition of independence for that board committee.

The 2006 rules require a company that has adopted its own definitions of independence for directors and committee members to disclose whether those definitions are posted on the company's web site, or include the definitions as an appendix to the company's proxy materials at least once every three years or if the policies have been materially amended since the beginning of the company's last fiscal year.

In addition, the new rules require, for each independent director or director nominee, a description of any transactions, relationships, or arrangements (by specific category or type) not disclosed pursuant to Item 404(a) that were considered by the board of directors of the company in determining that the applicable independence standards were met.

In a departure from prior rules, the independence disclosure is required for any person who served as a director of the company during any part of the year for which disclosure must be provided, even if the person no longer serves as a director at the time of filing the registration statement or report or, if the information is in a proxy statement, even if the director's term of office as a director will not continue after the meeting.

In addition to the disclosures currently required regarding audit and nominating committees of the board of directors, the new rules require similar disclosure regarding compensation committees. For example, the company must disclose whether the compensation committee's authority is set forth in a charter or other document, and if so, the company's web site address at which a current copy is available if it is so posted. If the company's compensation committee charter is not so posted, the company must attach the charter to the proxy statement once every three years (in the same manner that the audit committee charter may be made available).

The company is also required to describe its processes and procedures for the determination of executive and director compensation including:

- The scope of authority of the compensation committee (or persons performing the equivalent functions)
- The extent to which the compensation committee may delegate any authority to other persons, specifying what authority may be so delegated and to whom
- Any role of executive officers in determining or recommending the amount or form of executive and director compensation
- Any role of compensation consultants in determining or recommending the amount or form of executive and director compensation, identifying such

consultants, stating whether such consultants are engaged directly by the compensation committee (or persons performing the equivalent functions) or any other person, describing the nature and scope of their assignment, the material elements of the instructions or directions given to the consultants with respect to the performance of their duties under the engagement, and identifying any executive officer within the company the consultants contacted in carrying out their assignment

PLAIN ENGLISH

The SEC is serious about having companies communicate with their shareholders in a manner that is straightforward and understandable to the average investor. The new rules require that most of the disclosure required by Items 402, 403, 404, and 407 regarding executive and director compensation, related person transactions, beneficial ownership, and corporate governance disclosures be provided using the "plain English" principles currently required for prospectuses.

AFTERMATH OF THE FIRST PROXY SEASON UNDER THE NEW RULES

The first slate of proxy statements adhering to the 2006 disclosure rules were filed in March 2007. In an address made on March 23, 2007, at the University of Southern California Corporate Governance Summit, SEC Chairman Christopher Cox publicly expressed his disappointment with the length and complexity of the compensation disclosures. In particular, he was concerned that CD&As were not sufficiently in "plain English" as required by the rules. In his words:

> In the past, the disclosure about executives' pay has been among the most complicated for investors to decipher. That's why the SEC is so adamant that the new Compensation Discussion and Analysis be written in plain English. But now that the proxy season is well under way, and we've reviewed the first of this year's crop, alarm bells are ringing. Already we're seeing examples of over-lawyering that are leading to 30- and 40-page long executive compensation sections in proxy statements.

> I have to report that we are disappointed with the lack of clarity in much of the narrative disclosure that's been filed with the SEC so far. Based on the early returns, the average Compensation Disclosure and Analysis section isn't anywhere close to plain English. In fact, according to objective third-party testing, most of it's as tough to read as a Ph.D. dissertation. ... If I leave you with no other message from today's talk, I hope it will be this: The SEC is dead serious about shedding 70 years of accumulated bad habits in writing.

The SEC's message is loud and clear. But the execution is easier said than done. When the new rules first came out, the SEC's mantra was that under the new "principles-based" disclosure regime, *everything* in the nature of compensation must be disclosed—when in doubt, disclose it. The SEC's rules provide a *nonex-haustive* list of 21 topics to address in the CD&A alone. This open-ended requirement, coupled with the fact that the CD&A is now "filed" disclosure, which makes it subject to the liabilities of Section 18 of the Exchange Act and covered by the CEO and CFO certifications under the Sarbanes-Oxley Act, give rise to a natural desire to provide language that is thorough, exacting, and unambiguous. It will be quite interesting to see how companies and their advisors and regulators learn to walk this fine line over the next few years.

In terms of the public reaction to the expansive compensation disclosures in the 2006 proxy statements, investor groups and the press have had a field day with the information. *The New York Times*, the *Wall Street Journal*, and other major publications have featured a wealth of articles reacting to the new disclosures, most of which—not surprisingly—focus in on the new "total compensation" figures, perquisites, and exit pay packages. Some interesting observations:

- Even though one of the hallmarks of the new disclosure rules is the "total compensation" column in the Summary Compensation Table, many observers (including certain national press organizations) are ignoring that number and instead calculating "total compensation" in a manner that they deem to present a more realistic picture of the value bestowed on an executive in a given year. For example, the Associated Press reportedly totals (1) the figures in the Salary, Bonus, Non-Equity Incentive Plan Compensation, and All Other Compensation columns of the Summary Compensation Table, (2) above-market earnings on nonqualified deferred compensation (from a footnote to the Change in Pension Value and Nonqualified Deferred Compensation Earnings column), and (3) the "estimated value" of stock and option awards (which it obtains from the last column in the Grants of Plan-Based Awards Table). With new interactive disclosures available on the SEC's reporting system, it is increasingly easy to slice and dice public information in this manner.

- There seems to be a fascination with the word count of compensation disclosures. Articles have been written comparing the length of the Declaration of Independence (1,500 words), the U.S. Constitution (8,100 words), and even *Hamlet* (31,900 words), with the average executive compensation disclosures in the 2007 proxy statements (in the neighborhood of 14,000 words among the Fortune 50 companies). Berkshire Hathaway achieved an exemplary level of simplicity in its 2007 proxy disclosures: 487 words in its CD&A and only one table (the Summary Compensation Table). But by its own admission, its executive officer compensation program is different from most public company programs, with no incentive awards tied to company performance or stock price, no retirement plans, no perquisites, no employment or severance arrangements, and a CEO and Vice Chairman whose salaries have been fixed at $100,000 for the last 25 years.

- The tables required by the new rules pack a lot of information. This makes them almost indecipherable without lengthy supplementary disclosure. In fact, at the end of the 15 pages of rules for the summary compensation and equity grant tables alone, the instructions end with the admonition to "provide a narrative description of any material factors necessary to an understanding of the information disclosed in the tables. . . ." For any company with an average amount of "moving parts" in its compensation program, it is hard to see how the disclosures can be both legally compliant and simple as pie.

DISCLOSURE OF EQUITY COMPENSATION PLANS

BACKGROUND

Item 201(d) of Regulation S-K, adopted by the SEC in 2002, requires disclosure regarding a company's equity compensation plans. The disclosure must appear in the annual report on Form 10-K every year, and it must also be included in the proxy statement in years in which the company is submitting any compensation plan proposal, including a plan amendment, for stockholder approval. The disclosure is designed to reveal the potential dilutive effect of a company's equity compensation plans on stockholder value and to afford stockholders a clearer understanding of all equity-based compensation paid by the company.

CONTENT AND FORM OF THE DISCLOSURE

The rules require disclosure relating to equity compensation plans in effect as of the end of the company's last completed fiscal year. An equity compensation plan is one that provides for the award of the company's securities or the grant of options, warrants, or rights to purchase the company's securities to any person. The disclosure is required for all arrangements under which equity compensation may be issued, including arrangements for non-employees, such as directors, consultants, advisors, vendors, customers, suppliers, or lenders, and for individual arrangements even if not pursuant to a broader plan. The disclosure is not required for plans that are intended to meet the qualification requirement of Section 401(a) of the Internal Revenue Code or arrangements that provide for the issuance of rights to all security holders of the issuer on a pro rata basis (such as a dividend reinvestment plan).

Tabular Plan Disclosure

The rules require disclosure in tabular form of all employee stock options and other rights to acquire securities of the company under all equity compensation plans and arrangements of the company. The table must include the number and

Exhibit 6.1   Equity Compensation Plan Information

	(a)	(b)	(c)
Plan category	Number of securities to be issued upon exercise of outstanding options, warrants, and rights	Weighted-average exercise price of outstanding options, warrants, and rights	Number of securities remaining available for future issuance under equity compensation plans (excluding securities reflected in column (a))
Equity compensation plans approved by security holders			
Equity compensation plans not approved by security holders			
Total			

weighted-average exercise price of outstanding options, warrants and rights, and the number of securities available for future issuance under the company's existing equity compensation plans. The disclosure must be given separately for plans that have already been approved by stockholders and for plans that have not been approved by stockholders. Exhibit 6.1 is an example of how the table should look.

Certain information that does not readily fit into the table is to be disclosed in a footnote. For example, any "evergreen" formula that automatically increases the number of securities available for issuance under a plan is to be described in a footnote to the table. In addition, with respect to any individual options, warrants, or rights assumed in connection with a merger or other acquisition transaction where no future options may be granted under the plan, the information required by table columns (a) and (b) is to be disclosed in a footnote. If the assumed plan is ongoing, however, it should be disclosed as a non-stockholder-approved plan (unless the stockholders have separately approved it) in columns (a) and (c). To the extent that the number of securities remaining available for future issuance set forth in table column (c) includes securities available for issuance other than upon the exercise of an option, warrant, or right, the company should describe such other securities in a footnote.

In addition to the table, the rules also provide that the material features of each non-stockholder-approved plan be described briefly in narrative form. If the company's financial statements contain such a narrative description, this requirement may be satisfied by cross-referencing the appropriate financial statement disclosure.

Plan Filing Requirements

A company must file with the SEC a copy of each non-stockholder-approved plan in which any employee participates, unless immaterial in amount or significance. If a particular non-stockholder-approved plan is not set forth in a formal written document, the company must file a written description of the plan. Any non-stockholder-approved plan assumed in connection with a merger, consolidation, or other acquisition transaction is subject to this filing requirement if the company is able to make additional grants or awards of its equity securities under the plan.

DISCLOSURE TIPS

Restricted Stock and Restricted Stock Units

Restricted stock should not be included in the table in either column (a) or column (c), because these shares, once issued, are already reflected as outstanding in a company's financial statements. Restricted stock units, however, represent an obligation to issue shares in the future, and therefore shares subject to restricted stock units should be included in column (a) of the 201(d) table, with an explanatory footnote.

Employee Stock Purchase Plans

Shares authorized for future issuance under an employee stock purchase plan should be included in column (c) of the 201(d) table, but outstanding purchase rights that are accruing mid–purchase period may be disregarded and need not be transferred to column (a) and (b). Because employee stock purchase plans are generally perceived favorably, companies may want to show in a footnote how many of the shares in column (c) are reserved under an employee stock purchase plan.

401(k) Plans

Shares issuable pursuant to a qualified 401(k) plan do not need to be disclosed in the 201(d) table.

Options Assumed in a Merger

Options assumed in a merger, where no future options may be granted under a plan of the acquired company, do not need to be included in column (a), but should be disclosed in a footnote that would include the weighted-average exercise price. If the company retains the ability to grant future awards under an acquired company's plan, then the assumed options must be shown in column (a) and the remaining shares shown in column (c). In addition, the assumed plan will be considered non-stock-holder approved (and subject to the narrative description requirement) unless the company's stockholders have separately approved the assumption of the plan.

Expired Plans

Any outstanding grants should be reflected in column (a), even if the plan under which the grants were made has expired.

SELECTED PROVISIONS REGULATION S-K

The full texts of Items 201(d), 401, 402, 403, 404, 405, 406, 407, and 601(b)(10) of Regulation S-K are reproduced in Appendix A. Very brief descriptions of those sections are set out below. Items 402, 404, and 407 in particular embody many of the disclosure requirements described in more detail elsewhere in this chapter.

ITEM 201(D): SECURITIES AUTHORIZED FOR ISSUANCE UNDER EQUITY COMPENSATION PLANS

Item 201(d) of Regulation S-K requires disclosure of rights outstanding and shares available for issuance under the company's equity compensation plans, separately as between those plans that have been approved by shareholders and those that have not.

ITEM 401: DIRECTORS, EXECUTIVE OFFICERS, PROMOTERS, AND CONTROL PERSONS

Item 401 of Regulation S-K requires disclosure of certain personal and background information about the company's directors and executive officers, including information that would likely be relevant to stockholders in assessing such persons' ability to serve the company.

ITEM 402: EXECUTIVE COMPENSATION

Item 402 of Regulation S-K is designed to furnish shareholders with an understandable presentation of the nature and extent of executive and director compensation. It does so by consolidating the requisite disclosure in a series of tables and narrative setting forth each compensatory element for a particular fiscal year and requiring a CD&A articulating the company's compensation philosophy and basis for its compensation decisions.

ITEM 403: SECURITY OWNERSHIP OF CERTAIN BENEFICIAL OWNERS AND MANAGEMENT

Item 403 of Regulation S-K requires disclosure of beneficial ownership of company securities held by (1) persons that own more than 5% of any class of the company's voting securities, and (2) each director and director nominee, each of the named executive officers, and the directors and executive officers of the company as a group.

ITEM 404: TRANSACTIONS WITH RELATED PERSONS, PROMOTERS, AND CONTROL PERSONS

Item 404 of Regulation S-K requires disclosure of transactions and indebtedness involving amounts in excess of $120,000 between the company and "related persons." It also requires disclosure of the company's policies and procedures for the review, approval, or ratification of related person transactions.

ITEM 405: COMPLIANCE WITH SECTION 16(A) OF THE EXCHANGE ACT

Item 405 of Regulation S-K requires disclosure of any of the company's Section 16 Reporting Persons who failed to file a Form 3, 4, or 5 on a timely basis during the most recent fiscal year or prior fiscal years. The disclosure must include the number of late reports, the number of transactions that were not reported on a timely basis, and any known failure to file a form.

ITEM 406: CODE OF ETHICS

Item 406 of Regulation S-K requires a company to disclose whether it has adopted a code of ethics that applies to its principal officers or explain why it has not done so.

ITEM 407: CORPORATE GOVERNANCE

Item 407 of Regulation S-K was added in 2006. It consolidates former corporate governance disclosure requirements and requires disclosure regarding the independence of directors.

ITEM 601(b)(10): EXHIBITS—MATERIAL CONTRACTS

Item 601(b)(10) of Regulation S-K sets forth criteria for identifying the company's material contracts that must be filed as exhibits to the company's public filings. Compensation committees should note that material contracts that must be filed include any management contract or any compensatory plan, contract, or arrangement in which any director or any named executive officer of the company participates, and any other management contract or compensatory plan in which any other executive officer participates, unless it is immaterial in amount or significance.

Chapter 7

Other Securities Issues

This chapter discusses certain specific securities issues that should be of particular interest to compensation committees of public companies, in addition to the disclosure issues discussed in Chapter 6. The first section contains a discussion of special rules regarding insider trading, including (1) the reporting system and short-swing profit liability provisions of Section 16 of the Securities Exchange Act of 1934 (Exchange Act), (2) the prohibition against trading on "inside information," (3) the prohibition against insider trades during pension fund blackout periods, and (4) sales of restricted and control stock under Rule 144 of the Securities Act of 1933 (Securities Act). The next section addresses New York Stock Exchange (NYSE) and The Nasdaq Stock Market (NASDAQ) rules regarding shareholder approval of equity compensation plans. The chapter concludes by highlighting the effect of certain other provisions of the Sarbanes-Oxley Act of 2002 on executive compensation, including the prohibition on loans to directors and executive officers (Section 402) and the requirement to disgorge profits from equity awards upon certain financial restatements (Section 304).

SPECIAL RULES AFFECTING INSIDER TRADING

SECTION 16 OF THE EXCHANGE ACT

Background

Section 16 of the Exchange Act was adopted in response to perceived abuses by corporate insiders thought to be trading on material nonpublic information. Section 16 operates without regard to the insider's awareness or use of material nonpublic information, achieving its intended deterrent effect by (1) requiring certain officers, all directors, and all shareholders beneficially owning more than 10 percent of the issuer's equity securities (collectively, "Reporting Persons") to file reports indicating their present beneficial ownership of the issuer's equity securities and reporting all subsequent changes in such beneficial ownership; and (2) allowing the issuer's shareholders to sue on behalf of the issuer to recapture all "short-swing" profits realized by a Reporting Person from any nonexempt purchase and sale (or sale and purchase) of the issuer's equity securities within any six-month period.

An officer will be considered a Reporting Person if he or she performs policy-making functions within the issuer—including the chief executive officer (CEO), president, principal accounting officer, principal financial officer, and officers in charge of significant subsidiaries, business units, or divisions. The board should designate its Section 16 officers each year, based on the changing roles and responsibilities of the issuer's officers. In addition to permitting private actions to require a Reporting Person to disgorge any short-swing profit, the securities laws also permit the Securities and Exchange Commission (SEC) to seek court orders imposing civil monetary penalties of up to $500,000 for each violation of federal securities law. In addition, all late Section 16 reports (and/or the failure to file a report) must be disclosed in the issuer's Form 10-K and proxy statement, identifying the late filer by name and number of late transactions.

Reporting Requirements

Initial Report—Form 3. Each Reporting Person is required to file with the SEC an "Initial Statement of Beneficial Ownership of Securities" on Form 3 within 10 days after becoming a director, executive officer, or 10 percent shareholder. Form 3 establishes the Reporting Person's baseline securities ownership position for reporting purposes. A Form 3 must be filed even if the director or officer does not own shares of company stock.

Subsequent Reports—Form 4. A Reporting Person must keep the information on file with the SEC up to date by filing reports on Form 4 ("Statement of Changes in Beneficial Ownership of Securities") and Form 5 ("Annual Statement of Changes in Beneficial Ownership of Securities"). A Form 4 must be filed electronically with the SEC no later than the second business day following the day on which the transaction has been executed that results in a change in the Reporting Person's "beneficial ownership" (discussed in the following section) of issuer equity securities, unless the transaction falls into one of two narrow exceptions for which a slightly longer Form 4 filing period is permitted, or unless an exemption is available that allows for deferred reporting on Form 5. There are two narrow exceptions for delayed Form 4 filings: (1) transactions that meet the conditions set forth in Rule 10b5-1(c) (discussed later in this chapter) are eligible for slightly delayed reporting on Form 4, as long as the Reporting Person does not select the date of execution; and (2) "discretionary transactions" in employee benefit plans also are eligible for slightly delayed Form 4 reporting as long as the Reporting Person does not select the date of execution. Discretionary transactions are defined specifically in Rule 16b-3 and are limited to transactions pursuant to an employee benefit plan that result in either an intraplan transfer involving an issuer securities fund or a volitional cash distribution from an issuer securities fund.

Annual Reports—Form 5: Alternative Written Statement. A Form 5 must be filed with the SEC annually on or before the 45th day after the end of the issuer's fiscal year for any person who was a Reporting Person at any time during the year, *unless* (1) such person had no transactions in the issuer's securities during the fiscal year, or (2) all holdings and transactions required to be reported for the fiscal year have already been reported on Form 3 or Form 4. If a Reporting Person is not required to file a Form 5 for any year for either of these reasons, he or she should provide a written representation to the issuer that no Form 5 is required. Otherwise, the issuer may be forced to disclose that such person failed to file a Form 5 for that year in its annual meeting proxy statement. Only a small number of transactions, such as gifts and *de minimis* purchases, are eligible for reporting on Form 5.

Determining Beneficial Ownership

The "beneficial ownership" reported on Forms 3, 4, and 5 has a special meaning under Section 16, and may often be different from simple record ownership. For purposes of the Section 16(a) reporting requirements, a Reporting Person is regarded as the beneficial owner of securities if such person, directly or indirectly, through any contract, arrangement, understanding, relationship, or otherwise, has or shares a direct or indirect "pecuniary interest" therein (essentially an opportunity to profit from a transaction in the securities). For instance, such person will be deemed to have an indirect pecuniary interest in shares held by a family member who shares the same household (this is in addition to the family member's own direct pecuniary interest). Such person may also be regarded as the beneficial owner of securities owned by a partnership or corporation if such person is a member of the partnership or a shareholder in the corporation. The rules relating to beneficial ownership are complicated. This is particularly true because the SEC has adopted one set of rules for reporting beneficial ownership under Section 16(a), as described previously, and a different set of rules governing beneficial ownership of securities for purposes of reporting the officers' and directors' beneficial ownership of shares in registration statements filed by the issuer with the SEC and in the issuer's proxy statements.

Derivative Securities

A Reporting Person must also report such person's beneficial ownership of all types of "derivative securities." Included among "derivative securities" are puts, calls, options, warrants, stock appreciation rights, or other securities convertible into, exchangeable for, or that otherwise derive value from the issuer's common or preferred stock. Such derivative securities and underlying equity securities are considered part of the same class of equity security, and, if not exempt, the acquisition or disposition of a derivative security must be reported and can be matched with a disposition or acquisition of an identical derivative security or underlying equity security within six months to establish liability under Section 16(b). Exercises, exchanges, and conversions of derivative securities for or into underlying equity securities are also reportable events. A Reporting Person is required to report the acquisition or disposition of a derivative security on Form 4 by the close of business on the second business day following the day on which the acquisition or disposition occurs. In addition, the exercise, exchange, or conversion of a derivative security must be reported on Form 4 by the close of business on the second business day after such event.

Short-Swing Profit Liability

As indicated previously, nonexempt purchases and sales (or sales and purchases) of issuer equity securities by a Reporting Person occurring within any six-month period in which a profit is realized result in "short-swing profits" that may be recovered by the issuer or a shareholder acting on its behalf. Most securities granted to officers or directors by an issuer, while reportable under Section 16(a), would be exempt from short-swing profit liability under Rule 16b-3 if the grant is approved by a *fully independent* compensation committee or by the full board of directors or, more rarely, is approved or ratified by the shareholders. The most common nonexempt transactions that are subject to short-swing liability include open market purchases and sales (including broker-assisted cashless exercises of stock options, where shares are sold into the market to cover the exercise price or to satisfy the optionee's tax withholding obligation) and "Discretionary Transactions" (as defined under Rule 16b-3) pursuant to employee benefit plans.

For purposes of Section 16, short-swing profit is generally calculated to provide the maximum recoverable amount. The measure of damages is the profit derived from any nonexempt purchase and sale or any nonexempt sale and purchase within the six-month, short-swing period, without regard to any setoffs for losses or any first-in, first-out rules. This approach is sometimes referred to as the "lowest price in, highest price out" rule.

Insiders also may be liable for the receipt of short-swing profits in transactions involving the purchase or sale of derivative securities, such as options to purchase company common stock. As noted earlier, most derivative securities granted by the issuer would be exempt from Section 16(b) short-swing liability under Rule 16b-3 if the awards are properly granted by a fully independent compensation committee or the full board. Third-party derivatives written on company securities are not eligible for this exemption, however. For the purpose of determining liability, transactions involving derivative securities may be matched against transactions involving the underlying securities (i.e., the stock itself) because ownership of the derivative securities constitutes "beneficial ownership" of the underlying securities for purposes of Section 16. For example, the purchase of a call option on the issuer's stock and the sale of either the option or the shares of underlying stock within six months could result in short-swing profit liability.

The imposition of liability under Section 16(b) is not dependent upon proving the intent to violate that provision. Any profit (by a purchase and subsequent sale within six months at a higher price) or avoidance of loss (by a sale and subsequent purchase within six months at a lower price) whatsoever that falls within the mechanical test of Section 16(b) is recoverable, regardless of intentions and whether the sale or purchase was made on the basis of any inside information. Recall that:

- Only *nonexempt* transactions are subject to short-swing profit liability.
- Filing reports on Forms 3, 4, or 5 does not protect a Reporting Person from short-swing profit liability.
- Purchases and sales do not have to relate to the same shares for liability to arise.

Experience indicates that in the event of a violation of the short-swing profit provisions, it is *very likely* that an action will be brought, mainly because Form 4 and 5 reports will bring every violation to the attention of shareholders, particularly those professional shareholders and their attorneys who vigorously pursue Section 16(b) claims.

RULE 10b-5 OF THE EXCHANGE ACT

General

A second type of trading-related liability occurs when an insider (including not just Reporting Persons for Section 16 purposes, but also any employee or other person, whether or not employed by the issuer, who acquires material nonpublic information) trades in the issuer's common stock while in possession of material nonpublic information. Rule 10b-5 prohibits such persons from trading upon undisclosed material information to their advantage, and also prohibits them from providing such information to any other person (a practice known as *tipping*).

Penalties

Insider trading is a serious offense, vigorously pursued by the SEC, that may result in imprisonment, criminal fines and civil money penalties, as well as civil liability to a potentially large class of plaintiffs for damages bearing no relation to the insider's or tippee's profit. In addition, an insider trading violation constitutes a violation of one of the antifraud provisions for which an insider may be barred from serving as a corporate officer or director. Therefore, if a director, officer, or employee has material nonpublic information, such person should not disclose that information (except through public dissemination) or trade in securities of the issuer until the information has been effectively disclosed to and digested by the investing public. Because a director, officer, or employee will likely be unable to disclose the information (as disclosure may be against the issuer's interest and could constitute a violation of a fiduciary duty to the issuer), the safest course is to refrain from trading when any such person is in possession of material undisclosed information.

Trading Policies

Because of the seriousness of the offense, it is common for issuers to adopt an insider trading policy that requires directors, executive officers, and certain other designated individuals who desire to buy or sell the issuer's common stock to obtain preclearance from one of several compliance officers (usually the general counsel and/or one or more attorneys in the issuer's legal department) before engaging in any transaction in the issuer's securities. Typically, individuals covered by the policy will be prohibited from trading in issuer securities during quarterly blackout periods related to the compilation and public disclosure of quarterly earnings information and during event-specific blackout periods. In this manner, independent safeguards will exist to ensure that persons likely to be in possession of material nonpublic information are unable to knowingly or unknowingly buy or sell stock while there exists material nonpublic information about the issuer. Such a policy will also help the issuer and its "controlling persons" avoid liability that arises from insider trading by a director, officer, or employee of the issuer.

Having mentioned the risks of insider trading, it is also possible to identify circumstances in which information has been sufficiently disseminated to permit an insider to trade. The proper time when insiders may trade depends both on how thoroughly and how quickly inside information is disseminated by the news services and the press after public disclosure. Insiders should, as a general rule, always wait until a release has appeared in the press before making a purchase or sale and should further refrain from trading following dissemination until the public has had an opportunity to evaluate the information thoroughly. The waiting period depends on the circumstances, but it is typical to require that insiders must wait until the second business day after release before commencing any trading. Furthermore, trading even at that time is prohibited if the person is aware of additional undisclosed material information that was not the subject of the release. In addition, officers of the issuer will continually be faced with the very sensitive question of when and to what extent the officers inform the board of directors of corporate developments. Insufficient and untimely delivery of information to the board could result in numerous problems, including subjecting the directors to allegations of insider trading violations since the SEC will likely presume that the board members are aware of all material nonpublic information relating to the issuer.

Rule 10b5-1

Rule 10b5-1 under the Exchange Act provides an affirmative defense to shield an insider from liability for insider trading if certain conditions are satisfied. Rule 10b5-1 provides that a person (such as a corporate insider) may, during a time that he or she is *not* in possession of material nonpublic information, enter into a binding contract, arrangement, or plan (a "Rule 10b5-1 plan") for effecting subsequent sales or purchases of the issuer's stock, even if the person *is* in possession of material nonpublic information at the time of the sale or purchase. Such Rule 10b5-1 plans must (1) specify the amount of securities to be purchased or sold and the price at which and the date on which such sales or purchases are to take place, or (2) include a written formula or algorithm or a computer program for determining the amount of securities to be purchased or sold and the price at which and the date on which such sales or purchases are to take place, or (3) otherwise prohibit such persons from exercising any subsequent influence over how, when, or whether to effect purchases or sales (provided that any person who *is* permitted to exercise such influence must not have been aware of material nonpublic information when doing so). It is also a requirement of the rule that the purchase or sale actually occurs pursuant to the Rule 10b5-1 plan and not in a manner that altered or deviated from such program. In addition, the insider cannot make hedging transactions or positions with respect to the securities traded pursuant to the Rule 10b5-1 plan. The insider may change or terminate a Rule 10b5-1 plan at any time that he or she is not in possession of material nonpublic information.

Note that Rule 10b5-1 does not shield an insider from short-swing profit liability or reporting obligations under Section 16, and that trading pursuant to a Rule 10b5-1 plan does not necessarily mean that the trade is exempt under Section 16(b). In fact, it is most likely the Rule 10b5-1 plan would involve nonexempt sales on the open market. If a Section 16 insider entered into such a Rule 10b5-1 plan that called for annual or more frequent sales in the market, that person could never make a nonexempt purchase without incurring short-swing profit liability under Section 16(b). Therefore, officers and directors should be ever thoughtful in designing a preestablished trading program under Rule 10b5-1.

Insider trading has long been a primary focus of the SEC's enforcement efforts. Now, even company executives and insiders trading pursuant to Rule 10b5-1 plans are being subjected to scrutiny by the SEC. On March 8, 2007, the director of the SEC's Division of Enforcement, Linda Chatman Thomsen, announced in a speech that the SEC intends to investigate trading under Rule 10b5-1 plans that yield suspicious results.

The SEC's interest seems to have been triggered by a recent study conducted by Professor Alan D. Jagolinzer of Stanford University's Graduate School of Business. Professor Jagolinzer found a high incidence of executives entering into Rule 10b5-1 selling plans immediately prior to significant declines in the company's stock price. In addition, the study indicates that trades by individuals pursuant to Rule 10b5-1 stock trading plans outperformed non–Rule 10b5-1 trades by almost 6 percent, a possible implication of which is the manipulation or misuse of such plans to take advantage of material nonpublic information in making trades. (It is interesting to note that, as discussed in Chapter 15, a similar academic study in 2005 first drew the SEC's attention to the options backdating phenomenon.)

During her speech in March 2007, Ms. Thomsen announced that the SEC intends to prevent unfair exploitation of Rule 10b5-1 stock trading plans. She said that the "safe harbor" is designed "to give executives regular opportunities to liquidate their stock holdings—to pay their kid's college tuition, for example—without risk of inadvertently facing an insider trading inquiry. If executives are in fact trading on inside information and using a plan for cover, they should expect the 'safe harbor' to provide no defense." The SEC's recent comments suggest that insiders trading under Rule 10b5-1 plans should not be overly complacent.

Since the adoption of Rule 10b5-1 plans in 2000, it has been important to avoid the temptation to deviate from such plans for any reason or even no reason. Now, in light of the announced regulatory focus on insiders' sales under such plans, it is even more important to consult counsel when modifying or creating a new Rule 10b5-1 trading plan. All of the circumstances surrounding the original adoption of a plan, the reasons for modifying or adopting a new plan, and the historical and current circumstances surrounding the performance and activities of the subject company, must be carefully evaluated to avoid regulatory suspicion or scrutiny of an insider's Rule 10b5-1 plan and his or her trades pursuant to such plan.

INSIDER TRADES DURING PENSION FUND BLACKOUT PERIODS— DISGORGEMENT OF PROFITS

Background

Section 306 of the Sarbanes-Oxley Act is divided into two related but distinct parts. Section 306(a) prohibits a director or executive officer of a public company from trading in issuer equity securities during a blackout period during which pension plan participants are unable to effect transactions involving company stock. Section 306(b) of the Sarbanes-Oxley Act requires a 30-day advance notice to plan participants and beneficiaries of a more broadly defined set of blackout periods. The discussion in this chapter is limited to the provisions of Section 306(a), as Section 306(b) has no direct effect on stock trading by directors and executive officers.

Generally, during a pension fund blackout period, plan participants can contribute to their accounts, but cannot switch their account funds between investment options. This effectively locks them into their existing investment choices for a period of time, which can be worrisome when an unforeseen event, such as a sudden stock price decline, occurs during that period of time.

Enron and other highly publicized cases demonstrated the catastrophic consequences that can befall employees who have invested substantially all of their retirement savings in their employer's equity securities when the market price of such securities falls sharply. There have been allegations that, at a time when rank-and-file employees were precluded from selling their employer's equity securities held in their individual pension plan accounts, corporate executives were exercising and cashing out employee stock options and selling other securities acquired through the company's equity compensation plans.

Section 306(a) is intended to address the apparent unfairness of an issuer's directors and executive officers being able to sell their equity securities when the issuer's nonexecutive employees cannot. It does this by prohibiting directors and executive officers from trading in equity securities of the issuer when a substantial number of the issuer's employees are subject to a blackout period under their individual pension plan accounts.

Regulation BTR

In 2002, the SEC adopted Regulation BTR (Blackout Trading Restriction) to implement the statutory trading prohibitions of Section 306(a). By using many of the same concepts that have been developed under Section 16 of the Exchange Act,

Regulation BTR provides a broad scope to the trading prohibition of Section 306(a), takes advantage of a well-established body of rules and interpretations concerning the trading activities of corporate insiders, and facilitates enforcement of Section 306(a) by generally allowing reference to Section 16 trading reports (i.e., Forms 3, 4, and 5, discussed previously).

Regulation BTR prohibits a director or executive officer of an issuer from purchasing, selling, or otherwise acquiring or transferring any equity security of the issuer during a pension plan blackout period, if the equity security was acquired in connection with the director's or executive officer's service or employment as a director or executive officer. Therefore, the scope of the trading prohibition is limited to:

- An acquisition of equity securities during a blackout period if the acquisition is in connection with service or employment as a director or executive officer

- A disposition of equity securities during a blackout period if the disposition involves equity securities acquired in connection with service or employment as a director or executive officer

The Section 306(a) trading prohibition is limited to equity securities that a director or executive officer acquires in connection with his or her service or employment as a director or executive officer. Therefore, it does not completely preclude a director or executive officer from trading in equity securities of the issuer during a blackout period. This raises the difficulty of determining whether a particular transaction during a blackout period, such as a sale on the open market, involves equity securities that are subject to Section 306(a) or equity securities that are not so subject. To avoid this problem, Regulation BTR establishes an irrebuttable presumption that *any* equity securities sold or otherwise transferred during a blackout period were acquired in connection with service or employment, to the extent that the director or executive officer holds such securities, without regard to the actual source of the securities disposed of. However, to avoid an overly broad application of the presumption, in a given blackout period, equity securities held by a director or executive officer that were acquired in connection with service or employment could only count once against a disposition transaction during that blackout period.

Generally, equity securities acquired by an individual before he or she became a director or executive officer would not be subject to Section 306(a). This would exclude from the trading prohibition any equity securities acquired under a plan or arrangement while the individual was an employee, but not a director or executive officer, of the issuer. However, shares acquired in a director or executive officer capacity before January 26, 2003 (the effective date of Section 306) or before the company becomes a public "issuer" would be subject to the trading prohibition.

Transactional Exemptions

Similar to several familiar Section 16 transactional exemptions, Regulation BTR exempts from the trading restriction of Section 306(a):

- Acquisitions of equity securities under broad-based dividend or interest reinvestment plans
- Purchases or sales of equity securities pursuant to valid Rule 10b5-1(c) programs, as long as the advance election was not made or modified during the blackout period or at a time the director or executive officer was aware of the impending blackout
- Purchases or sales of equity securities pursuant to certain "tax-conditioned" plans, other than discretionary transactions (such terms are defined similarly to the Rule 16b-3 definitions of such terms)
- Increases or decreases in the number of equity securities held as a result of a stock split or stock dividend applying equally to all equity securities of that class

There is not, however, a complete parallel between the transactional exemptions under Regulation BTR and those available under Section 16. For example, there is no exemption under Regulation BTR for preapproved transactions directly with the issuer, as in Rule 16b-3(d) and Rule 16b-3(e).

Blackout Period Defined

Section 306(a) defines the term *blackout period* to mean any period of more than three consecutive business days during which the ability of not fewer than 50 percent of the participants or beneficiaries under all individual account plans maintained by the issuer to purchase, sell, or otherwise acquire or transfer an interest in any equity security of such issuer held in such an "individual account plan" is temporarily suspended by the issuer or by a fiduciary of the plan.

A blackout period does not include (1) a regularly scheduled trading suspension that is incorporated into the plan and timely disclosed to employees before becoming participants or as a subsequent plan amendment, or (2) any suspension that is imposed solely in connection with persons becoming participants or beneficiaries in such plan by reason of a corporate merger, acquisition, divestiture, or similar transaction involving the plan or plan sponsor.

Common administrative reasons for imposing blackout periods include changes in investment alternatives, changes in record keepers for the plan or other service providers, and mergers, acquisitions, or spin-off transactions that affect the coverage group of plan participants. For example, in the case of a change in record keepers, plan activities might be suspended to provide time for reconciliation of participant accounts and conversion of accounts to the new record keeper's system. Some blackout periods, however, are not within the control of the plan administrator, such as those caused by computer failure.

Individual Account Plan

In general, an "individual account plan" is a pension plan in which an individual account is maintained for each participant, which provides benefits based solely on the amounts contributed to the account (either by the participant or the issuer, through forfeitures or otherwise) and any earnings or losses thereon. For example, typical individual account plans would include 401(k) plans, profit-sharing and savings plans, stock bonus plans, and money purchase pension plans. Defined-benefit pension plans are not likely to be individual account plans.

Notice Requirement

Section 306(a) requires a company to timely notify its directors and executive officers, as well as the SEC, of the existence of a blackout period during which they would be prohibited from trading in issuer equity securities.

Remedies for Noncompliance; Disgorgement of Profits

Section 306(a) contains two distinct remedies. First, a violation is subject to a possible SEC enforcement action. This would include possible civil injunctive actions, cease-and-desist proceedings, civil penalties, and all other remedies available to the SEC to redress violations of the Exchange Act. Under appropriate circumstances, a director or executive officer also could be subject to possible criminal liability.

In addition, where a director or executive officer realizes a profit from a prohibited transaction during a blackout period, the issuer, or a shareholder on the issuer's behalf, may bring an action to recover the profit. This remedy reflects a standard of strict liability (regardless of the intent of the director or executive officer in entering into the transaction) that is similar to the standard under Section 16(b) of the Exchange Act.

As under Section 16(b) of the Exchange Act, the concept of realized profit would mean that the director or executive officer received a direct or indirect pecuniary benefit from the prohibited transaction. The SEC acknowledged the potential complexity of determining whether a transaction has resulted in the realization of recoverable profits, especially in the case of a purchase or other acquisition of equity securities during a blackout period. Therefore, Regulation BTR provides a straight-forward standard:

- Where a transaction involves a purchase, sale, or other acquisition or transfer (other than a grant, exercise, conversion, or termination of a derivative security) of a regularly traded equity security, recoverable profit is measured by comparing the difference between the amount paid or received for the equity security on the date of the transaction during the blackout period and the average market price of the equity security calculated over the first three trading days after the ending date of the blackout period.

- For any other transaction, profit is to be measured in a manner consistent with the objective of identifying the amount of any gain realized or loss avoided as a result of the transaction taking place during the blackout period rather than taking place outside of the blackout period.

For example, assume that during a blackout period, a director acquired, for $10 per share, in connection with service as a director, 1,000 shares of issuer stock. The average price of the issuer stock over the first three trading days after the blackout period was $12. The recoverable profit is $2 per share, or $2,000. If the average price of the issuer stock over the first three trading days after the blackout period had been less than $10, there would have been no recoverable profit, but the director would still be subject to potential sanctions, including SEC enforcement action.

Similarly, assume that during a blackout period, a director sold 1,000 shares of option-acquired stock for $20 per share. The average price of the issuer stock over the first three trading days after the blackout period was $12. The recoverable profit is $8 per share, or $8,000. If the average price of the issuer stock over the first three trading days after the blackout period had been more than $20, there would have been no recoverable profit, but the director would still be subject to potential sanctions, including SEC enforcement action.

Practical Considerations

As a practical matter, temporary pension plan blackout periods that will trigger a need to halt insider trading under Section 306(a) should be infrequent. Moreover, there are many exemptions that will keep the rule from being a complete bar to trading, and appropriately so. Still, the new Section 306(a) trading restrictions add another layer of complexity to the maze of rules that make insider trading in issuer securities a challenge of timing and judgment.

SALES OF RESTRICTED AND CONTROL STOCK UNDER RULE 144

Background

A fundamental premise of the Securities Act is that securities may not be sold without registration unless an exemption from the registration requirements of the Securities Act is available for the transaction. This rule applies both to original issuances of common stock by the issuer and to trading on the secondary level by the issuer's shareholders.

With respect to secondary trading, registration or an exemption from registration is necessary for (1) every sale of "restricted securities" (i.e., securities received in an unregistered private placement or an equivalent transaction) by any shareholder, and (2) every sale by an "affiliate" of any common stock of the issuer, whether or not the common stock was previously registered under the Securities Act. Shares of common stock that were purchased by affiliates in the open market or pursuant to a registered offering by the issuer and that are not "restricted securities" are referred to as *control securities* (referring to ownership by the affiliate, who is presumed to "control" the issuer). The distinction between restricted securities and control securities is important in determining which conditions of Rule 144 apply to a particular sales transaction.

The term *affiliate* refers to persons controlling, controlled by, or under common control with the issuer and presumptively includes executive officers, directors, greater than 10 percent shareholders, and the immediate relatives of all of the foregoing. Depending on the factual circumstances, however, certain of these persons may not actually have the ability to control the issuer and, therefore, may not be affiliates in all cases. Conversely, persons outside of these categories nevertheless may have control capabilities and, therefore, may be deemed affiliates in certain instances.

Rule 144

Because of the expense of a registration and in view of serious potential liabilities, it is important to assure that any sales made by an affiliate come within an applicable registration exemption. Although other exemptions may be available in some limited circumstances, the most commonly used exemption is a sale in a brokers' transaction under Rule 144. Rule 144 permits affiliates to sell common stock, whether characterized as "restricted securities" or "control securities," of the issuer if each of the following conditions is met:

- The affiliate must have owned any "restricted securities" (as described earlier) for at least one year prior to resale.

- The amount of common stock that an affiliate may sell during any three-month period may not exceed the greater of (1) 1 percent of the outstanding common stock or (2) the average weekly trading volume of the common stock for the four-week period prior to the date of the sale.

- The issuer must have been subject to the reporting requirements of the Exchange Act for at least 90 days and must have filed all required reports during the 12 months preceding the sale.

- The common stock must be sold in a "brokers' transaction" (a transaction where the activity of the selling broker is limited) or in a transaction with a "market maker" in the common stock.

- A notice of sale on Form 144 must be filed at the time of the sale, unless sales in the three-month period of the sale involve 500 or fewer shares and an aggregate sales price of less than $10,000. The affiliate must mail Form 144, if required, to the SEC contemporaneously with placing an order to sell common stock with the affiliate's broker. This form is usually provided by the brokerage firm when an affiliate places a sell order.

If for any reason a sale does not comply with the Rule 144 requirements, the broker may insist that the transaction be broken at the affiliate's expense. The affiliate should make sure that any broker used is experienced in Rule 144 trades.

The Rule 144 conditions may be disregarded in certain limited circumstances. A shareholder who is not an affiliate of the issuer at the time of the sale and has not been an affiliate during the preceding three months may sell or otherwise dispose of restricted securities under Rule 144(k) without complying with the conditions noted previously, provided he or she has held such securities for at least two years. Gifts of restricted securities that satisfy the two-year holding period to charitable or other similar types of institutions, or to adult family members not living with the donor and not dependent upon the donor generally, may be sold immediately under Rule 144(k) by the donees, provided the donees are not affiliates of the issuer at the time of the sale of the stock and were not affiliates for the three months preceding the date of sale.

NYSE/NASDAQ RULES: APPROVAL OF EQUITY COMPENSATION PLANS

BACKGROUND

Effective June 30, 2003, the SEC approved new NYSE and NASDAQ rules that significantly broadened shareholder approval requirements for equity-based compensation plans, including material revisions to such plans, subject to certain limited exceptions described later. Among other things, the new rules eliminate exceptions formerly available for broadly based plans and certain *de minimis* equity grants. In addition, the NYSE rule prohibits brokers holding shares on behalf of customers from voting such shares on equity compensation plan matters without specific voting instructions from the customers. Because the final NYSE and NASDAQ rules are significantly similar, the following discussion applies to both the NYSE and the NASDAQ rules, except as otherwise noted.

EQUITY COMPENSATION PLANS DEFINED

The NYSE rule defines *equity-compensation plan* as a plan or other arrangement that provides for the delivery of equity securities (either newly issued or treasury shares) to any employee, director, or other service provider as compensation for services (including compensatory grants of options or other equity securities that are not made under a plan). The NASDAQ rule requires shareholder approval when a stock option or stock purchase or other equity compensation plan or arrangement is to be established or materially amended pursuant to which options or stock may be acquired by officers, directors, employees, or consultants. Neither the NYSE rule nor the NASDAQ rule permits companies to avoid the shareholder approval requirements by funding options with repurchased or treasury shares.

Under the NYSE and NASDAQ rules, the following plans or arrangements are excluded from the shareholder approval requirement:

- Plans that are made available to shareholders generally (such as dividend reinvestment plans or plans involving the distribution of shares or purchase rights to all shareholders).

- Plans that merely allow employees, directors, and other service providers to purchase shares on the open market or from the company at fair market value (regardless of whether shares are delivered immediately or on a deferred basis or whether payments for shares are made directly or through deferral of compensation).

- Arrangements under which employees receive cash-only payments based on the value of the company's stock (such as phantom stock payable in cash).

EXCEPTIONS TO SHAREHOLDER APPROVAL REQUIREMENT

In addition to excluded plans as just described, the following arrangements are exempt from the NYSE and NASDAQ shareholder approval requirements, provided they are made with the approval of the company's compensation committee or a majority of the company's independent directors.

Employment Inducement Awards

Shareholder approval is not required for the grant of options or other equity-based compensation as a material inducement to a person being hired, or being rehired after a bona fide period of employment interruption (including grants to new employees in connection with a merger or acquisition), by a company or any of its subsidiaries. Promptly following the grant of an inducement award, a company must disclose the material terms of the award in a press release.

Plans or Arrangements Relating to a Merger or Acquisition

Shareholder approval is not required for:

- Options and other awards that are made or adopted to convert, replace, or adjust outstanding options or other equity compensation awards of another company in connection with the acquisition of that other company.

- Shares available under preexisting plans of a company acquired in a merger or acquisition by a listed company that are used for certain post-transaction grants, provided: (1) the plan originally was approved by the shareholders of the target company; (2) the number of shares available for grants is adjusted to reflect the transaction; (3) the time during which those shares are available is not extended; and (4) the options or other awards are not granted to individuals who were employed by the acquiring company or its subsidiaries at the time the merger or acquisition was consummated.

  ○ For purposes of this exemption, a plan adopted by the acquired company in contemplation of a merger or acquisition transaction would not be considered "preexisting."

  ○ Any additional shares available for issuance under a plan or arrangement acquired in connection with a merger or acquisition would be counted by the

NYSE or NASDAQ, as applicable, in determining whether the transaction involved the issuance of 20 percent or more of the company's outstanding common stock, thus triggering the shareholder approval requirements under NYSE Listed Company Manual Section 312.03(c) and NASDAQ Rule 4350(i)(1)(C).

Plans Intended to Meet the Requirements of Sections 401(a) or 423 of the Internal Revenue Code and Parallel Excess Plans

Shareholder approval is not required for these plans, as such plans are regulated by the Internal Revenue Code (IRC) and Treasury Department regulations.

The NYSE rule uses the term *parallel excess plan*, and the NASDAQ rule uses the term *parallel nonqualified plan*, both of which are defined to mean a plan that is a "pension plan" within the meaning of the Employee Retirement Income Security Act of 1974 that is designed to work in parallel with a plan intended to be qualified under IRC Section 401(a) to provide benefits that exceed the limits set forth in IRC Section 402(g) (the section that limits an employee's annual pre-tax contributions to a 401(k) plan), IRC Section 401(a)(17) (the section that limits the amount of an employee's compensation that can be taken into account for plan purposes), and/or IRC Section 415 (the section that limits the contributions and benefits under qualified plans), and/or any successor or similar limitations that may be enacted. A plan will not be considered a parallel excess plan or a parallel nonqualified plan unless: (1) it covers all or substantially all employees of an employer who are participants in the related qualified plan whose annual compensation is in excess of the limit of IRC Section 401(a)(17) (or any successor or similar limits that may be enacted); (2) its terms are substantially the same as the qualified plan that it parallels except for the elimination of the limits described in the preceding sentence and the limitation described in clause (3); and (3) no participant receives employer equity contributions under the plan in excess of 25 percent of the participant's cash compensation.

Companies must notify the NYSE or NASDAQ in writing when relying on one of the foregoing exceptions to the shareholder approval requirement.

MATERIAL REVISIONS/AMENDMENTS

Material revisions/amendments to equity-compensation plans and arrangements require shareholder approval. The NYSE and NASDAQ rules provide that a material revision/amendment includes, but is not limited to:

- A material increase in the number of shares available under the plan (other than solely to reflect a reorganization, stock split, merger, spin-off, or similar transaction)
- An expansion of the types of awards available under the plan
- A material expansion of the class of employees, directors, or other service providers eligible to participate
- A material extension of the term of the plan

In addition, the NYSE rule states that a material revision includes any material change to the method of determining the strike price of options under the plan and any deletion or limitation of any provision prohibiting repricing of options. Similarly, the NASDAQ rule provides that a material amendment would include any material increase in benefits to participants, including any reduction in the exercise price of outstanding options or the price at which shares or options to purchase shares may be offered.

Under the NYSE rule, if a plan has an "evergreen" provision that provides for automatic increases in the number of shares available under the plan, or the plan provides for automatic formula grants (in either case, a "formula plan"), each increase or grant is considered a revision requiring shareholder approval unless the plan has a term of not more than 10 years. Under the NASDAQ rule, a formula plan cannot have a term in excess of 10 years unless shareholder approval is obtained every 10 years.

The NYSE rule provides examples of formula plans, which include annual grants to directors of restricted stock having a certain dollar value, and company "matching contributions" whereby stock is credited to a participant's account based upon the amount of compensation a participant elects to defer. The NASDAQ rule describes formula plans as providing for automatic grants pursuant to a dollar-based formula, such as annual grants based on a certain dollar value, or company matching contributions based on compensation a participant elects to defer.

If a plan has no limit on the number of shares available and is not a formula plan (a "discretionary plan"), then under both the NYSE and NASDAQ rules, each grant under the plan is considered a material revision/amendment requiring separate shareholder approval regardless of whether the plan has a term of not more than 10 years. As a practical matter, very few plans were "discretionary" plans even before these new shareholder approval requirements came into effect.

OPTION REPRICINGS

In addition to treating a repricing as a material revision/amendment requiring shareholder approval, the NYSE rule provides that a plan that does not contain a provision specifically permitting the repricing of options will be considered to prohibit repricing. A *repricing* is defined in the NYSE rule to include any of the following or any other action that has the same effect: (1) lowering the exercise price of an option after it is granted; (2) any other action that is treated as a repricing under generally accepted accounting principles (GAAP); or (3) canceling an underwater option in exchange for another option, restricted stock, or other equity, unless in connection with a merger, acquisition, spin-off, or similar transaction.

Moreover, according to the NYSE rule, any actual repricing of options will be considered a material revision of a plan even if the plan itself is not revised. The NASDAQ rule treats repricings as material amendments requiring shareholder approval.

EFFECTIVE DATE

As a general rule, under both the NYSE and NASDAQ rules, plans that were adopted before June 30, 2003, are grandfathered and do not require shareholder approval unless and until they are materially revised or amended. Equity compensation plans and arrangements adopted (or materially revised or amended) on or after June 30, 2003, are subject to these rules regarding shareholder approval.

LIMITATION ON BROKER VOTING

The SEC noted that the existing rules of the National Association of Securities Dealers, Inc. prohibited discretionary voting by broker-dealers without explicit instructions from the beneficial owner. Under amended NYSE Rule 452, brokers holding shares for the accounts of customers are no longer permitted to vote those shares with respect to equity compensation plan matters unless the beneficial owner of the shares (i.e., the customer) has given the broker specific voting instructions. This change has significantly raised the bar for obtaining the requisite shareholder vote to approve equity compensation plans.

SELECTED SARBANES-OXLEY PROVISIONS RELATING TO EXECUTIVE COMPENSATION

SECTION 402: PROHIBITION ON LOANS TO DIRECTORS AND EXECUTIVE OFFICERS

Background

Section 402 of the Sarbanes-Oxley Act introduced a sweeping prohibition of personal loans by a public company to its directors and executive officers. The broad language used in Section 402 has raised many questions regarding the intended scope of the prohibition, and it remains unclear when or if the SEC will offer interpretive guidance. Public companies should carefully review anything that could be viewed as an extension of, or arrangements for an extension of, credit with its directors and executive officers.

Section 402 prohibits a public company from directly or indirectly extending, maintaining, arranging, or renewing a personal loan to or for a director or executive officer. Specifically, it amended Section 13 of the Exchange Act by adding a new Section 13(k):

> It shall be unlawful for any issuer ... directly or indirectly, including through any subsidiary, to extend or maintain credit, to arrange for the extension of credit, or to renew an extension of credit, in the form of a personal loan to or for any director or executive officer (or equivalent thereof) of that issuer. An extension of credit maintained by the issuer on [July 30, 2002] shall not be subject to the provisions of this subsection,

provided that there is no material modification to any term of any such extension of credit or any renewal of any such extension of credit on or after [July 30, 2002].

The Section 402 prohibition extends only to the extension or arrangement of credit that takes the form of a personal loan, but the act does not define the relevant terms. Because the SEC and the board of governors of the Federal Reserve System have broadly interpreted the concepts of arranging and extending credit in other contexts, the Section 402 prohibition could be interpreted to apply to a wide variety of transactions that are not commonly considered loans.

Certainly, public companies are prohibited under Section 402 from directly lending or cosigning or otherwise guaranteeing or providing security for an insider's personal loan. However, other common practices may or may not be prohibited, including such things as selecting a lending institution for an insider, making salary advances, awarding bonuses that are repayable in certain circumstances, using company funds to advance an insider's tax withholding obligations, and even advancement of litigation expenses.

Cashless Exercise Programs

One of the more common areas of concern that flared up in the immediate aftermath of the passage of Section 402, but seems to have subsided almost completely in the ensuing years of no enforcement activity, is the issue of whether certain broker-assisted cashless stock option exercises would violate the loan prohibition.

Many stock option arrangements provide for the exercise of an option through a broker-assisted cashless exercise. In a typical arrangement, the broker, upon receipt of exercise instructions, will sell a sufficient number of shares to remit the exercise price and applicable tax withholding amounts to the company, with the remaining shares or sales proceeds being delivered to the optionee (less applicable commissions). If the broker pays the company the exercise price on the date of exercise but does not receive the proceeds of the stock sale until the settlement date (typically on the third following business day, or T+3), the company may be considered to have "arranged for" the broker's margin loan to the insider, particularly if the company required or encouraged the optionee to use that particular broker to effect the cashless exercise. Or, if the company releases the shares to the broker upon exercise but does not receive payment until the T+3 settlement date, the company may be considered to have provided a short-term loan of the shares to or for the insider, although this is certainly not an unassailable theory. In either event, a potential Section 402 problem exists. There are arguments to be made (some based on legal theory, others on policy grounds) that most broker-assisted cashless exercises are not prohibited by the Sarbanes-Oxley Act, but there is as yet no binding authority or guidance from the SEC or Congress.

In light of this uncertainty, many companies soon after the enactment of the loan prohibition instructed their directors and executive officers not to engage in any form of broker-assisted cashless exercise of options until further guidance is provided or until "safe" cashless exercise structures have been identified and become widely accepted. While most companies now are reasonably comfortable that a properly constructed broker-assisted cashless exercise will not be prosecuted as a violation of Section 402, as an alternative, companies may consider encouraging their directors and executive officers to pay the option exercise price and withholding tax obligation by surrendering to the company shares of company stock they already own or by engaging in a "net exercise" in which option shares are withheld by the company to cover the exercise price and minimum tax obligation. Because a "net exercise" was a problem under former accounting rules (as explained in Chapter 13), many older option plans still prohibit that method of exercise. Before offering that as an alternative, a company should ensure that its option plans have been updated to allow that method of exercise. In addition, Section 402 does not prohibit the exercise of an option for cash, even where the director or executive officer obtained financing for such exercise (without company involvement).

Penalties for Violation of Section 402

The prohibitions of Section 402 apply to the issuer, rather than to the individual directors and executive officers. However, a director or executive officer could be subject to a state law derivative action to recover proceeds of illegal loans, and aiding and abetting claims may be possible. The issuer could be subject to civil or criminal sanctions under the Exchange Act, including administrative and civil remedies. For example, the SEC could seek injunctive remedies or monetary penalties of up to $500,000 under Section 21 of the Exchange Act, or could issue a cease-and-desist order or impose a temporary freeze on "extraordinary payments" during investigation under Section 21C of the Exchange Act. The Department of Justice could institute a criminal proceeding under Section 32 of the Exchange Act for willful violations and/or impose criminal fines of up to $25 million for corporate violations of the Exchange Act. It is unlikely that a right to a private civil action would be implied under the Exchange Act for Section 402 violations.

SECTION 304: FORFEITURE OF BONUSES AND PROFITS TRIGGERED BY RESTATEMENTS OF FINANCIAL REPORTS

Background

Section 304 of the Sarbanes-Oxley Act provides that if "misconduct" results in material noncompliance with SEC financial reporting requirements, and as a result of such noncompliance the company is required to restate its financial statements, then the CEO and chief financial officer (CFO) must disgorge both:

- Any bonuses or other incentive-based or equity-based compensation that he or she received during the 12-month period following the first public issuance or filing (whichever is earlier) of a financial document embodying such financial reporting requirement.

- Profits on the sale of company securities during such 12-month period.

While Section 304 has not received as much use or publicity as some of the other executive compensation provisions of the Sarbanes-Oxley Act (such as the prohibition of loans to insiders and the shortened Section 16 reporting rules), public companies should take special notice of the breadth of its potential application and its required penalties.

Events Triggering Disgorgement

Section 304's disgorgement requirement is triggered when a public company is required to prepare an accounting restatement due to material noncompliance with SEC financial reporting requirements as a result of misconduct. Unfortunately, Section 304 does not define several key terms critical to the application of this provision. While the Sarbanes-Oxley Act grants the SEC authority to adopt exemptions from Section 304 for certain persons, it does not require the SEC to adopt regulations that implement or interpret Section 304. Thus, it is not clear when or whether the SEC will provide interpretive guidance on the scope of these terms.

Key Terms Lack Definition

As with many other areas, it is impossible to know with certainty how this provision of the Sarbanes-Oxley Act will be applied. Among the terms that lack definition are:

- *Required.* First, the circumstances under which a company will be deemed to have been *required* to prepare an accounting restatement are unclear. For example, a restatement might be prepared voluntarily upon the advice of a new accounting firm, or pursuant to comments and suggestions from the SEC in connection with a securities offering. In many cases, the decision whether to prepare a restatement may be a judgment call by the company, driven by the interpretation of accounting principles, rather than any mandate or clear-cut requirement. Until the SEC provides guidance, it may be reasonable to assume that a restatement is *required* when the company's accounting firm cannot complete its interim review or deliver its audit opinion unless the restatement is made.

- *Misconduct.* Whatever the source of the "requirement" that financial statements be restated, Section 304's disgorgement provisions only apply when the requirement to restate arises from *misconduct* that results in material noncompliance with SEC financial reporting requirements. The Sarbanes-Oxley Act does not define "misconduct" or describe the necessary link between the misconduct and the restatement requirement. While Section 304's disgorgement provisions apply only to CEOs and CFOs, there is no specific requirement that such officers be the actual source of the misconduct. However, it is consistent with the general theme of the Sarbanes-Oxley Act that the ultimate responsibility for the integrity of a company's financial reporting rests with the CEO and the CFO.

- *Result.* Presumably the determination of whether a financial restatement was required *as a result of* misconduct would be a matter of proof in an enforcement action, much as causation is a required element of an action based on negligence. The Sarbanes-Oxley Act does not assign a presumption of causation.

Compensation to Be Disgorged

Disgorgement under Section 304 applies to any bonus or other incentive-based or equity-based compensation received by the CEO or CFO from the issuer during the 12 months following the first public issuance or filing of the tainted financial document. It is not clear whether this includes compensation received from affiliates of the issuer. It also is not clear whether the issuance of an earnings press release, for example, would start the 12-month clock running. While an earnings press release is not itself subject to financial reporting requirements, it typically contains selected information that will subsequently be included in a financial document embodying a financial reporting requirement, such as Form 10-Q or 10-K. Just as the events that trigger the disgorgement obligations are ill defined, several key terms relating to what must be disgorged are also open to question. For example:

- *Received.* It is unclear what compensation will be deemed to have been *received* by the executives during the applicable 12-month period. Certainly, cash bonuses paid during the period would be "received" and subject to disgorgement. However, awards subject to multiyear vesting could be deemed "received" either upon grant or upon vesting or upon exercise or settlement. It is possible that the SEC or the courts could take the position, for example, that options *granted* during the 12-month period are tainted, and any profits obtained upon their future exercise must be disgorged, even if the exercise occurred outside the 12-month period. It is also unclear how the "receipt" requirement would be applied to cash bonuses or other awards accrued during the 12-month period but paid or payable on a later date under a deferral arrangement.

- *Profits.* Section 304 requires disgorgement of profits from the executive's sale of company equity securities during the 12-month period. However, in order to calculate profit from the sale of securities, it is necessary to compare the sale price to a purchase price of a matching acquisition. Section 304 gives no guidance as to the time period for the matching acquisition. Note that unlike Section 306(a) of the Sarbanes-Oxley Act relating to insider trading during pension fund blackout periods (as discussed earlier), the securities related to a possible disgorgement under Section 304 are not limited to securities acquired by the executive in connection with the performance of service to the company. It also is unclear whether avoidance-of-loss principles will apply (as in Section 16 short-wing profit rules) such that a matching acquisition may either precede or follow the sale to produce a recoverable profit.

Salary is Not at Risk

The compensation that must be reimbursed is limited to bonuses or other incentive-based or equity-based compensation. Therefore, Section 304 may have the anomalous consequence of encouraging CEOs and CFOs to insist that a greater percentage of their pay be in the form of salary. This cuts against recent corporate governance initiatives to create more of a link between executive compensation and performance.

Enforcement

Unlike the disgorgement provisions of Section 306(a) of the Sarbanes-Oxley Act and Section 16(b) of the Exchange Act, there are no enforcement procedures set forth in Section 304. It is unclear whether enforcement will be limited to SEC action or whether Section 304 is intended to create a new private right of action. However, so far, a few federal district court cases have ruled that only federal authorities can sue under Section 304, not private plaintiffs. And there is no evidence that any enforcement action has been brought by the SEC under Section 304 to date.

SECTION 306(a): INSIDER TRADES DURING PENSION FUND BLACKOUT PERIODS—DISGORGEMENT OF PROFITS

See the section "Special Rules Affecting Insider Trading" in this chapter for a discussion of this provision of the Sarbanes-Oxley Act.

Chapter 8

Tax Rules and Issues

This chapter discusses relevant and important tax law, rules, and related issues that compensation committees need to know in order to properly structure and administer executive compensation arrangements. It does not present all of the rules and issues that compensation committees will face. However, it does present those common issues that arise when dealing with executive employment and compensation arrangements. Accordingly, this chapter will provide compensation committees with a working knowledge of relevant tax law and tax-related issues.

This chapter is divided into the following topics:

- Overview and brief background of U.S. federal tax law
- Major U.S. tax laws affecting executive compensation
- Other relevant U.S. tax law affecting executive compensation

OVERVIEW

When dealing with tax law issues, it is important to distinguish between the various taxing regimes, which generally can be broken down into the following:

- U.S. federal tax law
- State tax law
- Local tax law
- International tax law

Of course, most tax issues presented to compensation committees will concern U.S. federal tax law. However, the other taxing authorities will also need to be taken into account. Thus, in many cases compensation committees will need to consult their tax advisors for all tax effects (and in some cases, appropriate local and/or expert counsel).

The compensation tax issues encountered by compensation committee members generally concern the following questions:

- Will the payment or benefit be deductible by the company?
- Will the payment be treated as ordinary income or as capital gain?
- What are the company's withholding and Federal Insurance Contributions Act (FICA) obligations?

- If the payment is deferred, is there constructive receipt?
- Is there a tax penalty, and if so, what could it be?
- Will the arrangement impact an executive's estate planning?

As mentioned above, in many cases, compensation committees will need to engage tax counsel to help analyze and work through these issues. Note that all references to "Sections" in this chapter are to U.S. federal tax code sections.

ORGANIZATIONS RESPONSIBLE FOR FEDERAL TAX

First and foremost, Congress is responsible for the laws of the Internal Revenue Code (IRC or Code). Legislative history with respect to the enactment of the various sections of the IRC may become relevant. Indeed, language and concepts from the legislative history very often become part of the administrative regulations promulgated under the statute. The Treasury Department is responsible for the promulgation of the regulations interpreting the tax law. These regulations generally are first proposed and sometimes amended (Proposed Regulations). Then, after notice and comment, the Proposed Regulations are reissued as final regulations (Regulations). In some cases, the Treasury Department may issue temporary regulations to address transition issues or those issues that require immediate guidance.

The Internal Revenue Service (IRS or Service) usually is the author of or main contributor to the Regulations. The IRS, however, has its own set of guidance and standards that presents the IRS position with respect to certain issues. The IRS issues Revenue Rulings that generally address a specific issue or set of issues and which are applicable to all taxpayers. Similarly, the IRS may issue a Revenue Procedure that is also applicable to all taxpayers, but which explains the IRS position by "process," not through "ruling." In some cases, there is a fine line substantively between Revenue Rulings and Revenue Procedures, as both have the effect of influencing taxpayer behavior. The IRS also issues Private Letter Rulings (PLRs) that address a specific set of facts with respect to a specific taxpayer who has requested such a ruling. However, as PLRs have no precedential power, their importance is of limited value. Primarily, PLRs can be used to gain an understanding of what the IRS is "thinking" with respect to like issues. Similar to PLRs are Technical Advice Memoranda (TAMs) that typically are written by IRS national officials to IRS field agents. As with PLRs, they are limited to their specific issues and facts and have no precedential power. As part of the IRS's examinations of specific issues, the IRS's General Counsel may issue General Counsel Memoranda (GCMs) analyzing the specific legal issues in detail.

Finally, U.S. tax law ultimately is decided by U.S. federal courts. Most cases are first litigated in U.S. Tax Court, which is a national court system resolving only tax law cases. Most disputes are first brought to Tax Court because the taxpayer is not obligated to pay the disputed amount. If, however, the taxpayer is willing to pay the disputed amount before trial, then the case may be brought to a U.S. District Court or

U.S. Court of Federal Claims (presumably, the taxpayer has decided that this court would be better for the taxpayer than Tax Court). A decision rendered in either the Tax Court, Court of Federal Claims, or District Court may be appealed to the applicable U.S. Circuit Court of Appeals. A decision rendered in a Circuit Court may be appealed to the U.S. Supreme Court. A decision by the U.S. Supreme Court is, of course, final and nonappealable.

MAJOR U.S. TAX LAW AND ISSUES

The following are the major tax law sections and topics covered by this section:

- Deferred compensation, as regulated primarily by Sections 409A and 451
- The $1 million deductibility cap on executive compensation, as regulated by Section 162(m)
- The golden parachute restrictions, as regulated by Sections 280G and 4999
- The transfer of compensatory property, as regulated by Section 83

DEFERRED COMPENSATION

Prior to October 2004, deferred compensation was regulated by the constructive receipt rules under Section 451 (see related section below) and a judicial/administrative doctrine known as the "economic benefit" doctrine. In addition, Congress had limited the IRS in its regulation of deferred compensation under Section 132 of the Revenue Act of 1978, which effectively "froze" the existing rules that regulated deferred compensation and precluded the IRS from adopting or implementing any new rules. These "frozen" rules regulated deferred compensation for the next 26 years until 2004.

On October 11, 2004, Congress passed the American Jobs Creation Act of 2004 (the Jobs Act), which President Bush signed into law on October 22, 2004, and which generally was effective beginning on January 1, 2005. Section 885 of the Jobs Act added a new Section 409A to the IRC entitled "Inclusion in Gross Income of Deferred Compensation Under Nonqualified Deferred Compensation Plans." Generally, Section 409A provides that deferred compensation must satisfy the stringent require-ments under Section 409A. In addition, Section 409A also proscribes the use of certain offshore trusts as permissible funding arrangements for deferred compen-sation arrangements. Many practitioners believe that Section 409A was more or less a direct result of the increasing corporate "abuses" of deferred compensation, best evidenced by the activities at Enron Corporation. Indeed, the Congressional Joint Committee on Taxation issued a report on April 7, 2003, entitled: "JCX-36-03: Written Testimony of the Staff of the Joint Committee on Taxation on Executive Compensation and Company-Owned Life Insurance Arrangements of Enron

Corporation and Related Entities," which recommended major changes to deferred compensation tax law.

Simply put, Section 409A not only put deferred compensation arrangements "in a box," but "it's a very small box." If a deferred compensation arrangement does not satisfy the very strict Section 409A rules, then the compensation will be treated as constructively received in the year of deferral. Specifically, the heading to Section 409A(a) is "Rules Relating to Constructive Receipt," and that section provides that "[i]f at any time during a taxable year a nonqualified deferred compensation plan fails to meet the requirement of [Section 409A] or is not operated in accordance with [the Section 409A requirements], all compensation deferred under the plan for the taxable year and all preceding taxable years shall be includible in gross income for the taxable year to the extent not subject to a substantial risk of forfeiture and not previously included in gross income."

Deferred compensation that fails to comply with Section 409A produces onerous results. First, the noncompliant deferred compensation will be treated as taxable income with respect to the year in which the Section 409A violation occurs, and ordinary income tax applies to this compensation. Note that this tax becomes due even if the recipient of the deferred compensation has not yet received such compensation. Second, since Section 409A applies to compensation constructively received but never taxed in the same tax year, the taxpayer not only owes the ordinary income tax on this compensation but also interest on the underpayment of taxes, which for this purpose is set at 1 percent above the standard underpayment interest rate. Finally, and most importantly, the recipient of the deferred compensation will be subject to an additional 20 percent "penalty" tax on the deferred compensation.

It is important to note that Section 132 of the Revenue Act of 1978 was not repealed, which means that deferred compensation is still also subject to the old "frozen" rules. This means that all deferred compensation must be analyzed under the following three tests:

1. Does the deferred compensation pass the Section 409A test?
2. Does the deferred compensation pass the constructive receipt rules under Section 451?
3. Does the deferred compensation provide a benefit under the economic benefit doctrine?

Again, the deferred compensation must be subject to—and pass—all of the above three tests.

IRC Section 409A: Nonqualified Deferred Compensation Plans (NQDCP)

As of this writing, the following IRS guidance has been published with respect to Section 409A:

- Notice 2005-1, issued on December 20, 2004, modified on January 6, 2005, which set forth initial guidance with respect to the new tax law
- Section 409A Proposed Regulations, issued on September 29, 2005, but superseded by the final Regulations beginning January 1, 2008 (see below)
- Notice 2006-4, issued on January 4, 2006, which provided guidance with respect to stock options and stock appreciation rights granted before January 1, 2005
- Notice 2006-33, issued on March 21, 2006, which related to Section 409A compliance of offshore trusts due to technical corrections made to Section 409A(b) under the Gulf Opportunity Zone Act of 2005
- Notice 2006-64, issued on July 5, 2006, which provided relief for the acceleration of deferred compensation due to federal conflict-of-interest rules
- Notice 2006-79, issued on October 4, 2006, which extended Section 409A compliance for all written plans from December 31, 2006, to December 31, 2007, and foreclosed the substitution of certain stock options to achieve Section 409A compliance
- Notice 2006-100, issued on November 30, 2006, which provided interim reporting rules
- The final Regulations under Section 409A, issued on April 10, 2007
- Notice 2007-34, also issued on April 10, 2007, which provided guidance on the application of Section 409A to split-dollar life insurance arrangements
- Notice 2007-78, issued on September 10, 2007, which extended the deadline to bring plans into written compliance with Section 409A from December 31, 2007 to December 31, 2008.

Finally, it is important to note that FICA taxes (i.e., Social Security and Medicare tax) on deferred compensation imposed under Section 3121(v) generally are not impacted by Section 409A. Accordingly, payment of FICA taxes (which occurs when there is no longer a substantial risk of forfeiture regardless of whether the compensation is paid or continues to be deferred) is payable by taxpayers under the existing taxing regime established by the Regulation Sections 31.3121(v)(2)-1 and 1.3121(v)(2)-2.

Important and Immediate Action to Be Taken by Companies

The effective date for the Section 409A final Regulations was January 1, 2008. By that time, all nongrandfathered plans are required to be in compliance with Section 409A. Subject to Notice 2007-78, failure to do so could result in Section 409A penalties.

Companies should have already taken the following actions, but if they have not, then the following needs to be done immediately:

- Inventory:
  - All deferred compensation plans, programs, agreements, and arrangements

- All compensatory plans, programs, agreements, and arrangements (including cash-based and equity-based incentive compensation plans)
- All written and unwritten employment arrangements (including employment agreements, individual severance agreements (both change-in-control and non-change-in-control), severance plans (both change-in-control and non-change-in-control)
- Review all such plans, programs, agreements, and arrangements to determine if they are subject to Section 409A
- Amend all such plans, programs, agreements, and arrangements (other than grandfathered arrangements) to bring such arrangements into Section 409A compliance

It is important to understand that a deferred compensation arrangement subject to Section 409A may be contained not only in "traditional" deferred compensation plans and supplemental executive retirement plans (SERPs), but also in many different employment/compensation agreement or plans (e.g., an employment agreement, a change-in-control plan, a stock option agreement, or other equity-based incentive award).

A Section 409A Six-Step Analysis

Section 409A and the Section 409A final Regulations generally create an analytic framework involving six basic steps to determine whether compensation is deferred and subject to Section 409A, and if so, whether it complies with the Section 409A requirements:

Step 1. Determine whether the compensation is under a grandfathered arrangement. Generally, this means that the arrangement was in effect prior to October 4, 2004, and has not been materially modified since that date.

Step 2. Determine whether the compensation is actually deferred compensation under Section 409A. This requires an analysis of whether the compensation meets the regulatory definition of *deferral of compensation* or whether it meets any exemption such as either *short-term deferred compensation*, which generally is exempt from Section 409A, or as Section 83 property, which involves a careful analysis of whether the transferred property satisfies the strict requirements for Section 409A exemption.

Step 3. If the compensation meets the regulatory definition of *deferred compensation*, the next step is to determine whether the compensation is deferred under a nonqualified deferred compensation plan (NQDCP). If it is not (perhaps based on certain exemptions, such as for tax-qualified pension plans, certain welfare plans, certain separation pay plans, and certain foreign plans), then Section 409A would not apply.

Step 4. If the deferred compensation is deferred under a NQDCP, then the next step is to determine whether the NQDCP's provision relating to initial deferral elections and subsequent deferral elections with respect to the deferred compensation comply with Section 409A.

Step 5. The next step is to determine whether the NQDCP's provision relating to the distribution/payment of the deferred compensation comply with Section 409A.

Step 6. The final step is to determine whether the deferred compensation has been properly reported. This not only includes compliant deferred compensation, which has passed Steps 3 and 4 above, but also noncompliant deferred compensation.

Specific Section 409A Issues Important to Compensation Committees

While Section 409A has raised many issues for compensation committees, the following are perhaps the issues that they should be most familiar with:

- Definitions of *deferral of income, substantial risk of forfeiture*, and *performance-based compensation*
- Short-term (or 2½ month) deferral rule
- Written plan requirements
- Plan aggregation rules
- Initial deferral elections
- Subsequent deferral elections
- Anti-acceleration rule
- Permissible distribution/payment events
- Six-month delay-of-payment rule for executives of public companies
- Termination without Cause or for Good Reason
- Equity-based compensation
- Offshore trusts

The Section 409A Regulations use specific terminology. For example, the Regulations use the terms:

- *Service provider*, which generally refers to an executive/employee/independent contractor
- *Service recipient*, which generally refers to a company/employer
- *Separation of service*, which usually is equivalent to a termination of employment

The following discussion generally will use these specific terms.

Definitions

Deferral of compensation. Regulation Section 1.409A-1(b)(1) generally provides that there is a deferral of compensation (and thus, deferred compensation) if, under the terms of the compensation plan or arrangement and the relevant facts and circumstances, the service provider has a legally binding right during a taxable year to compensation that, pursuant to the terms of the plan, is or may be payable to (or on behalf of) the service provider in a later taxable year. A legally binding right to an amount that will be excluded from income when and if received does not constitute a deferral of compensation, unless the service provider has received the right in exchange for, or has the right to exchange the right for, an amount that will be includible in income (other than due to participation in a cafeteria plan described in Section 125). While the regulations do not precisely define what is a *legally binding right,* the preamble to the Regulations states that "[a] legally binding right includes a contractual right that is enforceable under the applicable law or laws governing the contract . . . and also includes an enforceable right created under other applicable law, such as a statute."

Note that an executive will not have a legally binding right to compensation if compensation may be reduced unilaterally or eliminated by the company after the services creating the right to the compensation have been performed (commonly referred to as *negative discretion.* However, an executive will be considered to have a legally binding right to the compensation if the facts and circumstances indicate that the discretion to reduce or eliminate the compensation is available or exercisable only upon a condition, or the discretion to reduce or eliminate the compensation lacks substantive significance. Whether the negative discretion lacks substantive significance depends on all of the relevant facts and circumstances, but the discretion to reduce or eliminate the compensation will not be treated as having substantive significance where the executive has effective control of the company with the discretion to reduce or eliminate the compensation. Compensation is not considered subject to unilateral reduction or elimination merely because it may be reduced or eliminated by operation of the objective terms of the plan, such as the application of a nondiscretionary, objective provision creating a substantial risk of forfeiture. Similarly, a service provider does not fail to have a legally binding right to compensation merely because the amount of compensation is determined under a formula that provides for benefits to be offset by benefits provided under another plan (including a plan that is qualified under Section 401(a)), or because benefits are reduced due to actual or notional investment losses, or in a final average pay plan, subsequent decreases in compensation.

Substantial risk of forfeiture. Deferred compensation that is subject to a substantial risk of forfeiture may take advantage of the short-term deferral rule (as discussed below), and thus, if it is paid within the 2½ month short-term deferral period following "vesting," the compensation is exempt from Section 409A. It also has its own rule relating to initial deferral elections. It is important to note that the substantial-risk-of-forfeiture standard used for purposes of Section 409A is quite different than the substantial-risk-of-forfeiture standard used for purposes of Sections 83 and 402(b), and at the time of this writing, Section 457(f).

Regulation Section 1.409A-1(d) provides that compensation is subject to a substantial risk of forfeiture if entitlement to the amount is conditioned on the performance of substantial future services by any person or the occurrence of a condition related to a purpose of the compensation, and the possibility of forfeiture is substantial. A condition related to a purpose of the compensation must relate to the service provider's performance for the service recipient or the service recipient's business activities or organizational goals (e.g., the attainment of a prescribed level of earnings or equity value or completion of an initial public offering). If a service provider's entitlement to the amount is conditioned on the occurrence of the service provider's involuntary separation from service without Cause, the right is subject to a substantial risk of forfeiture if the possibility of forfeiture is substantial.

An amount is not subject to a substantial risk of forfeiture merely because the right to the amount is conditioned, directly or indirectly, upon the refraining from the performance of services. Other than certain transaction-based compensation, the addition of any risk of forfeiture after the legally binding right to the compensation arises, or any extension of a period during which compensation is subject to a risk of forfeiture, is disregarded for purposes of determining whether such compensation is subject to a substantial risk of forfeiture.

An amount will not be considered subject to a substantial risk of forfeiture beyond the date or time at which the recipient otherwise could have elected to receive the amount of compensation, unless the present value of the amount subject to a substantial risk of forfeiture (disregarding, in determining the present value, the risk of forfeiture) is materially greater than the present value of the amount the recipient otherwise could have elected to receive absent such risk of forfeiture. This means that compensation that the service provider would receive for continuing to perform services regardless of whether the service provider elected to receive the amount that is subject to a substantial risk of forfeiture is not taken into account in determining whether the present value of the right to the amount subject to a substantial risk of forfeiture is materially greater than the amount the recipient otherwise could have elected to receive absent such risk of forfeiture. Thus, a salary deferral generally may not be made subject to a substantial risk of forfeiture. However, where a bonus plan provides an election between, for example, a cash payment or restricted stock units with a present value that is materially greater (disregarding the risk of forfeiture) than the present value of such cash payment and that will be forfeited absent continued services for a period of years, the right to the restricted stock units generally will be treated as subject to a substantial risk of forfeiture.

With respect to equity-based compensation that constitutes "stock rights" (see below), a stock right ceases to be subject to a substantial risk of forfeiture at the earlier of the first date the holder may exercise the stock right and receive cash or property that is substantially vested or the first date that the stock right is not subject to a forfeiture condition that would constitute a substantial risk of forfeiture. Accordingly, a stock option that the service provider may exercise immediately and receive substantially vested stock is not subject to a substantial risk of forfeiture, even if the stock option automatically terminates upon the service provider's separation from service.

Performance-based compensation. Under Section 409A, performance-based compensation, where the compensation does not vest or become payable until certain performance goals are met, is a variant of compensation subject to a substantial risk of forfeiture. It also has its own rule relating to initial deferral elections. It is important to note that performance-based compensation under the Section 409A Regulations is similar to—but not the same as—performance-based compensation under the Section 162(m) Regulations (discussed below).

The term *performance-based compensation* means compensation the amount of which, or the entitlement to which, is contingent on the satisfaction of preestablished organizational or individual performance criteria relating to a performance period of at least 12 consecutive months. Organizational or individual performance criteria are considered preestablished if established in writing by not later than 90 days after the commencement of the period of service to which the criteria relates, provided that the outcome is substantially uncertain at the time the criteria are established.

Performance-based compensation may include payments based on performance criteria that are not approved by a compensation committee of the board of directors (or similar entity in the case of a noncorporate service recipient) or by the stockholders or members of the service recipient. Performance-based compensation does not include any amount or portion of any amount that will be paid either regardless of performance, or based upon a level of performance that is substantially certain to be met at the time the criteria is established.

In addition, compensation generally is not performance-based compensation merely because the amount of such compensation is determined by reference to the value of the service recipient or the stock of the service recipient. Where a portion of an amount of compensation would qualify as performance-based compensation if the portion were the sole amount available under the plan, that portion of the award will not fail to qualify as performance-based compensation if that portion is designated separately or otherwise separately identifiable under the terms of the plan, and the amount of each portion is determined independently of the other.

Compensation may be performance-based compensation where the amount will be paid regardless of satisfaction of the performance criteria due to the service provider's death, disability, or a change in control (CIC), provided that a payment made under such circumstances without regard to the satisfaction of the performance criteria will not constitute performance-based compensation. Generally, a *disability* refers to any medically determinable physical or mental impairment resulting in the service provider's inability to perform the duties of his or her position or any substantially similar position, where such impairment can be expected to result in death or can be expected to last for a continuous period of not less than six months.

In addition, unlike under the Section 162(m) Regulations, the term *performance-based compensation* may include payments that are based on subjective performance criteria, provided that:

- The subjective performance criteria are bona fide and relate to the performance of the participant service provider, a group of service providers that includes the participant service provider, or a business unit for which the participant service provider provides services (which may include the entire organization); and

- The determination that any subjective performance criteria has been met is not made by the participant service provider or a family member of the participant service provider, or a person under the effective control of the participant service provider or such a family member, and no amount of the compensation of the person making such determination is effectively controlled in whole or in part by the service provider or such a family member.

With respect to equity-based compensation, compensation is performance-based compensation if it is based solely on an increase in the value of the service recipient, or a share of stock in the service recipient, after the date of a grant or award. However, compensation payable for a service period that is equal to the value of a predetermined number of shares of stock, and is variable only to the extent that the value of such shares appreciates or depreciates, generally will not be performance-based compensation.

The attainment of a prescribed value for the service recipient (or a portion thereof), or a share of stock in the service recipient, may be used as a preestablished organizational criterion for purposes of providing performance-based compensation, provided that the other requirements stated above are satisfied. In addition, an award of equity-based compensation may constitute performance-based compensation if entitlement to the compensation is subject to a condition that would cause the award to otherwise qualify as performance-based compensation, such as a performance-based vesting condition. A provision that allows a service provider to defer compensation that would be realized upon the exercise of a stock right generally constitutes an additional deferral feature for purposes of the definition of a *deferral of compensation* under the Regulations.

Short-Term or "2½ Month" Deferral Exemption

The basic rule is that even if compensation satisfies the definition of a *deferral of compensation*, if the deferred compensation is paid within a short period of time after certain events (e.g., the lapse of a substantial risk of forfeiture, the end of a performance period, the satisfaction of a performance goal), the compensation is exempt from Section 409A.

Regulation Section 1.409A-1(b)(4) provides that a deferral of compensation does not occur if the plan under which a payment is made does not provide for a deferred payment and the service provider actually or constructively receives such payment on or before the last day of the applicable 2½ month period.

The following rules apply for purposes of the 2½ month rule:

- The applicable 2½ month period is the period ending on the later of the 15th day of the third month following the end of the service provider's first taxable year in which the right to the payment is no longer subject to a substantial risk of forfeiture or the 15th day of the third month following the end of the service recipient's first taxable year in which the right to the payment is no longer subject to a substantial risk of forfeiture.

- A payment is treated as actually or constructively received if the payment is includible in income, including if the payment is includible in income under Section 83, the economic benefit doctrine, Section 402(b), or Section 457(f).

- A right to a payment that is never subject to a substantial risk of forfeiture is considered to be no longer subject to a substantial risk of forfeiture on the first date the service provider has a legally binding right to the payment.

- A plan provides for a deferred payment if the plan provides that any payment will be made or completed on or after any date, or upon or after the occurrence of any event, that will or may occur later than the end of the applicable 2½ month period, such as a separation from service, death, disability, a change in control, a specified time or schedule of payment, or an unforeseeable emergency, regardless of whether an amount is actually paid as a result of the occurrence of such a payment date or event during the applicable 2½ month period.

Written Plan Requirements

To be Section 409A compliant, a plan must comply with the following:

- *Initial deferral election provisions.* If a plan provides a service provider or a service recipient with an initial deferral election, the plan must set forth in writing, on or before the date the applicable election is required to be irrevocable the conditions under which such election may be made.

- *Subsequent deferral election provisions.* If a plan permits a subsequent deferral election, the plan must set forth in writing, on or before the date the election is required to be irrevocable the conditions under which such election may be made.

- *Payment accelerations.* A plan is not required to set forth in writing the conditions under which a payment may be accelerated if such acceleration is permitted under the Regulations.

- *Six-month delay for specified employees.* A plan must provide that distributions to a "specified employee" may not be made before the date that is six months after the date of separation from service or, if earlier, the date of death (see the "six-month payment delay" rule discussed below). The six-month delay rule, required for payments due to the separation from service of a specified employee, must be written in the plan. A plan does not fail to be established and maintained merely because it does not contain the six-month delay rule when the service provider who has a right to compensation deferred under such plan is not a specified employee. However, such provision must be set forth in writing on or before the date such service provider first becomes a specified employee. In general, this means the provision must be set forth in writing on or before the "specified employee effective date" (as discussed below) for the first list of specified employees that includes such service provider.

- *Plan amendments.* In the case of an amendment that increases the amount deferred under a NQDCP, the plan is not considered established with respect to the additional amount deferred until the plan, as amended, is established in accordance with the plan establishment rules above.

A legally enforceable unwritten plan that was adopted and effective before December 31, 2007, is treated as established under the Regulations as of the later of the date on which it was adopted or became effective, provided that the material terms of the plan are set forth in writing on or before December 31, 2007.

Plan Aggregation Rules

The basic rule is that a violation under one category of NQDCP of the service recipient is a violation of all NQDCPs of that service recipient of the same category. Generally, the Regulations divide NQDCPs into nine different categories:

Category 1. *Elective Account Balance Plans.* All deferrals of compensation at the election of that service provider under all plans of the service recipient that are account balance plans are treated as deferred under a single plan.

Category 2. *Nonelective Account Balance Plans.* All deferrals of compensation other than at the election of that service provider, including deferrals reflecting matching by the service recipient with respect to amounts a service provider elects to defer, under all plans of the service recipient that are account balance plans, are treated as deferred under a single plan.

Category 3. *Nonaccount Balance Plans.* All deferrals of compensation with respect to that service provider under all plans of the service recipient that are nonaccount balance plans, are treated as deferred under a single plan.

Category 4. *Separation Pay Plans.* All deferrals of compensation with respect to that service provider under all separation pay plans of the service recipient to the extent an amount deferred under the plans is not described in Category 5 and is payable solely upon an involuntary separation from service or as a result of participation in a window program, are treated as deferred under a single plan.

Category 5. *Reimbursement and In-Kind Benefits Arrangements.* All deferrals of compensation with respect to that service provider under all plans of the service recipient to the extent such amounts deferred consist of rights to in-kind benefits or reimbursements of expenses, such as membership fees, or expenses related to aircraft or vehicle usage, to the extent that the right to the in-kind benefit or reimbursement, separately or in the aggregate, does not constitute a substantial portion of either the overall compensation earned by the service provider for performing services for the service recipient or the overall compensation received due to a separation from service, are treated as deferred under a single plan.

Category 6. *Split-Dollar Life Insurance Arrangements.* All deferrals of compensation with respect to that service provider under all plans of the service recipient to the extent that the taxation of such compensation is governed by the split-dollar life insurance arrangements taxation rule are treated as deferred under a single plan.

Category 7. *Foreign Plans.* All deferrals of compensation with respect to that service provider under all agreements, methods, programs, or other arrangements of the service recipient to the extent the deferrals under the agreements, methods, programs, or other arrangements are deferrals of amounts that would be treated as modified foreign earned income if paid to the service provider at the time the amount is first deferred. This treatment presupposes that substantially all the participants in such agreements, methods, programs, or other arrangements and any substantially similar agreements, methods, programs, or other arrangements are nonresident aliens and that the service provider does not participate in a substantially identical agreement, method, program, or other arrangement that does not meet the requirements of a domestic arrangement, are treated as deferred under a single plan.

Category 8. *Stock Right Plans.* All deferrals of compensation with respect to that service provider under all plans of the service provider to the extent such plans are stock rights subject to Section 409A, are treated as deferred under a single plan.

Category 9. *All Other Plans.* All deferrals of compensation with respect to that service provider under all plans of the service recipient to the extent such plans are not described in Categories 1 through 8 are treated as deferred under a single plan.

Where an employee also is a member of the board of directors of the service recipient (or a similar position with respect to a noncorporate service recipient), the arrangements under which the employee participates as a director (director arrangements) are not aggregated with employee arrangements, provided that the director arrangements are substantially similar to arrangements provided to service providers providing services only as directors (or similar positions with respect to noncorporate service recipients). For example, an employee director who participates in an employee arrangement and a director arrangement generally may treat the two arrangements as separate plans, provided that the director arrangement is substantially similar to arrangements providing benefits to non-employee directors. To the extent a plan in which an employee director participates is not substantially similar to arrangements in which non-employee directors participate, such plan is treated as an employee plan. It should be noted that director plans and independent contractor plans are aggregated.

Initial Deferral Elections

The basic rule is that service provider elective deferrals must be made either in the year before the year of service (similar to the IRS-imposed rules under the principles of constructive receipt) or under the special rules relating to selected circumstance (e.g., a new plan or a new participant in a plan).

Generally, a plan that is, or constitutes part of, a NQDCP meets the requirements of Section 409A if under the terms of the plan, compensation for services performed during a service provider's taxable year (the service year) may be deferred at the service provider's election only if the election to defer such compensation:

- Is made not later than the close of the service provider's taxable year next preceding the service year, and
- Is made and becomes irrevocable not later than the latest date permitted under the initial deferral election rules.

An election will not be considered to be revocable merely because the service provider or service recipient may make an election to change the time and form of payment (as permitted under the Regulations) or the service recipient may accelerate the time of payment pursuant (as permitted under the Regulations).

Whether a plan provides a service provider an opportunity to elect the time or form of payment of compensation is determined based upon all the facts and circumstances surrounding the determination of the time and form of payment of the compensation. An election to defer includes an election as to the time of the payment, an election as to the form of the payment or an election as to both the time and the form of the payment, but does not include an election as to the medium of payment (e.g., an election between a payment of cash or a payment of property). Generally, an election will not be considered made until such election becomes irrevocable under the terms of the applicable plan.

Accordingly, a plan may provide that an election to defer may be changed at any time before the last permissible date for making such an election. Where a plan provides the service provider a right to make an initial deferral election, and further provides that the election remains in effect until terminated or modified by the service provider, the election will be treated as made as of the date such election becomes irrevocable as to compensation for services performed during the relevant service year. Thus, where a plan provides that a service provider's election to defer a set percentage will remain in effect until changed or revoked, but that as of each December 31 the election becomes irrevocable with respect to salary payable in connection with services performed in the immediately following year, the initial deferral election with respect to salary payable with respect to services performed in the immediately following year will be deemed to have been made as of the December 31 upon which the election became irrevocable. The reference to a service period or a performance period refers to the period of service for which the right to the compensation arises, and may include periods before the grant of a legally binding right to the compensation. For example, where a service recipient grants a bonus based on services performed in calendar year 2010, but retains the discretion to rescind the bonus until 2011 such that the promise of the bonus is not a legally binding right, the period of service or performance period to which the compensation relates is calendar year 2010.

Some NQDCPs do not provide for service provider deferral elections (e.g., SERPs). A plan that provides for a deferral of compensation for services performed during a service provider's taxable year that does not provide the service provider with an opportunity to elect the time or form of payment of such compensation must designate the time and form of payment by no later than the later of the time the service provider first has a legally binding right to the compensation or, if later, the time the service provider would be required to make such an election if the service provider were provided such an election. Such designation is treated as an initial deferral election. Where a plan permits a service recipient to exercise discretion to disregard a service provider election as to the time or form of a payment, any service provider election that is subject to such discretion will be treated as revocable so long as such discretion may be exercised.

Subsequent Deferral Elections

The basic rule is that changes in time or form of payment after an initial deferral election are permissible, but only if made 12 months before the payment would have been made and only if the new payment is delayed at least five additional years from the originally scheduled payment date.

A plan that permits under a subsequent election a delay in a payment or a change in the form of payment (referred to as a *subsequent deferral election*), including a subsequent deferral election made by a service provider or a service recipient, satisfies the requirements of Section 409A only if the below rules are met. Generally, a subsequent deferral election is not considered made until such election becomes irrevocable under the terms of the plan. Accordingly, a plan may provide that a subsequent deferral election may be changed at any time before the last permissible date for making such a subsequent deferral election. Where a plan permits a subsequent deferral election, this rule is satisfied only if the following conditions are met:

- The plan requires that such election not take effect until at least 12 months after the date on which the election is made.
- In the case of an election related to a payment other than on account of death, disability, or an unforeseeable emergency, the plan requires that the payment with respect to which such election is made be deferred for a period of not less than five years from the date such payment would otherwise have been paid (or in the case of a life annuity or installment payments treated as a single payment, five years from the date the first amount was scheduled to be paid).
- The plan requires that any election related to a payment at a specified time or pursuant to a fixed schedule be made not less than 12 months before the date the payment is scheduled to be paid (or in the case of a life annuity or installment payments treated as a single payment, 12 months before the date the first amount was scheduled to be paid).

Permissible Distribution/Payment Events

Deferred compensation may be either distributed in property (e.g., stock, an annuity contract) or paid in cash. Section 409A allows only six permissible distribution/payment events:

1. A specified time or a fixed schedule
2. Death
3. Disability
4. Unforeseeable emergency
5. Separation from service
6. A change in control.

It is critical to understand that these six distribution/payment events are the only permissible distribution/payment events, and that no other event will be treated as a permissible distribution/payment event.

With respect to a specified time or a fixed schedule, a plan provides for the payment upon a permissible distribution/payment event if the plan provides the date of the event is the payment date, or specifies another payment date that is objectively determinable and nondiscretionary at the time the event occurs. A plan may also provide that a payment upon a permissible distribution/payment event is to be made in accordance with a schedule that is objectively determinable and nondiscretionary based on the date the event occurs and that would qualify as a fixed schedule if the payment event were instead a fixed date, provided that the schedule must be fixed at the time the permissible payment event is designated.

In addition, a plan may provide that a payment, including a payment that is part of a schedule, is to be made during a designated taxable year of the service provider that is objectively determinable and nondiscretionary at the time the payment event occurs such as, for example, a schedule of three substantially equal payments payable during the first three taxable years following the taxable year in which a separation from service occurs. A plan may also provide that a payment, including a payment that is part of a schedule, is to be made during a designated period objectively determinable and nondiscretionary at the time the payment event occurs, but only if the designated period both begins and ends within one taxable year of the service provider or the designated period is not more than 90 days and the service provider does not have a right to designate the taxable year of the payment (other than an election that complies with the subsequent deferral election rules).

Where a plan provides for a period of more than one day following a payment event during which a payment may be made, such as within 90 days following the date of the event, the payment date for purposes of the subsequent deferral rules is treated as the first possible date upon which a payment could be made under the terms of the plan. A plan may provide for payment upon the earliest or latest of more than one event or time, provided that each event or time is a permissible distribution/payment event.

Death is treated as a separation from service. There are fairly precise rules pertaining to distributions/payments due to disability and unforeseeable emergencies, but generally compliance will be determined based on the facts and circumstances of each situation. Any separation from service is a permissible distribution/payment event (even a termination for Cause). A CIC must meet the definition of change in control under the Regulations, which generally is broken out into the following three events:

1. Change in the ownership of a corporation
2. Change in the effective control of a corporation
3. Change in the ownership of a substantial portion of a corporation's assets

The Regulations did "look to" the definition of *change in control* under the Section 280G Regulations, and thus the concepts are quite similar (but not exact).

Anti-Acceleration Rule

A NQDCP may not permit the acceleration of the time or schedule of any payment or amount scheduled to be paid pursuant to the terms of the plan, and no such accelerated payment may be made whether or not provided for under the terms of such plan.

An impermissible acceleration does not occur if payment is made in accordance with plan provisions or an election as to the time and form of payment in effect at the time of initial deferral or added in accordance with the rules applicable to subsequent deferral elections pursuant to which payment is required to be made on an accelerated schedule as a result of an intervening permissible distribution/payment. Thus, a plan may provide that a participant will receive six installment payments commencing at separation from service, and also provide that if the participant dies after such payments commence but before all payments have been made, all remaining amounts will be paid in a lump-sum payment. Additionally, it is not an acceleration of the time or schedule of payment of a deferral of compensation if a service recipient waives or accelerates the satisfaction of a condition constituting a substantial risk of forfeiture applicable to such deferral of compensation, provided that the requirements of Section 409A (including the requirement that the payment be made upon a permissible payment event) are otherwise satisfied with respect to such deferral of compensation. Thus, if a NQDCP provides for a lump-sum payment of the vested benefit upon separation from service, and the benefit vests under the plan only after 10 years of service, it is not a violation of the requirements of Section 409A if the service recipient reduces the vesting requirement to 5 years of service, even if a service provider becomes vested as a result and receives a payment in connection with a separation from service before the service provider would have completed 10 years of service. However, if such NQDCP had provided for a payment at a fixed date, rather than at separation from service, the date of payment could not be accelerated due to the accelerated vesting.

Generally, the addition of a permissible distribution/payment event, the deletion of a permissible distribution/payment event, or the substitution of one permissible distribution/payment event for another permissible distribution/payment event, results in an acceleration of a payment if the addition, deletion, or substitution could result in the payment being made at an earlier date than such payment would have been made absent such addition, deletion, or substitution. However, the addition of death, disability, or an unforeseeable emergency as a potentially earlier alternative payment event to an amount previously deferred will not be treated as resulting in an acceleration of a payment, even if such addition results in the payment being paid at an earlier time than such payment would have been made absent the addition of the payment event. However, the addition of such a payment event as a potentially later alternative payment event generally is subject to the rules governing changes in the time and form of payment.

The anti-acceleration rules apply to elections by beneficiaries with respect to the time and form of payment, as well as elections by service providers or service recipients with respect to the time and form of payment to beneficiaries. An election to change the identity of a beneficiary does not constitute an acceleration of a payment merely because the election changes the identity of the recipient of the payment, if the time and form of the payment is not otherwise changed. In addition, an election before the commencement of a life annuity to change the identity of a beneficiary does not constitute an acceleration of a payment if the change in the time of payments stems solely from the different life expectancy of the new beneficiary, such as in the case of a joint and survivor annuity, and does not change the commencement date of the life annuity.

The following are specific exceptions to the anti-acceleration rule:

- Domestic relations order
- Conflicts of interest
- Section 457(f)
- Limited cashouts
- Payment of employment taxes
- Payments upon income inclusion under Section 409A

- Cancellation of deferrals following an unforeseeable emergency or hardship distribution
- Termination and liquidation of a NQDCP
- Certain distributions to avoid a nonallocation year under Section 409(p)
- Linkage to qualified employer plans and certain other arrangements
- Payment of state, local, or foreign taxes
- Cancellation of deferral elections due to disability
- Certain offsets (generally under $5,000)
- Bona fide disputes as to a right to a payment
- Changes in elections under a Section 125 cafeteria plan

Six-Month Payment Delay Rule

The Regulations provides that in the case of any service provider who is a specified employee as of the date of a separation from service, the permissible distribution/payment requirements permitting a payment upon a separation from service are satisfied only if payments may not be made before the date that is six months after the date of separation from service (or, if earlier than the end of the six-month period, the date of death of the specified employee).

For this purpose, a service provider who is not a specified employee as of the date of a separation from service will not be treated as subject to this requirement even if the service provider would have become a specified employee if the service provider had continued to provide services through the next specified employee effective date. Similarly, a service provider who is treated as a specified employee as of the date of a separation from service will be subject to this requirement even if the service provider would not have been treated as a specified employee after the next specified employee effective date had the specified employee continued providing services through the next specified employee effective date.

However, this rule does not apply to a payment made with respect to:

- A domestic relations order
- A conflict of interest
- A payment of employment taxes

The required delay in payment is met if payments to which a specified employee would otherwise be entitled during the first six months following the date of separation from service are accumulated and paid on the first day of the seventh month following the date of separation from service, or if each payment to which a specified employee is otherwise entitled upon a separation from service is delayed by six months. A service recipient may retain discretion to choose which method will be implemented, provided that no direct or indirect election as to the method may be provided to the service provider. For an affected specified employee, a date upon which the plan or the service recipient designates that the payment will be made after the six-month delay is treated as a fixed payment date once the separation from service has occurred.

The term *specified employee* generally is a "key employee" under the Section 416 "top-heavy" pension plan rules. Specifically, the term *specified employee* means a service provider who, as of the date of the service provider's separation from service, is a key employee of a service recipient any stock of which is publicly traded on an established securities market or otherwise. A service provider is a key employee if the service provider meets the any of the requirements of Section 416(i)(1)(A) (applied in accordance with the regulations thereunder and disregarding Section 416(i)(5)) at any time during the 12-month period ending on a specified employee identification date:

- An officer of the employer having an annual compensation greater than $145,000 (increased from $140,000 in 2007 and subject to indexing)
- A 5 percent owner of the employer
- A 1 percent owner of the employer having an annual compensation from the employer of more than $150,000 (subject to indexing)

If a service provider is a key employee as of a specified employee identification date, the service provider is treated as a key employee for the entire 12-month period beginning on the specified employee effective date.

Termination of Employment without Cause or for Good Reason

Generally, any termination of employment is a permissible distribution/payment event, provided that the event was contained in the original written arrangement. If it is added after the date of the original arrangement, then it becomes subject to the subsequent election rule. Also, the termination must be real and not simply an arrangement.

Without Cause Termination   A "without Cause" termination (referred to in the Regulations as an *involuntary separation*) generally will be subject to the rules relating to a substantial risk of forfeiture. This means that severance payments may take advantage of the short-term or 2½ month rule. Termination of employment without Cause may provide a planning opportunity to take advantage of the short-term deferral rule. The Regulations generally provide that a separation from service with the employer if the employee dies, retires, or otherwise has a termination of employment with the employer.

Generally, whether a termination of employment has occurred (whether with or without Cause or with or without Good Reason) is determined based on whether the facts and circumstances indicate that the employer and employee reasonably anticipated that no further services would be performed after a certain date or that the level of bona fide services the employee would perform after such date (whether as an employee or as an independent contractor) would permanently decrease to no more than 20 percent of the average level of bona fide services performed (whether as an employee or an independent contractor) over the immediately preceding 36-month period (or the full period of services to the employer if the employee has been providing services to the employer less than 36 months). In other words, the separation from service must be real and not done merely to trigger the payment of deferred compensation.

Facts and circumstances to be considered in making this determination include, but are not limited to whether:

- The employee continues to be treated as an employee for other purposes (such as continuation of salary and participation in employee benefit programs).
- Similarly situated service providers have been treated consistently.
- The employee is permitted, and realistically available, to perform services for other service recipients in the same line of business.

The term *involuntary separation from service* means a separation from service due to the independent exercise of the unilateral authority of the service recipient to terminate the service provider's services, other than due to the service provider's implicit or explicit request, where the service provider was willing and able to continue performing services. An involuntary separation from service may include the service recipient's failure to renew a contract at the time such contract expires, provided that the service provider was willing and able to execute a new contract providing terms and conditions substantially similar to those in the expiring contract and to continue providing such services.

The determination of whether a separation from service is involuntary is based on all the facts and circumstances. Any characterization of the separation from service as voluntary or involuntary by the service provider and the service recipient in the documentation of the separation from service is presumed to properly characterize the nature of the separation from service. However, the presumption may be rebutted where the facts and circumstances indicate otherwise (e.g., if a separation from service is designated as a voluntary separation from service or resignation, but the facts and circumstances indicate that absent such voluntary separation from service the service recipient would have terminated the service provider's services, and that the service provider had knowledge that the service provider would be so terminated, the separation from service is involuntary).

Certain severance arrangement may be exempt from Section 409A if it satisfies what practitioners call the "two-times rule:"

- The severance amount does not exceed two times the lesser of:
  - ○ The sum of the executive's annualized compensation based on the annual rate of pay for services provided to the company for the taxable year of the executive preceding the taxable year of the executive in which the executive has a termination of employment
  - ○ The maximum amount that may be taken into account under a qualified plan pursuant to Section 401(a)(17) (which was increased from $220,000 to $225,000 in 2007) for the year in which the executive has a termination of employment
- The plan provides that the severance must be paid no later than the last day of the second taxable year of the executive following the taxable year of the executive in which the termination of employment occurs.

Good Reason Termination   The Regulations provide that a Good Reason termination by an executive will be treated as a "without Cause" termination by the company if the termination occurs under certain limited bona fide conditions. The avoidance of the requirements of Section 409A cannot be a purpose of the inclusion of these conditions in the agreement or plan, or of the actions by the executive in connection with the satisfaction of these conditions. In addition, the termination by the executive under such conditions must effectively constitute a without Cause termination. The Regulations require that such conditions be prespecified under an agreement, and that the Good Reason condition must be defined to require actions taken by the company resulting in a material negative change to the executive's employment relationship, such as the duties to be performed, the conditions under which such duties are to be performed, or the executive's compensation. Other factors taken into account in determining whether a Good Reason termination effectively constitutes a without Cause termination include:

- The extent to which the payments upon a Good Reason termination are in the same amount and are to be made at the same time and in the same form as payments available upon a without Cause termination
- Whether the executive is required to give the company notice of the existence of the Good Reason condition (presumably within a 90-day period following the occurrence of Good Reason) and a reasonable opportunity to remedy the condition (presumably at least 30 days after such notice).

The Regulations provide a "Good Reason Safe Harbor" that will always treat a Good Reason termination as a without Cause termination, thus completely exempting severance payments from Section 409A (assuming the short-term deferral rule is followed). This safe harbor requires the following three conditions:

1. The termination must occur during a predetermined limited period of time not to exceed two years following the initial existence of one or more of the following conditions arising without the consent of the executive:

- A material diminution:
  - In the executive's base compensation
  - In the executive's authority, duties, or responsibilities
  - In the authority, duties, or responsibilities of the supervisor to whom the executive is required to report, including a requirement that the executive report to a corporate officer or employee instead of reporting directly to the company's board of directors (or similar governing body with respect to an entity other than a corporation)
  - In the budget over which the executive retains authority
- A material change in the geographic location at which the executive must perform the services
- Any other action or inaction that constitutes a material breach by the company of the agreement under which the executive provides services

2. The amount, time, and form of payment upon the termination must be substantially identical to the amount, time, and form of payment payable due to a without Cause termination, to the extent such a right exists.
3. The executive must be required to provide notice to the company of the existence of the material diminution, change, or breach described above within a period not to exceed 90 days of the initial existence of the condition, upon the notice of which the company must be provided a period of at least 30 days during which it may remedy the condition and not be required to pay the amount.

Equity-Based Compensation

The general rule is that property transferred in connection with the performance of services and which is taxed under Section 83 is exempt from Section 409A.

If a service provider receives property from, or pursuant to, a plan maintained by a service recipient, there is no deferral of compensation merely because the value of the property is not includible in income by reason of the property being substantially nonvested (as defined under the Section 83 Regulations), or is includible in income solely due to a valid election under Section 83(b).

A transfer of property includes the transfer of a beneficial interest in a trust or annuity plan, or a transfer to or from a trust or under an annuity plan, to the extent such a transfer is subject to Section 83, Section 402(b), or Section 403(c). A right to compensation income that will be required to be included in income under taxability of a beneficiary of a nonexempt trust under Section 402(b)(4)(A) due to failure of the minimum coverage rules under Section 410(b) is not a deferral of compensation.

A plan under which a service provider obtains a legally binding right to receive property in a future taxable year where the property will be substantially vested at the time of transfer of the property may provide for the deferral of compensation. Thus, such a plan may constitute a NQDCP. A legally binding right to receive property in a future taxable year where the property will be substantially nonvested at the time of transfer of the property will not provide for the deferral of compensation and, accordingly, will not constitute a NQDCP unless offered in conjunction with another legally binding right that constitutes a deferral of compensation.

The term *stock right* means:

- A stock option (other than an incentive stock option [ISO] described in Section 422 or an option granted pursuant to an employee stock purchase plan [ESPP] described in Section 423)
- A stock appreciation right (SAR)

An option to purchase service recipient stock does not provide for a deferral of compensation if:

- The exercise price may never be less than the fair market value of the underlying stock on the date the option is granted and the number of shares subject to the option is fixed on the original date of grant of the option.
- The transfer or exercise of the option is subject to taxation under Section 83 and the Section 83 Regulations.
- The option does not include any feature for the deferral of compensation other than the deferral of recognition of income until the later of the following:
  - The exercise or disposition of the option under the Section 83 Regulations.
  - The time the stock acquired pursuant to the exercise of the option first becomes substantially vested.

A SAR does not provide for a deferral of compensation if:

- Compensation payable under the SAR cannot be greater than the excess of the fair market value of the stock on the date the SAR is exercised over an amount specified on the date of grant of the SAR (the SAR exercise price), with respect to a number of shares fixed on or before the date of grant of the right.
- The SAR exercise price may never be less than the fair market value of the underlying stock on the date the right is granted.
- The SAR does not include any feature for the deferral of compensation other than the deferral of recognition of income until the exercise of the SAR.

An option to purchase stock other than service recipient stock, or a SAR with respect to stock other than service recipient stock, generally will provide for the deferral of compensation. If, under the terms of an option to purchase service recipient stock (other than an ISO or an ESPP option), the exercise price is or could become less than the fair market value of the stock on the date of grant, the grant of the option generally will provide for the deferral of compensation.

If, under the terms of a SAR with respect to service recipient stock, the compensation payable under the SAR is or could be any amount greater than, with respect to a predetermined number of shares, the excess of the fair market value of the stock on the date the SAR is exercised over the fair market value of the stock on the date of grant of the SAR, the grant of the SAR generally will provide for a deferral of compensation.

To the extent a stock right provides a right other than the right to receive cash or stock on the date of exercise and such additional right would otherwise allow compensation to be deferred beyond the date of exercise, the entire arrangement (including the underlying stock right) provides for the deferral of compensation. Neither the right to receive substantially nonvested stock upon the exercise of a stock right nor the right to pay the exercise price with previously acquired shares constitutes a feature for the deferral of compensation.

Finally, the stock, with respect to the stock right, must satisfy a precise definition of *service recipient stock,* which generally is the stock of the employer corporation. In addition, there are very complex and technical rules associated with valuing the stock, which is critical to determine a "not-below" fair market value exercise price of the stock right.

Offshore Trusts

IRC Section 409A(b)(1) provides that in the case of assets set aside (directly or indirectly) in a trust (or other arrangement determined by the U.S. Treasury secretary) for purposes of paying deferred compensation under a nonqualified deferred compensation plan, IRC Section 83 will treat such assets as property transferred in connection with the performance of services whether or not such assets are available to satisfy claims of general creditors:

- At the time set aside if such assets (or such trust or other arrangement) are located outside of the United States
- At the time transferred if such assets (or such trust or other arrangement) are subsequently transferred outside of the United States

Section 409A(b)(1) provides further that these provisions do not apply to assets located in a foreign jurisdiction if substantially all of the services to which the nonqualified deferred compensation relates are performed in such jurisdiction.

In addition, IRC Section 409A(b)(2) provides that in the case of compensation deferred under a NQDCP, there is a transfer of property within the meaning of IRC Section 83 with respect to such compensation as of the earlier of:

- The date on which the plan first provides that assets will become restricted to the provision of benefits under the plan in connection with a change in the employer's financial health
- The date on which assets are so restricted, whether or not such assets are available to satisfy claims of general creditors

IRC Section 409A(b)(4) provides that in the event amounts are required to be included in income under Section 409A(b)(1) (due to the use of an offshore trust or similar arrangement) or Section 409A(b)(2) (due to a restriction on assets in connection with a change in the financial health of the service recipient), the tax imposed on such inclusion is increased by the sum of the amount equal to 20 percent of the amount required to be included in income, plus an interest charge based on the underpayment interest rate plus 1 percent determined on the underpayments of tax that would have occurred if the affected deferred amounts had been includible in income for the taxable year when first deferred.

IRC Section 451: Constructive Receipt and Economic Benefit

Nonqualified deferred compensation arrangements that are grandfathered under Section 409A are still subject to the constructive receipt rules. The discussion below is presented primarily for these grandfathered arrangements and for historical purposes, as many of the strict requirements of Section 409A now contain the rules that had been associated with constructive receipt tax law. In addition, as mentioned earlier, since Section 409A did not repeal Section 132 of the Revenue Act of 1978, these rules technically are still in effect and applicable to all deferred compensation.

Section 451 provides the general rules relating to what is known as *constructive receipt*. The concept of constructive receipt is that a taxpayer may not turn his, her, or its back on taxable income (usually through a deferral arrangement) to avoid taxation. Thus, while the payment is not actually received by the taxpayer, it still is constructively received (and thus taxable).

Section 451(a) provides a basic rule that any item of gross income will be included in the gross income of the taxpayer for the taxable year in which it was received unless under the taxpayer's method of accounting used in computing taxable income such amount is properly accounted for as of a different period. It is the Regulations that essentially explain what is meant by constructive receipt. Regulation Section 1.451-2(a) provides that income, although not actually reduced to a taxpayer's possession, is constructively received by the taxpayer in the taxable year in which it is credited to the taxpayer's account, set apart for the taxpayer, or otherwise made available so that the taxpayer may either draw upon it at any time, or could have drawn upon it during the taxable year if notice of intention to withdraw had been given. However, income is not constructively received if the taxpayer's control of its receipt is subject to substantial limitations or restrictions. It is this concept of substantial limitation or restrictions on which many deferred compensation arrangements build.

As mentioned above, Section 132 of the Revenue Act of 1978 (and still has) prohibits the IRS from issuing Revenue Rulings in this area. However, Revenue procedures are not prohibited, and the IRS has issued several Revenue Procedures to explain the minimum requirements it considers necessary in a deferred compensation arrangement before it will offer a favorable ruling through a PLR. Revenue Procedures 71-19 and 92-65 provide that:

- The election to defer compensation must be made before the beginning of the period of service for which the compensation is payable, regardless of the existence of forfeiture provisions in the plan.
- If any elections, other than the initial election referred to previously, may be made by an employee subsequent to the beginning of the service period, then the plan must set forth substantial forfeiture provisions that must remain in effect throughout the entire period of the deferral. A substantial forfeiture provision will not be considered to exist unless its conditions impose on the employee a significant limitation or duty that will require a meaningful effort on the part of the employee to fulfill and there is a definite possibility that the event that will cause the forfeiture could occur.
- New plans may allow new participants 30 days after adoption of the plan to make elections with respect to compensation earned after such election.
- New participants to an existing plan may have 30 days after becoming a participant of the plan to make elections with respect to compensation earned after such election.
- The plan may allow for earlier payout in the event of an unforeseeable emergency.
- The plan must provide that participants have the status of unsecured creditors.

In addition, since many deferred compensation arrangements were funded using a "rabbi trust" (called such because the first PLR to address whether this kind of trust resulted in constructive receipt concerned a trust created by a congregation for its rabbi), the IRS issued Revenue Procedure 92-64 at the same time it issued Revenue Procedure 92-65. This Revenue Procedure presented a "model" rabbi trust that needed to be followed if a taxpayer was requesting a PLR as to whether the trust caused constructive receipt. A rabbi trust generally is a "grantor trust" (within the meaning of the grantor-trust rules under Sections 671-679) established by the company that holds company assets for payment of the deferred compensation benefit; however, if there is a bankruptcy or insolvency, the trustee must then hold the trust's assets for the benefit of the company's general unsecured creditors.

Historically, there have been differing views with respect to whether the IRS's position on deferred compensation would be upheld by the courts. First is the issue of how far in advance the election to defer must be made. Most companies provide that salary deferral be made in the year before the salary is earned. Some companies, however, allow that bonus deferrals can be made just before the bonus is calculated and paid. Another example of a questionable technique is something called a *haircut*, where the amount of deferred compensation will be reduced if the taxpayer elects an earlier payout. Some believe that a substantial haircut tracks the language of the Regulations since it results in a substantial limitation or restriction. For example, assume that Executive X has $1 million in a deferred compensation account, and can elect an earlier payout but will forfeit 10 percent (or $100,000) of the deferred amount. Not only is there no consensus on whether 10 percent (or even a smaller percentage) is enough to trigger the substantial limitation or restriction requirement, but there is even a question as to whether at least $900,000 is constructively received. Another issue is whether an election once made may be changed (e.g., Executive X made a deferral election on January 1, 2005 to defer $1 million until January 1, 2015, and then on January 1, 2010, Executive X changes the payout date to January 1, 2014). Based on the Tax Court case of *Martin v. Commissioner*, there is a position that a change made at least a year before payout is permissible.

Finally, deferred compensation may be deemed to be constructively received under what is known as the *economic benefit doctrine*, which is separate and distinct from the constructive receipt doctrine under Section 451. This doctrine, not a product of the Tax Code or the IRS but created by the courts, provides generally that if a taxpayer receives any economic or financial benefit or property as compensation for services, the value of the benefit or property is currently includible in the individual's gross income. More specifically, the doctrine requires an employee to include in current gross income, the value of assets that have been unconditionally and irrevocably transferred as compensation into a fund for the employee's sole benefit, if the employee has a nonforfeitable interest in the fund.

IRC SECTION 162(m): The $1 Million Cap on Executive Compensation

In response to criticism involving what was perceived as excessive executive compensation in the early 1990s, Congress enacted Section 162(m) to cap the amount of compensation that could be deducted by a public company paid to its top five executives. Section 162(m) was enacted in 1993. The Proposed Regulations were released in 1993, and the Regulations were released in 1995.

Terminology used in the application of Section 162(m) includes:

- Publicly held corporation
- Applicable employee remuneration
- Covered employee
- Performance-based compensation
- Outside director

For whatever reason, the drafters of Section 162(m) repeatedly chose to use the word *remuneration* instead of the word *compensation*; however, for all intents and purposes, they are synonymous, and the statute's use of the word *remuneration* should not be a distraction.

Section 162(m)(1) provides that in the case of any publicly held corporation, no deduction will be allowed for applicable employee remuneration with respect to any covered employee to the extent that the amount of such remuneration for the taxable year with respect to such employee exceeds $1 million. The $1 million cap is not indexed. Thus, due to inflation, the cap effectively is reduced every year and most likely becomes applicable to more executives.

Section 162(m)(2) defines *publicly held corporation* as any corporation issuing any class of equity securities required to be registered under Section 12 of the Securities Exchange Act of 1934 (Exchange Act). A corporation is not considered publicly held if the registration of its securities is voluntary. Determination is based solely on whether, as of the last day of the corporation's taxable year, it is subject to the reporting obligations of Section 12 of the Exchange Act.

Section 162(m)(3) defines *covered employee* as any employee of the corporation who, as of the close of the taxable year, is the CEO of the corporation (or an individual acting in such capacity), or whose total compensation for the taxable year is required to be reported to shareholders under the Exchange Act by reason of such employee being among the four highest compensated officers for the taxable year (other than the CEO). Thus, covered employees generally are the "named executive officers" listed in the Summary Compensation Table found in a company's annual proxy statement or Form 10-K. Of importance is that in June 2007 in response to the new executive compensation disclosure rules issued in August 2006, the IRS released Notice 2007-47 which stated that:

> The IRS will interpret the term "covered employee" for purposes of § 162(m) to mean any employee of the taxpayer if, as of the close of the taxable year, such employee is the principal executive officer (within the meaning of the amended disclosure rules) of the taxpayer or an individual acting in such a capacity, or if the total compensation of such employee for that taxable year is required to be reported to shareholders under the Exchange Act by reason of such employee being among the 3 highest compensated officers for the taxable year (other than the principal executive officer or the principal financial officer). Accordingly, the term covered employee for purposes of § 162(m) does not include those individuals for whom disclosure is required under the Exchange Act on account of the individual being the taxpayer's principal financial officer (within the meaning of the amended disclosure rules) or an individual acting in such a capacity.

In addition, it is interesting to note that termination of employment of an employee immediately before the close of the taxable year results in that employee not being treated as a covered employee. Thus, for example, a company might want an executive who is a covered employee and who plans to retire at the end of the company's tax year to instead retire immediately before the close of the company's tax year. It is important to note, however, that at the time of this writing, Congress is considering changing this rule to provide that any executive who is ever a covered employee will always remain a covered employee, whether still a named executive officer or whether even employed by the company. Thus, this planning technique of delaying payment until after termination of employment would be eliminated.

Accordingly, it is critical for compensation committee members to be fully aware of the current status of the definition of *covered employee* under Section 162(m).

Section 162(m)(4) provides that *applicable employee remuneration* means, with respect to any covered employee, the aggregate amount allowable as a deduction under the IRC for such taxable year (determined without regard to Section 162(m)) for remuneration for services performed by such employee (whether or not during the tax year). *Remuneration* generally means cash and property. Excluded from the definition of *applicable employee remuneration* are:

- Commissions based on individual performance
- Any payment that generally relates to a payment from a tax-qualified pension plan
- Any benefit provided to or for the benefit of an employee if at the time such benefit is provided it is reasonable to believe that the employee will be able to exclude such benefit from his or her gross income
- Performance-based compensation

Section 162(m)(4)(C) provides the rules relating to "performance-based compensation" It means remuneration payable solely on account of the attainment of one or more performance goals, but only if:

Step 1. The performance goals are determined by a compensation committee of the board of directors of the corporation, which is comprised solely of two or more "outside directors."

Step 2. The material terms under which the remuneration is to be paid, including the performance goals, are disclosed to shareholders and approved by a majority of the vote in a separate shareholder vote before the payment of such remuneration.

Step 3. Before any payment of such remuneration, the compensation committee certifies that the performance goals and any other material terms were in fact satisfied.

Thus, it is a three-step test for compensation to qualify as performance based. First, compensation committee members must satisfy the "outside director" requirement.

The term *outside director* is not defined by Section 162(m), but is defined in the Regulations. A director qualifies as an outside director by satisfying all of the following four conditions:

- He or she is not a current employee of the corporation.
- If he or she is a former employee of the corporation, then he or she is not receiving compensation for prior services (other than benefits under a tax-qualified retirement plan) during the taxable year.
- He or she has never been an officer of the corporation.

- He or she does not receive remuneration from the corporation, either directly or indirectly, in any capacity other than as a director.

Remuneration received includes remuneration paid:

- Directly or indirectly to a director personally or to an entity in which the director has a more than 50 percent beneficial ownership interest
- To an entity in which the director has a 5 percent to 50 percent beneficial ownership interest (other than *de minimis* remuneration)
- To an entity by which the director is employed or self-employed other than as a director (other than *de minimis* remuneration)

De minimis remuneration is defined as remuneration received by the entity that is less than 5 percent of the gross revenue of such entity, so long as the remuneration received does not exceed $60,000 if paid (1) to an entity that the director has a 5 percent to 50 percent beneficial ownership interest or (2) for personal services if the director is employed or self-employed by the entity.

Second, performance goals must be both "preestablished" and "objective." Goals are "preestablished" if they are established in writing by the compensation committee not later than 90 days after the performance period begins or within the first 25 percent of the performance period if such period is shorter than one year. The outcome must be substantially uncertain at the time the goal is established. Goals are "objective" if a third party having knowledge of the relevant facts could determine whether the goal is met. Increasing the amount of compensation over the compensation levels set by the preestablished performance goals (usually referred to as *positive discretion*) is not permitted. However, a compensation committee may unilaterally reduce, with or without reason, the amount of compensation below the compensation levels set by the preestablished performance goals (usually referred to as *negative discretion*), assuming this can be done under the terms and conditions of the arrangement. Acceleration of payment must be discounted to reasonably reflect the time value of money. Restricted stock that vests based solely on service will not qualify as performance-based compensation. Stock options and SARs that are granted with an exercise price at or above current stock fair market value on the date of grant generally will qualify as performance-based compensation.

Third, shareholder approval is valid only if the following material terms are disclosed as part of the voting process:

- Those employees who are eligible to receive compensation
- A description of the business criteria on which the performance goal is based
- The maximum amount of compensation that can be paid to any employee
- Any other material terms of a performance goal as required under the same standards applicable under the Exchange Act

If the compensation committee can change the targets under a performance goal, shareholder reapproval is required every five years. Since most plans today have a menu of performance metrics (e.g., earnings, revenue growth, stock price, total shareholder return, return on assets, return on equity, etc.), compensation committees need to ensure that the plans they administer are reapproved by shareholders every five years.

Finally, the compensation committee must make sure that it certifies in writing that the performance goals (and all other material terms and conditions) were met.

The Regulations provide an exemption for privately held companies that become publicly held companies. In such a situation, compensation paid by a publicly held corporation pursuant to a compensation plan or agreement that existed during the period in which the corporation was not publicly held is exempt from Section 162(m). However, if the privately held corporation becomes publicly held through an initial public offering (IPO), then the previous exemption applies only if the prospectus accompanying the IPO discloses information concerning those plans or arrangements that satisfy all applicable securities laws then in effect. The exemption applies until the earliest of the following four occurrences:

1. The expiration of the plan or agreement
2. A material modification of the plan or agreement (a material modification occurs when the plan or agreement is amended to increase the amount of compensation payable to the employee)
3. The issuance of all employer stock and other compensation that has been allocated under the plan
4. The first meeting of shareholders at which directors are to be elected that occurs after the close of the third calendar year following the calendar year in which the IPO occurs, or in the case of a privately held corporation that becomes publicly held without an IPO, the first calendar year following the calendar year in which the corporation becomes publicly held

There are two methods to qualify compensation as performance-based compensation for corporations created by a spin-off transaction. Under a "prior establishment and approval" method, where the compensation qualified as performance-based compensation prior to the spin-off date, the compensation remains qualified if the compensation committee (comprised of two or more outside directors) of the spin-off company certifies that the performance goals have been met. Under a "transition period exemption" method, where all requisite elements of performance-based compensation are met other than the shareholder-approval requirement, the compensation will be qualified until the first regularly scheduled meeting of the spin-off's shareholders that occurs more than 12 months after the date the corporation becomes a publicly held corporation.

The $1 million cap is reduced by the amount (if any) that would have been included in the compensation of the covered employee for the taxable year but, because of the golden parachute tax rules, was disallowed as an excess parachute payment under Section 280G (discussed immediately below).

Example: Executive X receives $1,500,000, of which none is exempt from Section 162(m). Of the $1,500,000, $600,000 is an excess parachute payment (and thus the $600,000 becomes nondeductible under Section 280G). Thus, the corporation can deduct only $400,000 ($1 million minus the already nondeductible $600,000) of the $1,500,000 payment.

IRC SECTIONS 280G AND 4999: GOLDEN PARACHUTES

In the early 1980s, there was public outcry regarding some very large (at the time) golden parachutes made to certain executives. Accordingly, this public outcry was translated into tax law that generally eliminated a tax deduction for a company that paid golden parachutes and applied a 20 percent penalty tax on the executive who received a golden parachute. Sections 280G and 4999 were enacted in 1984. The Proposed Regulations were first released in 1989, and then reproposed in 2002. The Regulations were released in 2003. It is important to note that unlike Section 162(m), Section 280G applies to both public and private corporations.

The term *golden parachutes* generally refers to either severance-related payments or transaction-bonus payments made to executives, usually but not necessarily contingent on or in connection with a change in control of the company. The Regulations provide that a payment is treated as being contingent on a change in control if the payment would not, in fact, have been made had no CIC occurred, even if the payment is also conditioned on the occurrence of another event. Additionally, a payment generally is treated as one that would not, in fact, have been made in the absence of the CIC unless it was substantially certain, at the time of the change, that the payment would have been made whether or not the change occurred.

The key definitions and terms used in applying Sections 280G and 499 are:

- Parachute payments
- Excess parachute payments
- Base amount
- Base period
- Disqualified individual
- Annual includible compensation for the base period
- Reasonable compensation
- Change in control or ownership
- Safe harbor amount (Note that while this is not a term used under Section 280G, it is a term used by most practitioners in the golden parachute area, and thus is included.)

Section 280G(a) provides that a company will lose a tax deduction for all excess parachute payments. Section 280G(b)(1) defines an *excess parachute payment* as an amount equal to the excess of any parachute payment over the portion of the base amount allocated to such payment. Section 4999 imposes a 20 percent excise (penalty) tax on the recipient of any excess parachute payment. Section 4999 also requires that a company must withhold in many cases an amount equal to the excise tax imposed.

Section 280G(b)(2) provides that a *parachute payment* is a payment in the nature of compensation to or for a disqualified individual if such payment is contingent on a change in control or ownership and the aggregate present value of the payments in the nature of compensation to or for the disqualified individual equals or exceeds 300 percent of the base amount.

Section 280G does not define what a change in control or ownership is. The Regulations provide that a *de facto* change in control occurs if a person or group acquires either more than 50 percent of the voting stock of a corporation or one-third of the assets of the corporation. The Regulations presume that a change in control occurs if a person or group acquires 20 percent or more of a corporation's voting stock or if there is a change in the majority of directors of the corporation; however, this presumption may be rebutted by establishing that there has been no transfer of power to control the management and policies of the company.

Section 280G(b)(3) provides that the *base amount* is the disqualified individual's annualized includible compensation for the base period. Section 280G(c) provides that a disqualified individual is an employee or independent contractor of the corporation, and who is also an officer, shareholder, or highly compensated individual of the company. The Regulations provide that a highly compensated individual is a highly compensated employee as defined by Section 414(q) under the pension laws (which currently in 2007 is an employee earning $100,000 a year or more). In addition, a disqualified individual includes only a shareholder who owns stock of a corporation with a fair market value that exceeds 1 percent of the fair market value of the outstanding shares of all classes of the corporation's stock. Section 280G(d)(1) provides that the annualized includible compensation for the base period is the average compensation that was payable by the corporation undergoing the change in control or ownership and was includible in the gross income of the disqualified individual for taxable years in the base period. Section 280G(d)(2) provides that the base period is the period consisting of the most recent five taxable years ending before the date on which the change in control or ownership occurs. The Regulations provide that the base period may be less than five years if the disqualified individual did not work for the company for all five years.

Simply put, determining whether there is a loss of deduction and penalty tax under Sections 280G and 4999 is a two-step test. The first step is to test whether all payments that could be characterized as parachute payments equal or exceed 300 percent of the base amount. This is why many arrangements have come to use the number 299 percent as the "magic" threshold level; however, sometimes in these arrangements this threshold level is erroneously applied to current compensation or current cash compensation and not as it should be to the base amount (which usually is less than the current annual compensation). Practitioners usually will determine this threshold, called the *safe harbor amount*, as 300 percent of the base amount less $1. The second step is to test whether the parachute payments exceed the safe harbor amount (even by $1), and if they do, then all parachute payments above the base amount (i.e., everything over 100 percent of the base amount, not 300 percent of the base amount) are called *excess parachute payments*. It is only the excess parachute payment that is used to calculate the lost tax deduction and penalty tax.

Finally, Section 280G(b)(4) provides that parachute payments do not include any payments that the taxpayer establishes by clear and convincing evidence are reasonable compensation for personal services, whether rendered before or after the change in control. Reasonable compensation rendered after the CIC is completely disregarded. However, reasonable compensation rendered before the CIC is included in the parachute calculations and then used to reduce the excess parachute payments after first being applied to the base amount.

Example 1: CEO has a base amount of $1 million. Thus, the safe harbor amount is $2,999,999 ($1 million×300% = $1). There is a CIC, and the CEO receives $10 million as a transaction bonus. Assume none of the $10 million can be shown by clear and convincing evidence to be reasonable compensation. This is the only payment made in the nature of compensation and in connection with the change in control. The full $10 million is a parachute payment (because the payment exceeded the safe harbor amount of $2,999,999); $9 million is the excess parachute payment. The company loses $9 million as a tax deduction, and the CEO must pay $1.8 million ($9,000,000×20%) as penalty tax.

Example 2: Same as Example 1, but the CEO receives $3 million as a transaction bonus. The full $3 million is a parachute payment (because the payment still exceeded the safe harbor amount of $2,999,999); $2 million is the excess parachute payment. The company loses $2 million as a tax deduction, and the CEO must pay $400,000 as penalty tax.

Example 3: Same as Example 2, but the company and the CEO agree that the CEO will forego $1 of the $3 million payment. Thus, CEO receives $2,999,999 as a transaction bonus. The $2,999,999 payment is *not* a parachute payment since it did not exceed the safe harbor amount. Since the payment is not a parachute payment, there are no excess parachute payments, and thus no loss of deduction and no penalty tax.

Generally, there is a seven-step analysis when applying the golden parachute rules:

Step 1. Determine if a change in control or ownership has occurred under the Regulations. If not, then Section 280G does not apply and no further steps are required.

Step 2. Identify all individuals who qualify as a disqualified individual.

Step 3. Determine the base period for each disqualified individual.

Step 4. Calculate the base amount for each disqualified individual.

Step 5. Calculate the potential parachute payments that will be or have been made to each disqualified individual. This would include cash payments, stock-based compensation payments, accelerated payment of existing cash-based awards (e.g., retention programs), accelerated vesting of equity-based compensation, accelerated vesting/payment of deferred compensation, triggering of pension enhancers (e.g., additional years and service), continued welfare benefits, and so forth. These amounts are each present-valued as of the CIC date, and then totaled.

Step 6. Test the total amount against the safe harbor amount. If the total amount does not exceed the safe harbor amount, then the payments are not parachute payments and no further steps are required. If the total amount exceeds the safe harbor amount, then determine whether the parachute payments and/or the excess parachute payments may be reduced by various techniques (such as treating some of the payments as reasonable compensation).

Step 7. Calculate tax gross-up amounts for the penalty tax amounts (if required by agreement), or identify and calculate what amounts and actual payments will be reduced (if required by agreement).

Finally, while not a part of Section 280G *per se*, many companies have tried to "manage" the golden parachute issue through a variety of practices. The following market practices regarding Section 280G are noted:

- Full reduction of parachute payments to the safe harbor amount
- Mandatory reduction only if the executive is in a better after-tax position from the reduction
- Full tax gross-up (i.e., reimbursement of the excise tax, and then continued reimbursement of all excise, income, employment, and other taxes resulting from payment of the reimbursements)
- Partial tax gross-up (e.g., the company pays only the first excise tax, not the resulting tax impositions due to the reimbursement of the first excise tax; or a "corridor" is established so that no tax gross-up is paid if the parachute payments do not exceed a specific percentage or dollar amount above the safe harbor amount; or the company agrees to pay a percentage of a full tax gross-up, such as 50 percent)
- Nothing (usually referred to as the "let the chips fall where they may" approach)

Most public companies are now trying to effectively manage their golden parachute arrangements, particularly in light of the new disclosure requirements, which requires a quantification every year. This "Section 280G management" primarily concerns keeping a close eye on each disqualified individual's base amount and the amount (if any) that such disqualified individual's CIC payments exceed the safe harbor amount.

IRC SECTION 83: TAXATION OF PROPERTY TRANSFERRED IN CONNECTION WITH THE PERFORMANCE OF SERVICES

When property (e.g., stock) is transferred to an employee in connection with the performance of services, Section 83 is the Code section containing rules as to how and when the compensation will be taxed. Section 83 was enacted in 1969. The Regulations were released in 1976.

Section 83(a) generally provides that property transferred in connection with the performance of services will be taxed at the first time such property is transferable or is no longer subject to a substantial risk of forfeiture. The amount to be taxed is the fair market value (FMV) of the property at such time, less any amount paid for the property by the employee or other service   provider.

Section 83(b) provides an "election" to have the FMV of the property subject to the transfer taxed at the time of transfer, even if the property is still subject to restrictions on transfer and/or a substantial risk of forfeiture. This election closes out the compensatory element to the transfer. Future appreciation in the FMV of the property (if any) would then be taxed as capital gain. This election, of course, requires the employee or other service provider to pay taxes before the compensation associated with the transferred property is paid. It should be noted that these paid taxes would not be recoverable if the property depreciates.

Section 83(e) generally provides that options that have a "readily ascertainable FMV" will be treated as property under Section 83, and options that do not have a "readily ascertainable FMV" will not be treated as property under Section 83. A "readily ascertainable FMV" is not defined by the Code, but it is defined (to some extent) by the Regulations. It means that the option is actively traded on an established exchange, or that the option can be valued based on a list of factors. At the moment, compensatory options generally do not have a "readily ascertainable FMV" on the date of grant. Thus, most compensatory options are not covered by Section 83 on the date of grant. However, the Regulations provide that an option without a "readily ascertainable FMV" on the date of grant will be taxed under Section 83 when the option is exercised or otherwise disposed of in an arm's-length transaction. The value to be taxed will be the FMV as determined under Section 83 methodology; in other words, the spread in the option, or if the option is sold, then the sale price.

Section 83(h) generally provides that a company may take a corresponding deduction for the value of the property transferred when the employee or other service provider is taxed on the compensation. However, the company must file a Form W-2 or Form 1099, as applicable, to qualify for the deduction.

The Regulations provide that dividends or other income paid with respect to stock that has not yet been taxed under Section 83 will be treated as first being paid to the company and then paid by the company to the employee or other service provider as compensation. The Regulations also provide that if a shareholder transfers property to an employee or other service provider in connection with the performance of services, it will be treated as first being a transfer from the shareholder to the company, and then transferred from the company to the employee or other service provider. The Regulations also provide definitions and examples of what is meant by the terms *transfer of property, fair market value*, and *substantial risk of forfeiture*.

OTHER RELEVANT TAX CODE SECTIONS

The following sections of the U.S. federal tax code are also relevant to compensation committee members:

- IRC Section 55-59: Alternative Minimum Tax
- IRC Section 61: Taxation of Split-Dollar Life Insurance, Other
- IRC Section 101(a): Life Insurance Death Benefits
- IRC Section 105(h): Executive Medical Benefits
- IRC Section 132: Certain Fringe Benefits
- IRC Section 162(a): Reasonable Compensation
- IRC Section 401 and 402: Qualified Pension Plans
- IRC Section 404: Tax Deductions for Bonuses and Deferred Compensation
- IRC Section 421-424: Incentive Stock Options and Employee Stock Purchase Plans
- IRC Section 1032: Exchange of Stock for Property
- IRC Section 2001, 2501, 260: Gift and Estate Planning
- IRC Section 3101: FICA Tax
- IRC Section 3401: Withholding
- IRC Section 7702 and 7702A: Definition of Life Insurance
- IRC Section 7872: Below-Market Loans and Split-Dollar Life Insurance

Again, as stated earlier, the preceding list is not exhaustive, so compensation committees may be faced with issues arising from other sections of the tax code.

IRC Sections 55-59: Alternative Minimum Tax

Sections 55 through 59 contain the laws on the alternative minimum tax (AMT). Congress originally created the AMT in the Tax Reform Act of 1986 to ensure that wealthy taxpayers pay some tax. This is accomplished by eliminating many of the deductions that may be taken by individuals under the standard income tax calculation process and by including other income that would otherwise not be subject to income tax. Of particular importance to executives is Section 56(b)(3), which requires that compensation attributable to the exercise of incentive stock options (see Section 421-424) be included as income under AMT; otherwise, these options are not normally taxed until the underlying stock is sold.

IRC Section 61: Taxation of Split-Dollar Life Insurance, Other

Section 61 generally defines *gross income,* which includes "compensation for services, including fees, commissions, fringe benefits, and similar items." Thus, it contains some rules applicable to what (and how) certain executive compensation is taxed (e.g., personal use of corporate-owned or corporate-provided aircraft). In addition, Regulations under Section 61 provide one of the two tax treatments applied to split-dollar life insurance arrangements (the other treatment is found under Section 7872). Section 61 treatment is applied to split-dollar life insurance arrangements where the company (not the executive or his or her trust) is the owner of the policy. This generally is known as the *economic benefit* treatment. Under this treatment, the value of one-year term life insurance is deemed the economic benefit under the split-dollar life insurance arrangement, and the value of such insurance, based on either the actual cost of the term life insurance or the rates contained in a table issued by the IRS, is included in an employee's annual compensation. In addition, any other economic benefit (such as policy dividends paid to the executive or increases in the policy's cash value over the amount required to be paid back to the company) is also included in an employee's annual compensation and subject to tax.

IRC Section 101(a): Life Insurance Death Benefits

Section 101(a) generally provides that life insurance death benefits are not taxable to the recipient of such benefits. But it also provides that a life insurance policy that is transferred for valuable consideration, whether by assignment or otherwise, will have some or all of the death benefits taxed. However, this will not apply if the transfer is to the insured, to a partner of the insured, to a partnership in which the insured is a partner, or to a corporation in which the insured is a shareholder or officer.

IRC Section 105(h): Executive Medical Benefits

Section 105(h) imposes income tax on certain highly compensated employees who participate in a self-insured medical expense reimbursement plan that violates the discrimination rules contained in Section 105(h).

IRC Section 132: Certain Fringe Benefits

Section 132 contains the rules regarding whether certain fringe benefits (generally certain travel and security-related perquisites) will be included in the employee's gross income.

IRC Section 162(a): Reasonable Compensation

Section 162(a) provides that there is a deduction for all ordinary and necessary business expenses, including a "reasonable allowance for salaries or other compensation for personal services actually rendered." The Regulations provide, among other things, that "the test of deductibility in the case of compensation payments is whether they are reasonable and are in fact payments purely for services." This creates what is now known as the *amount test*, where the question to be answered is whether the amount of the compensation is reasonable (i.e., not excessive), and the *intent test*, where the question to be answered is whether the parties intended that the payments be compensation for actual services. While Section 162(a) has been the subject of much litigation, IRS challenges have been confined to compensation at private companies, not public companies. Presumably, the IRS believes there are enough checks and balances at public companies to prevent the payment of excessive compensation (both now and even before the enactment of Section 162(m)). However, there may come a time when the IRS, for whatever reason, might challenge the reasonableness of compensation paid to executives at a public company, and compensation committee members of public companies should be aware of this possibility no matter how remote. Compensation committee members of private companies, however, need to be acutely aware of Section 162(a) and the various issues associated with it:

- Disguised dividends (i.e., payment of compensation that otherwise should have been paid as dividends)
- Phantom income (i.e., payment of compensation that in substance should be treated as a gift)
- Contingent compensation arrangements (i.e., payment of compensation based on questionable contingencies the nonpayment of which might otherwise increase a company's taxable earnings)

Most disputes involve the application of the amount test not the intent test since the amount test is an objective test and the intent test generally is regarded as a subjective test. Moreover, most disputes almost always involve cash compensation, not stock-based compensation, but there may come a time when stock-based compensation at private companies similarly will be examined.

Courts have developed various approaches for testing reasonable compensation based on a myriad of factors. For example, there is a "5-factor" test (9th Circuit in the *Elliotts, Inc. v. Commissioner* case), a "7-factor" test (7th Circuit in the *Edwin's, Inc. v. Commissioner* case), a "9-factor" test (6th Circuit in the *Mayson Manufacturing Company v. Commissioner* case), and even a "21-factor" test (Tax Court in the *Foos v. Commissioner* case). Some of the factors usually considered by courts are:

- Employee's qualifications
- Nature, extent, and scope of employee's work
- Employee's work and salary scale
- Prevailing rates of compensation in the industry
- Size and complexity of the business
- Ratio of compensation to income of the business
- Contingent nature of the salary agreement
- General economic conditions
- Compensation paid in prior years
- Date of determination of the compensation
- Existence of action by the board of directors
- Comparison of compensation with distributions to shareholders
- Whether compensation is paid in proportion to the stock interest of employees of closely held corporations
- Time contributed to the business

Note that generally no one factor is controlling. The IRS has developed its own "12-factor" test, which was published in a former version of the Internal Revenue Manual (IRM) at 4233.232.2(3):

- Nature of duties
- Background and experience
- Knowledge of the business
- Size of the business
- Individual's contribution to profit making
- Time devoted
- Economic conditions in general and locally
- Character and amount of responsibility
- Time of year when compensation is determined
- Relationship of stockholder-officer's compensation to stockholdings
- Whether alleged compensation is in reality in whole or in part payment for a business or assets acquired
- The amount paid by similar size businesses in the same area to equally qualified employees for similar services

This "12-factor" test apparently has been amplified and/or replaced in May 1999 by new IRM 4.3.1.5-2.5.2.2, which list eight steps to test the reasonableness of officers' salaries in the context of partnerships and S corporations:

Step 1. Determine total compensation paid or accrued to principal officers.

Step 2. Determine if and to what extent each principal officer's compensation is unreasonable.

Step 3. The examiner should take into account the IRS "12-factor" test.

Step 4. Be alert to closely held multiple corporate situations.

Step 5. Determine that accruals payable to controlling shareholders are paid within the prescribed limit.

Step 6. Determine if executives have received substantial bonuses under the guise that the proceeds would be used by the recipient to make significant political contributions.

Step 7. Be aware of excessive compensation to S corporation officer/shareholders with respect to Section 1375.

Step 8. Be aware of inadequate salaries paid to officer/shareholders who receive substantial nontaxable distributions.

Current judicial trend has been to apply an *independent investor* test. This test generally examines whether an independent investor would approve the compensation paid, based on the actual return on equity and taking into account all the facts and circumstances. Thus, this test for excessive compensation is whether the compensation would unacceptably decrease the corporation's rate of return on equity for a substantial independent shareholder who is not actively engaged in the business. The proper base against which the rate of return is often measured is the initial investment in the corporation plus any additional capital contributions and any appreciation in the value of the stock. In using the independent investor test, many courts have thus rejected the automatic dividend theory; however, lack of payment of dividends may arouse IRS and judicial scrutiny. Courts are mixed as to how much weight to assign to the independent investor test.

Finally, as stated previously, public company compensation committees most likely will not be faced with a Section 162(a) issue. However, it is interesting to note that a 2003 Tax Court case (*Square D Company v. Commissioner*) applied Section 162(a) principles to an analysis of whether golden parachute payments under Section 280G qualified as reasonable compensation.

IRC Section 401 and 402: Qualified Pension Plans

Sections 401 and 402 generally contain many of the rules necessary to qualify a pension plan for special tax treatment. Section 401(a)(17) is the section that limits the amount of annual compensation taken into account for purposes of computing a pension benefit; for 2007, this amount is $225,000, and this amount will be increased in $5,000 increments thereafter based on cost-of-living adjustments (COLA). Section 402(g) is the section that limits annual elective deferrals to certain pension plans (notably 401(k) plans); for 2007, this amount is $15,500, and this amount will be increased in $500 increments thereafter based on COLA.

IRC Section 404: Tax Deduction for Bonuses and Deferred Compensation

Section 404(a) provides the rules associated with when a company may take a deduction for contributions made under a stock bonus, pension, profit-sharing, or annuity plan. Under 404(a)(5), the general rule for most executive plans is that the company may take a deduction for the year relating to the year when the compensation is taken into income by the executive. Under the Regulations for Section 404(b), a bonus paid within 2½ months of the year for which it was earned will not be treated as deferred compensation, and will relate to the year in which it was earned for purposes of deductibility.

IRC Section 415: Limitations on Benefits from and Contributions to Pension Plans

Section 415(b) generally provides that annual benefits under a defined-benefit pension plan will be capped. For 2007, this amount is $180,000, and this amount will be increased in $5,000 increments thereafter based on COLA. Section 415(c) generally provides that annual contributions to a defined-contribution pension plan will be capped. For 2007, this amount is $45,000, and this amount will be increased in $1,000 increments thereafter based on COLA.

IRC Sections 421-424: Incentive Stock Options and Employee Stock Purchase Plans

Sections 421 through 424 provide the rules relating to ISOs and ESPPs. Section 421 provides the general rule that if an award of stock or stock options qualifies as an ISO or an ESPP option under the applicable arrangement, then the taxable event will occur when the stock is sold, and the applicable tax rate will be the current long-term capital gain rate.

Section 422 provides the rules for ISOs. Generally, these rules are:

- Optionees must be employees of the company (or parent or subsidiary).
- The stock underlying the option must be held for at least more than two years from the date of grant *and* more than one year from the date of exercise.
- The option must be granted under a plan that was approved by shareholders within one year of the adoption of the plan.
- Options granted under the plan must be granted within 10 years of the earlier of the adoption of the plan or shareholder approval.
- The option term cannot exceed 10 years.

- The option must be nontransferable (other than by the laws of descent and distribution).
- The option must have an exercise price at or above the stock FMV on the date of grant.
- The option must have a post-employment exercise period not longer than 90 days (one year if termination is due to a disability as defined under Section 22(e)).
- Only options with an aggregate value of up to $100,000 (based on the stock FMV on the date of grant) may become exercisable in any calendar year (options that vest and which exceed this $100,000 limit lose their qualification as ISOs).
- If the optionee owns more than 10 percent of the stock, then the exercise price must be at least 110 percent of the stock FMV and the option term cannot exceed five years.

Section 423 provides the rules for ESPPs. While the arrangement is referred to as a Purchase plan, it operates very much as an option arrangement, and the law refers to these vehicles as "options." Generally, the rules are:

- Optionees must be employees of the company (or parent or subsidiary) and cannot own 5 percent or more of the stock.
- All employees (with some exceptions) must be able to participate in the plan.
- The stock underlying the option must be held for at least more than two years from the date of grant *and* more than one year from the date of exercise.
- The option must be granted under a plan that was approved by shareholders within one year of the adoption of the plan.
- The option term cannot exceed five years.
- The option must be nontransferable (other than by the laws of descent and distribution).
- The option must have an exercise price at least equal to 85 percent of the stock FMV on the date of grant or the date of exercise.
- The option must have a postemployment exercise period not longer than 90 days (one year if termination is due to a disability as defined under Section 22(e)).
- Only options with an aggregate value of up to $25,000 (based on the stock FMV on the date of grant) may be granted to any individual in any calendar year.

Section 424 provides a variety of rules applicable to ISOs and ESPPs. Section 424(a) and the Regulations provide that in the context of a corporate reorganization or liquidation, ISOs substituted or converted into options on a surviving company's stock (a rollover) will continue to qualify as ISOs provided that the rollover passes the spread test and the ratio test, and that the optionee does not receive additional and/or more favorable benefits under the new ISO. The spread test is satisfied if the spread in the prerollover option equals the spread in the postrollover option. The ratio test is satisfied if the ratio used to convert the prerollover ISO shares into postrollover ISO shares is the inverse of the ratio used to convert the prerollover exercise price into the postrollover exercise price. The additional/more favorable benefit test is a facts-and-circumstances test, but one example offered by the Regulations is that additional exercise methods (e.g., allowing a stock-for-stock exercise in addition to cash exercise) would be treated as an additional/more favorable benefit. Section 424 also provides that an ISO that is modified, extended, or renewed results in the deemed new grant of an option. The concern here is that if there is existing spread in the option, the deemed new option will not qualify as an ISO since the exercise price was below stock FMV on the date of grant. However, accelerating the vesting date of an existing ISO will not result in a deemed new grant.

IRC Section 1032: Exchange of Stock for Property

Section 1032 generally provides that no gain or loss is recognized by a corporation if the corporation receives cash or property in exchange for stock of the corporation. The Regulations provide that there must be an immediate transfer of the stock and that it cannot be held for any period of time. This rule impacts transfers of company stock to subsidiaries through the use of rabbi trusts.

IRC Sections 2001 et seq., 2501 et seq., and 2601 et seq.: Gift and Estate Planning

While an executive's personal estate planning generally is not an area of concern for the compensation committee, there may be instances where the design of a compensation program is affected by the executive's estate plan. In many cases, this will involve transfers of life insurance, options or other equity-based compensation, or deferred compensation to family trusts or other similar entities. The issue for most compensation committees will be whether the company is negatively impacted by structuring a certain program a certain way for the benefit of the executive. Generally, compensation committees should be aware of the sections of the tax code that relate to estate-planning issues. Sections 2001 through 2210 provide the rules with respect to federal estate tax. Sections 2501 through 2524 provide the rules with respect to gift tax. Sections 2601 through 2664 provide the rules for generation-skipping transfers. Finally, Sections 2701 through 2704 provide special valuation rules.

IRC Sections 3101 et seq.: FICA Tax

Sections 3101 through 3128 contain the rules relating to the tax imposed under the Federal Insurance Contributions Act (i.e., Social Security and Medicare taxes). Of note is Section 3121, which generally defines *wages*. In addition, Section 3121(v) provides that deferred compensation generally will be subject to FICA tax at the later of when the services are performed or when there is no substantial risk of forfeiture of the rights to such amount. Finally, it is noted that there is still an issue whether compensation attributable to ISOs or ESPPs (in whole or in part) should be treated as wages and subject to FICA tax.

IRC Sections 3401 et seq.: Withholding

Sections 3401 through 3406 contain the rules relating to the company's obligation to withhold on wages. Of note is Section 3401(a), which generally defines *wages*. This definition is very close but not identical to the definition of *wages* under FICA. In addition, it is noted that there is still an issue whether compensation attributable to ISOs or ESPPs (in whole or in part) should be treated as wages and subject to withholding, but generally the IRS issued a Notice in 2002 imposing an "administrative moratorium indefinitely," which stated that, with respect to ISOs and ESPPs, it will not assess FICA tax and will not require withholding until it completes its review of these issues.

IRC Sections 7702 and 7702A: Definition of Life Insurance

Section 7702 provides the definition of a *life insurance contract,* and requires that the contract either pass a cash value accumulation test or meet a guideline premium requirement and fall within the cash value corridor. Section 7702A generally provides that a life insurance contract will fail to be treated as a life insurance contract and instead will be treated as a modified endowment contract if it fails to pass the seven-pay test, which generally measures how much of the investment is used to buy life insurance. A modified endowment contract does not receive the tax advantages that a life insurance contract receives.

IRC Section 7872: Below-Market Loans and Split-Dollar Life Insurance

Section 7872 was enacted under the Tax Reform Act of 1986, generally to address interest-free loans. In the employer-employee context, Section 7872 requires that an interest-free loan or even a below-market loan be treated as compensation. The amount of imputed compensation is the amount of interest that the employee would otherwise have had to pay if the loan had an interest rate equal to the applicable federal rate which is an interest rate published monthly by the IRS. Section 7872 does differentiate between *term* loans and *demand* loans, and does provide a *de minimis* exemption of $10,000 for employer-employee loans. Regulations that were issued several years ago apply Section 7872 to split-dollar life insurance arrangements where the owner of the policy is the executive (or a related trust). In this situation, the amount of the premium paid by the company is treated as an interest-free loan to the executive. Thus, this Regulation dramatically altered past market practices prior to with respect to using this kind of split-dollar life insurance (usually called *equity split dollar*), and companies will need to determine whether applying Section 7872 is cost-effective and does not violate the federal securities law prohibiting a company from making personal loans to executives.

Chapter 9

Accounting Rules and Issues

This chapter discusses relevant and important accounting standards that compensation committees need to know in order to carry out their duties and responsibilities to the company and its shareholders. Of primary importance is the treatment of equity-based compensation and performance-based (both equity-based and cash-based) incentive compensation. The rules relating to the expense charges associated with incentive compensation changed dramatically when Statement of Financial Accounting Standards No.123 (Revised) (referred to as FAS 123R) became effective in December 2005.

This chapter is divided into the following topics:

- Overview of accounting rule-making organizations and standards, pronouncements and other rules issued by such organizations
- The new equity-based compensation accounting rules
- The old equity-based compensation rules, which are no longer applicable, but which are provided for current issues involving stock option back-dating and financial restatements
- Other significant accounting rules

OVERVIEW

This chapter provides a fundamental working knowledge of the relevant accounting principles, standards, and issues that most compensation committee members will encounter in discharging their committee duties. It is not intended to be complete; rather, it attempts to familiarize the compensation committee member with the accounting regulatory and organizational framework and the various relevant accounting pronouncements and their origins. Specific application and examples of these rules are contained in Part Three of this *Handbook*.

Accounting issues for compensation committees generally will involve the value of compensation expense and the timing of such expense. Major changes in equity-based compensation accounting standards both in the United States and internationally have caused compensation committees to compare the attributes and detriments of equity-based compensation with cash-based compensation. While stock options may no longer have the allure that they once had (since there usually was no impact on a company's financial statements), equity-based compensation still retains some advantages over cash-based arrangements. For example, a grant of stock generally is valued as of the grant date and expensed over the service period, and subsequent appreciation in the stock price (and thus increases in the value of the grant) is disregarded. A grant of cash, however, is valued by the amount paid. Another example is that equity-based compensation that was subject to performance requirements used to be "marked-to-market" until the performance goals were achieved; thus, such awards were limited in use and most financial performance arrangements used only cash-based awards. Now, adding nonstock financial performance goals to equity-based compensation preserves grant-date expensing values.

ORGANIZATIONS RESPONSIBLE FOR ACCOUNTING STANDARDS (PAST AND PRESENT)

Accounting standards that now comprise U.S. generally accepted accounting principles (GAAP) originally were promulgated by the American Institute of Certified Public Accountants (AICPA), a national trade organization for accountants that traces its beginnings back to 1887. Following the creation of the Securities and Exchange Commission (SEC) in 1934, the SEC also became involved in the process relating to creation of U.S. GAAP standards.

In 1939, the AICPA, with SEC encouragement, established the Committee on Accounting Procedures (CAP). From 1939 to 1959, the CAP issued 51 Accounting Research Bulletins (ARBs), of which ARB 43 was a compilation of the prior 42 ARBs. The general purpose of the ARBs was to address specific accounting issues that arose from time to time. Although it has been said that ARB 43 created U.S. GAAP, the ARBs did not, in fact, create a comprehensive set of accounting rules.

In 1959, the AICPA replaced the CAP with the Accounting Principles Board (APB). The APB issued a total of 31 Opinions and 4 Statements. For all intents and purposes, US GAAP was created through these Opinions and Statements. However, some felt that the APB, partly due to the fact that it was a part of the AICPA (i.e., a trade association), was not as effective as it should be, since the rulemaking body was part of the trade association representing those who would be affected by these rules. Thus, in 1971, the Wheat Commission (chaired by former SEC Commissioner Francis M. Wheat) examined whether the APB was the best accounting rulemaking structure. The Wheat Commission concluded that the APB should be replaced, and recommended that an independent organization be entrusted with the responsibility of setting U.S. accounting standards.

Following these recommendations, the Financial Accounting Standards Board (FASB) was established in 1974. So far, the FASB has issued 159 Statements of Financial Accounting Standards (FAS), 48 FASB Interpretations (FIN), and various Technical Bulletins and Statements of Concepts. In 1984, the FASB created the Emerging Issues Task Force (EITF), whose membership consists of the FASB Director of Research and Technical Activities (EITF chairman) and various individuals from public accounting firms, large companies, and certain relevant associations (e.g., the Financial Executives Institute, the Institute of Management Accountants). The EITF releases interpretations (or what is referred to as a Consensus) on specific issues under U.S. GAAP. In addition, the FASB staff also releases from time to time its interpretations on specific issues through FASB Staff Bulletins.

The AICPA thus is no longer responsible for setting most new accounting standards. It still does contribute to the process, however, through issuance of its own Statements of Positions (SOPs), very few of which would impact compensation committees. In addition, the SEC, while it has delegated accounting standards setting to the FASB, does issue Staff Accounting Bulletins (SABs), very few of which directly impact compensation committee members.

Outside the United States, the International Accounting Standards Committee (IASC), formed in 1973, was the organization involved in setting worldwide accounting standards. The IASC issued 41 International Accounting Standards (IAS), which are similar in concept to FAS pronouncements issued by the FASB, and 33 Standing Interpretations Committees (SIC), which are similar in concept to FIN pronouncements issued by the FASB. In 2001, the IASC was replaced by the International Accounting Standards Board (IASB). The IASB so far has issued eight International Financial Reporting Standards (IFRS), which are similar to—and a replacement for—an IAS, and will also be issuing International Financial Reporting Interpretations Committees (IFRIC), which are similar to—and a replacement for— a SIC. Compensation committee members should be aware of a concept called *convergence*, through which the FASB and the IASB are attempting to reconcile and essentially merge accounting standards so that U.S. GAAP is fundamentally the same as international GAAP.

Finally, because financial statements of state and local governments are so different from private and public businesses, the Governmental Accounting Standards Board (GASB) was created in 1984 to set the accounting standards for state and local governments; however, it is unlikely that compensation committee members will need to know anything more about the GASB other than its existence.

NEW EQUITY-BASED COMPENSATION ACCOUNTING RULES

The new equity-based compensation accounting rules generally involve the release of:

- FAS 123 in 1995
- IFRS 2 in 2004
- FAS 123R (the "R" is for revised) in 2004

FAS 123R completely replaced APB 25, along with its related FINs and EITFs, which had been the equity-based compensation accounting standard since 1972.

The result was that all equity-based compensation, including stock options, was now subject to mandatory expensing. It also substituted the concept of *fixed* versus *variable* accounting with the concept of *equity* versus *liability* accounting.

The primary importance is that since 2005 for international GAAP companies and since 2006 for U.S. GAAP companies, all stock option grants directly impact the earnings figure reported in the company's financial statements. At the time of this writing, companies have been and are still exploring and analyzing the impact of this requirement on its equity-based and other incentive compensation programs.

The old equity-based compensation accounting rules, where stock options did not impact the earning figure reported in a company's financial statements (other than earnings-per-share (EPS) calculations) are still included in this edition and presented below, primarily because some companies are involved in stock option backdating issues and/or financial restatements. Accordingly, the old equity-based compensation rules are applicable with respect to financial statements issued prior to the company's adoption of the new equity-based compensation accounting rules.

FAS 123: ACCOUNTING FOR STOCK-BASED COMPENSATION (1995)

When it was released in 1995, FAS 123 was a controversial accounting standard that was originally intended to require mandatory expensing of all equity-based compensation (including options) using a concept called *fair value*, which generally uses a stock's fair market value (FMV) to value stock awards and a recognized option pricing model (basically, the Black-Scholes option-pricing model) to value options. However, due to political pressures from both the business community and Congress, the FASB decided that companies could elect to adopt FAS 123 or continue to expense equity-based compensation under APB 25. The only new requirement applicable to all companies was that if a company elected to continue to expense under APB 25, then the financial statements must contain pro forma disclosure of what the equity-based compensation expense would have been if the company had adopted FAS 123. In addition, if a company elected to use FAS 123, it could never later change back to use APB 25.

In the late 1990s and early 2000s, any company that had adopted FAS 123 and that had granted stock options would thus have had its earnings reduced, even if the stock option's exercise price was at or above the stock's FMV on the grant date. Accordingly, prior to 2002, only a handful of companies had adopted FAS 123. The important aspect of FAS 123 was that the valuation of a stock option did not take into account vesting, forfeitability, nontransferability, and performance conditions. Thus, an option with a 10-year term and that vested 25 percent per year based only on continued employment was valued the same as a 10-year option that only vested if EPS growth targets were achieved.

In the FASB's view, this "leveled the playing field" between performance-based awards and time-based awards, and eliminated the distinctions between "fixed accounting" and "variable accounting." However, the FASB's new standard actually caused companies to not adopt FAS 123 and also to not use performance-based awards. In addition, FAS 123 did not contain rules on vesting, but some rules relating to vesting were provided in EITF 96-18 (discussed later in this chapter), which was released shortly after FAS 123 was issued. Essentially, for employee compensatory awards, the amount of expense would be expensed over the service period.

Thus, for example, assume that two equity-based awards are exactly the same, except that one is a time-based award vesting ratably over four years and the other is a performance-based award with a four-year performance period, and are made at the same time. The fair value of both would be the same. In addition, the value of a time-based award that vested 25 percent per year would be expensed over four years. The value of a performance-based award where the performance goals were achieved at the end of the fourth year would similarly be expensed (through restatement or otherwise and in accordance with FAS 5) over the same four years. Thus, the expense charge would be the same, and the only difference would be the timing of the expense recognition. The end result was—logically—that most companies continued to use APB 25, and only granted at-the-money time-vesting stock options throughout the 1990s.

Then came the corporate scandals of 2001 and 2002. A derivative result of these scandals was that a sea change occurred in the minds of the business community and the public with respect to stock options. Many corporate watchdog organizations (such as The Conference Board and various institutional investor groups) concluded that unexpensed option grants fueled executive greed. Within a short period of time, over 200 major corporations adopted FAS 123 in the spirit of good corporate citizenship.

However, on March 12, 2003, the FASB decided to add a new project on equity-based compensation accounting to its agenda. A little over a year later, on March 31, 2004, the FASB released a proposal to amend FAS 123 (these FASB proposals generally are referred to as *Exposure Drafts*). As stated in the summary of the Exposure Draft, the amendments to FAS 123 address the accounting for transactions in which an enterprise exchanges its valuable equity instruments for employee services and transactions in which an enterprise incurs liabilities that are based on the fair value of the enterprise's equity instruments or that may be settled by the issuance of those equity instruments in exchange for employee services. The Exposure Draft stated that it did not change the accounting for (1) business transactions, (2) similar transactions involving parties other than employees, or (3) employee stock ownership plans (which are subject to AICPA SOP 93-6, "Employers' Accounting for Employee Stock Ownership Plans").

FAS 123R: SHARE-BASED PAYMENT

FAS 123R was issued in December 2004. Its purpose was to establish standards for the accounting for transactions in which an entity exchanges its equity instruments for goods or services. FAS 123R addresses transactions in which an entity incurs liabilities in exchange for goods or services that are based on the fair value of the entity's equity instruments or that may be settled by the issuance of those equity instruments. FAS 123R focuses primarily on accounting for transactions in which an entity obtains employee services in share-based payment transactions.

FAS 123R does not change the accounting guidance regarding measurement date considerations for share-based payment transactions with parties other than employees provided in FAS 123 as originally issued and EITF Issue No. 96-18, "Accounting for Equity Instruments That Are Issued to Other Than Employees for Acquiring, or in Conjunction with Selling, Goods or Services." In addition, as with the Exposure Draft, FAS 123R did not address the accounting for employee share ownership plans, which are subject to AICPA SOP 93-6.

Key Reasons for FAS 123R

The FASB has stated the following reasons for revising FAS 123:

- *Addressing concerns of users and others.* Users of financial statements, including institutional and individual investors, as well as many other parties expressed to the FASB their concerns that using APB 25's intrinsic value method results in financial statements did not faithfully represent the economic transactions affecting the issuer, namely, the receipt and consumption of employee services in exchange for equity instruments. Financial statements that do not faithfully represent those economic transactions can distort the issuer's reported financial condition and results of operations, which can lead to the inappropriate allocation of resources in the capital markets. Part of the FASB's mission is to improve standards of financial accounting for the benefit of users of financial information. FAS 123R addresses users' and other parties' concerns by requiring an entity to recognize the cost of employee services received in share-based payment transactions, thereby reflecting the economic consequences of those transactions in the financial statements.

- *Improving the comparability of reported financial information by eliminating alternative accounting methods.* Over the last few years, approximately 750 public companies have voluntarily adopted or announced their intention to adopt FAS 123's fair value based method of accounting for share-based payment transactions with employees. Other companies continue to use APB 25's intrinsic value method. The FASB believed that similar economic transactions should be accounted for similarly (that is, share-based compensation transactions with employees should be accounted for using one method). Consistent with the conclusion in the original FAS 123, the FASB believed that those transactions should be accounted for using a fair value based method. By requiring the fair value based method for all public entities, FAS 123R eliminates an alternative accounting method; consequently, similar economic transactions will be accounted for similarly.

- *Simplifying U.S. GAAP.* The FASB believed that U.S. GAAP should be simplified whenever possible. Requiring that all entities follow the same accounting standard and eliminating APB 25's intrinsic value method and its related detailed and form-driven implementation guidance simplifies the authoritative literature.

- *Converging with international accounting standards.* FAS 123R will result in greater international comparability in the accounting for share-based payment transactions. In February 2004, the IASB, whose standards are followed by entities in many countries, issued IFRS 2, "Share-based Payment." IFRS 2 requires that all entities recognize an expense for all employee services received in share-based payment transactions, using a fair value–based method that is similar in most (but not all) respects to the fair value–based method established in FAS 123 and the improvements made to it by FAS 123R. Converging to a common set of high-quality financial accounting standards for share-based payment transactions with employees improves the comparability of financial information around the world and makes the accounting requirements for entities that report financial statements under both U.S. GAAP and international accounting standards less burdensome.

Key Provisions of FAS 123R

FAS 123R requires a public entity to measure the cost of employee services received in exchange for an award of equity instruments based on the grant-date fair value of the award (with limited exceptions). That cost will be recognized over the period during which an employee is required to provide service in exchange for the award—the requisite service period (usually the vesting period). No compensation cost is recognized for equity instruments for which employees do not render the requisite service. Employee share purchase plans will not result in recognition of compensation cost if certain conditions are met; those conditions are much the same as the related conditions in FAS 123.

A nonpublic entity, likewise, will measure the cost of employee services received in exchange for an award of equity instruments based on the grant-date fair value of those instruments, except in certain circumstances. Specifically, if it is not possible to reasonably estimate the fair value of equity share options and similar instruments because it is not practicable to estimate the expected volatility of the entity's share price, a nonpublic entity in most instances is required to measure its awards of equity share options and similar instruments based on a value calculated using the historical volatility of an appropriate industry sector index instead of the expected volatility of its share price. In some cases, a nonpublic company may use an alternative valuation, but which could be subject to "variable" accounting up through the date of settlement.

A public entity will initially measure the cost of employee services received in exchange for an award of liability instruments based on its current fair value; the fair value of that award will be remeasured subsequently at each reporting date through the settlement date. Changes in fair value during the requisite service period will be recognized as compensation cost over that period. A nonpublic entity may elect to measure its liability awards at their intrinsic value through the date of settlement.

The grant-date fair value of employee share options and similar instruments will be estimated using option-pricing models adjusted for the unique characteristics of those instruments (unless observable market prices for the same or similar instruments are available). If an equity award is modified after the grant date, incremental compensation cost will be recognized in an amount equal to the excess of the fair value of the modified award over the fair value of the original award immediately before the modification. Excess tax benefits, as defined by FAS 123R, will be recognized as an addition to paid-in capital. Cash retained as a result of those excess tax benefits will be presented in the statement of cash flows as financing cash inflows. The write-off of deferred tax assets relating to unrealized tax benefits associated with recognized compensation cost will be recognized as income tax expense unless there are excess tax benefits from previous awards remaining in paid-in capital to which it can be offset.

The notes to financial statements of both public and nonpublic entities will disclose information to assist users of financial information to understand the nature of share-based payment transactions and the effects of those transactions on the financial statements.

How FAS 123R Changes Practice and Improves Financial Reporting

According to the FASB, FAS 123R eliminated the alternative to use APB 25's intrinsic value method of accounting that was provided in FAS 123. Under APB 25, issuing stock options to employees generally resulted in recognition of no compensation cost. FAS 123R requires entities to recognize the cost of employee services received in exchange for awards of equity instruments based on the grant-date fair value of those awards (with limited exceptions). Recognition of that compensation cost helps users of financial statements to better understand the economic transactions affecting an entity and to make better resource allocation decisions. Such information specifically will help users of financial statements understand the effect that share-based compensation transactions have on an entity's financial condition and results of operations. FAS 123R also will improve comparability by eliminating one of two different methods of accounting for share-based compensation transactions and thereby also will simplify existing U.S. GAAP. Eliminating different methods of accounting for the same transactions leads to improved comparability of financial statements because similar economic transactions will be accounted for similarly.

The fair-value-based method in FAS 123R is similar to the fair value based method in FAS 123 in most respects. However, the following are the key differences between the two:

- Public entities are required to measure liabilities incurred to employees in share-based payment transactions at fair value. Nonpublic entities may elect to measure their liabilities to employees incurred in share-based payment transactions at their intrinsic value. Under FAS 123, all share-based payment liabilities were measured at their intrinsic value.

- Nonpublic entities are required to account for awards of equity instruments using the fair value based method unless it is not possible to reasonably estimate the grant-date fair value of awards of equity share options and similar instruments because it is not practicable to estimate the expected volatility of the entity's share price. In that situation, the entity will account for those instruments based on a value calculated by substituting the historical volatility of an appropriate industry sector index for the expected volatility of its share price. FAS 123 permitted a nonpublic entity to measure its equity awards using either the fair value based method or the minimum value method.

- Entities are required to estimate the number of instruments for which the requisite service is expected to be rendered. FAS 123 permitted entities to account for forfeitures as they occur.

- Incremental compensation cost for a modification of the terms or conditions of an award is measured by comparing the fair value of the modified award with the fair value of the award immediately before the modification. FAS 123 required that the effects of a modification be measured as the difference between the fair value of the modified award at the date it is granted and the award's value immediately before the modification determined based on the shorter of (1) its remaining initially estimated expected life or (2) the expected life of the modified award.

- FAS 123R also clarifies and expands FAS 123's guidance in several areas, including measuring fair value, classifying an award as equity or as a liability, and attributing compensation cost to reporting periods.

In addition, FAS 123R amends FAS 95, "Statement of Cash Flows," to require that excess tax benefits be reported as a financing cash inflow rather than as a reduction of taxes paid.

Costs and Benefits

The mission of the FASB is to establish and improve standards of financial accounting and reporting for the guidance and education of the public, including preparers, auditors, and users of financial information. In fulfilling that mission, the FASB endeavors to determine that a proposed standard will fill a significant need and that the costs imposed to meet that standard, as compared with other alternatives, are justified in relation to the overall benefits of the resulting information. The FASB's consideration of each issue in a project includes the subjective weighing of the incremental improvement in financial reporting against the incremental cost of implementing the identified alternatives. At the end of that process, the FASB considers the accounting provisions in the aggregate and assesses the perceived benefits and the related perceived costs on a qualitative basis.

Several procedures were conducted before the issuance of FAS 123R to aid the FASB in its assessment of the expected costs associated with implementing the required use of the fair value based accounting method. Those procedures included a review of the comment letters received on the Exposure Draft, a field visit program, a survey of commercial software providers, and discussions with members of the

Option Valuation Group that the FASB established to provide information and advice on how to improve the guidance in FAS 123 on measuring the fair value of share options and similar instruments issued to employees in compensation arrangements. That group included valuation experts from the compensation consulting, risk management, investment banking, and academic communities. The FASB also discussed the issues in the project with other valuation experts, compensation consultants, and numerous other constituents. After considering the results of those cost-benefit procedures, the FASB concluded that FAS 123R will sufficiently improve financial reporting to justify the costs it will impose.

Effective Date

FAS 123R is effective:

- For public entities that do not file as small business issuers—as of the beginning of the first interim or annual reporting period that begins after June 15, 2005
- For public entities that file as small business issuers—as of the beginning of the first interim or annual reporting period that begins after December 15, 2005
- For nonpublic entities—as of the beginning of the first annual reporting period that begins after December 15, 2005

FAS 123R applies to all awards granted after the required effective date and to awards modified, repurchased, or canceled after that date. The cumulative effect of initially applying FAS 123R, if any, is recognized as of the required effective date.

Specific Issues and Topics

FAS 123R presented the following specific issues and topics:

- Equity versus liability accounting
- What is fair value?
- Determination of grant date
- When is compensation expense recognized?
- What is a service condition and how is it expensed?
- What is a market condition and how is it expensed?
- What is a performance condition and how is it expensed?
- Tax issues

Each is discussed in more detail below.

Equity versus Liability   In 2003, the FASB issued FAS 150, _Accounting for Certain Financial Instruments with Characteristics of both Liabilities and Equity._

FAS 150 generally excludes from its scope "instruments" (i.e., equity-based compensation) that are accounted for under FAS 123R. Nevertheless, FAS 123R provides that an entity shall apply the classification criteria in FAS 150, as they are effective at the reporting date, in determining whether to classify as a liability a "freestanding financial instrument" given to an employee in a share-based payment transaction. FAS 123R provides criteria for determining when instruments subject to FAS 123R subsequently become subject to FAS 150 or to other applicable GAAP.

Generally, cash-settled instruments are treated as liability instruments and stock-settled instruments will be treated as equity instruments. Thus, a cash-settled stock appreciation right SAR will be subject to liability accounting, resulting in a charge to earnings equal to the "spread" in the SAR received as compensation. This is basically the same "mark-to-market" method used under the APB 25 concept of "variable" accounting. However, a SAR that is settled in shares of stock will be treated as an equity instrument (essentially, the same as a stock option), and will result in a charge to earnings based on the stock-settled SAR's fair value (as determined under FAS 123R).

Fair Value FAS 123R defines *fair value* as the "amount at which an asset (or liability) could be bought (or incurred) or sold (or settled) in a current transaction between willing parties, that is, other than in a forced or liquidation sale." Generally, fair value will be the fair market value of the stock for "full-value" awards, and a Black-Scholes, binomial, or other acceptable option-pricing model or method for an "appreciation-type" award. Some companies have explored creating a "market" (either real or artificial) to value their employee stock options, but this concept has not yet been generally accepted by the business community.

Grant Date FAS 123R defines *grant date* as:

> the date at which an employer and an employee reach a mutual understanding of the key terms and conditions of a share-based payment award. The employer becomes contingently obligated on the grant date to issue equity instruments or transfer assets to an employee who renders the requisite service. Awards made under an arrangement that is subject to shareholder approval are not deemed to be granted until that approval is obtained unless approval is essentially a formality (or perfunctory), for example, if management and the members of the board of directors control enough votes to approve the arrangement. Similarly, individual awards that are subject to approval by the board of directors, management, or both are not deemed to be granted until all such approvals are obtained. The grant date for an award of equity instruments is the date that an employee begins to benefit from, or be adversely affected by, subsequent changes in the price of the employer's equity shares.

This definition created an uncertainty in 2005 as to whether an awardee actually had to consent to the award, and what would be the accounting result if the awardee consented days after the company made the award. On October 18, 2005, the FASB staff provided in Staff Position No. FAS 123(R)-2, "Practical Accommodation to the Application of Grant Date as Defined in FASB Statement No. 123(R)," that:

- As a practical accommodation, in determining the grant date of an award subject to FAS 123R, assuming all other criteria in the grant date definition have been met, a mutual understanding of the key terms and conditions of an award to an individual employee shall be presumed to exist at the date the award is approved in accordance with the relevant corporate governance requirements (that is, by the Board or management with the relevant authority) if both of the following conditions are met:

  ○ The award is a unilateral grant and, therefore, the recipient does not have the ability to negotiate the key terms and conditions of the award with the employer.

  ○ The key terms and conditions of the award are expected to be communicated to an individual recipient within a relatively short time period from the date of approval.

Expense Recognition   FAS 123R continued to allow companies to expense compensation costs either under a "straight-line" approach or under an "accelerated" or "tranche" approach. Under the straight-line approach, expenses were recognized equally over the service period, which typically is the vesting period. Thus, an award that vested ratably over four years or that cliff-vested at the end of four years would be expensed similarly. The accelerated approach was first introduced in FIN 28 with respect to expensing cash-settled SARs, but it became applicable to other equity-based compensation. Under the accelerated approach, an award that vested ratably over four years would be broken down into four awards, one that cliff-vested at the end of Year 1, one that cliff-vested at the end of Year 2, one that cliff-vested at the end of Year 3, and one that cliff-vested at the end of Year 4. Thus, the accelerated method "front-loaded" compensation expense. The example below shows the difference accounting treatment:

Example: Award is 100 shares of restricted stock each with a per-share FMV of $10 (total FMV= $1,000) on date of grant.

Vesting:	Traditional Straight-Line Vesting		Accelerated Vesting	
	4-Year Cliff	25% per Year	4-Year Cliff	25% per Year[*]
End of Year 1	$ 250.00	$ 250.00	$ 250.00	$ 520.83
End of Year 2	$ 250.00	$ 250.00	$ 250.00	$ 270.83
End of Year 3	$ 250.00	$ 250.00	$ 250.00	$ 145.84
End of Year 4	$ 250.00	$ 250.00	$ 250.00	$ 62.50
TOTAL	$1,000.00	$1,000.00	$1,000.00	$1,000.00

[*]Accelerated vesting at 25% per year using the tranche-vesting method as shown next. 100 share grant vesting 25% per year is treated as 4 separate grants of 25 shares each, with each tranche cliff-vesting at the end of Year 1, 2, 3, and 4, respectively:

	End of Year 1	End of Year 2	End of Year 3	End of Year 4
Tranche 1	$250.00	$ 0.00	$ 0.00	$ 0.00
Tranche 2	$125.00	$125.00	$ 0.00	$ 0.00
Tranche 3	$ 83.33	$ 83.33	$ 83.34	$ 0.00
Tranche 4	$ 62.50	$ 62.50	$ 62.50	$62.50
TOTAL	$520.83	$270.83	$145.84	$62.50

While the FASB had been leaning toward allowing only the accelerated approach, FAS 123R allows both. However, the straight-line approach applies to awards with only a service condition (see below), and a company must make a policy decision as to which approach to use. The caveat is that a company must be consistent with the approach that it uses. It is noted that IFRS 2 issued by the IASB generally requires companies to use the accelerated approach.

Service Condition FAS 123R defines a *service condition* as:

> a condition affecting the vesting, exercisability, exercise price, or other pertinent factors used in determining the fair value of an award that depends solely on an employee rendering service to the employer for the requisite service period. A condition that results in the acceleration of vesting in the event of an employee's death, disability, or termination without cause is a service condition.

Generally, a service condition is the same as "time vesting." For purposes of expense recognition, a service condition will result in expensing over the service period, either under a straight-line or accelerated approach (whichever method the company consistently uses). With respect to forfeitures, compensation expenses previously recognized will be reversed. However, compensation expense associated with a stock option that is never exercised and subsequently expires unexercised is not reversed.

Market Condition FAS 123R defines a *market condition* as:

> a condition affecting the exercise price, exercisability, or other pertinent factors used in determining the fair value of an award under a share-based payment arrangement that relates to the achievement of (i) a specified price of the issuer's shares or a specified amount of intrinsic value indexed solely to the issuer's shares or (ii) a specified price of the issuer's shares in terms of a similar (or index of similar) equity security (securities).

Thus, a market condition is any performance metric that uses a stock's price to measure performance. Examples of a market condition would be a stock price hurdle, where a stock option or restricted share would only vest if a certain stock price is achieved for a set period of consecutive trading days. Total shareholder return (i.e., stock price plus dividend) is also an example of a market condition.

The importance is that a market condition can be taken into account when determining fair value. Thus, for example, an "at-the-money" stock option that can be exercised only when the stock price is equal to 150 percent of the exercise price for at least 30 consecutive trading days will have a lower fair value than the same at-the-money option that does not have such a stock price hurdle.

And, more importantly, compensation expense associated with an equity instrument that has a market condition will *not* be reversed if the performance goal of the market condition is *not* achieved. This is a fundamental difference between a market condition and a performance condition (discussed below).

Performance Condition   FAS 123R defines a *performance condition* as:

> a condition affecting the vesting, exercisability, exercise price, or other pertinent factors used in determining the fair value of an award that relates to both (i) an employee's rendering service for a specified (either explicitly or implicitly) period of time and (ii) achieving a specified performance target that is defined solely by reference to the employer's own operations (or activities). Attaining a specified growth rate in return on assets, obtaining regulatory approval to market a specified product, selling shares in an initial public offering or other financing event, and a change in control are examples of performance conditions for purposes of FAS 123R. A performance target also may be defined by reference to the same performance measure of another entity or group of entities. For example, attaining a growth rate in earnings per share that exceeds the average growth rate in earnings per share of other entities in the same industry is a performance condition for purposes of FAS 123R. A performance target might pertain either to the performance of the enterprise as a whole or to some part of the enterprise, such as a division or an individual employee.

Thus, performance metrics other a metric related to stock price will be a performance condition. This would include such performance metrics as:

- Revenues (actual or growth percentage)
- Earnings before interest, taxes, depreciation, and amortization (EBITDA) (actual or growth percentage)
- Net income (actual or growth percentage)
- EPS (actual or growth percentage)
- Profit margin
- Operating margin

The performance condition is *not* taken into account when determining the fair value of an equity instrument that has a performance condition.

Compensation expense with respect to an equity instrument with a performance condition will be recognized under the principles contained in FAS 5, which generally means when it becomes likely or probable that the performance goal will be achieved. However, unlike an equity instrument with a market condition, if the performance condition is never met, then there will be no compensation expense recorded (or reversed if previously recorded in accordance with FAS 5).

Exhibit 9.1 shows a flow chart illustrating the accounting for awards with service, market, and performance conditions.

Tax Issues   FAS 123R makes the observation that the:

> amount deductible on the employer's tax return may be less than the cumulative compensation cost recognized for financial reporting purposes. The write-off of a

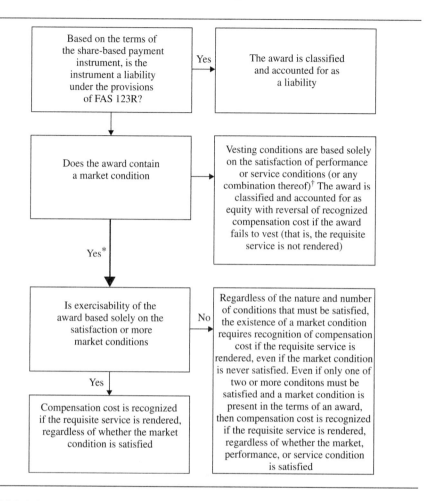

Exhibit 9.1 Accounting for Awards with Service, Market, and/or Performance Conditions

*The award should be classified and accounted for as equity. Market conditions are included in the grant-date fair value estimate of the award.

†Performance and service conditions that effect vesting are not included in estimating the grant-date fair value of the award. Performance and service conditions that effect the exercise price, contractual term, conversion ratio, or other pertinent factors affecting the fair value of an award are included in estimating the grant-date fair value of the award.

deferred tax asset related to that deficiency, net of the related valuation allowance, if any, shall first be offset to the extent of any remaining additional paid-in capital from excess tax benefits from previous awards accounted for in accordance with FAS 123R or FAS 123. The remaining balance, if any, of the write-off of a deferred tax asset related to a tax deficiency shall be recognized in the income statement.

FAS 123R defines an *excess tax benefit* as:

the realized tax benefit related to the amount (caused by changes in the fair value of the
entity's shares after the "measurement date" for financial reporting) of deductible
compensation cost reported on an employer's tax return for equity instruments in
excess of the compensation cost for those instruments recognized for financial reporting purposes.

This is a highly technical issue that involves the question of whether and when a
tax benefit will be treated as additional paid-in capital (APIC) and which needs to be
allocated to an APIC pool. This essentially was a concept based on the possibility that
with respect to a specific equity-based compensation award, the dollar amount of the
tax deduction might exceed the dollar amount of the compensation expense recognized for that award.

To help companies begin establishing APIC pools, the FASB staff issued a staff
position in November 2005 that stated the following:

- Upon adoption of FAS 123R, the beginning balance of the APIC pool related to
  employee compensation shall be calculated as follows:

  ○ The sum of all net increases of additional paid-in capital recognized in an entity's
    annual financial statements related to tax benefits from stock-based employee
    compensation during fiscal periods subsequent to the adoption of FAS 123 but prior
    to the adoption of FAS 123R, less

  ○ The cumulative incremental pretax employee compensation costs that would have
    been recognized if FAS 123 had been used to account for stock-based employee
    compensation costs, multiplied by the entity's blended statutory tax rate upon
    adoption of FAS 123R, inclusive of federal, state, local, and foreign taxes.
    Cumulative incremental compensation costs are the total stock-based employee
    compensation costs included in pro forma net income as if the fair value–based
    method had been applied to all awards pursuant to the provisions of FAS 123, less
    the stock-based compensation costs included in the entity's determination of net
    income as reported.

Tax benefits related to an employee award that is fully vested prior to the adoption
of FAS 123R that have been both (1) realized in accordance with footnote 82 of FAS
123R and (2) recognized in equity subsequent to the adoption of FAS 123R shall
increases the APIC pool. The impact on the APIC pool of an employee award that is
partially vested upon or granted after the adoption of FAS 123R should be determined
in accordance with the guidance in FAS 123R. That is, the compensation deduction for
tax purposes for a partially vested award should be compared with the sum of
compensation cost recognized or disclosed for that award under FAS 123 and FAS
123R. The tax effect of any resulting excess deduction for tax purposes should
increase the APIC pool; the tax effect of any resulting deficient deduction for tax
purposes should be deducted from the APIC pool.

An entity that elects the alternative transition method described in the FASB staff position should classify the tax benefits related to an employee award that is fully vested prior to the adoption of FAS 123R that have been both (1) realized in accordance with footnote 82 of FAS 123R and (2) recognized in equity subsequent to the adoption of FAS 123R as a cash inflow from financing activities and a cash outflow from operating activities within the statement of cash flows. The impact on cash flows of an employee award that is partially vested upon or granted after the adoption of FAS 123R should be determined in accordance with the guidance in FAS 123R. That is, any tax benefit excess should be determined as if the entity had always followed a fair value based method of recognizing compensation cost in its financial statements and should be included as a cash inflow from financing activities and a cash outflow from operating activities within the statement of cash flows.

Practical Considerations

Finally, from a practical standpoint, FAS 123R has been substantially altering compensation committee's design and use of equity-based compensation, and the following trends are noted:

- More use of "full-value awards" (e.g., restricted stock and restricted stock units) over stock options and SARs
- More use of SARs payable in stock
- Less use of broad-based equity-based compensation programs
- Less use of performance goals based on stock price
- Elimination of reload options
- More use of shorter option terms
- More use of cliff vesting or staggered, back-ended vesting rather than pro rata graded vesting

IFRS 2: SHARE-BASED PAYMENTS (2004)

Even before the FASB issued its Exposure Draft on FAS 123R, the IASB "upstaged" the FASB by releasing its final international standard that generally requires options to be expensed when granted. IFRS 2 is effective for periods beginning on or after January 1, 2005. It applies to grants of shares, share options, or other equity instruments that were granted after November 7, 2002 and had not yet vested at the effective date of the IFRS. It applies retrospectively to liabilities arising from share-based payment transactions existing at the date effective as of January 1, 2005. It uses a "fair value" approach to value the compensatory aspect of the option, and requires the six input assumptions of stock price, exercise price, volatility, option term, dividend yield, and risk-free interest rate of the Black-Scholes option-pricing model. IFRS 2 explicitly allows the use of other option-pricing models, and allows the valuation to take into account early exercise or variations of the other inputs over the option's life. SARs settled only in stock will be accounted for as an option. Compensation expense is not recognized if service or performance conditions are not met, but will be recognized (and not reversed) if a "market condition" (i.e., a performance condition using stock price as the measure) is not met. Compensation expense similarly will not be reversed if underwater options expire unexercised. Thus, many of the concepts contained in IFRS 2 were carried over in FAS 123R.

The main requirements of IFRS 2 are:

- An entity must recognize share-based payment transactions in its financial statements, including transactions with employees or other parties to be settled in cash, other assets, or equity instruments of the entity. There are no exceptions to IFRS 2, other than for transactions to which other IFRS rules apply.

- In principle, transactions in which goods or services are received as consideration for equity instruments of the entity should be measured at the fair value of the goods or services received, unless that fair value cannot be estimated reliably. If the entity cannot estimate reliably the fair value of the goods or services received, the entity is required to measure the transaction by reference to the fair value of the equity instruments granted.

- For transactions with employees and others providing similar services, the entity is required to measure the fair value of the equity instruments granted, because it is typically not possible to estimate reliably the fair value of employee services received. The fair value of the equity instruments granted is measured at grant date.

- For transactions with other parties (i.e., other than employees and those providing similar services), there is a rebuttable presumption that the fair value of the goods or services received can be estimated reliably. That fair value is measured at the date the entity obtains the goods or the counterparty renders service. In rare cases, if the presumption is rebutted, the transaction is measured by reference to the fair value of the equity instruments granted, measured at the date the entity obtains the goods or the counterparty renders service.

- For goods or services measured by reference to the fair value of the equity instruments granted, IFRS 2 specifies that, in general, vesting conditions are not taken into account when estimating the fair value of the shares or options at the relevant measurement date (as specified previously). Instead, vesting conditions are taken into account by adjusting the number of equity instruments included in the measurement of the transaction amount so that, ultimately, the amount recognized for goods or services received as consideration for the equity instruments granted is based on the number of equity instruments that eventually vest.

- The fair value of equity instruments granted must be based on market prices, if available, and to take into account the terms and conditions upon which those equity instruments were granted. In the absence of market prices, fair value is estimated, using a valuation technique to estimate what the price of those equity instruments would have been on the measurement date in an arm's length transaction between knowledgeable, willing parties.

- IFRS 2 also sets out requirements if the terms and conditions of an option or share grant are modified (e.g., an option is repriced) or if a grant is cancelled, repurchased, or replaced with another grant of equity instruments.

- For cash-settled share-based payment transactions, an entity must measure the goods or services acquired and the liability incurred at the fair value of the liability. Until the liability is settled, the entity is required to remeasure the fair value of the liability at each reporting date and at the date of settlement, with any changes in value recognized in profit or loss for the period.

- IFRS 2 also sets out requirements for share-based payment transactions in which the terms of the arrangement provide either the entity or the supplier of goods or services with a choice of whether the entity settles the transaction in cash or by issuing equity instruments.

- IFRS 2 prescribes various disclosure requirements to enable users of financial statements to understand:

  a. The nature and extent of share-based payment arrangements that existed during the period
  b. How the fair value of the goods or services received, or the fair value of the equity instruments granted, during the period was determined
  c. The effect of share-based payment transactions on the entity's profit or loss for the period and on its financial position

- Before IFRS 2 was issued, there was no existing International Financial Reporting Standard on the recognition or measurement of share-based payment. The requirements in IFRS 2 replaced the disclosure requirements in IAS 19, "Employee Benefits," with respect to equity compensation benefits.

As with IFRS 1, the IASB has released IFRS 2 as three separate booklets: the first booklet contains the mandatory requirements of IFRS 2; the second booklet contains the IASB's Basis for Conclusions, which sets out the IASB's reasoning behind the requirements in IFRS 2; and the third booklet consists of implementation guidance, including various illustrative examples.

There are differences between IFRS 2 and the FAS 123R, including the accounting for nonpublic enterprises, income tax effects, and certain modifications. The scope of IFRS 2 includes accounting for all share-based payment arrangements, regardless of whether the counterparty is an employee. In contrast, FAS 123R did not specify the measurement date for share-based payment transaction with non-employees, and the FASB continues to apply EITF 96-18 to grants of share options and other equity instruments to non-employees, and requires that they be measured at the earlier of (1) the date at which a commitment for performance by the counterparty to earn the equity instruments is reached, or (2) the date at which the counterparty's performance is complete. Thus, for many grants, the measurement date under EITF 96-18 may be different from the measurement date prescribed by IFRS 2.

OLD EQUITY-BASED COMPENSATION ACCOUNTING RULES

APB 25: ACCOUNTING FOR STOCK ISSUED TO EMPLOYEES (1972)

Prior to the FAS 123R, APB 25 had been the accounting standard most companies used to expense equity-based compensation. Similar to principles underlying ARB 43, the overarching principle was to value the stock award (i.e., a restricted stock award or a stock option) on the date of grant, and then to expense that amount over the service period. Thus, for example, a grant of restricted stock with a total FMV of $1,000 on the date of grant, which vests 25 percent per year, would result in a compensation expense of $250 expensed over the next four years.

With respect to stock options, APB 25 acknowledged that stock options indeed have a value, but essentially conceded that valuation was too problematic. It should be remembered that the Black-Scholes valuation methodology first appeared in 1974, and for that matter, it took almost 20 years before it was applied to compensatory stock options. Accordingly, APB 25 created the concept of *intrinsic value*, which simply meant the difference between the FMV of the stock award and any purchase price (i.e., spread). Thus, a stock award of FMV $100 where the grantee paid $10 would have an intrinsic value of $90. Similarly, a stock option with an exercise price of $10 granted when the stock FMV was $100 would also have an intrinsic value of $90. However, a stock option with an exercise price of $100 granted when the stock FMV was $100 would have an intrinsic value of $0.

This, perhaps, is what was most misunderstood about APB 25. Many believed that APB 25 provided that stock options have no value. In reality, however, the rule was that a "fixed" stock option granted with an exercise price equal to or greater than the stock FMV on the date of grant resulted in $0 compensation expense, and a "fixed" stock option with an exercise price less than the stock FMV on the date of grant (i.e., a discounted stock option) resulted in a compensation charge equal to the intrinsic value on the date of grant.

The concept of "fixed" equity-based awards and "variable" equity-based awards was another confusing issue relating to equity-based compensation. These terms sometimes were referred to as *fixed-plan accounting* versus *variable-plan account-ing*, which generally referred to older style nondiscretionary stock plans where all the terms and conditions (e.g., vesting schedule, option term, termination of employment, etc.) were "fixed" in the plan document, and where the award agreement merely listed the number of shares and the exercise price. Usually, these concepts were simply referred to as *fixed accounting* and *variable accounting*. However, as stock plans changed over the years, and provided more and more for a variety of terms and conditions, it became possible for some awards granted under the plan to be "fixed" and some awards granted under the same plan to be "variable"; thus, *fixed-award accounting* and *variable-award accounting* became the preferred terms.

Essentially, a fixed award was an award where the number of shares and the purchase/exercise price were known on the date of grant (this point in time is referred to as the *measurement date* in APB 25). An award was treated as fixed even if there was a vesting schedule, so long as the vesting schedule was time-based and not performance-based. If the number of shares was not known on the date of grant, then there was no measurement date until the number of shares became known (e.g., in a performance-based award, the measurement date occurred when the performance goals were achieved and the equity-based award vested or became payable). If an award was "variable," then the intrinsic value is measured each reporting period and is marked-to-market (i.e., if a stock award, then the stock FMV on the recording date is used; if an option, then the option's spread on the recording date is used) and then recorded in accordance with FAS 5 (discussed later). Obviously, variable accounting generally eliminates the accounting advantages of granting equity-based awards under APB 25 if, in fact, the stock FMV increases after the date of grant.

Using a concept known as the *ultimate vest*, some companies used plans with names such as TARSAPs (for Time Accelerated Restricted Stock Award Plans) or PASOPs (for Performance Accelerated Stock Option Plans) where the vesting of the stock award or stock option would occur at the end of the award's life, usually near the 10th anniversary of the date of grant, but would vest earlier if certain preestablished performance goals were achieved. The SEC examined this issue, and over the years, the ultimate cliff vest date had been reduced from 10 years to approximately seven years. Basically, the issue was whether the ultimate cliff vest date was illusory, and if it were, then the award would be subject to variable accounting. APB 25 applied only to employee compensatory plans and not to employee noncompensatory plans, an example of which was an employee stock purchase plan that met the qualifications of Internal Revenue Code Section 423 (discussed in Chapter 8). While APB 25 did not explicitly allow non-employee directors to be treated as employees, these rules were extended to non-employee directors who received stock option grants. Finally, APB 25 provided that if an option term was extended, then a new measurement date occurred, and if there was spread in the option on this new measurement date, then such intrinsic value would be recorded as a compensation expense; in substance, such amendment would be treated as a cancellation of the existing stock option and a grant of a new option.

FIN 28: ACCOUNTING FOR STOCK APPRECIATION RIGHTS AND OTHER VARIABLE STOCK OPTION OR AWARD PLANS (1978)

FIN 28 established the principle that SARs and other equity-based compensation awards payable in cash should be treated more as cash-based awards rather than as equity-based awards. This led to the principle of variable accounting for SARs, phantom stock, and the like, which required that the value or spread of the award be marked-to-market each recording period and taken as a compensation expense. It also introduced the concept of accelerated or tranche expensing that for the first time distinguished between cliff vesting (i.e., 100 percent of the stock award vested on one single date) and graded vested (i.e., various percentages of the stock award vested on various dates). FIN 28 required that tranche expensing be applied to all SARs. The application of tranche expensing results in compensation expense being front-loaded so that more of the total expense is recorded up-front than equally over the service period.

FIN 44: ACCOUNTING FOR CERTAIN TRANSACTIONS INVOLVING STOCK COMPENSATION (2000)

Within a few years following the issuance of the original FAS 123, the FASB decided to review APB 25 under what was known as the *maintenance and repairs* project. Essentially, the FASB examined specific practices that it felt exceeded the authority of APB 25. Some of these practices and a description of the changes were:

- *Repricing.* Any direct or indirect cancellation of an outstanding "underwater" option (i.e., an option where the exercise price is greater than the current stock FMV) and a grant of a new "repriced" option would result in variable accounting for the new repriced option.

- *Employees.* APB 25 applies only to common-law employees and a company's non-employee directors.

- *Business combinations.* Rollover of options in business combinations may result in compensation expense using FAS 123 valuation methodologies.

- *Accelerated vesting.* Discretionary accelerated vesting may cause additional compensation expense based on facts and circumstances.

- *Withholding.* Companies may only withhold the statutory minimum with respect to equity-based awards.

- *Puts and calls.* Stock (including stock received after the exercise of an option) must be held at least six months before it is cashed out by the issuer, or else it will be treated as a variable award.

- *Employee stock purchase plan (ESPP).* An ESPP that qualifies under IRC Section 423 will continue to be treated as a "noncompensatory plan."

- *Reloads.* A stock option with a reload feature as of the date of grant will be a fixed award; an existing stock option that is subsequently amended to provide a reload feature will be a variable award; the grant of the reload stock option itself will be treated as a new grant.

FIN 44 superseded EITF 87-33 and EITF 90-9.

ACCOUNTING STANDARDS THAT COMPENSATION COMMITTEE MEMBERS MAY NEED TO KNOW

While a company's audit committee, independent auditors, and financial departments will be the key players addressing accounting issues and will be primarily involved in all aspects of the compensation committee decisions impacting the financial statements, the following list contains most of the other major relevant accounting standards that compensation committees might encounter in discussing and addressing the financial impact of compensation committee decisions (some of which have been replaced and generally are no longer applicable):

Accounting Principles Board Opinions

- ARB 43: Compensation Involved in Stock Option and Stock Purchase Plans
- APB 12: Omnibus Opinion (Deferred Compensation Contracts)
- APB 15: Earnings Per Share
- APB 16: Business Combinations

FASB Financial Accounting Statements

- FAS 5: Accounting for Contingencies
- FAS 87: Employers' Accounting for Pensions
- FAS 88: Employers' Accounting for Settlements and Curtailments of Defined-Benefit Pension Plans and for Termination Benefits
- FAS 106: Employers' Accounting for Postretirement Benefits Other than Pensions
- FAS 128: Earnings per Share
- FAS 132: Employers' Disclosures about Pensions and Other Postretirement Benefits
- FAS 133: Accounting for Derivative Instruments and Hedging Activities
- FAS 141: Business Combinations
- FAS 142: Goodwill and Other Intangible Assets
- FAS 148: Accounting for Equity-Based Compensation Transition and Disclosure
- FAS 150: Accounting for Certain Financial Instruments with Characteristics of Both Liabilities and Equity
- FAS 158: Employers' Accounting for Defined-Benefit Pension and Other Post-retirement Plans

FASB Interpretations

- FIN 31: Treatment of Stock Compensation Plans in EPS Calculations
- FIN 38: Determining the Measurement Date for Stock Option, Purchase, and Award Plans Involving Junior Stock
- FIN 48: Accounting for Uncertainty in Income Taxes

Emerging Issues Task Force Releases

- EITF 84-13: Purchase of Stock Options and Stock Appreciation Rights in a Leveraged Buyout
- EITF 84-18: Stock Option Pyramiding
- EITF 84-34: Permanent Discount Restricted Stock Purchase Plan
- EITF 85-1: Classifying Notes Received for Capital Stock
- EITF 85-45: Business Combinations: Settlement of Stock Options and Awards
- EITF 86-27: Measurement of Excess Contributions to a Defined Contribution Plan
- EITF 87-6: Adjustments Related to Stock Compensation Plans
- EITF 87-23: Book Value Stock Purchase Plans
- EITF 87-33: Stock Compensation Issues Related to Market Decline
- EITF 88-6: Book Value Stock Plans in an Initial Public Offering
- EITF 90-7: Accounting for a Reload Stock Option
- EITF 90-9: Changes to Fixed Employee Stock Option Plans as a Result of Equity Restructuring
- EITF 94-6: Accounting for a Buyout of Compensatory Stock Options
- EITF 95-16: Accounting for Stock Compensation Arrangements with Employer Loan Features under APB 25
- EITF 96-18: Accounting for Equity Instruments that Are Issued to Other than Employees for Acquiring, or in Conjunction with Selling, Goods or Services
- EITF 97-5: Accounting for Delayed Receipt of Option Shares upon Exercise under APB 25
- EITF 97-14: Accounting for Deferred Compensation Arrangements Where Amounts Earned Are Held in a Rabbi Trust and Invested
- EITF 00-12: Accounting by an Investor for Stock-Based Compensation Granted to Employees of an Equity Method Investee
- EITF 00-23: Issues Related to the Accounting for Stock Compensation under APB 25 and FIN 44
- EITF 02-8: Accounting for Options Granted to Employees in Unrestricted, Publicly Traded Shares of an Unrelated Entity

SEC Staff Accounting Bulletins

- SAB 1 (Topic 4E): Receivables from Sale of Stock
- SAB 79 (Topic 5T): Accounting for Expenses or Liabilities Paid by Principal Stockholder(s)
- SAB 83 (Topic 4D): Cheap Stock
- SAB 107 (Topic 14): Interpretation of FAS 123R

It is noted again that many of the preceding standards will no longer have any applicability to future financial reporting (e.g., APB 25 will soon be obsoleted); however, for historical perspective and to help explain past practices, most relevant accounting standards impacting executive compensation are included.

ACCOUNTING PRINCIPLES BOARD OPINIONS

ARB 43, Chapter 13B: Compensation Involved in Stock Option and Stock Purchase Plans (1953)

ARB 43 generally was a compilation of the previous 42 ARBs. Chapter 13B was the first pronouncement with respect to equity-based compensation. Generally, it provided that market value was to be used in determining expense. For purposes of options, grant-date spread (i.e., the difference between the exercise or strike price of the option and the grant-date value of the underlying stock, if positive) was considered market value.

APB 12: Omnibus Opinion (Deferred Compensation Contracts) (1967)

This was the accounting standard used to measure deferred compensation costs. Generally, APB 12 requires the accrual of an employer's obligation under an individual deferred compensation arrangement pursuant to the terms of the arrangement; this meant that the obligation would be measured by the life expectancy of the employee using "best estimates." This vagueness caused inconsistent application and eventually led to an amendment in 1990 contained in FAS 106 (discussed later in this section).

APB 15: Earnings per Share (1969)

Earnings per share generally is calculated by dividing total earnings of the company by the number of outstanding shares. This accounting standard was important because it took into account the impact of stock options and similar instruments (called "common stock equivalents") in computing "fully diluted" EPS. This is accomplished by using a concept called the *treasury stock method*, which presumes that all options (vested and unvested) are exercised as of the EPS calculation date, and the proceeds presumed to be received from the company due to such fictional exercise are used to buy shares on the open market at the current FMV of a share of the company's common stock (stock FMV). Thus, for example, if a company had 3 million shares outstanding and 100,000 outstanding stock options with an exercise price of $10 when the stock FMV was $16, then the EPS denominator would be 3,037,500 shares computed as follows:

1. $100,000 option shares x $10 exercise price = $1,000,000 presumed proceeds
2. $1 million/$16 = 62,500 "fictional" additional shares
3. 3 million outstanding shares + 100,000 "exercised" shares − 62,500 "repurchased" shares = 3,037,500.

APB 16: Business Combinations (1970)

APB 16 was the accounting standard that established two types of accounting for transactions. The first was purchase accounting, where the transaction was treated as a purchase of one company by another. This resulted in the creation of the intangible asset called *goodwill*, which was amortized as an expense over a specific time period and reduced a company's earnings. The second was pooling-of-interest accounting, where the two companies were treated for accounting purposes as always having been one company. This eliminated goodwill, and thus a going-forward company's earnings were not negatively impacted. While the rules involving pooling-of-interest accounting were strict, and many companies were forced to use purchase accounting, many companies specifically (and sometimes aggressively) structured their business combinations to fit the preferred pooling-of-interest accounting. In 2001, APB 16 was replaced by FAS 141 (discussed later in this section), which eliminated pooling-of-interest accounting.

FASB FINANCIAL ACCOUNTING STATEMENTS

FAS 5: Accounting for Contingencies (1975)

FAS 5 established the accounting principle that estimated expense from a loss contingency will be recorded if and when it is probable that an asset has been impaired or a liability has been incurred, provided that the amount of loss can be reasonably estimated. This principle has been applied to determining when a performance cash-based or equity-based award will be recorded as an expense. The result is that a performance cash-based or equity-based award will not be expensed until it is probable that the contingency (i.e., the performance goal) will be achieved. At that point, the value of the award is measured (actual dollar amount if a cash award or dollar amount based on fair market value of the underlying stock at the time of measurement if an equity-based award) and expensed over the applicable period.

FAS 87: Employers' Accounting for Pensions (1985)

FAS 87 generally applies to expensing and disclosure of broad-based employee defined-benefit and defined-contribution pension plans. A fundamental objective of FAS 87 is to recognize the compensation cost of an employee's pension benefits over that employee's approximate service period. FAS 87 continues past practices of delaying the recognition of certain events, reporting net cost, and offsetting liabilities and assets. Compensation committees may need to consider FAS 87 if they become involved with new or existing pension plans.

FAS 88: Employers' Accounting for Settlements and Curtailments of Defined-Benefit Pension Plans and for Termination Benefits (1985)

FAS 88 established the accounting standards for an employer's accounting for settlement of defined-benefit pension obligations, for curtailment of a defined-benefit pension plan, and for termination benefits, and is closely related to FAS 87. Compensation committees may need to consider FAS 88 in the context of any executive's termination of employment.

FAS 106: Employers' Accounting for Postretirement Benefits Other than Pensions (1990)

FAS 106 establishes the accounting standards for an employer's accounting for postretirement benefits other than pension benefits (which commonly are referred to by the acronym OPEB for Other Postretirement Employee Benefits or sometimes Other Post Employment Benefits). Prior to FAS 106, OPEBs were accounted for when paid (similar to the "pay-as-you-go" standard under the federal Social Security system). Instead, FAS 106 required recognition of the accrued obligation. Generally, the standards under FAS 106 are similar to the standards under FAS 87. FAS 106, however, amended APB 12 to explicitly require that an employer's obligation under deferred compensation arrangements be accrued following the terms of the individual contract over the required service periods to the date the employee is fully eligible for the benefits. This eliminated the vagueness of the best-estimates provision contained in APB 12. Other significant aspects of FAS 106 are:

- In estimating future costs, anticipated plan changes may be considered in certain circumstances.
- Benefit/years-of-service actuarial method is mandated; actuarial valuation of obligation must be as of a date within three months of year-end, while current year expense shall be based on beginning of year assumptions.
- Employer must estimate its health care cost trend rate and assume current Medicare law continues.
- The discount rate selected should reflect current rates of return available on high-quality bonds.
- Prior service cost is amortized over the future service period of active employees.
- Delayed recognition of actuarial gains and losses is permitted; if unrecognized amount exceeds 10 percent of assets or obligation, minimum amortization of the excess amount over average remaining service of active employees is required.
- The obligation or asset upon adopting FAS 106 is either expensed or amortized over the remaining service life of active employees (or 20 years if longer); if amortized and total expense is less than cash payments, additional amortization is required.
- The annual expense for a multiemployer plan is generally the contribution called for that period.
- Balance sheet reflects the difference between cumulative amounts expensed and amounts funded (no minimum liability rules).
- The full liability net of any plan assets should be recorded at the date of a purchase business combination.

FAS 128: Earnings per Share (1997)

FAS 128 replaced APB 15 as the accounting standard for EPS. The concept of primary EPS was replaced with basic EPS, and fully diluted EPS was replaced by diluted EPS. Essentially, the concept of converting common-stock equivalents into additional fictional shares using the treasury stock method was retained.

FAS 132: Employers' Disclosures about Pensions and Other Postretirement Benefits (1998, Revised 2003)

This statement was revised in 2003 to address concerns that users of financial statements did not receive sufficient pension information. The statement replaces the disclosure provisions of FAS 87, 88, and 106. The statement applies to defined benefit plans and other retirement benefits and requires that the following information be provided annually:

- A breakdown of plan assets held in equity securities, debt securities, real estate, and other assets
- A description of the plan's investment strategies, policies, and target investment allocations
- Projections of the expected future benefit payment for the next five years
- The accumulated benefit obligation
- Estimated contributions for the next year
- Measurement dates
- A table of the key assumptions that the plan uses to determine its benefit obligation, net periodic benefit cost, and assumed health care cost trend rates

In addition, companies must report pension and other postretirement benefit costs quarterly. Domestic retirement plans must provide the preceding information, except estimated future benefit payments, for fiscal years ending after December 15, 2003. Estimated future benefit payments must be reported for years ending after June 15, 2004. Foreign plans and nonpublic entities must provide the information for years ending after June 15, 2004. The quarterly information is required for quarters beginning after December 15, 2003 for all plans.

FAS 133: Accounting for Derivative Instruments and Hedging Activities (1998)

FAS 133 establishes accounting and reporting standards for derivative instruments, including certain derivative instruments embedded in other contracts (collectively referred to as derivatives), and for hedging activities. It requires that an entity recognize all derivatives as either assets or liabilities in the statement of financial position and measure those instruments at fair value. If certain conditions are met, a derivative may be specifically designated as (a) a hedge of the exposure to changes in the fair value of a recognized asset or liability or an unrecognized firm commitment, (b) a hedge of the exposure to variable cash flows of a forecasted transaction, or (c) a hedge of the foreign currency exposure of a net investment in a foreign operation, an unrecognized firm commitment, an available-for-sale security, or a foreign-currency-denominated forecasted transaction.

FAS 141: Business Combinations (2001)

FAS 141 replaced APB 16 as the accounting standard for business combinations. The most important aspect of FAS 141 is that it eliminated pooling-of-interest accounting.

FAS 142: Goodwill and Other Intangible Assets (2001)

In conjunction with the adoption of FAS 141, the concept of amortizing goodwill as an expense under a purchase-accounting transaction and disregarding goodwill as an expense under a pooling-of-interest accounting transaction was replaced by the FAS 142 concept that goodwill will be expensed as it becomes impaired. While this did not provide the advantages of pooling-of-interest accounting, it helped to some degree reduce the disadvantages of using APB 16 purchase accounting. The concepts of how and when goodwill actually becomes impaired and when the expense must be recorded are still being discussed.

FAS 148: Accounting for Equity-Based Compensation Transition and Disclosure—an Amendment of FASB Statement No. 123 (2002)

Under the original FAS 123, a company that adopted FAS 123 was not required to restate prior years' financial statements but would record equity-based compensation expense on a going-forward basis (this was called the *prospective-only approach*). In 2002, as more and more companies began to adopt FAS 123, some companies wanted to restate prior years financial statements to avoid the appearance that the company had a large decrease in earnings (i.e., companies wanted to ramp up the presentation of equity-based expenses due to the adoption of FAS 123). FAS 128 amended the original FAS 123 to provide that companies could transition over from APB 25 to FAS 123 under three transition scenarios. The first was simply to restate all prior years as if the company had always been under FAS 123. The second was to expense new awards and prior awards that were unvested on the adoption date. The third was to use the prospective-only approach as contained in FAS 123, but which would now only be available to companies that adopted FAS 123 on or prior to their fiscal years ending on or before December 15, 2003.

FAS 150: Accounting for Certain Financial Instruments with Characteristics of both Liabilities and Equity (2003)

FAS 150 establishes standards for how an issuer classifies and measures certain financial instruments with characteristics of both liabilities and equity. It requires that an issuer classify a financial instrument that is within its scope as a liability (or an asset in some circumstances). Many of those instruments were previously classified as equity. Some of the provisions of FAS 150 are consistent with the current definition of liabilities in FASB Concepts Statement No. 6, "Elements of Financial Statements." The remaining provisions of FAS 150 are consistent with the FASB's proposal to revise that definition to encompass certain obligations that a reporting entity can or must settle by issuing its own equity shares, depending on the nature of the relationship established between the holder and the issuer.

FAS 158: Employers' Accounting for Defined-Benefit Pension and Other Postretirement Plans (2006)

FAS 158 improves financial reporting by requiring an employer to recognize the overfunded or underfunded status of a defined-benefit postretirement plan (other than a multiemployer plan) as an asset or liability in its statement of financial position and to recognize changes in that funded status in the year in which the changes occur through comprehensive income of a business entity or changes in unrestricted net assets of a not-for-profit organization. This Statement also improves financial reporting by requiring an employer to measure the funded status of a plan as of the date of its year-end statement of financial position, with limited exceptions.

FAS 158 requires an employer that is a business entity and sponsors one or more single-employer defined-benefit plans to:

- Recognize the funded status of a benefit plan—measured as the difference between plan assets at fair value (with limited exceptions) and the benefit obligation—in its statement of financial position. For a pension plan, the benefit obligation is the projected benefit obligation; for any other postretirement benefit plan, such as a retiree health care plan, the benefit obligation is the accumulated postretirement benefit obligation.

- Recognize as a component of other comprehensive income, net of tax, the gains or losses and prior service costs or credits that arise during the period but are not recognized as components of net periodic benefit cost pursuant to FAS 87 or FAS 106. Amounts recognized in accumulated other comprehensive income, including the gains or losses, prior service costs or credits, and the transition asset or obligation remaining from the initial application of FAS 87 and FAS 106, are adjusted as they are subsequently recognized as components of net periodic benefit cost pursuant to the recognition and amortization provisions of those Statements.

- Measure defined-benefit plan assets and obligations as of the date of the employer's fiscal year-end statement of financial position (with limited exceptions).

- Disclose in the notes to financial statements additional information about certain effects on net periodic benefit cost for the next fiscal year that arise from delayed recognition of the gains or losses, prior service costs or credits, and transition asset or obligation.

FAS 158 also applies to a not-for-profit organization or other entity that does not report other comprehensive income. This Statement's reporting requirements are tailored for those entities. FAS 158 amends FAS 87, FAS 88, FAS 106, and FAS 132, and other related accounting literature.

FASB INTERPRETATIONS

FIN 31: Treatment of Stock Compensation Plans in EPS Calculations (1980)

Funds used in applying the treasury stock method are the sum of the cash to be received upon exercise, the currently measurable compensation to be charged to expense in the future, and any tax benefit to be credited to capital. The interpretation also provides guidance on how to treat variable plans, combination plans, or plans payable in cash or in stock.

FIN 38: Determining the Measurement Date for Stock Option, Purchase, and Award Plans Involving Junior Stock (1984)

FIN 38 addressed a situation involving the accounting for a class of stock known as *junior stock*. Junior stock was a special class of stock issued to executives that was convertible to a company's common stock if certain performance goals were achieved. Because of a variety of restrictions and limitation of other rights, junior stock was expensed at a fraction of the stock FMV. FIN 38 applied variable accounting and required valuation and recording of the expense at the time the performance goals were achieved and with the value equal to the common stock. Essentially, FIN 38 shut down the use of junior stock.

FIN 48: Accounting for Uncertainty in Income Taxes—an Interpretation of FASB Statement No. 109 (Issued 2006)

FIN 48 clarifies the accounting for uncertainty in income taxes recognized in an enterprise's financial statements in accordance with FAS 109, "Accounting for Income Taxes." FIN 48 prescribes a recognition threshold and measurement attribute for the financial statement recognition and measurement of a tax position taken or expected to be taken in a tax return. FIN 48 also provides guidance on derecognition, classification, interest and penalties, accounting in interim periods, disclosure, and transition.

The evaluation of a tax position in accordance with FIN 48 is a two-step process. The first step is recognition: The enterprise determines whether it is more likely than not that a tax position will be sustained upon examination, including resolution of any related appeals or litigation processes, based on the technical merits of the position. In evaluating whether a tax position has met the more-likely-than-not recognition threshold, the enterprise should presume that the position will be examined by the appropriate taxing authority that would have full knowledge of all relevant information. The second step is measurement: A tax position that meets the more-likely-than-not recognition threshold is measured to determine the amount of benefit to recognize in the financial statements. The tax position is measured at the largest amount of benefit that is greater than 50 percent likely of being realized upon ultimate settlement. Differences between tax positions taken in a tax return and amounts recognized in the financial statements will generally result in one or both of the following:

- An increase in a liability for income taxes payable or a reduction of an income tax refund receivable
- A reduction in a deferred tax asset or an increase in a deferred tax liability

An enterprise that presents a classified statement of financial position should classify a liability for unrecognized tax benefits as current to the extent that the enterprise anticipates making a payment within one year or the operating cycle, if longer. An income tax liability should not be classified as a deferred tax liability unless it results from a taxable temporary difference (i.e., a difference between the tax basis of an asset or a liability as calculated using FIN 48 and its reported amount in the statement of financial position). FIN 48 does not change the classification requirements for deferred taxes.

Tax positions that previously failed to meet the more-likely-than-not recognition threshold should be recognized in the first subsequent financial reporting period in which that threshold is met. Previously recognized tax positions that no longer meet the more-likely-than-not recognition threshold should be derecognized in the first subsequent financial reporting period in which that threshold is no longer met. Use of a valuation allowance as described in FAS 109 is not an appropriate substitute for the derecognition of a tax position. The requirement to assess the need for a valuation allowance for deferred tax assets based on the sufficiency of future taxable income is unchanged by FIN 48.

EMERGING ISSUES TASK FORCE RELEASES

EITF 84-13: Purchase of Stock Options and Stock Appreciation Rights in a Leveraged Buyout (1984)

This EITF reached the consensus that a target company must record as compensation expense the amount it pays to acquire options and rights.

EITF 84-18: Stock Option Pyramiding (1984)

When an employee exercises an option by exchanging shares, unless the employee has held the shares for at least six months (i.e., the shares are mature), the option award is, in substance, a variable plan (or a SAR) requiring compensation charges. EITF 84-18 is the source of the six-month mature share rule applied to stock-for-stock cashless exercise programs.

EITF 84-34: Permanent Discount Restricted Stock Purchase Plan (1984)

In these plans, the company has a right of first refusal to repurchase the shares at the current market price less the original discount. Although no consensus was reached, most EITF members believe the plan is compensatory. Most of those believe compensation is fixed at the grant date. Others believe variable accounting is appropriate if buyback is likely or the employer must repurchase the stock (such as when the employee has a put).

EITF 85-1: Classifying Notes Received for Capital Stock (1985)

The EITF reached a consensus that when an enterprise receives a note rather than cash as a contribution to equity, reporting the note as an asset is generally inappropriate, except in very limited circumstances when there is substantial evidence of ability and intent to pay within a reasonably short period of time. The SEC (see SAB 1, discussed later) requires that public companies report such notes receivable as a deduction of shareholders' equity unless collected in cash prior to the issuance of the financial statements.

EITF 85-45: Business Combinations: Settlement of Stock Options and Awards (1985)

If a target company settles stock options voluntarily, at the direction of the acquiring company, or as part of the plan of acquisition, the target must recognize compensation expense. No consensus was reached on the issue of how the target should account for reimbursement from the acquiring company for the settlement cost.

EITF 86-27: Measurement of Excess Contributions to a Defined Contribution Plan (1986)

An employer terminates a plan and contributes the excess assets to an employee stock option plan (ESOP) that purchases stock. The amount in excess of the annual contribution is not allocated to participants. The unallocated shares should be reported as treasury stock. Compensation expense should be recognized at the allocation date at the then-current market price; any difference from the purchase price is reflected in equity. Dividends used to purchase more stock should be charged to treasury stock rather than retained earnings. Dividends paid to participants on unallocated shares should be charged to compensation expense. The sponsor should report its own debt securities owned by the ESOP as both an asset and debt. Unallocated shares will not be outstanding shares for earnings-per-share purposes.

EITF 87-6: Adjustments Related to Stock Compensation Plans (1987)

The EITF addressed four separate issues:

1. *EITF 87-6A: "Changes to Stock Option Plans Arising from the Tax Reform Act of 1986."* Minor technical changes linked to the 1986 act would not create a new measurement date if the aggregate effect on the value of the option is *de minimis* from the perspective of the employee. Changes to the option beyond the minimum necessary for disqualification would presumptively lead to a new measurement date. Because eliminating or changing a sequential exercise requirement may give the employee an economic benefit, such a change may not be de minimis.
2. *EITF 87-6B: "Stock Option Plan with Tax-Offset Cash Bonus."* Plans with tax offset cash bonuses must be accounted for as variable plans. However, for grants outstanding before April 7, 1987, that were granted with tax-offset cash bonuses or that are modified before that date to add a tax-offset cash bonus in connection with the employer's disqualification of the option and that meet certain other requirements, split accounting treatment (option and bonus accounted for separately, with option treated as a fixed plan) is appropriate.
3. *EITF 87-6C: "Use of Stock Option Shares to Cover Tax Withholding."* An option plan that allows the use of option shares to meet tax withholding requirements may be considered a fixed plan. Compensation expense must be recorded for all shares used to satisfy withholding if the fair value of the shares withheld exceeds the required tax withholding.
4. *EITF 87-6D: "Phantom Stock-for-Stock Exercise."* An employee presents mature shares (see EITF 84-18) to satisfy the exercise price. The enterprise allows the employee to retain the shares presented and issues a certificate for the net shares. This plan remains a fixed plan.

EITF 87-23: Book Value Stock Purchase Plans (1987)

This consensus addresses private company plans that set the purchase price based on a formula such as book value or earnings and provide for a repurchase upon termination or a determinable date using the same formula. If the employee makes a substantive investment that will be at risk for a reasonable period of time, no compensation expense should be recorded for changes in the formula. Variable plan accounting must be used between the grant date and the exercise date for options to purchase restricted stock based on the formula price; no substantive investment is at risk prior to exercise. Formula stock option plans for public companies are variable plans, although fixed plan accounting is permitted for grants prior to January 28, 1988, that had been previously accounted for as fixed plans.

EITF 87-33: Stock Compensation Issues Related to Market Decline (1987)

The EITF addressed five separate issues:

1. If the exercise price of an option is reduced, or an option is cancelled in exchange for the issuance of a new option that contains identical terms except for a reduced exercise price, (a) any originally measured compensation is not reversed; any unamortized amount should continue being amortized, and (b) a new measurement date occurs; compensation is measured using the current market price and the new exercise price. Any compensation in excess of the original amount measured should be amortized over the remaining vesting period.
2. If an option is repurchased in contemplation of the issuance of a new option containing identical terms to the remaining terms of the old option, the guidance in 1 should be applied. The cash paid represents additional compensation that should be expensed.
3. The conclusions in 1 and 2 also apply to restricted stock awards.
4. A new option is granted for a proportionately fewer number of shares at a lower exercise price, with a stipulation that each share acquired under the new grant cancels a proportionate number of shares under the original grant and vice versa. These awards are variable plans because the number of shares and the exercise price is not known. Compensation is measured as the amount by which the market price exceeds the exercise price under the new grant. No additional compensation is recognized after the point that the employee will receive more value under the original grant.
5. If an option contains a tandem stock indemnification right, the right should be accounted for separately only if the individual is subject to the SEC's six-month insider trading restrictions and the right is effective for six months. Under this approach, during the six months following exercise, compensation should be measured as the decrease in the market price from the exercise date. If the two criteria are not met, the entire arrangement (option plus right) is accounted for as a variable plan.

EITF 88-6: Book Value Stock Plans in an Initial Public Offering (1988)

A book value stock purchase plan of a public company is a performance plan; variable plan accounting must be used (see EITF 87-23).

Book value options in an IPO: For book value stock options that do not change after the IPO, the company should continue variable plan accounting and expense any increase in book value due to the IPO. For book value stock options that convert to market value options, compensation expense should be recognized for the difference between market value and book value at the date of the IPO. Because the conversion to a market value option establishes a new measurement date, no further compensation cost would be recognized.

Book value stock in an IPO: If the stock retains its book value buyback provisions after the IPO, no compensation is recognized as a result of the IPO. However, compensation expense should be recognized for subsequent changes in book value. If the restrictions lapse so that the book value stock converts to market value stock, no compensation expense is recognized at the date of the IPO or in future periods. In either case, if the shares were issued within one year of or in contemplation of the IPO, compensation expense must be recognized for the increases in book value since the issuance date.

EITF 90-7: Accounting for a Reload Stock Option (1990)

A reload stock option automatically awards additional options at the then current market price whenever existing options are exercised by tendering owned shares. These plans should be accounted for as fixed plans provided that shares tendered are mature as defined in EITF 84-18 and that the total number of shares that can be issued net of shares tendered is limited to the shares in the original grant.

EITF 90-9: Changes to Fixed Employee Stock Option Plans as a Result of Equity Restructuring (1990)

As a result of a restructuring in the form of a spin-off or a large, special, nonrecurring dividend, an employer changes outstanding options to offset the effects of the resulting dilution. Any consideration paid should be expensed. Other changes do not result in a new measurement date if (1) the aggregate intrinsic value does not increase, (2) the ratio of the option price to the market price of the shares is not reduced, and (3) the vesting and other provisions do not change.

EITF 94-6: Accounting for a Buyout of Compensatory Stock Options (1994)

This EITF requires that a buyout of a stock option will result in a compensation expense equal to the amount paid for the option.

EITF 95-16: Accounting for Stock Compensation Arrangements with Employer Loan Features under APB 25 (1995)

EITF 95-16 examined the situation where a stock option is exercised using a nonrecourse note with the employer. The conclusion was that use of the nonrecourse note was similar in substance to the use of an option, because if the stock price decreased below the value of the note, then there would not be reason to repay the note.

Thus, repayment would be similar to exercising the option. If the term of the note was longer than the original term of the option, then the option's term was extended and a new measurement date occurred.

EITF 96-18: Accounting for Equity Instruments that Are Issued to Other than Employees for Acquiring, or in Conjunction with Selling, Goods or Services (1996)

The original FAS 123 (issued in 1995) did not address vesting nor measurement date determinations. EITF 96-18 addressed vesting and measurement date considerations generally for independent contractors. However, many of the principles are believed to be applicable to employee stock options.

EITF 97-5: Accounting for Delayed Receipt of Option Shares Upon Exercise under APB Opinion No. 25 (1997)

This EITF addressed a compensation technique where unrealized gain in a stock option was, in substance, converted into a deferred compensation account. All or a portion of the account would then be invested in employer stock; any amount not invested in employer stock would be invested in other securities and vehicles for purposes of diversification. EITF 97-5 concluded that the conversion to a deferred compensation payable only in employer stock was a nonevent; however, if the account were diversified, then the award became variable since the number of shares delivered under the option was not known on the date of grant.

EITF 97-14: Accounting for Deferred Compensation Arrangements Where Amounts Earned Are Held in a Rabbi Trust and Invested (1997)

The EITF analyzed whether employer stock held by a rabbi trust should be treated as fixed or variable. EITF 97-14 concluded in part that the stock should be treated as fixed. This is the authority used to support fixed accounting for restricted stock units payable only in stock.

EITF 00-12: Accounting by an Investor for Stock-Based Compensation Granted to Employees of an Equity Method Investee (2000)

Both the investor and the investee companies are to recognize compensation cost (in the same amount and over the same vesting period) equal to the fair value of the stock compensation as ultimately measured on the award's vesting date (in accordance with FAS 123 and EITF 96-18), with a corresponding credit to each company's capital account. Further, there are no net changes to the asset or equity accounts on the balance sheets of the investor and the investee companies, and the income statements and balance sheets of other investor companies (if any) are not affected by the recognition of the stock compensation cost.

EITF 00-23: Issues Related to the Accounting for Stock Compensation under APB 25 and FIN 44 (2000)

Almost immediately after the release of FIN 44 in March 2000, the EITF (prodded by the SEC) began examining a list of fact patterns and issues relating to repricings, reloads, modifications, puts and calls, and many of the same issues that FIN 44 was to address and settle. This EITF is divided into some 50 separate issues, some of which are further divided into subissues. It is now virtually impossible to apply APB 25 without FIN 44, and it is equally impossible to apply FIN 44 without EITF 00-23. Since many fact patterns and examples are presented in EITF 00-23, compensation committee members should, when analyzing an APB 25/FIN 44 issue, first ask whether EITF addresses the specific issue.

EITF 02-8: Accounting for Options Granted to Employees in Unrestricted, Publicly Traded Shares of an Unrelated Entity (2002)

This EITF requires that a company that grants its employees options not on company stock but on shares of an unrelated entity should account for such grants in accordance with the guidance provided in FAS 133, "Accounting for Derivative Instruments and Hedging Activities."

SEC STAFF ACCOUNTING BULLETINS

SAB 1 (Topic 4E): Receivables from Sale of Stock

Deferred compensation or receivables arising from the issuance of stock or options to employees should be presented in the balance sheet as a deduction from stockholders' equity.

SAB 79 (Topic 5T): Accounting for Expenses or Liabilities Paid by Principal Stockholder(s)

When a principal stockholder pays an expense for a registrant, the registrant should reflect the expense and a corresponding capital contribution, unless the stockholder's action is caused by a relationship or obligation completely unrelated to his position as a stockholder or the registrant clearly does not benefit from the transaction.

SAB 83 (Topic 4D): Cheap Stock

If stock or options have been issued below the IPO price within one year of filing an IPO registration statement or in contemplation of the IPO, the stock or options should be considered outstanding for all periods presented for the purposes of computing earnings per share. The SEC staff will permit the use of the treasury stock method to determine the dilutive effect of options. Registrants must also consider whether compensation expense should be recognized for these awards.

SAB 107 (Topic 14): Interpretation of FAS 123R

SAB 107 express views of the SEC staff regarding the interaction between FAS 123R and certain SEC rules and regulations and provide the SEC staff's views regarding the valuation of share-based payment arrangements for public companies. In particular, SAB 107 provides guidance related to share-based payment transactions with non-employees, the transition from nonpublic to public entity status, valuation methods (including assumptions such as expected volatility and expected term), the accounting for certain redeemable financial instruments issued under share-based payment arrangements, the classification of compensation expense, non-GAAP financial measures, first-time adoption of FAS 123R in an interim period, capitalization of compensation cost related to share-based payment arrangements, the accounting for income tax effects of share-based payment arrangements upon adoption of FAS 123R, the modification of employee share options prior to adoption of FAS 123R, and disclosures in Management's Discussion and Analysis (MD&A) subsequent to adoption of FAS 123R.

Chapter 10

ERISA and Labor Law, Rules, and Issues

This chapter provides a general overview of the applicable laws, rules, regulations, and other legal or rule-making authority with respect to the Employee Retirement Income Security Act of 1974 (ERISA) and selected labor issues with which compensation committee members will need to be familiar. It does not present all of the rules and issues that compensation committees might encounter in these areas, but those common issues that arise when dealing with executive employment and compensation arrangements.

ERISA LAW AND REGULATIONS

ERISA was Congress's attempt at federalizing pension law in the United States. It accomplished this by creating a comprehensive set of laws relating to pensions and other employee-benefit arrangements. When enacted in 1974, ERISA amended both the Internal Revenue Code (IRC) and federal labor law. An important element of ERISA is its "preemption doctrine," which is contained in Section 514, which provides that ERISA "shall supersede any and all State laws insofar as they may now or hereafter relate to any employee benefit plan." Thus, in most cases, the ERISA preemption doctrine results in ERISA overriding most other laws.

   While ERISA generally applies to broad-based rank-and-file benefit plans, there are aspects of the law that compensation committee members will need to know. Essentially, the threshold issue usually involves whether the executive compensation or benefit arrangement is subject to ERISA, or whether it is exempt (in whole or in part) from ERISA. Thus, the definitions of the following terms are critical to the analysis:

- Employee benefit plan
- Pension benefit plan
- Welfare benefit plan
- Excess benefit plan
- Top-hat plan

In addition, most executive benefit plans are concerned only with the first five "parts" under Subtitle B of Title I of ERISA:

- Part 1, dealing with disclosure and reporting requirements
- Part 2, dealing with participation and vesting requirement
- Part 3, dealing with funding requirements
- Part 4, dealing with fiduciary responsibility
- Part 5, dealing with administration and enforcement

BASIC ERISA DEFINITIONS

ERISA Section 3(3) defines *employee benefit plan* or *plan* as "an employee welfare benefit plan, or an employee pension benefit plan, or a plan that is both an employee welfare benefit plan and an employee pension benefit plan."

ERISA Section 3(1) defines *employee welfare benefit plan* and *welfare plan* as:

Any plan, fund, or program that was heretofore or is hereafter established or maintained by an employer or by an employee organization, or by both, to the extent that such plan, fund, or program was established or is maintained for the purpose of providing for its participants or their beneficiaries, through the purchase of insurance or otherwise, (A) medical, surgical, or hospital care or benefits, or benefits in the event of sickness, accident, disability, death, or unemployment, or vacation benefits, apprenticeship or other training programs, or day care centers, scholarship funds, or prepaid legal services, or (B) any benefit described in Section 302(c) of the Labor Management Relations Act, 1947 (other than pensions on retirement or death, and insurance to provide such pensions).

ERISA Section 3(2) defines *employee pension benefit plan* and *pension plan* as:

Any plan, fund, or program that was heretofore or is hereafter established or maintained by an employer or by an employee organization, or by both, to the extent that by its express terms or as a result of surrounding circumstances, such plan, fund, or program provides retirement income to employees, or results in a deferral of income by employees for periods extending to the termination of covered employment or beyond, regardless of the method of calculating the contributions made to the plan, the method of calculating the benefits under the plan, or the method of distributing benefits from the plan.

The preceding three definitions are a starting point for any ERISA analysis, because in some cases, a compensation arrangement (such as an equity-based plan), either by its own terms or operationally, may fall within the definition of an ERISA employee benefit plan. Moreover, an executive severance plan will need to be analyzed as to whether it properly is characterized as a pension plan or as a welfare plan. In addition, there is case law that defines what is meant by the word *plan*; thus, some arrangements may be outside of ERISA because they do not rise to the level of an ERISA plan. Generally, most courts apply what is known as the "Donovan" test," from the 1982 11th Circuit Court of Appeals case *Donovan v. Dillingham*, which provided for a five-factor analysis. The *Donovan* test simply asks whether there is:

1. A plan, fund, or program,
2. Established or maintained,
3. By an employer or by an employee organization, or by both,
4. For the purpose of providing medical, surgical, hospital care, sickness, accident, disability, death, unemployment or vacation benefits, apprenticeship or other training programs, day care centers, scholarship funds, prepaid legal services, or severance benefits,
5. To participants or their beneficiaries?

If all five of these factors are not met, then there is no ERISA plan. In addition, in order to determine whether a plan has been "established," the Donovan test inquires whether, from the surrounding circumstances, "a reasonable person can ascertain the intended benefits, a class of beneficiaries, the source of financing, and procedures for receiving benefits." Finally, all plans are subject to the "Fort Halifax" test, as described by the U.S. Supreme Court in the 1987 case *Fort Halifax Packing Co. v. Coyne*, which generally requires that there must be *ongoing administration* of the arrangement for it to be subject to ERISA.

EXCESS BENEFIT PLANS

ERISA Section 3(36) defines *excess benefit plan* as:

> A plan maintained by an employer solely for the purpose of providing benefits for certain employees in excess of the limitations on contributions and benefits imposed by [IRC Section 415], without regard to whether the plan is funded. To the extent that a separable part of a plan (as determined by the Secretary of Labor) maintained by an employer is maintained for such purpose, that part shall be treated as a separate plan that is an excess benefit plan.

ERISA Section 4(b)(5) provides that Title I of ERISA does not apply to any employee benefit plan that meets the definition of an excess benefit plan. Thus, excess benefit plans (which may include plans also referred to as "restoration" or "restorative" plans, "add-back" plans, and/or "wraparound" plans) are not subject to the reporting and disclosure requirements of Part 1 of Subtitle B of Title I of ERISA, the participation and vesting requirements of Part 2, the funding requirements of Part 3, the fiduciary responsibility requirements of Part 4, and the administration and enforcement requirements of Part 5. It should be noted that while excess benefit plans are allowed to uncap the benefit limits ($180,000 in 2007) and contribution limits ($45,000 in 2007) contained in IRC Section 415, it does not expressly provide for uncapping the compensation limit ($225,000 in 2007) contained in IRC Section

401(a)(17). Thus, a plan that uncaps both the Section 415 and 401(a)(17) limits may actually be a top-hat plan and not an excess benefit plan.

TOP-HAT PLANS

The term *top-hat plan* is not defined in ERISA. Nor is it explicitly defined in the ERISA regulations. However, Labor Regulation Section 2520.104-23 essentially provides such a definition. It generally refers to a plan that is unfunded and is maintained by an employer primarily for the purpose of providing deferred compensation for a select group of management or highly compensated employees. These executive benefit programs are usually referred to as *top-hat plans* since that is the term used by the Department of Labor (DOL).

Unlike an excess benefit plan, which is exempt from ERISA, top-hat plans are subject to some, but not all, of ERISA's requirements. For example, top-hat plans are subject to the reporting and disclosure requirements under Part 1 and the enforcement and administration requirements of Part 5. However, top-hat plans are exempt from the participation and vesting requirements of Part 2, the funding requirements of Part 3, and the fiduciary responsibility requirements of Part 4.

With respect to the reporting and disclosure requirements of Part 1, Labor Regulation Section 2520.104-23 provides an "alternative" method of compliance for pension plans in which certain selected employees participate. An employer may satisfy all Part 1 reporting and disclosure requirements with respect to any of its top-hat plans by filing with the DOL within 120 days after the adoption of such plan a statement that contains:

- The name and address of the employer
- The Internal Revenue Service (IRS) employer identification number
- A declaration that the employer maintains the plan primarily for the purpose of providing deferred compensation for a select group of management or highly compensated employees
- A statement of the number of such plans (if more than one) and the number of employees in each
- A copy of the plan or plans, if requested by the DOL

This filing (commonly referred to by practitioners as the *top-hat plan one-pager*) is all a company needs to do to relieve itself of ERISA's Part 1 burdens. Compensation committees should check with their legal or HR departments to make sure that these one-pagers have been filed.

Issues arising under top-hat plans often involve whether or not the plan is "unfunded" and whether the plan is for management or highly compensated employees. Various case law on these issues provides some clarification, but overall, each situation is a facts-and-circumstances test and will need to be specifically analyzed.

LABOR LAWS AND REGULATIONS

Compensation committees generally have little interaction with labor laws, since most of such laws are with respect to rank-and-file employees and not executives. However, issues concerning executives usually arise with respect to:

- Over age 40 discrimination under the Age Discrimination in Employment Act of 1967 (ADEA), as amended by the Older Workers Benefit Protection Act of 1991 (OWBPA)
- Sex, race, religion, color, or national origin discrimination under Title VII of the Civil Rights Act of 1964, as amended by the Civil Rights Acts of 1972 and 1991
- Disability discrimination under the Americans with Disabilities Act of 1990
- Equal Pay Act
- Fair Labor Standards Act
- Family and Medical Leave Act
- For executives serving in the military, the Uniformed Services Employment and Reemployment Rights Act (USERRA)
- Various similar statutes under state and local laws

Generally, the issue is whether the executive has—or could have—a claim under any of the preceding laws. If the executive has a claim (e.g., a sex discrimination claim), then it usually becomes a matter for the company and its legal department and not for the compensation committee. However, if the executive is willing to waive any and all claims, then the compensation committee needs to know the applicable rules involving waivers and releases, as discussed in the following section.

ADEA LAW

Section 623(a) of Title 29 of the United States Code (otherwise referred to as "ADEA") provides that it is unlawful for an employer to:

- Fail or refuse to hire or to discharge any individual or otherwise discriminate against any individual with respect to his compensation, terms, conditions, or privileges of employment, because of such individual's age.
- Limit, segregate, or classify his employees in any way which would deprive or tend to deprive any individual of employment opportunities or otherwise adversely affect his status as an employee, because of such individual's age.
- Reduce the wage rate of any employee in order to comply with ADEA.

ADEA Section 631(a) provides that the prohibitions against age discrimination are limited to individuals who are at least 40 years of age.

ADEA Section 631(c) provides that compulsory retirement of any employee who has attained 65 years of age, and who for the two-year period immediately before retirement is employed in a bona fide executive or a high policy-making position, is permissible, but only if such employee is entitled to an immediate nonforfeitable annual retirement benefit from a pension, profit-sharing, savings, or deferred compensation plan, or any combination of such plans, of the employer of such employee, which equals, in the aggregate, at least $44,000.

Since most executives are age 40 or over, ADEA is the starting point for all discrimination claims by executives. Presumably, compensation committees become involved in executive discrimination claims only as part of the severance process. In determining the ultimate value of the severance package, a waiver and release of all employment-related claims (and many times, any and all claims) by the terminated executive is required before any severance will be paid.

WAIVERS AND RELEASES UNDER ADEA

ADEA Section 626 contains the rules relating to waiver and release of age discrimination claims. Since severance agreements typically do not separate out various discrimination claims and all other claims that are being waived, the Section 626 requirements usually are applied across the board. However, there are a few examples, due to the revocation period discussed below, in which the waiver and release of all of an executive's claims against the company is bifurcated into ADEA releases and non-ADEA releases.

ADEA Section 626(f) provides that an individual may not waive any right or claim under ADEA unless the waiver is knowing and voluntary. Generally, the waiver will not be considered knowing and voluntary unless at a minimum:

- The waiver is part of an agreement between the individual and the employer that is written in a manner calculated to be understood by such individual, or by the average individual eligible to participate.
- The waiver specifically refers to rights or claims arising under ADEA.
- The individual does not waive rights or claims that may arise after the date the waiver is executed.
- The individual waives rights or claims only in exchange for consideration in addition to anything of value to which the individual already is entitled.
- The individual is advised in writing to consult with an attorney prior to executing the agreement.
- The individual is given a period of at least 21 days within which to consider the agreement; or if a waiver is requested in connection with an exit incentive or other employment termination program offered to a group or class of employees, the individual is given a period of at least 45 days within which to consider the agreement.

- The agreement provides that for a period of at least seven days following the execution of such agreement, the individual may revoke the agreement, and the agreement shall not become effective or enforceable until the revocation period has expired.

- If a waiver is requested in connection with an exit incentive or other employment termination program offered to a group or class of employees, the employer (at the commencement of the applicable 45-day period mentioned previously) informs the individual in writing in a manner calculated to be understood by the average individual eligible to participate, as to any class, unit, or group of individuals covered by such program, any eligibility factors for such program, and any time limits applicable to such program; and the job titles and ages of all individuals eligible or selected for the program, and the ages of all individuals in the same job classification or organizational unit who are not eligible or selected for the program.

EXECUTIVE WAIVERS AND RELEASES

The 1991 OWBPA amendments to ADEA requiring the above conditions to have an enforceable ADEA release changed the way most executive general releases were drafted. It is now quite common for most of the above provisions to be explicitly contained in an executive separation or termination agreements or in the actual waiver and release. More importantly, these releases are usually drafted so that these provisions apply to the entire release, which is for *all* claims against the company, not just for age discrimination claims. The termination document may be drafted so that the above provisions only apply to the release of the ADEA claims and not to any other claims, but that is very uncommon. In addition, applying the ADEA Section 626(f) provisions only to ADEA can be cumbersome. Thus, many termination arrangements incorporate the ADEA Section 626(f) provisions and apply them to all claims.

While all of the ADEA Section 626(f) provisions listed above are important (e.g., 21-day review period, advisement to consult with an attorney prior to execution of the release), perhaps the most critical is the seven-day revocation period. This generally means that most severance payments will never be made (or begin if installments) until the expiration of the seven-day revocation period. Executives sometimes insist that payment be made on the termination date, which of course compensation committees cannot approve.

Finally, the compensation committee should be aware of a situation that occurs from time to time. The fact pattern typically involves a termination of the executive, in which all of the terms and the conditions of the termination arrangement have been negotiated and agreed to by the company and the executive but where the executive will continue working or otherwise still be involved with the company for some time after the execution of the termination agreement. Because the executive cannot release future claims, it becomes necessary for the executive to sign two releases:

1. The first release is signed on the date the termination agreement is executed, and which becomes effective after the expiration of the seven-day revocation period, and releases all claims prior to the date of the execution of the termination date, and

2. A second release, which is executed on the date of the executive's termination from the company, and which becomes effective after the expiration of the seven-day revocation period, and releases all claims that the executive might have for the period beginning on the date of the first release and ending on the date of the second release.

Example: On November 1, Company X terminates Executive Y and both parties agree that Executive Y will continue to be employed by Company X until December 31. The termination agreement and general release are both executed on November 1. The terms of the termination agreement provide for a $1 million severance payable in two equal installments. The first installment of $500,000 will be paid on the expiration of the seven-day revocation period under the general release, which releases all of Executive Y's claims against Company X up through November 1. The second installment will be paid only after Executive Y signs a second release, which releases all of Executive Y's claims against Company X from November 1st through December 31. In addition, the second installment of $500,000 will not be paid until the expiration of the second release's seven-day revocation period (e.g. – January 7).

Part Three

Practical Applications

Chapter 11

Executive Employment, Severance, and Change-in-Control Arrangements

This chapter discusses the compensation committee's primary role in the structuring, negotiation, and implementation of employment, severance, and change-in-control arrangements for a company's top executives. It also discusses current market-based practices and attitudes with respect to whether and why a company—primarily through its compensation committee—would consider entering into these arrangements.

This chapter is divided into the following topics:

- Background
- The process involved in determining whether a company should enter into formal employment, severance, and/or change-in-control arrangements for its top executives
- Types and forms of employment arrangements
- Terms and conditions, and other elements of these arrangements

Generally, this chapter assumes that the compensation committee is establishing and implementing employment arrangements for the company's CEO and other senior executives, not rank-and-file employees.

BACKGROUND

Essentially, there are two basic and distinct employment arrangements:

1. An "at-will" employment arrangement, generally evidenced by the *lack* of a written agreement
2. A "contract" or written employment arrangement, generally evidenced by some written agreement and/or plan, or a group of written agreements and/or plans

Thus, an employment arrangement that is *not* at-will typically is evidenced by a formal written employment agreement. However, compensation committees must recognize that these "non-at-will" arrangements may be evidenced by many other types of agreements and plans. Thus, for example, many of the elements contained in an individual executive employment agreement could be contained in an executive severance plan.

AT-WILL EMPLOYMENT ARRANGEMENTS

An at-will employment arrangement is an arrangement in which the employee serves at the unilateral pleasure of the employer. It means simply that an employee may be terminated by his or her employer at any time without notice for any reason or for no reason. A "true" at-will employment arrangement means that there are no written employment agreements, plans, letters, or similar writing. In an at-will employment arrangement, the employer makes no promises to the employee, and thus the employer has no legal obligation to the employee (e.g., minimum salary level, severance) other than what is required by state or federal law (e.g., state wage laws, federal and state employee benefit laws, federal and state discrimination laws, etc.). In an at-will arrangement, the employer basically can do "what, where, when, how and why" it wants with the employee. For example, the employer could relocate the employee from one state to another. Or the employer could significantly reduce the employee's base salary. Or the employer could change the employee's title or duties and responsibilities. In any of these situations, unless protected by law, the employee's only recourse—if he or she does not agree with the changes—is to quit.

The only instance in which a true at-will employment arrangement is evidenced by a written document is where there is an employment offer letter. This document typically states that the employer offers employment to the employee-candidate, and usually states the beginning salary. However, these letters generally do not contain any promises that the employee-candidate will be employed for any period of time. Similarly, there are no promises that the salary (or other compensation and benefits) will be at any minimum levels. Thus, an employment offer letter is not in and of itself a contract. It becomes a contract only if it contains promises by the company that are enforceable under law.

There is a recent trend to provide in formal contractual employment arrangements that the employer-employee relationship is *at-will*. The intent of such term is to allow the employer the right to terminate the employee's employment at any time and to not technically breach the employment agreement, which could give rise to legal action. However (as discussed below), the use of such provision is not completely accurate and can be somewhat disingenuous. Suffice it to say that some references to an "at-will" employment arrangement where there is a written contract may simply mean that the form follows a "modern" employment agreement (as discussed in more detail below).

While many shareholders and other corporate governance groups are against the use of employment agreements, the fact remains that most top executives who are contemplating joining a new company often will not agree to an at-will employment arrangement. Accordingly, compensation committees will need to take this into account at the beginning of any executive recruiting process and negotiation. As discussed below, from the executive's perspective, the risk that the new employer will have a "change of heart" and prematurely terminate the executive (i.e., before bonuses are paid or equity-based compensation vests) will be seriously considered by the executive in determining whether he or she will leave the current employer. Thus, most top executives joining a new company will arduously seek to have some kind of written employment arrangement. Obviously, this will depend on the bargaining position and strength of the parties. But even if the company's culture is not to have any written employment arrangements, in most cases in which a new top executive is recruited from outside the company, it is likely that the company will have to make some promises to the executive with respect to the basic elements of the employment arrangement (i.e., sign-on compensation, compensation during employment, and postemployment compensation).

CONTRACTUAL EMPLOYMENT ARRANGEMENTS

Over the past few decades, there has been a dramatic change in the written executive employment agreement. Specifically, since the late 1980s, contract employment agreements have consisted of two distinct types:

1. The "classic" or "traditional" employment agreement
2. The "modern" employment agreement

It should be noted that the classic employment agreement generally has been replaced by the modern employment agreement.

THE CLASSIC EMPLOYMENT AGREEMENT

The "classic" or "traditional" employment agreement is a written agreement whereby the employer and the employee (or independent contractor) simply agree to a specific type of employment over a set period of time. Set forth in the agreement is the amount of compensation (whether fixed or variable) that will be paid over such time period. In a classic employment agreement, the employer cannot "fire" the employee and the employee cannot "quit" unless the employment agreement is amended or terminated by both parties. If the employer were to fire the employee or if the employee were to quit under a classic employment agreement, such action would constitute a breach of the employment agreement. And as with any material breach of a provision in a contract, the nonbreaching party may sue the breaching party in a court of law for money damages that flow from such breach. Thus, under a classic employment agreement, if the employee is fired, the damage amount typically would be calculated based on the unpaid compensation under the contract, and not based on a concept of severance or wage continuation (although the end result might be the same).

THE MODERN EMPLOYMENT AGREEMENT

The vast majority of current executive employment arrangements do not follow the classic employment agreement form. The fundamental difference is that the contract provides for what would have been specific "liquidated damages" (i.e., severance payments and other benefits) if there had been a specific breach of the agreement (i.e., a termination of employment by the company without Cause). This generally means that failure by the company or by the executive to fulfill certain of its or his/her promises is not a breach of the agreement *per se* but a trigger that allows the other party to terminate the employment arrangement. Accordingly, both the executive and the company generally are free to terminate the employment arrangement at any time (perhaps subject to a reasonable notice requirement) or for any reason. This essentially simulates the at-will employment arrangement with one major difference: that it is a specific type of termination of employment, whether by the company or by the executive, that will determine what benefits (if any) the executive will be entitled to receive as a direct result of such termination.

FUNDAMENTAL ELEMENTS OF A WRITTEN EMPLOYMENT ARRANGEMENT

There are three primary elements of a written employment arrangement:

1. The promises made by the parties to one another that are in effect during the period of employment (including sign-on compensation)
2. The promises made by the parties to one another in effect after the termination of employment
3. Miscellaneous provisions that generally are applicable at all times

The promises made by the parties during the employment period generally are:

- From the company's perspective, the compensation and benefits that the company will pay to the executive for doing his or her job during the employment period
- From the executive's perspective, the promises he or she makes to the company regarding how, when, and/or where he or she will perform his or her job during the employment period

Thus, for example, the company might promise to provide to the executive an annual grant of a long-term incentive (LTI) compensation award equal to *x* percent of base salary. Under a classic employment agreement, if the company did not pay to the executive that LTI compensation award, there would be a breach of the contract and the executive could sue the company. Under a modern employment agreement, while there still would be a breach (which still allows the executive to sue), the failure to pay the annual LTI compensation award typically would provide a "Good Reason" for the executive to terminate his or her employment and receive severance payments as if the executive had been terminated by the company without Cause.

The promises made by the parties for the period following employment generally are:

- From the company's perspective, the compensation (i.e., severance) and benefits that the company will pay to the executive for having prematurely terminated the executive's employment

- From the executive's perspective, the promises he or she makes to the company regarding post-termination behavior and activity (e.g., confidentiality, noncompetition, nonsolicitiation, nondisparagement, cooperation, and other restrictive covenants)

The miscellaneous provisions contained in a written employment agreement typically cover:

- Indemnification

- Dispute resolution

- Representations

- Notices

- Amendment

- Assignment

- Various legal "boilerplate" provisions.

PROCESS

The threshold question that a compensation committee must first ask and answer is whether the company should even enter into a written agreement with the company's executives regarding the employment arrangement. Similar to a company's "compensation policy/philosophy" that is developed by the compensation committee and disclosed in the company's proxy statement, the compensation committee should develop an "executive employment policy/philosophy" for the company to follow.

Years ago, the process typically was that the company, usually acting through a board member and/or general counsel for chief executive officer (CEO) hirings, and through its CEO for all other executive hirings, would negotiate and structure an employment arrangement. After the negotiations were finalized, it would be presented to the board. In many cases, for CEOs and some top executives, this meant the execution of a formal employment agreement, which the board was supposed to review. It was too often the case that the board simply rubber-stamped the arrangement. The compensation committee may or may not have reviewed the arrangement before it was presented to the board, whether due to timing concerns, a *laissez-faire* attitude, or simply that such activities in the past were not part of the compensation committee's duties and responsibilities. Those days, for all intents and purposes, are over.

Today, either the compensation committee, a search committee, or some other committee of the board will take the lead in the search for the executive recruit. More importantly, this committee will also take the lead in negotiating the employment arrangement with the executive. This generally means that the chair of that committee will engage and have complete interaction with the executive recruiter (if one is used) and with the executive recruit. This also means that the decision as to whether to enter into an at-will employment arrangement, a contract employment arrangement, or something in between will be made by the committee. For the rest of this chapter, it will be assumed that it is the compensation committee that has been charged with the search for and selection of the executive.

The compensation committee generally will need any or all of the following professionals at its disposal to effectively carry out its duties and responsibilities in hiring an executive:

- Executive recruiter
- Executive compensation lawyer
- Executive compensation consultant

Experienced professionals are essential to help the committee through this process. Executive compensation market data—with respect to both compensation levels and other terms and conditions of these arrangements—need to be reviewed by the committee. This data should be taken into account in formulating an employment and compensation package; however, it should never be the sole driver of the package. Finally, the written documents will need to be straightforward and precise, reflecting the true intent of the parties to the employment arrangement and with an eye to public disclosure.

Extreme care should be taken if the compensation committee selects the company's general counsel to represent the committee. Simply put, it has often been said by many attorneys who represent CEOs that the best lawyer to represent the company in these CEO negotiations was the company's General Counsel, since the attorney's CEO client would ultimately (if hired) be the General Counsel's boss. Similarly, the use of the company's outside legal counsel may present a conflict or independence issue, particularly if the new CEO will have (as is often the case) decision-making authority with respect to the continued use of that specific outside legal counsel by the company.

Throughout this process, issues relating to tax law, accounting, securities law, and other regulatory authority most likely will impact the design and structure of an employment arrangement. In addition, if the executive recruit would violate a noncompetition provision if he or she were to become an employee of the company, then the cause and effect of such violation will need to be addressed, discussed, and resolved. In some cases, the resolution will be to pass on the executive recruit. In other cases, the compensation committee may decide to go forward with such recruit; however, then the issue of who bears the risk if the noncompetition provision is enforced will need to be addressed and resolved.

Finally, confidentiality is extremely important during this process, as there are countless examples of potential hirings that have been scuttled by "leaks." Accordingly, for both the company and the executive, caution and care will need to be taken. Of course, maintaining such confidentiality can be a Herculean task, and will always assert time pressure on both the executive recruit and the compensation committee during the negotiations.

TYPES OF EMPLOYMENT ARRANGEMENTS

Employment arrangements may be memorialized in writing in a wide variety of types and forms. The first distinction is whether the arrangement should be individual (i.e., an "agreement") or group (i.e., a plan, program, scheme, or similar arrangements).

INDIVIDUALIZED ARRANGEMENTS

Individual arrangements generally consist of one or more of the following:

- Employment offer letter
- Employment agreement
- Severance agreement
- Change-in-control severance agreement
- Incentive compensation document
- Transaction compensation agreement
- Supplemental executive retirement plan (SERP) or deferred compensation arrangement
- Retention agreement

GROUP ARRANGEMENTS

Group arrangements generally consist of one or more of the following:

- Severance plans
- Change-in-control severance plans
- Incentive compensation plans
- Transaction compensation plan
- SERP or deferred compensation plans

- Executive welfare-benefit plans
- Retention plans

INDIVIDUAL VERSUS GROUP ARRANGEMENTS

Many compensation committees prefer to work with group arrangements rather than individual arrangements. In a group arrangement, the compensation committee will discuss and approve the material terms and conditions of the arrangement only once. After that, the decision-making actions with respect to a specific executive generally will involve determining the plans in which the executive will participate and the compensation and benefit levels that the executive will receive. Thus, the paperwork to be reviewed and approved typically involves a "term sheet," an employment offer letter, and one or more "participation" agreements in the applicable plans, all of which are each one or two pages long.

The advantages of using a group arrangement are that the arrangement is "institutionalized" and formalized through the plan document. For example, assume that the company has an Executive Severance Plan (ESP), and the plan document contains a definition for *Cause*. When the company hires a new CEO, instead of negotiating the definition of *Cause* with the CEO recruit, the company simply offers to have the CEO recruit become a participant in the ESP. As a participant in the ESP, the new CEO would automatically accept that definition of *Cause*. The underlying rationale, of course, is that this definition applies to all of the members of the executive team who participate in the ESP. While this rationale is often used in negotiating individual agreements (e.g., the definition of *Cause* is what is used in the current CEO's employment agreement), the fact remains that negotiating changes to an individual agreement always is easier than negotiating changes to a plan.

However, there may be instances in which an executive that the committee is absolutely intent on hiring simply will not accept the terms of the existing plan. This forces the compensation committee to:

- Provide for the "different" definitions, terms, and conditions in the participation agreement (e.g., some plans provide that "unless otherwise defined in another written agreement between the company and the participant, *Cause* shall mean . . .).
- Amend the plan (which may result in the application of the new definitions, terms and conditions to other participants).
- Enter into an individual agreement rather than have the executive be a participant in the plan (which defeats the overarching reason for using group arrangements).

Finally, a company that uses only group employment arrangement may be able to state its public disclosures that it does not have "individual employment agreements." Although this may be somewhat disingenuous, certainly there is a distinction (small though it may be) between negotiating and entering into an individual employment agreement each time a new executive is hired (and which could contain significantly different terms and conditions than those in the last employment agreement) compared with having the terms and conditions of employment institutionalized and spread over a variety of group arrangements. Ultimately, the compensation committee will need to determine which course best fits its philosophy, but taking into account the facts and circumstances of the particular situation.

TERMS AND CONDITIONS CONTAINED IN EMPLOYMENT ARRANGEMENTS

While the type of form of the employment arrangements may differ, the terms and conditions of the employment arrangement are applicable to all written arrangements, whether contained in a specific formal employment agreement or spread over several different group arrangements.

Below are the terms and conditions that typically are addressed in most employment agreements. Some, of course, are also addressed in severance, change-in-control, and other written arrangements. For example, executive severance plans usually contain only those terms and conditions in connection with post-termination promises, although may in some cases provide that a change of the status quo (e.g., reduction of base salary) is a Good Reason.

PARTIES

Identification of the parties in most written arrangements generally will be a fairly easy matter. If the arrangement is an individual arrangement, then the parties will be the company and the executive. If the arrangement is a group arrangement, then the company will have established and adopted a plan, and the executive will become a participant in the plan through board or committee action, which usually will be evidenced by some form of participation agreement or letter.

However, complex corporate structures involving subsidiaries, parents, holding companies, joint ventures, and so on, may require that the documents provide more specificity as to who all the parties are. Executives sometimes insist that the parent or holding company be a party to and a signatory of a contract, or that the parent or holding company agree in the document or in another writing that it will guarantee the compensation and benefits obligated to be provided by the subsidiary or operating company.

TERM OF ARRANGEMENT/EMPLOYMENT PERIOD

Traditional employment agreements used the concept of a "term of the agreement," which usually related to the period of employment. The problem with using a "term of the agreement" is that following the termination of the agreement (which also almost always terminates the employment period), there still can be post-termination of employment obligations on the part of both the company and the executive. This then requires what is known as a "survival provision," which provides that certain obligations continue beyond the termination of the term of the agreement. It is not uncommon for this kind of agreement to recite that "Sections 8, 9, 10, 12, and 13 shall survive the termination of this Agreement" or that "any provision by its own terms that should survive the termination of this Agreement shall so survive."

Most modern employment agreements have moved away from the concept of a term of the agreement and now focus on the concept of the term of employment (commonly referred to simply as the *employment period*). This then raises the following questions:

- Is the intent of the parties to have a fixed employment period, which terminates on a date certain (or earlier if the executive quits or is fired)? This is commonly referred to as a *fixed-term arrangement*. Under a fixed-term agreement, there are three scenarios that can play out at the end of the employment period:

  1. The parties will actively and affirmatively negotiate a new agreement regarding a new employment period (which may be done before or even after the expiration of the existing fixed term).

  2. There is no negotiation, and the last day of the employment period becomes the last day of the executive's employment.

  3. The parties negotiate but agree that although the executive's employment will continue after the end of the employment period, it will do so without a written agreement or other document (i.e., after the end of the fixed term, the executive's employment will be a true at-will employment arrangement).

- Is it the intent of the parties to have a variable employment period that is subject to some automatic renewal trigger (commonly referred to as an "evergreen" arrangement) unless the parties notify the other that the employment period will not renew? In this situation, the evergreen may occur once or be successive. It could trigger at the end of the "initial" employment period for the same number of years (e.g., a three-year employment period will automatically renew into another three-year employment period) or could renew for a shorter period of time (e.g., many executive employment agreements begin with a three-year employment period and then automatically renew for successive one-year periods). Or the employment period could be a "rolling" employment period, which generally means that the employment period renews daily or monthly so that the employment period always remain the same number of days or months (e.g., the employment period is for a three-year period which automatically renews daily for one day, resulting in a "perpetual" three-year employment period).

- Is it the intent of the parties that the executive will be an employee until he or she either quits (including retirement) or is fired? If this is the situation, then the contract usually recites that the employment period begins on an "effective date" (typically the first day of employment) and ends on the date of a termination of employment. The result, of course, is that there is no stated employment period.

The reason that most executives and compensation committees become fixated on an employment period is to determine severance benefits. Under the classic employment agreement, the severance period was measured by the remaining employment period (or term of the agreement). Thus, the severance period would "burn down" as the executive continued working. For example, if the executive were terminated in the 35th month of a 36-month employment period under a classic employment agreement, he or she would receive a severance based on a severance period of just one month.

As mentioned above, the concept of severance as it applied under a classic employment agreement has been transformed under the modern employment agreement. A modern employment agreement typically provides for a severance based on a specific severance period (e.g., 24 months), even if—theoretically—the termination occurs shortly before the end of the fixed employment period. Thus, in the example above in which the executive was terminated in the 35th month, he or she would get the full severance benefit (e.g., 24 months of severance). A combination of the classic employment agreement and the modern employment agreement is where the contract provides that the severance will be measured by the greater of the remaining term of the employment period (or term of the agreement) or a fixed severance period. For example, if the employment period were five years, the severance might be the greater of (1) the remaining employment period or (2) three years. And a variation of that combination is a "burn-down" severance period where the severance period is the shorter of the remaining employment period or a fixed severance (e.g., the lesser of (1) two years or (2) the remainder of the employment period, but no less than six months).

However, some modern employment agreements simply recite a severance period irrespective of the remaining employment period, and thus the only impact that the employment period seems to have is whether or not the parties renew the arrangement, and if not then what severance (if any) the executive is entitled to receive. However, if the intent of the parties is to have the executive work until that point in time when his or her employment is terminated (for whatever reason), then the employment period is illusory and should most likely be discarded.

TITLES, DUTIES, RESPONSIBILITIES, AUTHORITY, REPORTING, AND OFFICE LOCATION

Employment agreements and employment letters almost always recite the titles, duties, responsibilities, authority, and reporting arrangements associated with the position. The reasons for this are several. First, it tells the executive what the company expects of him or her during employment. Second, it provides the parameters of authority associated with the position. Finally, it defines from the executive's perspective the scope of the executive's titles, duties, responsibilities, reporting obligations, and office location, and assures the executive that any material change of these items would be a breach of the agreement by the company.

Following is a brief discussion of each:

- *Titles.* These are typically straightforward and without controversy, and generally are used for executive ranking and grouping purposes. Sometimes the title will include subsidiary company titles as well as parent company titles (e.g., Executive Vice President and Chief Operating officer of Parent X and Chairman and Chief Executive Officer of Subsidiary Y). Care should be taken with titles that require approval from outside the management or committee level (e.g., a member of the board of directors of the company may need to be elected by shareholders, an Executive Chairman of the Board will need to be appointed by the full board, etc.). Finally, there are arrangements in which the executive is hired at one title and position, but is promised another or additional title and position within a set period of time (e.g., the executive was hired as President and Chief Operating Officer, but will become CEO before the end of the first year of employment). A typical provision might recite that "the Executive shall be President and CEO of the Company at all times after the Effective Date, and the Company shall cause the Executive to become Chairman of the Board on or prior to the second anniversary of the Effective Date."

- *Duties, responsibilities, and authority.* These provisions detail the executive's job functions. This may be with specificity or may be general and broad (e.g., the CEO will be responsible for the general affairs of the company). In addition, these provisions typically will recite some or all of the following promises by the executive that he or she will:
  - Devote substantially all of his/her time to the business of the company.
  - Use his/her best efforts in carrying out his/her duties.
  - Perform in the best interests of the company.

It is quite common to have a provision that exempts "permissible outside activities," so long as such activity does not "materially interfere" with the executive's duties and responsibilities, such as:

  - Serving on corporate and noncorporate boards (sometime subject to board approval and sometimes limited in number)
  - Working for charitable organizations or public service agencies
  - Speaking or teaching
  - Managing the executive's personal/financial affairs

- *Reporting.* Most executives are concerned with to whom he or she will report, and—in a few instances—who will report to the executive. For CEOs, the concern is to report directly (and sometimes solely) to the board, unless another arrangement has been negotiated (e.g., to the Chairman or to the Lead Director). Most senior executives will want to report directly to the CEO and not allow the company to deviate (e.g., without an explicit provision, a senior vice president of human resources who had been a direct report to the CEO could be later "rerouted" to directly report to the executive vice president and general counsel of the company). A change in the reporting relation usually will serve as "Good Reason."

- *Office location.* Some arrangements will specify the office location while others will not, which usually indicates whether office location is a material term of the arrangement. In some cases, the provision will recite merely that the executive's office will be at the company's headquarters or at its executive offices. In other cases, it will even state that the executive will have a "suitable and appropriate office commensurate with the executive's title and duties." Thus, this provision typically arises either because the executive believes there is a legitimate concern with respect to office location or, in more cases, simply because the provision found its way into one of the company's agreements and now has been imbedded as "company culture." A change in the office location (whether stated or not) or relocation of the office to a location that is a set number of miles away from the existing location usually will serve as a "Good Reason."

COMPENSATION AND BENEFITS

Generally, the payment or delivery of compensation and benefits are the company's major promises to the executive during the employment period, and consist of the following:

- Base salary
- Annual (or short-term) bonus
- Long-term incentive compensation (either cash or equity)
- Special compensation
- Employee benefits
- Executive benefits
- Perquisites
- Reimbursement of expenses
- Vacation

Base Salary

A promise regarding base salary is usually found only in employment offer letters or employment agreements. In an employment offer letter, the promise may be that the starting salary is $x per year with a guarantee that the salary will never be decreased, or might even contain an incremental salary schedule. Employment agreements typically contain one or more of the following:

- A promise of a minimum "base salary" during the employment period, and if such "base salary" is increased, then such increased amount will become the new "base salary" for purposes of the agreement
- A promise that the base salary will be periodically reviewed (usually at least annually) by either the board or the compensation committee, but the decision to increase the base salary lies solely in the discretion of the board or the committee
- A built-in cost-of-living-adjustment provision

A change in the base salary (and, for that matter, any set compensation or benefit level promised in the agreement) will serve as a "Good Reason"; however, sometimes the company is allowed to reduce the base salary if such reduction is applied across-the-board to all senior executives (although typically the reduction has a floor, such as 10 percent).

Annual/Short-Term Incentive Compensation

This promise usually is found in employment offer letters, employment agreements, or stand-alone compensation arrangements (which may include a plan and/or an award document). The elements are as follows:

- Formula to determine minimum (also called "threshold"), target, and maximum bonus, typically based on a percentage of base salary, but also can be a fixed dollar amount
- The date of payment of the bonus and when the bonus is "earned" (i.e., in some instances the bonus is earned on the last day of the company's fiscal year (assuming the executive is still employed on such date) or, in other instances, the bonus is earned on the date that the bonus is paid)
- Any guaranteed amounts (typical for new hires)
- Whether a pro rata bonus will be paid if there is a termination without Cause or for Good Reason, or a termination due to death, disability, or retirement.

Annual Grant of Long-Term Incentive Compensation

As with the annual bonus, this promise usually is found in employment offer letters, employment agreements, or stand-alone compensation agreements. The various arrangements (whether contained in an individual agreement or letter or in written group arrangements) are as follows:

- The terms of the arrangement provides a set annual level and perhaps a set type of LTI compensation, similar to what is typically provided under the annual bonus arrangement. Thus, a typical provision might provide that "the CEO shall be entitled to receive an annual LTI award with a target equal to x percent of Base Salary and a maximum equal to y percent of Base Salary, 50 percent of which will be full-value awards and 50 percent will be at-the-money appreciation-type awards, with such grant-date award values determined based on FAS 123R fair value valuation methodology."

- The terms of the arrangement will provide only for participation in LTI compensation program. Thus, a typical provision might provide that "the Executive shall be entitled to participate in the Company's LTI compensation plans, programs, and arrangements in effect from time to time and subject to revision or termination by the Board in its sole discretion at any time, and such participation shall be commensurate with his or her position as [CFO] and Executive shall be entitled to receive award levels similar to those granted to other similarly situated senior executives."
- No provision whatsoever.

Special Compensation

This usually relates to "sign-on" compensation that consists of two elements:

1. A portion representing the amount that the executive is forfeiting from his or her current employer in order to take the position with the new company.
2. A portion (if any) representing an inducement for the executive to take the position.

The form of this compensation can be cash or equity or a combination of the two. Typically, with respect to the make-whole amount, the type of compensation forfeited is replaced with the same type of compensation. For example, if an executive is giving up $x of restricted stock, then $x of restricted stock of the new company is awarded (and usually with a similar vesting schedule). What has become more complex is replacing vested and unvested appreciation-type awards with similar vested and unvested appreciation-type awards. While there are cases in which unvested underwater stock options at the current employer were replaced with at-the-money stock options at the new employer (which was to some degree a functional equivalent of a "repricing"), many compensation committees have embraced the concept that is often used in corporate transaction, in which the rules underlying the assumption and substitution of Internal Revenue Code (IRC) Section 422 "incentive stock options" are applied pursuant to IRC Section 424(a) (discussed in Chapter 8). This means that the economics are preserved by using both a "ratio test" and a "spread test." Another method is to use option pricing models (such as Black-Scholes) to equally value the forfeited and make-whole options, but in which the aggregate positive or negative spread in the option is generally maintained.

There may be a trend developing in which sign-on bonuses (whether cash or full-value awards) are being used to "replace" a severance obligation. For example, a compensation committee is committed to not having formal severance arrangements (whether individual or group), but has a CEO recruit that will not join unless there is some form of severance protection during the first few years. Thus, the company pays a fixed-cash amount or makes a special equity-compensation grant. The cash amount is subject to repayment by the executive (commonly referred to as a "clawback") if he or she terminates employment without Good Reason or is terminated for Cause. Similarly, the equity award is subject to a cliff-vesting schedule and will be fully forfeited if the executive terminates employment without Good Reason or is terminated for Cause. Thus, under this arrangement, there is a retention arrangement coupled with a "prepaid" severance. For example, assume that Company X wants to recruit Executive Y as its CEO, who would be leaving an established position with a formal employment agreement. Assume that Company X's policy is not to have employment agreements or executive severance plans. Finally, assume that Executive X, who is being offered a base salary of $1 million and an annual target bonus of 150 percent of base salary, is insisting on a severance level equal to 200 percent of the sum of base salary and target bonus. The solution might be to provide a sign-on bonus of $5 million in cash or full-value awards that will vest at the earlier of four years or a termination of employment without Cause or for Good Reason. While such arrangement certainly can be seen as having "severance-like" elements, it does not rise to a formal severance arrangement.

Employee/Executive Benefits and Perquisites

The basic provision is to provide the executive with participation in all of the company's rank-and-file employee-benefit plans, programs, and arrangements. In many cases, the provision will also provide that executive with participation in all of the company's benefit and perquisite plans, programs, and arrangements applicable to senior executives. It may also recite specific individual benefits (such as SERPs or other deferred compensation arrangements, special life insurance, or other insurance arrangements) and special perquisites (such as relocation, security, business travel, or club membership). Of course, as executive perquisites and other executive benefits are being scrutinized by shareholders and the press, it is important to make sure that these arrangements generally are appropriate and market-based, recognizing that each case must be examined under its particular and specific facts and circumstances.

Reimbursement of Expenses

This is typically recited in employment agreements and employment letter agreements, and simply provides that the executive will (usually promptly) be reimbursed for all reasonable business expenses incurred by the executive in the performance of his or her duties, and in accordance with the company's business reimbursement policy in effect from time to time.

Vacation

Vacation provisions usually are found in employment offer letters and employment agreements, and typically state that the executive will subject to company's vacation policy in effect from time to time. However, some executives may seek a minimum number of vacation days, as well as the retention of unused vacation days (particularly if the company has a "use-it-or-lose-it" vacation day policy).

TERMINATIONS OF EMPLOYMENT

For the obvious reason, almost all executive employment arrangements contain termination-of-employment provisions. Employment agreements and severance plans (both non-change-in-control plans and change-in-control plans) will address most or all of the following "10 Terminations":

1. Termination due to death
2. Termination due to disability
3. Termination by the company for Cause
4. Termination by the company without Cause
5. Termination by the executive for Good Reason
6. Termination by the executive without Good Reason
7. Retirement
8. Nonrenewal of the employment term by the company
9. Nonrenewal of the employment term by the executive
10. Termination in connection with a change in control (discussed in the next section)

Under a classic employment agreement, these terminations (other than death or disability and nonrenewal) would be a breach of the agreement. As mentioned above, the modern employment agreement provides for some or all of these terminations and explicitly provides that the termination is permitted under the agreement or arrangement (but with resulting consequences).

Death

Most employment documents will specify that the death of the executive terminates the employment period. Post-termination compensation and benefits can vary from nothing beyond what rank-and-file employees receive to continuation of salary, payment of bonus (full or pro rata), vesting of equity-based and other incentive (full or partial).

Many compensation committees use life insurance to provide a cash death benefit to the executive's designated beneficiary in lieu of continued salary, payment of incentive compensation, and so on. Depending on the insurability of the executive, insurance can be a logical and inexpensive solution for a company compared with "self-funding" a death benefit through continued compensation and vesting of incentive awards.

Disability

Most employment agreements will allow the company (and sometimes the executive) to terminate employment due to a *disability*, which usually is defined in the agreement as a disability under the company's long-term disability (LTD) program or the inability to perform the executive's duties and responsibilities for a set number of consecutive days or a set number of nonconsecutive days in any set period of time. The purpose is for the company to be able to terminate the executive who can no longer effectively serve the company, although some contracts explicitly or implicitly provide that the executive also has the right to terminate his or her employment for disability. Sometimes these arrangements only provide for benefits under the company's rank-and-file LTD program. As these LTD benefits usually are capped and thus inadequate for highly compensated executives, companies may provide additional LTD benefits through an executive program or directly through the employment agreement.

For Cause or Poor Performance

Typically, terminations for Cause in most arrangements will be driven by the definition of Cause contained in the written agreement. In almost all cases, Cause represents egregious actions on the part of the executive. Common definitions of Cause include some or many of the following actions by the executive:

- Commission/indictment/conviction for a felony; typically a conviction is required
- Commission/indictment/conviction for a misdemeanor (usually this is qualified by requiring a misdemeanor involving some level of "fraud, dishonesty, misappropriation, etc." or "moral turpitude," and typically this also requires a conviction)
- Commission/indictment/conviction for a securities law violation (usually this requires a conviction or an indictment)
- Refusal to cooperate with authorities
- Material breach of the contract or plan provision
- Acts constituting misconduct (typically "willful") or negligence (typically "gross")
- Failure to follow the reasonable lawful directions of the company's board of directors or the executive's supervisor
- Failure to perform, but usually subject to written notification and that the failure is continued and/or willful
- Violation of company policy, code of ethics, or other internal regulation
- For certain industries, loss of license necessary to perform the executive's duties (e.g., in the casino industry, a gaming license)

Many times the above items may be qualified by use of the word *material*, *substantial*, *significant*, *gross*, *willful*, and so on. *Willful* is sometimes defined as the executive acting or failing to act in bad faith and/or not in the best interests of the company. In addition, sometimes the activity needs to result in some kind of harm or damage to the company (usually material or substantial, sometimes limited to demonstrable economic harm, etc.). Finally, often there is a "cure" provision if the action is curable, as well as a "due process" provision that requires the board to provide the executive with notice and an opportunity to be heard (usually with counsel) before the board.

As can be seen by the above list, the concept of Cause is that the executive has acted or failed to act in a malicious or egregious manner. Generally, it is not for poor performance. Thus, upon a termination for Cause, an executive is entitled to receive only earned base salary, unreimbursed expenses, and vested benefits (in other words, only those items that would be guaranteed by federal or state law). All other compensation and benefits are forfeited, which usually includes all vested and unvested equity compensation award.

There is a trend among compensation committees to seek to include the concept of "poor performance" in the definition of Cause. However, most executives (as well as some compensation consultants and attorneys) strenuously object to this concept due to the subjectivity and vagaries of what would constitute "poor performance." Some compensation committees, when hiring an executive to achieve certain results, may be able to set reasonable objective standards that would not constitute Cause but rather "Poor Performance." For example, assume an executive was hired to achieve annual sales of $1 billion. The arrangement might provide that failure to achieve the $1 billion annual sales target would be treated as poor performance. However, usually in such a case, the result is that the termination for poor performance is treated as a termination without Cause but resulting in reduced severance compensation and benefits.

Without Cause or for Good Reason

A termination without Cause generally results in some or most of the following termination compensation and benefits, depending on the position and the culture of the company; the severance period typically is expressed as a time period (e.g., 2 years or 24 months or as a multiple or percentage, e.g., as a "2 × " severance or a "200 percent severance"):

- Earned base salary, earned but unpaid bonuses, unreimbursed business expenses, cashout of unused vacation time

- Full or pro rata bonus (at target, last paid bonus, or average of recently paid bonuses) with respect to the year of termination (sometimes only if performance goals are actually met)

- Salary severance, payable in a lump sum or over the severance period

- Bonus severance (using target, last paid bonus, or average of recently paid bonuses), payable in a lump sum or over the severance period

- Continuation of some or all welfare-benefit arrangements over the severance period

- For full-value equity compensation awards, some additional benefit ranging from 100 percent immediate vesting to continued vesting over the severance period
- For appreciation-type equity compensation awards, the same vesting applied to full-value equity compensation award and sometimes with an extended exercise period
- For long-term incentive compensation awards that are purely cash-based, full or pro rata vesting and payout as if the target amount had been achieved or based on actual performance
- Continued indemnification

Some arrangements may or may not include the concept of Good Reason; however, if the arrangement does include the concept of Good Reason, the termination benefits for a termination for Good Reason generally are the same as the termination benefits for a termination without Cause.

The notion of a termination for Good Reason arose from the legal concept of a "constructive termination"; that is, when the executive's employment was not actually terminated, but nevertheless the company changed his or her job so dramatically, if not egregiously, that the executive was no longer performing for—or being treated by—the company for which he or she had been hired. Generally, the test is marginalization. The underlying purpose of a constructive termination is simply that the company wants to make the executive's working life so miserable that the executive surely will quit. For example, an international company with its headquarters in New York City—and for no apparent business purpose—assigns its CEO to an office in another country. Or the company assigns its chief financial official the addition of running the custodial services. If there were no Good Reason provision associated with the executive's employment contract, the executive could only claim constructive termination and/or breach of contract. But the important point is that the executive generally cannot quit until the constructive termination is proved. However, if there is a Good Reason provision associated with the executive's employment arrangements, then the executive could notify the company of the Good Reason event, and then—based on the precise wording of the provision—terminate his or her employment for Good Reason and collect severance benefits.

Typical provisions for Good Reason include some of the following events or actions that would constitute a Good Reason:

- Reduction/diminution (sometimes adverse and/or material) in title, duties, responsibilities, authority, or change in title
- Assignment of duties and responsibilities that are inconsistent (sometimes material and/or adverse) with the executive's current title and position
- Reduction of salary and/or target bonus (but sometimes with an "across-the-board" exception)
- Reduction of the aggregate compensation and benefits
- Failure to promote the executive to a specific title or position within a set period of time

- Failure to elect/reelect the executive to the board, or the removal of the executive from the board
- Failure for a successor company to assume the agreement or the plan
- Relocation of the executive more than x miles from his or her current office location
- Material breach of the contract by the company
- Change in control of the company

Many of the above items will not constitute Good Reason if the company obtains written consent prior to the occurrence of the Good Reason event. In addition, it is common to have a "cure" provision so that a company can correct an inadvertent Good Reason event, particularly if the executive has a cure provision in the termination-for-Cause provision. Finally, the IRC Section 409A deferred compensation regulations have imposed certain conditions on the definition of Good Reason and the operation of termination-for-Good Reason provisions (e.g., a minimum 30-day cure period), which now need to be incorporated in all employment arrangements containing Good Reason provisions. See Chapter 8 for a "Good Reason Safe Harbor."

Without Good Reason or Retirement

A termination by the executive without Good Reason simply means that the executive quits. Most arrangements permit executives to quit, and most agreements explicitly state that a termination without Good Reason is not a breach of the agreement. If they do not, then they resemble the classic employment agreement discussed above. Thus, the company could have a cause of action for breach of the employment agreement and could sue the executive for money damages resulting from that breach. However, most employment arrangements explicitly require that the executive provide notice with a minimum time period (typically between 30 and 90 days).

The termination benefits for a termination without Good Reason are similar to the termination benefits under a termination for Cause. The major difference usually is that only unvested stock options—not all stock options—immediately terminate on the date of the termination without Good Reason, with vested options subject to a short post-termination exercise period (typically from 30 to 90 days).

A termination due to retirement (including an early retirement) under the company's retirement program or policy usually provides the same benefits as a termination without Good Reason, and may include a full or pro rata bonus (usually depending on when the retirement occurs) and continued vesting and exercisability of appreciation-type awards.

Nonrenewal of the Employment Period by the Company

This has become a major issue over the past few years, and relates to the concept of "term of employment." As discussed above, many employment agreements have "evergreen" provisions in which the employment period automatically renews unless either party notifies the other of his, her, or its intent not to renew within a set period of time before the expiration of the employment period. In these situations, a failure to give notice of nonrenewal has the same result as an affirmative act to renew an employment period.

The various approaches with respect to a nonrenewal by the company are as follows:

- Treated the same as if the executive terminated without Good Reason and with post-termination restrictive covenants remaining in effect.
- Treated the same as if the executive terminated without Good Reason but with no (or modified) post-termination restrictive covenants remaining in effect. Examples of such modifications could be a shortened restrictive covenant period, or elimination of the noncompetition provision but retention of the nonsolicitation of employees provision.
- Treated the same as if the executive were terminated by the company without Cause.
- Treated the same as if the executive were terminated by the company without Cause, but with reduced severance benefits (e.g., a 1 × severance benefit instead of a 2 × severance benefit).

In addition, some companies have a unilateral "option" to impose post-termination restrictive covenants following a nonrenewal by the company, but only if severance benefits are paid as consideration for the restrictive covenants. As mentioned above, there is no "right" or "wrong" arrangement. The arrangement that the compensation committee selects will depend on the specific facts and circumstances associated with the specific hiring.

Nonrenewal of Employment Period by the Executive

A nonrenewal of the employment period by the executive almost always is treated the same as a termination by the executive without Good Reason. A nonrenewal may occur based on an affirmative act of nonrenewal, or on the failure to give notice of renewal, depending on the terms and conditions of the specific arrangements. Thus, an arrangement that requires the affirmative act of renewal by the executive might provide that the executive must renew at least 60 days before the end of the employment period (this simulating the notice requirement under a termination without Good Reason).

As discussed above, a nonrenewal of the employment period by the executive might provide for all, some, or none of the restrictive covenants that are in effect, might provide for a reduced restrictive covenant period, or might allow the company to "buy" a noncompete period with a predetermined severance package.

OTHER PROVISIONS REGARDING TERMINATION OF EMPLOYMENT

The following are other provisions that compensation committees should be aware are contained in many employment arrangements:

- Waiver and release
- Resignations
- Cooperation
- Return of property
- Mitigation
- Offset

Each is briefly discussed below:

- *Waiver and release.* As a condition to receiving any severance benefits, most arrangements will require the executive to sign a waiver and release of all claims that he or she may have against the company as of the termination date. Sometimes (depending on the bargaining position of the executive and the company's past practices), these releases are mutual, although companies should not release any act by the executive involving willful misconduct or other egregious behavior. Often, the company attaches its standard form of waiver and release to the employment agreement or plan document.

- *Resignations.* Most employment arrangements will require the executive to resign from all officer and director positions as of the termination date.

- *Cooperation.* Companies sometime include a cooperation provision in which the executive agrees to cooperate with the company if asked to do so and involving any lawsuit, investigation, or other proceeding. However, these provisions typically are subject to a "reasonability standard" and reimbursement of the executive's expenses incurred during this cooperation, and sometimes payment of compensation if the cooperation is substantial.

- *Return of property.* Most employment arrangements will provide that the terminated executive must return all company property immediately.

- *Mitigation.* Most—but not all—executive employment arrangements provide that the terminated executive is *not* required to seek new employment in order to "mitigate" the severance benefits. The purpose of these provisions is to "contract around" the laws of many states that impose a "duty to mitigate." Most states that do impose this duty allow the parties to expressly provide in the contract that there is no duty to mitigate.

- *Offset.* Generally, there are two types of offset provisions. First is where the executive employment arrangements explicitly provide that a company may offset its obligations to the executive (i.e., severance) with amounts that the executive owes to the company. The other is where, even if the executive is not obligated to seek new employment, he or she is obligated to reduce continued severance benefits (e.g., salary continuation) being paid by the company with any post-termination compensation if he or she does become employed by a new employer. Both provisions are usually subject to negotiation.

CHANGE IN CONTROL AND CHANGE-IN-CONTROL TERMINATIONS

Change-in-control (CIC) employment arrangements usually are an extremely high priority with most executives. Even if the company will not agree to enter into a formal employment agreement with the executive, executives typically will push to have CIC protection. The justifications for these arrangements are that they:

- Eliminate distraction on the part of the executive if a CIC begins to happen
- Attempt to place the executive in a "neutral" position vis-à-vis the CIC

CIC arrangements may be contained in an employment agreement or in a separate CIC agreement or plan. CIC plans (as compared with the use of many similar or "form" individual agreements) have become quite popular, for the reasons stated above. Some companies are still using what practitioners call "springing employment agreements," which simply refers to a formal employment agreement that becomes effective only upon the occurrence of a CIC. Finally, most incentive compensation arrangements (particularly equity-based compensation) and retention arrangements contain CIC provisions.

When dealing with a CIC under a written employment arrangement, it is necessary to define the term *change in control*. Companies often have already defined this term in some plan or other agreement (usually an equity-based compensation plan), and the definition may be incorporated by reference into the new arrangement. Or the term may be defined differently in the individual agreement than in the other document (although this usually is not a good idea). Typical definitions of "change in control" provide that a CIC occurs when:

- A person or a group acquires beneficial ownership of x percent of the company's stock.
- A person or a group no longer has beneficial ownership of x percent of the company's stock.
- x percent of the "Incumbent Board of Directors" (i.e., the existing directors and any new director "approved" by the existing directors) are replaced during a set time period, usually 12 months.
- Certain business combination (e.g., a merger).
- A sale of all or substantially all of the company's assets.
- A liquidation of the company.

Some definitions contain other events. It is important to note that most *change-in-control* definitions will need to take into account the definition of *change in control* or similar term defined in:

- The golden parachute tax regulations under IRC Section 280G
- The deferred compensation tax regulations under IRC Section 409A

If these definitions are not taken into account, then there may be a disconnect from the desired result (e.g., an event that is a CIC under the employment arrangement that pays out deferred compensation must be a CIC under the Section 409A deferred compensation regulations). See Chapter 8 for a discussion of these tax effects.

The occurrence of a CIC may result in an immediate benefit (e.g., immediate full vesting of all unvested equity-based compensation awards, payment of a transaction compensation award). Such a result is referred to as a "single-trigger" arrangement, as the CIC is the only required trigger.

Most compensation and benefits that are triggered by a CIC require two events (referred to as a *double-trigger arrangement*). The second trigger in almost all instances is a termination without Cause or a termination for Good Reason. Again, both events (i.e., the CIC *and* the termination of employment) must occur. The double-trigger arrangement usually has a set time period, typically from one to three years following the CIC, which is often referred to as a *Protection Period*. In some arrangements, it is recognized that a termination of employment occurring prior to the change in control most likely was in connection with a change in control, and thus some arrangements provide that the Protection Period includes the six-month period preceding the date of the CIC.

Some arrangements also provide for the right for the executive to terminate without Good Reason during a set "window period," typically at any time during the 7th to 13th month following the CIC. This is referred to as a *walk-away right* or a *quit right*. The justification for this is that it requires the executive to remain at the acquired company for a reasonable transition period, and then, having fulfilled that responsibility, he or she is allowed to quit (if he or she wants to) and collect full CIC severance benefits. Its purpose is to eliminate the recurring dispute as to whether a Good Reason has occurred with respect to a particular executive. It should be noted that years ago, the definition of *Good Reason* sometimes contained CIC as a Good Reason, which essentially created an immediate quit right; however, such a definition has become less common (and usually is heavily negotiated if used).

Finally, most CIC employment arrangements provide for the effects of the golden parachute excise tax related to IRC Section 280G. Often, these provisions have provided a full tax gross-up for any golden parachute excise tax. Other provisions have required an automatic reduction of parachute payments, or require this reduction only if the aggregate payments do not exceed a set or formulaic amount. And other arrangements are completely silent as to golden parachute excise tax, which effectively means that the executive is responsible for the payment of any golden parachute excise tax. Ultimately, whether the CIC arrangement should contain a provision relating to the golden parachute excise tax, and if so, then what kind, is a matter that each compensation committee will need to address and resolve.

RESTRICTIVE COVENANTS

From a company's perspective, the most important promises that a company can extract from an executive under a written employment arrangement are the various restrictive covenants. These covenants can be found in almost all written employment and compensation arrangements. With respect to individual arrangements, these provisions usually are subject to negotiation; however, if, for instance, the restrictive covenants are contained in a plan and are not subject to negotiation, then the executive may choose not to participate in the plan.

The breach of any or selected provisions usually results in the following:

- Most severance payments will cease and might be subject to reclamation (commonly referred to as a *clawback*).
- Most equity arrangements will cease and might be subject to a clawback.
- The company may seek to restrain the executive from continuing the breach (i.e., a court might enjoin the executive from competing or enjoin a company from hiring an employee).

Noncompetition

The most important—and emotional—restrictive covenant is the "noncompete." Generally, this provision states that for a period of time (commonly called the *restricted* or *restriction period* and often tied to the severance period), the executive cannot directly or indirectly compete with the company. Definitions of *competing* or *competition* vary. Some are very broad and some are narrow. Typically, these definitions impose several elements to narrow the application of the covenant, usually referred to as *carve-outs*, such as working for a competitor:

- With a certain minimum annual revenue,
- But in a subsidiary, division, segment, business unit, etc. of the competitor that does not compete with the company, and/or
- Was not a competitor of the company as of the date that the executive's employment was terminated.

Obviously, non-competes impact different executives differently. A noncompete on a CEO who is specialized in one particular industry would have a greater impact than a noncompete on a CEO whose managerial skills could be applied across industries. In addition, certain executives such as general counsels and chief financial officers may not be severely limited in their ability to gain new employment. However, certain sales, marketing, or system executives may find non-competes to be quite onerous.

Finally, whenever a company seeks to enter into a noncompete with an executive, a careful analysis as to the state of the applicable case law is required. In some states, an "overbroad" noncompete will not be enforced by the courts. In other states, an overbroad noncompete may be "blue penciled," meaning the court will redraft the provisions of the noncompete (e.g., the court on its own may reduce a three-year noncompete period to a one-year noncompete period, or a restriction against competing anywhere in the United States may be reduced to just one or several states). And in some states, an overbroad noncompete that completely fails will cause the other restrictive covenants to fail as well.

Nonsolicitation

There are two types of non-solicits. The first has to do with directly or indirectly soliciting or hiring employees. Here, the issues surround whether the "soliciting" activity occurs. A blanket "no-hire" provision may be used by some companies, but there is always a question as to whether such a provision is enforceable under state law. Usually, the provision tracks the noncompete period, but sometimes it is longer. There are usually limitations as to when a company's employee can be hired by the executive, typically some two to six months after that employee's termination of employment.

The second type of non-solicit is a restriction against directly or indirectly soliciting customers or clients of the company. To some degree—this creates its own noncompete, since depending on the fact and circumstance, the inability of soliciting a company with a great many customers may for all intents and purposes preclude the executive from doing any business at all.

Noninterference

A variation of the non-solicit is a noninterference provision. Here, the executive agrees to not do anything that would cause the company to have a change in any of its relationships with its customers, clients, suppliers, or any other entity that has a business relationship with the company. In certain instances in which the customer/client pool is quite small, this may rise to a level of a noncompete.

Nondisparagement

Nondisparagement provisions generally require the executive not to say anything disparaging about the company with no stated time period. Most executives will object to the non-mutuality of the provision and the fact that the restriction is in perpetuity. Often, executive will seek and get mutual nondisparagements, but with the understanding that it applies only to the top executives and directors at a company.

Confidentiality

Many written employment arrangements (as well as employee handbooks and other hire documents) provide a confidentiality provision that generally states that the executive will not disclose a company's trade secrets and other confidential information. Typically, these provisions provide the following carve-outs for executives with respect to some or all confidential information:

- Disclosure with respect to the executive's performance of his or her job during the ordinary course of business
- Disclosures of confidential information that has become public knowledge but through no fault of the executive
- Disclosure as required by law (including, but not limited to, subpoena issued by any authority with apparent authority), but with a requirement that the executive immediately notify the company prior to such disclosure
- Disclosure to the executive's spouse, attorney, or tax advisors (but with the understanding that any disclosure by such individuals to a third party will be deemed to be a disclosure by the executive).

Usually, confidentiality provisions are not subject to a time period, although in certain instance (either due to state law or otherwise) a time period may be applied.

Dispute Resolution

Dispute resolutions fall under two types: court and arbitration. Sometimes the arrangement will specify only one type. Other arrangements will specify both types but at the unilateral or bilateral election of the parties. Sometimes the provision will recite that the executive waives the right to a jury trial. A typical provision is to provide for mandatory arbitration (other than with the enforcement of restrictive covenants), usually under the rules of the American Arbitration Association, with the parties mutually selecting an arbitrator, and if they cannot agree to select one arbitrator, then there is a "tie-breaker" provision in which each picks its own arbitrator and these arbitrators either pick a third arbitrator to form a panel or simply pick another arbitrator to be the sole arbitrator.

Payment of fees and expenses range from each party's paying its own expenses, with arbitration costs being split, to the company's paying all fees and expenses, including reasonable attorneys' fees. Sometime the provision will use what is referred to as the *English rule*, which means that the losing party pays. And sometimes the provision will provide for something referred to as a *modified English rule*, in which the company pays if the executive prevails and, if not, then each party pays its own fees and expenses and arbitration costs are split. Usually, the executive has to prevail on at least one material issue in dispute to receive payment of his or her fees and expenses by the company. There are examples of companies paying all of the fees and expenses no matter who prevails, but these provisions have become less common.

Indemnification

Most senior executives will be covered by the company's indemnification provision contained in company documents such as the bylaws. However, it is quite typical to have a provision that requires indemnification, and may provide for additional elements including:

- Advancement of fees
- Requirement to have a directors and officers' indemnification insurance policy
- A presumption that the executive's act or omission is not in bad faith or due to misconduct.

Miscellaneous and Boilerplate

Most agreements and plans will contain (usually at the end of the document) a slew of miscellaneous or "boilerplate" provisions with respect to the following:

- *Representations.* This generally provides that both parties have the authority to enter into the agreement, and sometimes states specific concerns that either the company or the executive have (e.g., that the executive is not under a non-competition agreement that would be violated by entering into the employment agreement, that the company has not misstated its financial condition). Sometime these representations can become contentious, and at times have been deal-breakers.

- *Survival.* If the agreement provides that it can be terminated, then a survival provision provides that certain provisions will continue after the termination of the agreement. In agreements where only the term of employment ends, these survival provisions are generally unnecessary.

- *Notices.* As in most contracts, the parties will provide how notices should be sent, to whom the notice should be sent, and when the notice will be considered received by the other party.

- *Amendment.* As in most contracts, this provision provides that the contract cannot be amended unless done so in writing and signed by both parties.

- *Merger clause.* This is also a typical provision in most contracts, which states that the contract is the only evidence of the intent of the parties, and thus any previous contract or writings will generally have no probative effect. This means that it will be important to identify any contract or writing that will need to be excepted from the merger clause, usually by what is called *incorporation by reference*.

- *Severability.* Another typical provision that states that if a court rules that a provision (or provisions) of the contract is unenforceable, the remaining provisions are unaffected by such ruling.

Chapter 12

Incentive Compensation

Most executive compensation arrangements consist of annual base salary, short-term incentives (e.g., annual bonus), long-term incentives (e.g., equity awards or multiyear cash awards), retirement arrangements, welfare benefits, perquisites, and sometimes severance benefits. This chapter provides a general overview of the design of short-term and long-term incentives, while a more detailed focus on equity-based incentives is covered in Chapter 13. This chapter also presents ideas, issues, and market practices that compensation committees should consider with respect to any kind of incentive arrangements. Finally, while not an incentive arrangement *per se*, retention-only plans are discussed at the end of this chapter.

The following items are covered in this chapter:

- Useful definitions when discussing incentive arrangements
- General comparison of using cash-based or equity-based incentive compensation
- Typical plan and award types and features
- Shareholder approval requirements
- Retention-only plans

USEFUL DEFINITIONS

The following is a list of definitions that may be helpful in discussing incentive arrangements. Note that these definitions are neither universal nor absolute, but generally are part of the executive compensation "lexicon" and will be used for purposes of this chapter:

- *Award:* A compensatory grant under a plan.

- *Award agreement or award letter:* A written document between the grantee and the company memorializing the terms and conditions of an award (including the terms and conditions that are incorporated from the plan under which the award was granted).

- *Cash-based arrangement:* An arrangement wherein the compensation is determined solely based on a specified dollar amount and does not in any way relate to or take into account company shares (e.g., an annual bonus program that provides a cash bonus expressed as a percentage of base salary).

- *Equity-based arrangement or stock-based arrangement:* An arrangement wherein the compensation is determined solely based on or measured by company shares, rather than a specified dollar amount (e.g., a grant of stock appreciation rights payable in stock or cash, or a grant of restricted stock units payable in stock or cash).

- *Grantee:* A person who has been granted an award.
- *Holding period:* The time period over which nonforfeitable compensation will be held before the payout date. (*Note:* While not entirely accurate, some may use the term *holding period* but actually should use the term *vesting period* if the compensation is subject to forfeiture.)
- *Hybrid arrangement:* An arrangement that has elements of both a cash-based arrangement and an equity-based arrangement.
- *Long term:* A time period longer than one year.
- *Market condition:* An accounting term under FAS 123R, which is a condition affecting the exercise price, exercisability, or any other factor used in estimating the fair value of an award, if the condition relates to the attainment of a specified stock price or increase in stock value, in absolute or relative terms. For example, a vesting condition based on a company's total shareholder return (TSR) over a certain period, or the company's TSR as compared to the TSR of a peer group, might be a market condition. See *service condition* and *performance condition.*
- *Midterm:* A time period generally between one and three years (*midterm* is not used very often by practitioners, and most often is used interchangeably with *long term*).
- *Omnibus plan or master plan:* A plan or program that authorizes the grant of several types of compensatory awards, which can be used to make individual grants or to create specialized incentive compensation subplans or programs, such as, for example, a compensation plan for non-employee directors or an executive cash incentive plan for a particular year or performance cycle (see *subplans*).
- *Payout date:* The date that the compensation from an award is paid (if cash) or delivered (if property) to the grantee.
- *Performance-based compensation:* Generally refers to compensation in which payout occurs only if and to the extent that one or more performance goals are reached (e.g., a cash bonus that is payable if the executive reaches preestablished personal performance goals for the year). Technically, a stock option or stock appreciation right is performance-based compensation in the sense that the award has value only if the stock price increases over the life of the award, while restricted stock that vests only if there is continued employment is not performance-based compensation. This term is also used to refer to compensation that meets the requirements for the performance-based compensation exemption from Section 162(m) of the Internal Revenue Code (IRC).
- *Performance measure or performance metric:* The measure used to rate performance with respect to a particular performance-based award, such as "earnings per share" or "total shareholder return."

- *Performance goal or performance target or performance objective:* A definable and measurable level of performance with respect to a performance metric, such as "earning per share of at least $2.35" or "total shareholder return of at least 8 percent."

- *Performance vesting:* Refers to an award in which vesting occurs only if a performance goal is reached.

- *Performance condition:* An accounting term under FAS 123R which is a vesting condition that is dependent on the attainment by the grantee or the company of one or more specified performance targets based on the company's operations (such as attaining a certain earnings target completing an IPO, or a change in control). See *service condition* and *market condition.*

- *Performance period or performance cycle:* The time period over which performance is measured with respect to a performance-based award.

- *Plan or program:* A written document detailing a particular compensation arrangement. While the term *plan* is most often used to describe a general plan document, such as an omnibus plan or a director subplan, it is sometimes used in an accounting sense to refer to a single award or a series of similar awards, such as "the plan vests ratably over 4 years and has a term of 10 years."

- *Plan life:* The time period during which awards may be made under a particular plan (Note that in many cases, the plan life is 10 years, but as a practical matter plans are usually depleted or replaced before they expire).

- *Plan period:* In the case of a hybrid arrangement, the plan period refers to the time period consisting of both the initial performance period (if applicable) and the subsequent time-vesting period (if applicable).

- *Service condition:* An accounting term under FAS 123R, which is a vesting condition that relates solely to the grantee's continued service to the company, or earlier triggering event such as death, disability or other qualifying terminations of employment. See *performance condition* and *market condition.*

- *Short term:* A time period equal to or less than one year.

- *Subplan or subprogram:* A plan or program the terms and conditions of which are subject to an omnibus plan. Examples of subplans would include (i) a subplan for the grant of awards to non-employee directors or (ii) a subplan consisting of performance-based stock unit awards for 2007-2009, or (iii) a Section 162(m) annual cash bonus subplan for 2009.

- *Time vesting or service vesting:* Refers to an award in which vesting occurs only if there is continued employment/service by the grantee.

- *Vest:* Generally an award is vested when the compensation becomes nonforfeitable; however, in the case of stock options or stock appreciation rights, vesting usually refers to the time after which the award may be exercised (even if it is subject to forfeiture in whole or in part after that date).

- *Vesting period or restricted period or restriction period:* The time period over which continued employment is required in order to vest in an award.

CASH VERSUS EQUITY

There is no "right" answer to the question of whether to use cash or equity as the basis of an incentive award. Each has its own attributes and detriments. As discussed more fully in Chapter 13, time-based stock options are losing their edge over performance-based equity awards (of any type) and over cash-based compensation since all now result in compensation expense under FAS 123R. However, equity-based awards that pay out solely in stock generally result in a fixed accounting expense calculated as of the grant date, while cash-based awards and equity-based awards payable in cash are treated as variable liability awards under applicable accounting rules, which is less predictable.

In contrast to cash-based compensation, the performance measure for equity-based compensation generally is the price of the stock. As a performance measure, stock price is easily understood by the grantee and can be readily tracked if the company is publicly traded. It also (at least on the surface) directly aligns the interests of the grantee with the interests of shareholders. For an equity-based incentive program at a private company, the stock most likely will need to be valued on a fairly regular basis (usually once a year, or perhaps even each quarter) if the company wants to imitate a public company stock incentive program and maintain a "line of sight" to the value of the enterprise. If it does not (usually because the "exit strategy" is a sale or IPO), then the grantee does not need a continuing line of sight since the focus is on the "end of the tunnel" when the sale or IPO occurs. Also, in the case of stock that is not publicly traded, there are difficult stock valuation issues for purposes of complying with exemptions from the new deferred compensation requirements under IRC Section 409A.

With the executive compensation scandals and controversies stemming from the massive corporate failures in the early 2000s, most of which focused on the use of "plain vanilla" stock options, the current thinking is that companies should be focusing on performance measures other than stock price. The list of performance measures presented later in this chapter should be reviewed by compensation committees and their senior executives to see if (and which of) these measures or others may be proper drivers of performance for their particular businesses.

Finally, it is noted that some incentive plans are "hybrid" or "combination" arrangements that are both cash-based and equity-based or both performance-based and time-based. This is not to be confused with a cash-based plan that pays out in stock (e.g., an annual bonus plan that pays 50 percent in cash and 50 percent in fully vested company stock), or an equity-based plan that pays out in cash (e.g., a stock appreciation right that pays in cash). A hybrid plan is a plan in which the compensation delivered is determined by the price of the stock and some other performance measure. For example, a hybrid plan could be a plan in which there is a three-year performance period with a performance goal based on increases in earnings per share (EPS) and that pays out at the end of the performance period 50 percent in cash and 50 percent in restricted stock that cliff vests at the end of a two-year service-based vesting period beginning at the end of the three-year performance period. Thus, while the total plan period is five years, for the first three years it is essentially a cash-based plan, and for the last two years it is essentially an equity-based plan.

TYPICAL PLAN FEATURES AND DESIGNS

Incentive plans come in all shapes and sizes, and, similar as to whether to use cash or equity, there is no "right" plan. Compensation committees should examine all elements of incentive compensation plans and decide which plan features and design are best for their companies.

The following are incentive compensation plan features and designs that compensation committees generally will need to consider:

- Type of awards and type of plan
- Purpose of plan
- Administration of plan
- Eligibility and participation
- Award levels
- Performance periods
- Performance measures
- Performance goals
- What happens if a participant's employment is terminated due to:
  - Death
  - Disability
  - Retirement
  - For Cause
  - Without Cause
  - For Good Reason
  - Without Good Reason
- What happens on a change in control
- Payout in cash or stock or both
- Other miscellaneous issues

TYPES OF AWARDS AND TYPES OF PLANS

When speaking of a "type" of incentive plan, the first type to consider is whether the plan is a "specific" or a "general" plan. A specific type of plan usually is an arrangement in which the delivery of compensation is limited to a specific type of award. Types of awards include:

- Incentive stock options (options qualified under IRC Section 422)
- Nonstatutory stock options (options that are not intended to qualify as incentive stock options)
- Stock appreciation rights (which may be payable in cash or stock or both)
- Stock
- Restricted stock
- Restricted stock units (which may be payable in cash or stock or both)
- Deferred stock units (which may be payable in cash or stock or both)
- Performance shares
- Performance units (which may be payable in cash or stock or both)
- Cash
- Property (other than company stock)

Thus, a plan may be, for example, a "Stock Option Plan," which provides only for the grant of stock options, a "Shareholder Value Plan," which provides only for the grant of performance units based on TSR, or an "Executive Bonus Plan," which provides only for the grant of annual cash bonuses. The point is that all these plans are limited in design and function.

A plan type may be further defined by the performance period. Thus, a plan may be, for example, the "2007 Annual Incentive Plan," which would correspond to the company's fiscal year 2007, or it may be the "2007–2009 Shareholder Value Plan," which would provide for a grant of performance units over a performance period from the beginning of the company's fiscal year 2007 and ending at the end of the company's fiscal year 2009. These types of specific plans are limited in design and function.

Moreover, a specific type of cash-based plan may provide the performance measure to be used to determine compensation. For example, an "EVA Plan" is a long-term cash-based arrangement that uses *economic value added* as a performance measure (and which typically has a feature in which the compensation is banked and subject to loss or reduction if future performance is poor). Alternatively, the plan may be an "EPS Growth Plan," in which cash or stock compensation is paid if EPS growth targets are achieved.

Overall, a *specific* plan, being limited in scope and function, does not allow the committee administering the plan a wide degree of discretion in setting the terms and conditions of the awards. This may have utility in some situations, but often such plans can be overly restrictive, particularly as current accounting rules are opening the field for more and different types of incentive arrangements.

While some companies still prefer to have a specific plan document for each compensation program, most companies are using *omnibus* plans that provide wide flexibility and discretion in devising and implementing compensation programs. Committees can satisfy any desire to compartmentalize different arrangements by creating a series of subplans under the umbrella of one shareholder-approved omnibus plan. Shareholders are not averse to approving omnibus plans, as their focus is on the overall cost and potential dilution of all awards. In other words, whether shareholders are presented with proposals to approve several separate specific plans or one omnibus plan, they look to all arrangements in the aggregate to determine whether the plan or plans meet their costs analyses and voting guidelines. Now that the stock exchange rules require shareholder approval for almost all equity arrangements, having an omnibus plan is an efficient manner of satisfying that requirement. In terms of documentation in the case of an omnibus plan, grantees would receive a copy of the omnibus plan (which would contain some, but not many, terms and conditions associated with the award), a copy of the subplan, if applicable (which would contain more of the specifics associated with the particular compensation program), and a copy of an individual award agreement (which is often a one- or two-page document that contains terms and conditions specific to that particular award and grantee).

PLAN PURPOSE

It is always important to establish and communicate the purpose of an incentive plan. Not only must the compensation committee understand how a particular plan fits into the company's overall compensation strategy, the plan, purpose, and fit must be communicated effectively to plan participants and other interested parties. The company's human resources and finance departments are key to this part of the process. For example, finance can help the committee understand the financial metrics that are important to the company's business plan and help assess the appropriateness of performance goals based on selected metrics. Human resources can help make sure that the plan participants understand what the plan is designed to reward and how it does so. If participants fail to understand the purpose of the incentive plan, it will be an ineffective driver of performance and a weak retention vehicle. Moreover, as part of the new expanded executive compensation disclosure rules, the Compensation Discussion and Analysis is required to include a discussion of each elements of compensation (including incentive compensation) and how it fosters the company's overall compensation philosophy and strategy.

ADMINISTRATION OF THE PLAN

A person or a committee will need to administer each incentive plan. For public companies, that committee should be comprised solely of directors who satisfy the *outside director* requirements for purposes of IRC Section 162(m), the *non-employee director* requirements under Rule 16b-3 of the Securities Exchange Act of 1934, and the *independent director* rules under the appropriate stock exchanges. This plan administration committee usually is the compensation committee, but it also could be a subcommittee of the compensation committee or could be the entire board of directors or all independent directors. The plan administration committee should have broad authority in administering and interpreting the terms and conditions of the plan, and the decisions of the committee should be final and binding on all grantees. The committee should be able to delegate some of its responsibilities and hire outside advisors. Committee members should be indemnified (other than for bad faith or gross negligence). It is also important that the committee understand its duties, responsibilities, and obligations under federal law and applicable state law (primarily the state's corporation law). More information on these responsibilities and duties is found in Chapters 5 and 6.

ELIGIBILITY AND PARTICIPATION

While *eligibility* and *participation* may appear to be (and for that matter may be) the same thing, there can be a difference. While all employees may be eligible to participate in the plan, in most cases only some employees do in fact become participants. For example, if the plan is a broad-based annual cash bonus plan in which all employees are eligible to participate, then all employees would likely be participants. Alternatively, the plan may be a three-year cash-based plan in which executives above a specific salary grade are automatic participants and other eligible employees may be selected by the committee in its sole discretion to be participants. Essentially, this will be driven by the purpose of the plan. Sometimes, employees will be divided into groups or "tiers" of employees, which determines who will participate in the plan. For example, employees in Tiers 1, 2, 3, and 4 will be participants in the company's annual bonus plan, but only employees in Tiers 1 and 2 will be participants in the company's long-term incentive plan.

In addition, a plan may or may not have a waiting period for new hires to become participants. For example, assume a company has overlapping three-year performance period EPS-growth programs, and a new CEO is hired in the middle of the fiscal year. The plan could allow the new CEO to "cycle into" the company's overlapping performance cycles so that he or she would receive 1/6 of the award for the performance period that is 2½ years complete, one-half of the award for the performance cycle that is 1½ years complete, and 5/6 of the award for the performance cycle that is only six months complete.

AWARD LEVELS

Award levels may be specified in the plan (e.g., a percentage of base salary), or may be determined through the use of a "pool" in which percentages of the pool are allocated to participants, or may simply be left to the discretion of the committee in creating specific award levels with respect to a specific subplan (e.g., under the XYZ Company Executive Annual Bonus Plan, the 2007 subplan determined award levels as a percentage of actual base salaries, while the 2008 subplan determined award levels based on salary grade). Award levels may be set at a single level (i.e., if the performance goal is met, the employee will receive $100,000). Or, more commonly, award levels may be expressed as a range from "minimum payout," which correlates to threshold performance; to "target payout," which correlates to target performance; to "maximum payout," which correlates to "outstanding" performance, typically with some method of interpolating between points on the scale. While relatively easy to conceptualize, the description of how performance plans work can be challenging, as evidenced by the lengthy descriptions of such common arrangements in the 2007 proxy statement disclosures. Ultimately, a performance-based incentive plan is effective only if the participants understand and are motivated by the performance goals and feel that they have the ability to make a difference in the outcome. Therefore, compensation committees have a serious responsibility to design and implement plans that have the right balance of performance metrics, performance goals, and payout opportunities.

PERFORMANCE PERIODS AND RESTRICTED PERIODS

Performance periods may be specified in the plan or left to the discretion of the committee to determine performance periods with respect to specific subplans (e.g., under the XYZ Company Omnibus Plan, which allows committee discretion in setting performance periods, the company created the XYZ Company Annual Bonus Plan with a performance period of one year, the XYZ Company 2007–2009 Long-Term Incentive Plan with a performance period of three years, and the XYZ Company Retention Plan with a vesting period of two years). Performance periods, for the most part, should be established in direct coordination with the company's business plan.

PERFORMANCE MEASURES

The following are common performance measures (other than stock price) that some companies might use (and in some cases a description of the measure):

- *Revenue.* Typically, this would relate to a target revenue amount, or revenue growth; may include all revenue or may carve out certain types of revenue (e.g., investment income), or may apply only to certain types of revenue (e.g., North American revenue).
- *Sales.* Same as revenue, but normally exclude non–sales revenue.
- *Pretax income.* before allocation of corporate overhead and bonus.
- *Budget.*
- *Cash flow.* Simply, the cash that a company takes in (cash inflow) and pays out (cash outflow).
- *Earnings per share.* Measures a company's performance; calculated by dividing net profit by number of common shares outstanding (basic EPS), or includes "common-stock equivalents" like stock options and warrants (diluted EPS).
- *Net income.*

- *Division, group, or corporate financial goals.*
- *Dividends.*
- *Total shareholder return.* The return based on increases in stock price plus dividend payments.
- *Return on shareholders' equity.* A measure of profitability; ROE = net profit after taxes/stockholders' equity.
- *Return on assets.* A measure of profitability and efficiency (i.e., how a company generates profits from assets); ROA = net profit after taxes/total assets.
- *Return on investment.* Similar to ROE; measures how efficiently the financial resources available to a company are used; ROI = annual profit/average amount invested.
- *Internal rate of return.* A present value–based measure used for determining the compounded annual rate of return on investments held for a time period of one year or more.
- *Attainment of strategic and operational initiatives.*
- *Market share.*
- *Operating margin.* This is equal to the ratio of operating income to sales revenue.
- *Gross profits.*
- *Earnings before interest and taxes (EBIT).* Also known as *operating profit,* as it is income from a company's ordinary business activities.
- *Earnings before interest, taxes, depreciation, and amortization (EBITDA).* Used by many to measure cash flow.
- *Economic value-added (EVA) models.* A measure of the superiority of the return a company is able to realize on invested capital above the baseline return expected by the investment community. The formula to calculate EVA is EVA = NOPAT – (C – K(c)), where NOPAT is net operating profit after taxes, C is the amount of capital a company plans to invest in a project, and K(c) is the cost of capital.
- *Comparisons with various stock market indices.*
- *Increase in number of customers.*
- *Reduction in costs.*
- *Bringing assets to market.*
- *Resolution of administrative or judicial proceedings or disputes.*
- *Funds from operations.*

While some arrangements will focus on only one performance measure, it is not uncommon for companies to use two, three, or more performance measures to calculate a payout. But a performance formula that is too complex may not be as effective as one that is more easily understood by participants. Typically, the use of two performance measures (e.g., revenue and EBITDA) may be presented using a

Exhibit 12.1   Example of Payouts Percentages Using Multiple Performance Measures

		50%	60%	70%	80%	90%	100%
	$180 m	50%	60%	70%	80%	90%	100%
R	**$170 m**	40%	50%	60%	70%	80%	90%
E	**$160 m**	30%	40%	50%	60%	70%	80%
V	**$150 m**	20%	30%	40%	50%	60%	70%
E	**$140 m**	10%	20%	30%	40%	50%	60%
N	**$130 m**	0%	10%	20%	30%	40%	50%
U	**$120 m**	0%	0%	10%	20%	30%	40%
E	**$110 m**	0%	0%	0%	10%	20%	30%
	$100 m	0%	0%	0%	0%	10%	20%
	EBITDA	**$30 m**	**$35 m**	**$40 m**	**$50 m**	**$65 m**	**$70 m**

matrix as shown in Exhibit 12.1. Overall, as with determining performance periods, the determination of which performance measure to use must be based on the company's business plan.

PERFORMANCE GOALS

Performance may be specified in the plan (e.g., a 10 percent annual growth in EPS) or left to the discretion of the committee in creating specific award levels with respect to a specific subplan (e.g., under the XYZ Company Executive Annual Bonus Plan, the performance goal is a 10 percent annual growth in EPS). As shown in Exhibit 12.1, a program may use more than one performance measure and thus more than one performance goal. While two or three measures are not uncommon, the use of more than three performance measures is unusual. Since the purpose of the performance measure is to focus the employee achieving specific performance levels with respect to that measure, introducing a myriad of measures may confuse the "line of sight" needed to properly motivate and incent most employees.

While some plans use an all-or-nothing approach to achieving a performance goal (e.g., minimum award is paid if 90 percent of the goal is achieved, target if 100 percent of the goal is achieved, and maximum if 150 percent of the goal is achieved), many plans will use interpolation to award amounts that fall in between the specific performance goals.

The matrix in Exhibit 12.1 shows how a company would pay out using two performance measures.

Thus, in this example, a grantee with a salary of $200,000 who has a "target" award of 50 percent of salary would receive $100,000 (i.e., 100 percent of target award) if revenue at the end of the performance period equaled $180 million and EBITDA at the end of the performance period equaled $70 million. He would receive $50,000 if revenue equaled $130 million and EBITDA equaled $70 million. The plan design shown in Exhibit 12.1 might provide that the percentages only reflect achievements of the specific goals; thus, revenue of $149 million and EBITDA of $39 million would result in an award level of 20 percent. However, if straight-line interpolation were applied, the award level would be 28.8 percent. Exhibit 12.1 shows a maximum award level of 100 percent of goal; it could, of course, show award levels exceeding 100 percent of goal. Indexing of the performance goal is also used by some companies, on the theory that a company's performance must be compared with the performance of its competitors to determine true performance. While the actual application can be complex, there is a purity in the concept of using relative performance comparisons, and to determine true underperformance or overperformance with respect to a defined market.

TERMINATION OF EMPLOYMENT

The consequences of the various types of termination of employment can range from total forfeiture of any award to full payment of the award. The applicable standard will be determined by the committee on either an employee-by-employee or group-by-group basis. In some cases, an employment agreement may control the consequence. The following list shows the various terminations and some comments:

- *Death.* Since this termination is an "act of God," neither the company nor the employee is "at fault." Complete forfeiture is typical, but this should take into account whether there is adequate company-provided life insurance (either paid in whole or in part by the company). However, there is an argument that the employee works for some portion of the performance period, and thus is entitled to a pro rata award, either based on target at time of termination or actual payout as if the employee had not died. Market practice appears to be leaning toward a pro rata award.

- *Disability.* Similar to death, this is a termination in which neither the company nor the employee is at fault. Complete forfeiture is typical, but this should take into account whether there are company-provided disability benefits (either paid in whole or in part by the employee). The pro rata argument similarly exists, and market practice appears to be leaning that way.

- *Retirement.* Retirement is not always addressed in these programs, and in those cases it usually is treated as a termination without Good Reason. However, if such is the case, an employee may decide to postpone retirement until a performance cycle ends, if the award is meaningful. In recognition of this motivation, companies oftentimes provide for a pro rata award for an employee who retires prior to the end of a performance period.

- *For Cause.* A termination of the employee's employment by the company for Cause (whether defined in the plan, in the award letter or agreement, in an employment agreement, or under common-law principles) almost always results in complete forfeiture of the award. Note that Cause generally means that the employee engaged in some type of egregious behavior and generally does not mean poor individual performance.

- *Without Cause.* A termination of the employee's employment by the company without Cause may result in total forfeiture, complete payment, or a pro rata payment. Factors considered are the salary grade of the employee, the number of days the employee was employed in the performance period, provisions in an employment agreement, and so forth. From the employee's perspective, the argument generally is that the company has taken away the employee's opportunity to earn the compensation, through no fault of the employee. From the company's perspective, the argument is that the compensation was never guaranteed and that the employee's employment was "at will," meaning that it could be terminated at any time for any reason or for no reason. However, companies must keep an eye on local law to make sure that the incentive compensation will not be treated as earned wages, which the employee has a legal right to receive. Another issue is when a termination of employment occurs after the end of the performance period. From the employee's perspective, the argument is that the termination of employment after the end of the performance period but before payout (usually within 2½ months of the end of the performance period) "robs" the employee of the compensation. However, many companies require that the employee be employed as of the payout date, not just through the entire performance period. Here again, if the employee has been told what the compensation is, and then is fired, there is a concern that it may be earned wages and subject to receipt under state law. Finally, as noted previously, some companies have applied a concept that falls somewhere between "Cause" and "without Cause"—a termination due to poor performance. In such a case, the employee generally forfeits 100 percent of the award, but in some cases may be entitled to a portion of the award.

- *For Good Reason.* The term *Good Reason* usually means that the company has "constructively" (but not actually) terminated the employee's employment without Cause. For example, the company may relocate the employee to a desolate working location, reduce the employee's compensation, or assign duties that are materially inconsistent with the employee's title and position. Thus, as a constructive termination, the same logic and standards applicable to a termination without Cause would exist, and it is a matter of prior company practice and/or company culture whether a Good Reason termination will be treated as a termination without Cause.

- *Without Good Reason.* A termination without Good Reason simply means that the employee quit his or her job, and almost always, there is a complete forfeiture of the compensation, unless the compensation has been earned but deferred.

CHANGE IN CONTROL

Some plans may contain specific terms and conditions relating to a change in control. If so, the plan usually contains a definition of change in control (although not always). Typically, a plan may require that all outstanding awards vest or are paid out at target (or sometimes at actual performance or at maximum) if there is a change in control. Sometimes, the plan may contain provisions relating to IRC Section 280G golden parachutes, either providing for a tax gross-up or a reduction in the award if it would be treated by the Internal Revenue Service (IRS) as an excess parachute payment.

Alternatively, the plan may provide complete committee discretion, which may be exercised on the date of grant and contained in individual award agreements, or when there is a change in control. If committees do exercise discretion after the date of grant, the consequences of award modification need to be taken into account. Also, under the new deferred compensation rules of IRC Section 409A, the payment of an award triggered by a change in control may present issues, depending on whether the award is exempt from or subject to IRC Section 409A and depending on whether the controlling plan definition of *change in control* meets the definition of a "change-in-control event" for purposes of IRC Section 409A.

PAYOUT IN CASH OR STOCK OR BOTH

Generally, payout is not a determining factor as to whether a plan is a cash-based arrangement or an equity-based arrangement. Using either cash or stock is a matter of what "currency" the company prefers to use to pay out the compensation. Additionally, design of the award may influence whether the payout is in cash or stock; for example, a stock appreciation right may pay out only in stock so as to receive "favorable" accounting treatment.

SHAREHOLDER APPROVAL REQUIREMENTS

If the company's stock is publicly traded, then IRC Section 162(m) will apply and may limit the amount of deductible compensation paid to the company's top executives. Thus, for publicly traded companies, all incentive plans will need to be approved by shareholders in order to qualify for the performance-based exemption under IRC Section 162(m). The shareholders may be asked to approve a single performance metric (as in a single purpose plan) or, more typically, a laundry list of performance metrics. In addition, the maximum compensation payable to any single participant must be disclosed in the shareholder approval materials. If the plan is an omnibus-type plan, it may be necessary to break out the various types of cash compensation that may be paid. For example, the plan may state that the maximum amount of compensation (measured by a dollar amount) that may be paid is $2 million for any arrangement in which the performance period is short-term, and $10 million for any arrangement in which the performance period is long-term. Moreover, plans that have a laundry list of performance metrics will need to be reapproved by shareholders every five years in order to preserve the performance-based compensation exemption under IRC Section 162(m). Finally, if a plan is materially amended or revised, shareholders will need to approve the amendment or revision.

RETENTION-ONLY PLANS

Retention-only plans were very popular in the late 1990s when merger and acquisition activity was at a peak. The rationale for these plans was that the management team (whether consisting of the most senior executives or all of management) was a valuable asset of the company, and the preservation of that team was necessary to preserve and increase the value of the company. Generally, the design of these arrangements was fairly straightforward: the executive would receive a cash amount over a specified period of time, based solely on his or her continued employment. The time period usually was between one and two years, and the cash amount would be a percentage or multiple of base salary. For example, the CEO might receive a cash payment of 2 × base salary at the end of a two-year period, and an executive vice president might receive 1 × base salary at the end of such two-year period. Some arrangements (generally based on the notion that the payment of the retention award was too far off in the future), might pay a portion of the award over the retention period; for example, participants in a two-year program might receive 30 percent at the end of the first year, another 30 percent at the end of 18 months, and the remaining 40 percent at the end of the two-year retention period. Because retention-only plans were not performance based, they generally were negatively perceived by shareholders. Pure retention plans are not as common today, but are still used by companies and typically are put in place when there is a particular threat or expectation of a corporate transaction that could engender wholesale employee attrition at a critical phase in the company's life.

Chapter 13

Equity-Based Compensation

The chapter describes some of the most common forms of equity-based compensation vehicles, with a focus on their tax and accounting consequences, Section 16 reporting and liability issues under federal securities laws, an overview of principal advantages and disadvantages, and predictions of future trends. It also discusses trends in stock ownership and retention guidelines.

EQUITY-BASED INCENTIVE AWARDS

There is no doubt that equity will continue to play an essential role in the compensation of executives of public companies. While stock options have been the gold standard of employee compensation for the last two decades, the mandatory expensing of stock options beginning in 2006 eliminated the compelling cost advantage of "plain vanilla" stock options over other types of equity awards. This change in accounting rules has already led to a much broader use of other types of equity-based incentives—in particular, those that focus on the achievement of specific performance objectives rather than simple increase in stock price. Given this evolution, it makes sense for a compensation committee to adopt a flexible incentive plan that permits a variety of award types (often referred to as an *omnibus* plan). Having a more flexible plan in place allows the committee to more precisely tailor individual awards to address the objectives of both the company and its employees.

This part of the chapter describes some of the most common forms of equity-based compensation vehicles, with a focus on their tax and accounting treatment, Section 16 reporting and liability issues, an overview of principal advantages and disadvantages, and a look into the future as to possible trends. Most equity-based awards are long-term incentives in that they provide compensation for performance measured over a period longer than 12 months. However, any of the equity-based incentives discussed in this chapter could be structured as short-term awards, measuring performance over a period of 12 months or less.

STOCK OPTIONS

Description of Stock Options

A stock option permits the holder to purchase stock at a predetermined price for a specific period of time. Options can be tax-advantaged incentive stock options (ISOs) or nonstatutory stock options (NSOs). Options that do not comply with the requirements for an ISO or that are otherwise stated not to be ISOs are NSOs.

In order to be considered an ISO, an option must meet all of the following requirements, which are specified in Section 422 of the Internal Revenue Code (IRC) and applicable regulations:

- Only a corporation (including an S corporation, a foreign corporation, or a limited liability company treated as a corporation) may grant ISOs.

- Only persons who are employees of the corporation granting the option (or employees of a related parent or subsidiary corporation) are eligible to receive ISOs—consultants and non-employee directors cannot receive ISOs.

- An ISO must be granted pursuant to a plan that has been approved by the company's shareholders within 12 months before or after the plan is adopted (certain plan amendments also require shareholder approval).

- An ISO must be granted within 10 years of the earlier of the date the plan was adopted by the board or the date the plan was approved by the shareholders.

- The plan under which ISOs are granted must designate a maximum aggregate number of shares that may be issued under the plan in the form of ISOs.

- The plan under which ISOs are granted must designate the employees or class or classes of employees eligible to receive options or other awards under the plan.

- The exercise price of an ISO may not be less than 100 percent of the fair market value (FMV) of the company's stock as of the date of grant of the option (or 110 percent in the case of an optionee who possesses more than 10 percent of the combined voting power of all classes of stock of the employer corporation or any related parent or subsidiary corporation).

- An ISO, by its terms, may not be exercisable more than 10 years from the date of grant (or 5 years in the case of an optionee who is a 10 percent shareholder) or more than 90 days after termination of employment (other than for death or disability).

- An ISO may not be transferable except in the event of the optionee's death, and is exercisable only by the optionee as long as he or she is living.

- For any one person, the maximum FMV of stock subject to ISOs that become exercisable for the first time in any calendar year may not exceed $100,000, which value is measured as of the date of grant.

Tax Treatment of Stock Options

The tax treatment of an option hinges on whether it is an ISO or an NSO.

ISOs The holder of an ISO is not taxed on the option spread when the option is exercised (but the spread is included for purposes of calculating the optionee's alternative minimum tax for the year of exercise). Instead, the holder of an ISO is taxed when the acquired stock is eventually sold. In short, ISOs provide a tax advantage to optionees that NSOs do not provide—automatic deferral of tax on the gain resulting from the exercise of the option.

Moreover, if stock acquired through the exercise of an ISO is held for a specified period of time—the longer of two years from the date the option is granted or one year after the option is exercised—then any gain on the sale of the stock will be taxed as long-term capital gain. If the stock is not held for the required holding period, the difference between the exercise price and the lesser of (1) the FMV of the stock on the date of exercise, and (2) the sales price, will be taxed as ordinary income. Any additional gain will be taxed as long-term or short-term capital gain depending on how long the stock was held.

The employer is not entitled to a tax deduction upon the exercise of an ISO or upon the subsequent sale of the stock if the required holding period is met. If the optionee does not hold the stock for the required holding period, however, the employer will be entitled to a tax deduction equal to the amount of ordinary income recognized by the optionee.

NSOs The holder of an NSO recognizes taxable income at the time the option is exercised, in an amount equal to the excess of the FMV of the stock on the exercise date over the exercise price. This amount is taxed at ordinary income tax rates. Any further appreciation in the value of the stock will be taxed when the stock is sold and will be either long-term capital gain or short-term capital gain depending on how long the stock has been held prior to sale. The company is entitled to a tax deduction equal to the amount of ordinary income recognized by the optionee on the exercise of the NSO. Unlike ISOs, the exercise price of an NSO can be less than the FMV on the grant date. However, an NSO that is "discounted" is not exempt from IRC Section 409A, as discussed below.

IRC Section 409A IRC Section 409A was added to Federal tax law as part of the American Jobs Creation Act of 2004, which imposes a host of new restrictions on nonqualified deferred compensation arrangements. Section 409A defines *deferred compensation* very broadly, so that it covers not only traditional nonqualified deferred compensation plans, but also arrangements that are not usually thought of as deferred compensation, such as certain equity awards. Section 409A is in large part a reaction of Congress to the Enron experience in which many executives were able to accelerate the payment of deferred compensation to themselves shortly before the corporation filed for bankruptcy. To counter this, Section 409A imposes strict new requirements designed to limit the control an employee has over the timing of income recognition.

Because stock options and stock appreciation rights (SARs) allow the holder to "time" the income recognition by choosing when to exercise, such stock rights typically provide a level of control that Congress was trying to avoid. Fortunately, most stock options and SARs are *exempt* from Section 409A. However, options or

SARs that have an exercise price that is or may become less than the FMV of the stock as of the grant date are *not exempt* from Section 409A. This means they must comply with the requirement of Section 409A for deferred compensation or they will be subject to the following very adverse tax treatment:

- In the year that each tranche of a noncompliant option or SAR vests, the employee will recognize ordinary income equal to the excess of the FMV of the stock as of the exercise date (or the last day of the year if the option is not exercised) over the exercise price—that is, generally, the option or SAR "spread."

- The employee will owe tax on the spread at the ordinary income rate, plus an additional 20 percent income tax (the "20 percent tax"), *plus* a second additional tax equal to the interest on unpaid taxes from year of vesting, calculated at the underpayment rate plus 1 percent (the "underpayment tax"). The 20 percent tax and the underpayment tax are not avoided by the fact that the employee recognizes and pays income tax on the spread in the year of vesting.

Limited Ability to Avoid the Consequences of Noncompliance with Section 409A. During calendar year 2007 only, a discounted option or SAR may be amended (1) to *avoid being subject* to Section 409A by increasing the exercise price to the FMV as of the date of grant, or (2) to *comply* with Section 409A by eliminating the ability to exercise at the discretion of the holder and instead having the option or SAR be exercised only in specified calendar year after 2007 (or a schedule of calendar years beginning after 2007). However, this relief is not available with respect to an option or SAR held by an executive officer or director of a public company if the company has reported or reasonably expects to report a financial expense due to the issuance of such discounted option or SAR. In other words, if a backdating incident results in a financial restatement to record expense for misdated options or SARs, then this transition relief is not available for officers or directors of that company who hold discounted options or SARs.

See Chapter 8 for an expanded discussion of IRC Section 409A.

Limits on Deductibility   IRC Section 162(m) prohibits a public company from deducting more than $1 million in compensation paid in any one calendar year to its chief executive officer (CEO) or any of the next three (or four) most highly compensated executive officers (each a "covered employee"). See Chapter 8 for detail about the evolving definition of *covered employee* under IRC Section 162(m). However, compensation that meets the definition of *performance-based compensation* within the meaning of IRC Section 162(m) and applicable tax regulations is exempt from the $1 million annual deduction limit. A special rule under IRC Section 162(m) treats stock options (both ISOs and NSOs) and SARs as performance-based compensation exempt from the deduction limits of IRC Section 162(m), provided the award meets all of the following three requirements:

1. The option or SAR is granted under a plan that has been approved by the share-holders of the company, and the plan specifies the maximum number of options or SARs that may be granted to any covered employee in a specified time period.
2. The option or SAR has an exercise price (or base price) of not less than the FMV of the company's stock on the date the award is granted.
3. The option or SAR is granted by a committee consisting solely of two or more "outside directors," as defined in the IRC Section 162(m) tax regulations. (Most public companies take care to assure that each member of the compensation committee qualifies as an outside director for this purpose.)

Accounting Treatment of Stock Options

The favorable accounting treatment for time-vesting, market-priced stock options was the primary design determinant in equity-based compensation programs prior to the mandatory expensing of options in 2006. Other types of cash and equity awards, all of which require recognition of expense, simply could not compete with the allure of "free" accounting for stock options.

Beginning in 2006, all U.S companies are required to use Financial Accounting Statement No. 123, revised 2004 (FAS 123R), to account for all equity-based awards, including stock options. Prior to 2006, corporations were able to elect to account for equity-based compensation under either the intrinsic value method pursuant to Accounting Principles Board Opinion No. 25 (APB 25) or the fair value method under Financial Accounting Statement No. 123 (FAS 123). Most companies elected to follow APB 25 for as long as possible. The discussion in this chapter about APB 25 is primarily of historical relevance. However, an appreciation of the contrast between accounting treatment under APB 25 and FAS 123R is useful to understanding the evolution of plan design. For a detailed description of these two accounting regimes, see Chapter 9.

Generally, under APB 25, the company would record a compensation expense on its income statement equal to the excess, if any, of (1) the FMV of the option stock on the "measurement date" (usually the date of grant), over (2) the exercise price of the option (often resulting in a charge of zero). Thus, market-priced, time-vesting stock options accounted for under APB 25 enjoyed a financial accounting advantage over all other equity-based and cash-settled compensation programs.

In contrast, under FAS 123R, the company records as a compensation expense the "fair value" of a stock option on the date of grant (determined by reference to a standard option-pricing model), and such charge is expensed ratably over the service period (usually the vesting period). This treatment of options is more in line with the historical accounting treatment of restricted stock.

Companies following APB 25 generally attempted to avoid "variable account-ing" of options. Variable accounting required that the company accrue a compensation expense based on changes in the market price of the underlying stock. Periodic adjustments were made, until the option was exercised or forfeited, to reflect changes in the market price of the stock (in other words, a mark-to-market approach). While most options accounted for under APB 25 could easily be structured to avoid variable accounting (i.e., to maintain "fixed accounting"), certain design features resulted in variable accounting, such as having a variable exercise price or making vesting solely contingent on the satisfaction of performance goals. In general, any feature that created uncertainty in either the number of shares that could be granted upon exercise, or the exercise price of the option, gave rise to variable accounting under APB 25.

Moreover, certain modifications to an otherwise fixed option resulted in variable accounting under APB 25. For example, any repricing of an option, either by lowering the exercise price or canceling the option and replacing it with a new lower-priced option within six months before or after the cancellation, would cause the repriced or replacement option to be a variable award under APB 25, as would any amendment of an option to add a reload feature.

Certain other types of modifications to an outstanding option could result in a new "measurement date" for the option, which under APB 25 would not result in variable accounting but would cause the employer to record a fixed compensation charge equal to the excess of the FMV of the stock on the date of the modification over the exercise price of the option. Examples of these types of modifications are (1) an acceleration of vesting that was not provided for in the original option agreement, or (2) an extension of the post-employment exercise period.

Under FAS 123R, there is much more flexibility in the ability to amend outstanding options without costly accounting effects. For example, under FAS 123R, if an option is materially amended, it is to be deemed a new grant. If the option was already fully vested at the time of the amendment, the compensation cost would be the excess, if any, of the fair value of the option immediately after the amendment over the fair value of the option immediately before the amendment, which should be considerably less than the option spread at the date of the amendment (the accounting cost measure under APB 25). To the extent that the option was not fully vested at the time of the amendment, the company must also recognize the previously unexpensed portion of the original grant-date fair value of the option.

Section 16 Reporting and Liability Related to Stock Options

As discussed more fully in Chapter 7, Section 16 of the Securities Exchange Act of 1934 (Exchange Act) imposes short-swing profit liability and reporting requirements on a company's executive officers, directors, and 10 percent shareholders. A stock option is a derivative security of the company subject to Section 16. The grant of an option to an executive officer or director will generally be treated as an *exempt* acquisition of a derivative security, provided the grant of the option is approved in advance by either the full board of directors or a committee consisting solely of two or more non-employee directors, as defined in Rule 16b-3. Most public companies take care to assure that each member of the compensation committee qualifies as a non-employee director for this purpose. Two other alternatives for exemption are (1) holding the option or the underlying stock for six months, or (2) having the individual grant approved or ratified by the shareholders (which is rarely done).

Whether or not exempt, the grant of an option to a Section 16 insider must be reported electronically to the SEC on a Form 4 within two business days after the grant of the option.

The exercise of an option by a Section 16 insider is generally an exempt transaction, but must be reported within two business days after the exercise. The sale of any acquired shares will not be exempt and must be reported within two business days after the sale. For example, a broker-assisted cashless exercise of an option involves a nonexempt public sale of some of the option shares, which is matchable with any nonexempt purchase occurring within six months before or after such sale.

Advantages and Disadvantages of Stock Options

The primary advantage to the company of granting stock options, as opposed to other equity-based awards, historically has been the significant accounting advantage under APB 25, which allowed the company in most cases to avoid recognizing any compensation expense. This advantage was eliminated under FAS 123R. Under either accounting regime, the primary advantage of stock options to the employee is the risk-free right to appreciation in stock price and the ability to time the recognition of income.

Predictions for the Future of Stock Options

It is reasonable to expect a gradual decline in the use of plain vanilla time-vesting stock options. In the absence of the highly favorable free accounting for such options available under APB 25, there is less compulsion to use them, especially when, as discussed later, an SAR settled in stock can provide the same incentive using fewer shares and without the need to pay an exercise price. To the extent that options are used in the future, they may well include performance-vesting features, which would have resulted in variable accounting under APB 25 and therefore were rarely used. Examples of option variations that may become more prevalent in the level accounting playing field include:

- *Performance-vesting stock options*, in which the option is forfeited unless pre-determined performance criteria (other than based on stock price) are met. These are in contrast to performance-accelerated stock options with an ultimate vest date based solely on continued service, which were sometimes used under APB 25, because the ultimate vesting date preserved the fixed accounting treatment.

- *Premium priced options*, which have an exercise price above the market value at the time of grant. These options could have fixed accounting even under APB 25, but were never widely used. They may become more prevalent under FAS 123R if the above-market price results in a substantially lower fair value of the option on the date of grant, and thus a lower compensation expense than a traditional market-priced option.

- *Indexed options*, which have an exercise price that fluctuates over time depending on the company's stock price relative to a selected index. Because these options would require variable accounting under APB 25, they have been rarely used. Under FAS 123R that is less of an issue, but while indexed options may make sense from an incentive design perspective, they are complex to administer and may not be easily understood by the average employee. These factors may continue to curtail their popularity.

STOCK APPRECIATION RIGHTS

Description of SARs

A SAR entitles the grantee to a payment (either in cash or stock) equal to the appreciation in value of the underlying stock over a specified time. For example, if the base price of a SAR is equal to the FMV of the company's stock on the grant date, the grantee will be entitled to a payment upon exercise of the SAR equal to the excess, if any, of the FMV of the stock at the exercise date over the base price, times the number of SARs being exercised. If the appreciation is settled in cash, it is generally referred to as a cash-settled SAR; if the appreciation is settled in shares of stock, it is generally referred to as a stock-settled SAR.

Tax Treatment of SARs

The FMV of the consideration paid to the grantee upon exercise of a SAR (whether settled in cash or stock) constitutes ordinary income to the grantee. The company is entitled to a tax deduction equal to the amount of ordinary income recognized by the grantee at the time of exercise. See the previous discussion under "Tax Treatment of Stock Options" regarding the application of IRC Section 409A to discounted SARs, and the special designation of SARs as performance-based compensation for purposes of the $1 million deduction limit of IRC Section 162(m), provided certain conditions are met.

Accounting Treatment of SARs

Under APB 25, both cash-settled and stock-settled SARs were accorded variable accounting treatment, meaning that the company must accrue an expense over the life of the SAR based on changes in the market price of the underlying stock. Periodic adjustments were made, until the exercise date, to reflect changes in the market price of the stock. Under FAS 123R, the accounting treatment depends on whether the SAR is payable in cash or stock. SARs that may be settled in cash (in whole or in part) are accounted for as a liability, which requires mark-to-market adjustments over the life of the SAR, based on changes in the fair value of the SAR. In contrast, SARs that may be settled only in shares of stock result in a fixed compensation charge on the date of grant equal to the "fair value" of the award as of the date of grant, and such charge is expensed ratably over the service period.

Section 16 Reporting and Liability Related to SARs

Similar to options, SARs are derivative securities that must be reported to the SEC on Form 4 within two business days of the date of grant to a Section 16 insider. The grant of a SAR to an executive officer or director will be an exempt acquisition if approved in advance by either the full board of directors or a committee consisting solely of non-employee directors or if the SAR is held for at least six months from the date of grant or if the grant is approved or ratified by the shareholders. The exercise of a SAR that is settled in cash is deemed the simultaneous purchase from the company at the exercise price, and sale back to the company at the market price, of the stock underlying the exercised SAR. The exercise of a SAR that is settled in stock is deemed a purchase from the company of the underlying stock at the exercise price and the simultaneous sale back to the company of a number of shares having a market value equal to the exercise price. In cases where the grant of the SAR to an officer or director was approved in advance by the board of directors or a qualifying committee of non-employee directors (or approved or ratified by the shareholders), both the deemed purchase and sale of stock upon exercise of the SAR should be exempt from short-swing profit liability, but the exercise must be reported on Form 4 within two business days after the exercise date.

Advantages and Disadvantages of SARs

From the grantee's perspective, the principal advantage of a SAR is that the grantee may receive the benefit of appreciation in stock value without having to actually purchase stock. From the company's perspective, the principal advantage is that SARs use fewer shares to deliver essentially the same value as an option. The principal disadvantage of SARs historically has been the requirement of variable accounting under APB 25 and, going forward, the principal disadvantage would be liability accounting for cash-settled SARs under applicable accounting rules.

Predictions for the Future of SARs

As companies now use FAS 123R to account for equity-based compensation, the use of SARs payable in stock is likely to proliferate, and may even overtake options as the most prevalent form of appreciation-type awards. This is primarily due to the fact that SARs payable in stock use fewer shares to deliver the same value as a stock option, because only the net number of shares is issued upon exercise, while the accounting cost is the same as for options under FAS 123R. Moreover, the fact that the grantee (typically) does not have to pay an exercise price to exercise a SAR eliminates the sometimes troublesome aspects of option exercises. See Chapter 7 for a discussion of trading restrictions that can affect the ability of insiders to sell company shares in the market.

RESTRICTED STOCK

Description of Restricted Stock

Restricted stock is stock that is awarded to the grantee without cost or for a nominal price. During the restricted period, the shares are not transferable and are subject to a substantial risk of forfeiture. For example, the restricted stock is forfeited if the grantee terminates employment with the company without Good Reason during a specified period of time. The stock may vest ratably over a period of time ("graduated" vesting) or become 100 percent vested after a stated time period ("cliff" vesting). Alternatively, an award of restricted stock could have performance-related vesting triggers, in addition to or in lieu of an ultimate vesting date. (See the section "Predictions for the Future of Restricted Stock" that follows.) Restricted stock is an example of a full-value award, as opposed to an appreciation-type award such as options and SARs.

Tax Treatment of Restricted Stock

The grantee of a restricted stock award is normally taxed when the grantee becomes vested in the stock. The FMV of the stock at the time of vesting (less any amount paid for the stock) is taxable to the grantee as ordinary income, and the company is entitled to a corresponding tax deduction, subject to applicable limits under IRC Section 162(m). The grantee may accelerate the recognition of tax by filing a Section 83(b) election with the IRS within 30 days of receiving the restricted stock. If a Section 83(b) election is made, the grantee will recognize ordinary income in the year of grant equal to the FMV of the stock on the date of grant (less any amount paid for the stock), and the company will be entitled to a corresponding tax deduction, subject to applicable limits under IRC Section 162(m). Any subsequent appreciation is taxed as capital gain when the stock is sold. However, if the stock fails to vest and is forfeited, the grantee cannot recover the tax paid. Dividends paid on unvested restricted stock are taxed as compensation.

Restricted stock is exempt from the provisions of IRC Section 409A. This special exemption applies to property received from an employer that is excludable from income by reason of being substantially nonvested (as defined in IRC Section 83), or property that is includible in income solely due to a Section 83(b) election. See "Tax Treatment of Restricted or Deferred Stock Units" below for a surprisingly different treatment of restricted stock units under IRC Section 409A.

Accounting Treatment of Restricted Stock

Under FAS 123R, compensation cost for restricted stock is based on the FMV of the stock on the date of grant, whether the vesting is based on continued service alone or on other performance requirements. Generally, the cost is recognized over the service (vesting) period. If the award is forfeited before vesting, any compensation charge previously recognized would be reversed. Any dividends paid on unvested restricted stock do not result in additional compensation expense unless the stock is later forfeited and the dividends are not repaid to the company.

Under APB 25, restricted stock that vested solely on the basis of continued service was accorded fixed accounting treatment. The compensation cost was equal to the FMV of the shares as of the date of grant, and such cost was recognized over the vesting period. If the restricted stock vested solely on the basis of other performance goals, it was accorded variable accounting treatment (based on fluctuations in the stock price) until the goals were achieved.

Section 16 Reporting and Liability Related to Restricted Stock

The grant of restricted stock to a Section 16 insider must be reported on a Form 4 within two business days after the grant date. A grant to an executive officer or director will be an exempt acquisition if approved in advance by either the full board of directors or a committee consisting solely of non-employee directors or if the stock is held for at least six months from the date of grant or if the grant is approved or ratified by the shareholders. The vesting of the award is not reportable and is an exempt transaction.

Advantages and Disadvantages of Restricted Stock

The grantee's principal advantage is that he or she is treated as an owner of the stock from the date of grant (usually including the right to vote the stock and receive dividends), and the grantee typically does not pay anything for the stock award. In addition, the grantee has the ability to accelerate taxation on the shares to avoid a potentially higher tax as the shares vest. From the company's standpoint, the company is able to give an immediate benefit to the grantee and, by imposing performance or service restrictions on the shares, can use the shares to encourage the grantee to meet performance objectives or remain in service.

The principal disadvantage is that the company must withhold income taxes at the time the tax liability arises (i.e., when the restrictions lapse or a Section 83(b) election is made). Although the grantee is the owner of the stock, he or she might not have the cash to pay the withholding tax. Therefore, it is common for a company to withhold shares from the award in an amount sufficient to cover the tax liability, but this results in a cash-flow cost to the company, because it must remit cash to the IRS and cannot resell the shares absent registration or an applicable transaction exemption. In many cases, equity plans provide that shares withheld from an award to pay taxes are added back to the plan share reserve for future awards. This is not a universal plan design feature, however, as it is deemed to be liberal share counting and can therefore affect the way institutional investors assess the cost of the plan for voting recommendation purposes.

Predictions for the Future of Restricted Stock

There has been a significant increase in the use of restricted stock in the last few years. However, restricted stock, as a full-value award, does not provide as much leverage or as strong an incentive for performance as do stock options or SARs, because the restricted stock continues to have value even if the stock price decreases over the vesting period. A grantee would like to see the value increase, but does not lose all if the stock price declines. However, for this same reason, restricted stock has a stronger retention power than options. For example, an employee might be willing to walk away from an underwater option but not a restricted stock award, which always has value.

RESTRICTED STOCK UNITS OR DEFERRED STOCK UNITS

Description of Restricted Stock Units or Deferred Stock Units

Restricted stock units (RSUs) represent the right to receive stock in the future, subject to the satisfaction of vesting requirements. Deferred stock units (DSUs) represent the right to receive stock at the end of a designated deferral period. It is not unusual to combine the two, such that stock is not delivered at vesting, but is deferred to the grantee's termination of employment or some other deferred date. In both cases, until the stock is delivered, the grantee does not own actual shares of stock, and therefore does not have voting rights or the right to receive dividends. Because of this, such awards are often coupled with dividend equivalent rights, such that phantom dividends are paid in cash or reinvested in additional stock units credited to the grantee's account.

Tax Treatment of Restricted or Deferred Stock Units

The grantee of a stock unit award is normally taxed when he or she receives or has the right to receive the stock. The FMV of the stock (less any amount the grantee paid for it) is taxable to the grantee at that time as ordinary income, and the company is entitled to a corresponding tax deduction, subject to applicable limits under IRC Section 162(m). Because IRC Section 83 does not apply to a promise to pay cash or property in the future, unlike for restricted stock, the vesting of RSUs is not a taxable event, and it is not possible to make a Section 83(b) election.

Unlike restricted stock, stock units are not categorically exempt from IRC Section 409A. However, these stock units can easily be designed to comply with Section 409A by having them payout on one of the following permitted distribution events:

- A specified date in the future (or a schedule of dates)
- Separation from service (plus 6 months for most officers of public companies)
- Disability (as defined in Section 409A)
- Death

- The occurrence of a change in control (to the extent provided in regulations)
- The occurrence of an unforeseeable emergency (as defined in Section 409A)

Alternatively, RSUs can be made exempt from Section 409A as a "short-term deferral" by designing them to pay out within 2½ months after the end of the year in which the award vests.

Accounting Treatment of Stock Units

Under FAS 123R, compensation cost for stock units payable in stock is based on the FMV of the underlying stock on the date of grant (less any amount paid by the employee for such award), whether or not the unit is fully vested on the grant date, and whether vesting is based on continued service alone or on other performance requirements. Generally, the cost is recognized over the vesting period, if any. If the award is forfeited before vesting, any compensation charge previously recognized would be reversed. Cash-settled RSUs are treated as liability awards, which means that they have variable accounting.

Under APB 25, stock units that were payable only in stock and fully vested on grant, or that vested on the basis of continued service, were accorded fixed accounting treatment. The compensation cost was equal to the fair market value of the underlying shares as of the date of grant (less any amount paid by the employee for such stock), and such cost was recognized over the vesting period. If stock units vested solely on the basis of other performance goals, they were accorded variable accounting treatment (based on fluctuations in the underlying stock price) until the goals were achieved. Although no longer applicable, cash-settled stock units had variable accounting under APB 25.

Section 16 Reporting and Liability Related to Stock Units

The grant of stock units to a Section 16 insider must be reported on Form 4 within two business days after the grant date. A grant of stock units to an officer or director will be an exempt acquisition if approved in advance by either the full board of directors or a committee consisting solely of non-employee directors or if the units are held for at least six months from the date of grant or if the grant is approved or ratified by the shareholders. If the stock unit may be settled only in stock (as opposed to cash), the unit may be reported on Table I of Form 4 as if it were the acquisition of the actual shares of stock, in which case, the later vesting of the award is not reportable and is exempt. The forfeiture of a stock unit while the grantee is still an officer or director is reportable on Form 4, and would most likely be exempt as part of the terms of the original award. The reinvestment of dividend equivalents into additional stock units would be exempt from reporting and liability if the company maintains a qualifying dividend reinvestment plan for its shareholders that operates in a substantially similar manner. If not, the periodic reinvestment of dividend equivalents into additional stock units must be reported on Form 4, but would most likely be exempt as part of the terms of the original award.

Advantages and Disadvantages of Stock Units

The grantee's principal advantage is that he or she is able to defer taxation until the shares are delivered or are constructively received. The principal disadvantage is that the grantee does not have voting rights in the interim and may not receive dividends (unless the award includes a dividend equivalents feature). From the company's standpoint, (1) an award of stock units uses fewer shares than an option to deliver equivalent value; (2) deferral of taxation to termination of employment avoids IRC Section 162(m) deduction limits; and (3) by imposing performance or service restrictions on the stock units, the company can use the stock units to drive performance and retention. Another disadvantage to both parties is that stock units are not categorically exempt from IRC Section 409A and must be designed to either meet the short-term deferral exemption or to comply with the strict distribution requirements of Section 409A.

Predictions for the Future of Stock Units

Expect to see significant use of stock units in the coming years, as companies and their employees grow familiar with the versatility and tax-deferral aspects of stock units.

PERFORMANCE AWARDS

Description of Performance Awards

Performance awards are not really a separate type of award. Any of the equity awards described above (options, SARs, restricted stock, or RSUs) are referred to as "performance awards" if they have vesting criteria other than continued service. Cash awards that are based on performance are also performance awards. Under the new executive compensation disclosure rules discussed in Chapter 6, all performance awards, whether cash or stock-based, are referred to in the rules as *incentive* awards.

The compensation committee typically sets the performance goals and other terms or conditions of performance awards. As such, they are very flexible and can be used to directly correlate executive pay to strategically focused performance.

Tax Treatment of Performance Awards

Publicly traded companies may designate any award as a qualified performance-based award in order to make the award fully deductible without regard to the $1 million deduction limit imposed by IRC Section 162(m). Market-priced stock options and SARs have special treatment under IRC Section 162(m) as discussed earlier. In order for any other type of award to be a qualified performance-based award, a committee consisting entirely of outside directors must establish objectively determinable performance goals for the award based on one or more of the performance criteria that have been approved by the company's shareholders (typically such performance criteria are set out in the incentive plan). For example, the list might include some or all of the financial or nonfinancial metrics suggested in Chapter 12 (or others not listed), and the permissible performance targets might be expressed in terms of companywide objectives or in terms of objectives that relate to the performance of a division, affiliate, department, region, or function within the company or an affiliate.

In order to obtain the exemption from IRC Section 162(m) limits, the committee must establish the performance goals within the first 90 days (or the first 25 percent, if shorter) of the period for which such performance goals relate, and the committee may not increase any award or, except in the case of certain qualified terminations of employment, waive the achievement of any specified goal. Any payment of an award granted with performance goals must be conditioned on the written certification of the committee in each case that the performance goals and any other material conditions were satisfied. If the performance targets are not specifically set out in the plan, but are left to the discretion of the committee based on one or more shareholder-approved performance criteria, the plan's performance criteria must be reapproved by the shareholders every five years to maintain the availability of the performance-based exemption.

Accounting Treatment of Performance Awards

Under APB 25, equity-based performance awards (whether be settled in cash or stock) were generally accorded variable accounting treatment (based on fluctuations in the underlying stock price) until the goals were achieved. For that reason, they were used sparingly. FAS 123R, on the other hand, accords fixed accounting for performance-based awards under most circumstances. Therefore, we are seeing a marked increase in the use of performance awards.

Under FAS 123R, the accounting treatment of a performance award depends on whether it is an appreciation-type award (option or SAR) or a full-value award, and on whether it may be settled in cash or stock, all as described above. However, the accounting treatment for a performance-based award is further affected by whether the vesting condition is a performance condition or a market condition.

In contrast to a pure service condition (in which all the employee has to do to vest in the award is remain employed or terminate for an approved reason, such as death or disability), a performance condition is dependent on both the employee remaining employed (a service condition) and the attainment by the employee or the company of one or more specified performance targets based on the company's operations (such as attaining a certain earnings target, completing an IPO, or a change in control). Service and performance conditions that solely affect *vesting* are not considered when estimating grant-date fair value of an award. However, if the award fails to vest, any compensation expense previously recognized for that award is reversed.

A market condition, on the other hand, is a condition affecting exercise price, exercisability, or any other factor used in estimating the fair value of an award, if the condition relates to the attainment of a specified stock price or increase in stock value, in absolute or relative terms. For example, a vesting condition based on a company's total shareholder return (TSR) over a certain period, or the company's TSR as compared to the TSR of a peer group, might be a market condition. Unlike service and performance conditions, market conditions *are* considered when estimating the grant date fair value of an award. If the award fails to vest *solely* because the market condition was not met, there is no reversal of previously recognized compensation expense. But, if the employee forfeits the award due to failure to satisfy a service condition before the market condition is met (i.e., if the employee leaves the company before the market condition is met), then the previously recognized compensation cost is reversed.

All this is to say that accounting for equity compensation under FAS 123R is much more complex than under APB 25. Compensation committees should always consult accounting experts so that they fully understand the accounting ramifications of a proposed plan design.

Section 16 Reporting and Liability Related to Performance Awards

The Section 16 analysis of performance awards is complex because it depends on the terms of the award and involves a number of deemed transactions. A performance award whose value is tied solely to the market price of the company's equity securities is a derivative security, whether the award is payable in cash or stock. Such an award must be reported on Form 4 within two business days after grant. Upon settlement for stock, if applicable, a Form 4 must be filed within two business days, reporting both the exempt disposition of the derivative security and the exempt acquisition of the shares. Upon settlement for cash, if applicable, a Form 4 must be filed within two business days, reporting the exempt disposition of the derivative security, the exempt deemed acquisition of the underlying shares, and deemed resale of such shares back to the company. Both the grant of the award and the settlement would be exempt transactions if the award was approved in advance by either the full board of directors or a committee consisting solely of non-employee directors, or the award was approved or ratified by the company's shareholders. When a performance award is not tied solely to the market price of the company's equity securities, it is not a derivative security and need not be reported. However, if such an award is settled in stock, the acquisition of the stock must be reported on Form 4 within two days.

Advantages and Disadvantages of Performance Awards

Performance awards can provide an incentive for employees to accomplish a variety of targeted company and individual goals and objectives. In this sense, they can be tailored to encourage a longer-term focus than time-vesting awards, which are increasingly criticized as encouraging a short-term focus based solely on stock price. The principal disadvantage to the company is the challenge of designing meaningful and understandable performance objectives for the awards. Historically, variable accounting under APB 25 was an additional disadvantage.

Predictions for the Future of Performance Awards

Expect to see an increase in the use of performance awards that combine incentives based on tailored business and individual performance achievement with that of increases in stock value.

STOCK OWNERSHIP AND RETENTION GUIDELINES

The primary justification for equity-based compensation is to align management's interests with the long-term interests of shareholders. It was this mantra by institutional shareholders, along with their insistence on "pay for performance," that led to the proliferation of stock option grants in the 1990s. However, as it turned out, this intended link with shareholder interests was undermined by management's propensity to exercise options and dispose of the stock at the earliest opportunity. In an effort to strengthen the desired alignment with shareholder interests, many public companies adopted stock ownership policies, generally requiring directors and executive officers to acquire and retain a minimum amount of company stock—typically based on a multiple of their base compensation.

However, evolving practices revealed that many such stock ownership policies were anemic, both in terms of magnitude and enforcement. For example, in most cases, equity-based awards to executives far exceeded the required minimum ownership guidelines. Therefore, management was able to sell large quantities of stock while staying well above the minimum holding requirements. Many were couched as mere guidelines with no consequence for failure to comply. These realizations have led to a widespread retooling of equity ownership policies. Many companies have instituted stock *retention* policies, in addition to or in lieu of traditional minimum ownership guidelines.

Retention policies generally require an officer or director to retain a designated percentage of all "profit shares" resulting from equity incentive awards (meaning shares remaining after payment of the option exercise price and tax payment obligations) for a designated period of time. The required holding period varies—it could be a number of years after the vesting or exercise of the award, or could extend to termination of service or beyond. Generally, retention requirements apply to all shares of company stock acquired by the officer or director in the scope of service, even those in excess of the minimum shares required to be owned.

Like ownership guidelines, retention policies are only effective if they are followed. Consideration should be given to designing appropriate consequences for noncompliance, from forfeiture of profits to ineligibility to receive additional equity awards.

Companies are encouraged to talk about their stock ownership and retention policies in the new Compensation Discussion and Analysis section of the annual proxy statement, as discussed in Chapter 6.

Chapter 14

Executive Pension-Benefit, Welfare-Benefit, and Perquisite Programs

This chapter provides a general overview of pension-benefit, welfare-benefit, and perquisite programs in which executives generally participate and with which compensation committee members will need to be familiar. Overall, these programs are essential to any complete executive compensation package; however, there may be a perception that these programs are excessive. Therefore, it is important for the compensation committee to balance the full array of programs and to properly disclose the extent of these programs. The compensation committee should also review the necessity for such programs and whether full and transparent disclosure of the program under the new executive compensation disclosure rules released by the Securities and Exchange Commission (SEC) in 2006 would be negatively perceived by shareholders, by the business press, and by the public in general.

There are numerous examples in which the revelation of these programs has produced unwanted controversy (e.g., retirement arrangements at a utility company and a financial services company; apartments at an entertainment company and a conglomerate; miscellaneous "small" perquisites at several conglomerates and a lifestyle company). In addition, as discussed in Chapter 6, the SEC's new executive compensation disclosure rules focused on—among other things—increased disclosure of benefit plans and particularly executive perquisites. Some companies have chosen to eliminate all or many of these programs; however, such an approach may not be the best approach or the most cost efficient. Accordingly, compensation committees should examine the internal efficacy of the specific program with respect to a specific executive or group of executives, and then externally test the program for market reasonableness.

LIST OF PROGRAMS

The following is a summary of the three arrangements discussed in this chapter:

- Pension-benefit arrangements:
  - Defined-benefit supplemental executive retirement plans (SERPs)
  - Defined-contribution SERPs

- ○ Excess-benefit SERPs
- ○ Deferred compensation arrangements
- ○ Rabbi trusts and secular trusts
- ○ Other pension arrangements
- Welfare-benefit arrangements:
  - ○ Executive life insurance
  - ○ Key-person life insurance
  - ○ Split-dollar life insurance
  - ○ Executive medical
  - ○ Executive disability
  - ○ Other welfare arrangements
- Perquisites:
  - ○ Relocation and temporary housing
  - ○ Expense accounts
  - ○ Club memberships
  - ○ Air travel
  - ○ Ground travel
  - ○ Security-related arrangements
  - ○ Financial and tax counseling
  - ○ Tax gross-ups
  - ○ Charitable contributions
  - ○ Business machines
  - ○ Annual physicals
  - ○ Other perquisites

PENSION-BENEFIT ARRANGEMENTS

Generally, pension-benefit arrangements are those arrangements that provide for a retirement benefit on or after termination of employment for most or all employees. Pension plans are usually bifurcated into qualified plans, which apply to most or all employees, and nonqualified plans, which usually apply only to management. A qualified plan is a plan that is designed to qualify under Internal Revenue Code (IRC) Section 401, so that company contributions to the plan are tax deductible when made by the company, but taxation to the plan participants only occurs when the benefits are distributed. To be qualified under the IRC, the plan must pass a variety of requirements, such as nondiscrimination, minimum funding levels, and contribution and benefit limits.

A nonqualified plan generally is a pension plan that is designed to ignore these qualified plan requirements. Thus, nonqualified plans discriminate between employees (i.e., between executives and the rank-and-file) and ignore the compensation and benefit limits imposed by the IRC. In many cases, these nonqualified arrangements will be subject to some—but not most—of the rules under the Employment Retirement Income Security Act of 1974 (ERISA). In order to be outside of most ERISA rules, the nonqualified plan must qualify as a top-hat plan. This essentially means that the plan is both only for management and is unfunded. To be unfunded, the company cannot create a plan trust or do anything that segregates assets intended to be used to pay benefits. For income tax purposes, nonqualified pension benefits are usually taxed as income when the benefit is paid (or distributed) to the executive, and it is only then that the company can take a corresponding deduction. However, funding the arrangement could cause the benefit to be constructively received by the executive. Thus, the primary issue is the avoidance of constructive receipt under the tax law. Even if constructive receipt is avoided, under the Federal Insurance Contributions Act (FICA) rules, accrued benefits under these plans may be taxed as wages prior to the date of distribution if the benefit is no longer subject to a substantial risk of forfeiture. In addition, pension-benefit arrangements most likely will be subject to the strict rules with respect to deferred compensation under IRC Section 409A.

Pension-benefit arrangements designed for members of management are commonly known as SERPs or SRPs, which usually stands for supplemental executive retirement plan/program or sometimes just supplement retirement plan/program. Some practitioners distinguish between what are called *true SERPs* and *restoration*, *"waraparound,"* or *excess-benefit SERPs*. A true SERP is an arrangement that stands on its own and in which the benefit is calculated in accordance with the formula or contribution design contained in the plan. It may incorporate by reference definitions from the company's qualified plans, and the benefit is almost always offset by the benefits paid under the qualified plan. It may be a group arrangement (usually contained in a plan document) or an individual arrangement (very often contained in an employment agreement). The restoration SERP is an arrangement that restores benefit limitations imposed by the IRC (discussed in more detail later). Be aware that the term *SERP* has become somewhat generic, and some may refer to any executive pension arrangement, including basic deferred compensation plans, as a SERP.

DEFINED-BENEFIT SERP ARRANGEMENTS

Although rank-and-file defined-contribution plans, such as 401(k) plans and cash-balance plans, have become increasingly popular, the defined-benefit pension plan still is a common pension plan at many companies. A defined-benefit plan pays a lifetime annual pension benefit that is defined by a formula calculated at retirement. The usual formula is $A \times B \times C$, in which:

A = a percentage (e.g., 2 percent, 1.75 percent)
B = the number of years of employment service
C = the employee's final or average annual compensation

Defined-benefit SERP arrangements generally operate in the same way. Companies implement these plans for a variety of reasons, which include:

- Offering the new executive a replacement pension arrangement similar to his or her existing arrangement at the former employer
- Offering the executive payout options not available under the qualified plan (e.g., the qualified plan only offers joint and 50 percent survivorship, but the SERP also offers lump sum distributions and joint and 100 percent survivorship)
- Changing the normal retirement date from 65 to an earlier age (e.g., 62) so that there is no actuarial reduction of the benefit for retirement prior to age 65
- Providing different features or computational levels to determine the benefit (e.g., actuarial reduction is 1 percent per year compared with an actuarial reduction of 1.5 percent per year under the qualified plan; changes in the calculation of final or average compensation, etc.)
- Allowing an executive to have a defined-benefit arrangement while the company's qualified plan is a defined-contribution arrangement.

In many circumstances, the defined-benefit SERP benefit will be offset and reduced by:

- The pension benefit paid under the company's qualified rank-and-file pension plan (assuming the executive is a participant)
- The pension benefit paid by all other pension arrangements outside of the company in which the executive is vested and entitled to receive a benefit.

The percentage variable can be fixed (e.g., 2 percent per year) or variable (e.g., 1.5 percent for the first 10 years, 1.75 percent for the next 10 years, and 2 percent for all years of service over 20). Many defined-benefit SERP arrangements will simply use a "target" final percentage at a specific age (e.g., 60 percent of final or average compensation at age 62). These final percentages typically range from 50 percent to 70 percent, but since the actual benefit is based on the definition of *compensation*, these percentages can be misleading.

The number of years of service generally is straightforward in most cases, sometimes capped at 30, 35, or 40 years (usually if the qualified plan is so capped). Sometimes when an executive is hired from outside the company, the compensation committees may award the executive "credited" years of service as a make-whole arrangement. The reason for this is that under most defined-benefit formulas, the final benefit is back-end loaded, since final or average compensation at the end of an executive's career drives the benefit higher. The following examples illustrate this additional years of service:

Example 1: Executive X, who is 50 years old, leaves Company A, where he has worked for 20 years, for Company B. X is vested in Company A's qualified pension plan, but is unvested in

Company A's SERP (which has a cliff vest at age 60). Company B provides him with a SERP that credits him with 20 years of service from Day 1, but that cliff vests at age 60. Assuming X retires at age 60 from Company B, he will have accrued 30 years of service in computing his benefit.

Example 2: Same as Example 1, but the company allows Executive X to build up to the additional 20 years by crediting X with 4 years of service for each of the first 5 years of employment. This is in addition to age 60 vesting.

Example 3: Executive Y (who is Company C's chief operating officer (COO) and might become Company C's chief executive officer (CEO)) leaves Company C after 25 years of service with a fully vested SERP to become Company D's CEO. Her final or average compensation is $500,000 and the Company C SERP uses a 2 percent per year benefit formula. Thus, her annual benefit is $250,000. Company D has the exact same SERP arrangement as Company C. Y works for 5 years for Company D and retires with final or average compensation of $1 million. Without any credited years of service, Y would receive a $250,000 annual benefit from Company C and a $100,000 annual benefit from Company D. However, if Y had stayed at Company C, became CEO and retired with final or average compensation of $1 million, her annual benefit would have been $600,000 instead of $350,000. Therefore, Company D, as part of the inducement to bring Y on board, provides her with 25 years of additional credited service (offset by any Company C benefit she receives) to make up this gap.

Final or average compensation is determined in a myriad of ways, and there are several components to consider. First is what makes up the definition of *compensation*. It may be salary only (many times this is the case under old qualified pension plans), salary plus annual cash bonus (which is the common arrangement), or even salary and annual cash bonus plus all or some long-term incentives (such as vested restricted stock or exercised options). The second element is whether final or average compensation reflects compensation paid in the last year of employment (which would truly be final compensation), or the highest annual compensation paid in the last three or five years of employment prior to retirement (highest compensation), or the average of the last 36 or 60 consecutive months of employment prior to retirement (average compensation), or the highest average 36 months of compensation over the past 10 years (highest average compensation). In many cases, this compensation is calculated by taking the average of the highest three years of compensation paid in the 10 years prior to retirement. Finally, for executives hired outside of the company, there may be a minimum floor for final or average compensation.

As mentioned before, one of the reasons for a SERP is to provide payout options that may not be available under the qualified plan. For example, a lump-sum payout is a common feature of SERPs, and may not be permitted under the company's qualified pension plan. Some SERPs may allow a joint and 100 percent survivor benefit (as compared with a joint and 50 percent survivor benefit, which is the common payout under a company qualified pension plan), or may use a more favorable formula than under the qualified plan to determine lump sum amounts or actuarial reductions.

Finally, there are always issues associated with any termination of employment. If the executive quits or is terminated for Cause, then typically the executive is entitled to receive any vested portion of the SERP and all unvested portions are forfeited. Thus, many SERPs are designed to be retention devices and substantially vest at or near age 60 or 65. If, however, there is a termination without Cause (and usually this also applies to a termination for Good Reason), then there may be accelerated vesting, or additional years of service and/or age used to calculate the benefit. In some cases, the SERP's vesting may be the same as under the qualified plan (typically 100 percent vesting after five years of service) but may provide for benefits to begin only if a specified age and years of service has been achieved. This may be known as the *Rule of 65*, which means that benefits can begin only if the executive has 10 years of service and is at least 55, or if the executive is 60 and has at least five years of service, or perhaps if the executive is 50 and has 15 years of service. There are variations of this rule (e.g., Rule of 70, Rule of 75), and certain limitations may be imposed (e.g., minimum retirement age is 55).

Public companies are required to disclose defined-benefit SERP arrangements in which the company's named executive officers participate in a tabular presentation. Under the new SEC disclosure rules, reporting companies must include in the Summary Compensation Table, under a column heading of "Change in Pension Value and Nonqualified Deferred Compensation Earnings", the aggregate change in the actuarial present value of the named executive officer's accumulated benefit under all defined benefit and actuarial pension plans (including supplemental plans) from the pension plan measurement date used for financial statement reporting purposes with respect to the registrant's audited financial statements for the prior completed fiscal year to the pension plan measurement date used for financial statement reporting purposes with respect to the registrant's audited financial statements for the covered fiscal year. In addition, the company must provide a Pension Benefits Table that discloses:

- The name of all defined-benefit pension plans
- The number of years of years of service credited to the named executive officer under the plan, computed as of the same pension plan measurement date used for financial statement reporting purposes with respect to the registrant's audited financial statements for the last completed fiscal year
- The actuarial present value of the named executive officer's accumulated benefit under the plan, computed as of the same pension plan measurement date used for financial statement reporting purposes with respect to the registrant's audited financial statements for the last completed fiscal year
- The dollar amount of any payments and benefits paid to the named executive officer during the registrant's last completed fiscal year

Finally, the SERP plan document is required to be publicly filed as a material contract.

DEFINED-CONTRIBUTION SERP ARRANGEMENTS

Defined-contribution plans generally are plans in which the benefit is not calculated by a formula but by the value of an account designated to the employee. In these arrangements, the company makes a contribution into the employee's account (usually on an annual basis). The amount of the contribution may be based on salary, other compensation, profits, or a predetermined benefit amount (such as in a "money-purchase" or "target-benefit" pension arrangement). The account is invested in either a fixed or variable vehicle. At retirement, the account is paid out (either in installments, in a lump sum, or to purchase an annuity).

Defined-contribution SERP arrangements operate similarly except the account must be unfunded to avoid being subject to all of the ERISA rules. Thus, the accounts are "notional" bookkeeping accounts, in which money is hypothetically invested in the fixed or variable instrument. The hypothetical investments are tracked and reported to the executives, but the benefit is simply an unsecured promise to pay by the company. In many cases, a company will actually set up a true account using a rabbi trust (discussed later), but with care so that there is no constructive receipt under Federal tax law.

Similar to defined-benefit SERPs, these arrangements may be used to replace a similar arrangement at an executive's former employer, or if the company has converted to or implemented a defined-contribution arrangement for most or all employees. Issues relating to timing and form of payout, as well as vesting and what happens on a termination of employment are also similar to those issues under defined-benefit SERPs.

As with defined-benefit SERP arrangements, reporting companies must include in the Summary Compensation Table under the Change in Pension Value and Non-qualified Deferred Compensation Earnings column the value of above-market or preferential earnings on compensation that is deferred on a basis that is not tax qualified, including such earnings on nonqualified defined contribution plans. In addition, the company must provide a Nonqualified Deferred Compensation Table that discloses:

- The name of the executive officer

- The dollar amount of aggregate executive contributions during the registrant's last fiscal year

- The dollar amount of aggregate registrant contributions during the registrant's last fiscal year

- The dollar amount of aggregate interest or other earnings accrued during the registrant's last fiscal year

- The aggregate dollar amount of all withdrawals by and distributions to the executive during the registrant's last fiscal year

- The dollar amount of total balance of the executive's account as of the end of the registrant's last fiscal year.

These arrangements must also be publicly filed as material contracts.

EXCESS-BENEFIT SERP ARRANGEMENTS

These arrangements are simply "standard" qualified plans, but in which the limiting tax rules (i.e., the 2007 annual compensation cap of $225,000 under IRC Section 401(a)(17), the 2007 annual contribution cap of $15,500 under IRC Section 402(g), the 2007 annual contribution cap of $45,000 under IRC Section 415, and the 2007 annual benefit cap of $180,000 under IRC Section 415) are ignored. Thus, the benefit is determined as if these rules did not exist, and the SERP benefit is offset by the benefit paid from the qualified plan.

The appeal of these plans is that they are quite simple to design and implement, since the only change is to allow a higher level of contribution and/or a higher level of benefit. Generally, all other terms and conditions remain the same. However, defined-contribution excess benefit plans may become more complicated if there are a variety of investment choices, as is the case under most excess benefit 401(k) plans. If so, the company will need to establish notional or "bookkeeping" accounts to track the hypothetical investments, since creating actual accounts would cause the arrangement to be treated as funded and thus subject to all ERISA rules.

Public companies are required to disclose excess-benefit SERPs generally in accordance with the defined-benefit and defined-contribution pension plan disclosure rules, as well as the requirement that the plan document be publicly filed.

DEFERRED COMPENSATION ARRANGEMENTS

A deferred compensation arrangement, at its core, is when the executive elects to defer the payment or distribution of already earned salary, bonus, or other cash or equity compensation to a future point in time. This point in time could be a certain date (e.g., January 15, 2025), or a contemplated scheduled event (i.e., the first of the month following the executive's 62nd birthday, which is the date of the executive's planned retirement), or an unanticipated date (e.g., immediately following the executive's termination of employment, within 10 days of a change in control, or within 30 days of the date of the executive's death). Of course, as discussed in Chapter 8, all deferred compensation arrangements are now subject to the strict requirements with respect to deferral elections and distribution/payments under IRC Section 409A.

Generally, already earned compensation is not subject to forfeiture (and thus would be subject to FICA tax when accrued). In some arrangements, a company may contribute additional amounts of deferred compensation (generally known as matching contributions similar to Section 401(k) arrangements); however, these amounts are often subject to a vesting schedule and—if used as a retention device—such vesting may occur at age 55, 60, or 62.

RABBI TRUSTS AND SECULAR TRUSTS

Because ERISA require that any executive pension arrangement that is funded will be subject to the discrimination, minimum funding, and other rules, the vast majority of these arrangements are unfunded; in other words, the company's obligation is simply a "promise to pay." This means that the executive is vulnerable to either a refusal to pay (commonly referred to as a *change in heart*) or a company's inability to pay (i.e., due to insolvency or bankruptcy). To protect executives against a change-in-heart scenario (usually due to a change in control), many companies have set up "rabbi trusts." Generally, these are irrevocable grantor trusts established by the company that require the trustee to use the assets of the trust to pay the SERP benefits if the company fails to do so; however, if there is an insolvency or bankruptcy, the trustee is required to cease all benefit payments and to hold the trust assets for the benefit of the company's general unsecured creditors (which would also include the executives who are participants in the SERP). Because, from the executives perspective, the trust's assets are subject to a substantial risk of forfeiture (i.e., in the event of insolvency), the assets are treated as still belonging to the company, and thus the executive is not taxed on the amount until the benefit is distributed and received. Also, as discussed in Chapter 9, IRC Section 409A now proscribes the use of offshore rabbi trusts and any trust that uses a financial condition as a funding trigger.

A secular trust is an irrevocable grantor trust usually established by the executive in which the assets are not subject to a risk of forfeiture. The assets may indirectly be subject to a clawback if the executive quits or breaches a noncompetition provision or similar covenant. Secular trust contributions are taxed when made (either when actually paid to the executive or when contributed by the company to the trust), and thus the advantages of having a higher rate of return through tax deferral is lost; however, the executive's benefit is secure and the company does take a deduction when the contribution is made.

OTHER PENSION ARRANGEMENTS

There are, of course, a variety of pension and pension-related arrangements that may be called SERPs. For example, a grant of company restricted stock or restricted stock units that vest on retirement might be called a *stock SERP*. There could be a SERP that uses life insurance (discussed in the next section) to provide a benefit at retirement, and there could be an arrangement in which a large bonus is paid at or near retirement (which might be called a *bonus SERP*). In other words, there is no limit as to what could be a SERP, as long as the delivery of compensation is designed to begin at and/or after retirement. The important aspect of these nontraditional arrangements for compensation committees is to determine whether the compensation will be treated as pension-related and thus subject to ERISA, and the appropriate disclosure (if required).

WELFARE-BENEFIT ARRANGEMENTS

Executive welfare-benefit arrangements usually are enhanced welfare-benefit programs. Whether these programs are available to executives depends on the number of participants, the culture of the company, and specific individual executive employment arrangements. If treated as compensation, then public companies may need to disclose such arrangements in their public filings, usually in a footnote to the Summary Compensation Table. While these disclosure rules are not hard and fast, compensation committees should take note of the trend toward transparency with respect to all compensation and benefits paid or provided to top executives.

EXECUTIVE LIFE INSURANCE

Most company group life insurance plans have low death benefit levels, perhaps based on a 1 × or 2 × multiple of salary. Thus, it is common for companies to offer an executive a life insurance program in which the executive may be able to purchase a 3 × , 4 × , or 5 × multiple of salary. In these situations, the executive typically pays for the insurance.

Some executives, particularly those hired from outside the company, may negotiate for the company to provide (at its own expense) life insurance to the executive with a substantial death benefit. In many cases, this company-paid benefit is additional compensation, and it is not unusual for executives to ask (and sometimes to receive) a tax gross-up on this amount.

KEY-PERSON LIFE INSURANCE

While not an executive welfare-benefit arrangement program for the executive per se, key-person life insurance is an executive arrangement in which the company buys life insurance on a "key person" (e.g., an executive) for the company's benefit. In this arrangement, the company is the owner and the beneficiary of the death benefit. The rationale behind this type of insurance is that the company will have additional costs if the executive dies, and this death benefit helps pay for these costs. Note that in this situation, the executive does not receive any benefit. If companies are considering providing executives with life insurance, it might be appropriate to consider this key-person insurance (if the company wants itself to have this benefit) at the same time, to deal with underwriting and insurability concerns.

SPLIT-DOLLAR LIFE INSURANCE

Split-dollar life insurance has been around for many years, but has recently undergone radical changes due to regulations issued by the IRS in 2003 (see Chapter 8 for more detail). Essentially, a split-dollar life insurance arrangement is when the policy is shared by the company and the executive (or a trust established by the executive). In almost all situations, the company is entitled to receive all policy premiums it has paid, either through a surrender of the policy's cash value or through death benefits. In some arrangements, the company owns all the cash value (this is usually called *traditional* or *classic* split dollar), and in some cases, the executive (or his or her trust) owns the cash value that exceeds the aggregate of all policy premiums paid by the company (this is usually called *equity* split-dollar). In both arrangements, the company pays all or most of the policy premiums, and the executive pays none or a portion that represents the cost of one-year term life insurance. If the executive pays none, then he or she has imputed income based on the cost of one-year term life insurance. Finally, there was a concept known as reverse split-dollar, in which the roles of the company were reversed and artificial premium levels were assumed; however, IRS notices have effectively shut down these arrangements. In the time following the 2003 IRS regulations, many companies have revised their split-dollar life insurance programs to bring them into compliance with the regulations. On the other hand, many companies have also simply eliminated the programs.

The equity split-dollar arrangement may be phasing out for two reasons. First, many believe that equity split-dollar arrangements most likely violate Section 402 of the Sarbanes-Oxley Act of 2002, which prohibits personal loans to executive officers and directors. IRS regulations released in 2003 require that equity split-dollar be treated as a series of loans from the company to the executive. Thus, at least conceptually, the use of equity split-dollar might be regarded as providing personal loans to executives under federal securities laws. Second, the IRS regulations requiring below-market loan treatment may not be cost effective.

Traditional split-dollar may still be a viable program for some companies, particularly if it is used to fund nonqualified deferred compensation or pension-benefit arrangements, or to provide a life insurance SERP. In addition, traditional split-dollar may be adjusted to provide death benefits exceeding the aggregate premiums paid by the company, which would provide a key-person arrangement.

It is noted that the deferred compensation rules under IRC Section 409A apply to split-dollar life insurance, but the IRS has provided relief for any existing and grandfathered split-dollar life insurance arrangement that is amended to comply with Section 409A.

EXECUTIVE MEDICAL BENEFITS

It is not uncommon for executives to have their own medical plan, program, or arrangement. Usually, this is superimposed over the rank-and-file health plan. Compensation committees will need to determine whether such a plan is necessary (based on the benefits and coverage under the rank-and-file plan), is consistent with the company's culture, and will not be regarded as an excessive arrangement. In addition, if the company has these plans, care will be needed to make sure that it complies with IRC Section 105(h).

EXECUTIVE DISABILITY BENEFITS

Similar to executive medical benefits, many companies will offer executive disability benefits to its executives. The need for this benefit generally is based on the maximum benefit payable under the company's rank-and-file disability benefit program (which usually ranges from $100,000 to $250,000 per year). Based on a concept that an employee will need 50 percent to 60 percent of annual cash compensation if disabled, executives earning $1 million would need at least a $500,000 annual disability benefit. This benefit may be provided by self-insurance (i.e., the company obligates itself to continue salary—and perhaps bonus—during the disability period), or the company will pay the premiums on individual disability insurance policies. Design of these programs should take into account the general tax rule that premiums paid with after-tax dollars will result in tax-free benefits, while premiums paid by the company, or company-provided benefits, will result in taxable benefits.

OTHER EXECUTIVE WELFARE BENEFITS

There may be other executive welfare-benefits arrangements that compensation committees may encounter. However, in most cases (other than severance benefit programs that are discussed in Chapter 9), many of these arrangements most likely fall into the perquisite category and are discussed in the next section.

PERQUISITES

Executive perquisites has become an extremely controversial subject, so compensation committees should examine their needs and structure thoroughly before implementing such programs. In most instances, the program will apply to mid-level and senior executives, and thus the CEO may be involved with and be an advocate of the program. Nevertheless, any perquisite program that includes senior executives falls under the auspices of the compensation committee.

Essentially, perquisites need to be viewed as simply another way of delivering compensation to the executive. While there is no argument that certain perquisites are a necessity (e.g., car arrangements), the issue arises as to the level of the perquisite. In other words, there is no question that providing an executive with a car is an important perquisite if it is necessary for the executive to have a car in order to do his or her job. However, whether that executive should be driving a $50,000 car or a $150,000 car needs to be evaluated and ascertained.

Disclosure of perquisites is another factor. The 2006 executive compensation disclosure rules require that if the total value of the perquisites exceeds $10,000, then the total value of the perquisites must be disclosed. In addition, itemized perquisite disclosure is required for any perquisite value that exceeds 25 percent of the total value of perquisites. See Chapter 6 for a discussion about the disclosure of perquisites.

Finally, there is a thin line between providing an executive with an appropriate perquisite consummate with his or her position, title, duties, and responsibilities, and going over the top. Thus, compensation committees need to be prepared to justify their actions with regard to all perquisite programs.

RELOCATION AND TEMPORARY HOUSING

This perquisite usually applies to a new hire from outside the company, but it may apply to an internal promote. In taking the new job, and with the mutual understanding that the executive will need to move from his or her home in location X to a new home in location Y, the executive will be looking to the company to pay the costs of this relocation. This might consist only of actual moving costs; however, more likely, it will also consist of some or most of the following:

- Reimbursement for temporary housing and/or hotel accommodations not only for himself or herself but also for his or her spouse and other members of the executive's family during the house-hunting phase
- Reimbursement for travel from location X to location Y, not only for himself or herself but also for his or her spouse and other members of the executive's family (although these trips may be limited in frequency or capped in amount)
- Closing costs associated with the purchase of the new home
- An arrangement for the company to purchase the existing home (usually based on an appraisal by a reputable appraiser or the average of three appraisals)
- Other miscellaneous expenses (sometimes subject to a cap)

Finally, while some of these costs/reimbursements may be a working condition fringe benefit and thus not treated as compensation, some of these reimbursements may be treated as compensation and thus taxable. Accordingly, it is not unusual for the executive to ask for a tax gross-up so that the relocation has a neutral financial impact to the executive.

EXPENSE ACCOUNTS (INCLUDING SPORTING AND ENTERTAINMENT EVENTS)

Companies generally have established policies with respect to expense accounts, and reasonable expenses reasonably incurred by the executive in the course of conducting business is a standard and uncontroversial practice. This would even include sporting and entertainment events used for business purposes. However, some executives may ask to have the company obligate itself to specific events or provide a dollar amount to be applied to such events. For example, an executive in the music industry might ask for a commitment from the company for attendance at the Grammys for him or her and 10 clients. Other common examples would be contractual commitments to provide tickets for the World Series, the Super Bowl, major golfing events, and the like. In reviewing these kinds of arrangements, the compensation committee generally should focus on whether there is a legitimate business purpose associated with providing these kinds of perquisites.

CLUB MEMBERSHIPS

Generally, club memberships may be divided into country clubs, eating clubs, and health clubs. The company may have a policy that allocates a fixed dollar amount to be applied to a club (any club), or the company may simply provide that it will pay the membership fees and dues for a specific club or a club of the executive's choice. Current taxation of these expenses will need to be examined, since some programs might be structured in such a way that the expenses are not deductible and some programs in which the expenses are treated as compensation (and thus deductible).

AIR TRAVEL ARRANGEMENTS

Air travel is usually governed by an established company policy. However, it is not unusual for executives (particularly CEOs) to request and sometimes receive a contractual commitment to first-class air travel or priority rights to corporate aircraft. In addition, personal use of corporate-owned or corporate-provided aircraft may also be contained in such a contractual provision. This is an area in which some compensation committees will need to "keep their eye on the ball."

GROUND TRAVEL ARRANGEMENTS

Companies have a variety of automobile arrangements. The questions for most compensation committees will be whether to provide the executive with a car only, a car and driver, and what kind of car. In addition, the company may provide parking as a perquisite, particularly if the executive's office is located in a congested urban area.

Commuting is never tax deductible. However, there are exceptions and arrangements that incorporate the commute into business travel, and these should be explored.

SECURITY-RELATED ARRANGEMENTS

The tax regulations allow deductions for a bona fide security program. However, this security need must be clearly established. Thus, if a company determines that it needs to provide extra security to its executive (e.g., a car with bulletproof glass), such expense may be deductible, but only to the extent of the cost of the security-related expenses (e.g., the cost of bulletproofing the car's glass, not the entire cost of the car). This is a complex area in which compensation committees definitely will need advice from tax counsel.

FINANCIAL AND TAX COUNSELING

A common perquisite is to provide executives with financial and tax counseling. Sometimes, a company contracts with a firm to provide this to a group of executives. Sometimes, the company will provide an allowance (usually with a cap). Companies that are trying to minimize their perquisite programs may simply provide a higher base salary to replace this lost perquisite.

TAX GROSS-UPS

While not normally considered a perquisite, some executive employment arrangements will provide that if certain benefits or perquisites are treated as compensation (thus resulting in the imposition of income tax), the executive will be provided with a tax gross-up that will leave the executive in an after-tax neutral position. For example, suppose a company agrees to provide an executive with full relocation benefits. The total relocation reimbursements are $50,000, 50 percent of which will not be treated as compensation under the company's relocation policy, but 50 percent of which will result in compensation. Using a 45 percent aggregate tax rate, the company would pay an additional $20,455 to fully gross-up the $25,000 that is treated as compensation.

The typical tax gross-up is a golden parachute excise tax gross-up (see Chapter 8 for a discussion of golden parachute tax law). Next would be for benefits and perquisites that are treated as compensation (e.g., the relocation example in the above paragraph). There are some companies that have tax gross-up programs with respect to their equity-based compensation programs. For example, a few companies that have migrated from appreciation-type awards (e.g., stock options) to full-value awards (e.g., restricted stock) have a design feature in which a tax gross-up will be paid when the restricted stock vests. In some cases, this was to replace the company-provided loan to pay the tax if an IRC Section 83(b) election was made, as such loans became illegal in 2002 by Section 402 of the Sarbanes-Oxley Act. Finally, there has been some discussion about using a tax gross-up with respect to deferred compensation that becomes taxable under IRC Section 409A; however, this generally has remained at the discussion stage at most companies.

Overall, it appears likely that the use of tax gross-ups will trend down, and compensation committees that are considering using this benefit should carefully review the rationale for adding this design to any arrangement.

CHARITABLE CONTRIBUTIONS

Executives may suggest or have an arrangement in which the company makes a contribution to a charity selected by the executive. This practice appears to be phasing out, as there is a question as to the tax results and the overall optics.

BUSINESS MACHINES

As the business world becomes more dependent on laptops, fax machines, Black-Berries, personal digital assistants (PDAs), and so forth, more and more companies are providing these machines to their executives. In some cases, the arrangement is that the company simply lets the executive use the machine and that it always remains the property of the company, subject to return upon a termination of employment. Some companies, however, simply give these machines to their executives, or establish an allowance for the purchase of such machines. The tax ramifications will depend on the structure of the program.

ANNUAL PHYSICALS

Annual physicals for executives were a popular perquisite years ago, particularly because they were not provided under standard medical benefit programs. Today, however, most health benefit programs (whether indemnity-based, health mainten-ance organization (HMO), preferred provider organization (PPO), etc.) provide for annual physicals at little or no cost. However, some companies have continued this program, particularly if they have contracted with a doctor group that caters to these types of physicals. In addition, some company cultures prefer to have a comprehen-sive physical of its top executive each year (over and above the standard physical under the company's health plan).

OTHER PERQUISITES

Of course, there are always other uncommon perquisites that a company may provide its CEO and/or other executives. For example, a defense-related company might allow its CEO (who had been a fighter pilot in the military) to use a company jet fighter. Similarly, a recreational boat company might provide its CEO with use of one of its luxury boats. An insurance company might contractually agree to provide new golf clubs and other golfing equipment every year to its executive if the executive did most of his business on the golf course. A company whose CEO lives in another state and does not relocate might provide a housing allowance with a tax gross-up. Or a company might purchase a residence (perhaps near the company's headquarters, perhaps in a major city) ostensibly for business purposes but which might be used exclusively by the CEO. These types of nontraditional perquisites, along with any and all other perquisites, will simply need to be assessed by the compensation committee for cost, reasonableness, tax consequences, and perception by shareholders and the public.

Chapter 15

Special Issues

This chapter touches on three topical issues that may be of particular interest to compensation committees, whether or not they come into play at their particular companies. The chapter begins with a discussion of the widespread investigation into option grant practices, the practical implication of having backdated options, and the related option grant practices colloquially referred to as *spring-loading* and *bullet-dodging*. Next, the chapter addresses option repricing in the current environment—why is it done and the implications of doing it. The chapter closes with a look into "going dark"—the process whereby a public company steps out of the public disclosure system by having its shares deregistered.

OPTION GRANT PRACTICES

The subject of option grant practices has fascinated the legal and financial press since the spring of 2006. Stemming largely from a 2005 study of CEO option awards conducted by researchers from the University of Iowa and a series of subsequent *Wall Street Journal* articles, it was demonstrated that many companies issued stock options immediately prior to upward swings in the stock price. This link between the date of option grants and the subsequent increase in stock price led to wide speculation that companies were backdating options—obtaining a low exercise price by maintaining that the option was granted on a prior date when the stock price was at a low for the period.

Even where there is no evidence of *backdating*, companies have come under scrutiny for a practice that has come to be known as *spring-loading*, which refers to granting options shortly before the release of positive information, or *bullet-dodging*, which refers to postponing the grant of options until shortly after the release of negative information, in both cases in order to take advantage of a stock price anticipated to be low on the option grant date.

Investigations into option grant practices developed rapidly and are continuing. Well over 100 companies have been or are currently under governmental investigation from the Securities and Exchange Commission (SEC), Department of Justice (DOJ), or local authorities. Many more companies engaged in internal investigations instigated by their audit committees or otherwise.

Following formal or internal investigations, an alarmingly large number of companies reported that they would restate their financial statements for prior periods as a result of backdating or other "irregularities" in their option grant practices.

Shareholder derivative actions abound, and many companies received inquiries from institutional investors, insurers, and the press, asking them to affirmatively state that they have or have not backdated options.

In the first instance of federal prosecutorial action in the backdating scandal, in July 2006, the SEC and DOJ brought civil and criminal actions against the former chief executive officer (CEO) and vice president of human resources of Brocade Communications Systems, Inc., alleging that they actively backdated options over the course of several years in order to maximize option value. The chief financial officer (CFO) faced SEC civil action for knowingly signing off on misleading financial statements. The Brocade action resulted in the first criminal conviction in this area, when in August 2007 the CEO was convicted on 10 felony counts, including securities fraud, conspiracy, and filing false financial statements, which could result in imprisonment of up to 20 years and a fine of up to $5 million. At the time of this writing, the conviction is expected to be appealed.

The Brocade action made it clear that the SEC was targeting individuals who took actions to effect the backdating, whether or not they realized personal gain from the awards. Since that time, the SEC and DOJ have instituted a number of civil and criminal actions against individuals involved in backdating investigations.

Backdating an option could be intentional or unintentional. Intentional backdating involves purposely selecting a date when the stock price was low and maintaining that an option was granted as of that prior date. Unintentional backdating could result from lax corporate procedures, such as using unanimous consent actions for granting options but not having all directors sign on the same day, or the compensation committee failing to set all material terms on the intended date of grant (generally, date of grant is the date all material terms of the grant are set and approved by all necessary corporate action). Interestingly, as to this issue, SEC Commissioner Paul Atkins said in a July 6, 2006, speech:

> Backdating of options sounds bad, but the mere fact that options were backdated does not mean that the securities laws were violated. Purposefully backdated options that are properly accounted for and do not run afoul of the company's public disclosure are legal. Similarly, there is no securities law issue if backdating results from an administrative, paperwork delay. A board, for example, might approve an options grant over the telephone, but the board members' signatures may take a few days to trickle in. One could argue that the grant date is the date on which the last director signed, but this argument does not necessarily reflect standard corporate practice or the logistical practicalities of getting many geographically dispersed and busy, part-time people to sign a document. It also ignores that these actions reflect a true meeting of the minds of the directors, memorialized by executing a unanimous written consent.

Innocent or not, there are substantial accounting, tax, and securities compliance problems with backdated stock options, as described in the following paragraphs. See Chapters 8, 9, and 13 for a more thorough discussion of the accounting and tax rules that are mentioned in the following paragraphs.

ACCOUNTING ISSUES

Under option accounting rules in effect prior to 2006 (ABP 25), time-vesting stock options that had an exercise price at least equal to the fair market value of the shares on the grant date resulted in no compensation charge and, therefore, were highly favorable. But time-vesting options with an exercise price of less than the fair market value on the grant date (i.e., discounted options) resulted in a fixed compensation expense equal to the amount of the discount. If as a result of backdating, a company took advantage of the favorable accounting treatment for market-priced stock options when in fact such options were discounted, the company would have had inaccurate financial statements. If material, this could require restatement of financial statements for prior years.

Under option accounting rules that became mandatory in 2006 (FAS 123R), all stock options result in an accounting expense equal to the "fair value" of the award on the grant date. A discounted exercise price can result in a higher fair value for the award, but the expense discrepancy between a fair market value–priced option and a discounted option may not be material. That is why most of the backdating restatements relate to awards issued prior to the time that companies followed FAS 123R for stock option accounting.

TAX ISSUES

Incentive stock options(ISOs). If any backdated options were intended to be ISOs under Section 422 of the Internal Revenue Code (IRC), they will fail to qualify as ISOs if the exercise price was less than the fair market value on the actual grant date. Backdating generally resulted in the exercise price being at a discount to market (thus disqualifying the ISO), and for options that have already been exercised, may have resulted in under reporting of income for employees and the company losing tax deductions that it was otherwise entitled to.

$1 million deduction limit under IRC Section 162(m). Time-based options granted to top executive officers are exempt from the $1 million deduction limit under IRC Section 162(m), but only if the exercise price is at least equal to the fair market value on the date of grant. Backdating that resulted in discounted options would cause a loss of the Section 162(m) exemption and may lead to a loss of deduction in the year such options were or will be exercised. Because of the way Section 162(m) works (as explained in Chapter 13), this can be an ongoing problem for companies that backdated options.

Deferred compensation under IRC Section 409A. Discounted options that remained unvested as of December 31, 2004, are not exempt from the new deferred compensation rules under IRC Section 409A and would, therefore, be taxable immediately upon vesting and subject to the holder to a 20 percent additional tax, interest, and penalties. Company have until December 31, 2007 to amend discounted options to either increase the exercise price to the grant date fair market value or to impose a fixed schedule for exercises so as to comply with IRC Section 409A. However, this transitional relief is not available to executive officers and directors of public companies that had to restate financial results based on options having been backdated (even if the officer or director was not directly implicated in the back-dating).

SECURITIES COMPLIANCE ISSUES

Proxy statement disclosures. Public disclosures would most likely be deemed false and misleading if they indicated that backdated options were granted at fair market value on the grant date, because the true grant date (for tax and accounting purposes) would have been the date that the board or compensation committee took action to approve the grant.

Proxy disclosure rules in effect prior to 2007 required a separate column in the option grants table if the exercise price of an option to a named executive officer was less than fair market value on the date of grant. Few companies complied with this disclosure—probably on the belief, or at least the theory, that the "stated" grant date was in fact the true grant date.

New proxy rules adopted in July 2006, effective for proxy statements filed beginning in 2007 (as discussed at length in Chapter 6), require far more explicit disclosure that is designed to spotlight any option with an exercise price different than the closing price of the stock on the date the board or compensation committee took action to approve the grant. This more specific disclosure requirement will further quell option backdating, but, as a practical matter, option backdating has largely stopped for other reasons.

Section 16 reporting. Now that Section 16 rules under the Securities Exchange Act of 1934 require two-day reporting of option grants (as discussed in Chapter 7), there is less practical opportunity to backdate options. Options backdated by more than two business days cannot comply with Section 16 reporting on a timely basis. Before 2002, insiders could wait until the 45th day of the next calendar year to report the grant of an option, which provided a tempting opportunity to backdate options to a favorable date before the grant had to be publicly reported. That is why many of the instances of backdating that are being uncovered today took place prior to 2002.

PLAN PROVISIONS

Many incentive plans prohibit the grant of discounted stock options. If a backdated option results in a discounted price, one must determine what legal effect that has. There are a number of possibilities, none of which is ideal. For example:

- If the company did not grant the option in accordance with the shareholder approved terms of the plan, did it have the authority to make the grant at all? There is a possibility that the grant is invalid.

- If the company granted the option outside of the regular incentive plan, the grant would not have been covered by the Form S-8 registration statement for the plan, and therefore may have violated Section 5 of the Securities Act of 1933 unless an exemption was available at the time of the grant. If no registration exemptions were available, the company may need to consider a rescission offer. This will be difficult or impossible if the options have already been exercised and the shares sold.

- Even if a registration exemption were available for the grant of the option, the optionee would acquire restricted securities upon exercise of the options and would need to hold the shares for the applicable Rule 144 holding period prior to a public sale of the shares.

- Was the grant of discounted options in violation of the plan terms a *de facto* amendment of the plan? Such an amendment without shareholder approval would violate stock exchange rules, as explained in Chapter 5.

OTHER PROBLEMS

Personal liability. Intentional backdating of options, or even engaging in spring-loading or bullet-dodging grant practices, could lead to director and officer liability for breach of the duty of loyalty and good faith. Two recent Delaware cases in this regard, *Ryan v. Gifford*, C.A. No. 2213-N (Del. Ch. Feb. 6, 2007) and *In Re Tyson Foods, Inc. Consolidated Shareholder Litigation*, C.A. No. 1106-N (Del. Ch. Feb. 6, 2007), are discussed in detail in Chapter 5 in the context of fiduciary duties of corporate directors. Backdating can also lead to personal liability for those who knowingly assisted in the activity. As an example of this, the SEC brought an early civil action against the former vice president of human resources of Brocade Communications, who presumably was just following orders from management to change the hire dates of certain executives. Lawyers may also be at risk—witness the early criminal charges brought by the SEC against the general counsel of Comverse Technology and, more recently, against the former general counsel of Apple Inc.

Disgorgement of compensation. As mentioned above, backdating options could require a financial restatement, if the accounting irregularities were material. Such a restatement may trigger the need for the chief executive officer (CEO) and the chief financial officer (CFO) to disgorge compensation under the provisions of Section 304 of the Sarbanes Oxley Act of 2002, as discussed in greater detail in Chapter 7. Under that law, if a public company is required to restate financials due to noncompliance with financial reporting requirements under the securities laws as a result of misconduct, the company's CEO and CFO must reimburse the company for (1) any bonus, incentive-based, or equity-based compensation received during the 12 months prior to the filing or public issuance of the financial document embodying such reporting requirement; and (2) any profits from the sale of issuer securities during that period.

Internal controls. Even unintentional backdating could call into question the adequacy of internal controls under Section 404 of the Sarbanes-Oxley Act or otherwise.

SPRING-LOADING AND BULLET-DODGING

While *backdating* is clearly problematic on almost all fronts, the practices of timing options to precede the release of positive information (spring-loading) or to follow release of negative information (bullet-dodging) are also under intense scrutiny.

Not everyone agrees that spring-loading and bullet-dodging are illegal or even a bad practice. In his much-quoted speech on July 6, 2006, SEC Commissioner Paul Atkins said:

> In the best exercise of their business judgment, directors might very well conclude that options should be granted in advance of good news. What better way to maximize the value that the option recipient attaches to the option? Conversely, a board would avoid granting options right before bad news hits since recipients are likely to place a lower value on such options. A board that times its option grants wisely can achieve the same result that it would by granting more options at a time when the stock price is likely to stagnate or drop. A board that makes a consistent practice of timing options grants before the stock price rises would be able to pay lower cash salaries than a board that makes options grants without taking into consideration the likely prospective changes in the stock price, precisely because there is a greater chance of the options being worth something and achieving their intended objective.

There are many who disagree with Commissioner Atkins's views on this point. Some claim that such propitious timing of options is "fraud on the market," and several shareholder suits have been filed on that basis. There may be a claim that the *true* fair market value of stock on the eve of the publication of good news is not reflected by the closing price of the stock that day on the uninformed market, and therefore any options granted at that price are per se not granted at fair market value.

Most experts, however, believe that timing of options to precede good news is not insider trading under Rule 10b-5 under the Securities Exchange Act as long as the officer receiving the award and the board making the award are equally aware of the nonpublic information. But Rule 10b-5 is clearly at play if the board was unaware of the positive news and optionee knew of it. This is the fact pattern of the classic insider-trading case of *SEC v. Texas Gulf Sulphur, Co.*, 401 F.2d 833 (2d Cir. 1968), cert. denied, 394 U.S. 976 (1969).

As mentioned above and in Chapter 6, the SEC's new executive compensation disclosure rules require focused disclosure of a company's policy or practices regarding the timing of option grants. In its open meeting to announce the new rules, the SEC made clear that it is not taking a position on the appropriateness or inappropriateness of any particular option grant practice. Rather, its concern is that the company's practice, whatever it is, be fully disclosed to investors and properly accounted for in the company's financial statements. The SEC's disclosure rules specifically do not mention the terms *backdating, spring-loading*, or *bullet-dodging* which colloquialisms carry negative connotations.

Also significantly, early on in the investigative frenzy, the SEC's accounting arm encouraged outside audit firms to avoid a slate of restatements resulting from excessive zeal in the investigation of option grant practices. Audit firms were urged to distinguish between innocuous mistakes and nefarious activity. In a detailed letter dated September 19, 2006, from the SEC's chief accountant, Conrad Hewitt, to the Chairs of the Committee on Corporate Reporting of Financial Executives International and the Center for Public Company Audit Firms at the American Institute of Certified Public Accountants, Mr. Hewitt expressed the views of the SEC staff on the application of APB 25 to several fact patterns that may be implicated in the review of option grant practices. Notably, the letter concluded, among other things, that not every misdated option should have accounting consequences under APB 25. The staff openly recognized the possibility that certain innocent foot-faults, such as short delays in completing administrative procedures to finalize a grant, ought not to result in an accounting consequence. At the same time, the letter clearly acknowledged that the analysis is highly dependent on the facts and circumstances of every case and that many of the issues that have been uncovered in review of option grant practices resulted in the grant of in-the-money options and accordingly do have accounting consequences under APB 25.

THE EMERGENCE OF OPTION GRANT POLICIES

The Compensation Discussion and Analysis (CD&A) under the SEC's new executive compensation disclosure rules requires a discussion of the company's equity grant practices. The compensation committee should establish a written policy about the timing and procedure for its program for granting equity awards, including stock options. While there is no universally correct option grant policy, such a policy might include some of the following elements, for example, designed to avoid the practice or appearance of timing grants to take advantage of a particular stock price:

- Annual equity grants will be approved at the meeting of the compensation committee held in [specified month] of each year and will be granted on the third business day after the next release of year-end or quarterly earnings.

- The compensation committee may delegate to the chairman of the committee (for example) the ability to make grants at other times, such as in the case of new hires or promotions, within specified parameters. (In this case, the person delegated such authority should document his or her actions in writing contemporaneously with such grants in order to provide clear evidence of the grant date.)

- If equity awards are granted outside of these two situations, they will be made at an in-person or telephonic meeting of the compensation committee (which avoids possible foot-faults based on the difficulties of having all committee members sign a written consent action on the intended date of grant).

- If the policy allows equity awards to be granted by unanimous consent action, the consent action should explicitly state that it will be effective as of the date that the last signature is obtained, and each director should manually supply the date next to his or her signature.

REPRICING STOCK OPTIONS

As a result of the sharp decline in the stock markets in the early 2000s, many companies faced the dilemma of stock options that were seriously "underwater" in the sense that the exercise price (which was equal to the fair market value of the stock on the date the options were granted) far exceeded the fallen stock price. During this time, there was a rash of repricings to lower the exercise price of options in an effort to restore the incentive and retention value of the awards. This practice was not without controversy or regulatory complication. However, with the recovered health of the stock markets (at the time of this writing, the Dow Jones Industrial Average hovers above 13,000, an all-time high), the need for repricing options has become far less compelling, even though new accounting rules have made it procedurally less cumbersome.

Ironically, the option repricings that occurred more frequently in 2007 were to *increase* the price of options that were determined to have been misdated as a result of option backdating or otherwise, as discussed earlier in this chapter. Whether the price is being adjusted up or down, there are a number of fiduciary, tax, accounting, and securities issues to be considered.

GENERAL SHAREHOLDER AND FIDUCIARY DUTY CONSIDERATIONS

Whether the decision is to reprice, replace, or simply grant additional awards, the compensation committee should consider the following issues:

- Shareholders may well view the replacement of underwater options as an elimination of the risk in what is designed to be a risk-reward mechanism.
- Stock incentives almost universally are promoted as linking executives' interests with those of shareholders. Shareholders may object to the repricing or replacement of executives' options since they, as shareholders, do not get to walk away from losses.
- Many plans by their terms expressly prohibit option repricings without shareholder approval—this is especially true in plans adopted in the 2000s. Many other plans are silent about whether options can or cannot be repriced. Under current NYSE shareholder approval rules, a plan that is silent about repricing will be deemed to prohibit it, so that if the company does reprice it will be deemed a material plan amendment, which requires shareholder approval.

- Repricing of stock options, directly or indirectly, is a serious hot button among institutional investors. In general, a repricing proposal that does not include certain terms favored by shareholders (such as, for example, exclusion of directors and executive officers, imposition of new vesting hurdles on the replacement awards, and a less than one-for-one exchange factor) is not likely to be approved.

- Lawsuits alleging corporate waste or lack of plan authority are sometimes brought against issuers and their directors for replacing underwater options.

- Repricing or replacing options may create internal inequities among employees. For example, some employees may have already exercised their options but failed to sell the option stock prior to the stock price decline.

Decisions concerning repricings are highly situational. Nevertheless, such decisions should be made on a basis that takes into account a number of factors, including the accounting cost associated with the repricing, the number of underwater options, the exercise price of the underwater options, the responsibilities and performance of the optionholder, and other matters deemed relevant by the compensation committee. Minutes of the committee's meeting should reflect thorough and careful deliberation on these issues.

The process followed by the board or compensation committee in its deliberative and decision-making activity is important in connection with securing the protections of the business judgment rule for its actions in this and other areas. See Chapter 5 for a more in-depth discussion of the fiduciary duties of directors in the context of compensation decisions.

The following paragraphs discuss each of four typical repricing alternatives, with comments on the accounting, tax, and securities issues unique to each.

REPRICE UNDERWATER OPTIONS OR REPLACE CONCURRENTLY WITH NEW STOCK OPTIONS

Accounting Issues

Under FAS 123R, any modification to an outstanding award is treated as a cancellation of the award and the grant of a replacement award. The company incurs a compensation cost equal to (1) the unexpensed value of the original option, if any, based on its fair value as of the original date of grant, plus (2) the excess of the fair value of the new option immediately after the modification over the fair value of the original option immediately before the modification. Therefore, a value-for-value options exchange would result in no additional compensation cost.

Tax Issues

Section 162(m) limit. For public companies, IRC Section 162(m) limits the corporate tax deduction for compensation paid to certain executive officers to $1 million, except that certain performance-based compensation does not count toward the $1 million limit. One example of such exempt performance-based compensation is a stock option granted at fair market value (FMV) under a plan that has been approved by the shareholders and that, by its terms, limits the number of options that may be granted to any one person in a stated time period. The repricing of options is treated as a grant of new options, such that the repriced options would count double against the maximum grant to a covered employee in the same period. The same analysis would apply if the company simply cancelled the outstanding options and issued new options at FMV on the date of grant.

Incentive stock option (ISO) issues. An employee is eligible for ISO treatment only with respect to options that become exercisable for the first time in any calendar year for up to $100,000 worth of stock (based on the FMV on the date of grant). Replacing existing ISOs with the same number of new ISOs at a lower exercise price should not run afoul of this limit, because the measure would be based on the fair market value of the stock on the date of regrant (i.e., the lower number). However, the $100,000 limitation may restrict the company's ability to provide an accelerated vesting schedule for the replacement options to preserve the prior vesting of the replaced options.

Securities Law Issues

Proxy statement reporting. Under Item 402 of Regulation S-K, proxy statement reporting is required if options held by any of a company's named executive officers (generally the CEO, CFO, and three other highest-paid executives) are repriced or otherwise materially modified, whether through amendment, surrender and replacement, or any other means. The company must explain the mechanics of the repricing in reasonable detail in a narrative description following the tables. In addition, the company should include in its CD&A a discussion of the rationale for the repricing.

Section 16. Whether the existing options are actually surrendered and replaced, or the company simply reduces the exercise price of the underwater options, the transaction would be deemed a surrender of the old option and grant of a new option for purposes of Section 16 of the Securities Exchange Act of 1934 (Exchange Act). In either case, the surrender of outstanding options and grant of new options will be deemed *exempt* transactions under Section 16(b), provided the full board of directors or a committee consisting entirely of *non-employee directors* as defined in Rule 16b-3(b)(3) approves the same in advance, or the shareholders approve or ratify such action. Notwithstanding the Section 16(b) exemptions, both the surrender and replacement of options should be reported pursuant to Section 16(a) on Form 4 within two business days.

Tender offer issue. If the optionee is given a choice as to whether to exchange his or her existing options for differently priced options (as opposed to the company's unilaterally changing the exercise price), it is likely that this will involve an issuer tender offer. In March 2001, the SEC's Division of Corporation Finance issued an exemptive order regarding option exchange offers that are conducted for compensatory purposes (e.g., offers to exchange underwater options for new options, restricted stock, cash, or other consideration). The exemptive order was quite narrow in scope and, in practice, served to formalize the SEC's formerly unofficial view that such option exchange offers constitute "issuer tender offers." Issuer tender offers are subject to specific requirements of Rule 13e-4 under the Exchange Act, including the filing of a Schedule TO with the SEC.

Plan Language

A company's option plans would need to be reviewed to see whether they expressly prohibit, expressly permit, or are silent about the company's ability to reprice or replace options. In light of strong preferences of institutional investors, many recent plans have an express prohibition on repricing (or cancellation and replacement) of stock options. Under NYSE shareholder approval rules, a plan that is silent about repricing will be deemed to prohibit it, so that if the company does reprice, it will be deemed a material plan amendment that requires shareholder approval. The NASDAQ rules, although less explicit, would probably also require shareholder approval under these circumstances.

LEAVE UNDERWATER OPTIONS IN PLACE AND GRANT ADDITIONAL OPTIONS AT MARKET PRICE

Accounting Issues

Under FAS 123R, the fair value of the old options would continue to be expensed over their remaining vesting period. The company would have an additional compensation charge equal to the fair value of the new options measured as of the grant date, which would be recognized over the vesting period of the new options.

Tax Issues

The tax effects to the company and the optionee with respect to such additional options would be no different than for any grant of options to employees. The tax effects will vary, of course, on whether the new options are incentive stock options or nonstatutory.

Securities Law Issues

Proxy statement reporting. The grant of additional options should not implicate repricing disclosures under the proxy rules. However, the normal rules would apply for reporting option grants during the year to the named executive officers. In addition, the company should comment in the CD&A on the rationale for the special grant.

Section 16. The grant would be treated like any other grant of options for purposes of Section 16—exempt if approved in advance by either the full board of directors or a committee consisting entirely of non-employee directors as defined in Rule

16b-3(b)(3) or approved or ratified by the company's shareholders. Notwithstanding the Section 16(b) exemptions, the grant should be reported pursuant to Section 16(a) on Form 4 by the second business day after grant.

Dilution Concerns

If the stock price rebounds to a level above the higher exercise price of the underwater options, the resulting dilution from the increased option overhang could reach unacceptable levels. This would also result in double compensation.

Plan Share Availability

There may not be sufficient shares under the company's current option plans to double up on existing underwater grants. Under NYSE and NASDAQ shareholder approval rules, shareholder approval is required to adopt new plans or amend existing plans to add shares.

REPLACE UNDERWATER OPTIONS WITH GRANTS OF RESTRICTED STOCK

A number of companies have elected to offer optionees the right to surrender their underwater options in exchange for grants of restricted stock. Historically, this was a favored approach because it avoided a six-month waiting period under ABP 25. This method has the advantage of adding back to the plan share pool the shares covered by the options that are surrendered and reduces the possibility of an unacceptably high overhang. In most cases, the number of restricted shares offered would be less than the number of options surrendered.

Accounting Issues

Under FAS 123R, the new restricted stock awards would result in a fixed compensation charge to the company, based on the fair market value of the shares on the date of grant, less the fair value of the cancelled underwater options as of the date of grant of the replacement awards. This fixed charge would be expensed over the vesting period of the restricted stock. Any unrecognized expense associated with the original options would also be recognized.

Tax Issues

The surrender of the underwater options would have no tax effect to the optionee or the company. The grant of the restricted stock would have no tax effect to the grantee or the company, unless the grantee filed an election under IRC Section 83(b) to be taxed currently on the grant. In that case, the grantee would have ordinary income on the date of grant equal to the then fair market value of the restricted stock, and the company would have a corresponding deduction, subject to the limits of IRC Section 162(m).

If a Section 83(b) election is not filed within 30 days after the grant of the restricted stock, the grantee will have ordinary income as the shares vest, equal to the fair market value of the shares on the various vesting dates. The company would have a corresponding tax deduction at that time, subject to the limits of IRC Section 162(m). Note that the restricted stock will not be exempt from the IRC Section 162(m) limitations unless it is performance based.

Securities Law Issues

Tender offer issue. As discussed previously with respect to an options-for-options exchange, the SEC takes the position that an exchange offer for restricted stock is likely to be an issuer tender offer that would require the filing of a Schedule TO under the Exchange Act.

Proxy statement reporting. For the named executive officers, the grant of the new restricted stock awards would be reflected in the proxy statement. Also, the company's CD&A should discuss the rationale for the replacement of underwater options with restricted shares.

Section 16. The surrender of the underwater options would be an exempt disposition for purposes of Section 16(b) if it is approved in advance by the compensation committee or the full board, or the shareholders approve or ratify such action. Likewise, the grant of the restricted stock would be an exempt acquisition for purposes of Section 16(b) if it is approved in advance by the compensation committee or the full board, or the shareholders approve or ratify such grant. In both cases, the transactions must be reported on a Form 4 by the end of the second business day thereafter.

CASHOUT UNDERWATER OPTIONS

Accounting Issues

Under FAS 123R, the cash payment to repurchase the underwater options would be accounted for as a reduction to equity, to the extent the repurchase amount does not exceed the fair value of the options at the repurchase date. Any excess of the purchase price over the fair value of the options as of that date would be recognized as additional compensation cost. If the repurchased option was unvested, any previously measured compensation cost for that unvested portion would be recognized.

Securities Law Issues

Tender offer issue. The SEC takes the position that this type of exchange offer for cash is likely to be an issuer tender offer that would require the filing of a Schedule TO under the Exchange Act.

Section 16. The surrender of the underwater options would be an exempt disposition for purposes of Section 16(b) if it is approved in advance by the compensation committee or the full board, or the shareholders approve or ratify such action. The disposition must be reported on a Form 4 by the end of the second business day after the transaction.

"GOING DARK"

It should come as no surprise that the landslide of new regulations applied to U.S. public companies in the last five years, the high cost of compliance, stepped-up enforcement agendas at the SEC and DOJ, increases in shareholder litigation, and the risk of personal liability of officers and directors has driven many companies to conclude that the aggregate of these pressures outweighs the benefit of having free access to the public markets. There are two exit paths: going private and going dark.

While sometimes confused, these are two distinct strategies. *Going private* refers to an actual transaction in which cash is paid to existing shareholders and the number of shareholders is reduced to a level that allows the company to terminate its public company status. Such transactions could take any number of forms, and might include a merger with a new company formed by a control group or private equity firm, a tender offer and sale of stock to such a control group or private equity firm, a company self-tender followed by a reverse stock split and cashout of fractional interests, or a similar transaction. Often, a going private transaction will involve a transaction with management or current directors, which can raise issues of conflicting interests and can affect the standard of review. However structured, going private is generally a complex process in terms of planning, financing, approval, disclosure, and SEC filings. Such transactions are generally motivated by something other than the desire to cease public reporting.

In contrast, *going dark* does not involve a transaction at all. It requires delisting the company's securities from their exchange and filing an application with the SEC to suspend the obligation to comply with the reporting requirements of the Securities Exchange Act of 1934 (Exchange Act). To be eligible, a company that is listed on an exchange must delist first because it cannot have securities listed on a national securities exchange and should have fewer than 500 holders of record. If not listed on an exchange, a company must have either (1) fewer than 300 shareholders of record or (2) fewer than 500 record shareholders and less than $10 million in assets at the end of the last three fiscal years. After a company goes dark, it need not file proxy statements or periodic reports with the SEC, need not comply with the Sarbanes-Oxley Act, and is no longer subject to the regulations of the stock exchange on which the shares may have previously been listed. However, because the shareholder count for this purpose is exclusive of beneficial owners of shares held in street name, a company can find its shareholder count quickly jump back above the 500 holder threshold if a broker decides to cease holding the company's shares and transfers its street name shares to the beneficial owners. If this happens, even if the company's securities are not then listed on a stock exchange, a company with more than $1 million in assets will need to "turn the lights back on" unexpectedly. (In a going private transaction this is less of a risk because the ultimate number of beneficial owners is generally quite small after the going private transaction.)

A decision to go dark should not be taken lightly (so to speak). Investors tend to disfavor the action, for several reasons. First, they do not receive cash for their shares as they would in a going private transaction, although they do indirectly benefit from the company's compliance cost savings in going dark. Second, they lose the benefit of the transparency of corporate results and operations afforded by the extensive SEC disclosure system. Investors may fear that this could be used to obscure poor performance or unpopular management decisions. Third, going dark substantially reduces the liquidity of the company's stock, which is at that point traded in the "pink sheets" or over-the-counter market. Also, the company's loss of access to the public markets hinders its ability to raise capital. Likely candidates for going dark are smaller public companies already having difficulties meeting the continued listing requirements of their applicable stock exchange.

When considering whether to go dark, a board of directors should be protected by the business judgment rule, as discussed in Chapter 5, provided that the directors do not have a conflicting personal interest and employ a reasonably informed deliberation process. If the presumption of the business judgment rule is successfully rebutted, directors will have the burden of showing that the decision to go dark was entirely fair. In any event, boards considering going dark should recognize and carefully consider the costs and benefits, and be prepared to justify the decision, both on a procedural and substantive basis.

Epilogue

LOOKING AHEAD

Compensation committees have come a long way over the past two decades, particularly since the enactment of the Sarbanes-Oxley Act of 2002. However, a number of committees still have a way to go. There are initiatives that these committees, as well as every other compensation committee, can immediately take to improve their performance, many of which are outlined in this *Handbook*. Chapter 1, for example, suggests six precepts that can lead to more effective committee performance in the coming years:

1. Get organized.
2. Get and stay informed.
3. Keep an eye on the big picture.
4. Return to reason.
5. Consider the shareholders' perspective.
6. Communicate effectively.

We have found that companies whose compensation committees have adopted these precepts in some form or another have benefited from a more focused and efficient process.

Along with the continuing evolution of the role and purview of the compensation committee, executive compensation practices are undergoing monumental change. For example, the leveling of the playing field resulting from FAS 123R, where all forms of equity compensation are expensed, opens up whole new opportunities for creative design in equity-based compensation, as discussed in Chapter 13. And certain trends highlighted in both the first and second editions of this *Handbook* continue to gather momentum. Some, such as increased representation of outside directors on boards, are now mandated by the stock exchanges. Other trends continue because they foster better corporate governance, such as increased board diversity, regular evaluation of board and CEO performance, and closer scrutiny of the link between pay and performance. And overall, directors and compensation committee members are working harder and longer (and hopefully smarter), and their increasing pay levels directly reflect these increased work hours.

The following are some of the trends we see for the years ahead:

- *Increased profile for the compensation committee.* The compensation committee has become the new board committee (after the audit committee) to galvanize public attention. Fully independent compensation committees will expend time and attention in developing compensation strategies and incentive programs that support the committee's overall compensation philosophy and corporate objectives. There will be more engagement of compensation committees in the processes of CEO evaluation, board evaluation, succession planning, and other key governance processes.

- *Shareholder transparency will continue.* Shareholders will expect to be informed about the company's stance on major governance issues. Expect to see increasing communication in annual reports, proxy statements, and electronic bulletin boards about board practices and activities. There will be more interaction between boards and all corporate constituencies.

- *Say-on-Pay.* More and more companies will either voluntarily adopt (or be required to adopt, if Congress passes such a law) an annual nonbinding share-holder vote on the company's executive compensation programs. These votes will directly communicate to the compensation committee whether shareholders are pleased or displeased with the compensation committee's performance.

- *Emphasis on ethics.* Compensation committees should continue to be proactive in avoiding practices that may have even the appearance of impropriety. Directors are increasingly concerned about shareholders' perception of their actions, especially as they may relate to ethical issues.

- *Succession planning.* CEO turnover will continue as in the past and may even increase. Succession planning will move to the top of the list among the most important board functions. Ideally, succession planning will be a continuous process, integrated into the overall strategic plan. As a consequence, boards should become more willing to replace nonperforming CEOs.

- *CEO searches will be global and will continue to be industry-wide.* Companies will continue to seek the best CEO candidates, no matter who and where they are. While many companies are more comfortable with promoting from within, from both a culture and cost perspective, boards must use all resources in filling open management positions. A recent trend is to hire more international executives, and certainly to hire CEOs outside of the industry.

- *Executive compensation.* Companies will continue to pay significant amounts for executive talent, as there will be continued emphasis on innovation, creativity, and accountability of executives. The SEC's 2007 compensation disclosure overhaul, with its emphasis on discussion and analysis, will encourage the com-pensation committee to refine its compensation philosophy and make periodic adjustments to the compensation program to ensure that each element appro-priately furthers the stated philosophy. In particular, we expect to see periodic tailoring of performance-based incentives and a more critical look at severance pay and supplemental retirement plans.

- *Internal Revenue Code Section 409A.* Internal Revenue Code Section 409A, enacted in 2004, with its broad reach into nontraditional areas of deferred compensation, such as separation pay and equity arrangements, has and will continue to affect plan design. While Section 409A compliance is currently fairly straightforward, if Congress were to expand Section 409A to add a $1 million annual cap, as was proposed in Congress early in 2007, the importance of qualifying for an exemption will become paramount, even though this may be antithetical to notions of good corporate governance. For example, given the dire consequences of exceeding a Section 409A cap, we would expect to see more companies structuring severance agreements to meet the short-term deferral exemption by paying out severance in a lump sum at termination, rather than paying out over time to better enforce post-termination restrictive covenants or to ease cash-flow considerations (although many companies have or are considering short-term lump sum severance payments anyway to completely avoid Section 409A). Also, we expect that an annual Section 409A cap would accelerate the trend in which companies have been migrating from equity-based compensation subject to Section 409A (such as the restricted stock units and performance units) to equity-based compensation that is completely outside the purview of Section 409A (such as "plain vanilla" stock options and restricted stock).

- *Equity-based compensation.* With the mandatory expensing of stock options beginning in 2006, equity-based compensation is likely to be more concentrated at the upper levels of management, with a continuing reduction in broad-based equity programs. The level playing field created by option expensing has opened the door to wider use of other types of equity-based incentive awards. Stock-settled stock appreciation rights (SARs) may overtake stock options as the most prevalent form of appreciation-type incentive award, and restricted stock most likely will regain popularity over restricted stock units due to restrictions imposed by Section 409A. Reload stock options have virtually disappeared from stock option arrangements. Option repricing has become less painful from an accounting perspective and thus will still be used by some companies to "clean up" an underwater stock option or SAR program, but typically requires shareholder approval.

- *Evaluations will become standard practice.* Regular CEO evaluations should become standard practice in the ensuing years, and director evaluations will become more prevalent, especially boardwide evaluations. More and more compensation committees will use the CEO evaluation process to determine CEO pay.

- *Director compensation.* Increasingly higher compensation for directors is expected, as a reflection of increased obligations, time commitment, expertise requirements, and the risk of personal liability. Director compensation is likely to level off after a few years, once a new equilibrium is established.

- *Director recruitment.* The nominating committee is now an essential element of the public company board. Directors are more likely to be selected for how they think, what they know, and how they deliver their knowledge and experience, than for whom they know. Companies will likely turn more often to executive recruiting firms to find qualified independent directors. Even so, members of the nominating committee, and all outside directors, are likely to spend substantial time and energy in the recruitment of new directors.

- *Certification of directors.* Certification of directors is a significant trend outside the United States. While there is some support for this in the United States, there is unlikely to be a national certification signifying "professional" directors. However, institutional investors are encouraging directors of companies in which they invest to attend director orientation programs. The National Association of Corporate Directors (NACD) has a core curriculum for the initial certification of directors, including a continuing education requirement.

- *Diversity.* An increase in women and minority representation on boards is inevitable. For several years, women have made up a slight majority in law school populations. Women also make up a substantial, and increasing, percentage of business school enrollments. The large representation of women in business and law schools should result in a significant increase in their ranks among top corporate offices and on corporate boards. With the move to more fully independent boards, limitations on the number of boards on which a director can serve, higher prevalence of mandatory director retirement ages, and the increase in number of required board committees, the ascension of women and minorities is quite timely to assist public companies seeking to provide the best and brightest new talent to serve on their boards and compensation committees.

- *Director profiles.* For a variety of reasons, including the imposition of mandatory retirement age, directors are likely to be younger and have greater honed skills in finance, management, governance, and technology. There most likely will be more international representation on U.S. boards, and more U.S. executives likely will serve on non-U.S. boards.

- *Contested director elections.* Driven by shareholder activism and the ability to communicate more effectively and quickly over a large group, the election of directors will no longer be a "done deal" when it comes to the shareholder vote. Institutional investors and their advisors are achieving unprecedented efficiency in the review of proxy proposals, including election of directors.

- *Director training will increase.* Pension funds and pension advisory services rate regular director training as an important criterion for their investment. Director orientation programs have emerged across the country to serve the need for new director training. Ongoing training and enrichment will be integrated into the corporate governance process, including both off site professional training programs and programs provided as part of board or committee meetings or retreats.

- *Board cultures will change for the better.* Boards will be more business-like, more results oriented, more involved and productive, more efficient, more sensitive to time pressure with less tolerance for unprepared directors.

- *Global markets and economies will continue to merge.* The emphasis on corporate governance continues on a worldwide basis. To compete, every economy will be fostering better boards as a means to improve corporate performance. The 100-member Japanese board will be an antiquity. Other countries are evolving better board practices, symbolic of the breadth of the corporate governance revolution. Great Britain's reliance on independent nonexecutive chairs has already affected U.S. practices. The executive talent pools will tend to merge, allowing for more international CEO searches.

- *Shareholder litigation.* Shareholder lawsuits will attempt to show lack of good faith by the board, which, if successful, would eliminate reliance on the business judgment rule, and most likely would pierce the protections of charter exculpation provisions and make directors unindemnifiable and uninsurable. While the final resolution of the *Disney* litigation in mid-2006 absolving the directors of liability may have doused the flame somewhat, the Delaware Court of Chancery in February 2007 reintroduced the very real possibility that a compensation committee might step across the line into bad faith in the context of option grant practices. The best defense to an allegation of bad faith is to pay serious attention to decision making, including seeking outside expert advice and keeping meticulous minutes to document the process actually followed.

- *Increased responsiveness to shareholders.* The focus will remain on greater interaction with and responsiveness to shareholders. Many boards have formed shareholder relations committees. Shareholders will engage the board directly to encourage reforms of one type or another. Concurrently, directors will learn more about what motivates shareholders to buy or sell their stock holdings, and shareholders, analysts, and investment managers will gain an appreciation of the impact directors have on corporate growth.

- *Financial analyst activism.* Analysts on both the buy and sell sides will recognize the role governance can play in creating shareholder value, and they will prioritize governance as a measure of corporate success. The Association for Investment Management and Research includes corporate governance as part of its Chartered Financial Analyst curriculum. Moody's and Standard & Poors each have added a substantial corporate governance research group to make corporate governance an element of its review of debt and equity.

THE NEXT EXECUTIVE COMPENSATION CONTROVERSY

At the time of this writing, the executive compensation landscape has been recently and substantially "reengineered" by both the federal government and quasi-government organizations (such as the stock exchanges and the FASB). With their focus on executive compensation, new SEC compensation disclosure rules, FAS 123R, and Internal Revenue Code Section 409A have rounded out the reformation process begun with the corporate scandals of 2001 and 2002, which initiated the Sarbanes-Oxley Act in 2002, lead to new NYSE and NASDAQ listing rules in 2003, and focused intense attention on director independence and board/committee functions. Thus, other than the already proposed adoption of say-on-pay arrangements, proposed expansions of Internal Revenue Code Sections 162(m) and 409A, and SEC refinements of its new disclosure regime, we expect the executive compensation landscape to remain relatively stable for the forthcoming years.

However, if history has taught us anything, it is that executive compensation—and thus compensation committees—will be at the center of controversy approximately every 10 years. For example, in the early 1980s, executives receiving excessive severance packages in connection with mergers and acquisitions outraged both the public and politicians, and the result was the golden parachute tax rules enacted in 1984. The recession of the early 1990s focused the country on CEO pay, and the result was a complete redesign by the SEC in 1992 of the executive compensation disclosure rules, the $1 million cap under Internal Revenue Code Section 162(m) enacted in 1993, and the unsuccessful attempt (later successful) by the FASB to impose mandatory expensing of stock options. And, as mentioned above, the corporate scandals in the beginning of this decade, which made Enron, WorldCom, Adelphia, Global Crossing, Tyco, and Martha Stewart the "poster children" of that controversy, prompted drastic changes in securities and tax law, and caused the FASB to finally impose mandatory expensing for stock options.

We cannot be sure when the next "executive compensation controversy" will occur. Maybe, if the 10-year cycle stays constant, we can expect something to happen in 2011 or 2012. Or maybe this time it will go well beyond the 10-year cycle. But we are certain that at some point in time, there will be another "executive compensation controversy," with a new company or companies personifying the "poster children" of that controversy. We hope, however, that this *Handbook* will have helped compensation committees keep themselves and their boards, their CEOs, and their executives from becoming part of that poster.

Selected SEC Rules, Regulations, Schedules, and Forms

This appendix is a summary listing of SEC regulations, schedules, and forms and stock exchange rules that directly or indirectly impact the duties and responsibilities of compensation committees. The full text of items marked with an asterisk (*) is reproduced following the summary listing.

SECURITIES ACT OF 1933, AS AMENDED

This is the federal law requiring full and fair disclosure and the use of a prospectus in connection with the offer and sale of securities.

SELECTED RELEVANT RULES UNDER THE SECURITIES ACT OF 1933

Rule 144—Persons Deemed Not to be Engaged in a Distribution and Therefore Not Underwriters

Rule 701—Exemption for Offers and Sales of Securities Pursuant to Certain Compensatory Benefit Plans and Contracts Relating to Compensation

SECURITIES EXCHANGE ACT OF 1934, AS AMENDED

This is the federal law prohibiting manipulative and abusive practices in the issuance of securities; requires registration of stock exchanges, brokers, dealers, and listed securities; also requires disclosure of certain financial information and insider trading.

SELECTED RELEVANT RULES AND REGULATIONS UNDER THE SECURITIES EXCHANGE ACT OF 1934

Rule 10b-5—Employment of Manipulative and Deceptive Devices

Rule 10b5-1—Trading "On the Basis of" Material Nonpublic Information in Insider Trading Cases

Rule 10b-18—Purchases of Certain Equity Securities by the Issuer and Others
Rules 16a-1 through 16a-13—Reports of Directors, Officers, and Principal Stockholders
Rules 16b-1 through 16b-8—Exemption of Certain Transactions from Section 16(b)
Regulation 14A—Solicitation of Proxies
Schedule 14A (Rule 14a-101)—Information Required in Proxy Statement

FORMS

Form 8-K—Current Report Pursuant to Section 13 or 15(d) of the Securities Exchange Act of 1934
Form 10-Q—Quarterly Reports
Form 10-K—General Form of Annual Report
Form 144—Notice of Proposed Sale of Securities Pursuant to Rule 144 under the Securities Act of 1933
Form S-8—Registration Under the Securities Act of 1933 of Securities to Be Offered to Employees Pursuant to Certain Plans
Form 3—Initial Statement of Beneficial Ownership of Securities
Form 4—Statement of Changes of Beneficial Ownership of Securities
Form 5—Annual Statement of Beneficial Ownership of Securities
Regulation S-K—Standard Instructions for Filing Forms under the Securities Act of 1933 and the Securities Exchange Act of 1934
Item 201(d)—Securities Authorized for Issuance under Equity Compensation Plans (*)
Item 401—Directors, Executive Officers, Promoters, and Control Persons (*)
Item 402—Executive Compensation (*)
Item 403—Security Ownership of Certain Beneficial Owners and Management (*)
Item 404—Transactions with Related Persons, Promoters, and Certain Persons (*)
Item 405—Compliance with Section 16(a) of the Exchange Act (*)
Item 406—Code of Ethics (*)
Item 407—Corporate Governance (*)
Item 601(b)(10)—Exhibits—Material Contracts (*)

SARBANES-OXLEY ACT OF 2002

Section 304—Forfeiture of Certain Bonuses and Profits
Section 306—Insider Trades during Pension Fund Blackout Periods
Section 402—Enhanced Conflict of Interest Provisions
Section 403—Disclosures of Transactions Involving Management and Principal Stockholders

OTHER

Regulation BTR—Blackout Trading Restriction
NYSE Rule 303A.05—Compensation Committee Requirements (*)
NASDAQ Stock Market Rule 4350(c)(3)—Compensation of Officers (*)

UNITED STATES
SECURITIES AND EXCHANGE COMMISSION
Washington, D.C. 20549

SELECTED PROVISIONS OF REGULATION S-K

17 CFR Subpart 229.200—Securities of the Registrant
229.201 (Item 201) Market Price of and Dividends on the Registrant's Common Equity and Related Stockholder Matters

(d) *Securities authorized for issuance under equity compensation plans.*

17 CFR Subpart 229.400—Management and Certain Security Holders

229.401 (Item 401) Directors, Executive Officers, Promoters, and Control Persons
229.402 (Item 402) Executive Compensation
229.403 (Item 403) Security Ownership of Certain Beneficial Owners and Management
229.404 (Item 404) Transactions with Related Persons, Promoters and Certain Persons
229.405 (Item 405) Compliance with Section 16(a) of the Exchange Act
229.406 (Item 406) Code of Ethics
229.407 (Item 407) Corporate Governance

17 CFR Subpart 229.600—Exhibits

229.601 (Item 601) Exhibits
(c)(10) *Material contracts.*

REGULATION S-K
Subpart 229.200—Securities of the Registrant

Market Price of and Dividends on the Registrant's Common Equity and Related Stockholder Matters

Reg. §229.201. Item 201.

(d) Securities authorized for issuance under equity compensation plans.

1. In the following tabular format, provide the information specified in paragraph (d)(2) of this Item as of the end of the most recently completed fiscal year with respect to compensation plans (including individual compensation arrangements) under which equity securities of the registrant are authorized for issuance, aggregated as follows:

   i. All compensation plans previously approved by security holders; and

   ii. All compensation plans not previously approved by security holders.

Equity Compensation Plan Information			
Plan category	Number of securities to be issued upon exercise of outstanding options, warrants and rights **(a)**	Weighted average exercise price of outstanding options, warrants and rights **(b)**	Number of securities remaining available for future issuance **(c)**
Equity compensation plans approved by security holders			
Equity compensation plans not approved by security holders			
Total			

2. The table shall include the following information as of the end of the most recently completed fiscal year for each category of equity compensation plan described in paragraph (d)(1) of this Item:

   i. The number of securities to be issued upon the exercise of outstanding options, warrants and rights (column (a));

   ii. The weighted-average exercise price of the outstanding options, warrants and rights disclosed pursuant to paragraph (d)(2)(i) of this Item (column (b)); and

iii. Other than securities to be issued upon the exercise of the outstanding options, warrants and rights disclosed in paragraph (d)(2)(i) of this Item, the number of securities remaining available for future issuance under the plan (column (c)).

3. For each compensation plan under which equity securities of the registrant are authorized for issuance that was adopted without the approval of security holders, describe briefly, in narrative form, the material features of the plan.

Instructions to Paragraph (d).

1. Disclosure shall be provided with respect to any compensation plan and individual compensation arrangement of the registrant (or parent, subsidiary or affiliate of the registrant) under which equity securities of the registrant are authorized for issuance to employees or non-employees (such as directors, consultants, advisors, vendors, customers, suppliers or lenders) in exchange for consideration in the form of goods or services as described in Statement of Financial Accounting Standards No. 123, *Accounting for Stock-Based Compensation*, or any successor standard. No disclosure is required with respect to:

   i. Any plan, contract or arrangement for the issuance of warrants or rights to all security holders of the registrant as such on a pro rata basis (such as a stock rights offering) or

   ii. Any employee benefit plan that is intended to meet the qualification requirements of Section 401(a) of the Internal Revenue Code (26 U.S.C. 401(a)).

2. For purposes of this paragraph, an "individual compensation arrangement" includes, but is not limited to, the following: a written compensation contract within the meaning of "employee benefit plan" under §230.405 of this chapter and a plan (whether or not set forth in any formal document) applicable to one person as provided under Item 402(a)(6)(ii) of Regulation S-K (§229.402(a) (6)(ii)).

3. If more than one class of equity security is issued under its equity compensation plans, a registrant should aggregate plan information for each class of security.

4. A registrant may aggregate information regarding individual compensation arrangements with the plan information required under paragraph (d)(1)(i) and (ii) of this Item, as applicable.

5. A registrant may aggregate information regarding a compensation plan assumed in connection with a merger, consolidation or other acquisition transaction pursuant to which the registrant may make subsequent grants or awards of its equity securities with the plan information required under paragraph (d)(1)(i) and (ii) of this Item, as applicable. A registrant shall disclose on an aggregated basis in a footnote to the table the information required under paragraph (d)(2)(i) and (ii) of this Item with respect to any individual options, warrants

or rights assumed in connection with a merger, consolidation or other acquisition transaction.

6. To the extent that the number of securities remaining available for future issuance disclosed in column (c) includes securities available for future issuance under any compensation plan or individual compensation arrangement other than upon the exercise of an option, warrant or right, disclose the number of securities and type of plan separately for each such plan in a footnote to the table.

7. If the description of an equity compensation plan set forth in a registrant's financial statements contains the disclosure required by paragraph (d)(3) of this Item, a cross-reference to such description will satisfy the requirements of paragraph (d)(3) of this Item.

8. If an equity compensation plan contains a formula for calculating the number of securities available for issuance under the plan, including, without limitation, a formula that automatically increases the number of securities available for issuance by a percentage of the number of outstanding securities of the registrant, a description of this formula shall be disclosed in a footnote to the table.

9. Except where it is part of a document that is incorporated by reference into a prospectus, the information required by this paragraph need not be provided in any registration statement filed under the Securities Act.

Subpart 229.400 — Management and Certain Security Holders
Directors, Executive Officers, Promoters and Control Persons
Reg. §229.401. Item 401.

---

a. Identification of directors. List the names and ages of all directors of the registrant and all persons nominated or chosen to become directors; indicate all positions and offices with the registrant held by each such person; state his term of office as director and any period(s) during which he has served as such; describe briefly any arrangement or understanding between him and any other person(s) (naming such person(s)) pursuant to which he was or is to be selected as a director or nominee.

Instructions to Paragraph (a) of Item 401.

1. Do not include arrangements or understandings with directors or officers of the registrant acting solely in their capacities as such.

2. No nominee or person chosen to become a director who has not consented to act as such shall be named in response to this Item. In this regard, with respect to proxy statements, see Rule 14a-4(d) under the Exchange Act (§240. 14a-4(d) of this chapter).

3. If the information called for by this paragraph (a) is being presented in a proxy or information statement, no information need be given respecting any

director whose term of office as a director will not continue after the meeting to which the statement relates.

4. With regard to proxy statements in connection with action to be taken concerning the election of directors, if fewer nominees are named than the number fixed by or pursuant to the governing instruments, state the reasons for this procedure and that the proxies cannot be voted for a greater number of persons than the number of nominees named.

5. With regard to proxy statements in connection with action to be taken concerning the election of directors, if the solicitation is made by persons other than management, information shall be given as to nominees of the persons making the solicitation. In all other instances, information shall be given as to directors and persons nominated for election or chosen by management to become directors.

b. *Identification of executive officers.* List the names and ages of all executive officers of the registrant and all persons chosen to become executive officers; indicate all positions and offices with the registrant held by each such person; state his term of office as officer and the period during which he has served as such and describe briefly any arrangement or understanding between him and any other person(s) (naming such person(s)) pursuant to which he was or is to be selected as an officer.

Instructions to Paragraph (b) of Item 401.

1. Do not include arrangements or understandings with directors or officers of the registrant acting solely in their capacities as such.

2. No person chosen to become an executive officer who has not consented to act as such shall be named in response to this Item.

3. The information regarding executive officers called for by this Item need not be furnished in proxy or information statements prepared in accordance with Schedule 14A under the Exchange Act (§240.14a-101of this chapter) by those registrants relying on General Instruction G of Form 10-K under the Exchange Act(§249.310 of this chapter), *Provided,* That such information is furnished in a separate item captioned "Executive officers of the registrant" and included in Part I of the registrant's annual report on Form 10-K.

---

c. *Identification of certain significant employees.* Where the registrant employs persons such as production managers, sales managers, or research scientists who are not executive officers but who make or are expected to make significant contributions to the business of the registrant, such persons shall be identified and their background disclosed to the same extent as in the case of executive officers. Such disclosure need not be made if the registrant was subject to section 13(a) or 15(d) of the Exchange Act or was exempt from section 13(a) by section 12(g)(2)(G) of such Act immediately prior to the filing of the registration statement, report, or statement to which this Item is applicable.

d. Family relationships. State the nature of any family relationship between any director, executive officer, or person nominated or chosen by the registrant to become a director or executive officer.

Instruction to Paragraph (d) of Item 401.

The term "family relationship" means any relationship by blood, marriage, or adoption, not more remote than first cousin.

---

e. Business experience.

1. *Background.* Briefly describe the business experience during the past five years of each director, executive officer, person nominated or chosen to become a director or executive officer, and each person named in answer to paragraph (c) of Item401, including: each person's principal occupations and employment during the past five years; the name and principal business of any corporation or other organization in which such occupations and employment were carried on; and whether such corporation or organization is a parent, subsidiary or other affiliate of the registrant. When an executive officer or person named in response to paragraph (c) of Item 401 has been employed by the registrant or a subsidiary of the registrant for less than five years, a brief explanation shall be included as to the nature of the responsibility undertaken by the individual in prior positions to provide adequate disclosure of his prior business experience. What is required is information relating to the level of his professional competence, which may include, depending upon the circumstances, such specific information as the size of the operation supervised.

2. *Directorships.* Indicate any other directorships held by each director or person nominated or chosen to become a director in any company with a class of securities registered pursuant to section 12 of the Exchange Act or subject to the requirements of section 15(d) of such Act or any company registered as an investment company under the Investment Company Act of 1940, 15 U.S.C. 80a-1, *et seq.*, as amended, naming such company.

Instruction to Paragraph (e) of Item 401.

For purposes of paragraph (e)(2), where the other directorships of each director or person nominated or chosen to become a director include directorships of two or more registered investment companies that are part of a "fund complex" as that term is defined in Item 22(a) of Schedule 14A under the Exchange Act (§ 240.14a-101 of this chapter), the registrant may, rather than listing each such investment company, identify the fund complex and provide the number of investment company directorships held by the director or nominee in such fund complex.

---

f. Involvement in certain legal proceedings. Describe any of the following events that occurred during the past five years and that are material to an evaluation of the ability or integrity of any director, person nominated to become a director or executive officer of the registrant:

1. A petition under the Federal bankruptcy laws or any state insolvency law was filed by or against, or a receiver, fiscal agent or similar officer was appointed by a court for the business or property of such person, or any partnership in which he was a general partner at or within two years before the time of such filing, or any corporation or business association of which he was an executive officer at or within two years before the time of such filing;

2. Such person was convicted in a criminal proceeding or is a named subject of a pending criminal proceeding (excluding traffic violations and other minor offenses);

3. Such person was the subject of any order, judgment, or decree, not subsequently reversed, suspended or vacated, of any court of competent jurisdiction, permanently or temporarily enjoining him from, or otherwise limiting, the following activities:

   i. Acting as a futures commission merchant, introducing broker, commodity trading advisor, commodity pool operator, floor broker, leverage transaction merchant, any other person regulated by the Commodity Futures Trading Commission, or an associated person of any of the foregoing, or as an investment adviser, underwriter, broker or dealer in securities, or as an affiliated person, director or employee of any investment company, bank, savings and loan association or insurance company, or engaging in or continuing any conduct or practice in connection with such activity;

   ii. Engaging in any type of business practice; or

   iii. Engaging in any activity in connection with the purchase or sale of any security or commodity or in connection with any violation of Federal or State securities laws or Federal commodities laws;

4. Such person was the subject of any order, judgment or decree, not subsequently reversed, suspended or vacated, of any Federal or State authority barring, suspending or otherwise limiting for more than 60 days the right of such person to engage in any activity described in paragraph (f)(3)(i) of this Item, or to be associated with persons engaged in any such activity; or

5. Such person was found by a court of competent jurisdiction in a civil action or by the Commission to have violated any Federal or State securities law, and the judgment in such civil action or finding by the Commission has not been subsequently reversed, suspended, or vacated.

6. Such person was found by a court of competent jurisdiction in a civil action or by the Commodity Futures Trading Commission to have violated any Federal commodities law, and the judgment in such civil action or finding by the

Commodity Futures Trading Commission has not been subsequently reversed, suspended or vacated.

Instructions to Paragraph (f) of Item 401.

1. For purposes of computing the five year period referred to in this paragraph, the date of a reportable event shall be deemed the date on which the final order, judgment or decree was entered, or the date on which any rights of appeal from preliminary orders, judgments, or decrees have lapsed. With respect to bankruptcy petitions, the computation date shall be the date of filing for uncontested petitions or the date upon which approval of a contested petition became final.

2. If any event specified in this paragraph (f) has occurred and information in regard thereto is omitted on the grounds that it is not material, the registrant may furnish to the Commission, at time of filing (or at the time preliminary materials are filed pursuant to Rule 14a-6 or 14c-5 under the Exchange Act (§§240.14a-6 and 240.14c-5 of this chapter), as supplemental information and not as part of the registration statement, report, or proxy or information statement, materials to which the omission relates, a description of the event and a statement of the reasons for the omission of information in regard thereto.

3. The registrant is permitted to explain any mitigating circumstances associated with events reported pursuant to this paragraph.

4. If the information called for by this paragraph (f) is being presented in a proxy or information statement, no information need be given respecting any director whose term of office as a director will not continue after the meeting to which the statement relates.

g. Promoters and control persons.

1. Registrants, which have not been subject to the reporting requirements of Section 13(a) or 15(d) of the Exchange Act for the twelve months immediately prior to the filing of the registration statement, report, or statement to which this Item is applicable, and which were organized within the last five years, shall describe with respect to any promoter, any of the events enumerated in paragraphs (f)(1) through (f)(6) of this section that occurred during the past five years and that are material to a voting or investment decision.

2. Registrants, which have not been subject to the reporting requirements of Section 13(a) or 15(d) of the Exchange Act for the twelve months immediately prior to the filing of the registration statement, report, or statement to which this Item is applicable, shall describe with respect to any control person, any of the events enumerated in paragraphs (f)(1) through(f)(6) of this section that occurred during the past five years and that are material to a voting or investment decision.

Instructions to Paragraph (g) of Item 401.

1. Instructions 1. through 3. to paragraph (f) shall apply to this paragraph (g).
2. Paragraph (g) shall not apply to any subsidiary of a registrant which has been reporting pursuant to Section13(a) or 15(d) of the Exchange Act for the twelve months immediately prior to the filing of the registration statement, report or statement.

---

§229.402 (Item 402) Executive compensation.

---

a. General.

1. *Treatment of foreign private issuers.* A foreign private issuer will be deemed to comply with this Item if it provides the information required by Items 6.B and 6.E.2 of Form 20-F (17 CFR 249.220f), with more detailed information provided if otherwise made publicly available or required to be disclosed by the issuer's home jurisdiction or a market in which its securities are listed or traded.

2. *All compensation covered.* This Item requires clear, concise and understandable disclosure of all plan and non-plan compensation awarded to, earned by, or paid to the named executive officers designated under paragraph (a)(3) of this Item, and directors covered by paragraph (k) of this Item, by any person for all services rendered in all capacities to the registrant and its subsidiaries, unless otherwise specifically excluded from disclosure in this Item. All such compensation shall be reported pursuant to this Item, even if also called for by another requirement, including transactions between the registrant and a third party where a purpose of the transaction is to furnish compensation to any such named executive officer or director. No amount reported as compensation for one fiscal year need be reported in the same manner as compensation for a subsequent fiscal year; amounts reported as compensation for one fiscal year may be required to be reported in a different manner pursuant to this Item.

3. *Persons covered.* Disclosure shall be provided pursuant to this Item for each of the following (the "named executive officers"):

   i. All individuals serving as the registrant's principal executive officer or acting in a similar capacity during the last completed fiscal year ("PEO"), regardless of compensation level;

   ii. All individuals serving as the registrant's principal financial officer or acting in a similar capacity during the last completed fiscal year ("PFO"), regardless of compensation level;

   iii. The registrant's three most highly compensated executive officers other than the PEO and PFO who were serving as executive officers at the end of the last completed fiscal year; and

iv. Up to two additional individuals for whom disclosure would have been provided pursuant to paragraph (a)(3)(iii) of this Item but for the fact that the individual was not serving as an executive officer of the registrant at the end of the last completed fiscal year.

Instructions to Item 402(a)(3).

1. *Determination of most highly compensated executive officers.* The determination as to which *executive* officers are most highly compensated shall be made by reference to total compensation for the last completed fiscal year (as required to be disclosed pursuant to paragraph (c)(2)(x) of this Item) reduced by the amount required to be disclosed pursuant to paragraph (c)(2)(viii) of this Item, *provided, however,* that no disclosure need be provided for any executive officer, other than the PEO and PFO, whose total compensation, as so reduced, does not exceed $100,000.

2. *Inclusion of executive officer of subsidiary.* It may be appropriate for a registrant to include as named *executive* officers one or more executive officers or other employees of subsidiaries in the disclosure required by this Item. See Rule 3b-7 under the Exchange Act (17 CFR 240.3b-7).

3. *Exclusion of executive officer due to overseas compensation.* It may be appropriate in limited circumstances for a registrant not to include in the disclosure required by this Item an individual, other than its PEO or PFO, who is one of the registrant's most highly compensated executive officers due to the payment of amounts of cash compensation relating to overseas assignments attributed predominantly to such assignments.

4. *Information for full fiscal year.* If the PEO or PFO served in that capacity during any part of a fiscal year with respect to which information is required, information should be provided as to all of his or her compensation for the full fiscal year. If a named executive officer (other than the PEO or PFO) served as an executive officer of the registrant (whether or not in the same position) during any part of the fiscal year with respect to which information is required, information shall be provided as to all compensation of that individual for the full fiscal year.

5. *Omission of table or column.* A table or column may be omitted if there has been no compensation awarded to, earned by, or paid to any of the named executive officers or directors required to be reported in that table or column in any fiscal year covered by that table.

6. *Definitions.* For purposes of this Item:

   i. The term *stock* means instruments such as common stock, restricted stock, restricted stock units, phantom stock, phantom stock units, common stock equivalent units or any similar instruments that do not have option-like features, and the term *option* means instruments such as stock options, stock appreciation rights and similar instruments with option-like features. The term *stock appreciation rights* (*"SARs"*) refers to SARs payable in cash or stock, including SARs payable in cash or stock at the election of the registrant or a named executive officer. The term *equity* is used to refer generally to stock and/or options.

ii. The term *plan* includes, but is not limited to, the following: Any plan, contract, authorization or arrangement, whether or not set forth in any formal document, pursuant to which cash, securities, similar instruments, or any other property may be received. A plan may be applicable to one person. Registrants may omit information regarding group life, health, hospitalization, or medical reimbursement plans that do not discriminate in scope, terms or operation, in favor of executive officers or directors of the registrant and that are available generally to all salaried employees.

iii. The term *incentive plan* means any plan providing compensation intended to serve as incentive for performance to occur over a specified period, whether such performance is measured by reference to financial performance of the registrant or an affiliate, the registrant's stock price, or any other performance measure. An *equity incentive plan* is an incentive plan or portion of an incentive plan under which awards are granted that fall within the scope of Financial Accounting Standards Board Statement of Financial Accounting Standards No. 123 (revised 2004), *Share-Based Payment,* as modified or supplemented ("FAS 123R"). A *non-equity incentive plan* is an incentive plan or portion of an incentive plan that is not an equity incentive plan. The term *incentive plan award* means an award provided under an incentive plan.

iv. The terms *date of grant* or *grant date* refer to the grant date determined for financial statement reporting purposes pursuant to FAS 123R.

v. *Closing market price* is defined as the price at which the registrant's security was last sold in the principal United States market for such security as of the date for which the closing market price is determined.

b. Compensation discussion and analysis.

1. Discuss the compensation awarded to, earned by, or paid to the named executive officers. The discussion shall explain all material elements of the registrant's compensation of the named executive officers. The discussion shall describe the following:

   i. The objectives of the registrant's compensation programs;

   ii. What the compensation program is designed to reward;

   iii. Each element of compensation;

   iv. Why the registrant chooses to pay each element;

   v. How the registrant determines the amount (and, where applicable, the formula) for each element to pay; and

vi. How each compensation element and the registrant's decisions regarding that element fit into the registrant's overall compensation objectives and affect decisions regarding other elements.

2. While the material information to be disclosed under Compensation Discussion and Analysis will vary depending upon the facts and circumstances, examples of such information may include, in a given case, among other things, the following:

i. The policies for allocating between long-term and currently paid out compensation;

ii. The policies for allocating between cash and non-cash compensation, and among different forms of non-cash compensation;

iii. For long-term compensation, the basis for allocating compensation to each different form of award (such as relationship of the award to the achievement of the registrant's long-term goals, management's exposure to downside equity performance risk, correlation between cost to registrant and expected benefits to the registrant);

iv. How the determination is made as to when awards are granted, including awards of equity-based compensation such as options;

v. What specific items of corporate performance are taken into account in setting compensation policies and making compensation decisions;

vi. How specific forms of compensation are structured and implemented to reflect these items of the registrant's performance, including whether discretion can be or has been exercised (either to award compensation absent attainment of the relevant performance goal(s) or to reduce or increase the size of any award or payout), identifying any particular exercise of discretion, and stating whether it applied to one or more specified named executive officers or to all compensation subject to the relevant performance goal(s);

vii. How specific forms of compensation are structured and implemented to reflect the named executive officer's individual performance and/or individual contribution to these items of the registrant's performance, describing the elements of individual performance and/or contribution that are taken into account;

viii. Registrant policies and decisions regarding the adjustment or recovery of awards or payments if the relevant registrant performance measures upon which they are based are restated or otherwise adjusted in a manner that would reduce the size of an award or payment;

ix. The factors considered in decisions to increase or decrease compensation materially;

x. How compensation or amounts realizable from prior compensation are considered in setting other elements of compensation (*e.g.*, how gains from prior option or stock awards are considered in setting retirement benefits);

xi. With respect to any contract, agreement, plan or arrangement, whether written or unwritten, that provides for payment(s) at, following, or in connection with any termination or change-in-control, the basis for selecting particular events as triggering payment (*e.g.*, the rationale for providing a single trigger for payment in the event of a change-in-control);

xii. The impact of the accounting and tax treatments of the particular form of compensation;

xiii. The registrant's equity or other security ownership requirements or guidelines (specifying applicable amounts and forms of ownership), and any registrant policies regarding hedging the economic risk of such ownership;

xiv. Whether the registrant engaged in any benchmarking of total compensation, or any material element of compensation, identifying the benchmark and, if applicable, its components (including component companies); and

xv. The role of executive officers in determining executive compensation.

Instructions to Item 402(b).

1. The purpose of the Compensation Discussion and Analysis is to provide to investors material information that is necessary to an understanding of the registrant's compensation policies and decisions regarding the named executive officers.

2. The Compensation Discussion and Analysis should be of the information contained in the tables and otherwise disclosed pursuant to this Item. The Compensation Discussion and Analysis should also cover actions regarding executive compensation that were taken after the registrant's last fiscal year's end. Actions that should be addressed might include, as examples only, the adoption or implementation of new or modified programs and policies or specific decisions that were made or steps that were taken that could affect a fair understanding of the named executive officer's compensation for the last fiscal year. Moreover, in some situations it may be necessary to discuss prior years in order to give context to the disclosure provided.

3. The Compensation Discussion and Analysis should focus on the material principles underlying the registrant's executive compensation policies and decisions and the most important factors relevant to analysis of those policies and decisions. The Compensation Discussion and Analysis shall reflect the individual circumstances of the registrant and shall avoid boilerplate language and repetition of the more detailed information set forth in the tables and narrative disclosures that follow.

4. Registrants are not required to disclose target levels with respect to specific quantitative or qualitative performance-related factors considered by the compensation committee or the board of directors, or any other factors or criteria involving confidential trade secrets or confidential commercial or financial information, the disclosure of which would result in competitive harm for the registrant. The standard to use when determining whether disclosure would cause competitive harm for the registrant is the same standard that would apply when a registrant requests confidential treatment of confidential trade secrets or confidential commercial or financial information pursuant to Securities Act Rule 406 (17 CFR 230.406) and Exchange Act Rule 24b-2 (17 CFR 240.24b-2), each of which incorporates the criteria for non-disclosure when relying upon Exemption 4 of the Freedom of Information Act (5 U.S.C. 552(b)(4)) and Rule 80(b)(4) (17 CFR 200.80(b)(4)) thereunder. A registrant is not required to seek confidential treatment under the procedures in Securities Act Rule 406 and Exchange Act Rule 24b-2 if it determines that the disclosure would cause competitive harm in reliance on this instruction; however, in that case, the registrant must discuss how difficult it will be for the executive or how likely it will be for the registrant to achieve the undisclosed target levels or other factors.

5. Disclosure of target levels that are non-GAAP financial measures will not be subject to Regulation G (17 CFR 244.100 - 102) and Item 10(e) (§229.10(e)); however, disclosure must be provided as to how the number is calculated from the registrant's audited financial statements.

c. Summary compensation table.

1. *General.* Provide the information specified in paragraph (c)(2) of this Item, concerning the compensation of the named executive officers for each of the registrant's last three completed fiscal years, in a Summary Compensation Table in the tabular format specified below.

2. The Table shall include:

   i. The name and principal position of the executive officer (column (a));

   ii. Fiscal year covered (column (b));

   iii. The dollar value of base salary (cash and non-cash) earned by the named executive officer during the fiscal year covered (column (c));

   iv. The dollar value of bonus (cash and non-cash) earned by the named executive officer during the fiscal year covered (column (d));

Instructions to Item 402(c)(2)(iii) and (iv).

1. If the amount of salary or bonus earned in a given fiscal year is not calculable through the latest practicable date, a footnote shall be included disclosing that the amount of salary or bonus is not calculable through the latest practicable date and providing the date that the amount of salary or bonus is expected to be

SUMMARY COMPENSATION TABLE

Name and Principal Position	Year	Salary ($)	Bonus ($)	Stock Awards ($)	Option Awards ($)	Non-Equity Incentive Plan Compensation ($)	Change in Pension Value and Non-qualified Deferred Compensation Earnings ($)	All Other Compensation ($)	Total ($)
(a)	(b)	(c)	(d)	(e)	(f)	(g)	(h)	(i)	(j)
PEO									
PFO									
A									
B									
C									

determined, and such amount must then be disclosed in a filing under Item 5.02(f) of Form 8-K (17 CFR 249.308).

2. Registrants shall include in the salary column (column (c)) or bonus column (column (d)) any amount of salary or bonus forgone at the election of a named executive officer under which stock, equity-based or other forms of non-cash compensation instead have been received by the named executive officer. However, the receipt of any such form of non-cash compensation instead of salary or bonus must be disclosed in a footnote added to the salary or bonus column and, where applicable, referring to the Grants of Plan-Based Awards Table (required by paragraph (d) of this Item) where the stock, option or non-equity incentive plan award elected by the named executive officer is reported.

---

    v. For awards of stock, the dollar amount recognized for financial statement reporting purposes with respect to the fiscal year in accordance with FAS 123R (column (e));

    vi. For awards of options, with or without tandem SARs, the dollar amount recognized for financial statement reporting purposes with respect to the fiscal year in accordance with FAS 123R (column (f));

Instructions to Item 402(c)(2)(v) and (vi).

For awards reported in columns (e) and (f), disregard the estimate of forfeitures related to service-based vesting conditions. Include a footnote describing all forfeitures during the year, and disclosing all assumptions made in the valuation. Disclose assumptions made in the valuation by reference to a discussion of those assumptions in the registrant's financial statements, footnotes to the financial statements, or discussion in the Management's Discussion and Analysis. The sections so referenced are deemed part of the disclosure provided pursuant to this Item.

---

    vii. The dollar value of all earnings for services performed during the fiscal year pursuant to awards under non-equity incentive plans as defined in paragraph (a)(6)(iii) of this Item, and all earnings on any outstanding awards (column (g));

Instructions to Item 402(c)(2)(vii).

1. If the relevant performance measure is satisfied during the fiscal year (including for a single year in a plan with a multi-year performance measure), the earnings are reportable for that fiscal year, even if not payable until a later date, and are not reportable again in the fiscal year when amounts are paid to the named executive officer.

2. All earnings on non-equity incentive plan compensation must be identified and quantified in a footnote to column (g), whether the earnings were paid

during the fiscal year, payable during the period but deferred at the election of the named executive officer, or payable by their terms at a later date.

---

viii. The sum of the amounts specified in paragraphs (c)(2)(viii)(A) and (B) of this Item (column (h)) as follows:

A. The aggregate change in the actuarial present value of the named executive officer's accumulated benefit under all defined benefit and actuarial pension plans (including supplemental plans) from the pension plan measurement date used for financial statement reporting purposes with respect to the registrant's audited financial statements for the prior completed fiscal year to the pension plan measurement date used for financial statement reporting purposes with respect to the registrant's audited financial statements for the covered fiscal year; and

B. Above-market or preferential earnings on compensation that is deferred on a basis that is not tax-qualified, including such earnings on nonqualified defined contribution plans;

Instructions to Item 402(c)(2)(viii).

1. The disclosure required pursuant to paragraph (c)(2)(viii)(A) of this Item applies to each plan that provides for the payment of retirement benefits, or benefits that will be paid primarily following retirement, including but not limited to tax-qualified defined benefit plans and supplemental executive retirement plans, but excluding tax-qualified defined contribution plans and nonqualified defined contribution plans. For purposes of this disclosure, the registrant should use the same amounts required to be disclosed pursuant to paragraph (h)(2)(iv) of this Item for the covered fiscal year and the amounts that were or would have been required to be reported for the executive officer pursuant to paragraph (h)(2)(iv) of this Item for the prior completed fiscal year.

2. Regarding paragraph (c)(2)(viii)(B) of this Item, interest on deferred compensation is above-market only if the rate of interest exceeds 120% of the applicable federal long-term rate, with compounding (as prescribed under section 1274(d) of the Internal Revenue Code, (26 U.S.C. 1274(d))) at the rate that corresponds most closely to the rate under the registrant's plan at the time the interest rate or formula is set. In the event of a discretionary reset of the interest rate, the requisite calculation must be made on the basis of the interest rate at the time of such reset, rather than when originally established. Only the above-market portion of the interest must be included. If the applicable interest rates vary depending upon conditions such as a minimum period of continued service, the reported amount should be calculated assuming satisfaction of all conditions to receiving interest at the highest rate. Dividends (and dividend equivalents) on deferred compensation denominated in the registrant's stock ("deferred stock") are preferential only if earned at a rate higher than dividends on the registrant's common stock.

Only the preferential portion of the dividends or equivalents must be included. Footnote or narrative disclosure may be provided explaining the registrant's criteria for determining any portion considered to be above-market.

3. The registrant shall identify and quantify by footnote the separate amounts attributable to each of paragraphs (c)(2)(viii)(A) and (B) of this Item. Where such amount pursuant to paragraph (c)(2)(viii)(A) is negative, it should be disclosed by footnote but should not be reflected in the sum reported in column (h).

---

ix. All other compensation for the covered fiscal year that the registrant could not properly report in any other column of the Summary Compensation Table (column (i)). Each compensation item that is not properly reportable in columns (c)–(h), regardless of the amount of the compensation item, must be included in column (i). Such compensation must include, but is not limited to:

A. Perquisites and other personal benefits, or property, unless the aggregate amount of such compensation is less than $10,000;

B. All "gross-ups" or other amounts reimbursed during the fiscal year for the payment of taxes;

C. For any security of the registrant or its subsidiaries purchased from the registrant or its subsidiaries (through deferral of salary or bonus, or otherwise) at a discount from the market price of such security at the date of purchase, unless that discount is available generally, either to all security holders or to all salaried employees of the registrant, the compensation cost, if any, computed in accordance with FAS 123R;

D. The amount paid or accrued to any named executive officer pursuant to a plan or arrangement in connection with:

1. Any termination, including without limitation through retirement, resignation, severance or constructive termination (including a change in responsibilities) of such executive officer's employment with the registrant and its subsidiaries; or

2. A change in control of the registrant;

E. Registrant contributions or other allocations to vested and unvested defined contribution plans;

F. The dollar value of any insurance premiums paid by, or on behalf of, the registrant during the covered fiscal year with respect to life insurance for the benefit of a named executive officer; and

G. The dollar value of any dividends or other earnings paid on stock or option awards, when those amounts were not factored into the grant date fair value required to be reported for the stock or option award in column (l) of the Grants of Plan-Based Awards Table required by paragraph (d)(2)(viii) of this Item; and

Instructions to Item 402(c)(2)(ix).

1. Non-equity incentive plan awards and earnings and earnings on stock and options, except as specified in paragraph (c)(2)(ix)(G) of this Item, are required to be reported elsewhere as provided in this Item and are not reportable as All Other Compensation in column (i).

2. Benefits paid pursuant to defined benefit and actuarial plans are not reportable as All Other Compensation in column (i) unless accelerated pursuant to a change in control; information concerning these plans is reportable pursuant to paragraphs (c)(2)(viii)(A) and (h) of this Item.

3. Any item reported for a named executive officer pursuant to paragraph (c)(2)(ix) of this Item that is not a perquisite or personal benefit and whose value exceeds $10,000 must be identified and quantified in a footnote to column (i). This requirement applies only to compensation for the last fiscal year. All items of compensation are required to be included in the Summary Compensation Table without regard to whether such items are required to be identified other than as specifically noted in this Item.

4. Perquisites and personal benefits may be excluded as long as the total value of all perquisites and personal benefits for a named executive officer is less than $10,000. If the total value of all perquisites and personal benefits is $10,000 or more for any named executive officer, then each perquisite or personal benefit, regardless of its amount, must be identified by type. If perquisites and personal benefits are required to be reported for a named executive officer pursuant to this rule, then each perquisite or personal benefit that exceeds the greater of $25,000 or 10% of the total amount of perquisites and personal benefits for that officer must be quantified and disclosed in a footnote. The requirements for identification and quantification apply only to compensation for the last fiscal year. Perquisites and other personal benefits shall be valued on the basis of the aggregate incremental cost to the registrant. With respect to the perquisite or other personal benefit for which footnote quantification is required, the registrant shall describe in the footnote its methodology for computing the aggregate incremental cost. Reimbursements of taxes owed with respect to perquisites or other personal benefits must be included in column (i) and are subject to separate quantification and identification as tax reimbursements (paragraph (c)(2)(ix)(B) of this Item) even if the associated perquisites or other personal benefits are not required to be included because the total amount of all perquisites or personal benefits for an individual named executive officer is less than $10,000 or are required to be identified but are not required to be separately quantified.

5. For purposes of paragraph (c)(2)(ix)(D) of this Item, an accrued amount is an amount for which payment has become due.

x. The dollar value of total compensation for the covered fiscal year (column (j)). With respect to each named executive officer, disclose the sum of all amounts reported in columns (c) through (i).

Instructions to Item 402(c).

1. Information with respect to fiscal years prior to the last completed fiscal year will not be required if the registrant was not a reporting company pursuant to section 13(a) or 15(d) of the Exchange Act (15 U.S.C. 78m(a) or 78*o*(d)) at any time during that year, except that the registrant will be required to provide information for any such year if that information previously was required to be provided in response to a Commission filing requirement.

2. All compensation values reported in the Summary Compensation Table must be reported in dollars and rounded to the nearest dollar. Reported compensation values must be reported numerically, providing a single numerical value for each grid in the table. Where compensation was paid to or received by a named executive officer in a different currency, a footnote must be provided to identify that currency and describe the rate and methodology used to convert the payment amounts to dollars.

3. If a named executive officer is also a director who receives compensation for his or her services as a director, reflect that compensation in the Summary Compensation Table and provide a footnote identifying and itemizing such compensation and amounts. Use the categories in the Director Compensation Table required pursuant to paragraph (k) of this Item.

4. Any amounts deferred, whether pursuant to a plan established under section 401(k) of the Internal Revenue Code (26 U.S.C. 401(k)), or otherwise, shall be included in the appropriate column for the fiscal year in which earned.

d. *Grants of plan-based awards table.*

1. Provide the information specified in paragraph (d)(2) of this Item, concerning each grant of an award made to a named executive officer in the last completed fiscal year under any plan, including awards that subsequently have been transferred, in the following tabular format:

2. The Table should include:

   i. The name of the named executive officer (column (a));

   ii. The grant date for equity-based awards reported in the table (column (b)). If such grant date is different than the date on which the compensation committee (or a committee of the board of directors performing a similar function or the full board of directors) takes action or is deemed to take action to grant such awards, a separate, adjoining column shall be added between columns (b) and (c) showing such date;

   iii. The dollar value of the estimated future payout upon satisfaction of the conditions in question under non-equity incentive plan awards granted

GRANTS OF PLAN-BASED AWARDS

Name	Grant Date	Estimated Future Payouts Under Non-Equity Incentive Plan Awards			Estimated Future Payouts Under Equity Incentive Plan Awards			All Other Stock Awards: Number of Shares of Stock or Units (#)	All Other Option Awards: Number of Securities Underlying Options (#)	Exercise or Base Price of Option Awards ($/Sh)	Grant Date Fair Value of Stock and Option Awards
		Threshold ($)	Target ($)	Maximin ($)	Threshold (#)	Target (#)	Maximum (#)				
(a)	(b)	(c)	(d)	(e)	(f)	(g)	(h)	(i)	(j)	(k)	(l)
PEO											
PFO											
A											
B											
C											

in the fiscal year, or the applicable range of estimated payouts denominated in dollars (threshold, target and maximum amount) (columns (c) through (e)).

iv. The number of shares of stock, or the number of shares underlying options to be paid out or vested upon satisfaction of the conditions in question under equity incentive plan awards granted in the fiscal year, or the applicable range of estimated payouts denominated in the number of shares of stock, or the number of shares underlying options under the award (threshold, target and maximum amount) (columns (f) through (h)).

v. The number of shares of stock granted in the fiscal year that are not required to be disclosed in columns (f) through (h) (column (i));

vi. The number of securities underlying options granted in the fiscal year that are not required to be disclosed in columns (f) through (h) (column (j));

vii. The per-share exercise or base price of the options granted in the fiscal year (column (k)). If such exercise or base price is less than the closing market price of the underlying security on the date of the grant, a separate, adjoining column showing the closing market price on the date of the grant shall be added after column (k) and

viii. The grant date fair value of each equity award computed in accordance with FAS 123R (column (l)). If at any time during the last completed fiscal year, the registrant has adjusted or amended the exercise or base price of options, SARs or similar option-like instruments previously awarded to a named executive officer, whether through amendment, cancellation or replacement grants, or any other means ("repriced"), or otherwise has materially modified such awards, the incremental fair value, computed as of the repricing or modification date in accordance with FAS 123R, with respect to that repriced or modified award, shall be reported.

Instructions to Item 402(d).

1. Disclosure on a separate line shall be provided in the Table for each grant of an award made to a named executive officer during the fiscal year. If grants of awards were made to a named executive officer during the fiscal year under more than one plan, identify the particular plan under which each such grant was made.

2. For grants of incentive plan awards, provide the information called for by columns (c), (d) and (e), or (f), (g) and (h), as applicable. For columns (c) and (f), *threshold* refers to the minimum amount payable for a certain level of performance under the plan. For columns (d) and (g), *target* refers to the amount payable if the specified performance target(s) are reached. For columns (e) and (h), *maximum* refers to the maximum payout possible under the plan. If the award provides only for a single estimated payout, that amount must be reported as the *target* in columns (d) and (g). In columns (d) and (g),

registrants must provide a representative amount based on the previous fiscal year's performance if the target amount is not determinable.

3. In determining if the exercise or base price of an option is less than the closing market price of the underlying security on the date of the grant, the registrant may use either the closing market price as specified in paragraph (a)(6)(v) of this Item, or if no market exists, any other formula prescribed for the security. Whenever the exercise or base price reported in column (k) is not the closing market price, describe the methodology for determining the exercise or base price either by a footnote or accompanying textual narrative.

4. A tandem grant of two instruments, only one of which is granted under an incentive plan, such as an option granted in tandem with a performance share, need be reported only in column (i) or (j), as applicable. For example, an option granted in tandem with a performance share would be reported only as an option grant in column (j), with the tandem feature noted either by a footnote or accompanying textual narrative.

5. Disclose the dollar amount of consideration, if any, paid by the executive officer for the award in a footnote to the appropriate column.

6. If non-equity incentive plan awards are denominated in units or other rights, a separate, adjoining column between columns (b) and (c) shall be added quantifying the units or other rights awarded.

7. Options, SARs and similar option-like instruments granted in connection with a repricing transaction or other material modification shall be reported in this Table. However, the disclosure required by this Table does not apply to any repricing that occurs through a pre-existing formula or mechanism in the plan or award that results in the periodic adjustment of the option or SAR exercise or base price, an antidilution provision in a plan or award, or a recapitalization or similar transaction equally affecting all holders of the class of securities underlying the options or SARs.

---

e. *Narrative disclosure to summary compensation table and grants of plan-based awards table.*

1. Provide a narrative description of any material factors necessary to an understanding of the information disclosed in the tables required by paragraphs (c) and (d) of this Item. Examples of such factors may include, in given cases, among other things:

   i. The material terms of each named executive officer's employment agreement or arrangement, whether written or unwritten;

   ii. If at any time during the last fiscal year, any outstanding option or other equity-based award was repriced or otherwise materially modified (such as by extension of exercise periods, the change of vesting or forfeiture conditions, the change or elimination of applicable performance criteria, or the change of the bases upon which returns are determined), a description of each such repricing or other material modification;

iii. The material terms of any award reported in response to paragraph (d) of this Item, including a general description of the formula or criteria to be applied in determining the amounts payable, and the vesting schedule. For example, state where applicable that dividends will be paid on stock, and if so, the applicable dividend rate and whether that rate is preferential. Describe any performance-based conditions, and any other material conditions, that are applicable to the award. For purposes of the Table required by paragraph (d) of this Item and the narrative disclosure required by paragraph (e) of this Item, performance-based conditions include both performance conditions and market conditions, as those terms are defined in FAS 123R; and

iv. An explanation of the amount of salary and bonus in proportion to total compensation.

Instructions to Item 402(e)(1).

1. The disclosure required by paragraph (e)(1)(ii) of this Item would not apply to any repricing that occurs through a pre-existing formula or mechanism in the plan or award that results in the periodic adjustment of the option or SAR exercise or base price, an antidilution provision in a plan or award, or a recapitalization or similar transaction equally affecting all holders of the class of securities underlying the options or SARs.

2. Instructions 4 and 5 to Item 402(b) apply regarding disclosure pursuant to paragraph (e)(1) of target levels with respect to specific quantitative or qualitative performance-related factors considered by the compensation committee or the board of directors, or any other factors or criteria involving confidential trade secrets or confidential commercial or financial information, the disclosure of which would result in competitive harm for the registrant.

2. Reserved.

f. Outstanding equity awards at fiscal year-end table.

1. Provide the information specified in paragraph (f)(2) of this Item, concerning unexercised options; stock that has not vested; and equity incentive plan awards for each named executive officer outstanding as of the end of the registrant's last completed fiscal year in the following tabular format:

2. The Table shall include:

i. The name of the named executive officer (column (a));

ii. On an award-by-award basis, the number of securities underlying unexercised options, including awards that have been transferred other than for value, that are exercisable and that are not reported in column (d) (column (b));

OUTSTANDING EQUITY AWARDS AT FISCAL YEAR-END

	Options Awards					Stock Awards			
Name (a)	Number of Securities Underlying Unexercised Options (#) Exercisable (b)	Number of Securities Underlying Unexercised Options (#) Unexercisable (c)	Equity Incentive Plan Awards: Number of Securities Underlying Unexercised Unearned Options (#) (d)	Option Exercise Price ($) (e)	Option Expiration Date (f)	Number of Shares or Units of Stock That Have Not Vested (#) (g)	Market Value of Shares or Units of Stock That Have Not Vested ($) (h)	Equity Incentive Plan Awards: Number of Unearned Shares, Units or Other Rights That Have Not Vested (i)	Equity Incentive Plan Awards: Market or Payout Value of Unearned Shares, Units or Other Rights That Have Not Vested (j)
PEO									
PFO									
A									
B									
C									

iii. On an award-by-award basis, the number of securities underlying unexercised options, including awards that have been transferred other than for value, that are unexercisable and that are not reported in column (d) (column (c));

iv. On an award-by-award basis, the total number of shares underlying unexercised options awarded under any equity incentive plan that have not been earned (column (d));

v. For each instrument reported in columns (b), (c) and (d), as applicable, the exercise or base price (column (e));

vi. For each instrument reported in columns (b), (c) and (d), as applicable, the expiration date (column (f));

vii. The total number of shares of stock that have not vested and that are not reported in column (i) (column (g));

viii. The aggregate market value of shares of stock that have not vested and that are not reported in column (j) (column (h));

ix. The total number of shares of stock, units or other rights awarded under any equity incentive plan that have not vested and that have not been earned, and, if applicable the number of shares underlying any such unit or right (column (i)); and

x. The aggregate market or payout value of shares of stock, units or other rights awarded under any equity incentive plan that have not vested and that have not been earned (column (j)).

Instructions to Item 402(f)(2).

1. Identify by footnote any award that has been transferred other than for value, disclosing the nature of the transfer.

2. The vesting dates of options, shares of stock and equity incentive plan awards held at fiscal-year end must be disclosed by footnote to the applicable column where the outstanding award is reported.

3. Compute the market value of stock reported in column (h) and equity incentive plan awards of stock reported in column (j) by multiplying the closing market price of the registrant's stock at the end of the last completed fiscal year by the number of shares or units of stock or the amount of equity incentive plan awards, respectively. The number of shares or units reported in columns (d) or (i), and the payout value reported in column (j), shall be based on achieving threshold performance goals, except that if the previous fiscal year's performance has exceeded the threshold, the disclosure shall be based on the next higher performance measure (target or maximum) that exceeds the previous fiscal year's performance. If the award provides only for a single estimated payout, that amount should be reported. If the target amount is not determinable, registrants must provide a representative amount based on the previous fiscal year's performance.

4. Multiple awards may be aggregated where the expiration date and the exercise and/or base price of the instruments is identical. A single award consisting of a combination of options, SARs and/or similar option-like instruments shall be reported as separate awards with respect to each tranche with a different exercise and/or base price or expiration date.

5. Options or stock awarded under an equity incentive plan are reported in columns (d) or (i) and (j), respectively, until the relevant performance condition has been satisfied. Once the relevant performance condition has been satisfied, even if the option or stock award is subject to forfeiture conditions, options are reported in column (b) or (c), as appropriate, until they are exercised or expire, or stock is reported in columns (g) and (h) until it vests.

---

g. *Option exercises and stock vested table.*

1. Provide the information specified in paragraph (g)(2) of this Item, concerning each exercise of stock options, SARs and similar instruments, and each vesting of stock, including restricted stock, restricted stock units and similar instruments, during the last completed fiscal year for each of the named executive officers on an aggregated basis in the following tabular format:

OPTION EXERCISES AND STOCK VESTED

	Option Awards		Stock Awards	
Name **(a)**	**Number of Shares Acquired on Exercise (#)** **(b)**	**Value Realized on Exercise ($)** **(c)**	**Number of Shares Acquired on Vesting (#)** **(d)**	**Value Realized on Vesting ($)** **(e)**
PEO				
PFO				
A				
B				
C				

2. The Table shall include:

   i. The name of the executive officer (column (a));

   ii. The number of securities for which the options were exercised (column (b));

   iii. The aggregate dollar value realized upon exercise of options, or upon the transfer of an award for value (column (c));

   iv. The number of shares of stock that have vested (column (d)); and

   v. The aggregate dollar value realized upon vesting of stock, or upon the transfer of an award for value (column (e)).

Instruction to Item 402(g)(2).

Report in column (c) the aggregate dollar amount realized by the named executive officer upon exercise of the options or upon the transfer of such instruments for value. Compute the dollar amount realized upon exercise by determining the difference between the market price of the underlying securities at exercise and the exercise or base price of the options. Do not include the value of any related payment or other consideration provided (or to be provided) by the registrant to or on behalf of a named executive officer, whether in payment of the exercise price or related taxes. (Any such payment or other consideration provided by the registrant is required to be disclosed in accordance with paragraph (c)(2)(ix) of this Item.) Report in column (e) the aggregate dollar amount realized by the named executive officer upon the vesting of stock or the transfer of such instruments for value. Compute the aggregate dollar amount realized upon vesting by multiplying the number of shares of stock or units by the market value of the underlying shares on the vesting date. For any amount realized upon exercise or vesting for which receipt has been deferred, provide a footnote quantifying the amount and disclosing the terms of the deferral.

h. Pension benefits.

1. Provide the information specified in paragraph (h)(2) of this Item with respect to each plan that provides for payments or other benefits at, following, or in connection with retirement, in the following tabular format:

PENSION BENEFITS

Name (a)	Plan Name (b)	Number of Years Credited Service (#) (c)	Present Value of Accumulated Benefit ($) (d)	Payments During Last Fiscal Year ($) (e)
PEO				
PFO				
A				
B				
C				

2. The Table shall include:
   i. The name of the executive officer (column (a));
   ii. The name of the plan (column (b));
   iii. The number of years of service credited to the named executive officer under the plan, computed as of the same pension plan measurement date used for

financial statement reporting purposes with respect to the registrant's audited financial statements for the last completed fiscal year (column (c));

iv. The actuarial present value of the named executive officer's accumulated benefit under the plan, computed as of the same pension plan measurement date used for financial statement reporting purposes with respect to the registrant's audited financial statements for the last completed fiscal year (column (d)); and

v. The dollar amount of any payments and benefits paid to the named executive officer during the registrant's last completed fiscal year (column (e)).

Instructions to Item 402(h)(2).

1. The disclosure required pursuant to this Table applies to each plan that provides for specified retirement payments and benefits, or payments and benefits that will be provided primarily following retirement, including but not limited to tax-qualified defined benefit plans and supplemental executive retirement plans, but excluding tax-qualified defined contribution plans and nonqualified defined contribution plans. Provide a separate row for each such plan in which the named executive officer participates.

2. For purposes of the amount(s) reported in column (d), the registrant must use the same assumptions used for financial reporting purposes under generally accepted accounting principles, except that retirement age shall be assumed to be the normal retirement age as defined in the plan, or if not so defined, the earliest time at which a participant may retire under the plan without any benefit reduction due to age. The registrant must disclose in the accompanying textual narrative the valuation method and all material assumptions applied in quantifying the present value of the current accrued benefit. A benefit specified in the plan document or the executive's contract itself is not an assumption. Registrants may satisfy all or part of this disclosure by reference to a discussion of those assumptions in the registrant's financial statements, footnotes to the financial statements, or discussion in the Management's Discussion and Analysis. The sections so referenced are deemed part of the disclosure provided pursuant to this Item.

3. For purposes of allocating the current accrued benefit between tax qualified defined benefit plans and related supplemental plans, apply the limitations applicable to tax qualified defined benefit plans established by the Internal Revenue Code and the regulations thereunder that applied as of the pension plan measurement date.

4. If a named executive officer's number of years of credited service with respect to any plan is different from the named executive officer's number of actual years of service with the registrant, provide footnote disclosure quantifying the difference and any resulting benefit augmentation.

3. Provide a succinct narrative description of any material factors necessary to an understanding of each plan covered by the tabular disclosure required by this paragraph. While material factors will vary depending upon the facts, examples of such factors may include, in given cases, among other things:

   i. The material terms and conditions of payments and benefits available under the plan, including the plan's normal retirement payment and benefit formula and eligibility standards, and the effect of the form of benefit elected on the amount of annual benefits. For this purpose, normal retirement means retirement at the normal retirement age as defined in the plan, or if not so defined, the earliest time at which a participant may retire under the plan without any benefit reduction due to age;

   ii. If any named executive officer is currently eligible for early retirement under any plan, identify that named executive officer and the plan, and describe the plan's early retirement payment and benefit formula and eligibility standards. For this purpose, early retirement means retirement at the early retirement age as defined in the plan, or otherwise available to the executive under the plan;

   iii. The specific elements of compensation (*e.g.*, salary, bonus, etc.) included in applying the payment and benefit formula, identifying each such element;

   iv. With respect to named executive officers' participation in multiple plans, the different purposes for each plan; and

   v. Registrant policies with regard to such matters as granting extra years of credited service.

i. Nonqualified defined contribution and other nonqualified deferred compensation plans.

   1. Provide the information specified in paragraph (i)(2) of this Item with respect to each defined contribution or other plan that provides for the deferral of compensation on a basis that is not tax-qualified in the following tabular format:

NONQUALIFIED DEFERRED COMPENSATION

Name (a)	Executive Contributions in Last FY ($) (b)	Registrant Contributions in Last FY ($) (c)	Aggregate Earnings in Last FY ($) (d)	Aggregate Withdrawals/ Distributions ($) (e)	Aggregate Balance at Last FYE ($) (f)
PEO					
PFO					
A					
B					
C					

2. The Table shall include:

i. The name of the executive officer (column (a));

ii. The dollar amount of aggregate executive contributions during the registrant's last fiscal year (column (b));

iii. The dollar amount of aggregate registrant contributions during the registrant's last fiscal year (column (c));

iv. The dollar amount of aggregate interest or other earnings accrued during the registrant's last fiscal year (column (d));

v. The aggregate dollar amount of all withdrawals by and distributions to the executive during the registrant's last fiscal year (column (e)); and

vi. The dollar amount of total balance of the executive's account as of the end of the registrant's last fiscal year (column (f)).

Instruction to Item 402(i)(2).

Provide a footnote quantifying the extent to which amounts reported in the contributions and earnings columns are reported as compensation in the last completed fiscal year in the registrant's Summary Compensation Table and amounts reported in the aggregate balance at last fiscal year end (column (f)) previously were reported as compensation to the named executive officer in the registrant's Summary Compensation Table for previous years.

---

3. Provide a succinct narrative description of any material factors necessary to an understanding of each plan covered by tabular disclosure required by this paragraph. While material factors will vary depending upon the facts, examples of such factors may include, in given cases, among other things:

i. The type(s) of compensation permitted to be deferred, and any limitations (by percentage of compensation or otherwise) on the extent to which deferral is permitted;

ii. The measures for calculating interest or other plan earnings (including whether such measure(s) are selected by the executive or the registrant and the frequency and manner in which selections may be changed), quantifying interest rates and other earnings measures applicable during the registrant's last fiscal year; and

iii. Material terms with respect to payouts, withdrawals and other distributions.

j. Potential payments upon termination or change-in-control. Regarding each contract, agreement, plan or arrangement, whether written or unwritten, that provides for payment(s) to a named executive officer at, following, or in connection with any termination, including without limitation resignation, severance, retirement or a constructive termination of a named executive officer, or a change in control of the registrant or a change in the named executive officer's responsibilities, with respect to each named executive officer:

1. Describe and explain the specific circumstances that would trigger payment(s) or the provision of other benefits, including perquisites and health care benefits;
2. Describe and quantify the estimated payments and benefits that would be provided in each covered circumstance, whether they would or could be lump sum, or annual, disclosing the duration, and by whom they would be provided;
3. Describe and explain how the appropriate payment and benefit levels are determined under the various circumstances that trigger payments or provision of benefits;
4. Describe and explain any material conditions or obligations applicable to the receipt of payments or benefits, including but not limited to non-compete, non-solicitation, non-disparagement or confidentiality agreements, including the duration of such agreements and provisions regarding waiver of breach of such agreements; and
5. Describe any other material factors regarding each such contract, agreement, plan or arrangement.

Instructions to Item 402(j).

1. The registrant must provide quantitative disclosure under these requirements, applying the assumptions that the triggering event took place on the last business day of the registrant's last completed fiscal year, and the price per share of the registrant's securities is the closing market price as of that date. In the event that uncertainties exist as to the provision of payments and benefits or the amounts involved, the registrant is required to make a reasonable estimate (or a reasonable estimated range of amounts) applicable to the payment or benefit and disclose material assumptions underlying such estimates or estimated ranges in its disclosure. In such event, the disclosure would require forward-looking information as appropriate.
2. Perquisites and other personal benefits or property may be excluded only if the aggregate amount of such compensation will be less than $10,000. Individual perquisites and personal benefits shall be identified and quantified as required by Instruction 4 to paragraph (c)(2)(ix) of this Item. For purposes of quantifying health care benefits, the registrant must use the assumptions used for financial reporting purposes under generally accepted accounting principles.
3. To the extent that the form and amount of any payment or benefit that would be provided in connection with any triggering event is fully disclosed pursuant to paragraph (h) or (i) of this Item, reference may be made to that disclosure. However, to the extent that the form or amount of any such payment or benefit would be enhanced or its vesting or other provisions accelerated in connection

with any triggering event, such enhancement or acceleration must be disclosed pursuant to this paragraph.

4. Where a triggering event has actually occurred for a named executive officer and that individual was not serving as a named executive officer of the registrant at the end of the last completed fiscal year, the disclosure required by this paragraph for that named executive officer shall apply only to that triggering event.

5. The registrant need not provide information with respect to contracts, agreements, plans or arrangements to the extent they do not discriminate in scope, terms or operation, in favor of executive officers of the registrant and that are available generally to all salaried employees.

---

k. *Compensation of directors.*

1. Provide the information specified in paragraph (k)(2) of this Item, concerning the compensation of the directors for the registrant's last completed fiscal year, in the following tabular format:

DIRECTOR COMPENSATION

Name (a)	Fees Earned or Paid in Cash ($) (b)	Stock Awards ($) (c)	Option Awards ($) (d)	Non-Equity Incentive Plan Compensation ($) (e)	Change in Pension Value and Nonqualified Deferred Compensation Earnings (f)	All other Compensation ($) (g)	Total ($) (h)
A							
B							
C							
D							
E							

1. The Table shall include:

i. The name of each director unless such director is also a named executive officer under paragraph (a) of this Item and his or her compensation for service as a director is fully reflected in the Summary Compensation Table pursuant to paragraph (c) of this Item and otherwise as required pursuant to paragraphs (d) through (j) of this Item (column (a));

ii. The aggregate dollar amount of all fees earned or paid in cash for services as a director, including annual retainer fees, committee and/or chairmanship fees, and meeting fees (column (b));

iii. For awards of stock, the aggregate grant date fair value computed in accordance with FAS 123R (column (c));

iv. For awards of stock options, with or without tandem SARs, the dollar amount recognized for financial statement reporting purposes with respect to the fiscal year in accordance with FAS 123R (column (d));

Instruction to Item 402(k)(2)(iii) and (iv).

For each director, disclose by footnote to the appropriate column: the grant date fair value of each equity award computed in accordance with FAS 123R; for each option, SAR or similar option like instrument for which the registrant has adjusted or amended the exercise or base price during the last completed fiscal year, whether through amendment, cancellation or replacement grants, or any other means ("repriced"), or otherwise has materially modified such awards, the incremental fair value, computed as of the repricing or modification date in accordance with FAS 123R; and the aggregate number of stock awards and the aggregate number of option awards outstanding at fiscal year end. However, the disclosure required by this Instruction does not apply to any repricing that occurs through a pre-existing formula or mechanism in the plan or award that results in the periodic adjustment of the option or SAR exercise or base price, an antidilution provision in a plan or award, or a recapitalization or similar transaction equally affecting all holders of the class of securities underlying the options or SARs.

---

v. The dollar value of all earnings for services performed during the fiscal year pursuant to non-equity incentive plans as defined in paragraph (a)(6)(iii) of this Item, and all earnings on any outstanding awards (column (e));

vi. The sum of the amounts specified in paragraphs (k)(2)(vi)(A) and (B) of this Item (column (f)) as follows:

A. The aggregate change in the actuarial present value of the director's accumulated benefit under all defined benefit and actuarial pension plans (including supplemental plans) from the pension plan measurement date used for financial statement reporting purposes with respect to the registrant's audited financial statements for the prior completed fiscal year to the pension plan measurement date used for financial statement reporting purposes with respect to the registrant's audited financial statements for the covered fiscal year; and

B. Above-market or preferential earnings on compensation that is deferred on a basis that is not tax-qualified, including such earnings on nonqualified defined contribution plans;

vii. All other compensation for the covered fiscal year that the registrant could not properly report in any other column of the Director Compensation Table (column (g)). Each compensation item that is not properly reportable in columns (b)–(f), regardless of the amount of the compensation item, must be included in column (g). Such compensation must include, but is not limited to:

A. Perquisites and other personal benefits, or property, unless the aggregate amount of such compensation is less than $10,000;

B. All "gross-ups" or other amounts reimbursed during the fiscal year for the payment of taxes;

C. For any security of the registrant or its subsidiaries purchased from the registrant or its subsidiaries (through deferral of salary or bonus, or otherwise) at a discount from the market price of such security at the date of purchase, unless that discount is available generally, either to all security holders or to all salaried employees of the registrant, the compensation cost, if any, computed in accordance with FAS 123R;

D. The amount paid or accrued to any director pursuant to a plan or arrangement in connection with:

1. The resignation, retirement or any other termination of such director; or

2. A change in control of the registrant;

E. Registrant contributions or other allocations to vested and unvested defined contribution plans;

F. Consulting fees earned from, or paid or payable by the registrant and/or its subsidiaries (including joint ventures);

G. The annual costs of payments and promises of payments pursuant to director legacy programs and similar charitable award programs;

H. The dollar value of any insurance premiums paid by, or on behalf of, the registrant during the covered fiscal year with respect to life insurance for the benefit of a director; and

I. The dollar value of any dividends or other earnings paid on stock or option awards, when those amounts were not factored into the grant date fair value for the stock or option award; and

---

Instructions to Item 402(k)(2)(vii).

1. Programs in which registrants agree to make donations to one or more charitable institutions in a director's name, payable by the registrant currently or upon a designated event, such as the retirement or death of the director, are charitable awards programs or director legacy programs for purposes of the

disclosure required by paragraph (k)(2)(vii)(G) of this Item. Provide footnote disclosure of the total dollar amount payable under the program and other material terms of each such program for which tabular disclosure is provided.

2. Any item reported for a director pursuant to paragraph (k)(2)(vii) of this Item that is not a perquisite or personal benefit and whose value exceeds $10,000 must be identified and quantified in a footnote to column (g). All items of compensation are required to be included in the Director Compensation Table without regard to whether such items are required to be identified other than as specifically noted in this Item.

3. Perquisites and personal benefits may be excluded as long as the total value of all perquisites and personal benefits for a director is less than $10,000. If the total value of all perquisites and personal benefits is $10,000 or more for any director, then each perquisite or personal benefit, regardless of its amount, must be identified by type. If perquisites and personal benefits are required to be reported for a director pursuant to this rule, then each perquisite or personal benefit that exceeds the greater of $25,000 or 10% of the total amount of perquisites and personal benefits for that director must be quantified and disclosed in a footnote. Perquisites and other personal benefits shall be valued on the basis of the aggregate incremental cost to the registrant. With respect to the perquisite or other personal benefit for which footnote quantification is required, the registrant shall describe in the footnote its methodology for computing the aggregate incremental cost. Reimbursements of taxes owed with respect to perquisites or other personal benefits must be included in column (g) and are subject to separate quantification and identification as tax reimbursements (paragraph (k)(2)(vii)(B) of this Item) even if the associated perquisites or other personal benefits are not required to be included because the total amount of all perquisites or personal benefits for an individual director is less than $10,000 or are required to be identified but are not required to be separately quantified.

viii. The dollar value of total compensation for the covered fiscal year (column (h)). With respect to each director, disclose the sum of all amounts reported in columns (b) through (g).

Instruction to Item 402(k)(2).

Two or more directors may be grouped in a single row in the Table if all elements of their compensation are identical. The names of the directors for whom disclosure is presented on a group basis should be clear from the Table.

3. *Narrative to director compensation table.* Provide a narrative description of any material factors necessary to an understanding of the director

compensation disclosed in this Table. While material factors will vary depending upon the facts, examples of such factors may include, in given cases, among other things:

  i. A description of standard compensation arrangements (such as fees for retainer, committee service, service as chairman of the board or a committee, and meeting attendance); and

 ii. Whether any director has a different compensation arrangement, identifying that director and describing the terms of that arrangement.

Instruction to Item 402(k).

In addition to the Instruction to paragraphs 402(k)(2)(iii) and (iv) and the Instructions to paragraph (k)(2)(vii) of this Item, the following apply equally to paragraph (k) of this Item: Instructions 2 and 4 to paragraph (c) of this Item; Instructions to paragraphs (c)(2)(iii) and (iv) of this Item; the Instruction to paragraphs (c)(2)(v) and (vi) of this Item; Instructions to paragraph (c)(2)(vii) of this Item; Instructions to paragraph (c)(2)(viii) of this Item; and Instructions 1 and 5 to paragraph (c)(2)(ix) of this Item. These Instructions apply to the columns in the Director Compensation Table that are analogous to the columns in the Summary Compensation Table to which they refer and to disclosures under paragraph (k) of this Item that correspond to analogous disclosures provided for in paragraph (c) of this Item to which they refer.

Instruction to Item 402.

Specify the applicable fiscal year in the title to each table required under this Item which calls for disclosure as of or for a completed fiscal year.

Security Ownership of Certain Beneficial Owners and Management Reg. §229.403. Item 403.

a. Security ownership of certain beneficial owners. Furnish the following information, as of the most recent practicable date, insubstantially the tabular form indicated, with respect to any person (including any "group" as that term is used in section13(d)(3) of the Exchange Act) who is known to the registrant to be the beneficial owner of more than five percent of any class of the registrant's voting securities. The address given in column (2) may be a business, mailing or residence address. Show in column (3) the total number of shares beneficially owned and in column (4) the percentage of class so owned. Of the number of shares shown in column (3), indicate by footnote or otherwise the amount known to be shares with respect to which such listed beneficial owner has the right to acquire beneficial ownership, as specified in Rule 13d-3(d)(1) under the Exchange Act(§240.13d-3(d)(1) of this chapter).

(1) Title of Class	(2) Name and Address of Beneficial Owner	(3) Amount and Nature of Beneficial Owner	(4) Percent of Class

b. *Security ownership of management.* Furnish the following information, as of the most recent practicable date, in substantially the tabular form indicated, as to each class of equity securities of the registrant or any of its parents or subsidiaries, including directors' qualifying shares, beneficially owned by all directors and nominees, naming them, each of the named executive officers as defined in Item 402(a)(3) (§229.402(a)(3)), and directors and executive officers of the registrant as a group, without naming them. Show in column (3) the total number of shares beneficially owned and in column (4) the percent of the class so owned. Of the number of shares shown in column (3), indicate, by footnote or otherwise, the amount of shares that are pledged as security and the amount of shares with respect to which such persons have the right to acquire beneficial ownership as specified in §240.13d-3(d)(1) of this chapter.

(1) Title of Class	(2) Name of Beneficial Owner	(3) Amount and Nature of Beneficial Owner	(4) Percent of Class

c. *Changes in control.* Describe any arrangements, known to the registrant, including any pledge by any person of securities of the registrant or any of its parents, the operation of which may at a subsequent date result in a change in control of the registrant.

Instructions to Item 403.

1. The percentages are to be calculated on the basis of the amount of outstanding securities, excluding securities held by or for the account of the registrant or its subsidiaries, plus securities deemed outstanding pursuant to Rule 13d-3(d)(1) under the Exchange Act [17 CFR 240.13d-3(d)(1)]. For purposes of paragraph (b), if the percentage of shares beneficially owned by any director or nominee, or by all directors and officers of the registrant as a group, does not exceed one percent of the class so owned, the registrant may, in lieu of furnishing a precise percentage, indicate this fact by means of an asterisk and explanatory footnote or other similar means.

2. For the purposes of this Item, beneficial ownership shall be determined in accordance with Rule 13d-3 under the Exchange Act (§240.13d-3 of this chapter). Include such additional subcolumns or other appropriate explanation

of column (3) necessary to reflect amounts as to which the beneficial owner has (A) sole voting power, (B) shared voting power, (C) sole investment power, or (D) shared investment power.

3. The registrant shall be deemed to know the contents of any statements filed with the Commission pursuant to section 13(d) or 13(g) of the Exchange Act. When applicable, a registrant may rely upon information set forth in such statements unless the registrant knows or has reason to believe that such information is not complete or accurate or that a statement or amendment should have been filed and was not.

4. For purposes of furnishing information pursuant to paragraph (a) of this Item, the registrant may indicate the source and date of such information.

5. Where more than one beneficial owner is known to be listed for the same securities, appropriate disclosure should be made to avoid confusion. For purposes of paragraph (b), in computing the aggregate number of shares owned by directors and officers of the registrant as a group, the same shares shall not be counted more than once.

6. Paragraph (c) of this Item does not require a description of ordinary default provisions contained in the charter, trust indentures or other governing instruments relating to securities of the registrant.

7. Where the holder(s) of voting securities reported pursuant to paragraph (a) hold more than five percent of any class of voting securities of the registrant pursuant to any voting trust or similar agreement, state the title of such securities, the amount held or to be held pursuant to the trust or agreement (if not clear from the table) and the duration of the agreement. Give the names and ad dresses of the voting trustees and outline briefly their voting rights and other powers under the trust or agreement.

Transactions with related persons, promoters and certain control persons. Reg. §229.404. Item 404.

---

a. Transactions with related persons. Describe any transaction, since the beginning of the registrant's last fiscal year, or any currently proposed transaction, in which the registrant was or is to be a participant and the amount involved exceeds $120,000, and in which any related person had or will have a direct or indirect material interest. Disclose the following information regarding the transaction:

1. The name of the related person and the basis on which the person is a related person.

2. The related person's interest in the transaction with the registrant, including the related person's position(s) or relationship(s) with, or ownership in, a firm, corporation, or other entity that is a party to, or has an interest in, the transaction.

3. The approximate dollar value of the amount involved in the transaction.

4. The approximate dollar value of the amount of the related person's interest in the transaction, which shall be computed without regard to the amount of profit or loss.

5. In the case of indebtedness, disclosure of the amount involved in the transaction shall include the largest aggregate amount of principal outstanding during the period for which disclosure is provided, the amount thereof outstanding as of the latest practicable date, the amount of principal paid during the periods for which disclosure is provided, the amount of interest paid during the period for which disclosure is provided, and the rate or amount of interest payable on the indebtedness.

6. Any other information regarding the transaction or the related person in the context of the transaction that is material to investors in light of the circumstances of the particular transaction.

Instructions to Item 404(a).

1. For the purposes of paragraph (a) of this Item, the term *related person* means:

   a. Any person who was in any of the following categories at any time during the specified period for which disclosure under paragraph (a) of this Item is required:

      i. Any director or executive officer of the registrant;

      ii. Any nominee for director, when the information called for by paragraph (a) of this Item is being presented in a proxy or information statement relating to the election of that nominee for director; or

      iii. Any immediate family member of a director or executive officer of the registrant, or of any nominee for director when the information called for by paragraph (a) of this Item is being presented in a proxy or information statement relating to the election of that nominee for director, which means any child, stepchild, parent, stepparent, spouse, sibling, mother-in-law, father-in-law, son-in-law, daughter-in-law, brother-in-law, or sister-in-law of such director, executive officer or nominee for director, and any person (other than a tenant or employee) sharing the household of such director, executive officer or nominee for director; and

   b. Any person who was in any of the following categories when a transaction in which such person had a direct or indirect material interest occurred or existed:

      i. A security holder covered by Item 403(a) (§229.403(a)); or

      ii. Any immediate family member of any such security holder, which means any child, stepchild, parent, stepparent, spouse, sibling, mother-in-law, father-in-law, son-in-law, daughter-in-law, brother-in-law, or sister-in-law of such security holder, and any person (other than a tenant or employee) sharing the household of such security holder.

2. For purposes of paragraph (a) of this Item, a *transaction* includes, but is not limited to, any financial transaction, arrangement or relationship (including any indebtedness or guarantee of indebtedness) or any series of similar transactions, arrangements or relationships.

3. The amount involved in the transaction shall be computed by determining the dollar value of the amount involved in the transaction in question, which shall include:

   a. In the case of any lease or other transaction providing for periodic payments or installments, the aggregate amount of all periodic payments or installments due on or after the beginning of the registrant's last fiscal year, including any required or optional payments due during or at the conclusion of the lease or other transaction providing for periodic payments or installments; and

   b. In the case of indebtedness, the largest aggregate amount of all indebtedness outstanding at any time since the beginning of the registrant's last fiscal year and all amounts of interest payable on it during the last fiscal year.

4. In the case of a transaction involving indebtedness:

   a. The following items of indebtedness may be excluded from the calculation of the amount of indebtedness and need not be disclosed: amounts due from the related person for purchases of goods and services subject to usual trade terms, for ordinary business travel and expense payments and for other transactions in the ordinary course of business;

   b. Disclosure need not be provided of any indebtedness transaction for the related persons specified in Instruction 1.b. to paragraph (a) of this Item; and

   c. If the lender is a bank, savings and loan association, or broker-dealer extending credit under Federal Reserve Regulation T (12 CFR part 220) and the loans are not disclosed as nonaccrual, past due, restructured or potential problems (see Item III.C.1. and 2. of Industry Guide 3, Statistical Disclosure by Bank Holding Companies (17 CFR 229.802(c))), disclosure under paragraph (a) of this Item may consist of a statement, if such is the case, that the loans to such persons:

      i. Were made in the ordinary course of business;

      ii. Were made on substantially the same terms, including interest rates and collateral, as those prevailing at the time for comparable loans with persons not related to the lender; and

      iii. Did not involve more than the normal risk of collectibility or present other unfavorable features.

5.

    a. Disclosure of an employment relationship or transaction involving an executive officer and any related compensation solely resulting from that employment relationship or transaction need not be provided pursuant to paragraph of this Item if:

        i. The compensation arising from the relationship or transaction is reported pursuant to Item 402 (§229.402); or

        ii. The executive officer is not an immediate family member (as specified in Instruction 1 to paragraph (a) of this Item) and such compensation would have been reported under Item 402 (§229.402) as compensation earned for services to the registrant if the executive officer was a named executive officer as that term is defined in Item 402(a)(3) (§229.402(a)(3)), and such compensation had been approved, or recommended to the board of directors of the registrant for approval, by the compensation committee of the board of directors (or group of independent directors performing a similar function) of the registrant.

    b. Disclosure of compensation to a director need not be provided pursuant to paragraph (a) of this Item if the compensation is reported pursuant to Item 402(k) (§229.402(k)).

6. A person who has a position or relationship with a firm, corporation, or other entity that engages in a transaction with the registrant shall not be deemed to have an indirect material interest within the meaning of paragraph (a) of this Item where:

    a. The interest arises only:

        i. From such person's position as a director of another corporation or organization that is a party to the transaction; or

        ii. From the direct or indirect ownership by such person and all other persons specified in Instruction 1 to paragraph (a) of this Item, in the aggregate, of less than a ten percent equity interest in another person (other than a partnership) which is a party to the transaction; or

        iii. From both such position and ownership; or

    b. The interest arises only from such person's position as a limited partner in a partnership in which the person and all other persons specified in Instruction 1 to paragraph (a) of this Item, have an interest of less than ten percent, and the person is not a general partner of and does not hold another position in the partnership.

7. Disclosure need not be provided pursuant to paragraph (a) of this Item if:

    a. The transaction is one where the rates or charges involved in the transaction are determined by competitive bids, or the transaction involves the rendering of services as a common or contract carrier, or public utility, at rates or charges fixed in conformity with law or governmental authority;

b. The transaction involves services as a bank depositary of funds, transfer agent, registrar, trustee under a trust indenture, or similar services; or

c. The interest of the related person arises solely from the ownership of a class of equity securities of the registrant and all holders of that class of equity securities of the registrant received the same benefit on a pro rata basis.

---

b. Review, approval or ratification of transactions with related persons.

1. Describe the registrant's policies and procedures for the review, approval, or ratification of any transaction required to be reported under paragraph (a) of this Item. While the material features of such policies and procedures will vary depending on the particular circumstances, examples of such features may include, in given cases, among other things:

   i. The types of transactions that are covered by such policies and procedures;

   ii. The standards to be applied pursuant to such policies and procedures;

   iii. The persons or groups of persons on the board of directors or otherwise who are responsible for applying such policies and procedures; and

   iv. A statement of whether such policies and procedures are in writing and, if not, how such policies and procedures are evidenced.

2. Identify any transaction required to be reported under paragraph (a) of this Item since the beginning of the registrant's last fiscal year where such policies and procedures did not require review, approval or ratification or where such policies and procedures were not followed. *Instruction to Item 404(b).* Disclosure need not be provided pursuant to this paragraph regarding any transaction that occurred at a time before the related person became one of the enumerated persons in Instruction 1.a.i., ii., or iii. to Item 404(a) if such transaction did not continue after the related person became one of the enumerated persons in Instruction 1.a.i., ii., or iii. to Item 404(a).

c. Promoters and certain control persons.

1. Registrants that are filing a registration statement on Form S-1 or Form SB-2 under the Securities Act (§239.11 or §239.10 of this chapter) or on Form 10 or Form 10-SB under the Exchange Act (§249.210 or §249.210b of this chapter) and that had a promoter at any time during the past five fiscal years shall:

   i. State the names of the promoter(s), the nature and amount of anything of value (including money, property, contracts, options or rights of any kind) received or to be received by each promoter, directly or indirectly, from the registrant and the nature and amount of any assets, services or other consideration therefore received or to be received by the registrant; and

ii. As to any assets acquired or to be acquired by the registrant from a promoter, state the amount at which the assets were acquired or are to be acquired and the principle followed or to be followed in determining such amount, and identify the persons making the determination and their relationship, if any, with the registrant or any promoter. If the assets were acquired by the promoter within two years prior to their transfer to the registrant, also state the cost thereof to the promoter.

2. Registrants shall provide the disclosure required by paragraphs (c)(1)(i) and (c)(1)(ii) of this Item as to any person who acquired control of a registrant that is a shell company, or any person that is part of a group, consisting of two or more persons that agree to act together for the purpose of acquiring, holding, voting or disposing of equity securities of a registrant, that acquired control of a registrant that is a shell company. For purposes of this Item, shell company has the same meaning as in Rule 405 under the Securities Act (17 CFR 230.405) and Rule 12b-2 under the Exchange Act (17 CFR 240.12b-2).

Instructions to Item 404.

1. If the information called for by this Item is being presented in a registration statement filed pursuant to the Securities Act or the Exchange Act, information shall be given for the periods specified in the Item and, in addition, for the two fiscal years preceding the registrant's last fiscal year, unless the information is being incorporated by reference into a registration statement on Form S-4 (17 CFR 239.25), in which case, information shall be given for the periods specified in the Item.

2. A foreign private issuer will be deemed to comply with this Item if it provides the information required by Item 7.B. of Form 20-F (17 CFR 249.220f) with more detailed information provided if otherwise made publicly available or required to be disclosed by the issuer's home jurisdiction or a market in which its securities are listed or traded.

Compliance with Section 16(a) of the Exchange Act
Reg §229.405. Item 405.

Every registrant having a class of equity securities registered pursuant to Section 12 of the Exchange Act (15 U.S.C. 78(*l*), every closed-end investment company registered under the Investment Company Act of 1940 (15 U.S.C. § 80a-1 *et seq.*), and every holding company registered pursuant to the Public Utility Holding Company Act of 1935 (15 U.S.C. § 79a *et seq.*) shall:

a. Based solely upon a review of Forms 3 (§ 249.103) and 4 (§ 249.104) and amendments thereto furnished to the registrant pursuant to § 240.16a-3(e) during its most recent fiscal year and Forms 5 and amendments thereto (§ 249.105) furnished to the registrant with respect to its most recent fiscal year, and any written representation referred to in (b)(1) of this section:

1. Under the caption "Section 16(a) Beneficial Ownership Reporting Compliance," identify each person who, at any time during the fiscal year, was a director, officer, beneficial owner of more than ten percent of any class of equity securities of the registrant registered pursuant to section 12 of the Exchange Act with respect to the registrant because of the requirements of section 30 of the Investment Company Act ("reporting person") that failed to file on a timely basis, as disclosed in the above Forms, reports required by section 16(a) of the Exchange Act during the most recent fiscal year or prior fiscal years.

2. For each such person, set forth the number of late reports, the number of transactions that were not reported on a timely basis, and any known failure to file a required Form. A known failure to file would include, but not be limited to, a failure to file a Form 3, which is required by all reporting persons, and a failure to file a Form 5 in the absence of the written representation referred to in paragraph (b)(1) of this section, unless the registrant otherwise knows that no Form 5 is required.

Note: The disclosure requirement is based on a review of the forms submitted to the registrant during and with respect to its most recent fiscal year, as specified above. Accordingly, a failure to file timely need only be disclosed once. For example, if in the most recently concluded fiscal year a reporting person filed a Form 4 disclosing a transaction that took place in the prior fiscal year, and should have been reported in that year, the registrant should disclose that late filing and transaction pursuant to this Item 405 with respect to the most recently concluded fiscal year, but not in material filed with respect to subsequent years.

---

b. With respect to the disclosure required by paragraph (a) of this section, if the registrant:

1. Receives a written representation from the reporting person that no Form 5 is required; and

2. Maintains the representation for two years, making a copy available to the Commission or its staff upon request, the registrant need not identify such reporting person pursuant to paragraph (a) of this section as having failed to file a Form 5 with respect to that fiscal year.

Code of Ethics
Reg. §229.406. Item 406

---

a. Disclose whether the registrant has adopted a code of ethics that applies to the registrant's principal executive officer, principal financial officer, principal accounting officer or controller, or persons performing similar functions. If the registrant has not adopted such a code of ethics, explain why it has not done so.

b. For purposes of this Item 406, the term *code of ethics* means written standards that are reasonably designed to deter wrongdoing and to promote:

   1. Honest and ethical conduct, including the ethical handling of actual or apparent conflicts of interest between personal and professional relationships;
   2. Full, fair, accurate, timely, and understandable disclosure in reports and documents that a registrant files with, or submits to, the Commission and in other public communications made by the registrant;
   3. Compliance with applicable governmental laws, rules and regulations;
   4. The prompt internal reporting of violations of the code to an appropriate person or persons identified in the code; and
   5. Accountability for adherence to the code.

c. The registrant must:

   1. File with the Commission a copy of its code of ethics that applies to the registrant's principal executive officer, principal financial officer, principal accounting officer or controller, or persons performing similar functions, as an exhibit to its annual report;
   2. Post the text of such code of ethics on its Internet website and disclose, in its annual report, its Internet address and the fact that it has posted such code of ethics on its Internet Web site; or
   3. Undertake in its annual report filed with the Commission to provide to any person without charge, upon request, a copy of such code of ethics and explain the manner in which such request may be made.

d. If the registrant intends to satisfy the disclosure requirement under Item 10 of Form 8-K regarding an amendment to, or a waiver from, a provision of its code of ethics that applies to the registrant's principal executive officer, principal financial officer, principal accounting officer or controller, or persons performing similar functions and that relates to any element of the code of ethics definition enumerated in paragraph (b) of this Item by posting such information on its Internet website, disclose the registrant's Internet address and such intention.

Instructions to Item 406.

1. A registrant may have separate codes of ethics for different types of officers. Furthermore, a code of ethics within the meaning of paragraph (b) of this Item may be a portion of a broader document that addresses additional topics or that applies to more persons than those specified in paragraph (a). In satisfying the requirements of paragraph (c), a registrant need only file, post or provide the portions of a broader document that constitutes a code of ethics as defined in paragraph (b) and that apply to the persons specified in paragraph (a).

2. If a registrant elects to satisfy paragraph (c) of this Item by posting its code of ethics on its website pursuant to paragraph (c)(2), the code of ethics must remain accessible on its Web site for as long as the registrant remains subject to the requirements of this Item and chooses to comply with this Item by posting its code on its Web site pursuant to paragraph (c)(2).

---

§229.407 (Item 407) Corporate governance.

---

a. Director independence. Identify each director and, when the disclosure called for by this paragraph is being presented in a proxy or information statement relating to the election of directors, each nominee for director, that is independent under the independence standards applicable to the registrant under paragraph (a)(1) of this Item. In addition, if such independence standards contain independence requirements for committees of the board of directors, identify each director that is a member of the compensation, nominating or audit committee that is not independent under such committee independence standards. If the registrant does not have a separately designated audit, nominating or compensation committee or committee performing similar functions, the registrant must provide the disclosure of directors that are not independent with respect to all members of the board of directors applying such committee independence standards.

1. In determining whether or not the director or nominee for director is independent for the purposes of paragraph (a) of this Item, the registrant shall use the applicable definition of independence, as follows:

   i. If the registrant is a listed issuer whose securities are listed on a national securities exchange or in an inter-dealer quotation system which has requirements that a majority of the board of directors be independent, the registrant's definition of independence that it uses for determining if a majority of the board of directors is independent in compliance with the listing standards applicable to the registrant. When determining whether the members of a committee of the board of directors are independent, the registrant's definition of independence that it uses for determining if the members of that specific committee are independent in compliance with the independence standards applicable for the members of the specific committee in the listing standards of the national securities exchange or inter-dealer quotation system that the registrant uses for determining if a majority of the board of directors are independent. If the registrant does not have independence standards for a committee, the independence standards for that specific committee in the listing standards of the national securities exchange or inter-dealer quotation system that the registrant uses for determining if a majority of the board of directors are independent.

ii. If the registrant is not a listed issuer, a definition of independence of a national securities exchange or of an inter-dealer quotation system which has requirements that a majority of the board of directors be independent, and state which definition is used. Whatever such definition the registrant chooses, it must use the same definition with respect to all directors and nominees for director. When determining whether the members of a specific committee of the board of directors are independent, if the national securities exchange or national securities association whose standards are used has independence standards for the members of a specific committee, use those committee specific standards.

iii. If the information called for by paragraph (a) of this Item is being presented in a registration statement on Form S-1 (§239.11 of this chapter) or Form SB-2 (§239.10 of this chapter) under the Securities Act or on a Form 10 (§249.210 of this chapter) or Form 10-SB (§249.210b of this chapter) under the Exchange Act where the registrant has applied for listing with a national securities exchange or in an inter-dealer quotation system which has requirements that a majority of the board of directors be independent, the definition of independence that the registrant uses for determining if a majority of the board of directors is independent, and the definition of independence that the registrant uses for determining if members of the specific committee of the board of directors are independent, that is in compliance with the independence listing standards of the national securities exchange or inter-dealer quotation system on which it has applied for listing, or if the registrant has not adopted such definitions, the independence standards for determining if the majority of the board of directors is independent and if members of the committee of the board of directors are independent of that national securities exchange or inter-dealer quotation system.

2. Registrants shall provide the disclosure required by paragraph (a) of this Item for any person who served as a director during any part of the last completed fiscal year, except that no information called for by paragraph (a) of this Item need be given in a registration statement filed at a time when the registrant is not subject to the reporting requirements of section 13(a) or 15(d) of the Exchange Act (15 U.S.C. 78m(a) or 78o(d))

3. For each director and nominee for director that is identified as independent, describe, by specific category or type, any transactions, relationships or arrangements not disclosed pursuant to Item 404(a) (§229.404(a)), or for investment companies, Item 22(b) of Schedule 14A (§240.14a-101 of this chapter), that were considered by the board of directors under the applicable independence definitions in determining that the director is independent.

Instructions to Item 407(a).

1. If the registrant is a listed issuer whose securities are listed on a national securities exchange or in an inter-dealer quotation system which has requirements that a majority of the board of directors be independent, and also has exemptions to those requirements (for independence of a majority of the board of directors or committee member independence) upon which the registrant relied, disclose the exemption relied upon and explain the basis for the registrant's conclusion that such exemption is applicable. The same disclosure should be provided if the registrant is not a listed issuer and the national securities exchange or inter-dealer quotation system selected by the registrant has exemptions that are applicable to the registrant. Any national securities exchange or inter-dealer quotation system which has requirements that at least 50 percent of the members of a small business issuer's board of directors must be independent shall be considered a national securities exchange or inter-dealer quotation system which has requirements that a majority of the board of directors be independent for the purposes of the disclosure required by paragraph (a) of this Item.

2. Registrants shall provide the disclosure required by paragraph (a) of this Item for any person who served as a director during any part of the last completed fiscal year, except that no information called for by paragraph (a) of this Item need be given in a registration statement filed at a time when the registrant is not subject to the reporting requirements of section 13(a) or 15(d) of the Exchange Act (15 U.S.C. 78m(a) or 78o(d)) respecting any director who is no longer a director at the time of effectiveness of the registration statement.

3. The description of the specific categories or types of transactions, relationships or arrangements required by paragraph (a)(3) of this Item must be provided in such detail as is necessary to fully describe the nature of the transactions, relationships or arrangements.

---

b. Board meetings and committees; annual meeting attendance.

1. State the total number of meetings of the board of directors (including regularly scheduled and special meetings) which were held during the last full fiscal year. Name each incumbent director who during the last full fiscal year attended fewer than 75 percent of the aggregate of:

i. The total number of meetings of the board of directors (held during the period for which he has been a director); and

ii. The total number of meetings held by all committees of the board on which he served (during the periods that he served).

2. Describe the registrant's policy, if any, with regard to board members' attendance at annual meetings of security holders and state the number of board members who attended the prior year's annual meeting.

Instruction to Item 407(b)(2).

In lieu of providing the information required by paragraph (b)(2) of this Item in the proxy statement, the registrant may instead provide the registrant's Web site address where such information appears.

---

3. State whether or not the registrant has standing audit, nominating and compensation committees of the board of directors, or committees performing similar functions. If the registrant has such committees, however designated, identify each committee member, state the number of committee meetings held by each such committee during the last fiscal year and describe briefly the functions performed by each such committee. Such disclosure need not be provided to the extent it is duplicative of disclosure provided in accordance with paragraph (c), (d) or (e) of this Item.

c. *Nominating committee.*

1. If the registrant does not have a standing nominating committee or committee performing similar functions, state the basis for the view of the board of directors that it is appropriate for the registrant not to have such a committee and identify each director who participates in the consideration of director nominees.

2. Provide the following information regarding the registrant's director nomination process:

i. State whether or not the nominating committee has a charter. If the nominating committee has a charter, provide the disclosure required by Instruction 2 to this Item regarding the nominating committee charter;

ii. If the nominating committee has a policy with regard to the consideration of any director candidates recommended by security holders, provide a description of the material elements of that policy, which shall include, but need not be limited to, a statement as to whether the committee will consider director candidates recommended by security holders;

iii. If the nominating committee does not have a policy with regard to the consideration of any director candidates recommended by security holders, state that fact and state the basis for the view of the board of directors that it is appropriate for the registrant not to have such policy;

iv. If the nominating committee will consider candidates recommended by security holders, describe the procedures to be followed by security holders in submitting such recommendations;

v. Describe any specific minimum qualifications that the nominating committee believes must be met by a nominating committee-recommended nominee for a position on the registrant's board of directors, and describe any specific qualities or skills that the nominating committee believes are necessary for one or more of the registrant's directors to possess;

vi. Describe the nominating committee's process for identifying and evaluating nominees for director, including nominees recommended by security holders, and any differences in the manner in which the nominating committee evaluates nominees for director based on whether the nominee is recommended by a security holder;

vii. With regard to each nominee approved by the nominating committee for inclusion on the registrant's proxy card (other than nominees who are executive officers or who are directors standing for re-election), state which one or more of the following categories of persons or entities recommended that nominee: security holder, non-management director, chief executive officer, other executive officer, third-party search firm, or other specified source. With regard to each such nominee approved by a nominating committee of an investment company, state which one or more of the following additional categories of persons or entities recommended that nominee: security holder, director, chief executive officer, other executive officer, or employee of the investment company's investment adviser, principal underwriter, or any affiliated person of the investment adviser or principal underwriter;

viii. If the registrant pays a fee to any third party or parties to identify or evaluate or assist in identifying or evaluating potential nominees, disclose the function performed by each such third party; and

ix. If the registrant's nominating committee received, by a date not later than the 120th calendar day before the date of the registrant's proxy statement released to security holders in connection with the previous year's annual meeting, a recommended nominee from a security holder that beneficially owned more than 5% of the registrant's voting common stock for at least one year as of the date the recommendation was made, or from a group of security holders that beneficially owned, in the aggregate, more than 5% of the registrant's voting common stock, with each of the securities used to calculate that ownership held for at least one year as of the date the recommendation was made, identify the candidate and the security holder or security holder group that recommended the candidate and disclose whether the nominating committee chose to nominate the candidate, *provided, however,* that no such identification or disclosure is required without the written consent of both the security holder or security holder group and the candidate to be so identified.

Instructions to Item 407(c)(2)(ix).

1. For purposes of paragraph (c)(2)(ix) of this Item, the percentage of securities held by a nominating security holder may be determined using information set forth in the registrant's most recent quarterly or annual report, and any current report subsequent thereto, filed with the Commission pursuant to the Exchange Act (or, in the case of a registrant that is an investment company registered under the Investment Company Act of 1940, the registrant's most recent report on Form N-CSR (§§249.331 and 274.128 of this chapter)), unless the party relying on such report knows or has reason to believe that the information contained therein is inaccurate.

2. For purposes of the registrant's obligation to provide the disclosure specified in paragraph (c)(2)(ix) of this Item, where the date of the annual meeting has been changed by more than 30 days from the date of the previous year's meeting, the obligation under that Item will arise where the registrant receives the security holder recommendation a reasonable time before the registrant begins to print and mail its proxy materials.

3. For purposes of paragraph (c)(2)(ix) of this Item, the percentage of securities held by a recommending security holder, as well as the holding period of those securities, may be determined by the registrant if the security holder is the registered holder of the securities. If the security holder is not the registered owner of the securities, he or she can submit one of the following to the registrant to evidence the required ownership percentage and holding period:

   a. A written statement from the "record" holder of the securities (usually a broker or bank) verifying that, at the time the security holder made the recommendation, he or she had held the required securities for at least one year; or

   b. If the security holder has filed a Schedule 13D (§240.13d-101 of this chapter), Schedule 13G (§240.13d-102 of this chapter), Form 3 (§249.103 of this chapter), Form 4 (§249.104 of this chapter), and/or Form 5 (§249.105 of this chapter), or amendments to those documents or updated forms, reflecting ownership of the securities as of or before the date of the recommendation, a copy of the schedule and/or form, and any subsequent amendments reporting a change in ownership level, as well as a written statement that the security holder continuously held the securities for the one-year period as of the date of the recommendation.

4. For purposes of the registrant's obligation to provide the disclosure specified in paragraph (c)(2)(ix) of this Item, the security holder or group must have provided to the registrant, at the time of the recommendation, the written

consent of all parties to be identified and, where the security holder or group members are not registered holders, proof that the security holder or group satisfied the required ownership percentage and holding period as of the date of the recommendation.

Instruction to Item 407(c)(2).

For purposes of paragraph (c)(2) of this Item, the term *nominating committee* refers not only to nominating committees and committees performing similar functions, but also to groups of directors fulfilling the role of a nominating committee, including the entire board of directors.

---

3. Describe any material changes to the procedures by which security holders may recommend nominees to the registrant's board of directors, where those changes were implemented after the registrant last provided disclosure in response to the requirements of paragraph (c)(2)(iv) of this Item, or paragraph (c)(3) of this Item.

Instructions to Item 407(c)(3).

1. The disclosure required in paragraph (c)(3) of this Item need only be provided in a registrant's quarterly or annual reports.
2. For purposes of paragraph (c)(3) of this Item, adoption of procedures by which security holders may recommend nominees to the registrant's board of directors, where the registrant's most recent disclosure in response to the requirements of paragraph (c)(2)(iv) of this Item, or paragraph (c)(3) of this Item, indicated that the registrant did not have in place such procedures, will constitute a material change.

---

d. Audit committee.

1. State whether or not the audit committee has a charter. If the audit committee has a charter, provide the disclosure required by Instruction 2 to this Item regarding the audit committee charter.
2. If a listed issuer's board of directors determines, in accordance with the listing standards applicable to the issuer, to appoint a director to the audit committee who is not independent (apart from the requirements in §240.10A-3 of this chapter), including as a result of exceptional or limited or similar circumstances, disclose the nature of the relationship that makes that individual not independent and the reasons for the board of directors' determination.
3.
    i. The audit committee must state whether:
        A. The audit committee has reviewed and discussed the audited financial statements with management;

B. The audit committee has discussed with the independent auditors the matters required to be discussed by the statement on Auditing Standards No. 61, as amended (AICPA, *Professional Standards*, Vol. 1. AU section 380),[1] as adopted by the Public Company Accounting Oversight Board in Rule 3200T;

C. The audit committee has received the written disclosures and the letter from the independent accountants required by Independence Standards Board Standard No. 1 (Independence Standards Board Standard No. 1, *Independence Discussions with Audit Committees*),[2] as adopted by the Public Company Accounting Oversight Board in Rule 3600T, and has discussed with the independent accountant the independent accountant's independence; and

D. Based on the review and discussions referred to in paragraphs (d)(3)(i)(A) through (d)(3)(i)(C) of this Item, the audit committee recommended to the board of directors that the audited financial statements be included in the company's annual report on Form 10-K (17 CFR 249.310) (or, for closed-end investment companies registered under the Investment Company Act of 1940 (15 U.S.C. 80a-1 *et seq.*), the annual report to shareholders required by section 30(e) of the Investment Company Act of 1940 (15 U.S.C. 80a-29(e)) and Rule 30d-1 (17 CFR 270.30d-1) thereunder) for the last fiscal year for filing with the Commission.

ii. The name of each member of the company's audit committee (or, in the absence of an audit committee, the board committee performing equivalent functions or the entire board of directors) must appear below the disclosure required by paragraph (d)(3)(i) of this Item.

4.

i. If the registrant meets the following requirements, provide the disclosure in paragraph (d)(4)(ii) of this Item:

A. The registrant is a listed issuer, as defined in §240.10A-3 of this chapter;

B. The registrant is filing either an annual report on Form 10-K or 10-KSB (17 CFR 249.310 or 17 CFR 249.310b), or a proxy statement or information statement pursuant to the Exchange Act (15 U.S.C. 78a *et seq.*) if action is to be taken with respect to the election of directors; and

C. The registrant is neither:

1. A subsidiary of another listed issuer that is relying on the exemption in §240.10A-3(c)(2) of this chapter; nor

---

[1]Available at www.pcaobus.org/standards/interim_standards/index_au.asp?series=300&section=300.
[2]Available at www.0pcaobus.org/Standards/Interim_Standards/Independence_Standards/1SB1.pdf.

        2. Relying on any of the exemptions in §240.10A-3(c)(4) through (c)(7) of this chapter.

    ii.

        A. State whether or not the registrant has a separately-designated standing audit committee established in accordance with section 3(a)(58)(A) of the Exchange Act (15 U.S.C. 78c(a)(58)(A)), or a committee performing similar functions. If the registrant has such a committee, however designated, identify each committee member. If the entire board of directors is acting as the registrant's audit committee as specified in section 3(a)(58)(B) of the Exchange Act (15 U.S.C. 78c(a)(58)(B)), so state.

        B. If applicable, provide the disclosure required by §240.10A-3(d) of this chapter regarding an exemption from the listing standards for audit committees.

    5. *Audit committee financial expert.*

        i.

        A. Disclose that the registrant's board of directors has determined that the registrant either:

            1. Has at least one audit committee financial expert serving on its audit committee; or

            2. Does not have an audit committee financial expert serving on its audit committee.

        B. If the registrant provides the disclosure required by paragraph (d)(5)(i)(A)(*1*) of this Item, it must disclose the name of the audit committee financial expert and whether that person is *independent*, as independence for audit committee members is defined in the listing standards applicable to the listed issuer.

        C. If the registrant provides the disclosure required by paragraph (d)(5)(i)(A)(*2*) of this Item, it must explain why it does not have an audit committee financial expert.

Instruction to Item 407(d)(5)(i).

If the registrant's board of directors has determined that the registrant has more than one audit committee financial expert serving on its audit committee, the registrant may, but is not required to, disclose the names of those additional persons. A registrant choosing to identify such persons must indicate whether they are independent pursuant to paragraph (d)(5)(i)(B) of this Item.

---

ii. For purposes of this Item, an *audit committee financial expert* means a person who has the following attributes:

A. An understanding of generally accepted accounting principles and financial statements;

B. The ability to assess the general application of such principles in connection with the accounting for estimates, accruals and reserves;

C. Experience preparing, auditing, analyzing or evaluating financial statements that present a breadth and level of complexity of accounting issues that are generally comparable to the breadth and complexity of issues that can reasonably be expected to be raised by the registrant's financial statements, or experience actively supervising one or more persons engaged in such activities;

D. An understanding of internal control over financial reporting; and

E. An understanding of audit committee functions.

iii. A person shall have acquired such attributes through:

A. Education and experience as a principal financial officer, principal accounting officer, controller, public accountant or auditor or experience in one or more positions that involve the performance of similar functions;

B. Experience actively supervising a principal financial officer, principal accounting officer, controller, public accountant, auditor or person performing similar functions;

C. Experience overseeing or assessing the performance of companies or public accountants with respect to the preparation, auditing or evaluation of financial statements; or

D. Other relevant experience.

iv. *Safe harbor.*

A. A person who is determined to be an audit committee financial expert will not be deemed an *expert* for any purpose, including without limitation for purposes of section 11 of the Securities Act (15 U.S.C. 77k), as a result of being designated or identified as an audit committee financial expert pursuant to this Item 407.

B. The designation or identification of a person as an audit committee financial expert pursuant to this Item 407 does not impose on such person any duties, obligations or liability that are greater than the duties, obligations and liability imposed on such person as a member of the audit committee and board of directors in the absence of such designation or identification.

C. The designation or identification of a person as an audit committee financial expert pursuant to this Item does not affect the duties, obligations or liability of any other member of the audit committee or board of directors.

Instructions to Item 407(d)(5).

1. The disclosure under paragraph (d)(5) of this Item is required only in a registrant's annual report. The registrant need not provide the disclosure required by paragraph (d)(5) of this Item in a proxy or information statement unless that registrant is electing to incorporate this information by reference from the proxy or information statement into its annual report pursuant to General Instruction G(3) to Form 10-K (17 CFR 249.310).

2. If a person qualifies as an audit committee financial expert by means of having held a position described in paragraph (d)(5)(iii)(D) of this Item, the registrant shall provide a brief listing of that person's relevant experience. Such disclosure may be made by reference to disclosures required under Item 401(e) (§229.401(e)).

3. In the case of a foreign private issuer with a two-tier board of directors, for purposes of paragraph (d)(5) of this Item, the term *board of directors* means the supervisory or non-management board. In the case of a foreign private issuer meeting the requirements of §240.10A-3(c)(3) of this chapter, for purposes of paragraph (d)(5) of this Item, the term *board of directors* means the issuer's board of auditors (or similar body) or statutory auditors, as applicable. Also, in the case of a foreign private issuer, the term *generally accepted accounting principles* in paragraph (d)(5)(ii)(A) of this Item means the body of generally accepted accounting principles used by that issuer in its primary financial statements filed with the Commission.

4. A registrant *that* is an Asset-Backed Issuer (as defined in §229.1101) is not required to disclose the information required by paragraph (d)(5) of this Item.

Instructions to Item 407(d).

1. The information required by paragraphs (d)(1) – (3) of this Item shall not be deemed to be "soliciting material," or to be "filed" with the Commission or subject to Regulation 14A or 14C (17 CFR 240.14a-1 through 240.14b-2 or 240.14c-1 through 240.14c101), other than as provided in this Item, or to the liabilities of section 18 of the Exchange Act (15 U.S.C. 78r), except to the extent that the registrant specifically requests that the information be treated as soliciting material or specifically incorporates it by reference into a document filed under the Securities Act or the Exchange Act. Such information will not be deemed to be incorporated by reference into any filing under the Securities Act or the Exchange Act, except to the extent that the registrant specifically incorporates it by reference.

2. The disclosure required by paragraphs (d)(1)–(3) of this Item need only be provided one time during any fiscal year.

3. The disclosure required by paragraph (d)(3) of this Item need not be provided in any filings other than a registrant's proxy or information statement relating to an annual meeting of security holders at which directors are to be elected (or special meeting or written consents in lieu of such meeting).

---

e. *Compensation committee.*

1. If the registrant does not have a standing compensation committee or committee performing similar functions, state the basis for the view of the board of directors that it is appropriate for the registrant not to have such a committee and identify each director who participates in the consideration of executive officer and director compensation.

2. State whether or not the compensation committee has a charter. If the compensation committee has a charter, provide the disclosure required by Instruction 2 to this Item regarding the compensation committee charter.

3. Provide a narrative description of the registrant's processes and procedures for the consideration and determination of executive and director compensation, including:

   i.

   A. The scope of authority of the compensation committee (or persons performing the equivalent functions); and

   B. The extent to which the compensation committee (or persons performing the equivalent functions) may delegate any authority described in paragraph (e)(3)(i)(A) of this Item to other persons, specifying what authority may be so delegated and to whom;

   ii. Any role of executive officers in determining or recommending the amount or form of executive and director compensation; and

   iii. Any role of compensation consultants in determining or recommending the amount or form of executive and director compensation, identifying such consultants, stating whether such consultants are engaged directly by the compensation committee (or persons performing the equivalent functions) or any other person, describing the nature and scope of their assignment, and the material elements of the instructions or directions given to the consultants with respect to the performance of their duties under the engagement.

4. Under the caption "Compensation Committee Interlocks and Insider Participation":

   i. Identify each person who served as a member of the compensation committee of the registrant's board of directors (or board committee performing equivalent functions) during the last completed fiscal year, indicating each committee member who:

A. Was, during the fiscal year, an officer or employee of the registrant;

B. Was formerly an officer of the registrant; or

C. Had any relationship requiring disclosure by the registrant under any paragraph of Item 404 (§229.404). In this event, the disclosure required by Item 404 (§229.404) shall accompany such identification.

ii. If the registrant has no compensation committee (or other board committee performing equivalent functions), the registrant shall identify each officer and employee of the registrant, and any former officer of the registrant, who, during the last completed fiscal year, participated in deliberations of the registrant's board of directors concerning executive officer compensation.

iii. Describe any of the following relationships that existed during the last completed fiscal year:

A. An executive officer of the registrant served as a member of the compensation committee (or other board committee performing equivalent functions or, in the absence of any such committee, the entire board of directors) of another entity, one of whose executive officers served on the compensation committee (or other board committee performing equivalent functions or, in the absence of any such committee, the entire board of directors) of the registrant;

B. An executive officer of the registrant served as a director of another entity, one of whose executive officers served on the compensation committee (or other board committee performing equivalent functions or, in the absence of any such committee, the entire board of directors) of the registrant; and

C. An executive officer of the registrant served as a member of the compensation committee (or other board committee performing equivalent functions or, in the absence of any such committee, the entire board of directors) of another entity, one of whose executive officers served as a director of the registrant.

iv. Disclosure required under paragraph (e)(4)(iii) of this Item regarding a compensation committee member or other director of the registrant who also served as an executive officer of another entity shall be accompanied by the disclosure called for by Item 404 with respect to that person.

Instruction to Item 407(e)(4).

For purposes of paragraph (e)(4) of this Item, the term *entity* shall not include an entity exempt from tax under section 501(c)(3) of the Internal Revenue Code (26 U.S.C. 501(c)(3)).

---

5. Under the caption "Compensation Committee Report:"

  i. The compensation committee (or other board committee performing equivalent functions or, in the absence of any such committee, the entire board of directors) must state whether:

    A. The compensation committee has reviewed and discussed the Compensation Discussion and Analysis required by Item 402(b) (§229.402(b)) with management; and

    B. Based on the review and discussions referred to in paragraph (e)(5)(i)(A) of this Item, the compensation committee recommended to the board of directors that the Compensation Discussion and Analysis be included in the registrant's annual report on Form 10-K (§249.310 of this chapter), proxy statement on Schedule 14A (§240.14a-101 of this chapter) or information statement on Schedule 14C (§240.14c-101 of this chapter).

  ii. The name of each member of the registrant's compensation committee (or other board committee performing equivalent functions or, in the absence of any such committee, the entire board of directors) must appear below the disclosure required by paragraph (e)(5)(i) of this Item.

Instructions to Item 407(e)(5).

1. The information required by paragraph (e)(5) of this Item shall not be deemed to be "soliciting material," or to be "filed" with the Commission or subject to Regulation 14A or 14C (17 CFR 240.14a-1 through 240.14b-2 or 240.14c-1 through 240.14c-101), other than as provided in this Item, or to the liabilities of section 18 of the Exchange Act (15 U.S.C. 78r), except to the extent that the registrant specifically requests that the information be treated as soliciting material or specifically incorporates it by reference into a document filed under the Securities Act or the Exchange Act.

2. The disclosure required by paragraph (e)(5) of this Item need not be provided in any filings other than an annual report on Form 10-K (§249.310 of this chapter), a proxy statement on Schedule 14A (§240.14a-101 of this chapter) or an information statement on Schedule 14C (§240.14c-101 of this chapter). Such information will not be deemed to be incorporated by reference into any filing under the Securities Act or the Exchange Act, except to the extent that the registrant specifically incorporates it by reference. If the registrant elects to incorporate this information by reference from the proxy or information statement into its annual report on Form 10-K pursuant to General Instruction G(3) to Form 10-K, the disclosure required by paragraph (e)(5) of this Item will be deemed furnished in the annual report on Form 10-K and will not be deemed incorporated by

reference into any filing under the Securities Act or the Exchange Act as a result as a result of furnishing the disclosure in this manner.

3. The disclosure required by paragraph (e)(5) of this Item need only be provided one time during any fiscal year.

---

f. Shareholder communications.

1. State whether or not the registrant's board of directors provides a process for security holders to send communications to the board of directors and, if the registrant does not have such a process for security holders to send communications to the board of directors, state the basis for the view of the board of directors that it is appropriate for the registrant not to have such a process.

2. If the registrant has a process for security holders to send communications to the board of directors:

i. Describe the manner in which security holders can send communications to the board and, if applicable, to specified individual directors; and

ii. If all security holder communications are not sent directly to board members, describe the registrant's process for determining which communications will be relayed to board members.

Instructions to Item 407(f).

1. In lieu of providing the information required by paragraph (f)(2) of this Item in the proxy statement, the registrant may instead provide the registrant's Web site address where such information appears.

2. For purposes of the disclosure required by paragraph (f)(2)(ii) of this Item, a registrant's process for collecting and organizing security holder communications, as well as similar or related activities, need not be disclosed provided that the registrant's process is approved by a majority of the independent directors or, in the case of a registrant that is an investment company, a majority of the directors who are not "interested persons" of the investment company as defined in section 2(a)(19) of the Investment Company Act of 1940 (15 U.S.C. 80a-2(a)(19)).

3. For purposes of this paragraph, communications from an officer or director of the registrant will not be viewed as "security holder communications." Communications from an employee or agent of the registrant will be viewed as "security holder communications" for purposes of this paragraph only if those communications are made solely in such employee's or agent's capacity as a security holder.

4. For purposes of this paragraph, security holder proposals submitted pursuant to §240.14a-8 of this chapter, and communications made in connection with such proposals, will not be viewed as "security holder communications."

Instructions to Item 407.
1. For purposes of this Item:

   a. *Listed issuer* means a listed issuer as defined in §240.10A-3 of this chapter;

   b. *National securities exchange* means a national securities exchange registered pursuant to section 6(a) of the Exchange Act (15 U.S.C. 78f(a));

   c. *Inter-dealer quotation system* means an automated inter-dealer quotation system of a national securities association registered pursuant to section 15A(a) of the Exchange Act (15 U.S.C. 78o-3(a)); and

   d. *National securities association* means a national securities association registered pursuant to section 15A(a) of the Exchange Act (15 U.S.C. 78o-3(a)) that has been approved by the Commission (as that definition may be modified or supplemented).

2. With respect to paragraphs (c)(2)(i), (d)(1) and (e)(2) of this Item, disclose whether a current copy of the applicable committee charter is available to security holders on the registrant's Web site, and if so, provide the registrant's Web site address. If a current copy of the charter is not available to security holders on the registrant's Web site, include a copy of the charter in an appendix to the registrant's proxy or information statement that is provided to security holders at least once every three fiscal years, or if the charter has been materially amended since the beginning of the registrant's last fiscal year. If a current copy of the charter is not available to security holders on the registrant's Web site, and is not included as an appendix to the registrant's proxy or information statement, identify in which of the prior fiscal years the charter was so included in satisfaction of this requirement.

Subpart 229.600—Exhibits
Exhibits
Reg. §229.601. Item 601.

---

b. *Description of exhibits.* Set forth below is a description of each document listed in the exhibit tables.

10. *Material contracts—*

   i. Every contract not made in the ordinary course of business which is material to the registrant and is to be performed in whole or in part at or after the filing of the registration statement or report or was entered into not more than two years before such filing. Only contracts need be filed as to which the registrant or subsidiary of the registrant is a party or has succeeded to a party by assumption or assignment or in which the registrant or such subsidiary has a beneficial interest.

ii. If the contract is such as ordinarily accompanies the kind of business conducted by the registrant and its subsidiaries, it will be deemed to have been made in the ordinary course of business and need not be filed unless it falls within one or more of the following categories, in which case it shall be filed except where immaterial in amount or significance:

A. Any contract to which directors, officers, promoters, voting trustees, security holders named in the registration statement or report, or underwriters are parties other than contracts involving only the purchase or sale of current assets having a determinable market price, at such market price;

B. Any contract upon which the registrant's business is substantially dependent, as in the case of continuing contracts to sell the major part of registrant's products or services or to purchase the major part of registrant's requirements of goods, services or raw materials or any franchise or license or other agreement to use a patent, formula, trade secret, process or trade name upon which registrant's business depends to a material extent;

C. Any contract calling for the acquisition or sale of any property, plant or equipment for a consideration exceeding 15 percent of such fixed assets of the registrant on a consolidated basis; or

D. Any material lease under which a part of the property described in the registration statement or report is held by the registrant.

iii. A. Any management contract or any compensatory plan, contract or arrangement, including but not limited to plans relating to options, warrants or rights, pension, retirement or deferred compensation or bonus, incentive or profit sharing (or if not set forth in any formal document, a written description thereof) in which any director or any of the named executive officers of the registrant, as defined by Item 402(a)(3) (§ 229.402(a)(3)),participates shall be deemed material and shall be filed; and any other management contract or any other compensatory plan, contract, or arrangement in which any other executive officer of the registrant participates shall be filed unless immaterial in amount or significance.

B. Any compensatory plan, contract or arrangement adopted without the approval of security holders pursuant to which equity may be awarded, including, but not limited to, options, warrants or rights (or if not set forth in any formal document, a written description thereof), in which any employee (whether or not an executive officer of the registrant) participates shall be filed unless immaterial in amount or significance. A compensation plan assumed by a registrant in connection with a merger, consolidation or other acquisition transaction pursuant to which the registrant may make further grants or awards of its equity securities shall be considered a compensation plan of the registrant for purposes of the preceding sentence.

C. Notwithstanding paragraph (b)(10)(iii)(A) above, the following management contracts or compensatory plans, contracts or arrangements need not be filed:

1. Ordinary purchase and sales agency agreements.

2. Agreements with managers of stores in a chain organization or similar organization.

3. Contracts providing for labor or salesmen's bonuses or payments to a class of security holders, as such.

4. Any compensatory plan, contract or arrangement which pursuant to its terms is available to employees, officers or directors generally and which in operation provides for the same method of allocation of benefits between management and non-management participants.

5. Any compensatory plan, contract or arrangement if the registrant is a foreign private issuer that furnishes compensatory information under Item 402(a)(1) (§229.402(a)(1)) and the public filing of the plan, contractor arrangement, or portion thereof, is not required in the registrant's home country and is not otherwise publicly disclosed by the registrant.

6. Any compensatory plan, contract, or arrangement if the registrant is a wholly owned subsidiary of a company that has a class of securities registered pursuant to section 12 or files reports pursuant to section 15(d) of the Exchange Act and is filing a report on Form 10-K and Form 10-KSB or registering debt instruments or preferred stock which are not voting securities on Form S-2.

Instruction 1 to paragraph (b)(10). With the exception of management contracts, in order to comply with paragraph (iii) above, registrants need only file copies of the various remunerative plans and need not file each individual director's or executive officer's personal agreement under the plans unless there are particular provisions in such personal agreements whose disclosure in an exhibit is necessary to an investor's understanding of that individual's compensation under the plan.

Instruction 2 to paragraph (b)(10). If a material contract is executed or becomes effective during the reporting period reflected by a Form 10-Q or Form 10-K, it shall be filed as an exhibit to the Form 10-Q or Form 10-K filed for the corresponding period. *See* paragraph (a)(4) of this Item. With respect to quarterly reports on Form 10-Q, only those contracts executed or becoming effective during the most recent period reflected in the report shall be filed.

NASDAQ STOCK MARKET RULE 4350(C)(3)—COMPENSATION OF OFFICERS (C) INDEPENDENT DIRECTORS

3. Compensation of Officers

A. Compensation of the chief executive officer of the company must be determined, or recommended to the Board for determination, either by:

   i. a majority of the independent directors, or

   ii. a compensation committee comprised solely of independent directors.

The chief executive officer may not be present during voting or deliberations.

B. Compensation of all other executive officers must be determined, or recommended to the Board for determination, either by:

   i. a majority of the independent directors, or

   ii. a compensation committee comprised solely of independent directors.

C. Notwithstanding paragraphs 3(A)(ii) and (3)(B)(ii) above, if the compensation committee is comprised of at least three members, one director who is not independent as defined in Rule 4200 and is not a current officer or employee or a Family Member of an officer or employee, may be appointed to the compensation committee if the board, under exceptional and limited circumstances, determines that such individual's membership on the committee is required by the best interests of the company and its shareholders, and the board discloses, in the proxy statement for the next annual meeting subsequent to such determination (or, if the issuer does not file a proxy, in its Form 10-K or 20-F), the nature of the relationship and the reasons for the determination. A member appointed under this exception may not serve longer than two years.

NYSE RULE 303A.05—COMPENSATION COMMITTEE REQUIREMENTS

5.

   a. Listed companies must have a compensation committee composed entirely of independent directors.

   b. The compensation committee must have a written charter that addresses:

      i. the committee's purpose and responsibilities—which, at minimum, must be to have direct responsibility to:

         A. review and approve corporate goals and objectives relevant to CEO compensation, evaluate the CEO's performance in light of those goals and objectives and, either as a commit-tee or together with the other independent directors (as directed by the board), determine and approve the CEO's compensation level based on this evaluation; and

B. make recommendations to the board with respect to non-CEO compensation, incentive-compensation plans and equity-based plans; and

C. produce a compensation committee report on executive compensation as required by the SEC to be included in the company's annual proxy statement or annual report on Form 10-K filed with the SEC;

ii. an annual performance evaluation of the compensation committee.

Commentary: In determining the long-term incentive component of CEO compensation, the committee should consider the company's performance and relative shareholder return, the value of similar incentive awards to CEOs at comparable companies, and the awards given to the listed company's CEO in past years. To avoid confusion, note that the compensation committee is not precluded from approving awards (with or without ratification of the board) as may be required to comply with applicable tax laws (i.e., Rule 162(m)). Note also that nothing in Section 303A.05(b)(i)(B) is intended to preclude the Board from delegating its authority over such matters to the compensation committee.

The compensation committee charter should also address the following items: committee member qualifications; committee member appointment and removal; committee structure and operations (including authority to delegate to subcommittees); and committee reporting to the board.

Additionally, if a compensation consultant is to assist in the evaluation of director, CEO or senior executive compensation, the compensation committee charter should give that committee sole authority to retain and terminate the consulting firm, including sole authority to approve the firm's fees and other retention terms.

Boards may allocate the responsibilities of the compensation committee to committees of their own denomination, provided that the committees are composed entirely of independent directors. Any such committee must have a published committee charter.

Nothing in this provision should be construed as precluding discussion of CEO compensation with the board generally, as it is not the intent of this standard to impair communication among members of the board.

List of Organizations and Periodicals

Many organizations provide information of interest to compensation committees. This appendix lists organizations that provide information on compensation, roles of the board and directors, corporate governance, and shareholder issues of various types. Some of these organizations offer memberships for a nominal fee; others provide free access to their web sites. Also included is a list of relevant periodicals, some of which are free. Please also refer to the Bibliography for further reading on the similar subjects.

Exhibit B.1   List of Organizations

Organization	Address and Other Information	Contacts
American Management Association	1601 Broadway New York, NY 10019-7420 www.amanet.org Tel#: (800) 262-9699 Fax#: (518) 891-0368	Edward T. Reilly, President and CEO
Business Roundtable	1717 Rhode Island Ave., NW, Suite 800 Washington, DC 20036 Membership@businessround-table.org www.businessroundtable.org Tel#: (202) 872-1260 Fax#: (202) 466-3509	Johanna I. Schneider, Executive Director, External Relations
California Public Employees' Retirement System (CalPERS)	Lincoln Plaza North 400 Q Street Sacramento, CA 95814 www.calpers.org Tel#: (888) 225-7377 Fax#: (916) 326-3507	Fred Buenrostro, Chief Executive Officer
The Conference Board	845 Third Avenue New York, NY 10022-6679 info@conference_board.org www.conference-board.org Tel#: (212) 759-0900 Fax#: (212) 980-7014	Richard E. Cavanagh, President and CEO

Corporate Governance	9295 Yorkship Court Elk Grove, CA 95758 jm@corpgov.net www.corpgov.net Tel#: (916) 869-2402	James McRitchie
Corporate Governance Center at Kennesaw State University	1000 Chastain Road Kennesaw, GA 30144 www.kennesaw.edu/cgc Tel#: (770) 423-6587 Fax#: (770) 423-6606	Professor Paul Lapides
The Corporate Library	45 Exchange Street Suite 201 Portland, ME 04101 nminow@thecorporatelibrary.com www.thecorporatelibrary.com Tel#: (207) 874-6921 Fax#: (207) 874-6925	Nell Minow, Editor and Founder
Council of Institutional Investors	888 17th St., NW Suite 500 Washington, DC 20006 info@cii.org www.cii.org Tel#: (202) 822-0800 Fax#: (202) 822-0801	Ann Yerger, Executive Director
Foundation for Enterprise Development	1241 Care Street LaJolla, CA 92037 Inquire@fed.org www.fed.org Tel#: (858) 822-6030	Mary Ann Beyster, President Ray Smilor, Executive Vice-President
Institutional Shareholder Services, a Risk Metrics Group Subsidiary	2099 Gaither Road Suite 501 Rockville, MD 20850-4045 www.issproxy.com Tel#: (301) 556-0500 Fax#: (301) 556-0491	Martha L. Carter, PhD, Managing Director, Corporate Governance Patrick S. McGurn, Executive Vice President and Special Counsel
The International Association for Attorneys for Family-Held Enterprise	11357 Nuckols Rd. #115 Glenn Allen, VA 23059 afhe@afhe.com www.afhe.com Tel#: (757) 784-2312 Fax# (757) 282-5757	Sarah E. Spiers, Executive Director
National Association of Corporate Directors	Two Lafayette Centre 1133 21st Street NW Washington, DC 20036 info@nacdonline.org www.nacdonline.org Tel#: (202) 775-0509 Fax#: (202) 775-4857	Roger W. Raber, President and CEO Peter R. Gleason Chief Operating Officer and Director of Research

(Continued)

Exhibit B.1   (Continued)

Organization	Address and Other Information	Contacts
National Association of Stock Plan Professionals	P.O. Box 21639 Concord, CA 94521-0639 www.nasspp.com Tel#: (925) 685-9271 Fax#: (925) 930-9284	Barbara Baksa, Executive Director
The National Center for Employee Ownership	1736 Franklin Street 8th Floor Oakland, CA 94612-3445 nceo@nceo.org www.nceo.org Tel#: (510) 208-1300 Fax#: (510) 272-9510	Corey Rosen, Executive Director Pam Chernoff Director of Equity Compensation Projects
National Investor Relations Institute	8020 Towers Crescent Drive Suite 250 Vienna, VA 22182 info@niri.org www.niri.org Tel#: (703) 506-3576 Fax#: (703) 506-3571	Linda Y. Kelleher, Interim CEO
The New York Society of Security Analysts	1177 Ave of the Americas, 2nd Floor New York, NY 10086-2714 membership@nyssa.org www.nyssa.org Tel#: (212) 541-4530 Fax#: (212) 541-4677	Alvin Kressler, Executive Director Eileen Budd, Director of Programming and Education
The Society of Corporate Secretaries and Governance Professionals	521 Fifth Avenue New York, NY 10175 Dfox@governanceprofessionals.org www.governanceprofessionals.org Tel#: (212) 681-2000 Fax#: (212) 681-2005	David W. Smith, President Deborah Fox, Administrator, Membership
TIAA-CREF	730 Third Avenue New York, NY 10017-3206 www.tiaa-cref.org Tel#: (800) 842-2252	Herbert M. Allison, Jr., Chairman, President, and CEO
WorldatWork	14040 N. Northsight Boulevard Scottsdale, AZ 85260-3601 www.worldatwork.org Tel#: (480) 951-9191 (877) 951-9191 Fax#: (480) 483-8352	Anne C. Ruddy, CCP, CPCU President Jason Kovac, CCP, CBP Compensation Contact

Exhibit B.2   Periodicals

Name of Periodical	Publisher	Editor(s)	Frequency	Address/E-mail/Web Site/ Telephone Number
Across The Board	The Conference Board	A. J. Vogl	Monthly	845 Third Avenue New York, NY 10022-6679 www.conference-board.org Tel#: (212) 339-0345 Fax#: (212) 836-9740
Agenda	Money Media, Inc.	Eduardo Llull	Monthly	1430 Broadway, 12th Floor New York, NY 10018 www.boardalert.net Tel#: (212) 542-1200 Fax#: (212) 616-3882
Board Leadership: A bimonthly workshop	Jossey-Bass Publisher	John and Miriam Carver	Bi-monthly	P.O. Box 13007 Atlanta, GA 30324-0007 www.carvergoverance.com Tel#: (404) 728-9444 Fax#: (404) 728-0060
Boardroom INSIDER	Ralph Ward	Ralph Ward	Monthly	P.O. Box 196 Riverdale, MI 48877 www.boardroominsider.com Tel#: (989) 833-7615 Fax#: (989) 833-7615
BusinessWeek's Annual Executive Compensation Survey	Business Week	Louis Lavelle	Annually, published in early April	1221 Avenue of the Americas New York, NY 10020-1095 www.businessweek.com Tel#: (212) 512-2511 Fax#: (212) 512-4589
The Corporate Board	Vanguard Publications	Ralph D. Ward	Bi-monthly	4440 Hagadorn Road Okemos, MI 48864-2414 Info@corporateboard.com www.corporateboard.com Tel#: (517) 336-1700 Fax#: (517) 336-1705
Corporate Board Member	Corporate Board Member Magazine	Deborah Scally	Monthly	475 Park Ave. South 19th Floor New York, NY 10016 www.boardmember.com Tel#: (212) 686-1805 Fax#: (212) 686-3041
The Corporate Counsel	Executive Press, Inc.	Broc Romonek	Bi-monthly	P.O. Box 21639 Concord, CA 94521-0639 www.thecorporatecounsel.net Tel#: (925) 685-5111 Fax#: (925) 685-5402

(Continued)

Exhibit B.2   (Continued)

Name of Periodical	Publisher	Editor(s)	Frequency	Address/E-mail/Web Site/ Telephone Number
The Corporate Executive	Executive Press, Inc.	Broc Romonek	Bi-monthly	P.O. Box 21639 Concord, CA 94521-0639 www.thecorporatecounsel.net Tel#: (925) 685-5111 Fax#: (925) 685-5402
Corporate Governance	Corporate Governance. Net	James McRitchie	As needed	9295 Yorkship Court Elk Grove, CA 95758 Jm@corpgov.net www.corpgov.net Tel#: (916) 869-2402
Corporate Governance Bulletin	Investor Responsibility Research Center	Maryanne Moore	Quarterly	1350 Connecticut Avenue, Suite 700 Washington, DC 20036-1702 www.irrc.org Tel#: (202) 833-0700 Fax#: (202) 833-3555
Corporate Monitoring Newsletter	Mark Latham	Mark Latham	Quarterly	1755 Robson St. #469 Vancouver, B.C. Canada V6 G 387 www.corpmon.com Tel#: (604) 608-9779
The Corporate Secretary	The American Society of Corporate Secretaries	David Smith	Quarterly	521 Fifth Avenue New York, NY 10175 www.ascs.org Tel#: (212) 681-2000 Fax#: (212) 681-2005
Crystal Column	Bloomberg Information	Graef Crystal	Monthly	3519 Daybreak Court Santa Rosa, CA 95404-2042 www.crystalreport.com Tel#: (707) 591-0464 Fax#: (707) 591-0645
Directors & Boards Magazine	MLR Holdings LLC	James Kristie	Quarterly	P.O. Box 41966 Philadelphia, PA 19101-1966 www.directorsandboards.com Tel#: (800) 637-4464 Fax#: (215) 405-6078
Directors Monthly	The National Association of Corporate Directors	Deborah J. Davidson	Monthly	Two Lafayette Centre 1133 21st Street NW Suite 700 Washington, DC 20036 www.nacdonline.org Tel#: (202) 775-0509 Fax#: (202) 775-4857

Directorship	The Directorship Search Group, Inc.	William J. Holstein	Monthly	90 Park Avenue, 10th Floor New York, NY 10016 info@directorship.com www.directorship.com Tel#: (646) 289-4980 Fax#: (646) 289-4999
The Employee Ownership Report (NCEO Newsletter)	The National Center for Employee Ownership	Scott Rodrick	Bi-monthly	1736 Franklin Street 8th Floor Oakland, CA 94612-1217 www.nceo.org Tel#: (510) 208-1300 Fax#: (510) 272-9510
Executive Compensation Resources Newsletter	Towers Perrin, HR Services	Judith Fischer	Twice monthly	2107 Wilson Blvd Suite 500 Arlington, VA 22201 ecrinfo@ecronline.com www.ecronline.com Tel#: (800) 391-0045 Fax#: (703) 837-9501
Forbes' Magazine Annual Executive Compensation Survey	Forbes	Scott DeCarlo	Annually, published in May	60 Fifth Avenue New York, NY 10011 www.forbes.com Tel#: (212) 620-2338 Fax#: (212) 620-1863
Insights: The Corporate Securities Law Advisor	Aspen Publishers	Amy L. Goodman	Monthly	76 Ninth Avenue, 7th Floor New York, NY 10011 www.aspenpublishers.com Tel#: (212) 771-0600 Fax#: (212) 771-0885
Investor Relations Newsletter	Kennedy Information, Inc.	David Beck	Monthly	One Phoenix Mill Lane 5th Floor Petersborough, NH 03458 www.kennedyinfo.com Tel#: (800) 531-8007 Fax#: (603) 924-4460
Investor Relations Quarterly	National Investor Relations Institute	Hank Boerner	Quarterly	8020 Towers Crescent Drive Suite 250 Vienna, VA 22182 www.niri.org Tel#: (703) 506-3570 Fax#: (703) 506-3571
IR Update	National Investor Relations Institute	Hank Boerner	Monthly	8020 Towers Crescent Drive Suite 250 Vienna, VA 22182 www.niri.org Tel#: (703) 506-3572 Fax#: (703) 506-3571

(Continued)

Exhibit B.2 (Continued)

Name of Periodical	Publisher	Editor(s)	Frequency	Address/E-mail/Web Site/ Telephone Number
The ISS Friday Report	Institutional Shareholder Services	Stephen Deane	Weekly	2099 Gaither Road Suite 501 Rockville, MD 20850-8041 www.issproxy.com Tel#: (301) 556-0500 Fax#: (301) 556-0491
The Journal of Compensation and Benefits	West Publishers, Inc.	Jeffrey D. Manorsky	Bi-monthly	610 Opperman Drive Eagan, MN 55123 www.westthomson.com Tel#: (651) 687-7000
Journal of Employee Ownership Law and Finance	The National Center for Employee Ownership	Scott Rodrick	Quarterly	1736 Franklin Street 8th Floor Oakland, CA 94612-1217 www.nceo.org Tel#: (510) 208-1300 Fax#: (510) 272-9510
The Stock Plan Advisor	The National Association of Stock Plan Professionals	Broc Romanek	Monthly	P.O. Box 21639 Concord, CA 94521-0639 www.naspp.com Tel#: (925) 685-9271 Fax#: (925) 930-9284
The Wall Street Journal's Annual Chief Executive Officer Compensation Survey	The Wall Street Journal	Joann S. Lublin	Annually, published in early April	200 Liberty Street New York, NY 10281 www.wsj.com Tel#: (212) 416-2000 Fax#: (212) 416-2653
Workspan	WorldatWork	Andrea Ozias	Monthly	440 N. Northsight Boulevard Scottsdale, AZ 85260-3601 www.worldatwork.org Tel#: (480) 922-2038 (800) 951-9191 Fax#: (480) 483-8352
WorldatWork Journal	WorldatWork	Andrea Ozias	Quarterly	1440 N. Northsight Boulevard Scottsdale, AZ 85260-3601 www.worldatwork.org Tel#: (480) 922-2038 (800) 951-9191 Fax#: (480) 483-8352

List of Directors Colleges and Other Training Opportunities

Sponsoring Organization	The Conference Board
Name of Program	Directors' Institute
Length of Program	Varies, see contact information.
Description of Course	The Directors' Institute conducts highly interactive sessions for corporate directors only. Directors' Institute programs meet director education needs by providing high-level forums for public company directors to review real-world governance and business challenges. The Directors' Institute offers intensive, one-day Director Dialogue Sessions throughout the year focusing on corporate governance, audit committees, and compensation committees:

Corporate Governance Sessions & New Director Orientation:
- Fiduciary Responsibilities & Challenges
- Enterprise Risk Assessment
- Board Evaluation
- Director Liability Issues
- Institutional Investor Expectations

Audit Committee Sessions:
- Legislative & Regulatory Landscape
- Financial Risk Assessment
- Evaluation of the Audit Process
- Recognizing "Red Flags"
- Committee Effectiveness

Compensation Committee Sessions:
- Compensation Issues & Trends
- Structuring "Pay for Performance"
- Evaluating Management Performance
- Use of Compensation Consultants
- Committee Effectiveness

(Continued)

The Directors' Institute's intensive one-day sessions focus on interactive discussion among directors. Experienced public company directors serve as discussion leaders, supplemented by expert presentations in key areas such as legal, insurance, governance, ethics, regulations, finance, auditing, and accounting. Sessions are strictly limited to 25 directors.

Contact Information	Tina S. Van Dam Associate Director, Governance Center The Conference Board 845 Third Avenue New York, NY 10022 E-mail: tinavandam@conference-board.org Phone: 1-212-339-0343 Fax: 1-212-836-9765 www.conference-board.org/knowledge/govern/govInstitute.cfm

---

Sponsoring Organization	Harvard Business School Executive Education
Name of Program	Compensation Committees: New Challenges, New Solutions
Length of Program	3 days
Description of Course	The program is designed as a timely, action-oriented opportunity for directors to think deeply about the root causes of many compensation issues—and to identify possible solutions to the difficulties their particular boards and companies are facing.

Given these challenges, the program emphasizes the growing demand for compensation committees to exhibit greater knowledge, independence, and accountability.

This intensive learning experience provides an educational, interactive environment for directors to:

- Identify and address critical issues pertaining to employment agreements, overall pay, incentive compensation, stock ownership, and stock compensation—then determine to what extent their own board's compensation plans need to be demolished and rebuilt.

- Define the characteristics of a well-functioning compensation committee—then review and rethink their respective committee charters in regard to purpose, processes, roles, responsibilities, and review procedures.

- Prepare to operate successfully in the new age of accountability by becoming knowledgeable of current issues, acting independently of management, and diligently discharging all duties.

Contact Information	Executive Education Programs Harvard Business School Soldiers Field Boston, MA 02163-9986 E-mail: executive_education@hbs.edu Phone: 1-800-HBS-5577 (1-617-495-6555) Fax: 1-617-495-6999 www.exed.hbs.edu/programs

Sponsoring Organization	Harvard Business School Executive Education
Name of Program	Making Corporate Boards More Effective
Length of Program	3 days
Description of Course	The program addresses critical issues facing boards today, including:

- Changing legal responsibilities of directors
- Board composition and director selection
- Setting time-efficient agendas
- Conducting dynamic, constructive board meetings
- Effective use of committees
- Role of the board in strategic planning and as an agent of positive change
- Designing performance scorecards to monitor business strategy and management performance
- Role of the board and audit committee in formulating an external financial reporting and disclosure strategy
- CEO evaluation and compensation
- CEO succession
- Evaluation of the board and its members
- Director compensation and stock ownership

These issues will be examined in the overall context of structuring a corporate governance system that facilitates cooperation between the board and management, thereby achieving real benefits for the enterprise. Particular attention will be devoted to helping participants develop action plans for improving their own boards. Participants will have the opportunity to discuss their plans with both their peers and the faculty.

Contact Information	Executive Education Programs
	Harvard Business School
	Soldiers Field
	Boston, MA 02163-9986
	E-mail: executive_education@hbs.edu
	Phone: 1-800-HBS-5577 (1-617-495-6555)
	Fax: 1-617-495-6999
	www.exed.hbs.edu/programs

Sponsoring Organization	National Association of Corporate Directors
Name of Program	The NACD offers a variety of one-day programs for compensation committees and board directors in general. Current program offerings are listed below. Please check the NACD web site for availability.
Length of Program	1 day

(Continued)

Listing of Courses	• Effective Compensation Committees
	• Annual Corporate Governance Conference
	• Audit Committee: Improving Quality, Independence, and Performance
	• Director Finance: What Every Director Should Know
	• Director Professionalism
	• Role of the Board in Corporate Strategy and Risk Oversight
	• Role of the Governance Committee: Raising the Bar on Board Policies, Practices and Board Evaluations
	• Small Company Governance: Building Board Value
	• What the Board Really Expects from the General Counsel and Corporate Secretary
Contact Information	Catherine Nelson
	Director of Education
	National Association of Corporate Directors
	1133 21st Street, NW, Suite 700,
	Washington, DC 20036
	E-mail: cnelson@nacdonline.org
	Phone: 202-775-0509, ext 2081
	Fax: 202-775-4857
	www.nacdonline.org

Sponsoring Organization	Terry College of Business
	Executive Education
	(University of Georgia)
	and the National Association of Corporate Directors (Atlanta Chapter)
Name of Program	Terry/NACD Directors' College
Length of Program	2 days
Description of Course	The Terry College of Business/NACD Directors' College focuses on the increasingly critical and challenging role corporate boards play in business organizations. The program develops the skills and insight needed to function as an informed, contributing board director. By combining the practical knowledge of experienced business executives with conceptual frameworks developed by highly acclaimed Terry College of Business faculty, the program highlights the strategic significance of the corporate board and the tools required to effectively monitor company performance.

An overview of the course materials:

Compliance issues

• Shareholder law suits

• Business judgment rule

• Recent court cases and how they may apply to you

• Board minutes

• D&O liability coverage

What do financial statements show and what directors should know about them

- Brief overview of financial statements
- Case studies relating to fraud and legal actions
- Signs of trouble and indications of fraud
- What the board can do about it

Ways in which the board can improve corporate performance

- Relationship between corporate governance and corporate performance
- Executive compensation
- CEO evaluation
- Succession planning
- Board evaluation
- Importance of independence and diversity

Roles, responsibilities, and expectations of directors

- Legal obligations
- Duty of care and loyalty
- Different oversight committees

Emerging issues

- Regulation FD
- SEC actions and rules
- Institutional investor activism
- Stock analyst's focus on the board
- Size and composition of the board

Contact Information   Richard L. Daniels
Associate Dean for Executive Programs, Professor of Management
Terry College of Business
278 Brooks Hall
Athens, GA 30602-6262
E-mail: rdaniels@terry.uga.edu
Phone: 706-542-8393
Fax: 706-542-3835
www.terry.uga.edu/exec_ed/director_education/index.php

For additional Director training opportunities, Institutional Shareholder Services provides a list of accredited Director education programs at www.isscgq.com/programlist.asp.

Annotated Form and Samples of Compensation Committee Charter

This appendix contains an annotated form of compensation committee charter, as well as the compensation committee charters for Amgen, Apple Computer, Goldman Sachs, General Electric, and Revlon.

[CORPORATE NAME] COMPENSATION COMMITTEE CHARTER

PURPOSE AND RESPONSIBILITIES[1]

The Compensation Committee (the "Committee") shall be responsible for:

- Discharging the Board of Directors responsibilities relating to the compensation of [corporate name] (the "Company") executives.
- Reviewing and discussing with management the compensation discussion and analysis (CD&A) and producing an annual report thereon for inclusion in the Company's [proxy statement for the annual meeting of [stockholders] [shareholders[2]] [annual report filed on Form 10-K with the Securities and Exchange Commission], in accordance with applicable rules and regulations.

COMPOSITION OF THE COMMITTEE

The members of the Committee shall be independent[3] directors meeting the requirements of the [New York Stock Exchange[4]] [The NASDAQ Stock Market[5]] and appointed by the Board of Directors on the recommendation of the Nominating and Corporate Governance Committee.[6] The Chair of the Committee shall be designated by the Board of Directors. In the absence of the Chair, the members of the Committee

---

[1] *See* NYSE Rule 303A.5(b)(i).
[2] *See* corporate code of state of incorporation for proper term.
[3] *See* NYSE Rule 303A.5(a) and NASDAQ Rule 4350(c)(3)(A)(ii) and 4350(c)(3)(C).
[4] *See* NYSE Rule 303A.2(a) and (b) for independence requirements.
[5] *See* NASDAQ Rule 4200(a)(15) for independence requirements.

may designate a chair by majority vote. The Board of Directors may at any time remove one or more directors as members of the Committee and may fill any vacancy on the Committee.[7] The Committee may form and delegate authority to subcommittees when appropriate. At least two of the directors appointed to serve on the Committee shall be "nonemployee directors" (within the meaning of Rule 16b-3 promulgated under the Securities Exchange Act of 1934, as amended) and "outside directors" (within the meaning of Section 162(m) of the Internal Revenue Code of 1986, as amended, and the regulations thereunder).

OPERATIONS OF THE COMMITTEE

The Committee shall:

- Annually review and approve corporate goals and objectives relevant to the chief executive officer's compensation

- Annually evaluate the chief executive officer's performance in light of such corporate goals and objectives

- Annually [together with the other independent directors] (as directed by the Board) determine and approve the chief executive officer's base salary and incentive compensation levels based on the Committee's evaluation of the chief executive officer's performance relative to the relevant corporate goals and objectives[8]

- Annually review, evaluate and [determine] [make recommendations to the Board of Directors with respect to] the base salary level and incentive compensation levels of other executive officers of the Company[9]

- Make recommendations to the Board of Directors with respect to the Company's incentive-compensation plans and equity-based compensation plans[10]

---

[6] *See* NYSE Rule 303A.4. Also note that current NASDAQ rules do not require listed companies to have a nominating/corporate governance committee and do not require the adoption of corporate governance guidelines.

[7] *See* second paragraph of commentary to NYSE Rule 303A.5.

[8] *See* NYSE Rule 303A.5(b)(i)(A) and NASDAQ Rule 4350(c)(3)(A). Under NYSE standards, the compensation committee alone may approve the corporate goals and objectives relative to CEO compensation and evaluate the CEO's performance in light of such goals and objectives, but the Board may direct that the other independent directors may participate in determining and approving the CEO's compensation level based on this evaluation. Under NASDAQ standards, compensation of the CEO may be determined, or recommended to the Board for determination, either by the compensation committee or a majority of the independent directors, and the chief executive officer may not be present during voting or deliberations.

[9] *See* NYSE Rule 303A.5(b)(i)(A) and NASDAQ Rule 4350(c)(3)(B). Under NYSE standards, the compensation committee may itself determine, or may make recommendations to the Board with respect to, compensation of executive officers other than the CEO. Under NASDAQ standards, compensation of the non-CEO executive officers may be determined, or recommended to the Board for determination, either by the compensation committee or a majority of the independent directors, and the chief executive officer may be present during voting or deliberations.

[10] *See* NYSE Rule 303A.5(b)(i)(B).

- Make regular reports to the Board of Directors concerning the activities of the Committee[11]
- Perform an annual performance evaluation of the Committee[12]
- Perform any other activities consistent with this Charter, the Company's [Certificate][Articles][13] of Incorporation and Bylaws and governing law as the Committee or the Board of Directors deem appropriate

To these ends, the Committee shall have and may exercise all the powers and authority of the Board of Directors to the extent permitted under Section [Authorizing Statute of State of Incorporation] of the [State of Incorporation][General Corporation Law].

The Committee may determine, from time to time, the advisability of retaining a compensation consultant to assist in the evaluation of chief executive officer or other executive officer compensation. The Committee has the authority to retain, at Company expense, and terminate a compensation consultant, including sole authority to approve the consultant's fees and other retention terms.[14]

COMMITTEE MEETINGS

The Committee shall meet at least [two] times per year. One such meeting shall be held at a time when the Committee can review and recommend annual base salary and incentive awards as described previously. The other meeting[s] shall be held at the discretion of the Chairperson of the Committee. Minutes of each of these meetings shall be kept.

AMGEN, INC.

COMPENSATION AND MANAGEMENT DEVELOPMENT COMMITTEE CHARTER

As Amended December 12, 2006

Purpose

The Compensation and Management Development Committee (the "Committee") of the Board of Directors (the "Board") assists the Board in fulfilling its fiduciary responsibilities with respect to the oversight of the Company's affairs in the areas of compensation plans, policies and programs of the Company, especially those

---

[11] See second paragraph of commentary to NYSE Rule 303 A.5.
[12] See NYSE Rule 303A.5(b)(ii).
[13] See corporate code of state of incorporation for proper term.
[14] See third paragraph of commentary to NYSE Rule 303 A.5.

regarding executive compensation, employee benefits, and producing an annual report on executive compensation for inclusion in the Company's proxy materials in accordance with applicable rules and regulations and assists the Board in oversight of Executive Talent Management. The Committee shall ensure that compensation programs are designed to encourage high performance, promote accountability and adherence to Company values and the code of conduct, assure that employee interests are aligned with the interests of the Company's stockholders, serve the long-term best interests of the Company and that the Executive Management Development processes are designed to attract, develop and retain talented leadership to serve the long-term best interests of the Company.

The Committee shall have the authority to undertake the specific duties and responsibilities described below and the authority to undertake such other duties as are assigned by law, the Company's certificate of incorporation or bylaws or by the Board.

Membership

The Committee shall be composed of at least three (3) members of the Board, one of whom shall be designated by the Board as the Chair.

Each member of the Committee shall (1) qualify as independent under the NASDAQ listing requirements, (2) be a "non-employee director" within the meaning of Rule 16b-3 of the Securities Exchange Act of 1934, as amended, (3) be an "outside director" under the regulations promulgated under Section 162(m) of the Internal Revenue Code of 1986, as amended (the "Code"), and (4) be otherwise free from any relationship that, in the judgment of the Board, would interfere with his or her exercise of business judgment as a Committee member.

Meetings and Procedures

The Committee shall hold at least four (4) regularly scheduled meetings each year.

In discharging its responsibilities, the Committee shall have sole authority to, as it deems appropriate, select, retain and/or replace, as needed, compensation and benefits consultants and other outside consultants to provide independent advice to the Committee. In addition, the Committee shall have free access to Company staff personnel to provide data and advice in connection with the Committee's review of management compensation practices and policies and leadership development processes and practices.

The Committee shall maintain written minutes or other records of its meetings and activities. Minutes of each meeting of the Committee shall be distributed to each member of the Committee. The Secretary of the Company shall retain the original signed minutes for filing with the corporate records of the Company.

The Chair of the Committee shall report to the Board following meetings of the Committee and as otherwise requested by the Chairman of the Board.

Responsibilities

The Committee shall be responsible for:

1. Overseeing succession planning for senior management of the Company, including consulting on an ongoing basis with the Chief Executive Officer and the Board to remain abreast of management development activities, including a review of the performance and advancement potential of current and future senior management and succession plans for each and reviewing the retention of high-level, high potential succession candidates.

2. Assessing the overall compensation structure of the Company and adopting a written statement of compensation philosophy and strategy, selecting an appropriate peer group, and periodically reviewing executive compensation in relation to this peer group.

3. Reviewing and approving corporate goals and objectives relating to the compensation of the Chief Executive Officer, evaluating the performance of the Chief Executive Officer in light of the goals and objectives, and making appropriate recommendations for improving performance. The Committee shall establish the compensation of the Chief Executive Officer based on such evaluation. In performing the foregoing functions, the Chair of the Committee shall solicit comments from the other members of the Board and shall lead the Board in an overall review of the Chief Executive Officer's performance in an executive session of non-employee Board members. Final determinations regarding the performance and compensation of the Chief Executive Officer will be conducted in an executive session of the Committee and be reported by the Chair of the Committee to the entire Board during an independent session of the Board.

4. Reviewing and approving all compensation for all other officers of the Company; evaluating the responsibilities and performance of other executive officers and making appropriate recommendations for improving performance.

5. Recommending policies to the Board regarding minimum retention and ownership levels of Company common stock by officers.

6. Administering and reviewing all executive compensation programs and equity-based plans of the Company. The Committee shall have and shall exercise all the authority of the Board with respect to administering such plans, including approving amendments thereto.

7. Making recommendations to the Board with respect to incentive compensation plans and equity based plans.

8. Approving, amending and terminating ERISA-governed employee benefit plans.

9. Reviewing the Company's Compensation Discussion and Analysis to be included in the Company's annual proxy statement and preparing and approving the Report of the Compensation Committee to be included as part of the Company's annual proxy statement.

10. Conducting an annual evaluation of the effectiveness of the Committee.

The Committee shall have the authority to delegate its functions to a subcommittee thereof.

For purposes of this Charter, "compensation" shall include, but not be limited to, cash or deferred payments, incentive and equity compensation, benefits and perquisites, employment, retention and/or termination/severance agreements and any other programs which pursuant to the regulations of the Securities and Exchange Commission or Internal Revenue Service (or successor organizations, if applicable), would be considered to be compensation. In addition, "officer" shall be as defined in Section 16 of the Securities Exchange Act of 1934, and Rule 16a-1 thereunder.

The Committee shall review and reassess the Committee's charter on a periodic basis and submit any recommended changes to the Board for its consideration.

The Committee shall perform such other functions and have such other powers as may be necessary or convenient in the efficient discharge of the foregoing.

APPLE COMPUTER, INC.

COMPENSATION COMMITTEE CHARTER

2/2/06

There shall be a Committee of the Board of Directors to be known as the Compensation Committee with purpose, composition, duties and responsibilities, as follows:

Purpose of the Committee

The Committee shall (i) establish and modify compensation and incentive plans and programs, (ii) review and approve compensation and awards under compensation and incentive plans and programs for elected officers of the Corporation, and (iii) be the administering committee for certain stock option and other stock-based plans as designated by the Board.

Composition

The members of the Committee shall be appointed by the Board of Directors. The Committee will be composed of not less than three Board members. Each member shall be "independent" in accordance with applicable law, including the rules and regulations of the Securities and Exchange Commission and the rules of the NASDAQ Stock Market. The Chairman of the Committee shall be designated by the Board of Directors. The Chairman of the Board, any member of the Committee or the Secretary of the Corporation may call meetings of the Committee.

Authority and Resources

The Committee may request any officer or employee of the Corporation or the Corporation's outside counsel to attend a Committee meeting. The Committee has the right at any time to obtain advice, reports or opinions from internal and external counsel and expert advisors and has the authority to hire independent legal, financial and other advisors as it may deem necessary, at the Corporation's expense, without consulting with, or obtaining approval from, any officer of the Corporation in advance.

Duties and Responsibilities

The duties of the Committee shall include the following:

- Review periodically and approve all compensation and incentive plans and programs (other than those administered by the Benefits Committee).
- Conduct and review with the Board of Directors an annual evaluation of the performance of the Chief Executive Officer and review with the CEO and report to the Board annually on the performance of other executive officers.
- Review periodically and fix the salaries, bonuses and perquisites of elected officers of the Corporation and its subsidiaries, including the Chief Executive Officer.
- Act as administering committee of the Corporation's various bonus plans, stock plans and equity arrangements that may be adopted by the Corporation from time to time, with such authority and powers as are set forth in the respective plans' instruments, including but not limited to establishing performance metrics, determining bonus payouts and the granting of equity awards to employees and executive officers.
- Review for approval or disapproval special hiring or termination packages for officers and director-level employees of the Corporation and its subsidiaries that go beyond the Board's adopted criteria for management authority, if it is determined by the members of the Committee that approval by the full Board is not necessary.
- To the extent it deems necessary, recommend to the Board of Directors the establishment or modification of employee stock-based plans for the Corporation and its subsidiaries.
- To the extent it deems necessary, review and advise the Board of Directors regarding other compensation plans.
- To prepare an annual Compensation Committee Report for inclusion in the Corporation's proxy statement.
- Review the Committee charter, structure, process and membership requirements at least once a year.
- Report to the Board of Directors concerning the Committee's activities.
- The Committee can delegate any of its responsibilities to the extent allowed under applicable law.

Exceptions

Notwithstanding any implication to the contrary above:

- The Committee shall not be empowered to review or approve broad-based employee benefit plans (such as medical or insurance plans) not specifically delegated to the Committee, and the consideration and approval of any such plans shall remain the responsibility of the Board, the Benefits Committee or the officers of the Corporation and its subsidiaries, depending on the amounts involved.
- In making its determination regarding compensation and plans which it is responsible for administering, the Committee shall take into account compensation received from all sources, including plans or arrangements which it is not responsible to administer.
- The Committee should take into consideration the tax-deductibility requirements of Section 162(m) of the Internal Revenue Code when reviewing and approving compensation for executive officers and, if deemed advisable, have such compensation approved by no less than two outside Committee members. If the Committee does not have two outside directors as defined in Section 162(m) of the Internal Revenue Code, such compensation should be approved by a majority of the outside Board members.
- The Committee shall not be empowered to approve matters which applicable law, the Corporation's charter, or the Corporation's bylaws require be approved by a vote of the entire Board.

THE GOLDMAN SACHS GROUP, INC.

COMPENSATION COMMITTEE CHARTER

AMENDED AND RESTATED AS OF JANUARY 2007

Purpose of Committee

The purpose of the Compensation Committee (the "Committee") of the Board of Directors (the "Board") of The Goldman Sachs Group, Inc. (the "Company") is to:

a. Determine and approve the compensation of the Company's Chief Executive Officer (the "CEO") and other executive officers;
b. Make recommendations to the Board with respect to incentive compensation and equity-based plans that are subject to Board approval;
c. Assist the Board in its oversight of the development, implementation and effectiveness of the Company's policies and strategies relating to its human capital management function, including but not limited to those policies and strategies regarding recruiting, retention, career development and progression,

management succession (other than that within the purview of the Corporate Governance and Nominating Committee), diversity and employment practices; and

d. Prepare any report on executive compensation required by the rules and regulations of the Securities and Exchange Commission (the "SEC").

Committee Membership

The Committee shall consist of no fewer than three members of the Board. The members of the Committee shall each have been determined by the Board to be "independent" under the rules of the New York Stock Exchange, Inc. At least two members of the Committee should qualify as "Non-Employee Directors" for the purposes of Rule 16b-3 under the Securities Exchange Act of 1934, as in effect from time to time ("Rule 16b-3"), and as "outside directors" for the purposes of Section 162(m) of the Internal Revenue Code, as in effect from time to time ("Section 162(m)"). No member of the Committee may (except in his or her capacity as a member of the Committee, the Board or any other Board committee) receive, directly or indirectly, any consulting, advisory or other compensatory fee from the Company, other than fixed amounts of compensation under a retirement plan (including deferred compensation) for prior service with the Company (provided that such compensation is not contingent in any way on continued service). Members shall be appointed by the Board based on the recommendations of the Corporate Governance and Nominating Committee and shall serve at the pleasure of the Board and for such term or terms as the Board may determine.

Committee Structure and Operations

The Board, taking into account the views of the Chairman of the Board, shall designate one member of the Committee as its chairperson. The Committee shall meet at least three times a year, with further meetings to occur, or actions to be taken by unanimous written consent, when deemed necessary or desirable by the Committee or its chairperson.

The Committee may invite such members of management and other persons to its meetings as it may deem desirable or appropriate. The Committee shall report regularly to the Board summarizing the Committee's actions and any significant issues considered by the Committee.

Committee Duties and Responsibilities

The following are the duties and responsibilities of the Committee:

1. In consultation with senior management, to make recommendations to the Board as to the Company's general compensation philosophy and to oversee the development and implementation of compensation programs.

2. To review and approve those corporate goals and objectives established by the Board that are relevant to the compensation of the CEO, evaluate the performance

of the CEO in light of those goals and objectives, and determine and approve the CEO's compensation level based on this evaluation. As part of this evaluation, the Committee shall consider the evaluation of the CEO conducted by the Corporate Governance and Nominating Committee. In determining the long-term incentive component of CEO compensation, the Committee shall consider, among other factors, the Company's performance and relative shareholder return, the value of similar incentive awards to chief executive officers at the Company's principal competitors and other comparable companies, and the awards given to the CEO in past years.

3. To review and approve the annual compensation of the Company's executives and any new compensation programs applicable to such executives, to make recommendations to the Board with respect to the Company's incentive compensation and equity-based plans that are subject to Board approval, including the Amended and Restated Stock Incentive Plan, the Partner Compensation Plan and the Restricted Partner Compensation Plan, to oversee the activities of the individuals and committees responsible for administering these plans, and to discharge any responsibilities imposed on the Committee by these plans.

4. To review periodically, as it deems appropriate:
   • Benefits and perquisites provided to the Company's executives; and
   • Employment agreements, severance arrangements and change in control agreements and provisions relating to the Company's executives.

5. To review annually the application of the compensation process to the Company's investment research professionals and assess whether that process remains consistent with the Company's Investment Research Principles and the requirements of Section I.5 of Addendum A to the global research settlement to which the Company is a party.

6. To review the Company's policies on the tax deductibility of compensation paid to "covered employees" (as defined by Section 162(m)), and, as and when required, to administer plans, establish performance goals and certify that performance goals have been attained for purposes of Section 162(m).

7. To discuss with management periodically, as it deems appropriate:
   • Reports from management regarding the development, implementation and effectiveness of the Company's policies and strategies relating to its human capital management function, including but not limited to those policies and strategies regarding recruiting, retention, career development and progression, management succession (other than that within the purview of the Corporate Governance and Nominating Committee), diversity and employment practices;
   • Reports from management relating to compensation guarantees; and
   • Reports from management regarding the Company's regulatory compliance with respect to compensation matters.

8. To prepare and issue the report and evaluation required under "Committee Reports" below.

9. To discharge any other duties or responsibilities delegated to the Committee by the Board from time to time.

Committee Reports

The Committee shall produce the following report and evaluation and provide them to the Board:

1. Any report or other disclosures required to be prepared by the Committee pursuant to the rules of the SEC for inclusion in the Company's annual proxy statement.
2. An annual performance evaluation of the Committee, which evaluation shall compare the performance of the Committee with the requirements of this charter. The performance evaluation shall also include a review of the adequacy of this charter and shall recommend to the Board any revisions the Committee deems necessary or desirable, although the Board shall have the sole authority to amend this charter. The performance evaluation shall be conducted in such manner as the Committee deems appropriate.

Delegation to Subcommittee

The Committee may, in its discretion, delegate all or a portion of its duties and responsibilities to a subcommittee of the Committee, whether or not such delegation is specifically contemplated under any plan or program. In particular, the Committee may delegate the approval of award grants and other transactions and other responsibilities regarding the administration of compensatory programs to a subcommittee consisting solely of members of the Committee who are (i) "Non-Employee Directors" for the purposes of Rule 16b-3, and/or (ii) "outside directors" for the purposes of Section 162(m).

Resources and Authority of the Committee

The Committee shall have the resources and authority appropriate to discharge its duties and responsibilities, including the authority to select, retain, terminate and approve the fees and other retention terms of special counsel or other experts or consultants, as it deems appropriate, without seeking approval of the Board or management. With respect to compensation consultants retained to assist in the evaluation of CEO or executive compensation, this authority shall be vested solely in the Committee.

GENERAL ELECTRIC COMPANY

MANAGEMENT DEVELOPMENT AND COMPENSATION COMMITTEE CHARTER

The Management Development and Compensation Committee of the board of directors of General Electric Company shall consist of a minimum of three directors.

Members of the committee shall be appointed by the board of directors upon the recommendation of the Nominating and Corporate Governance Committee and may be removed by the board of directors in its discretion. All members of the committee shall be independent directors, and shall satisfy GE's independence guidelines for members of the Management Development and Compensation Committee.

The purpose of the committee shall be to carry out the board of directors' overall responsibility relating to executive compensation.

In furtherance of this purpose, the committee shall have the following authority and responsibilities:

1. To assist the board in developing and evaluating potential candidates for executive positions, including the chief executive officer, and to oversee the development of executive succession plans.

2. To review and approve on an annual basis the corporate goals and objectives with respect to compensation for the chief executive officer. The committee shall evaluate at least once a year the chief executive officer's performance in light of these established goals and objectives and based upon these evaluations shall set the chief executive officer's annual compensation, including salary, bonus and non-equity incentive compensation.

3. To review and approve on an annual basis the evaluation process and compensation structure for the Company's officers. The committee shall evaluate the performance of the Company's senior executive officers and shall approve the annual compensation, including salary, bonus and non-equity incentive compensation, for such senior executive officers. The committee shall also provide oversight of management's decisions concerning the performance and compensation of other Company officers.

4. To review the Company's equity incentive compensation and other stock-based plans and recommend changes in such plans to the board as needed. The committee shall have and shall exercise all the authority of the board of directors with respect to the administration of such plans.

5. To maintain regular contact with the leadership of the Company. This should include interaction with the Company's leadership development institute, review of data from the employee survey and regular review of the results of the annual leadership evaluation process.

6. To review and discuss with management the Company's compensation discussion and analysis (CD&A) and to recommend to the board that the CD&A be included in the Company's annual report and proxy statement.

The committee shall have the authority to delegate any of its responsibilities to subcommittees as the committee may deem appropriate in its sole discretion.

The committee shall have authority to retain such compensation consultants, outside counsel and other advisors as the committee may deem appropriate in its sole discretion. The committee shall have sole authority to approve related fees and retention terms.

The committee shall report its actions and any recommendations to the board after each committee meeting and shall conduct and present to the board an annual performance evaluation of the committee. The committee shall review at least annually the adequacy of this charter and recommend any proposed changes to the board for approval.

REVLON, INC.

COMPENSATION COMMITTEE CHARTER

Updated as of April 11, 2007

In accordance with Article IV of the By-Laws of Revlon, Inc. (the "Company") and applicable laws, rules and regulations, there will be a standing committee of the Board of Directors of the Company (the "Board") known as the Compensation and Stock Plan Committee (the "Compensation Committee").

I. Organization

The Compensation Committee will consist of three or more directors of the Company. The Board will, to the extent practicable, ensure that the Compensation Committee will at all times have at least two members who are "outside directors" pursuant to Section 162(m) of the Internal Revenue Code, as amended, and as defined in Treasury Reg. Section 1.162-27(e)(3), as may be amended from time to time. Further, the Board will, to the extent practicable, ensure that at least two members of the Compensation Committee are "nonemployee directors" pursuant to Rule 16b-3(b))(3)(i) under the Securities Exchange Act of 1934, as amended from time to time. The Board will appoint the members of the Compensation Committee annually. Each member will serve until his/her successor is appointed.

II. Meetings

The Compensation Committee will meet as often as it determines is necessary or desirable, and will endeavor to meet not less frequently than quarterly. The Compensation Committee may from time to time decide to act by unanimous written consent in lieu of a meeting. The Chairman of the Compensation Committee will preside at each meeting of the Compensation Committee and, in consultation with the other members of the Compensation Committee and the Company's Secretary, will set the agenda of items to be addressed at each upcoming meeting. Each member of the Compensation Committee may suggest the inclusion of items on such agenda, and may raise at any Compensation Committee meeting appropriate and relevant business subjects that are not on the agenda for that meeting. The Chairman of the Compensation Committee and the Company's Secretary will ensure, to the extent feasible, that the agenda for each upcoming meeting of the Compensation Committee is circulated to each member of the Compensation Committee in advance of the meeting.

III. Authority and Responsibilities

The Compensation Committee will have the following authority and principal direct responsibilities:

a. reviewing and approving corporate goals and objectives relevant to the compensation of the Company's Chief Executive Officer, evaluating the CEO's performance in light of those goals and objectives and determining, either as a committee or together with the Board, the CEO's compensation, including salary, bonus, incentive and equity compensation, based on such evaluation, as well as on the evaluation of the CEO's performance by the Nominating and Corporate Governance Committee and, if applicable, by the full Board;

b. reviewing and approving the compensation, incentive compensation plans and equity based plans established for the Company's and its subsidiaries' Executive Officers and such other employees of the Company as the Compensation Committee may determine to be necessary or desirable from time to time;

c. reviewing and discussing with the Company's appropriate officers the Compensation Discussion and Analysis required by the Securities and Exchange Commission rules and based on such review and discussion (i) determining whether to recommend to the Board that the Compensation Discussion and Analysis be included in the Company's annual report and/or annual proxy statement and (ii) producing the Board's annual Compensation Committee Report for inclusion in the Company's annual report and/or proxy statement, in accordance with applicable rules and regulations, or such other analyses, reports or discussions as may be required under applicable laws, rules and regulations, as may be amended and in effect from time to time;

d. Administering the Revlon, Inc. Stock Plan, the Revlon, Inc. Supplemental Stock Plan and the Revlon Executive Bonus Plan, in each case as may be amended and in effect from time to time, as well as any other stock plans, executive bonus plans or other incentive compensation plans or arrangements of the Company and its subsidiaries, as may be in effect from time to time, including establishing bonus objectives under any such plan, and assessing the achievement and performance of such bonus objectives by certain of the Company's executive officers;

e. Conducting an annual self-evaluation;

f. Periodically reviewing the Compensation Committee charter and recommending changes, if any, to the Board;

g. Appointing subcommittees to perform any or all of its functions and to delegate to appropriate Company officers execution of certain actions as may be appropriate from time to time; and

h. Performing any other activities consistent with this Charter and the Company's By-Laws or as required under the rules and regulations of the Securities and Exchange Commission and the New York Stock Exchange, as in effect from time to time.

IV. Resources

The Compensation Committee will have the sole authority to retain and terminate any compensation consultant or other advisors to assist in the evaluation of director, CEO or other Company or subsidiary Executive Officer compensation and to advise the Compensation Committee or its subcommittees as they determine necessary to carry out their duties, without seeking Board approval. The Nominating Committee will determine the extent of funding necessary for payment of compensation to any such compensation consultant or other advisor retained to advise the Compensation Committee or its subcommittees, which funds will be provided by the Company.

*   *   *

For purposes of the foregoing, the term "Executive Officer" means a president, principal financial officer, principal accounting officer (or, if there is no such accounting officer, the controller) of the Company, any vice president of the Company in charge of a principal business unit, division or function (such as sales, administration or finance), any other officer who performs a policymaking function, or any other person who performs similar policy-making functions for the Company. Officers of the Company's parent or subsidiaries shall be deemed "executive officers" of the Company if they perform such policy-making functions for the Company.

Last updated as of April 11, 2007.

Sample Compensation Discussion and Analysis (CD&A)

This appendix contains three examples of the first year of CD&As under the SEC's new proxy disclosures rules (eBay, Citigroup, and the inimitable Berkshire Hathaway). These samples illustrate the wide range of responses to the new principles-based disclosure regime. The SEC's "post mortem" of the first year of disclosure under the new rules will be of interest to all and will no doubt have a major impact on the second season's drafting.

eBAY

COMPENSATION DISCUSSION AND ANALYSIS

Introduction; Objectives of Compensation Programs

Our compensation programs are designed to align compensation with business objectives and performance, enabling us to attract, retain, and reward executive officers and other key employees who contribute to our long-term success and motivate executive officers to enhance long-term stockholder value. We also strive to design programs to position eBay competitively among the companies against which we recruit and compete for talent. We recognize that compensation programs must be understandable to be effective and that program administration and decision making must be fair and equitable. We also consider the financial obligations created by our compensation programs and design them to be cost effective. To meet these objectives, the principal components of executive compensation in 2006 consisted of base salary, short-term cash incentive awards, and long-term equity incentive awards. For 2006, the equity incentive awards were primarily stock options, and, in specific circumstances, restricted stock and restricted stock units. We do not have any pension plan for our U.S. employees, including our executive officers.

The Compensation Committee reviews and sets our overall compensation strategy for all employees on an annual basis. In the course of this review, the committee considers our current compensation programs and whether to modify them or introduce new programs or elements of compensation in order to better meet our overall compensation objectives. As a result of its 2006 review, the Compensation Committee decided to add performance-based restricted stock units as a part of the long-term compensation program for all employees who are at the level of senior vice president and above starting in 2007.

Role of the Compensation Committee

The Compensation Committee reviews and approves all compensation programs (including equity compensation) applicable to our executive officers and directors, our overall strategy for employee compensation, and the specific compensation of our CEO, other executive officers, our other employees who are senior vice presidents, and any vice president whose compensation exceeds approved guidelines for cash and equity compensation. The committee has the authority to select, retain, and terminate special counsel and other experts (including compensation consultants), as the committee deems appropriate. As discussed in more detail below, in 2006, the committee retained two compensation consultants, both of which reported directly to the committee.

Role of Executive Officers and Consultants in Compensation Decisions

While the Compensation Committee determines eBay's overall compensation philosophy and sets the compensation of our CEO and other executive officers, it looks to the executive officers identified below and the compensation consultants retained by the committee to work within the compensation philosophy to make recommendations to the committee with respect to both overall guidelines and specific compensation decisions. Our CEO also provides the Board and the Compensation Committee with her perspective on the performance of eBay's executive officers as part of the annual personnel review and succession planning discussions as well as a self-assessment of her own performance. The committee establishes compensation levels for our CEO in consultation with the compensation consultants it retains, and our CEO is not present during any of these discussions. Our CEO recommends to the committee specific compensation amounts for executive officers other than herself, and the committee considers those recommendations and makes the ultimate compensation decisions. Our CEO, CFO, Senior Vice President of Human Resources, and Senior Vice President, Legal Affairs & General Counsel regularly attend the Compensation Committee's meetings to provide perspectives on the competitive landscape and the needs of the business, information regarding eBay's performance, and technical advice. Members of the committee also participate in the Board's annual review of the CEO's performance and its setting of annual performance goals, in each case led by our lead independent director. See "Our Corporate Governance Practices" for further details.

As discussed above, in 2006 the committee retained Mercer Human Resources Consulting and Towers Perrin to provide advice, their opinions, and resources to help develop and execute our overall compensation strategy. As part of their engagements, the Compensation Committee has directed the compensation consultants to work with our Senior Vice President of Human Resources and other members of management to obtain information necessary for them to form their recommendations and evaluate management's recommendations. The compensation consultants also meet with the committee during the committee's regular meetings and in executive session, where no members of management are present, and with individual members of the committee outside of the regular meetings.

As part of its engagement in 2006, Mercer evaluated proposed performance goals under the eBay Incentive Plan, or eIP, and 2006 compensation levels recommended by management for executive officers. As part of its engagement in 2006, Towers Perrin evaluated and proposed a compensation strategy to start in 2007 and the related equity and cash compensation guidelines, which included an analysis of eBay's performance and that of specified peer groups. To facilitate making external compensation comparisons, both Mercer and Towers Perrin provided the Compensation Committee with competitive market data by analyzing proprietary third-party surveys provided to them by management and publicly-disclosed documents of companies in specified peer groups (see the section entitled "Competitive Considerations" below for a further discussion regarding these peer groups).

Competitive Considerations

To set total compensation guidelines, the Compensation Committee reviews market data of companies with which eBay competes for executive talent, business, and capital. The market data consists of publicly-disclosed data from companies in two peer groups (consisting of high-tech companies and consumer products companies) and proprietary third-party survey data. The committee believes that it is necessary to consider this market data in making compensation decisions in order to attract and retain talent. The committee also recognizes that at the executive level, we compete for talent against larger companies across the United States, not just technology companies based in Silicon Valley. As discussed in more detail below in the section entitled "Elements of Compensation/Executive Compensation Practices—Long-term Equity Incentive Awards," eBay also uses these peer groups as benchmarks against which to assess its performance. In 2006, the peer groups consisted of the following companies:

High-Tech Peer Group	Consumer Products Peer Group
• Adobe Systems Incorporated	• Coach, Inc.
• Amazon.com, Inc.	• The Coca-Cola Company
• Apple Inc.	• The Gap, Inc.
• Cisco Systems, Inc.	• General Mills, Inc.
• Dell Inc.	• Harley-Davidson, Inc.
• Electronic Arts Inc.	• The Hershey Company
• EMC Corporation	• Kellogg Company
• First Data Corporation	• Nike, Inc.
• Google Inc.	• PepsiCo, Inc.
• Intel Corporation	• Polo Ralph Lauren Corporation
• IAC/InterActiveCorp	• Charles Schwab & Co., Inc.
• Intuit Inc.	• Starbucks Corporation
• Microsoft Corporation	• Tiffany & Co.
• Qualcomm Incorporated	• Time Warner Inc.
• Symantec Corporation	• Wm. Wrigley Jr. Company
• Yahoo! Inc.	

In deciding whether a company should be included in one of the peer groups, the committee considers a number of screening criteria, which generally includes the company's revenue, market value, and historical growth rate, as well as the company's primary line of business, whether the company has a recognizable and well-regarded brand, and whether we compete with the company for talent. To ensure that these peer groups continue to reflect the markets in which we compete for executive talent, the committee reviews the peer groups annually. Before adding or deleting a company from a peer group, the committee considers how the change would impact the comparative market data. For 2006, two companies were deleted from, and one company was added to, the high-tech peer group and two companies were deleted from the consumer products peer group.

Elements of Compensation/Executive Compensation Practices

For 2006, the principal components of executive compensation consisted of base salary, short-term cash incentive awards, and long-term equity incentive awards. The equity awards were primarily stock options, and, in specific circumstances, restricted stock and restricted stock units. Our executive officers were also provided certain perquisites, as described below, and were also eligible to participate in our health and benefits plans, savings plans, and our employee stock purchase plan, which are generally available to our employees. Although the Compensation Committee has not established a policy for the allocation between cash and equity compensation or short-term and long-term compensation, as described below, the committee has policies for each component of compensation, and as part of its evaluation of the compensation of our executive officers, the committee reviews not only the individual elements of compensation, but also total compensation. In general, however, compensation of executive officers is weighted towards long-term equity incentives, as the committee wants the senior leadership team to have a long-term perspective on the company's affairs.

Base Salary

Base salary is the fixed portion of executive pay and is set to reward individuals' current contributions to the company and compensate them for their expected day-to-day performance. Our pay positioning strategy is to target annual base salary and short-term cash incentives of the executive group as a whole at median levels relative to our peer groups in the high-tech and consumer products sectors. The Compensation Committee then sets a salary range for each executive job level, with the midpoint of the salary range based on the median level of our peer groups, although more weight is given to the high-tech sector than the consumer product sector. For 2006, eBay's actual cash compensation pay position for executives was somewhat higher than the median level, in part due to the performance of individual members of the executive group and the cash compensation paid to recently-hired executives, as described below. The committee believes that paying higher cash compensation was necessary to attract new executives, particularly those who came to us from industries with higher cash compensation levels.

The committee meets at least once a year to review and approve each executive officer's salary for the upcoming year. When reviewing base salaries, the committee considers the pay practices of companies in our peer groups, individual performance against specified goals, levels of responsibility, breadth of knowledge, and prior experience. Of these factors, competitive pay practices are the primary determinant of the range within which individual salaries are set. For 2006, the committee set the base salaries of our executive officers named in the Summary Compensation Table below (which are referred to as our named executive officers) within these ranges, except for Mr. Donahoe, whose base salary was above the range for his job level. Mr. Donahoe's salary exceeded the high end of his range in large measure due to the salary he negotiated when he joined us in 2005, which in turn reflected the high cash compensation he received in his previous position. Base salaries of our named executive officers (other than our CEO) were $400,000 to $800,000, effective March 1, 2006, which represent increases of 6.0% to 9.9% over the prior year. For the third straight year, our CEO's salary was maintained at $995,016. In determining Ms. Whitman's salary, the committee gave particular attention to Ms. Whitman's request that her salary not be raised.

Short-term Cash Incentive Awards

eBay Incentive Plan (eIP). The eIP is a cash incentive program designed to align executive compensation with quarterly and annual performance and to enable eBay to attract, retain, and reward individuals who contribute to eBay's success and motivate them to enhance the value of eBay. The eIP was approved by our stockholders in 2005. The Compensation Committee believes that incentive payouts should be tightly linked to eBay's performance, with individual compensation differentiated based on individual performance. As a result, funding and payouts under the eIP are dependent and based on eBay's performance and individual performance.

The committee determines the quarterly, annual, or other performance period under the eIP. For each performance period, the committee establishes (1) performance measures based on business criteria and target levels of performance and (2) a formula for calculating a participant's award based on actual performance compared to the pre-established performance goals. Performance measures may be based on a wide variety of business metrics. Management recommends to the committee a proposed approach to setting the performance measures and targets. Under ordinary circumstances, the committee sets the annual targets within 90 days of the commencement of the year and other targets within the period that is the first 25% of the quarter or other performance period.

For 2006, the eIP provided for (1) quarterly incentives based upon non-GAAP net income targets for each quarter and individual performance, so long as both minimum revenue (calculated on a constant foreign exchange basis) and non-GAAP net income thresholds were met and (2) an annual incentive based upon non-GAAP net income targets for the year, so long as both minimum revenue (calculated on a constant foreign exchange basis) and non-GAAP net income thresholds were met. Non-GAAP net income excludes certain items, primarily stock-based compensation expense and related payroll taxes, amortization of acquired intangible assets, and income taxes related to these items. For the quarterly incentives, if the minimum revenue and non-GAAP net income thresholds have been met, half of the award is based on the company's performance, and half of the award is based on individual performance. The committee selected non-GAAP net income target and revenue as the company performance measures because it believes they are the strongest drivers of long-term value for the company.

The amount by which the eIP is funded is determined based on the company's actual performance measured against the targets set by the committee. Unless both the threshold revenue and non-GAAP net income levels for any given performance period are met, there is no payout for that period. After the end of each performance period, the company's actual performance is compared to the targets to determine the funding level, and our CEO presents the committee with her assessment of the performance of each of the other executive officers; the committee reviews her assessments and determines the level of performance for each of those executive officers. In addition, the committee reviews and determines the CEO's level of performance, based in part on her self-assessment. For executive officers other than the CEO, quarterly assessments are typically based on performance against financial performance measures for the executive's business unit or function, organizational development and leadership, and, as applicable, major product introductions, integration of acquisitions, and achievement of strategic and infrastructure objectives. For our CEO, quarterly assessments are based on the committee's subjective assessment of the company's overall financial performance, achievement of strategic objectives, and leadership of the executive team (which was a particularly important factor in 2006 given the substantial amount of change in the team over the course of the year) and of the company as a whole.

The committee sets the company performance measures with a goal of having the minimum threshold met approximately 90% of the time, the target level met approximately 50–60% of the time, and the maximum level met approximately 10% of the time. Target levels are generally set with reference to the company's annual budget (adjusted for actual financial performance year-to-date to a level expected to achieve the 50–60% probabilities of achievement referenced above). The minimum and maximum levels are set at an amount expected to result in the 10% probability of non-achievement and achievement, respectively, referenced above. The following table sets forth the 2006 performance measures set by the committee:

	Minimum	Target	Maximum
Annual 2006:			
Revenue threshold	$5.80B	—	—
Non-GAAP net income	$1.388B	$1.480B	$1.662B
Q1 2006:			
Revenue threshold	$1.365B	—	—
Non-GAAP net income	$315.1M	$333.0M	$361.6M
Q2 2006:			
Revenue threshold	$1.370 B	—	—
Non-GAAP net income	$317.3M	$347.0M	$376.9M
Q3 2006:			
Revenue threshold	$1.355B	—	—
Non-GAAP net income	$316.8M	$336.7M	$365.7M
Q4 2006:			
Revenue threshold	$1.671 B	—	—
Non-GAAP net income	$388.6M	$408.5M	$449.4M

In 2006, quarterly incentive amounts could range from 0% to 160% of an executive's target opportunity, based on financial and individual performance in the quarter. The maximum that could be paid on the annual component was 200% of target. Half of the total 2006 incentive target for executives was based on quarterly performance (12.5% per quarter), and half was based on annual performance. In 2006, total annual target incentive amounts for the named executive officers (other than the CEO) were 60% to 85% of base salary. The target incentive amount for the CEO remained 100% of base salary.

eBay paid incentive compensation for every quarter of 2006, which contributed, along with individual performance, to quarterly incentive payments to our named executive officers ranging from 91% to 152% of the quarterly target opportunity. Based on eBay's annual performance, the annual component for all executives, including the CEO, was paid out at 107% of the annual target opportunity.

Special Retention Bonus Plans. Messrs. Donahoe and Swan each have special retention bonus plans that were entered into in connection with their hiring. The Compensation Committee believed that it was necessary to enter into these special bonus plans to provide each of Messrs. Donahoe and Swan with a total compensation package that would be attractive to them and cause them to join eBay, in each case with particular reference to the compensation he had been receiving at his previous position. Under the terms of Mr. Donahoe's plan, he is eligible to receive a special retention bonus of up to $2,000,000 in cash, of which $500,000 was paid in each of 2005, 2006, and 2007. The plan provides that Mr. Donahoe will receive one additional bonus payment of $500,000, payable on the third anniversary of the date of his commencement of employment, assuming his continued employment with eBay. Under the terms of Mr. Swan's plan, he is eligible to receive a special retention bonus of up to $1,000,000 in cash, of which $200,000 was paid in each of 2006 and 2007. The plan provides that Mr. Swan will receive three additional bonus payments of $200,000, payable on each of the second, third, and fourth anniversaries of the date of his commencement of employment, assuming his continued employment with eBay. The amounts paid to Messrs. Donahoe and Swan under these bonus plans were in addition to their base salaries and cash incentives earned under the eIP.

Long-Term Equity Incentive Awards   During 2006, we granted our executive officers long-term equity incentives in the form of stock options to reward them for potential long-term contributions, align their incentives with the long-term interests of our stockholders, and provide a total compensation opportunity commensurate with our performance. Initial option grants for specific individuals also take into account specific recruitment needs. Following the initial hire grant, additional grants are made to participants pursuant to a periodic focal grant program or following a significant change in job responsibilities, scope, or title. See the section entitled "Equity Compensation Practices" below for a description of our equity grant practices. Focal grants are based upon a number of factors, including performance of the individual, job level, future potential contributions to eBay, competitive external levels of equity incentives, and the retention value associated with each individual's unvested equity. Vested equity held by the employee is generally not a factor in the Compensation Committee's consideration of equity grants. The number of shares subject to focal grants are determined within ranges established for each job level that are reviewed and approved by the committee on at least an annual basis. These job level ranges are established based on our desired pay positioning relative to the competitive market, with our CEO and Senior Vice President of Human Resources and the committee's compensation consultant involved in the process of recommending the job level ranges to the committee for approval. For both initial and focal grants, the committee approves the final sizes of awards for those employees who are at the level of senior vice president and above. The process and methodology for determining the size of awards for executives are generally the same as those used for our other employees. For 2006, the Compensation Committee set the stock option focal amounts for our named executive officers within the job level ranges, except for Mr. Donahoe, whose focal grant was above the range for his job level. The committee believed that it was necessary to set Mr. Donahoe's focal grant, which consisted of two option grants, one with slower than normal vesting, at the level it did to appropriately reflect the size of the business unit that Mr. Donahoe manages relative to eBay as a whole and his expected contributions to eBay's overall results.

Our pay positioning strategy for long-term incentive compensation varies, based on our performance. In setting annual long-term incentive award guidelines, the committee considers eBay's total stockholder return, revenue growth, and net income growth over trailing four-quarter and three-year periods relative to its peer groups of high-tech companies and consumer products companies. The committee also considers data from a proprietary third-party survey prepared by Buck Consultants that provides data on the equity guidelines of companies in the high-tech industry. From this survey, the committee can determine how eBay's long-term incentive award guidelines would likely compare against companies in the high-tech peer group. If eBay's performance compared to its peer group companies is average, the midpoints of long-term incentive award guidelines for the subsequent year are targeted to be positioned at the 50th percentile of the guidelines for the high-tech industry provided by the survey. If eBay's performance compared to its peer group companies is high, midpoints of long-term incentive award guidelines could be positioned as high as the 75th percentile. If eBay's performance compared to its peer group companies is low, midpoints of long-term incentive guidelines could be positioned as low as the 25th percentile. Once the midpoints of the long-term incentive guidelines are set, ranges around the midpoints are established to allow for differentiation of awards by individual. Individual awards may therefore be higher or lower than the pay positioning guidelines. The committee may also make special compensation-related decisions for performance, recognition, long-term retention value, and/or recruitment purposes that cause individual compensation to differ from the regular stated compensation strategy and guidelines. In addition to setting annual long-term incentive award guidelines, the committee determines a maximum dilution target rate for the year. The committee considers trends in the high-tech industry and dilution rates of companies in the high-tech peer group in setting the maximum dilution rate. In addition to following the guidelines described above, the company cannot grant awards in excess of the maximum dilution target without the committee's approval.

Given eBay's performance in 2005 (based on trailing four-quarter and three-year periods), the committee decided to position the midpoints of the long-term incentive award guidelines for 2006 at approximately the 75th percentile of the guidelines for the high-tech industry provided by the survey. This positioning was subject to a maximum gross dilution rate, including grants to existing employees and grants associated with anticipated growth in eBay's employee base. Consistent with the methodology described above, the committee reviewed eBay's performance in 2006 (based on trailing four-quarter and three-year periods) and determined that the midpoints of the guidelines for 2007 should be positioned at the 65th percentile, subject to a maximum gross dilution rate.

In connection with the commencement of his employment and in addition to his initial stock option grant, the committee granted Mr. Swan 50,000 shares of restricted stock. The committee granted Mr. Swan this special award to enhance the overall compensation package being offered to him.

As discussed above, as a result of its 2006 review of our compensation strategy and programs, the Compensation Committee decided that, while it expects that the company will continue to use stock options as a significant vehicle for long-term compensation for at least the most highly-compensated half of its employees, it would award, in addition to stock options, performance-based restricted stock units to all employees who are at the level of senior vice president and above, starting in 2007. The committee's decision was based on a number of factors, including its desire to more strongly link equity awards to key financial performance metrics for executive officers, reduce the dependence of rewards on stock price appreciation while preserving the ability to have larger awards for outstanding company performance, recognize the volatility of eBay's stock price, and facilitate actual stock ownership. The committee also considered the impact on dilution and the accounting consequences associated with performance-based restricted stock units in light of the adoption of Financial Accounting Standard Board's Statement of Financial Accounting Standards 123(R). For employees awarded performance-based restricted stock units, which are all employees who are at the level of senior vice president and above, the performance-based restricted stock units are expected to constitute approximately 20% of their long-term incentive value in 2007, with the remaining 80% being stock options. The percentage of the long-term incentive value attributable to performance-based restricted stock units is expected to increase over time. For 2007, employees below the level of senior vice president will generally receive a mix of stock options and time-vested restricted stock units.

For 2007, performance-based restricted stock units were awarded with both a one-year performance period and a two-year performance period. After this transition year, all performance-based restricted stock units will have a two-year performance period, which will provide a longer time horizon than the one-year time horizon of our existing eIP incentive plan. The amount of the awards granted for the 2007 and 2007–2008 performance periods will be determined based on company performance under non-GAAP operating margin and revenue growth measures, which, in turn, will be modified by a return on invested capital performance metric, all set by the committee. Non-GAAP operating margin excludes certain items, primarily stock-based compensation expense and related payroll taxes, amortization of acquired intangible assets, and income taxes related to these items. If the performance criteria are satisfied, the performance-based restricted stock units will vest one-half on the first of March following the end of the performance period and one-half one year later.

Perquisites We provide certain executive officers with perquisites and other personal benefits that the Compensation Committee believes are reasonable and consistent with our overall compensation programs and philosophy. These benefits are provided in order to enable us to attract and retain these executives. The committee periodically reviews the levels of these benefits provided to our executive officers. Of these benefits, the most significant is allowing certain executive officers to use the corporate aircraft for personal use and providing these executives with bonuses to cover related income taxes. In 2006, the committee authorized our CEO to use the corporate aircraft up to 200 hours for personal use and granted her a bonus to cover related income taxes.

In addition, we have (1) assisted certain executive officers with expenses they have incurred in connection with relocations, both when they join eBay and, if appropriate, when they take on new assignments within eBay that involve a geographic relocation and (2) provided executive officers with cost of living, housing, and automobile allowances in connection with overseas assignments. Mr. Swan's relocation assistance included assistance with selected costs and expenses related to moving from Texas to the San Francisco Bay Area (including transportation and temporary housing) and the sale of his home and related tax reimbursements. Mr. Swan's relocation assistance was negotiated as part of the terms of his offer to join eBay, and the committee later agreed to provide Mr. Swan with additional relocation assistance, which included an agreement to pay Mr. Swan the difference between $3,000,000 and the sales price of Mr. Swan's home, to preserve the intent of the relocation assistance included in his original offer in light of the condition of the real estate market in Plano, Texas. The committee believes it was necessary to offer Mr. Swan relocation assistance in order to attract him to join eBay. In connection with Mr. Dutta's appointment as President, Skype, we provided him with relocation assistance, which included assistance with the costs and expenses related to moving from the San Francisco Bay Area to the United Kingdom (including transportation and temporary housing) and a cost of living allowance. The committee believes it was appropriate to provide Mr. Dutta with this assistance in light of this appointment.

Equity Compensation Practices

We do not have any program, plan, or practice to select option grant dates in coordination with the release of material non-public information, nor do we time the release of information for the purpose of affecting value. We do not backdate options or grant options retroactively. Initial grants of stock options are made to eligible employees in connection with the commencement of employment. The company has maintained a rules-based approach to new hire option grants since inception. From January 2004 to

July 2006, grants were made on the Friday of the first week of employment for employees whose first day of employment was the first business day of the week and the following Friday if the employee started on a different day. Beginning in June 2005, grants of 100,000 shares or more (which we refer to as sizeable new hire grants) were split into two tranches, with the first tranche granted on the Friday following the employee's first full week of employment and the second tranche granted on the date 26 weeks from the date of the first grant. In July 2006, we changed our grant practices to provide that new hire options are granted on the second Friday of the month following the month in which employment commences. In all cases, the options are priced at the closing price of the company's stock on the date of grant. These grants generally become fully vested after four years, with 1/4th of the grant vesting on the first anniversary of the date of commencement of employment and 1/48th of the grant vesting monthly thereafter. Sizeable new hire grants are made in two equal tranches, with the first grant made and priced as described above and the second grant made and priced at the closing market price on the date 26 weeks from the date of the first grant. Both tranches vest with respect to 1/4th of the shares on the first anniversary of the date of commencement of employment and 1/48th of the shares vesting monthly thereafter. For all stock options granted after January 1, 2006, employees have seven years from the date of the grant to exercise vested options, assuming they remain an employee of an eBay company and subject to any requirements of local law.

Focal stock option grants are awarded on March 1 of each year (or if March 1 is not a trading day, the next trading day with vesting effective as of March 1) and are priced at the closing market price on the date of the grant. We selected the March 1 date to allow eBay to close its financial statements for the prior year, announce earnings for the prior year, and finalize the performance ratings of employees prior to the determination of the awards. In addition, we cluster our promotions semiannually to coincide with our focal grant date and September 1 (or if September 1 is not a trading day, the next trading day with vesting effective as of September 1) and most promotional grants are therefore made on those two dates.

Focal and promotional stock option grants generally become fully vested after four years, with 1/8th of the grant vesting six months after the date of the grant and 1/48th of the grant vesting monthly thereafter. For all stock options granted after January 1, 2006, employees have seven years from the date of the grant to exercise vested options, assuming they remain employees of eBay and subject to any requirements of local law.

Focal stock option grants awarded to executives are priced and granted to executives on the same date and at the same price that they are priced and granted to the rest of our employees and have the same four-year vesting schedule.

Employment Agreements, Change-in-Control Arrangements, and Severance Arrangements with Executive Officers

We do not have individual employment arrangements or change-in-control arrangements with any of our executive officers. We do not have any severance payment arrangements with any of our executive officers, except for our CEO, who was given a severance provision when she was initially hired in 1998. Under this provision, she is entitled to receive her base salary for six months if she is terminated other than for cause; and if she remains unemployed at the end of such six-month period, she is eligible to receive additional base salary for the lesser of six months or commencement of other employment. If our CEO had been terminated other than for cause at December 31, 2006, she would have been entitled to receive $497,508 during the first six months of 2007, and if she remained unemployed at the end of such six-month period, she would have been entitled to receive an additional $82,918 per month for each month she remained unemployed (up to an aggregate of $497,508).

Stock Ownership Guidelines

In September 2004, the Board adopted stock ownership guidelines to better align the interests of eBay's executives with the interests of stockholders and further promote eBay's commitment to sound corporate governance. Under the guidelines, executive officers are required to achieve ownership of eBay common stock valued at three times their annual base salary (five times in the case of the CEO). The guidelines provide that the required ownership level for each executive officer is re-calculated whenever an executive officer changes pay grade and as of January 1 of every third year. Until an executive achieves the required level of ownership, he or she is required to retain 25% of the after-tax net shares received as the result of the exercise of eBay stock options or the vesting of restricted stock or restricted stock units. A more detailed summary of the stock ownership guidelines can be found on our website at *http://investor.ebay.com/governance*. All of our directors and all of our executive officers who began their employment with eBay prior to January 1, 2005 have achieved the level of stock ownership required under the guidelines. The ownership levels of our executive officers as of March 30, 2007 are set forth in the section entitled "Security Ownership of Certain Beneficial Owners and Management" above. We also have an insider trading policy that, among other things, prohibits employees from trading any instrument that relates to the future price of our stock.

Impact of Accounting and Tax Requirements on Compensation

We are limited by Section 162(m) of the Internal Revenue Code of 1986 to a deduction for federal income tax purposes of up to $1,000,000 of compensation paid to our named executive officers in a taxable year. Compensation above $1,000,000 may be deducted if, by meeting certain technical requirements, it can be classified as "performance-based compensation." The eIP was approved by stockholders in 2005 and satisfies the requirements of Section 162(m) for "performance-based" compensation. In 2004, the Board adopted and stockholders approved amendments to eBay's 1999 Global Equity Incentive Plan to allow awards under that plan to qualify as "performance-based compensation," and in Proposal 2 we are asking our stockholders to approve an amendment to the 1999 Plan to further satisfy the requirements of Section 162(m). Although the Compensation Committee uses the requirements of Section 162(m) as a guideline, deductibility is not the sole factor it considers in assessing the appropriate levels and types of executive compensation and it will elect to forego deductibility when the committee believes it to be in the best interests of the company and its stockholders.

In addition to considering the tax consequences, the committee considers the accounting consequences of, including the impact of the Financial Accounting Standard Board's Statement of Financial Accounting Standards 123(R), its decisions in determining the forms of different awards.

Conclusion

In evaluating the individual components of overall compensation for each of our executive officers, the Compensation Committee reviews not only the individual elements of compensation, but also total compensation. Through the compensation programs described above, a significant portion of the compensation awarded to our executive officers is contingent upon individual and eBay performance. The committee remains committed to this philosophy of pay-for-performance and will continue to review executive compensation programs to ensure the interests of our stockholders are served.

CITIGROUP, INC.

COMPENSATION DISCUSSION AND ANALYSIS

Objectives of Citigroup's Executive Compensation Programs

Citigroup pays its senior executives according to its longstanding philosophy of compensating senior executives for objectively demonstrable performance. Senior management compensation programs at Citigroup are intended to align the interests of management with those of stockholders in the creation of long-term stockholder value by providing pay for performance. The programs are designed to attract and retain the best talent, and to motivate executives to perform by linking incentive compensation to demonstrable performance-based criteria.

Citigroup seeks to attract and retain a highly qualified global workforce to deliver superior short-term and long-term performance to stockholders. Compensation for management is based on pay for performance, so that individual compensation awards reflect the performance of Citigroup overall, the particular business unit and individual performance. Performance goals for management are designed to balance short-term and long-term financial and strategic objectives that build stockholder value. Compensation levels are competitive with the marketplace in order to attract and retain high-performing executives.

Citigroup compensates its executives based not only on how well its businesses perform from a financial standpoint, but on *how* Citigroup does business. Superior performance encompasses achievement of financial goals as well as objective excellence in other key areas, such as exemplifying Citigroup's Shared Responsibilities, including the maintenance of sound regulatory relationships around the world.

When an executive achieves superior results, the executive is rewarded. Conversely, inferior performance by an executive leads to a reduction in, or elimination of, incentive compensation for the subject period. Inferior performance is also evaluated to determine the underlying causes and the executive, as well as his or her staff, will be incentivized to address the issues and will be rewarded for improved performance, or, where appropriate, replaced.

Elements of Compensation

Set forth below is a discussion of each element of compensation, the reason Citigroup pays each element, how each amount is determined, and how that element fits into Citigroup's overall compensation philosophy.

- *Base pay.* Annual base salary is capped at $1,000,000 for the named executive officers. Base salary, while not specifically linked to Citigroup performance, is necessary to compete for talent and is a relatively small component of overall compensation for the named executive officers (less than 10% of the total compensation awarded to any named executive officer for 2006).
- *Bonus and equity compensation awards.* The named executive officers receive discretionary annual incentive and retention awards based on their performance as described in more detail in this Compensation Discussion and Analysis. Forty percent of the nominal amount of the incentive and retention awards is made in shares of restricted or deferred stock under the terms of CAP. These awards vest over a four-year period, thereby aligning the executives' interests with the long-term interests of stockholders and placing ultimate compensation for our senior executives at risk through the performance of Citigroup and its stock. Citigroup believes that the current allocation formula is the appropriate mix of cash and non-cash incentives for senior management, as well as the appropriate balance between short-term and long-term compensation. The terms of CAP are discussed in detail in the General Discussion of the Summary Compensation Table and Grants of Plan-Based Awards Table.
- *Bonus and equity compensation awards.* The named executive officers receive discretionary annual incentive and retention awards based on their performance as described in more detail in this Compensation Discussion and Analysis. Forty percent of the nominal amount of the incentive and retention awards is made in shares of restricted or deferred stock under the terms of CAP. These awards vest over a four-year period, thereby aligning the

executives' interests with the long-term interests of stockholders and placing ultimate compensation for our senior executives at risk through the performance of Citigroup and its stock. Citigroup believes that the current allocation formula is the appropriate mix of cash and non-cash incentives for senior management, as well as the appropriate balance between short-term and long-term compensation. The terms of CAP are discussed in detail in the General Discussion of the Summary Compensation Table and Grants of Plan-Based Awards Table.

○ As part of Citigroup's Stock Ownership Commitment, the named executive officers are required to retain at least 75% of the equity awarded to them as long as they are members of the Citigroup Management Committee. While stock ownership commitments are now considered to be in the vanguard of good corporate governance, Citigroup has had some form of stock ownership commitment for well over a decade. The policy is intended to align the interests of the named executive officers even further with the interests of stockholders.

○ CAP awards are granted to a significant percentage of Citigroup's global workforce. Approximately 53,700,000 shares were awarded to approximately 36,700 employees in 82 countries around the world under CAP in January 2007 in respect of 2006 performance. Of the total number of CAP shares granted in January 2007, approximately 609,270 shares were granted to the named executive officers, representing 1.1% of the total number of shares granted.

• *Retirement and other deferred compensation plans.* The named executive officers participate or are eligible to participate in the Citigroup Pension Plan and the Citigroup 401(k) Plan, which are broad-based, tax-qualified retirement plans. The purpose of these programs is to provide all employees with tax-advantaged savings opportunities and income after retirement or other termination from Citigroup. Basic broad-based, tax-qualified retirement benefits are provided to assist employees in saving and accumulating assets for their retirement. Eligible pay under these plans is limited to IRC annual limits ($220,000 for 2006). More information on the terms of Citigroup's retirement plans is provided in the narrative following the Pension Benefits Table.

○ As a general rule, Citigroup does not rely on nonqualified deferred compensation to provide substantial compensation to its executives.

○ Some named executive officers have accrued benefits under legacy nonqualified retirement plans, as described in detail in the narrative following the Pension Benefits Table. Accruals for the named executive officers under these supplemental plans ceased in 1993 for one supplemental plan and in 2001 for another plan. After 2001, the only retirement benefits accrued by the named executive officers were those available generally to all salaried employees.

○ Nonqualified deferred compensation plans are not generally available to named executive officers at Citigroup. Mr. Rubin is a party to an employment agreement dated as of October 26, 1999 (as amended), and pursuant to this agreement, the cash component of Mr. Rubin's annual incentive awards from

1999 though 2005 was deferred into a nonqualified trust established by Citigroup. The deferral arrangement was entered into at the request of Citigroup primarily to facilitate Citigroup's tax planning. The amount deferred for each such year has been previously disclosed in the Summary Compensation Table in the applicable prior year's proxy statement as annual bonus compensation. The arrangement does not result in an increase to Mr. Rubin's total compensation from Citigroup, as explained in more detail in connection with the Nonqualified Deferred Compensation Table.

- *Health and insurance plans.* The named executive officers are eligible to participate in company-sponsored benefit programs on the same terms and conditions as those made available to salaried employees generally. Basic health benefits, life insurance, disability benefits and similar programs are provided to ensure that employees have access to healthcare and income protection for themselves and their family members. Under Citigroup's medical plans, higher paid employees are required to pay a significantly higher amount of the total premiums, while the premiums paid by lower paid employees receive a higher subsidy from Citigroup.

- *Other compensation.* As demonstrated in the Summary Compensation Table, Citigroup pays additional compensation to its named executive officers in the form of personal benefits only in limited circumstances. A discussion of personal benefits is provided in the footnotes to the Summary Compensation Table.
  - As authorized by its stockholder-approved stock incentive plans, Citigroup pays dividend equivalents on nonvested restricted or deferred stock awards on the same basis to all employees receiving such awards, which, as stated above, includes a significant percentage of all employees worldwide. The dividend rate is the same for the named executive officers as for other stockholders. This practice is consistent with and furthers the goal of aligning the interests of employees with those of stockholders.

Process for Determining Executive Officer Compensation

The Role of the Personnel and Compensation Committee. The committee is responsible for evaluating the performance of and determining the compensation for the CEO and approving the compensation structure for senior management, including the operating committee, members of the business planning groups, the most senior managers of corporate staff and other highly paid professionals, in accordance with guidelines established by the committee from time to time. The committee regularly reviews the design and structure of Citigroup's compensation programs to ensure that management's interests are aligned with stockholders and that the compensation programs are aligned with Citigroup's strategic priorities.

In furtherance of these goals, the committee has retained Independent Compensation Committee Adviser, LLC, to provide independent evaluations and advice regarding executive compensation. The independent consultant reports directly to the chair of the committee and meets with the committee in executive session, without the presence of management. The committee also relies on Mercer Human Resource Consulting to provide data, evaluations and advice regarding executive compensation.

Benchmarking   Near and after the end of 2006, benchmarking information on performance of peer companies and compensation at peer companies was obtained from publicly available sources and third-party proprietary databases, and reviewed with the compensation consultants. Compensation paid to the named executive officers is intended to be competitive with pay for comparable performance at peer companies, recognizing that the combination of lines of business at Citigroup is not replicated at any other company. The companies considered to be peers for compensation benchmarking purposes were ABN AMRO, AIG, American Express, Bank of America, Bank of New York, Credit Suisse Group, Deutsche Bank, General Electric, Goldman Sachs, HSBC, JP Morgan Chase, Merrill Lynch, Morgan Stanley, UBS, Wachovia and Wells Fargo. The criteria benchmarked were earnings, earnings per share growth, revenue growth, return on common equity, and criteria relating to stock price (five-year and one-year total returns, price to book value ratio, and 2006 price/earnings ratio).

Performance Evaluations   Mr. Prince presented an evaluation of the executive officers who report directly to him to the committee and the independent compensation consultant. The evaluation was based on performance by each of the executive officers against the criteria set forth in detail below. The committee then evaluated the performance of Mr. Prince and Mr. Rubin, using the same criteria. The committee received an evaluation of CEO compensation from the independent compensation consultant in executive session, and then determined incentive and retention awards for the CEO and the other named executive officers based on this input, the performance results, and benchmarking data.

Each of the factors comprising the performance results was considered in determining each executive's compensation. Formulaic approaches were not used to weight these factors, consistent with the committee's and Citigroup's belief that the adoption of any given formula could inadvertently encourage undesirable behavior (e.g., favoring one financial measure to the exclusion of other important values). Accordingly, each named executive officer's incentive and retention compensation was determined using a balanced approach that considered, in the context of a competitive marketplace, factors contributing to the financial performance of Citigroup and the executive's individual leadership.

Performance Criteria Used in Evaluations   For 2006, Citigroup and individual performance were measured by evaluating the following factors against actual performance, in accordance with Citigroup's Senior Executive Compensation Guidelines:

Business Practices Performance

Developing and maintaining positive regulatory relationships around the world, and the absence of any new significant regulatory enforcement actions. Citigroup generally maintained very positive regulatory relationships around the world in 2006, and there were no major new regulatory enforcement matters last year. It is noteworthy that the Federal Reserve approved several significant acquisitions by Citigroup.

In objective surveys, year-over-year improvements on employee-focused matters such as living the Shared Responsibilities. Employee survey scores have risen for two years, and overall employee satisfaction continued to improve on these surveys.

Excellence in talent development, including the development of diverse talent. Citigroup demonstrated strong performance in this area by, for example, increasing exposure of members of the operating committee to Board members.

Performance on audit and control measures improving year-over-year and exceeding Citigroup-wide audit and control performance ratings. Internal audit and control scores continued to improve during 2006 across Citigroup.

Financial Performance

Organic revenue growth, in the mid-to-high single digit range for Citigroup. Revenues grew 7%, almost all of which was organic.

Net income growth faster than revenue growth. Net income from continuing operations grew at about the same rate as total revenues (about 7% in each case).

Return on equity in the 18–20% range for 2006 for Citigroup. The 2006 return on equity was 18.8%.

Total return to stockholders compared to the peer companies listed above. Total return to stockholders was 19.6%, which was lower than many of the listed peer companies but comparable to large money center banks.

Strategic Performance

Continued execution of Citigroup's strategic plan. Highlights included the opening of over 1,100 retail bank and consumer finance branches, partnerships with 7-Eleven, Expedia, Shell and Home Depot, and exceeding the targeted reduction in data centers.

Performance of strategic investment initiatives, measured by contribution to earnings, returns on equity and franchise development. Performance of new investments exceeded expectations for both financial results and franchise development.

Continued successful implementation of Citigroup's acquisition strategy, including consideration of the impact on earnings and credit ratings. In 2006, announced strategic acquisitions or significant ownership stakes included HDFC, Akbank, Grupo Uno, Guangdong Development Bank, Grupo Cuscatlan and Quilter. In addition, certain credit ratings were upgraded in 2006.

After the committee determined each named executive officer's incentive and retention compensation, the independent compensation consultant retained by the committee reviewed the committee's decisions to determine whether the compensation paid to each executive was reasonable, based on these criteria and related results. In particular, the independent review of CEO compensation took into account positive and negative factors in Citigroup's financial performance, the success of strategic initiatives, and the market competitiveness of total CEO compensation. Based on its review of these factors, the consultant determined that the compensation paid to each named executive officer was reasonable. Before finalizing the decisions, the committee determined that the awards were permitted under the Executive Performance Plan. For more detail on the plan, see "Tax deductibility of the named executive officers' incentive and retention compensation" below.

Equity Awards

Once the committee determined the nominal amount of the named executive officers' incentive and retention compensation, the cash and equity components of the awards were determined under the equity plans, such that the named executive officers received 40% of their awards in restricted or deferred stock under CAP. As stated above, CAP awards are long-term incentives designed to increase retention and their value relates directly to the enhancement of stockholder value. The terms and conditions of CAP awards, including the vesting periods, the stock option election and provisions regarding termination of employment, are the same for the named executive officers as for all other CAP participants, and are described in more detail in the General Discussion of the Summary Compensation Table and Grants of Plan-Based Awards Table and the discussion of Potential Payments Upon Termination or Change in Control below.

Awards Made by the Committee

Based on the foregoing, in January 2007 the committee approved the following incentive awards to the named executive officers for their performance in 2006:

Name	Bonus	Stock Awards	Options	Total
Charles Prince	$13,200,000	10,633,333	$0	$23,833,333
Sallie Krawcheck	$5,820,000	4,688,333	$0	$10,508,333
Robert E. Rubin	$8,400,000	6,766,666	$0	$15,166,666
Robert Druskin	$8,100,000	6,525,000	$0	$14,625,000
Stephen Volk	$5,670,000	4,567,500	$0	$10,237,500

This table reflects the way in which the committee analyzed and made awards to the named executive officers for performance in 2006. The values for the stock awards in the above table differ from the values disclosed in the Summary Compensation Table (appearing later in this section) for the same awards, as shown in the table below.

Name	Stock Awarded in January 2007 for 2006 Performance	Value of Stock Awards Shown in 2006 Summary Compensation Table	Difference Between Stock Awarded and Summary Compensation Table Values
Charles Prince	$10,633,333	$10,633,333	$0
Sallie Krawcheck	$4,688,333	$2,946,251	$1,742,082
Robert E. Rubin	$6,766,666	$6,766,666	$0
Robert Druskin	$6,525,000	$6,555,103	$(30,103)
Stephen Volk	$4,567,500	$3,915,520	$651,980

The differences are largely attributable to the fact that the Summary Compensation Table, prepared in accordance with SEC regulations issued in December 2006, values equity awards based principally on the treatment of compensation expense in the income statement of the employer under the applicable accounting rule, Statement of Financial Accounting Standards (SFAS) No. 123 (revised 2004), "Share-Based Payment" (SFAS 123(R)). In general under that rule, an equity award is expensed over the vesting period of the equity award, unless the employee is eligible to retire. If the employee is eligible to retire, then the award must be expensed on the grant date or accrued over a service period prior to the grant date. Although Citigroup's equity programs do not expressly contain retirement provisions, they do have terms that result in retirement treatment under the applicable accounting standards.

At Citigroup, if an employee's age and years of service total at least 75, all of his or her equity awards will continue to vest on schedule after termination of employment under most circumstances. Accordingly, under SFAS 123(R), awards made to individuals who meet this "Rule of 75" must be expensed on or prior to the grant date. If an employee's age and service total at least 60 and certain other service requirements are satisfied, a portion of his or her equity awards will continue to vest on schedule after termination of employment under most circumstances. Accordingly, under SFAS 123(R), that portion of the awards made to an individual who meets this "Rule of 60" must be expensed on or prior to the grant date.

The differences between the stock awards made by the committee and the values in the Summary Compensation Table may be explained as follows:

Mr. Prince: Mr. Prince meets the Rule of 75. Accordingly, under SFAS 123(R), his awards must be expensed on or prior to the grant date. In 2006, Citigroup accrued in full an expense in respect of the CAP awards made to him in January 2007.

Ms. Krawcheck: Ms. Krawcheck is not eligible for the Rule of 60 or the Rule of 75, which means that under SFAS 123(R), her CAP and other equity awards are expensed over their vesting periods, and accordingly, the amount shown in the Summary Compensation Table for Ms. Krawcheck is the aggregate amortization charges for the awards made in prior years that are still vesting.

Mr. Rubin: Mr. Rubin meets the Rule of 75. Accordingly, under SFAS 123(R), his awards must be expensed on or prior to the grant date. In 2006, Citigroup accrued in full an expense in respect of the CAP awards made to him in January 2007.

Mr. Druskin: Mr. Druskin meets the Rule of 60. Accordingly, under SFAS 123(R), a portion of his awards must be expensed on or prior to the grant date, and in 2006, Citigroup accrued the related expense in respect of this portion of his 2007 compensation. In addition, some of Mr. Druskin's awards from prior years are still vesting, and under SFAS 123(R), the amount shown in the Summary Compensation Table for Mr. Druskin includes the amortization charges for awards made in prior years that are still vesting.

Mr. Volk: Mr. Volk is not eligible for the Rule of 60 or the Rule of 75, which means that under SFAS 123(R), his CAP and other stock awards are expensed over their vesting periods, and accordingly, the amount shown in the Summary Compensation Table for Mr. Volk is the aggregate amortization charges for the awards made in prior years that are still vesting.

The values for the stock option awards disclosed in the Summary Compensation Table (appearing later in this section) also differ from committee action in January 2007 in respect of 2006 performance, as shown in the table below.

Name	Value of Stock Options Awarded in 2007 for 2006 Performance	Value of Stock Options Shown in 2006 Summary Compensation Table
Charles Prince	$0	$746,607
Sallie Krawcheck	0	645,701
Robert E. Rubin	0	828,342
Robert Druskin	0	467,680
Stephen Volk	0	0

In accordance with SEC rules, the value of stock options shown in the 2006 Summary Compensation Table includes certain SFAS 123(R) charges for options granted in prior years plus the SFAS 123(R) value of 2006 reload options.

Under SFAS 123(R), the fair value of a stock option granted to a retirement-eligible employee will be expensed earlier than an identical stock option granted to an employee who is not retirement-eligible. Citigroup expenses the full fair value of the reload options granted to a retirement-eligible employee in the month following the grant. Conversely, the fair value of a reload option granted to an employee who is not retirement-eligible is amortized over the six-month vesting period beginning in the month following the grant. The Rule of 75 applies to Citigroup stock options, and accordingly, the foregoing accounting treatment for stock options awarded to individuals eligible for the Rule of 75 applies to the grant of Citigroup stock options.

In accordance with SFAS 123(R), reload options granted to Mr. Prince and Mr. Rubin were expensed in 2006, and to the extent required by SFAS 123(R), these values are included in the Summary Compensation Table. The fair values of stock options granted to Ms. Krawcheck and Mr. Druskin in current and prior years were expensed in Citigroup's income statement in 2006 over the applicable vesting periods, and accordingly, the amount disclosed in the Summary Compensation Table for Ms. Krawcheck and Mr. Druskin includes some expense recorded in 2006 in respect of their prior years' awards.

In the view of the committee and Citigroup, the December 2006 SEC release regarding reporting of equity compensation in the Summary Compensation Table does not reflect the way the committee and Citigroup analyze and make equity awards. Under the new rules, the treatment in the Summary Compensation Table of awards with the same terms for all the named executive officers may differ depending on age and length of service with Citigroup, and accordingly, may make it difficult to discern the committee's judgments about executive performance for 2006. The purpose of the foregoing discussion and disclosure is to make it clear that the committee made incentive awards for 2006 and in prior years based on the fair value of the awards and not on the accounting treatment of those or prior awards on Citigroup's financial statements under SFAS 123(R) or other applicable accounting standards.

Other Important Compensation Policies Affecting Named Executive Officers

Timing of Awards Equity incentive and retention awards are made at the regularly scheduled Board meeting in January, which is the grant date for annual incentive and retention awards made to all employees. Citigroup sets the date of the Board meeting a year or more in advance of the actual meeting, and Citigroup's practice for several years has been to hold the meeting on the third Tuesday of the month. In January 2006 and January 2007, fourth quarter earnings were released a few days later; in 2006 the closing share price declined between the date the awards were priced and the date of the earnings release, and in 2007, the closing share price increased in this time frame.

Citigroup does not coordinate awards with the release of earnings for any purpose, including the purpose of affecting executive compensation.

Grants of Stock Options   None of the named executive officers received a discretionary grant of stock options as part of his or her incentive and retention awards for 2006. Certain named executive officers received reload options whose issuance resulted from rights that were granted to them as part of an earlier option grant and were made under Citigroup's stockholder-approved equity compensation plans. Since 2003, Citigroup has not granted reload options except to the extent required by the terms of previously granted options.

Pricing of Stock Options   Citigroup's equity plans provide that the exercise price of options is no less than the closing price of a share of Citigroup common stock on the NYSE on the trading date immediately preceding the date on which the option was granted. However, starting in 2007, the exercise price of a reload or extraordinary option will be the closing price of a share of Citigroup common stock on the NYSE on the date on which the option is granted. Citigroup believes that both pricing approaches are appropriate measures of fair market value.

Tax Deductibility of the Named Executive Officers' Incentive and Retention Compensation   To secure the deductibility of incentive and retention compensation awarded to the named executive officers, each named executive officer's incentive and retention compensation for 2006 is awarded under the Executive Performance Plan. While Citigroup currently seeks to preserve deductibility of compensation paid to the named executive officers under Section 162(m) of the Internal Revenue Code, flexibility to provide compensation arrangements necessary to recruit and retain outstanding executives is maintained. The plan was approved by stockholders in 1999 and establishes criteria for determining the maximum amount of bonus compensation available for executives covered by the plan.

Change in Control Agreements   In 2002, Citigroup's Board of Directors adopted a resolution specifically prohibiting cash payments to a departing executive officer in the event of a change in control that would equal or exceed three times the executive officer's annual income.

Citigroup generally does not provide for change in control protection as part of individual employment arrangements. Mr. Rubin is party to an employment agreement dated as of October 26, 1999 (as amended), under which he has agreed, among other things, to serve as a Director and as Chairman of the Executive Committee. Mr. Rubin's agreement provides that in the event of a change in control of Citigroup, Mr. Rubin will be accorded no less favorable treatment in terms of compensation and awards under Citigroup compensation and benefit plans and arrangements as those applying to Mr. Prince and he will also be entitled to payments sufficient to reimburse him fully on an after-tax basis for any tax under Section 4999 of the IRC as well as any costs associated with resolving the application of such tax to him.

None of the other named executive officers has change in control arrangements other than those applicable to their equity awards under Citigroup's stockholder-approved equity plans, as described in detail below under Potential Payments Upon Termination or Change in Control.

Recoupment of Unearned Compensation   As part of Citigroup's Corporate Governance Guidelines, the board has adopted a policy requiring reimbursement, in all appropriate cases, of any bonus or incentive compensation awarded to an executive officer or effecting the cancellation of nonvested restricted or deferred stock awards previously granted to the executive officer if: (a) the amount of the bonus or incentive compensation was calculated based upon the achievement of certain financial results that were subsequently the subject of a restatement, (b) the executive engaged in intentional misconduct that caused or partially caused the need for the restatement, and (c) the amount of the bonus or incentive compensation that would have been awarded to the executive had the financial results been properly reported would have been lower than the amount actually awarded.

Policy on Employment Agreements   Citigroup will enter into a new employment agreement with an executive officer or a candidate only when necessary to attract or retain exceptional personnel. Any employment agreement with an executive officer (a) must be approved by the committee; (b) should have as short a term as possible and provide as few terms and conditions as are necessary to accomplish its purpose; and (c) if required by law to be available for public review, must be filed promptly with the appropriate regulatory authority. Employment agreements with executive officers may not provide for post-retirement personal benefits of a kind not generally available to employees or retirees, except with the express prior approval of the board.

BERKSHIRE HATHAWAY INC.

COMPENSATION DISCUSSION AND ANALYSIS

Berkshire's program regarding compensation of its executive officers is different from most public company programs. Mr. Buffett's compensation is reviewed annually by the Governance, Compensation and Nominating Committee ("Committee") of the Corporation's Board of Directors. Due to Mr. Buffett's desire that his compensation remain unchanged, the Committee has not proposed an increase in Mr. Buffett's compensation since the Committee was created in 2004. Prior to that time Mr. Buffett recommended to the Board of Directors the amount of his compensation. Mr. Buffett's annual compensation has been $100,000 for over the last 25 years and he would not expect or desire it to increase in the future.

The Committee has established a policy that: (i) neither the profitability of Berkshire Hathaway nor the market value of its stock are to be considered in the compensation of any executive officer; and (ii) all compensation paid to executive officers of Berkshire Hathaway be deductible under Internal Revenue Code Section 162 (m). Under the

Committee's compensation policy, Berkshire does not grant stock options to executive officers. The Committee has delegated to Mr. Buffett the responsibility for setting the compensation of Berkshire's two other executive officers.

Like Mr. Buffett, Mr. Munger has been paid an annual salary of $100,000 for over the last 25 years. Mr. Buffett does not anticipate that Mr. Munger's compensation will be increased in the future. Both Mr. Buffett and Mr. Munger will on occasion utilize Berkshire personnel and/or have Berkshire pay for minor items such as postage or phone calls that are personal. Mr. Buffett and Mr. Munger reimburse Berkshire for these costs by making an annual payment to Berkshire in an amount that is equal to or greater than the costs that Berkshire has incurred on their behalf. During 2006, Mr. Buffett reimbursed Berkshire $50,000 and Mr. Munger reimbursed Berkshire $5,500. Mr. Buffett and Mr. Munger do not use Company cars or belong to clubs to which the Company pays dues. It should also be noted that neither Mr. Buffett nor Mr. Munger utilizes corporate-owned aircraft for personal use. Each of them is personally a fractional NetJets owner, paying standard rates, and they use Berkshire owned aircraft for business purposes only.

Factors considered by Mr. Buffett in setting Mr. Hamburg's salary are typically subjective, such as his perception of Mr. Hamburg's performance and any changes in functional responsibility. Mr. Buffett also sets the compensation for each of the CEO's of Berkshire's significant operating businesses. He utilizes several different incentive arrangements, with their terms dependent on such elements as the economic potential or capital intensity of the business. The incentives can be large and are always tied to the operating results for which a CEO has authority. These incentives are never related to measures over which the CEO has no control.

Glossary

ABA   Abbreviation for *American Bar Association.*

Accounting Principles Board (APB)   A board convened in 1959 by the American Institute of Certified Public Accountants (AICPA) to determine and publish accounting principles. This group was terminated in 1973 and replaced by the Financial Accounting Standards Board (FASB). All opinions of the APB remain in effect unless superseded by FASB announcements.

accredited investors   Sophisticated investors who, under the securities laws, can participate in private placements of unregistered securities. Individuals fall into this category if they have certain wealth and income characteristics, such as a net worth (alone or with a spouse) of $1 million.

accrued compensation expense   Incurred and charged expense that has not yet been paid. This expense would be reflected on the balance sheet and will show on the income statement.

actuarial assumptions   An actuary's prediction of future measures that will have an impact on pension cost. Examples include life expectancy, investment returns, inflation, and mortality rates.

actuary   Mathematician usually employed by a life insurance company or consulting firm to calculate life insurance premiums, reserves, policy dividend payments, insurance, pension amounts, pension balances, annuity rates, and the like, using mortality rates and other risk factors obtained from experience.

ADEA   Abbreviation for *Age Discrimination in Employment Act of 1967.*

ADR   Abbreviation for *American depositary receipt.*

affiliate   An affiliate of a corporation is a person who controls, is controlled by or is under common control with the corporation, and typically includes the corporation's directors, officers, and 10 percent or more shareholders.

AFL-CIO   Voluntary federation of America's labor unions, formed in 1955 by the merger of the American Federation of Labor and the Congress of Industrial Organizations.

AFR   Abbreviation for *applicable federal rate.*

Age Discrimination in Employment Act (ADEA) of 1967, as amended   Treats nonfederal employees age 40 and over as a protected class relative to treatment in pay, benefits, and other personnel actions. The 1990 amendment is called the *Older Workers Benefit Protection Act.*

agency theory   A theory of motivation that depicts exchange relationships in terms of two parties: agents and principals. According to the theory, both sides of the exchange will seek the most favorable exchange possible, and will act opportunistically if given a chance.

agent   Individual authorized by another person, called the principal, to act on the latter's behalf in transactions involving a third party.

aggregate exercise price   The exercise or strike price of an option times the number of underlying securities subject to the option.

alternative minimum tax (AMT)   An alternative method of calculating income tax liability that requires the taxpayer to include in his or her taxable income certain tax preference items that are deductible under the regular income tax rules.

American Bar Association (ABA)   An association of the legal profession in the United States.

American depositary receipt (ADR)   Receipt for the shares of a foreign-based corporation held in the care of a U.S. bank and entitling the shareholder to all dividends and capital gains of the stock. Instead of buying shares directly on the foreign stock exchange, ADR shareholders buy shares in the United States in the form of an ADR. ADRs are available on hundreds of stocks on numerous exchanges. The SEC requires limited disclosure for ADRs. ADRs are also called *"American depositary shares."*

American Institute of Certified Public Accountants (AICPA)   The national, professional organization for all certified public accountants. Its mission is to supply members with the resources, information, and leadership that enable them to provide valuable services in the highest professional manner, to benefit the public as well as employers and clients.

American option   An option contract that may be exercised at any time between the date of purchase or vesting date and the expiration date of the option.

American Stock Exchange (AMEX)   An open-auction market similar to the New York Stock Exchange, where buyers and sellers compete in a centralized marketplace. The AMEX typically lists small- to medium-cap stocks of younger or smaller companies. Until 1921 it was known as the New York Cumulative Exchange. The AMEX merged with NASDAQ in the late 1990s.

AMEX   Abbreviation for *American Stock Exchange.*

AMT   Abbreviation for *alternative minimum tax.*

analyst   Person in a brokerage house, bank trust department, or mutual fund group who studies a number of companies and makes buy or sell recommendations on the securities of particular companies and industry groups.

annual incentive   A lump-sum payment (cash, stock, etc.) made in addition to base salary for a fiscal year, based on achievement of performance goals.

annual meeting Once-a-year meeting at which the managers of a company report to shareholders on the year's results and directors stand for election for the next year.

annual report An SEC filing made annually by a public company, which contains the company's audited financial statements and other information of interest to security holders.

annuity A contract sold by life insurance companies that guarantees a fixed or variable payment to the annuitant at some future time, usually retirement. In a fixed annuity, the amount will ultimately be paid out in regular installments, varying with the payout method elected. In a variable annuity, the payout is based on a guaranteed number of units; unit values and payments depend on the value of the underlying investments. All capital in the annuity grows tax deferred.

APB Abbreviation for *Accounting Principles Board.*

applicable federal rate (AFR) Interest rates, which are published monthly, set by the U.S. Treasury for determining imputed interest and for other specified purposes.

appreciation Increase in value of an asset (typically the price of stock).

appreciation rights The right to receive the appreciation in value of an instrument (typically common stock) over time, which appreciation can be paid in the form of cash or stock.

arbitrage A technique used by stock traders, now aided by sophisticated computer programs, to profit from minute price differences for the same security on different markets.

arm's-length transaction An exchange between parties who are independent of each other, and who are acting in their own best interests.

articles of incorporation (also called certificate of incorporation or charter) Document filed with a U.S. state by the founders of a corporation setting forth such information as the corporation's legal name, business purpose, number of authorized shares, and number and identity of directors. The corporation's powers derive from the laws of the state of incorporation and the provisions of the charter.

attestation An affidavit or declaration of share ownership by which an option holder exercising an option by a stock swap can avoid surrendering a physical stock certificate for the shares used to exercise the option.

audit report Often called the "accountant's opinion"; the statement of the auditor as to whether the company's financial statements present fairly the results of its operations in conformity with GAAP.

average Arithmetic mean of reported data; sum of the values divided by the number of cases.

backdating options The practice of obtaining a low exercise price by maintaining that the option was granted on a prior date when the stock price was at a low for the period.

balance sheet   A financial statement that shows total assets, total liabilities, and owners' equity. Also referred to as a "statement of financial position."

Barone-Adesi and Whaley value   The value derived by a method for pricing tradable call options on dividend-paying stock. Uses the stock price, the exercise price, the risk-free interest rate, the time to expiration, the expected standard deviation of the stock return, and the dividend yield. Developed by Giovanni Barone-Adesi and Robert E. Whaley. See Giovanni Barone-Adesi and Robert E. Whaley, "Efficient Analytic Approximation of American Option Values," *Journal of Finance* 42 (1987): 301–320.

base salary   A core element of compensation; the basic compensation that an employer pays for work performed.

basis   See *tax basis.*

bear   An investor who believes that a stock price or the overall market will decline.

bear market   Any market in which prices are in a declining trend, usually accompanied by a drop in stock prices of 20 percent or more.

bearish   A viewpoint that anticipates a price decline, referring either to an individual security or to the entire market.

benchmarking   A company's use of information about other firms in the same industry; used for comparisons and to set standards and goals.

beneficial owner   For most purposes under the federal securities laws, any person or entity with sole or shared power to vote or dispose of the stock. This SEC definition is intended to include a holder who enjoys the economic benefits of ownership although the shares may be held in another's name. For example, one spouse is generally deemed the beneficial owner of shares held by the other spouse.

beta   A mathematical measure of the sensitivity of rates of return on a stock compared with the broader stock market. Higher betas indicate higher stock price volatility. In specific, a coefficient measuring a stock's relative volatility. The beta is a covariance of the stock in relation to the rest of the stock market. The Standard & Poor's 500 Stock Index has a beta coefficient of 1. Any stock with a higher beta is more volatile than the market, and any with a lower beta can be expected to rise and fall more slowly than the market.

binomial option pricing model   A model for pricing stock options. Fundamental to the binomial option pricing model is the idea that stock price movements are well approximated by assuming the stock price can only move to two possible values in a short interval of time. A price tree is constructed that describes the probability of future stock price movements.

Black-Scholes model   A "closed" option pricing model that incorporates both the intrinsic value (the spread in the option) and the time value of the option (the term of the option) to determine the option's total market value.

blackout period   A period of time prior to the release of annual or quarterly financial information by a publicly held company during which insiders are restricted from trading the company's stock.

BLS   Abbreviation for *Bureau of Labor Statistics*.

blue chip   An adjective to describe stock of a nationally known company that has a long record of profit growth and dividend payments and a reputation for quality management, products, and services. Blue-chip stocks typically are relatively high priced and low yielding.

blue sky laws   A popular name for state corporation laws, in particular those enacted to protect the public against securities fraud.

board of directors   The governing body of a corporation, as elected by the shareholders.

board of trustees   Often the name of the governing body of a nonprofit organization. Similar to a board of directors.

bonus plan   An annual program established to regulate the funding and distribution of annual or short-term cash bonus payments. Also referred to as "short-term incentive plan."

book-value stock (BVS)   Stock for which the value is based on book value.

book-value stock option (BVSO)   Options for which the exercise price is based on book value.

broad-banding   A compensation strategy that collapses salary grades or classes into a few salary bands. The bands are usually 70 percent to 150 percent wide and encompass numerous occupational groups at a comparable organizational level. Broad-bands are often used to support skill/competency-based or -influenced pay programs. The effect of broad-banding is to shift the focus from vertical to horizontal career movement and place more responsibility for salary administration at the manager level.

bullet-dodging   Refers to the practice of postponing the grant of options until shortly after the release of negative information, in order to take advantage of a stock price anticipated to be low on the option grant date.

Bureau of Labor Statistics (BLS)   The principal fact-finding agency for the federal government in the broad field of labor economics and statistics. The BLS is a source of certain compensation data, including the Consumer Price Index.

burn rate   The annual rate at which a company issues shares as incentive compensation, expressed as a percentage of its shares outstanding.

buy-sell agreement   An arrangement between two or more parties that obligates one party to buy and another party to sell in accordance with a formula or process; typically used in shareholder agreements of privately held companies to regulate the transfer of shares upon the death, disability, or termination of employment of one or more of the owners.

bylaws A corporation's self-imposed rules governing the management of the corporation, including the election of directors, the appointment and duties of executives, the duties of officers, and other fundamental corporate functions and processes.

cafeteria plan A benefit plan that gives employees a choice from among a number of offered benefits, which usually includes health, disability, retirement, and death benefits and elective programs from which the employee may elect a set dollar amount. Also referred to as a "flexible benefit plan."

call option (call) A derivative security giving the holder the right to buy the underlying securities at a fixed price. An employee stock option is a type of call option, in that the employee has the right to buy the stock at a fixed price for a set number of years (see *put option*).

capital Permanent money invested in a business. Also can mean the long-term assets of a company.

capital asset pricing model (CAPM) A model used to evaluate a publicly held stock. The underlying principle of the model is that investors demand a return that equals the risk-free rate of return plus a nominal risk premium for equity investment times the risk factor (beta) of the particular stock.

capital gain (loss) Profit (or loss) from the sale of a capital asset. Capital gains may be short term (held 12 months or less) or long term (held more than 12 months). Capital losses are used to offset capital gains to establish a net position for tax purposes.

capital loss limitation Net long-term capital losses and net short-term capital losses may be used to offset up to $3,000 of ordinary income.

CAPM Abbreviation for *capital asset pricing model.*

carried interest Total shares in which an owner or option holder has an interest or financial stake in the appreciation of the value of the company.

cash balance pension plan A defined benefit plan that maintains individual employee accounts like a defined contribution plan.

cash flow Total funds that are generated internally for investment and working capital.

cash surrender value The amount that an insurance policyholder is entitled to receive when he or she discontinues coverage.

cashless exercise/same-day sale A brokerage transaction in which an option holder exercises a stock option and simultaneously sells some or all of the shares, with a portion of the sale proceeds delivered to the company by the broker to pay the exercise price and/or tax withholding.

CBOE Abbreviation for *Chicago Board Options Exchange.*

CBOT Abbreviation for *Chicago Board of Trade.*

CEO Abbreviation for *chief executive officer.*

certified public accountant (CPA) An accountant who has met specified professional requirements established by the AICPA and local state societies.

CFO Abbreviation for *chief financial officer.*

change-in-control (CIC) agreement A contractual agreement that provides certain payments or benefits to an employee based on a change in control of the employer. Can be a single-trigger (CIC only) or double-trigger (CIC and termination of employment) arrangement. This is sometimes referred to as a "change-of-control (COC) agreement."

charitable remainder trust Involves the irrevocable transfer of assets, such as company stock, to a trust. The income stream from the assets goes to an individual or individuals (who may include the transferee of the assets); a qualified charity receives the assets at the expiration of the trust period. The contributor of the assets receives a charitable tax deduction at the time of the transfer, equal to the present value of the charity's remainder interest. The transferred property will escape federal estate tax, as it is removed from the donor's estate.

cheap stock Stock options granted to employees at a low exercise price relative to a planned IPO offering price.

Chicago Board of Trade (CBOT) A futures exchange formed in 1948 as a central marketplace for the midwestern grain trade.

Chicago Board Options Exchange (CBOE) Founded in 1973, the CBOE was established for the trading of call options on listed stock.

chief executive officer (CEO) The principal executive officer of a company.

chief financial officer (CFO) The principal financial officer of a company, often placed in charge of accounting, finance, budgeting, tax, and cash management functions of the company.

chief operating officer (COO) The principal operating officer of a company.

CIC or COC Abbreviation for *change in control* or *change of control.* Used interchangeably.

Civil Rights Act Title VII of the Civil Rights Act of 1964, which prohibits discrimination in terms and conditions of employment (including benefits), based on race, color, religion, sex, or national origin.

classified board A corporate board structure in which only a portion of the board of directors is elected each year, often used to discourage takeover attempts.

closing price The last price paid for a security on any trading day.

COBRA Abbreviation for *Consolidated Omnibus Budget Reconciliation Act.*

Code   Abbreviation for *Internal Revenue Code of 1986, as amended.*

coefficient of correlation (r)   Measures the strength of a relationship between the independent and dependent variables in a *regression* (e.g., an element of compensation and revenues). This figure of merit ranges from −1 to 1. A correlation of 0 denotes that there is no relationship between the independent and dependent variables. A correlation of −1 denotes that there is a perfect inverse relationship, and a correlation of +1 denotes that there is a perfect positive relationship.

coefficient of determination (r^2)   Measures the ability of the regression to explain the variance in a regression. It is equal to the square of the coefficient of correlation.

COLA   Abbreviation for *cost-of-living-adjustment.*

COLI   Abbreviation for *corporate-owned life insurance.*

common stock   Units of ownership of a corporation. Common shareholders are typically entitled to vote on the selection of directors and other matters. Distinguished from *preferred stock,* which generally has more favorable dividend and liquidation rights, although often has more limited voting rights.

compa-ratio   An index that helps assess how managers actually pay employees in relation to the midpoint of the pay ranges established for jobs. It estimates how well actual practices correspond to intended policy.

compensable factors   Job attributes that provide the basis for evaluating the relative worth of jobs inside an organization.

compensation   All forms of financial returns and tangible services and benefits employees receive as part of an employment relationship. Compensation elements include salary, bonus, long-term incentive, health and welfare benefits, pension entitlements, and perquisites.

compensation committee   At many companies, a committee of the board of directors, generally made up of outside directors, that is responsible for executive compensation matters, including stock plans.

competency   Basic units of knowledge and abilities employees are expected to acquire or demonstrate in order to successfully perform their duties, satisfy customers, and achieve business objectives.

compression   Narrow pay differentials among jobs at different levels as a result of wages for jobs filled from the outside increasing faster than the internal pay structure.

Consolidated Omnibus Budget Reconciliation Act (COBRA)   A federal law requiring employers with more than 20 employees to offer terminated or retired employees the opportunity to continue their health insurance coverage for 18 months at the employee's expense. Coverage may be extended to the employee's dependents for up to 36 months in certain circumstances.

constructive receipt   Refers to the time that compensation is taxable to the employee because he or she has control over and access to the payment.

constructive sale   Tax term referring to when the IRS recharacterizes as a sale a transaction that eliminates the risk of loss and the opportunity for gain.

Consumer Price Index (CPI)   An index published by the Bureau of Labor Statistics U.S. Department of Labor. The CPI measures the changes in prices of a fixed basket of goods and services purchased by a typical average family.

control stock   Stock held by affiliates of the corporation; a term used under Rule 144.

COO   Abbreviation for *chief operating officer.*

corporate owned life insurance (COLI)   An insurance policy of which an organization is the owner and beneficiary. Should the insured executive die while covered, the company pays a comparable noninsured sum to selected survivors. Policy loans associated with the insurance typically are accessible to the organization.

cost of living adjustment (COLA)   Across-the-board wage and salary increases or supplemental payments based on changes in some index of prices, usually the Consumer Price Index.

Council of Institutional Investors   Founded in 1985, the Council of Institutional Investors (CII) is an organization of large public, Taft-Hartley and corporate pension funds formed to address investment issues that affect the size or security of plan assets.

covered employee   Under Internal Revenue Code Section 162(m)(3), any employee of a company who, as of the close of a taxable year, is the CEO of the company (or an individual acting in such capacity), or whose total compensation for the taxable year is required to be reported to shareholders under the Securities Exchange Act of 1934 by reason of such employee being among the four highest compensated officers for the taxable year. May change to coincide with 2006 changes to the definition of "named executive officers" for proxy reporting purposes.

CPA   Abbreviation for *certified public accountant.*

CPI   Abbreviation for *Consumer Price Index.*

credited service   A length of employment prior to or subsequent to the effective plan date that is recognized as service for plan purposes. This would include such issues as determination of benefit amounts, benefits entitlement, and/or vesting.

cumulative voting   A method of stock voting that permits shareholders to cast all votes for one candidate. A voting system that gives minority shareholders more power, by allowing them to cast all of their board-of-director votes for a single candidate, as opposed to regular or statutory voting, in which shareholders must vote for a different candidate for each available seat.

current ratio Current assets divided by current liabilities. This ratio measures liquidity as it measures a company's ability to pay current liabilities from current assets.

CUSIP The trademark for a system that uniquely identifies securities trading in the United States. It was developed in the late 1960s by the American Bankers Association as a way to standardize the identification and tracking of securities. The CUSIP number consists of nine digits—the first six identify the issuer and the last three identify the issue. CUSIP numbers are a trademark of the American Bankers Association.

Davis-Bacon Act of 1931 Requires most federal contractors to pay wage rates prevailing in the area where the work is performed.

DCF Abbreviation for *discounted cash flow.*

dead-hand poison pill An anti-takeover device designed to prevent the acquisition of a company even if a majority of shareholders favor the acquisition. Dead-hand poison pills can be removed only by incumbent directors or their chosen successors.

deferred compensation Compensation as to which a service provider incurs a legally binding right in one year to be received in a future year. Under Code Section 409A, deferred compensation is defined very broadly to include certain types of severance pay and equity compensation arrangements.

defined-benefit pension plan A pension plan that promises to pay a specified amount to a service provider who retires after certain age and years of service.

defined-contribution pension plan A pension plan in which the retirement benefit consists of cumulative contributions may by the service recipient and/or the service provider over a number of years.

Department of Labor (DOL) A department in the U.S. executive branch, responsible for the administration and enforcement of more than 180 federal statutes. In specific, the DOL protects workers' wages, health and safety, employment and pension rights; equal employment opportunity; job training, unemployment insurance, and workers' compensation programs. It also collects, analyzes, and publishes labor and economic statistics.

Depository Trust Company (DTC) The world's largest securities depository, with more than $10 trillion of securities in custody. DTC is a national clearinghouse for the settlement of trade in corporate and municipal securities and performs securities custody-related services for its participating banks and broker-dealers.

derivative security An option, warrant, convertible security, stock appreciation right, or similar right with an exercise or conversion privilege at a price related to an *equity security,* or similar securities with a value derived from the value of an equity security.

dilution Refers to the effect that the grant of equity awards has upon the other shareholders of a company. For example, each time an option is granted, an existing shareholder's ownership interest in the company is potentially reduced, because at exercise, the value of the stock is greater than the cash paid to exercise the option. In effect, this results in a transfer of economic value from existing shareholders to the option holder.

direct compensation Pay received directly in the form of cash (e.g., salary and annual bonus).

directors and officers (D&O) liability insurance Professional liability coverage for legal expenses and liability to shareholders, bondholders, creditors, or others due to actions or omissions by a director or officer of a corporation or nonprofit organization.

discount stock option The opposite of premium options; discount stock options have an exercise price *below* market value at the time of grant.

discounted cash flow (DCF) Present value of future expected cash flow of a company.

discretionary bonus An incentive award made on a purely subjective basis, not based on a performance-related formula or specific measurable criteria.

disqualifying disposition (of incentive stock options) A sale, gift, or exchange of ISO shares within two years from the grant date or one year from the exercise date. Upon a disqualifying disposition, the employee recognizes taxable ordinary income, and the company is entitled to claim a deduction equal to the excess of the fair market value on the exercise date or the sale price, whichever is lower, over the exercise price.

dividend The payment designated by the board of directors to be distributed pro rata among the shares outstanding.

dividend equivalent rights The right to be credited with cash or additional shares under an equity award, such as restricted stock units, for the value of dividends that the company has paid on its shares while the award is outstanding.

DJIA Abbreviation for *Dow Jones Industrial Average.*

D&O Abbreviation for directors & officers. Usually used in context of *D&O liability insurance.*

DOL Abbreviation for *Department of Labor.*

dollar cost averaging A system of buying securities at regular intervals with a fixed dollar amount. Under this system, investors buy by the dollars' worth rather than by the number of shares. If each investment is of the same number of dollars, payments buy more shares when the price is low and fewer when it rises. Temporary downswings in price benefit investors if they continue periodic purchases in both good times and bad and the price at which the shares are sold is more than their average cost.

double trigger   A term used in connection with a change in control of ownership; refers to how a CIC, together with a subsequent event, such as termination of the employee by the company or termination by the employee for good reason, might trigger severance payments or other benefits. A *double* trigger means that vesting or payment will not occur until the second event takes place.

Dow Jones Industrial Average (DJIA)   An index used to measure the performance of the U.S. financial markets. Introduced on May 26, 1896, by Charles H. Dow, it is the oldest stock price measure in continuous use. Over the past century, "the Dow" has become the most widely recognized stock market indicator in the United States and probably in the world.

DTC   Abbreviation for *Depository Trust Company.*

due diligence   An investigation into the financial, legal, and business affairs of a company undertaken by underwriters and their counsel prior to a public offering by the company, or by the buyer in the purchase of a company.

early exercisable options   Options that are immediately exercisable (i.e., before vesting), but that typically do not start vesting until six months to a year after grant. The underlying shares received at exercise are restricted and subject to a repurchase right by the company at the exercise price until they are vested. Early exercise starts the capital gain clock ticking for a later resale. No gains are realized on the spread from the option exercise until vesting or until a Section 83(b) election is filed. Sometimes referred to as *reverse vesting.*

earnings before interest and taxes (EBIT)   All profits (operating and nonoperating) before deduction of interest and income taxes.

earnings before interest, taxes, depreciation, and amortization (EBITDA)   Concerns the cash flow of a company; by not including interest, taxes, depreciation, and amortization, one can see clearly the amount of money a company is bringing in.

earnings per share (EPS)   Net income for the fiscal year divided by the total number of shares outstanding, with adjustments for common stock equivalents.

EBIT   Abbreviation for *earnings before interest and taxes.*

EBITDA   Abbreviation for earnings before interest, taxes, depreciation, and amortization.

EBP   Abbreviation for *excess benefit plan.*

economic indicator   A key statistic in the overall economy that may be used as a yardstick to predict the performance of the stock market.

economic profit   A calculation of profits that exceed the expected return to shareholders. Normally calculated by subtracting the cost of capital from an adjusted profit number. Many variations of the calculation exist.

economic value added (EVA)   A concept copyrighted by Stern Stewart & Co. EVA is net operating profit minus an appropriate charge for the opportunity cost of all capital invested in an enterprise. As such, EVA is an estimate of true "economic" profit, or the amount by which earnings exceed or fall short of the required minimum rate of return that shareholders and lenders could get by investing in other securities of comparable risk.

EDGAR—electronic data gathering, analysis, and retrieval system The system through which companies electronically file reports and registration statements with the SEC. Allows public access to SEC filings on the Internet.

EEOC Abbreviation for *Equal Employment Opportunity Commission.*

EITF Abbreviation for *Emerging Issues Task Force.*

Emerging Issues Task Force (EITF) Organization affiliated with FASB that addresses new and emerging accounting issues. The EITF was formed in 1984 in response to the recommendations of the FASB's task force on timely financial reporting guidance and an FASB Invitation to Comment on those recommendations.

employee stock purchase plan (ESPP) A type of broad-based plan that permits employees to purchase stock of the company, usually at a discount price and by payroll deduction. ESPPs may or may not qualify as tax-advantaged plans under Section 423 of the Code.

employment agreement A legal agreement between a company and an executive that sets forth the terms and conditions of employment, often including severance arrangements.

EPA Abbreviation for *Equal Pay Act.*

EPS Abbreviation for *earnings per share.*

Equal Employment Opportunity Commission (EEOC) A commission of the federal government charged with enforcing the provision of the Civil Rights Act of 1964 and the EPA of 1963 as it pertains to sex discrimination in pay.

Equal Pay Act (EPA) of 1963 An amendment to the Fair Labor Standards Act of 1936, prohibiting pay differentials on jobs that are substantially equal in terms of skills, efforts, responsibility, and working conditions, except when the variances are the result of bona fide seniority, merit, or production-based systems, or any other job-related factor other than gender.

equity collar Hedging strategy involving offsetting puts and calls on an equity position, often used to diversify concentrated stock positions. The collar can be structured so that the premium received for the sale of the call and the money paid for purchase of the put net each other out (a "zero-cost" collar). This strategy allows an executive to hold stock after an option exercise for long-term capital gains, minimizes the risk of stock price fluctuations, finances the cost of the put (zero-cost collar), or brings in more or less cash than the cost of the put.

equity incentive plan   For purposes of Item 402 of Regulation S-K, an incentive plan or portion of an incentive plan under which awards are granted that fall within the scope of FAS 123R.

equity security   An ownership interest in a company. Common and preferred stock are types of equity securities. Equity securities can be distinguished from debt securities, such as bonds, and from derivative securities, such as stock options.

ERISA   Abbreviation for *Employee Retirement Income Security Act of 1974.*

ERISA excess plan   A type of pension plan for key executives to restore benefits that were reduced by the enactment of ERISA. The company makes up the difference between what an executive accrues under the company pension plan and the amount he or she is allowed to receive under ERISA restrictions.

ESOP   Abbreviation for *employee stock ownership plan.*

ESPP   Abbreviation for *employee stock purchase plan.*

European option   A stock option that may be exercised only on its expiration date.

EVA   Abbreviation for *economic value added.*

evergreen agreement   An agreement that does not expire. The agreement is usually automatically renewed if not canceled by a certain date each year.

evergreen stock option reserve   An employee stock plan funding mechanism that authorizes annual increases (generally expressed as a percentage of outstanding common stock) to the number of shares available for stock grants and awards.

excess benefit plan   See *ERISA excess plan.*

ex-dividend   A synonym for "without dividend." The buyer of an ex-dividend stock is not entitled to the next dividend payment. Dividends are paid on a set date to all those shareholders recorded on the books of the company as of a previous date of record. For example, a dividend may be declared as payable to stockholders of record on a given Friday. Since three business days are allowed for delivery of stock in a regular transaction on the New York Stock Exchange, the NYSE would declare the stock "ex-dividend" as of the opening of the market on the preceding Wednesday. That means anyone who bought it on or after that Wednesday would not be entitled to that dividend. When stocks go ex-dividend, the stock tables include the symbol "x" following the name.

executive perquisite   Special benefit made available to executives (and sometimes other managerial employees). May be taxable income to the employee. Company-related perquisites may include company-paid club memberships, first-class air travel, use of corporate aircraft, company car, home computer, cellular phone, and other amenities related to work. Personal perquisites include such items as personal tax planning and legal counsel. Since 1978, the IRS has required companies to value these special benefits and require executives to pay tax on the imputed income associated with the benefit.

exercisable   Describes options that, because of the passage of time or the meeting of specified performance targets, have vested and may now be exercised by the option holder. Options often become exercisable in increments over time.

exercise   The act of acquiring the underlying securities subject to a stock option by paying the exercise price.

exercise period   The period during which specific stock options are available for exercise (usually the period between the vesting date and the option expiration date).

expatriate   Employee assigned outside of the base country for any period of time in excess of one year.

face value   Refers to the number of shares times the share price. For example, 100 shares at $50 per share have a face value of $5,000.

Fair Labor Standards Act of 1936 (FLSA)   A federal law that establishes minimum wage, overtime pay, recordkeeping, and child labor standards. FLSA applies to enterprises that have employees who are engaged in interstate commerce; producing goods for interstate commerce; or handling, selling, or working on goods or materials that have been moved in or produced for interstate commerce.

fair market value (FMV)   The value that would as closely as possible approximate the value of a particular instrument or share of stock as determined by a willing buyer and a willing seller in an arms' length transaction. For public companies, FMV is often determined by, or based on, the quoted market price. With a private company, the fair market value measure is more subjective, and often may be based on a recent round of financing or set by an outside valuation.

fair value   The amount for which an asset could be bought or sold in a current transaction between willing parties; that is, other than in a forced liquidation sale. Quoted market prices in active markets are the best evidence of fair value and are to be used as the basis for measurement, if available. If quoted market prices are not available, the estimate of fair value is based on the best information available. The estimate of fair value considers prices for similar amounts and the results of valuation techniques to the extent available. Examples of valuation techniques include the present value of estimated future cash flows using a discount rate commensurate with the risks involved, option-pricing models, matrix pricing, option-adjusted spread models, and fundamental analysis. As used in FAS 123R with respect to share-based payments, "fair value" mean the value of equity award based on an accepted valuation model, such as Black-Scholes or a binomial option pricing model in the case of an option or stock appreciation right.

Family Medical Leave Act (FMLA) of 1993   Entitles an eligible employee to receive unpaid leave of up to 12 weeks per year for specified family or medical reasons, such as caring for ill family members or adopting a child.

FAS   Abbreviation for *Financial Accounting Statement*.

FAS 123R   Abbreviation for Financial Accounting Standards Board Statement of Financial Accounting Standards No.123 (revised 2004), "Share-Based Payments," as modified or supplemented.

FASB   Abbreviation for *Financial Accounting Standards Board.*

Federal Insurance Contributions Act (FICA)   The statute that established social security contribution withholding requirements. The FICA payments are made equally by the employer and employee.

Federal Unemployment Tax Act (FUTA)   A law enacted more than 60 years ago to guarantee financing for a national employment security system. The idea was that employers would pay the cost of administering the new unemployment compensation system, along with a national job placement system, to help them recruit new workers and to get laid-off workers and unemployment compensation claimants into new jobs as quickly as possible. FUTA is administered by the DOL.

FICA   Abbreviation for *Federal Insurance Contributions Act.*

Financial Accounting Standards Board (FASB)   An organization that develops accounting standards on a wide range of financial topics, including stock compensation. Since 1973, the FASB has been the designated organization in the private sector for establishing standards of financial accounting and reporting. Those standards govern the preparation of financial reports. These accounting standards are officially recognized as authoritative by the Securities and Exchange Commission (Financial Reporting Release No. 1, Section 101) and the American Institute of Certified Public Accountants (Rule 203, Rules of Conduct, as amended May 1973 and May 1979).

Financial Accounting Statement No. 123 (FAS 123)   Accounting standard that originally recommended expensing of all stock-based compensation using stock fair market value to value stock awards and a recognized option-pricing model (typically Black-Scholes) to value options. FAS 123, however, was not mandatory, and companies could elect to continue to expense stock-based compensations under APB 25. In its revised form, beginning in 2006, FAS 123R became the mandatory method for accounting for share-based payments, including stock options.

financial statements   The balance sheet, income statement, statement of changes in financial position, statement of changes in owners' equity accounts, and notes thereto.

fiscal year   Any consecutive 12-month period of financial accountability for a corporation or government.

fixed accounting   A method of accounting for share-based employee compensation under which a nonvarying charge to earnings is recorded and amortized over the service period. FAS 123R uses the term *fixed award* in a somewhat different sense than APB Opinion 25, which distinguishes between fixed awards and variable awards. FAS 123R distinguishes between fixed awards and liabilities.

fixed award   See *fixed accounting.*

fixed grant guidelines   Guidelines under which a company determines grant size according to a set number of shares or a set percentage of shares outstanding rather than a value for the shares granted.

FLSA   Abbreviation for *Fair Labor Standards Act of 1936.*

FMLA   Abbreviation for *Family Medical Leave Act of 1993.*

FMV   Abbreviation for *fair market value.*

Form 3   The initial form filed with the SEC pursuant to Section 16(a) of the Securities Exchange Act of 1934 by directors, officers, and 10 percent owners to report initial holdings in company equity securities.

Form 4   Form filed with the SEC to report changes in an insider's beneficial ownership of shares of a public company, such as a purchase or sale.

Form 5   Year-end form filed with the SEC pursuant to Section 16(a) of the Securities Exchange Act of 1934 to report certain transactions exempt from Form 4 reporting and any changes not previously reported by the insider on Form 3 or Form 4.

Form 8-K   A current report required to be filed with the SEC to publicly disclose certain material corporate events, such as a change in control, a significant acquisition, a bankruptcy, a change in the company's fiscal year or accounting firms, changes in management, and certain developments in management compensation.

Form 10-K   Annual report required to be filed with the SEC after the end of the fiscal year. The 10-K includes a description of the company's business and properties, the audited financial statements, and management's discussion and analysis (MD&A) of the financials.

Form 10-Q   Quarterly report required to be filed with the SEC after the end of each of the first three fiscal quarters. Form 10-Q is less comprehensive than the Form 10-K annual report and does not require that financial statements be audited. It covers the specific quarter and the year to date.

Form 144   The notice of sale required when an executive officer, director, or other affiliate of a company sells that company's stock. It must be filed with the SEC at the time an order is placed with a broker to sell the stock. Form 144 is not required if both the number of shares does not exceed 500 *and* the aggregate sale price does not exceed $10,000.

Form 1099-B   Form provided by a broker detailing the amount received from securities sales, such as the proceeds from a cashless exercise. This amount, along with the person's tax basis, is used to calculate gain or loss for tax purposes on Schedule D.

Form 1099-MISC   Tax form provided to nonemployees (e.g., consultants, independent contractors) that reports income/compensation.

Form S-1   A registration statement under the Securities Act of 1933, which a company files with the SEC to register its stock for sale. Form S-1 is generally the form used by a private company that is going public. It contains the prospectus, along with a number of exhibits and other information about the company. The SEC staff reviews the Form S-1 and provides comments that must be resolved with the staff before the public offering can go forward.

Form S-3   A shorter form of registration statement than the Form S-1 that can be used by certain already-public companies to sell additional shares. It is also the form most often used to cover resales of restricted securities by selling shareholders.

Form S-4   A form of registration statement used when a company is issuing its shares in connection with a merger or acquisition.

Form S-8   A brief form of registration statement filed with the SEC to register shares to be issued under an employee benefit plan. Does not require filing of a prospectus.

Form W-2   See *W-2*.

Form W-8   See *W-8*.

Form W-9   See *W-9*.

formula plan   A plan in which both the recipients and the number of shares to be granted are set by the terms of the plan itself rather than being left to the discretion of the compensation committee.

formula-value stock   Simulated stock, also called *phantom stock*, used to measure the performance of companies or business units that do not have publicly traded shares. The value of the stock is determined by a formula.

founders' stock   A pre-IPO stock grant.

fundamental research   Analysis of industries and companies based on such factors as sales, assets, earnings, products or services, markets, and management. As applied to the economy, fundamental research includes consideration of gross national product, interest rates, unemployment, inventories, savings, and so forth.

funding formula   The performance level required, as defined by the board, for bonuses to be paid and the percentage of profits above the threshold that will go toward bonuses.

FUTA   Abbreviation for *Federal Unemployment Tax Act.*

going public   When a privately held company first offers its shares to the investing public; also known as an IPO or initial public offering.

golden bungee   Refers to executive "severance" benefits after a change in control of ownership when the executive agrees to stay with the new organization and receive additional pay in various forms.

golden handcuffs   Refers to compensation and benefits that could be lost upon voluntary termination of the executive.

golden hello   See *sign-on bonus.*

golden parachute   A phrase commonly used to refer to a severance arrangement between a company and an employee that provides benefits triggered by termination of employment in connection with a change in control of the company.

grant   The issuance of an award under a stock plan, such as a stock option or shares of restricted stock.

grant date   The date on which a stock award is granted. For purposes of Item 402 of Regulation S-K, the term grant date refers to the grant date determined for financial statement reporting purposes pursuant to FAS 123R.

grant multiple   The multiple of aggregate stock option award (options shares times option exercise price) as a function of the grantee's salary.

grant price   The price per share at which a stock option is granted and that must be paid to exercise the stock option. The grant price is typically the fair market value of the stock on the date of grant. Also known as the *exercise price* or *strike price.*

hedging   Investments made in an attempt to reduce the risk of adverse price fluctuations in a security, by taking an offsetting position in a related security.

hold   Refers to an exercise transaction in which the option holder holds the shares received upon exercise (rather than selling them for cash).

immaculate option exercise   A form of cashless exercise in which the option exercise price is paid by instructing the company to withhold from the total number of shares issuable upon an option exercise a number of shares equal to the exercise price. The option holder is left with just the number of shares equal to the option spread. The effect is the same as a stock-settled stock appreciation right.

imputed interest   Interest that the IRS assumes has been paid on a loan if the stated interest is below a minimum interest rate (the applicable federal rate).

incentive plan   For purposes of Item 402 of Regulation S-K, the term incentive plan means any plan providing compensation intended to serve as incentive for performance to occur over a specified period, whether such performance is measured by reference to financial performance of the company or an affiliate, the company's stock price or any other performance measure.

incentive stock option (ISO)   A stock option that has met certain tax requirements that entitle the option holder to favorable tax treatment. Such an option is free from regular tax at the date of grant and the date of exercise (when a nonqualified option would become taxable). If two holding-period tests are met (two years after the date and one year after the exercise date), the profit on the option qualifies as a long-term capital gain rather than ordinary income. If the holding periods are not met, there has been a disqualifying disposition, and the holder incurs ordinary income.

indexed stock option   Option that has an exercise price which may fluctuate *above* or *below* market value at grant, depending on the company's stock price performance relative to a specified index (e.g., the Standard & Poors 500 Stock Index) or the movement of the index itself. Indexed options differ from performance options in that the exercise price of indexed options typically remains variable until the option is exercised. Indexed options will rarely be used now that Code Section 409A applies to discounted options.

Individual Retirement Account (IRA)   An individual pension fund that anyone may open with a bank. An IRA permits investment of contributed funds, through intermediaries such as mutual funds, insurance companies, and banks; or directly in stocks and bonds, through stockbrokers. Because it is intended for retirement, money in an IRA enjoys many tax advantages over traditional investments, but may not be withdrawn early without heavy penalty fees.

initial public offering   The process of first issuing a company's stock to the public in a registered public offering.

insider   An officer, director, or principal shareholder of a publicly owned company and members of his or her immediate family. The term may also include other people who obtain nonpublic information about a company and owe a duty not to use it for personal gain.

insider trading   Trading in a company's securities by company insiders or others while in possession of material, nonpublic information.

Insider Trading and Securities Fraud Enforcement Act of 1988   Federal legislation that greatly increased the penalties for trading on material inside information.

installment exercise   A form of stock option exercise right that can be executed at certain times and with certain limits during its term.

institutional investor   Organization whose primary purpose is to invest its own assets or those entrusted to it by others. The most common such investors are employee pension funds, insurance companies, mutual funds, university endowments, and banks.

internal equity   Refers to the pay relationships among jobs or skill levels within a single organization and focuses attention on employee and management acceptance of those relationships. It involves establishing equal pay for jobs of equal worth and acceptable pay differentials for jobs of unequal worth.

Internal Revenue Service (IRS)   U.S. agency charged with collecting federal taxes, including personal and corporate income taxes, social security taxes, and excise, estate, and gift taxes. The IRS administers the rules and regulations that are the responsibility of the U.S. Treasury Department and investigates and prosecutes (through the U.S. Tax Court) tax illegalities.

intrinsic value The difference between the exercise price and/or strike price of an option and the market value of the underlying security.

Investment Advisers Act of 1940 This act, which falls under the purview of the SEC, regulates investment advisers. With certain exceptions, this act requires that firms or sole practitioners compensated for advising others about securities investments must register with the SEC and conform to regulations designed to protect investors.

investment bank Also known as underwriter; investment banks serve as intermediaries between corporations issuing new securities and the buying public. Normally one or more investment banks buy the new issue of securities from the issuing company for a negotiated price. The company retains this new supply of capital, while the investment banks form a syndicate and resell the issue to their customer base and the investing public. Investment banks perform a variety of other financial services, such as merger and acquisition advice and market analysis.

Investment Company Act of 1940 This act, which falls under the purview of the SEC, regulates the organization of companies, including mutual funds that engage primarily in investing, reinvesting, and trading in securities and whose own securities are offered to the investing public. The regulation is designed to minimize conflicts of interest that arise in these complex operations. The act requires these companies to disclose their financial condition and investment policies to investors when stock is initially sold and, subsequently, on a regular basis.

IRA Abbreviation for *individual retirement account.*

IRC Abbreviation for *Internal Revenue Code.*

irrevocable trust Trust that cannot be changed or terminated by the one who created it without the agreement of the beneficiary of the trust.

IRS Abbreviation for *Internal Revenue Service.*

ISO Abbreviation for *incentive stock option.*

job evaluation The process for determining the relative worth of a position within an organization based on the factors valued by the organization. The end result of the job evaluation process is the assignment of jobs to some form of pay hierarchy.

job family A collection of jobs that have common skills, occupational qualifications, technology, working conditions, and so on. Often, a job family represents increasingly complex levels of a job.

joint and survivor (J&S) annuity A common form of pension plan payout, which pays over the life of the retiree and his or her spouse after the retiree dies.

J&S   Abbreviation for *joint & survivor*.

junior stock   Stock with limited or no voting stock or dividend rights; convertible into regular common stock if performance goals (or other stated events such an initial public offering) are met.

Labor-Management Reporting and Disclosure Act   Law dealing with the relationship between a union and its members. It safeguards union funds and requires reports on certain financial transactions and administrative practices of union officials, labor consultants, and the like. The Office of Labor-Management Standards administers the act, which is part of the Employment Standards Administration. This act is also known as the *Landrum-Griffin Act*.

LCN   Abbreviation for *Local Country National*.

legend   A notice on a stock certificate that the shares represented by that certificate are restricted in some manner.

leverage   Any means of increasing value and return by borrowing funds or committing less of one's own. For corporations, it refers to the ratio of debt (in the form of bonds and preferred stock outstanding) to equity (in the form of common stock outstanding) in the company's capital structure. The more long-term debt there is, the greater the financial leverage. Shareholders benefit from this financial leverage to the extent that the return on the borrowed money exceeds the interest costs of borrowing it. Because of this effect, financial leverage is popularly called "trading on the equity." For individuals, leverage can involve debt, as when an investor borrows money from a broker on margin and so is able to buy more stock than he or she otherwise could. If the stock goes up, the investor repays the broker the loan amount and keeps the profit. By borrowing money, the investor has achieved a higher return on his or her investment than if he or she had paid for all the stock personally. Rights, warrants, and option contracts also provide leverage, not through debt but by offering the prospect of a high return for little or no investment.

leveraged stock option   Often used after the restructure of a corporation; the company will match some multiple of stock options to the employee's purchase of a fixed number of shares (e.g., company provides four options for one share purchased).

liquidity   (1) The ability to convert an asset into cash quickly and without any price discount. (2) The ability of the market in a particular security to absorb a reasonable amount of buying or selling at reasonable price changes.

limited offering   Sales of securities exempt from registration pursuant to certain exemptions that limit the size of the offering and the number of purchasers.

limited stock appreciation right (LSAR)   Similar to a SAR, but only exercisable in the case of a change in control or up to a certain value. Usually granted in tandem with a stock option.

listed stock   The stock of a company that is listed for trading on a securities exchange.

living trust   A trust created by a person during his or her lifetime.

Local Country Nationals (LCNs)   Citizens of countries in which a U.S. foreign subsidiary is located. LCNs' compensation is tied either to local wage rates or to the rate of U.S. expatriates performing the same job. Each practice of paying LCNs has different internal equity and external equity implications.

lock-up   An agreement between investment bankers and the companies that they take public. This agreement restricts the resale of shares owned by founders, employees, and venture capitalists immediately after the IPO. Typically lasts for 180 days, but could last for a shorter or longer period.

look-back feature   Option provision typically used in a Code Section 423 employee stock purchase plan (ESPP). The purchase price (with or without a discount) is based on the *lower* of the market price at the beginning or end of the purchase period (a typical plan purchase period might run for six months). For example, for a plan with a look-back feature and a 15 percent discount, if the stock price is $10 at the beginning of the purchase period and goes up to $20 at the end, the purchase price is just $8.50 ($10–15 percent).

margin   The amount paid by the customer when using a broker's credit to buy or sell a security.

market share   Sales of a particular product or product line as a percentage of total sales of the product or product line.

material information   Information that would affect a reasonable investor's decision to buy or sell a security if the information was known to him or her. Examples might include a corporate takeover, a divestiture, significant management changes, and new product introductions.

mean   The sum of a set of data reported divided by the number of observations. Also referred to as the average.

measurement date   When the fair value of a stock-based employee award is known and fixed, according to current FASB rules, the first date on which the stock award can be measured. It is the first date on which both the number of shares and the option or purchase price are known.

median   The middle value of a variable in a distribution of numbers. Thus, the median of (1, 2, 3, 10, and 100) is 3. The mean (or average) of these values is 23.2. The median is generally preferred to the mean as a measure of typical values, because extreme values (very high or very low) will tend to skew the mean.

mega-grant   An exceptionally large share-based award.

monetize   To convert illiquid value such as stock option spread to cash. See *hedging, costless collar,* and *zero premium collar.*

mutual fund A portfolio of stocks, bonds, or other securities administered by a team of one or more managers from an investment company who make buy and sell decisions on component securities. Capital is contributed by smaller investors who buy shares in the mutual fund rather than the individual stocks and bonds in its portfolio. The return on the fund's holdings is distributed back to its contributors, or shareholders, minus various fees and commissions. This system allows small investors to participate in the reduced risk of a large and diverse portfolio that they could not otherwise build themselves. They also have the benefit of professional managers overseeing their money who have the time and expertise to analyze and pick securities.

named executive officers (NEOs) The CEO, CFO, and next three highest paid executive officers of a public company, whose compensation is reflected in the company's annual proxy statement, pursuant to SEC disclosure requirements.

National Association of Securities Dealers (NASD) An association of securities broker/dealers, including all of the major brokerage firms as members. The NASD establishes uniform practices in the securities industry for trading in the over-the-counter market in order to protect investors. The NASDR is the regulatory arm of the NASD.

NASDAQ The NASDAQ Stock Market.

national market system A system mandated by the Securities Act Amendments of 1975.

Eight markets—the American, Boston, Cincinnati, Chicago, New York, Pacific, Philadelphia, and NASD over-the-counter markets—are linked electronically by computers. This allows traders at any exchange to seek the best available price on all other exchanges that a particular security is eligible to trade on. The national market system also includes a consolidated electronic tape, which combines last-sale prices from all markets into a single stream of information.

negative discretion Provision in an incentive plan that permits the compensation committee to reduce, but not to increase, an employee's formula-generated bonus payment.

New York Stock Exchange (NYSE) Oldest (established in 1792) and largest securities exchange in the United States. Liquidity in the NYSE auction market system is provided by individual and institutional investors, member firms trading for their own accounts, and assigned specialists. The NYSE is linked with other markets trading listed securities through the Intermarket Trading System (ITS). NYSE-assigned dealers, known as specialists, are responsible for maintaining a fair and orderly market in the securities assigned to them. Most trading, however, is conducted by brokers acting on behalf of customers, rather than by dealers trading for their own account. For this reason, the NYSE is often described as an agency auction market. The interaction of natural buyers and sellers determines the price of an NYSE-listed stock.

nonequity incentive plan   This term has a specialized meaning for purposes of Item 402 of Regulation S-K: a non-equity incentive plan is an incentive plan or portion of an incentive plan that is not an equity incentive plan. See *incentive plan* and *equity incentive plan*.

nonqualified deferred compensation plan   A nonqualified plan is an employer-sponsored retirement or other deferred compensation plan that does not meet the tax-qualification requirements under the Code. Under Code Section 409A (effective in 2005), nonqualified deferred compensation is defined very broadly to include certain types of severance pay and equity compensation arrangements.

nonqualified stock option (NQSO)   An employee stock option not meeting the IRS criteria for ISOs (incentive stock options) and therefore triggering a tax upon exercise. This type of option requires withholding of state and federal income tax, Medicare, and FICA/FUTA on the excess of the fair market value over the exercise price on the exercise date. Also referred to as a *nonstatutory stock option (NSO)*.

NQSO   Abbreviation for *nonqualified stock option*.

NSO   Abbreviation for *nonstatutory stock option*.

NYSE   Abbreviation for *New York Stock Exchange*.

NYSE Composite Index   A market-value weighted index of all stocks on the NYSE. The Composite Index consists of all common stocks listed on the NYSE and four subgroup indexes—Industrial, Transportation, Utility, and Finance.

Occupational Safety and Health Act (OSH Act)   The law administered by the Occupational Safety and Health Administration (OSHA). Safety and health conditions in most private industries are regulated by OSHA or OSHA-approved state systems.

off-hours trading   Trading that takes place after the close of the regular session. In June 1991, the NYSE introduced off-hours trading in the form of two post-4:00 PM crosses. Crossing Session I introduced a 5:00 PM cross in individual stocks at the NYSE regular day closing price; Crossing Session II facilitates the crossing of portfolios until 5:15 PM.

omnibus incentive plan   An incentive plan that provides the flexibility to use a number of equity and non-equity incentive vehicles, such as stock options, stock appreciation rights, restricted stock, performance shares, performance units and cash awards. A list of performance measures often is included in such a plan to satisfy Code Section 162(m) purposes.

option   The legal right to purchase shares at a fixed price at designed time or period in the future. For purposes of Item 402 of Regulation S-K, the term *option* is used to describe all instruments with option-like features, such as stock options and stock appreciation rights.

option holder   A person who has been granted a stock option. Also referred to as an *optionee*.

option spread   The amount by which the value of stock underlying an option grant exceeds the exercise price. The aggregate spread is determined by multiplying the number of shares by the amount by which the market price per share exceeds the option's exercise price per share. Also referred to as *intrinsic value*.

optionee   A person who has been granted a stock option. Also referred to as an *option holder*.

out-of-the-money   A term used to describe an employee stock option when the current market price is below the option exercise price. When an option is out of the money, it would cost more than the underlying stock is worth to exercise the option. Such options are also described as being *underwater*.

outside director   A board member who is neither a current employee nor a former employee. Also refers to a director who meets the independence requirements under Code Section 162(m).

over the counter   A market, including NASDAQ, in which securities transactions are conducted through a computer network connecting dealers in stocks and bonds, rather than on the floor of an exchange.

OWBPA   Abbreviation for *Older Workers Benefit Protection Act.*

ownership guidelines   Requirements at some companies that executives, directors, and key employees own a specified amount of company stock so that their financial interests are clearly aligned with those of shareholders. The most commonly used guidelines require stock ownership with a value based on some multiple of salary (e.g., 3 × salary). A minority of companies express ownership as a specific number of shares. The guidelines are usually tiered by position so that the CEO has the highest-level ownership requirement.

PARSAP   Abbreviation for *performance-accelerated restricted stock award plan.*

pay differential   Pay differences among levels within the organization, such as the difference in pay between adjacent levels in career path, between supervisors and subordinates, and between executive and nonexecutive employees.

penny stocks   Low-priced issues, often highly speculative, selling at less than $1 a share.

performance condition (performance award)   An award of stock-based employee compensation for which vesting depends on both (a) an employee's rendering services to the employer for a specified period of time, and (b) the achievement of a specified performance target. A performance condition may pertain either to the performance of the enterprise as a whole or to some part of the enterprise, such as a division.

performance share   Grants of actual shares of stock or phantom stock whose payment is contingent on performance as measured against predetermined objectives over a period of time; same as performance units except that the value paid fluctuates with stock price changes as well as performance against objectives. Payout may be settled in cash or stock.

performance stock option   Options for which some aspect of vesting or exercise price is subject to specified performance criteria.

performance unit   Similar to performance shares, except that payments are not necessarily related to stock price and units are earned on the basis of internal financial performance measures. Payout may be settled in cash or stock.

performance-accelerated restricted stock award plan (PARSAP)   Also known as *performance-accelerated restricted stock* (PARS) and *time-accelerated restricted stock award plans* (TARSAPs). Grants of restricted stock or restricted stock units that may vest early upon attainment of specified performance objectives. Otherwise, a time-vesting schedule would remain in effect.

performance-based compensation   Under Code Section 162(m)(4)(C), remuneration that is payable solely on account of the attainment of one or more performance goals, but only if the performance goals are determined by a compensation committee of the board of directors, which is comprised solely of two or more "outside directors," the material terms under which the remuneration is to be paid (including the performance goals) are disclosed to and approved by stockholders, and the compensation committee certifies that the performance goals and any other material terms were satisfied before any payment of such remuneration.

perquisites   See *executive perquisite.*

phantom stock award   A type of incentive grant in which the recipient is not issued actual shares of stock on the grant date, but instead receives an account credited with a certain number of hypothetical shares. The value of the account increases or decreases over time based on the appreciation or depreciation of the stock price and sometimes including the crediting of dividend equivalents. Payout may be settled in cash or stock.

plan   For purposes of Item 402 of Regulation S-K, the term plan includes, but is not limited to, any plan, contract, authorization, or arrangement, whether or not set forth in any formal document, pursuant to which cash, securities, similar instruments, or any other property may be received. A plan may be applicable to one person.

poison pill   A device designed to prevent a hostile takeover by increasing the takeover cost, usually through the issuance of new preferred shares that carry severe redemption provisions.

pooling of interests   A merger accounting method (now obsolete) whereby the balance sheets of the two merging companies are combined line by line without a tax impact.

preferred stock   A class of stock that typically pays a fixed dividend, regardless of corporate earnings, and has priority over common stock in the payment of dividends and/or liquidation. However, it often carries no voting rights. The fixed income stream of preferred stock makes it similar in many ways to bonds.

Pregnancy Discrimination Act of 1978 An amendment to Title VII of the Civil Rights Act, that requires a company to extend to pregnant employees or spouses the same disability and medical benefits provided other employees or spouses of employees.

premium-priced stock option Options that have an exercise price above market value at the time of grant.

present value (PV) Value today of a future payment, or stream of payments, discounted at some appropriate compound interest or discount rate. The present-value method, also called the discounted cash-flow method, is widely used to compare alternative investments of cash-flow streams.

price-earnings (P/E) ratio A popular measure for comparing stocks selling at different prices in order to single out over- or undervalued issues. The P/E ratio is the price per share divided by the company's earnings per share.

price index Overall measure of how much prices have increased over a period of time. Prices are expressed as some percentage of the prices prevailing during a base period.

primary offering An offering of as-yet unissued securities.

principal stockholder An investor that either (1) owns 10 percent or more of an entity's common stock or (2) has the ability, directly or indirectly, to control or significantly influence the entity.

private placement Sales of securities not involving a public offering.

program trading A wide range of portfolio trading strategies involving the purchase or sale of 15 or more stocks having a total market value of $1 million or more.

prospectus A legal document offering securities for sale, required by the Securities Act of 1933. The required contents of the prospectus is dictated by the form of registration statement being used. Also called "offering circular."

proxy Refers either to a person, such as a member of management, who is designated by a shareholder to vote on behalf of the shareholder at a meeting. Corporate matters are typically voted on via proxy because it would be impractical to assemble all of the shareholders at one time to vote in person.

proxy battle Strategy used by an acquiring company in a hostile takeover attempt, whereby the acquirer challenges the target company's management and solicits support from the target company's shareholders for proposals that would effectively give the acquiring company control of the target without having to pay a premium. Also known as a "proxy fight."

proxy fight See *proxy battle.*

proxy statement   Information document that the SEC requires to be provided to shareholders before they vote by proxy on corporate matters. The proxy statement contains biographical information on the members of the board of directors; information about the compensation of the directors and top executive officers; and any proposals from management or shareholders to be acted upon at the meeting.

Public Utility Holding Company Act of 1935   Interstate holding companies engaged, through subsidiaries, in the electric utility business or in the retail distribution of natural or manufactured gas are subject to regulation under this act.

put option (put)   A derivative security giving the holder the right to sell securities at a fixed price (see *call option*). A protective put strategy allows holders of concentrated stock positions to have protection against share price drops. By purchasing a put, if the stock price is below the strike price at expiration, the holder will receive a payment for the difference.

PV   Abbreviation for *present value*.

pyramid exercise   A type of stock swap option exercise in which a small number of previously owned shares is surrendered to the company to pay a portion of the exercise price, for which a slightly larger number of option shares may be purchased. The newly purchased shares are then immediately surrendered back to the company to pay additional amounts of the exercise price, and so on until the full option price has been paid and the option holder is left with just the number of shares equal to the option spread.

qualified plan   Generally, a plan that meets qualifications for favorable tax treatment under applicable sections of the Internal Revenue Code. For example, a qualified defined benefit pension allows a company to take a tax deduction for the accrual of a pension benefit.

qualified stock option   A stock option that meets the requirements established by Internal Revenue Code Section 422. Usually referred to as an ISO.

qualifying disposition   Transfer (e.g., by gift or sale) of ISO or ESPP shares after the required holding period of two years from the grant date and one year from the purchase/exercise date.

rabbi trust   A trust created for the purpose of supporting the nonqualified benefit obligations of employers to their *employees*; sometimes referred to as *grantor trusts*. These trusts are called rabbi trusts due to the first initial ruling made by the IRS on behalf of a synagogue. Rabbi trusts create security for employees because the assets within the trust are typically outside the control of the employers and are irrevocable. However, the *assets* of the trust are subject to the claims of the company's creditors in the event of insolvency.

real estate investment trust   See *REIT*.

record date   The date set by the board of directors for the transfer agent to close the company's books to further changes in registration of stock, in order to identify the shareholders entitled to receive the next dividend or to vote at an upcoming meeting. A shareholder must officially own shares as of the record date to receive the dividend or vote at the meeting.

record owner   The shareholder of record of shares of stock, which may be different from the beneficial owner of those shares.

registration   Before a company may make a public offering of new securities, the securities must be registered under the Securities Act of 1933. A registration statement is filed with the SEC by the issuer, which discloses pertinent information relating to the company's operations, securities, management, and purpose of the public offering. Before a security may be admitted for listing on a national security exchange, it must be registered under the Securities Exchange Act of 1934.

registration statement   A disclosure document filed with the SEC to register shares of stock for sale to the public. Forms S-1, S-3, S-4, and S-8 are common types of registration statements. Form S-8 is used for employee benefit plans.

regression   A common statistical approach used to determine the relationship between pay and factors that may affect pay, such as revenue size, number of employees, and so on.

Regulation T   Federal Reserve Board regulations governing the extension of credit by broker/dealers, including their participation in cashless exercise/same-day sale transactions.

REIT (real estate investment trust)   An organization similar to an investment company in some respects, but concentrating its holdings in real estate investments.

reload stock option   A replacement stock option granted to an option holder upon a stock swap exercise. The number of reload options granted typically is equal to the number of shares delivered to exercise the option plus, in some cases, any shares withheld for tax withholding obligations. The exercise price of the new option is the current market price; the reload option generally expires on the same date that the original option would have expired.

repricing   The exchange of previously granted, now out-of-the-money stock options for lower-priced options at the current market price. The actual exchange can be structured in different ways and with different ratios of old-to-new stock options. It is also possible to have an upward repricing, typically to adjust for options discounted as a result of backdating.

restricted securities   The term used under SEC Rule 144 for securities issued privately by the company or an affiliate, without the benefit of a registration statement. Restricted securities are subject to a holding period before they can be sold to the public under Rule 144.

restricted stock award   Grants of shares of stock subject to restrictions on transfer and risk of forfeiture until vested by continued employment or by reaching a performance target. Restricted stock typically vests in increments over a period of several years. Dividends may be paid, and award holders may have voting rights during the restricted period.

restrictive covenants   Covenants by an employee to refrain from certain activities, usually for a prescribed period of time after termination of employment. Typical restrictive covenants include covenants not to compete, not to solicit employees or customers, not to divulge confidential information or trade secrets, and not to disparage the former employer or its constituents.

return on assets (ROA)   A profitability ratio measured by net income divided by assets. This is equivalent to return on sales multiplied by capital turnover.

return on equity (ROE)   A profitability ratio measured by net income divided by equity. This is equivalent to return on assets (ROA) multiplied by leverage (the ratio of assets to shareholders' equity).

return on invested capital (ROIC)   Amount, expressed as a percentage, earned on a company's total capital.

return on sales (ROS)   Net income as a percentage of sales. ROS is a useful measure of overall operational efficiency when compared with prior periods or with other companies in the same line of business. ROS varies widely from industry to industry.

reverse vesting   A technique (also known as *early exercise*) most often found in stock option plans offered by pre-IPO companies. Under this type of arrangement, the optionee would be allowed to exercise options before they are vested. For each option exercised, the optionee would receive a share of restricted stock, which is subject to vesting based on the original vesting schedule of the option.

ROA   Abbreviation for *return on assets.*

ROC   Abbreviation for *return on capital.*

ROE   Abbreviation for *return on equity.*

ROIC   Abbreviation for *return on invested capital.*

ROS   Abbreviation for *return on sales.*

ROSE   Abbreviation for *return on shareholders' equity.*

RSO   Abbreviation for *reload stock option.*

Rule 10b-5   An SEC rule that prohibits trading by insiders while they are in possession of material nonpublic information.

Rule 13d   An SEC rule that requires holders of 5 percent or more of a company's stock to disclose their security holdings and any changes in a Schedule 13D filing.

Rule 144   An SEC rule that applies to public resales of restricted securities, as well as all sales by affiliates. The requirements include:

• Current public information about the issuer.

- A one-year holding period for restricted securities.
- Unsolicited brokers' transactions.
- An amount limitation—the greater of 1 percent of the outstanding stock or the average weekly trading volume may be sold during any three-month period.
- A Form 144 filing in most cases.

Rule 701   SEC registration exemption used for private company equity plans.

SAB   Abbreviation for *Staff Accounting Bulletin.*

same-day sale   A same-day option exercise and sale transaction, effected through a broker. The broker uses the proceeds of the sale to pay to (1) the company the exercise price and any tax withholding and (b) the option holder the net shares or cash (less any brokerage commissions or fees).

SAR   Abbreviation for *stock appreciation right.*

Schedule 13D, 13G   Disclosure forms required to be filed with the SEC and the company by a shareholder or group of shareholders that owns more than 5 percent of a public company. Schedule 13G is a short-form version of the 13D and may generally (but not always) be used only by institutional investors.

SEC   Abbreviation for *Securities and Exchange Commission.*

Section 16(a)   Provision of the Securities Exchange Act of 1934 that requires company insiders to file periodic reports disclosing their holdings and changes in beneficial ownership of the company's equity securities. See *Forms 3, 4,* and *5.*

Section 16(b)   Provision of the Securities Exchange Act of 1934 that requires any profit realized by a company insider from the purchase and sale, or sale and purchase, of the company's equity securities within a period of less than six months to be returned to the company. Section 16(b) is also known as the "short-swing profit rule."

Section 162(m)   The section of the Internal Revenue Code imposing a $1 million cap on deductible compensation paid by a publicly held corporation to its *named executive officers* (see also *named executive officers*).

Section 409A   Provision of the Internal Revenue Code added in 2005 as part of the American Jobs Creation Act of 2004, which imposes a host of new restrictions on nonqualified deferred compensation arrangements.

Section 423   The Internal Revenue Code section that regulates employee stock purchase plans.

Section 83(b) election   An election filed by an employee to be taxed on a restricted stock grant as of the date of grant. This voluntary election must be made within 30 days of the date of grant to be effective.

secular trust   A trust fund for holding deferred compensation. Differs from a rabbi trust in that contributions are taxable to the recipient as they accumulate. The trust usually begins to pay out when the trust beneficiary retires. The trust assets are not subject to claims of creditors in the event of a bankruptcy.

Securities Act of 1933 (Securities Act) Federal legislation enacted to protect potential purchasers of stock by requiring companies to register their public stock offerings and make full disclosure to purchasers. The Securities Act of 1933 has two basic objectives:

1. Require that investors receive financial and other significant information concerning securities being offered for public sale; and
2. Prohibit deceit, misrepresentations, and other fraud in the sale of securities.

Securities and Exchange Commission (SEC) The government agency responsible for the supervision and regulation of the securities industry and markets, as well as public securities offerings and the ongoing disclosure obligations of public companies.

Securities Exchange Act of 1934 (Exchange Act) The Exchange Act gives the SEC broad authority over all aspects of the securities industry, including the power to register, regulate, and oversee brokerage firms, transfer agents, and clearing agencies as well as the nation's securities self-regulatory organizations (SROs). The Exchange Act also identifies and prohibits certain types of conduct in the markets and provides the SEC with disciplinary powers over regulated entities and persons associated with them. The act also empowers the SEC to require periodic reporting of information by companies with publicly traded securities.

security Includes any note, stock, treasury stock, bond, debenture, evidence of indebtedness, certificate of interest, or participation in any profit-sharing agreement. Also includes collateral-trust certificate; preorganization certificate or subscription; transferable share; investment contract; voting-trust certificate; certificate of deposit for a security; fractional undivided interest in oil, gas, or other mineral rights; any put, call, straddle, option, or privilege on any security, certificate of deposit, or group or index of securities (including any interest therein or based on the value thereof); or any put, call, straddle, option, or privilege entered into on a national securities exchange relating to foreign currency. In general, any interest or instrument commonly known as a "security," or any certificate of interest or participation in, temporary or interim certificate for, receipt for, guarantee of, or warrant or right to subscribe to or purchase any of the foregoing.

self-funding/self-insurance A health care benefit financing technique in which an employer pays claims out of an internally funded pool, as permitted under ERISA. Self-funded companies might or might not also be self-administered, meaning they perform the administrative tasks associated with the benefit as opposed to purchasing such services from an outside firm.

sequential exercise The exercise of employee stock options in the order in which they were granted.

SERP Abbreviation for *supplemental executive retirement plan.*

share repurchase plan A program by which a corporation buys back its own shares in the open market. It is usually done when the common shares are undervalued. Because it reduces the number of shares and thus increases earnings per share, it tends to elevate the market value of the remaining shares held by shareholders.

shareholder proposal A recommendation or requirement, proposed by a shareholder holding at least $2,000 market value or 1 percent of the company's voting shares, that the company and/or its board of directors take action presented for a vote by other shareholders at the company's annual meeting.

shareholder value Usually calculated as market capitalization—the stock price multiplied by the number of shares. Changes in shareholder value reflect both dividends and appreciation of the stock.

shareholders' agreement An agreement among the shareholders of a company governing any of a number of possible topics, such as buy-out terms and voting rights.

shares outstanding The number of company shares currently held by shareholders, as tracked by the transfer agent.

short-against-the-box A short sale by an investor who also owns the stock being sold is referred to as a sale "against the box," meaning it is a sale versus the broker's "box" position, not the stock in the account of the person who is short-selling. Strategies of this type are generally referred to as hedging strategies.

short sale The sale of a security that is not owned by the seller at the time of the trade, necessitating a purchase or delivery some time in the future to cover the sale. Investors who believe the stock being sold will decline in value between the time it is sold short and the time it is covered use the strategy. By being able to cover at a price lower than the short sale price, the investor profits on the difference in price.

short-swing transaction Any purchase and sale (or sale and purchase) of the issuer's equity securities by an insider within a period of less than six months. See *Section 16(b).*

SIC Abbreviation for *Standard Industrial Classification code.*

Sign-on bonus An amount of cash or stock granted at the time an executive joins a company. Also referred to as a *golden hello.*

S&P 500 A capitalization weighted index of 500 stocks. Standard and Poor's 500 stock index represents the price trend movements of the major common stock of U.S. public companies. It is used to measure the performance of the entire U.S. domestic stock market.

spring-loading Refers to the practice of granting options shortly before the release of positive information, in order to take advantage of a stock price anticipated to be low on the option grant date.

specified employee   This term is relevant for purposes of internal Revenue Code Section 409A and generally means a "key employee" as defined in Code Section 416. An employee is a key employee if the employee meets the requirements of section 416(i)(1)(A) at any time during the 12-month period ending on an identification date. Generally, this is an employee who is either (1) an "officer" having "annual compensation" from the employer of greater than the then-current 415(d) limit ($140,000 for 2006; $145,000 for 2007); or (2) a 5 percent owner of the employer, or (3) a 1 percent owner of the employer having annual compensation from the employer of more than $150,000.

spin-off   The separation of a subsidiary or division of a corporation from its parent by issuing shares in a new corporate entity. Shareholders in the parent receive shares in the new company in proportion to their original holding, and the total value remains approximately the same.

split   The division of the outstanding shares of a corporation into either a larger or smaller number of shares, without any immediate effect on individual share-holders equity. For example, a 3-for-1 forward split by a company with 1 million shares outstanding results in 3 million shares outstanding. Each holder of 100 shares before the split would have 300 shares (each worth less) after the split, although the proportionate equity in the company would stay the same. A reverse split would reduce the number of shares outstanding and each share would be worth more.

split-dollar life insurance   An arrangement between a company and an executive whereby the parties agree to allocate the benefits and costs of a life insurance contract.

spread   Depending on the context, refers either to (1) the difference between the bid and ask prices for an over-the-counter stock, or (2) the difference between an option's exercise price and the market price of the underlying shares (i.e., the profit component of the option).

Staff Accounting Bulletin (SAB)   Promulgation that reflects the SEC staff's views regarding accounting-related disclosure practices. SABs represent interpretations and policies followed by the Division of Corporation Finance and the Office of the Chief Accountant in administering the disclosure requirements of the federal securities laws. SABs do not represent official positions of the SEC.

staggered board   A corporate board structure whereby only a portion of the board of directors is elected each year, often used to discourage takeover attempts.

stakeholders   All parties interested in the performance of a company. Stakeholders range from the owners of a company to the local taxing authorities, to company employees, and also to residents concerned about the company's impact on the environment.

Standard Industrial Classification code (SIC) Four-digit code used by the SEC to categorize and identify a company's type of business.

STI Abbreviation for *short-term incentive.*

stock appreciation right (SAR) A contractual right that allows an individual to receive cash or stock of a value equal to the appreciation of a share of stock from the grant date to the date the SAR is exercised.

stock award Generally refers to a grant of unrestricted common shares. However, for purposes of Item 402 of Regulation S-K, the term *stock award* refers to any equity compensation award that does not have option-like features, such as common stock, restricted stock, restricted stock units, phantom stock, phantom stock units, or common stock equivalent units.

stock bonus plan A plan that provides for periodic awards of stock based upon the company's performance.

stock dividend A dividend paid in securities rather than cash. The dividend may be additional shares of the issuing company, or shares of another company (usually a subsidiary) held by the company.

stock exchange Organized marketplace in which members of the exchange, acting as agents (brokers) and as principals (dealers or traders) trade stocks, common stock equivalents, and bonds. Each exchange sets its own requirements for membership.

stock grant See *stock award.*

stock option A contractual right granted by the company, generally under a stock option plan, to purchase a specified number of shares of the company's stock at a specified price (the exercise price) for a specified period of time (generally 5 or 10 years). The option will become more valuable if the market price goes up over the term of the option. The option effectively gives the option holder the right to buy stock in the future at a discount. This definition describes an employee stock option, as distinguished from a listed or exchange-traded option. Stock options come in several forms, including the following, each of which is defined separately in this glossary: *performance stock options, premium-priced stock options, discount stock options,* and *indexed stock options.*

stock swap Also known as a "stock-for-stock" exercise. A form of cashless exercise transaction in which shares of company stock already owned are delivered, either physically or by attestation, in lieu of cash to pay for the exercise of stock options.

stock withholding A cashless method of satisfying the exercise price or withholding taxes for an equity award, by authorizing the company to withhold from the shares otherwise due a number of shares the value of which is equal to the exercise price and/or taxes.

street name   Securities held in the name of a broker instead of a customer's name are said to be carried in "street name." This occurs when the securities have been bought on margin or when the customer wishes the security to be held by the broker.

strike price   Also known as the *exercise price* or *grant price*, the price per share at which a stock option is granted and that must be paid to exercise a stock option. The strike price is typically the fair market value of the stock on the date of grant.

substantial risk of forfeiture   Tax term that applies when rights to compensation will be forfeited unless certain condition are met such as a requirement that the holder perform substantial future services (e.g., working X years for a company) or the requirement that certain performance goals are met.

summary compensation table   A table that appears in the proxy statement of a publicly held company which summarizes the compensation paid to its "named executive officers" in each of the last three fiscal years.

supplemental executive retirement plan (SERP)   A nonqualified plan for retirement benefits or deferred compensation.

TARSAP   Abbreviation for *time-accelerated restricted stock award plan.*

tax basis   Cost of stock for calculating gains or losses for tax purposes. For equity compensation, the basis includes the costs plus any compensation income previously recognized with respect to the award (e.g., the amount recognized as ordinary income upon the exercise of an NQSO).

tax preference items   Various tax breaks available under the regular income tax system that are added back to income to determine alternative minimum tax (AMT).

technical market research   Analysis of the market and stocks based on supply and demand. The technician studies price movements, volume, trends, and patterns, which are revealed by charting these factors, and attempts to assess the possible effects of current market action or future supply and demand for securities and individual issues.

tender offer   An offer to purchase outstanding shareholders' securities, often made in an attempt to gain control of a company.

testamentary trust   A trust established by a will that takes effect upon death. A revocable trust is a trust in which the creator reserves the right to modify or terminate the trust; an irrevocable trust may not be modified or terminated by the trustor after its creation.

third-party administrator (TPA)   An independent company or person who contracts with an employer to provide administrative functions associated with a benefit or benefits, but does not assume or underwrite risk.

TIAA-CREF   Abbreviation for *Teachers Insurance and Annuity Association–College Retirement Equities Fund.*

tick   The direction in which the price of a stock moved on its last sale. An up-tick means the last trade was at a higher price than the one before it and a down-tick means the last sale price was lower than the one before it. A zero-plus tick means the transaction was at the same price as the one before, but still higher than the nearest preceding different price.

ticker symbol   A system of letters used to uniquely identify a stock or mutual fund.

time-accelerated restricted stock award (TARSAP)   A restricted stock plan that combines both time-lapse and performance vesting restrictions. Using such an approach, the restricted stock will vest at the earlier of a stated period of time or upon the achievement of certain performance targets.

top-hat plan   An ERISA term referring to a plan maintained by an employer that primarily provides deferred compensation for highly compensated or management employees.

total capital   Common and preferred equity plus long-term debt.

total cash compensation   The total of salary and bonus.

total compensation   The complete pay package for employees, including all forms of cash, stock, benefits, services, and in-kind payments. *Total direct compensation* refers to *salary, bonus,* and *long-term incentive.*

total reward system   Includes financial compensation, benefits, opportunities for social interaction, security, status and recognition, work variety, appropriate work load, importance of work, authority/control/autonomy, advancement opportunities, feedback, hazard-free working conditions, and opportunities for personal and professional development. An effective compensation system will use many of these rewards.

transfer agent   An agent who keeps a record of the name of each registered shareowner, his or her address, and the number of shares owned, and sees that the certificates presented for transfer are properly cancelled and new certificates issued in the name of the new owner.

transferable stock options   Options providing, by their terms, that they may be transferred by the option holder, generally only to a family member or to a trust, limited partnership, or other entity for the benefit of family members, or to a charity.

tranche   A set of stock options as part of a larger grant. For example, if options vest in 25 percent blocs over four years, each 25 percent bloc of options is a tranche.

treasury stock   Stock reacquired by the issuing company. Depending on state law variations, treasury stock is typically issued but not outstanding, cannot be voted, neither pays nor accrues dividends, and is not included in any of the financial ratios measuring values per common share.

trigger   As relates to stock compensation, an event that causes change or acceleration in the vesting or payout schedule. For example, some stock plans accelerate vesting upon a change in control. Other plans may require a double trigger of a change in control followed by termination of employment.

trust   A legal entity in which one person or institution holds the right to manage property or assets for the benefit of someone else. Types of trusts include:

- Testamentary trust—A trust established by a will that takes effect upon death.
- Living trust—A trust created by a person during his or her lifetime.
- Revocable trust—A trust in which the creator reserves the right to modify or terminate the trust.
- Irrevocable trust—A trust that may not be modified or terminated by the trustor after its creation.

Trust Indenture Act of 1939   This act, which falls under the purview of the SEC, applies to debt securities such as bonds, debentures, and notes offered for public sale. Even though such securities may be registered with the SEC, they may not be offered for sale to the public unless a formal agreement between the issuer of bonds and the bondholder, known as the *trust indenture,* conforms to the standards of this act.

trustee   An individual or institution appointed to administer a trust for its beneficiaries.

underwater   A term used to describe a stock option when the current market price is below the option exercise price. Also called an *out-of-the-money option.*

underwriter   An investment banking firm that actually buys the shares from the company in a public offering and then resells them to its customers.

Uniformed Services Employment and Reemployment Rights Act   The act giving certain persons who serve in the U.S. armed forces a right to reemployment with the employer they were with when they entered service. This includes those called up from the reserves or National Guard. The Veterans' Employment and Training Service administer these rights.

variable accounting   Under APB 25, "variable accounting" required that the issuer accrue a compensation expense over time based on changes in the market price of the underlying stock. FAS 123R does not use the concept of variable accounting for share-based payments that are settled only in stock. However, equity awards that may be settled in cash will be treated as "liability awards" under applicable accounting rules, which is a form of variable accounting.

variable annuity   An insurance policy under which the annuity premium (a set amount of dollars) is invested in units of a portfolio of stocks. Upon retirement, the policyholder is paid according to accumulated units, the dollar value of which varies according to the performance of the stock portfolio.

variable compensation   The portion of pay that is determined by performance. Typical variable compensation includes annual bonuses, long-term cash incentive awards, options, and performance shares and units. Also referred to as *variable incentive pay.*

variable grant guidelines   Under these guidelines, a company determines equity grant size according to a target dollar value rather than a target number of shares.

variable universal life insurance   A type of life insurance that combines a death benefit with a savings element that accumulates tax-deferred at current interest rates. Under a variable universal life insurance policy, the cash value in the policy can be placed in a variety of subaccounts with different investment objectives.

vesting period   The period between the grant date of an award and the time that is exercisable or no longer subject to a substantial risk of forfeiture.

vesting schedule   Schedule setting forth when, and to what extent, options or SARs become exercisable, or restricted stock or stock units are no longer subject to forfeiture (for example, 20 percent per year over five years). The schedule may be based on continued employment or may be based in whole or in part on meeting performance targets.

volatility   An amount, expressed as a percentage of the stock price, that reflects recent fluctuation of the stock price. The moving average of this parameter is used in certain option pricing models to calculate the fair value of options. Volatility is generally expressed as the annual standard deviation of the daily price changes in the security. The volatility of a stock is the standard deviation of the continuously compounded rates of return on the stock over a specified period. The higher the volatility, the more the returns on the stock can be expected to vary—up or down. Volatility is typically expressed in annualized terms that are comparable regardless of the time period used in the calculation (for example, daily, weekly, or monthly price observations).

volume   The number of shares or contracts traded in a security or an entire market during a given period. Volume is normally considered on a daily basis, with a daily average being computed for longer periods.

voting right   The common shareholders' right to vote their stock in the affairs of a company. Preferred stock usually has the right to vote when preferred dividends are in default for a specified period. The right to vote may be delegated by the shareholder to another person.

W-2   IRS form that reports income paid and taxes withheld by an employer for a particular employee during a calendar year.

W-8   Certificate of Foreign Status form required by the IRS to tell the payer, transfer agent, broker, or other intermediary that an employee is a nonresident alien or foreign entity that is not subject to U.S. tax reporting or backup withholding rules.

W-9 Request for Taxpayer Identification Number and Certification form required by the IRS to furnish the payer, transfer agent, broker, or other intermediary with an employee's social security or taxpayer identification number. The filing of this form allows the employee not to be subject to backup withholding because of underreporting of interest and dividends on his or her tax return.

WARN Abbreviation for *Worker Adjustment and Retraining Notification* act.

warrants Financial instruments that are usually given to financial backers, other corporations, and underwriters as part of a funding or business arrangement. In most respects, warrants are like stock options, but they usually have more complex provisions to reflect anti-dilution adjustments and other aspects of the business arrangement between the investors and the company.

when issued A short form of "when, as, and if issued." The term indicates a conditional transaction in a security authorized for issuance but not as yet actually issued. All "when issued" transactions are on an "if" basis, to be settled if and when the actual security is issued and the exchange rules the transactions are to be settled.

whole life insurance A type of life insurance that offers a death benefit and also accumulates cash value, tax-deferred, at fixed interest rates. Whole life insurance policies generally have a fixed annual premium that does not rise over the duration of the policy.

Wilshire 5000 A capitalization weighted index of all U.S. headquartered companies. The capitalization of the portfolio is the sum of the market capitalizations of all the companies.

Worker Adjustment and Retraining Notification Act (WARN) Mandates that employees be given early warning of impending layoffs or plant closings. The DOL's Employment and Training Administration administers this law.

yield In general, the amount of current income provided by an investment. For stocks, the yield is calculated by dividing the total of the annual dividends by the current price. For bonds, the yield is calculated by dividing the annual interest by the current price. The yield is distinguished from the return, which includes price appreciation or depreciation.

zero-premium collar Hedging strategy used for high-value, concentrated stock positions, sometimes referred to as a *zero-cost collar.*

Bibliography

Abelson, Reed. "Who Profits if the Boss Is Overfed?" *New York Times*, June 20, 1999: 9.

Ackerman, Elise. "Optionaires, Beware!" *U.S. News & World Report*, March 6, 2000: 25.

Alpern, Richard. *Guide to Change of Control: Protecting Companies and Their Executives.* Alexandria, Virginia: Executive Compensation Advisory Services, 2001.

American Bar Association. *Corporate Directors Guidebook*, 4th ed. Chicago: American Bar Association, Committee on Corporate Laws, Section of Business Law, 2004.

American Law Institute. *Principles of Corporate Governance: Analysis and Recommendations.* Vols. 1 and 2. St. Paul, Minn.: American Law Institute, 1994.

American Society of Corporate Secretaries. *Directors: Selection, Orientation, Compensation, Evaluation, and Termination.* New York: American Society of Corporate Secretaries, 2000.

American Society of Corporate Secretaries. *Compensation Committees.* New York: American Society of Corporate Secretaries, 2000.

American Society of Corporate Secretaries. *Board Committees: Considerations, Structures, and Uses in Effective Governance.* New York: American Society of Corporate Secretaries, 2000.

American Society of Corporate Secretaries. *Corporate Governance Principles: A Representative Sampling.* New York: American Society of Corporate Secretaries, 2000.

American Society of Corporate Secretaries. *Corporate Secretary's Resource Guide for the New Public Company.* New York: American Society of Corporate Secretaries, 2000.

American Society of Corporate Secretaries. *Current Board Practices, 3rd Study.* New York: American Society of Corporate Secretaries, 2000.

American Society of Corporate Secretaries. *Corporate Minutes: A Monograph for the Corporate Secretary.* New York: American Society of Corporate Secretaries, 1996.

Ang, James S., Shmuel Hauser, and Beni Lauterbach. "Top Executive Compensation under Alternative Ownership and Governance Structures: Evidence from Israel," in Hirschey and Marr, *Advances in Financial Economics* 3, 1997.

Balsam, Steven. *An Introduction to Executive Compensation.* San Diego: Academic Press, 2002.

Bernard, Tara Siegel. "It's Your Choice." *Wall Street Journal's Special Report on Executive Pay*, April 12, 2004: R3.

Bernstein, Peter. *Against the Gods: The Remarkable Story of Risk.* New York: John Wiley & Sons, 1996.

Bhagat, Sanjai, Dennis Carey, and Charles Elson. "Director Ownership, Corporate Performance, and Management Turnover." *Business Lawyer* 54, no. 3 (May 1999): 885–919.

Bickley, James M. and Gary Shorter. "Stock Options: The Backdating Issue." *Congressional Research Service Report for Congress*, March 15, 2007.

Bischoff, Bill. "Now That's an Interesting Option." *SmartMoney.com*, August 23, 2000.

Black, Fischer, and Myron Scholes. "The Pricing of Options and Corporate Liabilities." *Journal of Political Economy* 81 (May/June 1973): 637–654.

Blair, Margaret. *Ownership and Control: Rethinking Corporate Governance for the Twenty-First Century.* Washington, D.C.: The Brookings Institution, 1995.

Block, Stanley. "A Study of Financial Analysts: Practice and Theory." *Financial Analysts Journal* 55, no. 4 (July/August 1999): 86–95.

Bogan, Christopher, and Michael English. *Benchmarking for Best Practices: Winning Through Innovative Adaptation.* New York: McGraw-Hill, 1994.

Bogle, John. "Bogle on Mutual Fund Investment Policies and Corporate Governance." Speech before the New York Society of Security Analysts, Washington, D.C., October 20, 1999.

Bogle, John. "Creating Shareholder Value: BY Mutual Funds... or FOR Mutual Fund Shareholders ." Speech before the Annual Conference for the Investor Responsibility Research Center, Washington, D.C., October 26, 1998.

Bok, Derek. *The Cost of Talent: How Executives Are Paid and How It Affects America.* New York: Free Press, 1993.

Booth, Richard. "Seven Myths about Stock Options." *Directors & Boards*, Summer 1999: 35–38.

Brancato, C. K., ed., *Institutional Investor Report.* New York: The Conference Board, January 1998.

Brancato, C. K. and Alan A. Rudnick. *The Evolving Relationship Between Compensation Committees and Consultants*: The Conference Board Global Corporate Governance Research Center, January 2006.

Brickley, James, Clifford Smith, and Jerold Zimmerman. *Managerial Economics and Organizational Architecture.* Boston: Irwin-McGraw Hill, 1997.

Brinkley, Christina, and Joann Lublin. "ITT Brass to Get 'Golden Bungee' in Takeover." *Wall Street Journal*, February 12, 1998: B1.

Buck Consultants, Inc. *Review of CEO Employment Arrangements.* New York: Buck Consultants, 2001.

Bulkeley, William. "Decompensation: Executives Ordered to Return Millions; Computer Associates Forgot about Those Stock Splits; Still, 'No Mere Bagatelle.'" *Wall Street Journal,* November 10, 1999: A1.

Business Roundtable. "Statement of the Business Roundtable on the American Law Institute's Proposed 'Principles of Corporate Governance and Structure.'" New York: Business Roundtable, 1998.

Byrd, John, Robert Parrino, and Gunnar Pritsch. "Stockholder-Manager Conflicts and Firm Value." *Financial Analysts Journal* 54, no. 3 (May/June 1998): 14–30.

Byrne, John. "How to Reward Failure: Reprice Stock Options." *BusinessWeek*, October 12, 1998: 50.

Byrne, John. "The Teddy Roosevelts of Corporate Governance." *BusinessWeek*, May 31, 1999: 75–79.

Byrnes, Tracy. "Stock Options Lost Value? Little-Known Provision May Be a Life Preserver." TheStreet.com, May 11, 2000.

California Public Employees' Retirement Equities Fund Home Page. *Barriers to Good Corporate Governance*. 1999, www.calpers.com.

Carey, Dennis, Dayton Ogden, and Judith A. Roland. *CEO Succession: A Window on How Boards Can Get It Right When Choosing a New Executive*. New York: Oxford University Press, 2000.

Cartano, David. *Taxation of Compensation and Employee Benefits*. New York: Panel Publishers, Inc., 1999.

Carver, John, and Miriam Carver. *Reinventing Your Board: A Step-by-Step Guide to Implementing Policy Governance*. San Francisco: Jossey-Bass, 1997.

Carver, John. *Corporate Boards that Create Value*. San Francisco: Jossey-Bass, 2002.

Ceron, Gaston. "The Company We Keep." *Wall Street Journal's Special Report on Executive Pay*, April 12, 2004: R4.

Charan, Ram. *Boards at Work: How Corporate Boards Create Competitive Advantage*. San Francisco: Jossey-Bass, 1998.

Charan, Ram, and Geoffrey Colvin. "Why CEOs Fail." *Fortune*, June 21, 1999: 69–78.

Chew, Donald, and Stuart L. Gillan (eds.), *Corporate Governance at the Crossroads: A Book of Readings*. New York: McGraw-Hill Irwin, 2005.

Chingos, Peter, and KPMG Peat Marwick LLP. *Paying for Performance: A Guide to Compensation Management*. New York: John Wiley & Sons, 1997.

Ciampa, Dan, and Michael Watkins. "The Successor's Dilemma." *Harvard Business Review* (November/December 1999): 161–165.

Colvin, Geoffrey. "The Great CEO Pay Heist." *Fortune*, June 25, 2001: 64–68.

Conger, Jay, Edward Lawler, and David Finegold. *Corporate Boards: New Strategies for Adding Value at the Top*. San Francisco: Jossey-Bass, 2001.

Cook, Frederic. "Do Stock Options Dilute Shareholder Interests?" *ACA Journal* 7, no. 1 (Spring 1998): 67–72.

Council of Institutional Investors. *Does Shareholder Activism Make a Difference?* Washington, D.C.: Council of Institutional Investors Monograph, 1998.

Cox, John, and David Larcker. "Performance Consequences of Requiring Target Stock Ownership Levels." Philadelphia: Wharton School working paper, revised December 7, 1999.

Cox, John, S. A. Ross, and M. Rubenstein. "Option Pricing: A Simplified Approach." *Journal of Financial Economics* 7 (September 1979): 239–263.

Crystal, Graef, and Ira Kay. "Contrasting Perspectives: Do Stock Options Affect Performance?" *ACA Journal* 7 no. 1 (Spring 1998): 102–108.

Day, Kathleen. "Defying Gravity." *Washington Post*, April 1, 2001: B1.

"Does Good Governance Create Better Corporate Performance? Interview with Charles Elson." *Directorship* 25, no. 1 (January 1999): 5–6.

Delves, Donald P. *Stock Options and the New Rules of Corporate Accountability: Measuring, Managing, and Rewarding Executive Performance.* New York: McGraw-Hill, 2004.

Donaldson, Gordon, and Jay Lorsch. *Decision Making at the Top.* New York: Basic Books, 1983.

Duca, Diane. *Nonprofit Boards: Roles, Responsibilities and Performance.* New York: John Wiley & Sons, 1996.

Ellig, Bruce R. *The Complete Guide to Executive Compensation.* New York: McGraw-Hill Trade, 2001.

Ellin, Abby. "When the Glitter of Stock Options Turns to Dust." *New York Times,* August 22, 1999: C10.

Elson, Charles. "Director Compensation and the Management-Captured Board—The History of a Symptom and a Cure." *SMU Law Review* 50 no. 1 (September/October 1996): 127–174.

Elson, Charles. "Courts and Boards: The Top 10 Cases." *Directors and Boards,* Fall 1997: 26–32.

Ermann, David, and Richard Lundman. *Corporate and Governmental Deviance.* New York: Oxford University Press, 1978.

Fierman, Jaclyn. "The People Who Set the CEO's Pay. (Chief Executive Officer, The Compensation Committee)." *Fortune,* March 12, 1990: 58–62.

Frederic W. Cook & Co. *Reload Stock Options: The First 10 Years.* New York: Frederic W. Cook & Co., 1998.

Foundation for Enterprise Development. *The Entrepreneur's Guide to Equity Compensation,* 2nd ed. Washington, D.C.: Foundation for Enterprise Development, 1998.

Gay, Christopher. "Hard to Lose: Reload Options Promote Stock Ownership among Executives. But Critics Say They're a Lot More Costly than Shareholders Realize." *Wall Street Journal's Special Report on Executive Pay,* April 8, 1999: R6.

Gogoi, Pallavi. "False Impressions: More Companies Require Top Executives to Own Stock. The Result Isn't What Everybody Expected." *Wall Street Journal's Special Report on Executive Pay,* April 8, 1999: R3.

Gordon, Jeffrey N. *Executive Compensation: If There's a Problem, What's the Remedy? The Case for "Compensation Discussion and Analysis,"* Columbia Law School, The Center for Law and Economic Studies Working Paper No. 273/2006, *Journal of Corporation Law,* Summer 2006.

Gross, Bill. "The New Math of Ownership." *Harvard Business Review,* 76, no. 6 (November/December 1998): 68–74.

Hall, Brian J., and Kevin J. Murphy. "The Trouble with Stock Options." *Journal of Economic Perspectives 2003,* Vol. 17: 49–70.

Hallock, Kevin. "Reciprocally Interlocking Boards of Directors and Executive Compensation." *Journal of Financial and Quantitative Analysis* 32, no. 3 (September 1997): 331–334.

Hallock, Kevin. "Dual Agency: Corporate Boards with Reciprocally Interlocking Relationships," in *Executive Compensation and Shareholder Value: Theory and Evidence,* by Jennifer Carpenter, and Yermack, Kluwer, 1999: 55–75.

Hallock, Kevin, and Paul Oyer. "The Timeliness of Performance Information in Determining Executive Compensation," *Journal of Corporate Finance* 5, (December 1999): 303–321.

Hankins, Melissa. "Battle over the Boardroom: Should Directors Get Paid Based on Corporate Performance?" *Wall Street Journal*, April 12, 2001: R6.

Heath, Chris, Steven Huddart, and Mark Lang. "Psychological Factors and Stock Option Exercise." *Quarterly Journal of Economics* 114, no. 2 (May 1999): 601–627.

Heidrick, Robert. "Board Evaluations: Who Does Them, Who Doesn't and Why." *Corporate Board* 20, no. 115 (March/April 1999): 23–26.

Hemmer, T., S. Matsunaga, and T. Shevlin. "An Empirical Examination of Reload Employee Stock Options." Working paper, University of Washington, October 1996.

Hemmer, T., S. Matsunaga, and T. Shevlin. "Optimal Exercise and the Cost of Employee Stock Options with a Reload Provision." *Journal of Accounting Research* 36, (Fall 1998): 231–235.

Hewitt Associates LLC. *Research Report: Unleashing the Power of Employee Ownership.* Lincolnshire, Ill.: Hewitt Associates, 1998.

Hewitt Associates LLC. *Survey Findings: Executive Employment Contracts.* Lincolnshire, Ill.: Hewitt Associates, 1998.

Huddart, Steven. "Employee Stock Options." *Journal of Accounting and Economics* 18, (1994): 207–231.

Huddart, Steven. "Options 101: Planning for Stock Option Wealth." Presentation before the 55th Pennsylvania State University Tax Conference, May 2001.

Huddart, Steven. "Patterns of Stock Option Exercise in the United States." Durham, N.C.: The Fuqua School of Business working paper, revised November 24, 1997.

Huddart, Steven, Bin Ke, and Kathy Petroni. "What Insiders Know about Future Earnings and How They Use It: Evidence from Insider Trades." *Journal of Accounting & Economics* 35, no. 3 (August 2003): 315–346.

Huddart, Steven, and John S. Hughes. "Public Disclosure and Dissimulation of Insider Trades." *Econometrica* 69, no. 3 (May 2001): 665–681.

Huddart, Steven, and Mark Lang. "Employee Stock Option Exercises: An Empirical Analysis." *Journal of Accounting and Economics* 21 (1996): 5–43.

Huddart, Steven, and Mark Lang. "Information Distribution within Firms: Evidence from Stock Option Exercises." *Journal of Accounting & Economics* 34, no. 1–3 (January 2003): 3–31.

Jacobs, Karen. "Enough Is Enough: Computer Associates Offers a Cautionary Example of High Pay." *Wall Street Journal's Special Report on Executive Pay*, April 8, 1999: R8.

Jensen, Michael, and Kevin Murphy. "CEO Incentives—It's Not How Much You Pay, But How." *Harvard Business Review*, May 1, 1990.

Johnson, Carrie. "Some Shocked at Tax Bills on Options." *Washington Post*, March 16, 2001: E1.

Johnson, Mike. *Building and Retaining Global Talent: Towards 2002.* London: The Economist Intelligence Unit, 1998.

Keasey, Kevin, Steve Thompson, and Mike Wright. *Corporate Governance: Economic, Management and Financial Issues.* New York: Oxford University Press, 1997.

Khurana, Rakesh. "The Curse of the Superstar CEO." *Harvard Business Review*, September 2002: 23.

Kotter, John, and James Heskett. *Corporate Culture and Performance*. New York: Free Press, 1992.

Lavelle, Louis. "The Artificial Sweetener in CEO Pay." *BusinessWeek*, March 26, 2001: 102–103.

"Leapfrogging Pay Packages." *Executive Compensation Reports* 19 no. 15 (December 1, 1999): 1–2.

Lederer, Jack, Susan Lowry, and Dennis Carey. "Compensation Committee: 10 Best Practices." *Directors & Boards*, Summer 1999: 44–45.

Leonhardt, David. "Law Firms' Pay Soars to Stem Dot-Com Defections." *New York Times*, February 2, 2000: A1, E2.

Lipton, Martin, and Jay Lorsch. "A Modest Proposal for Improved Corporate Governance." *Business Lawyer* 70, no. 48 (November 1992): 59–72.

Lorsch, Jay, and Rakesh Khurana. "Changing Leaders: The Board's Role in CEO Succession." *Harvard Business Review* 77, no. 3 (May/June 1999): 96–105.

Lorsch, Jay, and Elizabeth MacIver. *Pawns or Potentates: The Reality of America's Corporate Boards*. Boston: Harvard Business School, 1989.

Lowenstein, Roger. "Heads I Win, Tails I Win." *New York Times Magazine*, June 9, 2002: 9.

Lublin, Joann. "Here Comes Politically Correct Pay." *Wall Street Journal's Special Report on Executive Pay*, April 12, 2004: R1.

Lublin, Joann. "In Whose Interest?: Compensation Committees Are Supposed to Be Independent. That May Be Tough When the CEO Is a Member." *Wall Street Journal's Special Report on Executive Pay*, April 8, 1999: R4.

Lublin, Joann, and Leslie Scism. "Stock Options at Firms Irk Some Investors." *Wall Street Journal*, January 12, 1999: C1, C4.

Lyons, Dennis. "CEO Casualties: A Battlefront Report." *Directors & Boards*, Summer 1999: 43–44.

MacDonald, Elizabeth. "Fears about Hidden Earnings Overstatements Caused by Stock Options Appear Overblown." *Wall Street Journal*, October 11, 1999.

Martin, Roger. "Taking Stock." *Harvard Business Review*, January 1, 2003.

McConnell, Pat, Janet Pegg, and David Zion. *Employee Stock Option Expense Pro Forma Impact on EPS and Operating Margins*. New York: Bear Stearns Equity Research, May 1, 1998.

Milkovich, George, and Jerry Newman. *Compensation*, 7th ed. Chicago: Irwin, 2001.

Millstein, Ira, and Paul MacAvoy. "The Active Board of Directors and Performance of the Large Publicly Traded Corporation." *Columbia Law Review* 98, no. 5 (June 1998): 1283–1321.

Monks, Robert. "Stock Options Don't Work: If CEOs Want Shares, Let 'Em Buy Some." *Fortune*, September 18, 1995: 230.

Monks, Robert, and Nell Minow. *Corporate Governance*, Malden, Mass: Blackwell Business, 1995.

Morgenson, Gretchen. "Why Not Restate Bonuses." *New York Times*, April 25, 2004: C1.

Morgenson, Gretchen. "Executive Pay: A Special Report; Two Pay Packages, Two Different Galaxies." *New York Times*, April 4, 2004: C1.

Morgenson, Gretchen. "Dispelling the Myth That Options Help Shareholders." *New York Times*, July 29, 2001: C1.

Morgenson, Gretchen. "Hidden Costs of Stock Options May Soon Come Back to Haunt." *New York Times*, June 13, 2000: A1.

Morgenson, Gretchen. "Holding Executives Answerable to Owners." *New York Times*, April 29, 2001: E1.

Morgenson, Gretchen. "Investors May Now Eye Costs of Stock Options." *New York Times*, August 29, 2000: E1.

Morgenson, Gretchen. "Options Seem to Be Coming Home to Roost." *New York Times*, October 8, 2000: E1.

Morgenson, Gretchen. "Rumblings of an Avalanche." *New York Times*, August 15, 1999: E1.

Morgenson, Gretchen. "Stock Options Are Not a Free Lunch." *Forbes*, May 18, 1999: 212–217.

Napolitano, Gabriel, and Abby Cohen. *The Controversy Surrounding Employee Stock Options*. New York: Goldman Sachs Investment Research, May 4, 1998.

Napolitano, Gabriel, and Abby Cohen. The NACD Blue Ribbon Commission on Executive Compensation and the Role of the Compensation Committee. Washington, D.C.: NACD, 2003.

National Association of Corporate Directors (NACD). *2003–2004 Public Company Governance Survey*. Washington, D.C.: NACD, 2003.

National Association of Corporate Directors (NACD). *Report of the NACD Blue Ribbon Commission on Director Professionalism*. Washington, D.C.: NACD, 2001.

National Association of Corporate Directors (NACD). *Report of the NACD Best Practices Council: Coping with Fraud and Other Illegal Activity*. Washington, D.C.: NACD, 1998.

National Association of Corporate Directors (NACD). *Report of the NACD Blue Ribbon Commission on Executive Compensation: Guidelines for Corporate Directors*. Washington, D.C.: NACD, 1993.

National Center for Employee Ownership. *The Stock Options Book*. Oakland, Calif: NCEO, 1999.

Neff, Thomas, James Citrin, and Paul Brown. *Lessons from the Top: The Search for America's Best Business Leaders*. New York: Currency Doubleday, 1999.

"Optional Logic." *Wall Street Journal*, September 21, 1998: A28.

Ottenstein, Robert, and Nina Scheller. *Paine Webber Specialty Chemicals Research Report. Corporate Governance: Update on Executive Compensation, Incentive Programs and Stock Ownership*. New York: Paine Webber, 1998.

Overton, Bruce, and Susan E. Stoffer. *Executive Compensation Answer Book*. 5th ed. New York: Panel, 2003.

Pastore, Robert. *Stock Options: An Authoritative Guide to Incentive and Nonqualified Stock Options*. San Francisco: PCM Capital Publishing, 1999.

Pearl Meyer & Partners, Inc. *2003 Equity Stake, Study of Management Equity Participation in the Top 200 Corporations*. New York: Pearl Meyer & Partners, 2004.

Peterson, Pamela, and David Peterson. *Company Performance and Measures of Value Added.* Charlottesville, Va.: The Research Foundation of the Institute of Chartered Financial Analysts, December 1996.

Phillips, Robert. *Stakeholder Theory and Organizational Ethics.* San Francisco: Berrett-Koehler Publishers, Inc., 2003.

Porter, Michael. *Competitive Advantage: Creating and Sustaining Superior Performance.* New York: Free Press, 1985.

Post, James E., et al. *Redefining the Corporation: Stakeholder Management and Organizational Wealth.* Stanford: Stanford University Press, 2002.

Rappaport, Alfred. *Creating Shareholder Value: A Guide for Managers and Investors.* New York: Free Press, 1998.

Rappaport, Alfred. "New Thinking on How to Link Executive Pay with Performance." *Harvard Business Review,* March/April 1999: 91–101.

Reda, James F. "Till Wealth Do Us Part: The Truth Behind Executive Employment Arrangements." *World at Work Journal,* 11, no. 2 (Second Quarter 2002): 34–43.

Reda, James F. "Committees: A Glimpse at the Future Boardroom." *Corporate Board* 23, no. 133 (March/April 2002): 21–25.

Reda, James F. "CEO Stock Ownership Guidelines." *Directors & Boards* 25, no. 1 (Fall 2000): 46–47.

Reda, James F. "Change-in-Control Severance Arrangements: Practical Considerations." *Journal of Compensation and Benefits* 15, no. 2 (September/October 1999): 21–26.

Reda, James F. "The Compensation Committee: A Potential Strategic Asset." *ACA Journal* 9, no. 1 (First Quarter 2000): 39–46.

Reda, James F. "Executive Pay Today and Tomorrow." *Corporate Board* 22, no. 126 (January/February 2001): 18–21.

Reda, James F. "The New World of the Compensation Committee." *Corporate Board* 20, no. 119 (November/December 1999): 18–21.

Reda, James F. "The Six Habits of a Highly Effective Compensation Committee." *Directorship* 26, no. 1 (January 2000): 6–9, 12–13, 16.

Reda, James F. "What's New in Accounting for Executive Stock Awards." *Journal of Taxation of Employee Benefits* 6, no. 5 (January/February 1999): 214–220.

Reda, James F. "What You Need to Know about Pooling of Interests Accounting." *Journal of Compensation and Benefits* 15, no. 2 (March/April 1999): 33–39.

Reda, James, and John Chandler. "Imperatives for Compensation Committees." *National Association of Corporate Directors' Monthly* 23, no. 10 (October 1999): 1–5.

Reda, James, and Thomas Hemmer. "Reload Stock Options: Facts and Fictions." *Journal of Compensation and Benefits* 14, no. 6 (May/June 1999): 38–43.

Reda, James, and Stewart Reifler. "Repricing Stock Options: Current Trends and Dangers." *Journal of Compensation and Benefits* 14, no. 3 (November/December 1998): 5–10.

Reda, James, James McMahon, and Eric Lane. *2000 Pay to Win: How America's Most Successful Companies Pay Their Executives.* San Diego: Harcourt, 2000.

Reda, James, James McMahon, and Eric Lane. "Repricing Stock Options: How to Win a Loser's Game." *Journal of Taxation of Employee Benefits* 7, no. 1 (May/June 1999): 45–48.

Reifler, Stewart. "New Golden Parachute Rules." *Mergers and Acquisitions* 3, no. 1 (May 2002): 3.

Reifler, Stewart. "New IRS Rules for Split-Dollar Life Insurance Arrangements." *Corporation Business Taxation Monthly* 4, no. 8 (May 2003): 20.

Reifler, Stewart. "New IRS Rules Will Impact Private Split-Dollar Life Insurance Arrangements." *Estate Tax Planning Advisor* 2, no. 4 (April 2003): 1.

Reifler, Stewart, and Atief Heermance. "SEC Adopts Revised Rules Requiring Shareholder Approval of Equity Compensation Plans." *Securities Regulatory Update* 6, no. 14 (July 21, 2003): 1.

Reifler, Stewart, and James Reda. "Repricing Stock Options: Surviving the Great American Blowout." *Director's Monthly* 22 (December 1998): 7.

Reifler, Stewart, Mary Hevener, Helyn Goldstein, and Rachel Rimland. "Section 162(m) Outside Director Sample Questionnaire." *Tax Executive* 48 (July/August 1996): 283.

Reifler, Stewart, and Mary Hevener. "Taxation: Section 162(m) Final Regulations." *National Law Journal*, March 25, 1996: B5.

Reifler, Stewart, and Mary Hevener. "Final Tax Regulations Issued Governing the $1 Million Deduction Limitation on Executive Compensation." *Metropolitan Corporate Counsel*, February 13, 1996: 13.

Reingold, Jennifer. "Nice Option If You Can Get It." *BusinessWeek*, May 4, 1998: 111, 114.

Reingold, Jennifer. "What Keeps the Pay Merry-Go-Round Whirling." *BusinessWeek*, April 19, 1999: 81.

Reingold, Jennifer. "Options Plan Your CEO Hates." *BusinessWeek*, February 28, 2000: 82–85.

Reingold, Jennifer. "As Long as You're Up, Get Me a Restricted Stock Grant: When Prices Fall, Execs Find Such Awards Preferable to Options." *BusinessWeek*, April 3, 2000: 42.

Richard, J. *Compensation Committee Manual.* Half Moon Bay, Calif.: J. Richard & Co., 1999.

Richtel, Matt. "Stock Option Blues: Slide Leaves Little but a Big Tax Bill." *New York Times*, February 18, 2001: C1.

Rothwell, William. *Effective Succession Planning: Ensuring Leadership Continuity and Building Talent from Within.* AMACOM: New York, 2001.

Sagalow, Ty. *Directors and Officers Liability Insurance: A Director's Guide.* Washington, D.C.: NACD, 2000.

Sahlman, William A. "Expensing Options Solves Nothing." *Harvard Business Review*, December 2002.

Salter, Malcolm S. "Tailor Incentive Compensation to Strategy." *Harvard Business Review*, March 1973.

Saly, Jane, Ravi Jagananathan, and Steven Huddart. "Valuing the Reload Features of Executive Stock Options." *Accounting Horizons* 13, no. 3 (September 1999): 219–240.

Schellhardt, Timothy. "More Directors Are Raking in Six-Figure Pay." *Wall Street Journal* 29 (October 1999): B1.

Schellhardt, Timothy. "National Presto Comes Under Microscope: Analysts Study Governance Issues." *Wall Street Journal*, July 28, 1999: C1, C4.

Schellhardt, Timothy. "Relocating Mom: A Primer of New Perks." *Wall Street Journal*, June 23, 1998: B1, B6.

Serven, Lawrence. *Value Planning: The New Approach to Building Value Every Day.* New York: John Wiley & Sons, 1998.

Sherman, Hugh, and Rajeswarao Chaganti. *Corporate Governance and the Timeliness of Change: Reorientation in 100 American Firms.* Westport, Conn.: Quorum Books, 1998.

Shorter, Gary, Mark Jickling, and Alison A. Raab. "Excessive CEO Pay: Background and Policy Approaches." *Congressional Research Service Report for Congress*, February 13, 2007.

Shultz, Susan. *The Board Book: Making Your Corporate Board a Strategic Force in Your Company's Success.* New York: AMACOM, 2001.

Smith, David. "The Case for a Chief Governance Officer." Speech before the National Association of Corporate Directors' Directors Summit, Madison, Wisconsin, September 6, 2001.

Sonnenfeld, Jeffrey. *The Hero's Farewell: What Happens When CEOs Retire.* New York: Oxford University Press, 1988.

Spellman, Howard. *Corporate Directors: A Treatise on the Principles of the Law Governing.* New York: Prentice-Hall, 1931.

Stanton, Elizabeth. "Executive Pay: A Power Behind the Pay Surge." *New York Times*, April 1, 2001: C2.

Strauss, Gary. "Good Year or Not, Execs Clean Up: Performance, Compensation Often Unlinked." *USA Today*, October 4, 2000: 3B.

Strauss, Gary. "CEO Pay: Fair or Foul." *USA Today*, April 6, 2001: 1B.

Strauss, Gary. "Forget the Brass Rings—Execs Grab for Gold: Golden Contracts Give Bigwigs Beaucoup Bucks to Stay . . . or Sometimes to Go." *USA Today*, March 20, 2001: 1B.

Strauss, Gary. "Many Execs Pocket Perks Aplenty." *USA Today*, June 20, 2001: 1B.

Strauss, Gary. "Spotlight on Corporate Performance Burns CEOs." *USA Today* November 14, 2000: 1B.

Teachers Insurance and Annuity Association—College Retirement Equities Fund. *TIAA-CREF Policy Statement on Corporate Governance.* New York: TIAA-CREF, 1999.

Teitelbaum, Richard. "Greenspan Weighs in on Options and Earnings." *New York Times*, August 29, 1999: C1.

Thatcher, Laura. "SEC's Amended Executive Compensation Disclosure Rules: Aligning Equity Reporting With FAS 123R" Journal Reports: Law and Policy, BNA Executive Compensation Library, March 2007.

Thatcher, Laura. "Analysis and Perspective: Prohibition on Trading During Blackout Periods under the Sarbanes-Oxley Act." *BNA, Inc. Daily Tax Report*, February 24, 2003.

Thatcher, Laura. "Analysis and Perspective: Executive Compensation Aspects of the Sarbanes-Oxley Act of 2002." *BNA, Inc. Daily Tax Report*, February 19, 2003.

Thatcher, Laura. "Analysis and Perspective: Prohibition on Trading During Blackout Periods under Section 306(a) of the Sarbanes-Oxley Act of 2002." *BNA, Inc. Corporate Accountability Report*, February 14, 2003.

Thatcher, Laura. "Analysis and Perspective: Executive Compensation Aspects of the Sarbanes-Oxley Act of 2002." *BNA, Inc. Corporate Accountability Report*, January 24, 2003.

Thatcher, Laura. "Special Report: Executive Compensation." *BNA, Inc. Corporate Accountability Report*, October 17, 2003.

Thatcher, Laura. "Insider Issues in Spin-off Transactions." *Executive Compensation Reports*, November/December 2000.

Thatcher, Laura. "Securities Considerations in Offering Company Stock as an Investment Alternative in Participant-Directed Plans." *Journal of Deferred Compensation*, Winter 1998.

Thatcher, Laura, Michael Brink, and Mark Williamson. "Legislative/Regulatory Developments: IRS Issues Notice on Split-Dollar Life Insurance." *Journal of Deferred Compensation*, Spring 2001.

Thatcher, Laura, Michael Brink, and Mark Williamson. "SERP Swap—Continuing the Evolution of Executive Benefits." *Journal of Deferred Compensation*, Winter 2001.

Thomas, Kaye. *Consider Your Options: Get Most from Your Equity Compensation.* Lisle, Ill.: Fairmark Press, 1999.

Varallo, Gregory, and Daniel Dreisbach. *Fundamentals of Corporate Governance: A Guide for Directors and Corporate Counsel.* Chicago: American Bar Association, 1996.

Wagner, Richard H. *Executive Compensation 2004 Guide.* New York: Kennedy Information, 2004.

Ward, John. *Creating Effective Boards for Private Enterprises.* Marietta, Ga.: Business Owner Resources, 1997.

Ward, Ralph. *Improving Corporate Boards: The Boardroom Insider Guidebook.* New York: John Wiley & Sons, 2000.

Ward, Ralph. *21st Century Corporate Board.* New York: John Wiley & Sons, 1997.

Watson Wyatt Worldwide. *Stock Option Overhang: Shareholder Boon? Or Shareholder Burden?* Bethesda, Md.: Watson Wyatt Worldwide, 1998.

Weisbach, M. S. "Outside Directors and CEO Turnover" *Journal of Financial Economics* 20, no. 1–2 (January/March 1988): 431–460.

Weston, Fred, Kwang Chung, and Juan Siu. *Takeovers, Restructuring, and Corporate Governance* Upper Saddle River, N.J.: Prentice-Hall, 1997.

Whittlesey, Fred. "Indexed Stock Options: A Solution to the Excessive Pay Issue." *ACA News*, September 1999: 6.

"Who Wants to Be a Billionaire? Stock Options Have Made Many American Bosses Rich—But Not Necessarily Any Better at Their Jobs." *Economist*, May 8, 1999: 12–15.

Williamson, Oliver. *The Mechanisms of Governance.* New York: Oxford University Press, 1996.

Worthy, James, and Robert Nueschel. *Emerging Issues in Corporate Governance.* Evanston, Il.: Northwestern University Press, 1983.

Yavitz, Boris, and William Neuman. *Strategy in Action: The Execution, Politics, and Pay of Business Planning.* New York: Free Press, 1982.

Zehnder, Egon. "A Simpler Way to Pay." *Harvard Business Review*, April 2001: 53.

Index